R

JUST WATCH ME

—

JOHN ENGLISH

JUST
WATCH ME

THE LIFE OF PIERRE ELLIOTT TRUDEAU

1968–2000

ALFRED A. KNOPF CANADA

PUBLISHED BY ALFRED A. KNOPF CANADA

Copyright © 2009 John English

All rights reserved under International and Pan-American Copyright
Conventions. No part of this book may be reproduced in any form or by any
electronic or mechanical means, including information storage and retrieval
systems, without permission in writing from the publisher, except by a reviewer,
who may quote brief passages in a review. Published in 2009 by
Alfred A. Knopf Canada, a division of Random House of Canada Limited,
and simultaneously in Quebec by Les Éditions de l'Homme, Montreal.
Distributed by Random House of Canada Limited, Toronto.

Knopf Canada and colophon are trademarks.

www.randomhouse.ca

Pages 756 to 758 constitute a continuation of the copyright page.

LIBRARY AND ARCHIVES CANADA CATALOGUING IN PUBLICATION

English, John, 1945–
Citizen of the world : the life of Pierre Elliott Trudeau / John English.
—1st ed.

Vol. 2 has title: Just watch me : the life of Pierre Elliott Trudeau,
1968–2000.
Includes bibliographical references and index.
ISBN-13: 978-0-676-97521-5 (bound : v. 1). —ISBN-10: 0-676-97521-6
(bound : v.1). —ISBN-13: 978-0-676-97523-9 (bound : v. 2)

1. Trudeau, Pierre Elliott, 1919–2000. 2. Canada—Politics and
government—1968–1979. 3. Canada—Politics and government—1980–1984.
4. Prime ministers—Canada—Biography. I. Title. II. Title: Just watch me.

FC626.T7E53 2006   971.064'4092   C2006-902597-5

Book design by CS Richardson

Printed and bound in the United States of America

2 4 6 8 9 7 5 3 1

To Bob English
Who never voted for Trudeau but now wishes he had

CONTENTS

—

—

CHAPTER ONE

TAKING POWER

The champagne sparkled, the boyish smile lingered as Pierre Elliott Trudeau waved to the cheering crowd at the Liberal convention in 1968. On April 6, a Saturday afternoon, the forty-eight-year-old Montrealer and Canada's reformist minister of justice was elected on the fourth ballot as the seventh Liberal leader since Confederation. His victory meant that he would become the sixth Liberal prime minister of Canada. Donning the mantle of Laurier and King, St. Laurent and Pearson, Trudeau prepared to address not only the delegates at Ottawa's Civic Centre but also the curious nation beyond, which, gathered around mostly black-and-white television sets, was about to witness the birth of "Trudeaumania." Whatever the meaning of the phenomenon, the evening seemed historic, for Trudeau would be the first Canadian prime minister born in the twentieth century, the youngest prime minister since the 1920s, and with fewer than three years in the House of Commons, the least experienced prime minister in Canada's history.

The Trudeau crowd was young but so were the times. Trudeau had begun his victorious campaign to capture the Prime Minister's Office just as the Beatles launched their Magical Mystery Tour and the musical *Hair* declared its discovery of sex, drugs, and rock and roll and headed for Broadway. The year blended magic and political shock as the fringe and the alternative merged with the mainstream. At the end of January, the Viet Cong had stunned American forces in Vietnam with its Tet offensive, and the American presidency of Lyndon Johnson suddenly began to crumble. Richard Nixon, the old Cold Warrior, returned from the political wilderness to become a serious Republican contender for the presidency as Democrats jostled to succeed Johnson. And the American dream had become a nightmare. That vision of promise, embodied in the young and eloquent John F. Kennedy, had entranced Canadians at the beginning of the decade, but Kennedy was gone, and on Thursday, April 4, the day before the Liberal leadership convention began, James Earl Ray had gunned down the Reverend Martin Luther King Jr., as the civil rights leader stood on a motel balcony in Memphis, Tennessee. The eruption of violence in America's largest cities following King's assassination shared front-page headlines in Canada's newspapers with the convention triumph of Pierre Trudeau.

The contrast was striking. Canada suddenly seemed different (*cool* in the argot of the day), a "peaceable kingdom" as some now called it. In this setting the candidacy of the parliamentarian of only three years became politically intriguing. His style and stance were unique in the history of Canada: an erstwhile socialist who cared what French intellectuals wrote, wore shoes without socks and jackets without ties and still looked elegant, drove the perfect Mercedes 300SL convertible, and flirted boldly with women a generation younger. That April weekend the American counterparts of the youth at the Ottawa Civic Centre were angrily demonstrating in the streets or on campuses. Bob Rae, then a hairy, rumpled student radical at the University of Toronto, later recalled how he went off to that convention, drawn to Trudeau's incisiveness, wit, "belief that ideas mattered in politics," and most of all, his "style." His roommate and fellow student activist, Michael Ignatieff, joined the Trudeau team and claimed, forty years later, that politics were never again as exciting for him as during those heady days in the spring of 1968. John Turner supporter Bruce Allen Powe took his thirteen-year-old son to the convention, where Bruce Jr. defied his father's allegiance, hid his Trudeau buttons beneath his jacket, and began a lifelong infatuation.

The infatuation was infectious. After the convention formally ended, Trudeau's supporters and thousands of others crammed into the new Skyline Hotel in downtown Ottawa, where the "curvaceous" Diamond Lil performed one of her livelier dances between two Trudeau campaign posters. Throngs of miniskirted teenagers screamed a welcome to the new leader, and older followers sang "For He's a Jolly Good Fellow." "Let's party tonight," a beaming Trudeau told the crowd, "but remember that Monday the party is over."

Before long, Trudeau spotted Bob Rae's striking young sister, Jennifer, across the room, and fastening his penetrating blue eyes on her, he came close and whispered, "Will you go out with me sometime?" She later did, but he also remembered the fetching teenager who had spurned him in Tahiti the previous December but had willingly accepted his eager kiss that afternoon as he left the convention floor. When reporters asked Margaret Sinclair, the daughter of a former Liberal Cabinet minister, "Have you eyes for Trudeau? Are you a girlfriend?" she replied, "No, I have eyes for him only as prime minister." The office had already brought Trudeau unanticipated benefits, and for the first time since Laurier, a Canadian prime minister was sexy.[1]

Trudeau knew that public expectations were too high, and he moved quickly to dampen them in his acceptance speech at the convention and at his next appearance. The acceptance speech reads poorly, but content mattered little, as Trudeau's words were submerged in the froth of victory. On April 7, the day after he became leader, Trudeau held a nationally televised press conference. Sporting the fresh red rose that had already become his trademark, he praised his opponents—particularly Robert Winters, who had finished second—and said he was considering how they would fit into his Cabinet. To the surprise of some commentators, he indicated there was no need for an immediate election. Then, unexpectedly, he denied that he was a radical or a "man of the left." "I am," he declared, "essentially a pragmatist." The comment confused many observers.

Not long before, Trudeau had proudly declared himself a leftist. Evidence of his "radicalism" and left-wing views abounded in old newspaper clippings; in the memories of many who knew him; and in *Cité libre*, the journal he had edited in the 1950s. New Democratic Party leader Tommy Douglas recalled trying to recruit Trudeau as a socialist candidate only a few years earlier. Trudeau knew that his future success rested on reassurance, which paradoxically required ambiguity, rather than strong assertions of principle. At the convention he'd talked about the "Just Society" he intended to construct, but its contours were thinly sketched and its foundations, apart from a commitment to the rights of individuals to make their own decisions, were barely visible.

Ambiguity or, perhaps more accurately, mystery was apparently alluring.* Even the *Spectator*, the British conservative magazine so often given to cynical observations about the oldest

---

* There was considerable mystery, for instance, about Trudeau's age. The biography in the official 1968 *Canadian Parliamentary Guide*, which Trudeau's own office had drafted, indicated that his year of birth was 1921. "Is he 46, 47, or 48?" a journalist asked. "Only his barber knows—and perhaps Mr. Trudeau himself." With a wry reference to Trudeau's true age, Conservative leader Robert Stanfield said the error suggested that Trudeau would never get numbers right. Trudeau himself teased the press about the discrepancy.

dominion, succumbed to the enthusiasm surrounding Trudeau: "It was as if Canada had come of age, as if he himself single handedly would catapult the country into the brilliant sunshine of the late 20th century from the stagnant swamp of traditionalism and mediocrity in which Canadian politics had been bogged down for years." In the spring of 1968, an intrigued William Shawn, the celebrated editor of the *New Yorker*, commissioned Edith Iglauer to write a long article on Canada's new prime minister. It took a year to complete, but it remains the best portrait of Trudeau as he took power and shaped his private self to the new demands of public life.

Leading Canadian journalists could not resist his charm, and many cast objectivity to the winds and signed a petition endorsing Trudeau. Historian Ramsay Cook, a traditional supporter of the New Democratic Party but a Trudeau speechwriter in 1968, retains a scrap of paper from that year which reads: "Pierre Trudeau is a good shit *(merde).*" It was signed by eminent leftist journalist June Callwood and her sportswriter husband, Trent Frayne; *Maclean's* editor Peter Gzowski and his wife, Jenny; and the brash young interviewer Barbara Frum. Peter C. Newman, the talented and bestselling political journalist at the *Toronto Star*, commented, "The whole house of clichés constructed by generations of politicians is demolished as soon as [Trudeau] begins to speak."[2]

When a radio interviewer in Wingham, Ontario, suggested gingerly that Trudeau was forty-eight, Trudeau replied, "Well, some say that. Some say other figures. I will have to ask my sister again. I am not too sure." *Canadian Parliamentary Guide 1968* (Ottawa: Pierre Normandin, 1968), 264; and *Le Devoir*, April 8, 1968. The Wingham interview is found in Brian Shaw, *The Gospel according to Saint Pierre* (Richmond Hill, Ont.: Pocket Books, 1969), 172; and *Le Devoir*, April 8, 1968.

—

Trudeau's freshness seemed to free him from the dense political foliage and sombre shades that had darkened Ottawa in the mid-1960s, when Canada, in Newman's famous term, suffered from political "distemper." Two veterans of the First World War, John Diefenbaker and Lester Pearson, fought pitched battles that both bored and infuriated Canadians. The Conservatives rejected Diefenbaker in a bitter convention in 1967 and turned to the Nova Scotia premier, Robert Stanfield, whose laconic style and careful ways contrasted strongly with the fiery Saskatchewan populist. The seventy-year-old Pearson stepped aside more gracefully just before Christmas 1967, when the polls were showing that Stanfield would trounce the Liberals should the government fall. The Liberal minority tottered as the candidates for Pearson's succession took their places in the winter of 1968. By that time Pearson had become convinced that his successor should be Pierre Trudeau, who had been his parliamentary secretary but had remained personally distant. Pearson told a close friend that "ice water" ran through Trudeau's veins. Still, his successor had to be a francophone, he thought, and Trudeau's intellect, his presence, and even his cold rationality made him the logical choice. Pearson's wife, Maryon, was openly smitten with the charm Trudeau so deftly and consciously revealed to women, and her affection for her husband's successor was obvious to all. A cartoonist wrote a caption on a photograph above Maryon as she gazed fondly at Trudeau: "Of course, Pierre, you realize that if you win, I go with the job."[3] She didn't, but the Victorian mansion on Sussex Drive did. It was the bachelor Pierre Trudeau's first house. With only two suitcases and his treasured Mercedes, he took possession when the Pearsons moved to the prime minister's official country retreat at Harrington Lake after the convention.

The two suitcases contained striking and elegant clothing,

his wrist bore a gold Rolex, and his thinning hair was artfully shaped to conceal bare skin. "Canadians," the *Winnipeg Free Press* declared, "are looking to Mr. Trudeau for great things, much in the manner that those Americans who elected John F. Kennedy as their leader expected great things from him."* The English-language press abounded with glowing references to Trudeau in the spring of 1968, but the French press, though almost always respectful, was more reserved and even critical. *Le Devoir's* Claude Ryan had known Trudeau since the 1940s, when he wrote an admiring article for a Catholic journal on the young Quebec intellectual, but he had endorsed Paul Hellyer for the leadership after his first choice, Mitchell Sharp, withdrew in favour of Trudeau. Although he never failed to acknowledge Trudeau's ability and political appeal, he was increasingly critical of his longtime acquaintance's constitutional arguments and especially his arch refusal of special status for Quebec. After dismissing suggestions that Trudeau lacked experience, Ryan said: "But Mr. Trudeau has developed to a very high level some significant qualities. He holds well-articulated personal thoughts. He speaks in the direct terms favoured by today's generation. He appears to fear no person or orthodoxy, whether official or not."[4] While disagreeing with his policies, Ryan acknowledged that there was a clarity to Trudeau's rejection of "special status" for Quebec. Trudeau's

---

* Over three decades later, Peter Gzowski, who had become fascinated with Trudeau in Montreal in the early years of the Quiet Revolution, recalled that "to those of us who had been swept up in the American promise of John F. Kennedy and still mourned his death, Trudeau was especially inspiring. He was glamorous, he was sexy, and he was ours—the perfect symbol of the newly invigorated Canada that had emerged from Expo and the centennial celebrations." "Watch Me," in *Trudeau Albums* (Toronto: Otherwise Editions, 2000), 67.

position differentiated him not only from Ryan himself but also from Quebec premier Daniel Johnson and Robert Stanfield, who in his first months as Conservative leader began to talk of "two nations"—a concept that was anathema to Trudeau.

Trudeau's rise to national political power was fundamentally a response, first by the Liberal Party and then by many Canadians, to Quebec's new challenge to Canadian confederation. The so-called Quiet Revolution of the early 1960s had shattered the foundations of Quebec's political structures, eroding the Roman Catholic faith that had provided the buttress for tradition. As a vibrant and activist secular state emerged in Quebec, the two political forces of nationalism and separatism exploded and pushed Quebec politicians and intellectuals toward different sides. Once a nationalist and for a brief time a separatist, Trudeau took his stand with those who believed that the future of French-speaking Canadians would be realized most fully within a renewed Canadian federalism. In 1965, as the Pearson-appointed Royal Commission on Bilingualism and Biculturalism was declaring that Canada was passing through "the greatest crisis" in its history, Trudeau joined with two old friends and collaborators, the journalist Gérard Pelletier and the labour leader Jean Marchand, to become one of "the three wise men" who would sort out the confusion the new Quebec had caused in Ottawa. By 1968 Trudeau had eclipsed his more celebrated colleagues and had become a charismatic leader fit for an extraordinary challenge.

Trudeau had first gained national attention in 1967 with his reforms to the Criminal Code, which he cleverly and memorably described as taking the state out of the bedrooms of the nation. He quickly framed his public character: candid, fresh, and alive with the spirit of the sixties. In a Montreal speech with a strong federalist message that troubled Ryan, Trudeau declared that he would speak "truth" in politics and that "*les Canadiens français*" must hear the truth. Some of them wanted to hesitate, others to obfuscate, but the choices had finally become clear. On the one hand, there was the view that a modern Quebec was incompatible with a united Canada. According to Trudeau this attitude would lead ineluctably to separatism. On the other hand, there was federalism, accompanied "by a new resolve and new methods, [and] the new resources of modern Quebec." For Trudeau, the choice was obvious. Canadian federalism "represents a more pressing, exciting, and enriching challenge than the rupture of separation because it offers to the Québécois, to the French Canadian, the opportunity, the historic chance to participate in the creation of a great political adventure of the future."[5] And so a great political adventure began.

As the tides of Trudeaumania, or *la Trudeaumanie*, as Quebec's milder version was termed, swept over the popular media, dissenters began to appear, particularly in his native province. Their ranks included many who had shared earlier adventures with Trudeau. From the left came complaints that the new "pragmatist" had abandoned his own core beliefs in favour of a naked thrust for power. *Le Devoir* carried a bitter attack from McGill historian, television host, and NDP activist Laurier LaPierre, who denounced Trudeau's constitutional rigidity, his opposition to Quebec nationalism, and his silence over the Vietnam War. LaPierre, later a Liberal senator, said that far from catalyzing change, the election of Trudeau would mean a return to the "do little" politics of Mackenzie King and the end of Canada. Trudeau became a regular target in the many radical journals that promoted the combined separatist and socialist cause. Some of his oldest friends were now among his most virulent critics: the sociologist Marcel Rioux, who had dined regularly with him when, as two lonely young Quebec intellectuals, they worked in Ottawa in the early 1950s; the brilliant Laval academic Fernand Dumont, who had written often for *Cité libre* when Trudeau was its editor in the 1950s; and the writer Pierre Vadeboncoeur, who had been Trudeau's close friend during childhood and adolescence.

From the right in Quebec and English Canada came rumours of Trudeau's homosexuality and his flirtations with Communism: the proof lay, it was said, in his trips to the Soviet Union and China. Although right-wing columnist Lubor Zink touched on these subjects in the mainstream *Toronto Telegram*, most Canadian journalists ignored or dismissed the tales as scatological.[6] To his credit, Claude Ryan sternly and admirably rebuked those, including some within the Church, who spread "*calomnies insidieuses*" about Trudeau. While declaring that he was increasingly opposed to Trudeau's policies, Ryan recalled that the two had shared "*une vieille amitié*" since the 1940s and that he could personally attest that such attacks had absolutely "no basis in fact."[7]

Some friends had left Trudeau, but he found new allies who, together with Marchand and Pelletier, reassured him that his course was correct. Friends and colleagues mattered a lot to Trudeau, but his first journey after gaining the Liberal leadership was to Montreal to visit his closest confidant—his mother, Grace Elliott Trudeau. Widowed in 1935, she had since devoted herself to her three children and doted especially on Pierre, her elder son, who shared her gracious home in the prosperous Montreal suburb of Outremont until he became prime minister. An easy banter had developed between them in the 1940s as Trudeau formed his adult personality, and in his mother's presence, he retained a wondrous blend of playfulness and serious purpose. They went to the symphony together, cruised the corniches of the Riviera on his Harley-Davidson, and shared the pain when Pierre's romantic life faltered, as it often did in the forties and fifties. Grace could be critical when women did not meet her standards, and most of Pierre's dates recall their trepidation as they mounted the steps at 84 McCulloch Avenue. In the mid-sixties, however, Grace's mind became cloudy. She probably did not know that her son became Canada's prime minister in 1968, although three decades before, she had dreamed that he might. She was, as always, dressed elegantly when he saw her on April 9, and she listened mutely as he held her hand, spoke softly, and told of their most recent and greatest triumph. In silence her strong presence abided.[8]

—

At first Trudeau hesitated to call an election. After the convention he suddenly disappeared, and a frantic press finally discovered him in Fort Lauderdale, Florida, with his colleagues Edgar Benson and Jean Marchand and their wives. Benson, a pipe-smoking accountant and early supporter of Trudeau's leadership bid, had co-chaired the Trudeau campaign, although few expected him to have a senior position in the new Cabinet. Marchand also smoked a pipe, but his ebullient nature and fiery oratory, crafted before tough, working-class audiences, contrasted strongly with the phlegmatic Benson's style. Trudeau was comfortable with both, a trait that served him well in politics and in life more generally. By the time he returned to Ottawa and met the Pearson Cabinet on April 17, he was still ambiguous about the election date. He spoke about an "alternative course" in which the House would meet quickly and then dissolve. Two days later the Cabinet's mood was one of "wide disenchantment" with "the present Parliament's effectiveness, and general agreement in the country that the present Parliament was no longer useful or meaningful." Faced with this turnaround, Pearson, who had settled at Harrington Lake with his fishing gear, was obliging when he was asked to resign, and Trudeau swore in his Cabinet on April 20, two days earlier than he had first indicated.[9]

Trudeau had a rich legacy on which to draw: Pearson's Cabinet was one of the most talented in Canadian history, with three future prime ministers in its ranks and several others who would make significant contributions to Canadian public life. Trudeau was cautious in his picks and, as he promised, pragmatic. Prime ministers normally ask their leadership opponents to join the Cabinet, and Trudeau complied. The brilliant and often difficult Eric Kierans was the sole exception—but only because he was not an MP. Joe Greene, whose folksy speech at the convention charmed the delegates and received high marks from the media, became minister of agriculture. John Turner had irritated Trudeau by his decision to remain on the last ballot, but his political talents could not be ignored and he was rewarded with the ministry of consumer and corporate affairs. Paul Hellyer, who had created huge controversy when he unified Canada's armed forces, became minister of transport. The wily and experienced Cape Bretoner Allan MacEachen, who was deeply committed to social Catholicism, became minister of national health and welfare.

The political veteran Paul Martin, who only a year previously had been considered the most likely successor to Pearson, now presented a problem. Trudeau thought poorly of Martin's leadership in the Department of External Affairs, and he blamed some of Martin's people for rumours about his socialism and his personal life. Still, Martin had a following and impressive political experience. The two men met and talked about the justice portfolio, but the devout Catholic Martin did not want to implement the reforms already planned for the Criminal Code, with their liberal approach to homosexuality and abortion. A bit grumpily, the good soldier Martin therefore accepted the position of government leader in the Senate. However, Trudeau's major opponent, Bay Street favourite Robert Winters, decided to step aside after two meetings with Trudeau. "Pierre," Winters said on April 17, "we have been talking for two hours on two successive days, and I still don't know if you want me in your government or if you don't." Trudeau replied, "Well, it's a decision you will have to make." In these laconic words, Trudeau revealed a persistent trait: he insisted that individuals make their own decision. Ardent wooing was not his game.[10]

He had no desire to woo former Pearson minister Judy LaMarsh, who at the convention, with microphone nearby, told

Hellyer to fight the "bastard" Trudeau to the end. She resigned abruptly as expected and muttered something about becoming an independent. Trudeau's first Cabinet had no female member, an appalling weakness given that Diefenbaker and Pearson both had female ministers. The influence of francophones and of Quebec was, however, striking. The Cabinet announced on April 20 had eleven ministers from Quebec and eleven francophones. This strong representation appears to have resulted in the assignment of the major offices, External Affairs and Finance, to the Ontarians Mitchell Sharp and Edgar Benson, respectively. The weakness of the Liberal Party in the West limited Trudeau's choices, with British Columbia's Arthur Laing being the only significant western Canadian minister. Charles "Bud" Drury, a superb administrator whose Montreal patrician style appealed to Trudeau, became industry minister, and the effervescent Jean-Luc Pepin, whom Trudeau had known since their university days in Paris in the forties, became minister of labour.

It was, as Trudeau said at the time, a "makeshift" Cabinet designed to emphasize continuity. He also told the press that he chose this particular Cabinet composition to allay any fears that his government "appeared to be that of a new bunch of outsiders coming into the party." Caution and continuity prevailed because an election loomed. Everyone knew the Cabinet that mattered would be formed after the election—a Cabinet that would fully reflect Trudeau's political agenda.[11]

—

Although the Cabinet was traditional, the mood and style in Ottawa were suddenly very different. Reporters were startled and photographers delighted when, on April 22, they spied Trudeau sprinting across Parliament Hill to his office to avoid a group of "girls" from Toronto who were pursuing him. The *Globe and Mail* featured three photographs of the chase on its front page, following a comment that Trudeau "is clearly savoring his new power and its fringe benefits—old ladies queuing up for his autograph, young girls clamoring to be kissed, mothers holding up their babies to see the great man pass, and traffic jams on the street as motorists stop to catch a glimpse." Cabinet colleagues soon learned, however, that Trudeau's public playfulness and frivolity were left behind at the door. At his first formal meeting, he sternly warned his new ministers that he would not tolerate any "leaks" about his political plans. A leak had apparently occurred the previous weekend, with stories about the "hawks" and the "chickens" in the Cabinet—the former favouring an election, the latter opposing it. He also served notice that he would "ensure improved discipline in the attendance of Ministers in the House of Commons and in the coordination of House business." He established the rudiments of a Cabinet committee system that would become a fundamental alteration in the method of government. From that first meeting, it was apparent that Trudeau meant business. To his political colleagues, he was no longer "Pierre"; he was now "Prime Minister."[12]

The next morning, April 23, he met the caucus on Parliament Hill after a meeting with Senators Dick Stanbury and John Nichol, the present and past Liberal Party presidents, to discuss the latest very good poll results. The caucus was raucous, and most Liberal MPs were ready for an election. So was Trudeau. He went immediately to his West Block office and slipped away via a secret staircase. Then, to avoid suspicion, he entered a car in which a puzzled Paul Martin was waiting. They travelled inconspicuously past the Parliament Buildings and along Rideau Street and soon arrived at Martin's residence at Champlain Towers, in Ottawa's east end. They descended to the basement garage, where yet another car awaited Trudeau. With the press completely tricked, his new driver took him to Rideau Hall, which he entered by the inconspicuous greenhouse entrance; there a bemused Governor General Roland Michener signed the order dissolving the House. As Martin later wrote, the "twist perfectly illustrated Trudeau's liking for the unexpected and his disdain for convention."[13]

Trudeau then returned to the House of Commons and announced that there would be an election on June 25. The twenty-seventh Parliament ended five minutes after it began, with order papers thrown wildly into the air amid yelps of joy and final embraces before the campaign. Stanfield was furious, and he said at his press conference that Trudeau's request for a mandate was absurd, given that there was "no record, no policy, and no proof of his ability to govern the country." But it was not only the opposition parties that were upset. The unexpected dissolution of Parliament left no time for tributes to Lester Pearson—and the revered former prime minister was denied the opportunity to make the gracious speech he had prepared in response to the expected generous praise of his friends, colleagues, and successor. To make matters worse, April 23 was his seventy-first birthday. Maryon Pearson's affection for Trudeau diminished—though not greatly. The slight was not deliberate, but it reflected a carelessness in personal interactions and manners that sometimes marked Trudeau's behaviour.[14]

Few commented on the oversight, however, and Canadians already seemed too eager to shed memories of Pearson and his stumbling government.* With excitement rising, the party that

---

* Pearson himself felt the slight but characteristically did not express anger. Although Trudeau was driven toward the election by events, notably the strong Liberal standing in polls and the argument with Quebec about the province's role in international affairs, Douglas Fisher, a former NDP politician turned journalist, was correct when he said that there was an "atmosphere of indifference for Mr. Pearson when he retired in April 1968; there was a notable keenness by his successor to separate his government distinctly from the bad Pearson years—scandals, leaks, messy staggering parliaments, and disorganized ventures." Douglas Fisher, "The Quick, Unusual Hallowing of Lester Pearson," *Executive* (July 1973), 8.

had so coyly embraced Trudeau now rushed to follow his colours. Trudeau recalled his Conservative father complaining bitterly in the thirties about the Liberal "campaign machine," but now the gears of that machine began to grind steadily in his support. Financial support, a considerable worry for the party, suddenly appeared as individual donations complemented substantial funds from the corporate world. Throughout the country MPs, senators, candidates, fundraisers, and others rallied behind their irreverent, unpredictable, puzzling, but wildly popular new leader. They knew, after six years of minority governments, that they finally had a winner. Suzette Trudeau Rouleau, who possessed a sister's skepticism, returned from one rally in shock and declared to a friend: "My goodness, Pierre is like a Beatle." There was even a popular song, "PM Pierre," with such lines as "PM Pierre with the ladies, racin' a Mercedes / Pierre, in the money, find him with a bunny."

Aware of the photographer's moment and the quick quip—the "sound bite" that slips neatly into TV news spots—Trudeau, like the Beatles, lived part of his life as a performance. The Canadian communications theorist Marshall McLuhan, then at the height of his international celebrity, was caught up in the campaign. He immediately declared that Trudeau perfectly fitted the sixties with its instant news, colour TV, and politics integrating quickly into the new technologies. "The story of Pierre Trudeau," he wrote, "is the story of the Man in the Mask. That is why he came into his own with TV. His image has been shaped by the Canadian cultural gap. Canada has never had an identity. Instead it has had a cultural interface of 17th-century France and 19th-century America. After World War II, French Canada leapt into the 20th century without ever having had a 19th century. Like all backward and tribal societies, it is very much 'turned on' or at home in the new electric world of the 20th century." Such comments appalled many of McLuhan's academic colleagues, but Trudeau himself was intrigued. He shared McLuhan's intuition that the new media had transformed not only politics but also what a politician represented to the electorate.* A correspondence between Trudeau and McLuhan, rich in irony and playfulness, began during the election campaign. When the CBC organized a leaders' debate—the first in Canadian history—McLuhan rightly criticized the format in a letter to Trudeau. "The witness box cum lectern cum pulpit spaces for the candidates was totally non-TV." "Total TV," however, was perfect for Trudeau's cool, detached, but vital image. "The age of tactility via television and radio is one of the innumerable interfaces or 'gaps' that replace the old connections, legal, literate, and visual," he told Trudeau.[15]

—

* Trudeau relied on physicist Jim Davey, a close assistant who was a "futurist," to interpret McLuhan to him, but sometimes even Davey admitted he had no idea what McLuhan meant. McLuhan's letter of April 16 had an impact upon Trudeau: "The men of the press can work only with people who have fixed points of view and definite goals, policies and objectives. Such fixed positions and attitudes are, of course, irrelevant to the electronic age. *Our world* [underlined by Trudeau] substitutes mosaics for points of view and probes for targets. Knowing of your acquaintance with De Tocqueville, I can understand why you have such an easy understanding of the North American predicament in the new electronic age." Trudeau asked Davey to call McLuhan to thank him for this letter, but they did not connect. The following month, when Davey wrote to McLuhan, he said that they had discussed the ideas set out in the letter and that Trudeau wanted to speak with him after the election. McLuhan to Trudeau, April 16, 1968; Davey to McLuhan, May 21, 1968, TP, MG 26 020, vol. 9, file 9–28, Library and Archives Canada (LAC).

In terms of the media, the 1968 election represents a historic divide. Seventeen million Canadians watched the Liberal convention, and almost as many watched the leaders' debate. Polling became constant, and American-style tours based on flights that jumped across the country became the norm. Trudeau flew in a DC-9 jet and followed a tight script: a brief statement, passage through the city centre in a convertible, followed by a shopping centre or hockey rink rally with cheerleaders clad in orange and white miniskirts. Cameras, of course, recorded Trudeau's progress. Journalist Walter Stewart, Tommy Douglas's sympathetic biographer, wrote that "beside Trudeau, Stanfield seemed lumpish and Tommy petulant. Stanfield flew in a propeller-driven DC-7 at half Trudeau's speed and made laconic, dull, and sensible speeches. Tommy Douglas flew economy on Air Canada and made provocative speeches that, in most cases, he might as well have shouted into the closet back in his Burnaby apartment."[16] The opposition leaders struggled to find an issue that would focus the campaign, but they were not successful.

Trudeau seemed bemused at the attention he received and remained so when he wrote his memoirs twenty-five years later. He recalled the "exceptional enthusiasm" of the crowds and the astonishing number of people who came to see. In Victoria, "a city of peaceful, respectable folk, many of them retired," he had to be lowered from a helicopter onto a hill, where he was surrounded by thousands. He decided that the crowds came not to hear his speeches but to see the "neo-politician who had made such a splash." It was "part of the spirit of the times," part of the post-Expo mood of "festivity."[17]

There was certainly spontaneous excitement during the campaign, but there was also careful staging as the Liberal strategists focused on their leader in a way that only the new media made possible. For the TV cameras, they even staged a fake fall down the stairs by the athletic Trudeau. They had used "consultants" in 1963 to try to remake Pearson's dowdy presence, but they were much more sophisticated five years later as they copied recent innovations in American politics. Richard Nixon loathed television, but he had learned from his ill-fated 1960 debate with John F. Kennedy, when he won among radio listeners but lost badly among those who watched his dark shadows on the screen, that politics had become principally the manipulation of images.[18] Television embraced Trudeau: the dramatic high cheekbones; the intense blue eyes; the quick change of moods from caustic to shy to affectionate; the striking retort; and the "cool" presence. Somehow the camera missed his pock-marked cheeks, the faintly yellow tinge to his complexion, and his less than average height.* A grudging Walter Stewart complained that "whatever quality it is that [makes] TV work for one person and not for another, Trudeau had it."[19]

A superb actor, Trudeau knew well what the crowd wanted: the expert jackknife into a pool, beautiful and brilliant young people, and stunning women in miniskirts surrounding him. In his memoirs, he tellingly chose a photograph of a buxom young woman wearing a T-shirt emblazoned with "Vote P.E.T. or Bust." George Bain, the *Globe and Mail*'s senior columnist, wrote

---

* One of his most frequent and tallest "dates" of the sixties, Carroll Guérin, recalls how Trudeau insisted that she wear flat shoes when they went out. Trudeau's television presence is preserved well by the CBC and Radio-Canada. Readers may consult them at http://archives.cbc.ca/IDD-1-73-2192/politics_economy/ trudeau/ in English and http://archives.radio-canada.ca/IDD-0-18-2076/ personnalites/trudeau/ in French. Trudeau's different speaking style in French and in English is visible—he is more animated in French, more modulated in English.

caustically of the Trudeau campaign: "If it puckers, he's there."
And, seemingly, he always was.

Trudeau enjoyed the attention, but he strongly resisted its
tendency to trivialize his political message. Perhaps in response to
Bain's effective jibe, Trudeau gave him a long interview in which
he tried to elaborate on the Liberals' platform and, in particular,
his call for a "Just Society." At the time, May 22, the English press
was becoming critical of the emphasis on style over substance in
the Trudeau campaign. When Bain demanded, "What is a just
society?" Trudeau replied:

> It means certain things in a legal sense — freeing an individ-
> ual so he will be rid of his shackles and permitted to fulfil
> himself in society in the way which he judges best, without
> being bound up by standards of morality which have nothing
> to do with law and order but which have to do with prejudice
> and religious superstition.
>
> Another aspect of it is economic, and, rather than develop
> that in terms of social legislation and welfare benefits, which
> I do not reject or condemn, I feel that at this time it is more
> important to develop in terms of groups of people . . . The
> Just Society means not giving them a bit more money or a bit
> more welfare. The Just Society for them means permitting
> the province or the region as a whole to have a developing
> economy. In other words, not to try to help merely the indi-
> viduals but to try to help the region itself to make all parts of
> Canada liveable in an acceptable sense . . .
>
> Another one, I think, is in terms of our relations with
> other countries. . . . Canada [is] . . . a country of modest
> proportions in world terms — not geographically, but eco-
> nomically and in terms of its population — we must make
> sure that our contribution to world order is . . . not only . . .
> to appear just [but] . . . to be just.[20]

The outlines of the "Just Society" remain faintly drawn in this interview, but the absence of sharp detail was intentional. Trudeau worried about expectations, and he took refuge in ambiguity and caution. He signalled that the great innovations in social welfare of the Pearson years—the Canada Pension Plan, medicare, and Canada Student Loans—would have no immediate successors. He would focus on "groups"; regions; and broad, incremental change. This comment took tangible form in the Trudeau years in new programs for regional economic development, special grants for youth and Aboriginals, recognition of the language rights of francophones throughout Canada, and the establishment of avenues through which francophones could more easily reach the pinnacle of the public service in Canada.

Despite the apparent modesty of the proposed programs, Trudeau believed that he represented a revolutionary innovation in Canadian politics. He urged Canadians to "take a chance" on him, even though he was unwilling to tell them yet what their wager would mean. He played with their hopes, artfully revealing little while raising expectations. He had rehearsed for this moment since adolescence. On New Year's Day 1938, he had written in his diary: "If you want to know my thoughts, read between the lines," and six months later, he was forthright in expressing his ambitions: "I would like so much to be a great politician and to guide my nation."[21] He knew that ambiguity, paradox, irony, and a seductive elusiveness were assets in achieving the goal he had so long cherished: to be a great politician guiding a nation and affecting destiny. Pierre Trudeau had never been as happy as he was in the spring of 1968, and he revelled in the first sips of power.

He loved the highest office, though he was wary, even fearful, of its personal costs and the flamboyant manner he had used to achieve it. He cherished his privacy, shunned close emotional attachment, and often took moments where no one could pierce his silence. Those around him quickly learned to retreat at those times. The campaign, moreover, was a long one, and the constant repetition of airport greetings, motorcades, and rallies began to bore him. He worried whether his legitimacy as an intellectual who had helped to shape his province in the postwar years might not be undermined by the trivialities of the campaign. He was especially annoyed in parts of Quebec when his sexual orientation was questioned. The Créditiste strength in rural Quebec drew on profound doubts about the Quiet Revolution—doubts that had led to defeat for the Lesage government in 1966 and, in 1968, threatened the federal Liberal appeal in those areas. The rumours about Trudeau's "Communism" and sexual tastes were so strong that he was forced to confront them directly in rallies in the Lac St-Jean region.

In English Canada and urban Quebec, the personal issues were ignored in the mainstream press. There was, as usual, a striking difference between the campaigns in French and English Canada, in terms of issues and reporting. A major cause of this situation dated back to the previous year, when the Johnson government in Quebec decided to build on France's willingness to give the province international stature by accepting invitations to international conferences. This had struck Trudeau and others as a dramatic and dangerous threat to Canadian federalism. Then, in mid-1967 French president Charles de Gaulle proclaimed, "*Vive le Québec libre!*" before a cheering crowd at Montreal's Hôtel de Ville, stunning Canadians who were joyously celebrating their Centennial and catalyzing the swelling forces of separatism in the province of Quebec. Paul Martin in External Affairs worried that a firm rebuke would accomplish little. There was, he reported to Cabinet, "no mistaking the enthusiasm for de Gaulle in Montreal and at Expo 67." Trudeau, who had spoken seldom in Cabinet since his appointment in April, quickly dismissed these concerns. "The people in France," he warned, "would think the Government was weak if it did not react; the General had not the support of the intellectuals in his country and the French press was opposed to him."[22] An angry Pearson backed Trudeau and rebuked de Gaulle, who immediately flew home to Paris. In this incident, Trudeau had made a strong impression on Pearson, the Cabinet, and even General de Gaulle—who concluded that Trudeau was "the enemy of the French fact in Canada."[23]

Now, Trudeau deliberately made Quebec's international ambitions a campaign issue—indeed, Cabinet records reveal that they were the principal reason he decided to call an early election. Moreover, the Quebec NDP and Conservative leaders, Robert Cliche and Marcel Faribault, respectively, both supported the idea of *"deux nations"* or *"statut particulier"* (two nations or special status) for Quebec—a position Trudeau had not only long opposed but regarded as the slippery slope heading directly to separatism. These various ambitions gave Trudeau his "issue." His Quebec speeches were more formal, with much more content and less political fluff than his speeches in the rest of Canada. In response, the Quebec press took what he said more seriously and, except in the tabloids, completely ignored the "puckering."

Trudeau also faced greater controversy and more strident and even vocal opposition in Quebec. The June 1 death of André Laurendeau, the co-chair of the Royal Commission on Bilingualism and Biculturalism, shocked Trudeau, and he wept openly at the June 4 funeral in Outremont. Laurendeau had been an early mentor, a frequent critic, and a shrewd observer of Trudeau's career.* Together, Trudeau, Marchand, and Pelletier attended the

---

* Laurendeau had counselled Trudeau on his career in the early forties; had been his party leader when Trudeau joined the Bloc populaire during the war; had written a long, critical, yet warm review of Trudeau's essay on Quebec on the eve of the Asbestos Strike; and had encouraged Trudeau to go to Ottawa in

funeral at Église Saint-Viateur, a church where Trudeau frequently prayed. As they left the church, a crowd confronted them, its leaders shouting, "Traitors! Goddamn traitors! Go back to Ottawa." The event jarred Trudeau. He became less comfortable with the campaign's demands on him and less willing to "pucker and run" during carefully staged events and scripted speeches. The following day, Trudeau was scheduled to give a speech in Sudbury on "Northern Problems and the Just Society," which even its author, Ramsay Cook, regarded as uninspiring. He threw away the speech and "passionately improvised before a large attentive audience." He spoke with feeling of Laurendeau and of his own commitment to tolerance and diversity. He angrily attacked those who had killed Bobby Kennedy earlier that day and linked them

---

1965. Yet Trudeau often irritated him. He refused to congratulate Trudeau on his election that year, not least because he discovered that Trudeau had openly criticized the Royal Commission on Bilingualism and Biculturalism. Nevertheless, he met Trudeau in Ottawa shortly after his election to the House in 1965 and "was struck by his good spirits, and his energy: it's been a long time since I've seen him so up." Marchand told him that Trudeau was "wonderfully successful" in Ottawa and would soon be the Liberals' "big man in French Canada, eclipsing all the others." Laurendeau was depressed by the radicalization of the nationalist and separatist movement in the later 1960s. He wrote in his diary that the future for him looked "thankless" and that those for whom he felt "the most natural and spontaneous affection, will be in the opposite camp"—namely, René Lévesque and the young. "There is only one thing that repels me more than being snubbed by the young, and that is to flatter them like demagogues." Life, he wrote, "is not going to smile on me much any more." Trudeau shared some of these feelings when he considered his own place in Quebec. See Patricia Smart, ed., *The Diary of André Laurendeau* (Toronto: James Lorimer, 1991), 154, 168.

with the terrorists in Quebec. Pearson phoned Marc Lalonde, his former assistant, who had urged Trudeau to enter politics, to tell him it was the best political speech he had ever heard. When Cook offered his own praise, Trudeau responded by "smiling wickedly" and saying, "And you didn't write it!"[24]

Trudeau increasingly resisted his advisers as the campaign progressed, and the adoring crowds in parts of English Canada caused him to ease his normal discipline. At a meeting for a new "star candidate" in the constituency of North York, Trudeau introduced Barney Danson as Barney Dawson. Danson corrected him, but minutes later Trudeau called him "Barry Danson." The errors did not matter: two days before the election, Danson's Conservative opponent informed him that he had given up: "This Trudeau thing is just too big." Trudeau's national opponents were similarly frustrated. His debate performance on June 9 was flat, and he seems unfairly to have blamed those who prepared him. He had followed the script, while Tommy Douglas and Créditiste leader Réal Caouette were humorous and spontaneous. Former Liberal Party president John Nichol recalls how, as the campaign progressed, Trudeau increasingly refused to go beyond the prearranged schedule and argued with campaign manager Bill Lee about every new demand. As Edith Iglauer, the *New Yorker* journalist, observed while travelling with Trudeau, the new prime minister, unlike Winston Churchill, Franklin Roosevelt, and most other politicians, insisted on at least eight hours' sleep at night.[25]

This regimen made campaigning difficult in a country that covers several time zones. On June 15 Nichol and other advisers had a bitter exchange with Trudeau when he refused to make one last western trip. A furious Nichol hollered that "hundreds of Liberals—candidates and their workers—had been working for weeks preparing for him to come." When he threatened to resign, Trudeau reluctantly gave in. With success and celebrity, the campaign had become bloated with assistants, advisers, and "hangers on." Richard Stanbury, who had replaced Nichol as Liberal Party president, wrote in his diary that Trudeau's popularity had attracted too many admirers eager to be near the coming Messiah. He even intervened himself to keep some Trudeau enthusiasts, including an exuberant Michael Ignatieff, at a greater distance from the leader.[26]

Whatever the campaign's flaws, the roar of the crowds and the excitement around the leader smothered any doubters among Liberals. Unlike the Conservatives, where sparring between former leader John Diefenbaker and Robert Stanfield marred the campaign, the Liberals seemed united, and no more so than on June 19 in Toronto. Over fifty thousand gathered on Nathan Phillips Square at noon to cheer Trudeau. Later in the day, he went to the riding of York Centre, where Lester Pearson introduced him with glowing words: "A man prepared to speak out loud and clear in favour of unity . . . A man who doesn't make idle promises . . . A man for today and a man for tomorrow . . . My friend, my former colleague, a man for all Canada — Pierre Elliott Trudeau." As the Liberal leader came forward, Pearson beamed at his successor and tears welled up in Trudeau's eyes.[27]

Perhaps because his welcome was so warm in English Canada, the increasingly hostile press coverage in Quebec angered Trudeau — and his combative instincts led him to respond more aggressively than his advisers thought wise. He would privately attack journalists as ignorant and boring, the news media as "the last tyranny" in free societies.[28] He engaged in an unseemly quarrel over whether Conservative star candidate Marcel Faribault had been personally involved in banning him from teaching at the Université de Montréal in the early fifties on the grounds that he was a socialist. Claude Ryan became more caustic as the campaign neared its end, and even the Montreal *Gazette* waxed critical. It was no surprise, then, when the *Gazette*, which had supported the Liberals in 1965, urged its readers to vote for "an enlightened Conservatism" that "does not attempt to dazzle without reason; or lead without explanation; act without steadiness; or discard without cause; or add without need."[29]

Stanfield's campaign had impressed many editorialists, especially in Quebec, where *Le Devoir*, *L'Action*, and the *Sherbrooke Record* all endorsed the Conservatives, and even the traditionally Liberal *La Presse*, *Le Droit*, and *Le Soleil* attached reservations to their support of Trudeau. In rural Quebec, Caouette campaigned relentlessly and successfully against Trudeau's liberal social programs and "socialist" economics, while rumours about Trudeau's sexual orientation continued to animate discussions at the rural *boucheries* and *dépanneurs*. In Montreal, Pierre Bourgault of the Rassemblement pour l'indépendance nationale (RIN) attacked Trudeau unrelentingly as a *vendu* and warned him not to attend the historic parade on Saint-Jean-Baptiste Day. Not surprisingly, Trudeau announced he would be there. He argued with close advisers and Montreal mayor Jean Drapeau, who told him that violence was certain if he went. When Richard Stanbury accompanied him to his house before the rally, a roughly dressed man who obviously knew Trudeau stopped him and warned him to stay at home. Trudeau told Stanbury that the man was a friend from his youth who was now close to violent separatists. Trudeau thanked his old chum but ignored his advice.[30]

As darkness fell on June 24, election eve, Trudeau arrived at the reviewing stand on Sherbrooke Street for the parade. He took his place between Archbishop of Montreal Paul Grégoire and Premier Daniel Johnson, two seats away from Mayor Drapeau. Despite the hundreds of police milling about, the crowd broke into chants of *"Tru-deau au pot-eau"* (Trudeau to the gallows), and suddenly, the hostile throng erupted into a violent riot, throwing bottles and stones. Sirens blared, ambulances and police cars sped in and out. Defiant, Trudeau stood up and waved, but the chants intensified. One police car was overturned; another was aflame. Demonstrators poured out of Lafontaine Park onto the streets, which by this time were sprinkled with shattered glass. Suddenly, a bottle came through the air toward the reviewing stand. Seeing its arc, Drapeau fled with his wife, Johnson escaped, and two RCMP officers moved quickly to shield the prime minister. One threw his raincoat over him, but Trudeau flung it aside, put his elbows on the railing, and stared defiantly at the melee below. He stood there alone, his visage stony.* The crowd, initially stunned, began slowly to applaud Trudeau's courage. The Mounties, realizing that he would not be moved, sat down beside him as he stayed to the parade's end at 11:20 p.m. The startling images of Trudeau confronting the rioters dominated the late television news throughout Canada. The following morning, the front pages of the newspapers featured photographs of Trudeau's icy defiance on the reviewing stand, while editorialists paid tribute to his character and strength. The whole performance embellished Trudeau's steely image and confirmed the impression that here was a leader.† And, in truth, it was election day.

Trudeau voted in an overcast Montreal that morning and then flew to Ottawa. There he visited Liberal headquarters

---

* Readers may see the event in detail in this clip from the CBC archives: http://archives.cbc.ca/IDC-1-73-2192-13270/politics_economy/trudeau/clip7. Donald Peacock includes an excellent account of this incident in his *Journey to Power: The Story of a Canadian Election* (Toronto: Ryerson, 1968), 372–77. This account draws on both of these sources as well as newspaper stories of the time.

† Trudeau's angry attacks on separatist hecklers undoubtedly strengthened English-Canadian belief that Trudeau would be "tough" on Quebec's "rowdies." At a meeting in Rouyn, Trudeau lashed out at separatists who were harassing him: "The men who killed Kennedy are purveyors of hate like you — those who refuse to discuss! There won't be free speech in your Québec libre,

and thanked the party workers before having dinner at his new home on Sussex Drive. After the polls closed, his driver took him to the historic Château Laurier hotel, where police held back the crowd as he made his way to the Liberal suites on the fifth floor. Campaign workers gathered below. Trudeau watched the returns and worked on his speech in a small bedroom at one end of the floor. He emerged briefly to greet Lester and Maryon Pearson, whom he had invited to join him. The night began badly with the loss of 6 Liberal seats in Newfoundland, followed by a Conservative sweep of Prince Edward Island's 4 seats and 10 of the 11 Nova Scotia seats—a testimony to the personal appeal of Bob Stanfield. Then the Conservative tide slowed dramatically as it reached the francophone constituencies of New Brunswick and collapsed in Quebec, where the Liberals took 53.3 percent of the vote and 56 of its 74 seats. Trudeaumania held in Ontario, where the Liberals took 64 of its 88 seats. When the night ended, the victory was decisive. Even Alberta, which had rejected the Liberal Party for over a generation, gave 4 seats to Trudeau. In British Columbia, Tommy Douglas lost his own seat as the Liberals won 16 in all—9 more than in 1965.

A later academic study of the election is especially revealing. The Liberals took 45.2 percent of the popular vote but 63.9 percent of "professionals," 72.2 percent of immigrants after 1946, 67.1 percent of francophones, and 59.2 percent of Canadians under the age of thirty. Large metropolitan areas gave 67.7 percent of their votes to the Liberals. The Conservatives led slightly among

---

monsieur . . . It's not me you're insulting. It's your fellow citizens . . . If you want to get rid of foreigners, of the English, of American capital, it's easy. You only have to continue the violence. But you're going to be left behind by the 20th century." *Ottawa Citizen*, quoted in George Radwanski, *Trudeau* (Toronto: Macmillan, 1978), 109.

rural Canadians, and the populist and rural Ralliement des Créditistes raised their party standing from 8 at dissolution to 14. However, bad economic conditions probably mattered more to Créditiste voters than the rumours about Trudeau's radical ways and sexual habits.[31] As Claude Ryan grudgingly admitted, most francophones reached the same conclusion they had earlier with Wilfrid Laurier and Louis St. Laurent: "After all, here's a French Canadian who has become prime minister. Why not give him a fair chance?"[32]

Given the chance, Trudeau was exultant. He waited for Stanfield to concede, which he did with his usual grace. Unfortunately, John Diefenbaker chose to make a national address as well, where he declared the result a "calamitous disaster for the Conservative Party" and seemed to relish the deluge that had come after him. Trudeau ignored Diefenbaker's remarks and praised both Stanfield and Douglas. Then he declared: "For me it was a great discovery. . . . We now know more about this country, which we did not know two months ago. . . . The election has been fought in a mood of optimism and confidence in our future. . . . We must intensify the opportunities for learning about each other."[33] He was unexpectedly solemn but clearly pleased. He knew his time had come.

But what exactly did "we" know? What had Canadians learned about themselves and their new prime minister? Trudeau's personal appeal to the young and the francophones was obvious. Interestingly, he increased Liberal support among men (from 39 percent in 1965 to 45 percent in 1968) more than among women (from 43 percent to 48 percent). As with John Kennedy, men apparently admired both Trudeau's manly courage and his sex appeal to women.[34] Whatever the psychological causes, both opponents and supporters gave Trudeau credit for the victory; Stanfield and Douglas later said that the die was cast against them when Pearson resigned and Winters' campaign failed. Nevertheless,

John Duffy, in his history of Canada's decisive elections, omits 1968 because, he argues, the election confirmed existing trends and created no dramatic rupture from the past.[35]

Trudeau himself minimized the extent of change that his government represented. His outline of the Just Society was faint in detail yet familiar in its references. He was, in his own words, a "pragmatist" among Canadians, who were "accustomed to deal with their problems in a pragmatic way." The erstwhile socialist and adolescent revolutionary bluntly rebuked an Ontario crowd: "You know that no government is a Santa Claus, and I thought as I came down the street and saw all the waves and the handshakes that I'd remind you that Ottawa is not a Santa Claus." There would be no great programs, his government would not raise taxes, and he would make no rash promises.[36]

Duffy is correct to suggest continuity and to point out how the foundations of Canadian electoral behaviour persisted in 1968. The Liberals were becoming ever more the urban, immigrant, and francophone party throughout the 1960s, while the Conservatives became more rural and anglophone. Unlike the historic elections of 1896, 1925–26, and 1957–58, no fundamental realignment and no great dividing issues characterized the election of 1968. Indeed, journalists struggled to find issues that separated the parties, especially in English Canada. In another sense, however, both Duffy and Trudeau misled by minimizing the change that Trudeau represented. Stanfield, Winters, or Hellyer would have been very different prime ministers, and if elected, any of them would have produced a very different Canada.

The significance of the 1968 election derives partly from Trudeau's unique personality, but the major distinction comes from the particular moment when the election occurred and the manner in which Trudeau reflected it: the spring of 1968.[37] The images endure: Paris aflame; the Tet offensive in Vietnam; Robert Kennedy and Martin Luther King gunned down; police clubbing Harvard students; the Beatles and the Stones; and the liberation of the Prague Spring. Into this collage, Trudeau, defiant on the platform and elegant on the diving board, fits perfectly. Pierre Trudeau's style mimicked the times—and forecast a new Canada.

—

NEW WINE IN NEW BOTTLES

The year 1968 was "the epicenter of a shift, of a fundamental change, the birth of our postmodern media-driven world," Mark Kurlansky writes in his history of the "year that rocked the world." "That is why the popular music of the time, the dominant expression of popular culture in the period, has remained relevant to successive generations of youth. It was the beginning of the end of the cold war and the dawn of a new geopolitical order. Within that order, the nature of politics and of leaders changed. The Trudeau approach to leadership, where a figure is known by style rather than substance, has become entrenched." Although American historians rarely cast their glance northward, Trudeau intrigued Kurlansky, who notes that "in a time of extremism, [Trudeau] was a moderate with a lefty style, but his exact positions were almost impossible to establish." Yet in the spring of 1968, while Americans contemplated the choice of Richard Nixon or Hubert Humphrey, Canada became "a weirdly happy place." Trudeau appealed, as Robert Fulford wrote forty years later, "to citizens who lived through a time of fractious partisanship and . . . [yearned] for a new era, with fresh energy and fresh optimism." In those times, style truly matters.[1]

In interpreting the Trudeau phenomenon, Kurlansky turns to Marshall McLuhan's prediction that politicians will abdicate in favour of image because the image will be more powerful than the politician could ever be. Trudeau's success in 1968 reflected and responded to broader forces within Canadian and North American politics and society. The choice of Trudeau as Liberal leader and then as prime minister arose from the transformation of politics caused by television. In the mid-sixties, news blended with entertainment to take the main stage in programs such as *This Hour Has Seven Days*, which taunted and mocked political leaders in songs by Dinah Christie and interviews by hosts Patrick Watson and Laurier LaPierre. When the CBC cancelled the program in May 1966, the public outcry led Prime Minister Pearson to appoint an inquiry.* It concluded that the producers had pushed the boundaries of journalistic traditions, ethics, and good taste, but in the late sixties, those boundaries were no longer fixed.[2] Colour television came quickly to Canada just as *Seven Days* ended, and the 1968 campaign, like the dramatic youth explosions in Paris, Prague, and New York, gained vibrancy and immediacy not only

---

* Trudeau had interviewed to be one of the hosts, but LaPierre got the position. Carroll Guérin, who was aware how much Trudeau wanted the position, commiserated with him: "What a pity the TV thing proved to be a flop. It goes to show that our apprehensions were not without reason. It is a pity that entertainment is placed prior to ideas — but what can you expect from Toronto?" On Trudeau and the CBC, see Eric Koch, *Inside Seven Days: The Show That Shook the Nation* (Scarborough: Prentice-Hall, 1986), 45; and Carroll Guérin to Trudeau, Dec.16, 1964, TP MG26 02, vol. 49, file 8, LAC. The significance of the program is recognized by the Chicago-based Museum of Broadcast Communication. Its appraisal of the program, written by William O. Gilsdorf,

because of their varied hues but also because of hand-held cameras and other technical advances.

Television was merciless for the bald and awkward Robert Stanfield. Trudeau cruelly mocked him as he told the press before a deliberately clumsy dive that he was doing a Stanfield imitation. Media historian Paul Rutherford concludes that Trudeau could not have "shot to stardom without television carrying his charisma into the homes of Canadians." His rapid ascent to power was the first indication of its "fast-forward effect" on politics. Although Trudeau's appearance and skills fitted TV especially well, the new importance of the medium meant that all political campaigns changed dramatically, as did the talents required of those who served political leaders.[3] Their entourage swelled, eventually including makeup artists, voice trainers, and professional direc-tors. Although earlier politicians such as Franklin Roosevelt and Adolf Hitler had used mass communications, these tools became essential for success in the 1960s when presidents had to be "sold," to use Joe McGinniss's famous term. Canada, George Radwanski shrewdly noted, "was peculiarly hungry for a leader like Trudeau." Its mood "was conditioned by nearly a decade of jealousy . . . [of] the presidency of John Kennedy," and it now sought a leader like

---

is lukewarm. While praising its technical innovations and creativity, Gilsdorf notes that "the *Seven Days* team often seemed to achieve the goal of involving the viewer in the emotion and actuality of television while innovating on and stretching the conventions of TV journalism. It is also clear that the team was often seduced by the power of television to embarrass guests or sensationalize issues through manipulative set-ups like the KKK interview. The series often entertained, perhaps more than it informed, foreshadowing the current concern and debate over the line between news and entertainment," http://www.museum.tv/archives/etv/T/htmlT/thishourhas/thishourhas.htm.

him: one who mastered television, surrounded himself with beautiful and intelligent women, communicated crisply, and conveyed excitement and energy.[4] In short, Canadians wanted a leader unlike Lester Pearson, Mackenzie King, and Bob Stanfield.

—

These were new times, and Trudeau's team fitted right into them. Gordon Gibson, who had played a major part in the leadership campaign, recalled the extraordinary energy around Trudeau that attracted brilliant and exciting people to him. His campaign team and his staff were relatively new acquaintances, collaborators who shared his distrust of Quebec's new nationalism—which he believed had replaced blind loyalty to the Church with an even more dangerous faith in the state. While rejecting separatism and nationalism, Trudeau embraced contemporary social science, with its postwar confidence in planning, rationality, and the rule of law. Born on the streets of Paris and in the lecture halls of the London School of Economics in the forties, Trudeau's "socialism" now possessed the qualities of the liberal salons of New York, where Harvard economist and Democratic Party activist John Kenneth Galbraith's still gentle critiques of American capitalism held sway and Le Monde's editorial writer (and Trudeau acquaintance) Claude Julien praised both North American technology and the welfare state.

In the new environment of the sixties, Trudeau's "functional politics," a term he had defined in the fifties as a rejection of ideological approaches, changed to fit with the secularism and nationalism that flowed vigorously into politics, economics, and the arts. Trudeau benefited politically from this surge of Canadian nationalism even as he was wary of its nature: "Nationalism will eventually have to be rejected as a principle of sound government," he wrote. "In the world of tomorrow, the expression 'banana republic' will not refer to independent fruit-growing nations but to countries where formal independence has been given priority over the cybernetic revolution. In such a world, the state — if it is not to be outdistanced by its rivals — will need political instruments which are sharper, stronger, and more finely controlled than anything based on mere emotionalism: such tools will be made up of advanced technology and scientific investigation, as applied to the fields of law, economics, social psychology, international affairs, and other areas of human relations; in short, if not a pure product of reason, the political tools of the future will be designed and appraised by more rational standards than anything we are currently using in Canada today." Canada was on a "collision course," he warned, and only "cold, unemotional rationality" held promise if the country was to avert disaster.[5]

In the same month that Trudeau wrote these comments, May 1964, he joined several other Quebec intellectuals in publishing "Pour une politique fonctionnelle" in *Cité libre*. Michael Pitfield, an Ottawa-based civil servant, translated the essay as "An Appeal for Realism in Politics" for *The Canadian Forum*, which left-leaning English Canadian intellectuals avidly read.[6] Trudeau and his co-authors, attracted to the possibilities of contemporary social science, were repelled by the bluster of Diefenbaker, the emotionalism of René Lévesque, and the inadequacy of the anglophone Ottawa mandarins to deal with the crisis of Quebec.

One of this manifesto's authors, Marc Lalonde, Pearson's chief policy adviser since 1965, was central to Trudeau's rise to power. He was, Peter C. Newman wrote, "the first of a new breed of brilliant French-Canadian technocrats to move into a position of high influence within the Ottawa hierarchy." Lalonde increasingly shared with Trudeau his concerns about the disorganization of Pearson's office, the chaos of his Cabinet, and the lack of strategic planning in Ottawa. Pitfield, who worked in the Privy Council Office in the mid-1960s, echoed these concerns about the crisis of

Canadian confederation and Pearson's ability to cope with it. Like Trudeau, both these men, born and educated in Montreal, were bilingual, with disciplined work habits and Cartesian minds.[7] They were also Liberal outsiders with Conservative roots.

Ramsay Cook, the editor of *The Canadian Forum* at the time the article was published, was an active New Democrat. In 1968, however, he, too, left his traditional political affiliation and supported Trudeau's political quest. Along with many other academics, he stepped down from the ivory tower, joined a constituency association, encouraged his students to become politically active, and published articles brimming with enthusiasm for Pierre Trudeau. Cook became a speechwriter for the Trudeau campaign, as did the elegant and perceptive writer Jean Le Moyne. They were joined by Roger Rolland, who had shared in some of Trudeau's most outrageous pranks in the forties, fought with him against Duplessis in the fifties, and promoted him at Radio-Canada (where he worked) in the sixties. Two other young academics who signed the manifesto were also important in shaping Trudeau's politics. They were the Breton brothers: Albert, an economist, and Raymond, a sociologist. Trudeau had met them in the early 1960s at the Université de Montréal, where they joined the Groupe de recherche sociale, founded by Fernand Cadieux, yet another prominent intellectual who took an active part in Trudeau's campaign.

It is significant that so many of those who now clustered around Trudeau had little previous political involvement—the newcomers, in fact, wore their inexperience and lack of Liberal background as a badge. Among the young academics and professionals who animated Trudeau's quest for the leadership and the first days of government, only Gordon Gibson had strong Liberal ties, though they were excused because they were inherited: his father, Gordon Sr. had been a Liberal member of the British Columbia legislature in the 1950s. Otherwise, Trudeau's supporters took pride in their recent conversions, and like most converts, they became passionate about the one cause they shared: Pierre.

While the Bretons and Cook remained in academic life after June 1968, Lalonde, Pitfield, Gibson, and Cadieux became a central part of Trudeau's personal staff when he took office. Other influential members included the British-born Montreal physicist Jim Davey, who shared Pitfield's fascination with planning and "scientific" approaches to policy making, and Tim Porteous, who had met Trudeau in Africa in 1957 but was best known for his role in McGill University's *My Fur Lady*, a satirical revue that went on to become a national hit. Prominent Montreal lawyer and academic Carl Goldenberg became a constitutional adviser, as did Ivan Head, a former External Affairs officer, who in 1963 had joined the law faculty of the University of Alberta. He took academic leave in 1967 to work for Trudeau and never returned.

Just as *My Fur Lady* mocked Canadian customs, Trudeau's staff and his new Cabinet shredded political traditions. They lacked party ties, were mostly from Quebec, and had little Ottawa experience. Lalonde and Pitfield had fretted about the absence of expertise on Quebec in Pearson's office and the difficulty of recruiting francophones to Ottawa, but things soon changed. Trudeau's office was much larger, bilingual, and thoroughly engrossed in Quebec politics. It reflected hope for the future, with little reference to Ottawa's past.

The Cabinet largely remained the one Trudeau had appointed after the convention, although some changes were necessary because of election losses (Maurice Sauvé) and others because of regional needs (the western provinces) and Trudeau's personal interests. Unlike the Office of the Prime Minister, the Cabinet had considerable political experience, yet it, too, was remarkably youthful, with twenty-two of its twenty-nine members under fifty. Several ministers were in their thirties, including two future prime ministers: Jean Chrétien (thirty-four) at Indian Affairs and Northern Development and John Turner (thirty-nine) at Justice, with crucial responsibility for continuing the reform of the Criminal Code begun by Trudeau. Trudeau appointed his newly elected former leadership opponent Eric Kierans as postmaster general—traditionally a minor patronage position but one that suddenly became critical because Canadian postal workers (along with almost all federal civil servants) had gained the right to strike and were about to take full advantage of it.

Trudeau also promoted Jean Marchand to Forestry and Rural Development—which was soon transformed into the key ministry of Regional Development—and he named the other "wise man," Gérard Pelletier, as secretary of state, responsible for the full range of government cultural policies. His old classmate Jean-Luc Pepin went to Industry, Trade, and Commerce—the most senior economic post ever held to that point by a francophone. The composition of this Cabinet allowed Trudeau to boast that he had brought French power to Canada—and he remained immensely proud of this achievement, even though it later became a political burden.

—

At the Cabinet's first meeting on July 8, Trudeau described how it would operate. There would be structure, records, efficiency, confidentiality, and responsibility. After welcoming the new ministers in his curiously flat but strong voice, Trudeau was blunt about his demands. First, he said, "was the matter of Cabinet solidarity. The oaths of Cabinet Ministers were to be taken very seriously. Policies would be hammered out in the Cabinet, and outside the Cabinet there must be complete solidarity. This was a very strict rule; if a Minister did not agree with a decision taken he had a right, and indeed a duty, to resign." The first sign of any erosion of Cabinet solidarity would cause concern: "Ministers' appointments were not forever, and it was possible to envisage movement out of the Cabinet

as well as into it." Trudeau was clear: the ministers served at his discretion. Recalling the damaging "leaks" of the Pearson years, he set
down the rule for the new Cabinet members: "If the source of any
leak of Cabinet information would be identified, the action taken
would have to be merciless." At the end of the meeting, he circulated a "work program" for the summer, which included an inten-
sive series of meetings until July 20. After that, the ministers could
take "three weeks' holidays" before work resumed in mid-August.[8]
Trudeau, the dilettante, now seemed a distant memory. The
Liberals had a leader, a majority government, and a mandate.

Trudeau and, more particularly, Lalonde, Davey, and Pitfield
had blamed the chaotic character of Pearson's Cabinet on its lack
of structure. Acting on their advice and his own growing fascination with systems analysis and futurology, Trudeau set out to
impose order on the tradition-encrusted system of Cabinet government. In truth, the system badly needed change as modern
communications, new technologies (especially photocopying),
and the expansion of government services had overwhelmed the
world that Mackenzie King's mandarins had carefully constructed.
In the mid-1960s the filing system that had developed in the 1940s
collapsed under the weight of expanded government functions
and mountains of paper. "When I came on the scene," Trudeau
wrote, "the volume of mail increased fourfold. . . . [It] meant I had
to respond to such uncontrollable situations by multiplying my
staff." He added that most governments based on the British parliamentary system, including Conservative Margaret Thatcher's,
expanded dramatically to meet the new challenges. Indeed,
Pitfield, Trudeau's chief architect of government machinery,
struck up a close friendship with Burke Trend, who bore the same
responsibility in the United Kingdom.[9] But Trudeau went further
than the British and undertook a thorough restructuring of the
Cabinet and caucus system. The controversial effects of those
reforms shaped Canadian government for decades.

First, he established "regional desks" within the Prime Minister's Office, creating a countervailing force to the ministers themselves. The notion of opposing forces increasingly attracted Trudeau in the sixties and deeply influenced his approach to government organization and politics generally. Next he expanded the role of the government caucus and permitted it to debate legislation before it was presented to Parliament. Caucus members could confront ministers directly—and they frequently did. He began a process through which MPs obtained funds for constituency offices and acquired greater office resources and support for family travel. Although the initial impulse was his call for "participatory democracy," the changes later responded to his need to keep MPs satisfied while power became more centralized. The centralization occurred through a system of eight Cabinet committees, the most significant being "Priorities and Planning," which Trudeau chaired. It served as the Cabinet's coordinator, and ministers were obliged to follow the priorities it set. In a significant break with the past, Cabinet committees could make decisions, and within committees, individual ministers debated the policies of their colleagues. At Cabinet itself, only controversial or major items came forward for discussion, and ministers had to defend them against their colleagues and the informed and sometimes intense questioning of Trudeau himself. Ministerial assistants could not attend Cabinet committee meetings, but public servants could. The result was a tough and demanding process that sought to impose consensus on ministers and clarity on decisions.

Later appraisals of the changes have been largely unfavourable—reflecting the often caustic comments of Cabinet members of the time. "It reinforced the weak and frustrated the strong," John Turner grumbled. Veterans Allan MacEachen and Paul Martin found the Cabinet meetings interminable and ineffective as tools of government—"the enemy of political common sense." The experienced civil servant, prime ministerial adviser, and Newfoundland politician Jack Pickersgill, whom many regarded as the shrewdest political analyst of his generation, "deplored" Trudeau's "lack of interest in good administration and his poor judgment of the suitability of men and women for membership in the Cabinet and high administrative posts"—an implicit criticism of Davey and Pitfield. The most extensive academic study of the attempt to bring a systems approach to Canadian government, by Dr. Jason Churchill, also concludes that expectations were not met and that achievements fell far short of what had been promised when the spirited band around Trudeau set out to remake Canadian government. Gordon Robertson, the experienced bureaucrat who became Trudeau's first secretary to the Cabinet, admits that the system limited certain ministers: he recalls how John Turner once exploded in a conversation with him, saying it was impossible to handle the Finance ministry "with twenty-three God-damned ministers of Finance." As for the systems analysis, Robertson "never discerned any advantage in any of it." Even Trudeau later concluded, "We may have gone a bit overboard at times."[10]

Perhaps—but governments in those times badly needed reform. Trudeau's attempts responded to the challenges of complexity that overwhelmed officials and politicians in democratic societies throughout the West. The political system, and participation in it, had lost their allure for Kennedy's "new generation" of Americans. In partial response, they turned initially to protest and even violence, and then inward to drugs or social movements such as feminism and sexual liberation. Trudeau's reforms of Cabinet and caucus, along with the many task forces, white papers, and discussion groups packaged as "participatory democracy," attempted to reinvigorate public space and citizen involvement. The intent was to create a mass party in which caucus members played leadership roles. Postwar optimism about the managerial revolution, Keynesian budgeting, and the welfare state was quickly eroding, and critics of the liberal consensus were increasingly influential, not only on the left with Noam Chomsky and Theodor Adorno but also on the right with Edward Banfield and Milton Friedman. The sixties began with a celebration of the long prosperity that followed the creation of the activist state in the forties. John F. Kennedy's New Frontier, Lyndon Johnson's Great Society, Harold Wilson's "white heat" of technological revolution, and late in the decade, Pierre Trudeau's Just Society all captured the confidence of liberal politicians committed to activist intervention for the general good.

The dream began to die with Vietnam and race riots on the one hand and slowing productivity growth and unsuccessful, expensive social programs on the other. "After 1968," American historian James Patterson writes, "there was no turning back to the higher hopes that liberals had had in 1964 and early 1965."[11] The backlash set in, and Americans lost faith in politicians and political action. Canada, characteristically, followed later, and the delay was fortunate for Trudeau. It meant that many able and brilliant young people followed him to Ottawa and formed a corps of remarkable public servants. One of them, Maureen O'Neil, later recalled the sense of excitement and experiment and the "tremendous energy" that drew her to public service in those years. Trudeau's Ottawa was very distant from what American historian Rick Perlstein has called "Nixonland," where public debate was rooted in anger and resentment and public service was demeaned by left and right.[12] Detailed studies of the 1968 election reveal that support for Trudeau's Liberals "varied directly with religiosity, moral liberalism, interest in foreign affairs, greater importance being attached to the central government," and a "general optimism about the future and economic expectations."[13] In Canada it remained the Liberal hour, if only briefly.

—

Trudeau's insistence on "pragmatism," his refusal to be "Santa Claus," and his vague description of the "Just Society" betrayed his own growing doubts about some parts of the Liberal legacy. Already the Pearson government had delayed the introduction of medicare because of economic pressures. In January 1968, as new health care costs loomed, Mitchell Sharp, the finance minister, had warned that Ottawa's resources were limited and that the provinces must consequently adopt policies of restraint. As estimates of the costs of medicare continued to rise, the quarrel between the provincial and federal governments over payment intensified. These differences mingled intimately with the ongoing discussions about constitutional reform. Soon after the election, the new finance minister, Edgar Benson, announced that the federal government would follow policies of restraint and that the expansion of government must come to an end. Trudeau warned his Cabinet that it was not enough to bring forward programs; their costs must always be understood as well. Montreal businessman and retired brigadier-general Charles "Bud" Drury, the secretary of the Treasury Board, gained early prominence in Trudeau's government as the enforcer of fiscal discipline, and he quickly became one of Trudeau's most trusted advisers. Drury's advice habitually erred on the side of caution, and Trudeau would find his arguments increasingly convincing.

In Trudeau's capacious mind, enthusiasm was always tempered by doubt, particularly as the social spending commitments of the sixties not only endured but grew. Beyond the closed Cabinet doors, however, the summer of 1968 remained a time for celebration—a political "honeymoon," even for many of Trudeau's campaign critics. In *Le Devoir*, Claude Ryan praised the new Cabinet, especially the strong Quebec representation, declaring that Trudeau had become "a calm leader, sure of himself, conscious of his power but resolved to employ it with moderation." He was cautious, yet aware of the "great desire for renewal which was the source of his success."[14] Trudeau no doubt smiled wryly: he knew the honeymoon would be brief.

With his popularity at its peak, Trudeau left on July 21 for a tour of Canada's Arctic—a region that had always fascinated him and had never before been visited by a prime minister. Travelling almost fifteen thousand kilometres—first in a Jetstar and then in a DC-3, an Otter, and a helicopter—he traversed the vast northern lands in a mere eight days. He went with a party of ten, including his brother, Charles; R.J. Orange, the MP for the Northwest Territories; and *New Yorker* writer Edith Iglauer.* Trudeau camped out on Ellesmere Island, attended church in Fort Chimo, fished for Arctic char, and even danced with Inuit "go-go girls" at Frobisher Bay (now Iqaluit). The journey strengthened the image of his intimacy with nature and the Canadian frontier. That image reflected the reality of his fascination with the wilds but also had

---

* When she sought an interview for her *New Yorker* profile, Iglauer had met Roméo LeBlanc, Trudeau's press secretary, and was told Trudeau was too busy to see her. She then learned about the trip from LeBlanc and told him she had written a book on the North. She sent the book to Trudeau, who asked Gordon Robertson, a former deputy minister of northern affairs, if she should go. Robertson apparently replied, "Take her with you. You won't be sorry." He wasn't. Iglauer was an engaging companion and wrote a fine sketch. On one occasion, at Cassiar Asbestos Mine, Trudeau rode a motorbike expertly in circles. Iglauer asked Charles, "What was it like to be his younger brother?" He laughed and replied, "Pierre always had to have the last word." She used these words as the opening for her article. Iglauer in Nancy Southam, ed., *Pierre: Colleagues and Friends Talk about the Trudeau They Knew* (Toronto: McClelland and Stewart, 2005), 81–82; and Iglauer, "Prime Minister / Premier Ministre," *New Yorker*, July 5, 1969, 36–60.

romantic appeal in the apartments of Canada's expanding cities. In an interview as the frantic trip ended, Trudeau claimed that the "Eskimos" were less "miserable" than they had been when he encountered them on canoe trips a decade earlier. Still, he concluded, the "North" was far from an economic "takeoff."[15]

As usual, Trudeau's travels and antics dominated the front pages that summer as the ministers in Ottawa busily put together their programs for the autumn. The records of their deliberations reveal much unfinished business from the Pearson years—notably, the Official Languages bill, the amendment of the Criminal Code begun by Trudeau himself in 1967, and the reform of Parliament. To these items were added a series of reviews, the most significant of which were in the areas of defence and foreign policy and, separately, taxation policy.[16] The tax review was needed to prepare a response to the massive Carter Commission report of 1967, which had recommended a radical restructuring of taxation in Canada. It immediately caused controversy in its emphasis on equity in the sense of fairness and the integration of all income, including capital gains, which Canada did not then tax. "A buck is a buck is a buck," it famously declared, to the despair of Bay Street and some parts of Main Street. Benson began to work on a specific program based on the Carter recommendations, but the task, as we shall see, took several years, caused enormous controversy, and resulted in a political firestorm late in the mandate of Trudeau's first government.[17]

The summer's end brought another foray into Canadian affairs on the part of French president Charles de Gaulle, who on September 9 compared Canada to Nigeria, which was in the middle of a bloody civil war. When asked whether the election of a francophone changed matters in Canada, he replied, "Definitely not." De Gaulle and his officials knew and despised Trudeau— "l'adversaire de la chose française au Canada"—and the contempt was mutual. Trudeau acidly rebuked de Gaulle on September 11 and went on to attack the activities of Philippe Rossillon, a French official working in Canada under a France-Canada cultural accord, as those of a "secret agent." His suspicions intensified when some French officials close to de Gaulle intrigued to support separatism and nationalism in Canada.[18] The Rossillon affair, which centred on this official's activities with Franco-Manitobans and Acadians, paralleled the struggle between Canada and France to exert economic and diplomatic influence within the Francophonie, an international francophone organization, and so advance the very separate national interests of Canada and France. The relationship between France and Quebec was, therefore, a central issue in Trudeau's first two years as prime minister.

Later, the shrewd political analyst Jim Coutts correctly pointed to the weakness of these early years. Trudeau, in rhetoric and belief, wanted to shatter the old system of political power brokers, and he dreamed of a new politics that was "participatory"—where citizens would come together with their leaders to choose reason over passion in the shaping of public policy. But Trudeau soon learned that citizens "do not want to participate in a national debate in which they have to find their own way." Rather, captured by his charisma, they expected him to lead, not debate. Trudeau's attempt to have public reviews and study groups examine "subjects from top to bottom" ended with "few initiatives" and considerable frustration. Most of these exercises "were counter-productive, squandering government resources and sapping the creative energies of both elected politicians and the public service." Trudeau would have been wiser, Coutts said, to have concentrated on four or five "very specific ideas" at most. Instead, in its first years, the government established a study group that brought forward twelve priorities—far too many even for a new majority government. Ironically, Trudeau was most successful not in his new initiatives but in ensuring the continuance of the rich legacy of his predecessor.[19]

That legacy meant that three central issues dominated Canadian politics in the fall of 1968: the Constitution and Quebec; the reform of social legislation to reflect the new Canada emerging in the 1960s; and Canada's role in the world as the Vietnam War and the rise of Europe profoundly altered international relations. There was also the need to adjust fiscally to the new demands on the federal treasury caused by the expansion of government. In the case of the Constitution and Quebec, Trudeau took a direct hand. He chaired the Cabinet committee formed to deal with federal-provincial relations, and his closest assistants devoted most of their attention to the issue: Marchand skillfully managed the Quebec Liberals; Pelletier gracefully gained entry to hostile editorial boardrooms and university seminars; and Marc Lalonde used his lawyer's sharp eye for detail and his Jesuit-trained mind for organization. Later, other members of Trudeau's Cabinets complained that a separate "Quebec group" had captured the constitutional issue. Although others, notably Gordon Robertson in the early years, penetrated this group, the nature of the constitutional question meant that inevitably there was a tendency to discuss it within the confines of a small group of old and close friends. Their closeness was initially a source of strength for Trudeau and his government, but later it became a source of weakness.[20]

—

Trudeau's personal life was a perpetual source of public and press interest, and in the spring of 1969, many saw him as the "No. 1 catch." *Chatelaine*, the leading magazine for women in Canada, ran numerous features on Trudeau, including one with the direct title "Whom Should Trudeau Marry?" The article was adorned with photographs of "some past and recent dates," notably the winsome young Montreal actress Louise Marleau, who had played Juliet at Stratford's Shakespeare Festival in the summer. Local newspapers had wondered whether Ottawa's Romeo would kiss his Juliet when he visited the festival. He did. Interestingly, Marleau's sister, Huguette, was Trudeau's Conservative opponent in Mount Royal in the 1968 election. Other dates mentioned in the article included Jennifer Rae and Carleton University professor Madeleine Gobeil. The article kept up the tease by submitting Trudeau's characteristics to a computer and asking what type of woman would suit the prime minister. The answer was trivial, but more interesting was the comment that "Trudeau requires extensive and high compatibility in a woman because he has lived for half a century; he has a distinctive (bachelor) lifestyle; he is more rigid and conservative than liberal for a number of reasons: his mother's rather than father's influence in mid-teens; his need for control and self-discipline; his basic shyness; the need to tame his impulses and temper. He does not seek completion with another, so that his tolerance for others and for nearness is low. . . . He is basically a loner."[21]

Neither Trudeau nor his friends would have disagreed with this perceptive computer. He was most certainly a loner, though he often appeared at theatres, in restaurants, on ski hills, and in the driveway of 24 Sussex Drive with many different but always beautiful women. The times, too, were changing—most dramatically in the traditional patterns of courtship throughout the West. Trudeau had dated widely and continually in the fifties, a decade when, as the novelist Ian MacEwan writes, "to be young was a social encumbrance, a mark of irrelevance, a faintly embarrassing condition for which marriage was the beginning of a cure." Like many men, Trudeau welcomed the greater sexual openness that suddenly blossomed, but Carroll Guérin recalls that there were limits to his embrace of new ways: pangs of jealously affected him when he learned that she had begun to date others in England at the end of the sixties, even though he declared he was not a jealous type.[22]

Immediately after the Liberal leadership convention, Trudeau got in touch with Jennifer Rae, and they began to date that very week. For several months they "went to movies, out to dinner, occasionally to cocktail parties, formal dinners, and public events like the Montreal Grand Prix." He was "inventive, passionate, and generous-spirited as a lover" if not so generous with funds. Frequently, Jennifer or the chauffeur had to buy the movie tickets, and the only gift Pierre ever gave her was a pair of old tennis shoes, which had obviously belonged to another girlfriend. They spent many weekends at Harrington Lake—Trudeau's romantic retreat throughout his prime-ministerial tenure.

One day in February 1969, they were in the kitchen preparing smoked oysters on wheat thins as an hors d'oeuvre before a dinner for four. Jennifer prepared the plate and squeezed some lemon juice over the oysters. Trudeau exploded, demanding to know what she was doing, and an "awful, between-clenched-teeth-so-the-guests-don't-hear argument" began. It was all about freedom to put lemon on one's own oysters: "The reason I am irritated is that each person has the right to decide whether he or she wants to have lemon juice on the oysters," Pierre fumed. "You have taken that right away." The relationship did not last much beyond that evening, and Jennifer soon married someone else. For Pierre, a most intriguing partner soon appeared from the south.[23]

Barbra Streisand and Elliott Gould, two American cinema giants, separated on February 13, 1969, just before Barbra tied for best actress at the Academy Awards for her performance in *Funny Girl*.* Although Elliott sat beside her at the gala on April 14 when

---

* The co-winner was Katharine Hepburn for her performance in *The Lion in Winter*. Barbra tripped on her pantsuit as she walked on stage and discovered later that the bright television lights seemed to make her striking outfit transparent.

she heard the good news, the marriage had come to an end. Her major interest, however, had become Pierre Trudeau, whom she had met at the London premiere of *Funny Girl* the previous fall. Before the gala, and knowing that her relationship with Gould had ended, Streisand and her close friend Cis Corman had been looking through the current *Life* magazine. As she explained, "We were jokingly checking if there might be a suitable candidate somewhere in the pages who would be right for me." They spotted a photograph of Trudeau wearing a trenchcoat and sandals and were immediately intrigued—he was so different from Richard Nixon, Spiro Agnew and other American politicians of the time. Shortly thereafter, she and Trudeau were placed at Princess Margaret's table at the *Funny Girl* premiere. "He was," Streisand later said, "everything my imagination had promised and more." Forty years later, she recalls Trudeau as a tantalizing blend of "Marlon Brando and Napoleon." Nevertheless, she refused to dance with him that night because she knew that a prime minister and a star would attract immediate attention. Cis Corman gladly obliged and appeared in the tabloids the next day as a Trudeau "flame."

Streisand and Trudeau's mutual celebrity quickly bonded them, and they both possessed an intensity and electricity that attracted all around them. They went public immediately as Canadian officials fretted about the open affair between the prime minister and a recently separated Jewish American who was a very liberal Democrat. At the very least, President Nixon would certainly not approve. Moreover, rumours of Barbra's fame, flamboyance, and perfectionism—apparent in everything she wore, did, and sang—made her risky in the eyes of many, who worried about what would happen if the affair broke up publicly and angrily, as celebrity affairs often did. Trudeau's top advisers met and debated the issue. Finally, Tim Porteous exploded: "We're debating whether Pierre should date the hottest star in the world. My God, this is political gold!"[24]

It's doubtful whether his advisers could have stopped Trudeau, but he went with their blessing for a weekend in New York with Streisand soon after. On the Friday evening they dined at Casa Brasil on the Upper East Side, at a small, intimate table, and then went to Raffles, the elite discotheque at the Sherry-Netherland Hotel. Their relationship was very romantic, and the next day they did not emerge from Streisand's apartment at all. On the Sunday, however, they reappeared as a glamorous couple at the theatre as the paparazzi swarmed around them. On subsequent meetings, they sometimes ate at a Chinese restaurant, where Trudeau particularly enjoyed the large snails. They talked easily about architecture, politics, and their different worlds. In Pierre, Barbra saw the qualities of her adored father, who was also highly intellectual and thoroughly athletic. In January 1970, after filming *The Owl and the Pussycat*, Streisand came to Ottawa. The event overheated the capital, which was then in the middle of its worst winter in memory. Bedecked in furs and with Cis Corman as her chaperone, Barbra's presence was royal in its grandeur, press coverage, and reception. She attended Question Period in the House of Commons, where the Speaker acknowledged her presence as Trudeau beamed up at the gallery. When the time came for her to depart, Trudeau quickly left a meeting, ran to her limousine, and bade a short farewell with hands joined and eyes intensely linked. On the evening of January 28, Barbra and Pierre attended the celebration of Manitoba's Centennial at the new National Arts Centre. They travelled separately to the hall, but once there, Pierre leapt from his limousine to open the door of hers and, arm in arm, they walked together into the theatre. She was resplendent in white mink, and reporters everywhere borrowed the famous opening line of *Funny Girl* to describe her: "You're gorgeous." There were restaurant sightings, amorous moments, and a fond farewell to make Ottawa, for once, more than a political capital.[25]

Trudeau and Streisand continued to date, and he invited her to Harrington Lake, where he impressed her by diving expertly into the chill of the lake. Trudeau approached the question of a lasting relationship, mentioned his desire for children, and basked in Streisand's extraordinary presence. But suddenly she found it "scary": her marriage had just ended; her career was gloriously successful; and however enchanting she found Trudeau, Canada was a foreign country. There were obviously many questions and problems. What about his Catholic religion and her Jewish beliefs? Must she learn French? What would happen to her film career if she was Trudeau's wife? She would never ask him to resign, strong liberal that she was. Her questions amounted to a refusal, and the affair came to an end later in the spring. They remained in contact and on friendly terms: Streisand sent a cable when the Quebec Liberals won the provincial election in April 1970 — "Congratulations for Quebec and Love for the Liberals" — and she sent birthday greetings in October later that year. "Amidst all of this chaos," she wrote, "I hope you have a happy birthday. My thoughts continue to be with you. Love, Barbra." The affection endured, and in Streisand's words, so did the exquisite memories of the way they were that winter of 1969–70: lovers who shared "mutual admiration and respect — and chemistry." They would meet again in November, and later in the eighties.[26]

Trudeau continued to date others, notably the engaging and intellectual Madeleine Gobeil, whom he had known for many years and who now taught French at Carleton University. She was often his close companion when he attended events at the National Arts Centre, and they sometimes spent evenings together, with dinner and conversation, at her home in Ottawa. He also continued to see Carroll Guérin, who was both amused and troubled by Trudeau's romantic escapades. Her remarkable ability to cut through his defensive layers meant that he was frequently drawn to her in crises, and while neither censorious nor possessive, she suspected that his addiction to serial dating could create such a crisis. And she was right.

Margaret Sinclair learned of the candlelit dinner with Barbra Streisand at 24 Sussex Drive in the morning papers on January 29, 1970. Furious, she slammed down the phone when Pierre asked her out after Barbra had left. "Go back to your American actresses," she screamed into the receiver. She had good reason to feel betrayed. They had begun dating in August 1969, when Trudeau asked her out during a visit to Vancouver after she'd returned from a torrid love affair with the young Frenchman Yves Lewis. She had chosen Yves over Pierre in Tahiti and then enjoyed a "hippie's" life in Morocco, where she sampled promiscuity and drugs. When Trudeau called her at home, Margaret hesitantly accepted his invitation and then, with the help of her mother and sisters, she turned the "flower child into a Barbie doll" in frenzied preparations for the date.*

Accompanied by two plainclothes officers, Margaret and Pierre dined at the Grouse's Nest, a touristy restaurant with compensating spectacular views of Vancouver. Their initial nervousness dissipated as Margaret enthralled Pierre with tales of Yves's time at Berkeley, where he had stashed hand grenades and

---

* Margaret's father, Jimmy Sinclair, seems to have welcomed the romance. He wrote to his former Cabinet colleague and Margaret's godfather, Doug Abbott, in February 1969 that of his children, Margaret was "the best scholar of the lot but has been very leftish." She had become interested in Trudeau and wanted to attend the Liberal convention for that reason. He noted that the family had gone to Tahiti at Christmas and "that's where . . . [Margaret and her sisters] met Trudeau and developed such a crush on him!" Sinclair to Abbott, Feb. 28, 1969, Abbott Papers MG 32 B6, vol. 4, LAC.

weapons while preparing for revolution, and of her own life on the edge in Marrakesh. The ever-curious Trudeau was intrigued, and he encouraged Margaret to talk: "It is in his nature to be charming and complimentary to women," she recalled, "and, away from that sort of old-fashioned gallantry for so long, I had quite forgotten how beguiling" it could be. And he questioned her continually. They danced closely together, and in that emotional moment, Margaret forgot that Pierre was two years older than her mother. They talked effortlessly and with some excitement about religion and a spiritual experience, perhaps induced by drugs, that she had had in Morocco. The night ended with a suggestion that she leave Vancouver, where she was unhappy, and move east. She considered his idea of going to Ottawa, but essentially took pleasure in an evening where she was "not battling with a young man's ego." She didn't think about what prospects there might be for two such very different people: "one cerebral, clear-headed, rational, devout and almost fifty; the other confused, scatty, certain of only one thing and that was to avoid all possible formality and social responsibility, and barely twenty." With an uncertain future, that fall she did decide to move to Ottawa.[27]

Their romance bloomed after she took a job as a sociologist with the new Department of Manpower and Immigration. At Pierre's request, their meetings were secret. Margaret loathed her job but adored Pierre more and more. She found him youthful, willing to listen, and understanding of a young person's dreams. Her views gained support when those champions of youth, the Beatle John Lennon and his companion, Yoko Ono, called on Trudeau at his parliamentary office on December 23, 1969. Clad entirely in black and grounded in Canada because Lennon had broken American drug laws, the two celebrities spent fifty minutes with Trudeau—forty minutes more than booked. They emerged and told a gaggle of reporters that they were enthralled. When asked whether Trudeau was "beautiful," Lennon responded,

"I think he is." Yoko Ono had had doubts when she came, she confessed, but no longer: he was "more beautiful than we expected."
He was, Lennon declared, a man who could bring "peace" to the
world. With Trudeau's popularity on the wane and many Canadian
newspapers complaining that he was unimaginative in policy, these
unexpected endorsements possessed real political weight.[28]

—

During the election campaign, Trudeau had frequently spoken
about the need to re-evaluate Canadian foreign policy. He took
office at the moment when public support for America's war in
Vietnam had collapsed, and Canadian critics expected he would
end the ambiguities that had marked Paul Martin's policy toward
that war. Had he not attacked Lester Pearson in 1963 when the
"defrocked prince of peace" committed a future Liberal government to accept nuclear weapons as part of its commitment to
NATO and NORAD? Trudeau mused openly about those commitments while he campaigned and reiterated his belief that
Canada's foreign and defence policies needed "review." Volume
One of this biography revealed how Trudeau's views differed from
Pearson's during the golden age of Canadian diplomacy in the late
1940s and in the 1950s. He had opposed the Korean War and speculated about Canadian neutrality in the Cold War. Pearson,
Trudeau claimed, believed that the role of Canada was to interpret
"London to Washington & vice versa, as if they needed a despicable mouthpiece." As in so much else, Trudeau changed his mind
once he came to power, and most Canadians accepted that the
new prime minister now belonged in the mainstream.[29]

But the mainstream became highly turbulent in the late
1960s, and Trudeau kept some of his earlier sentiments. First, he
retained the view that the Department of External Affairs was an
"Anglo-Saxon" preserve, an opinion sustained by the research of

the Royal Commission on Bilingualism and Biculturalism. Second, he still felt uneasy about the weight of the "U.S.–U.K. axis" in Canadian foreign and defence policies. His opposition to nuclear weapons was fundamental, and membership in NATO meant that Canada was a member of an alliance committed to their use. His closest political allies, Marchand and Pelletier, were inclined toward neutralism, and as a journalist, Pelletier had expressed strong opposition to U.S. Asian policies in the early 1960s. In Trudeau's view, NATO had dominated Canadian international policy, and that domination was wrong.

Third, Trudeau had long since concluded that Soviet Communism was authoritarian, hidebound, and dangerous, but he detested the virulent anti-Communism often expressed by the American right. His frequent visits to Sweden piqued his interest in neutrality, yet he recognized that Canada's relationship with the United States made neutrality unrealistic. Fourth, in *Two Innocents in Red China*, Trudeau had ridiculed China's exclusion from international organizations and its non-recognition by many Western democracies, including Canada. It would be a mark of the "independent foreign policy" many Canadian intellectuals and journalists were demanding if the Canadian government broke with the Americans and others and recognized China.*

---

* When the book was republished in 1968, Trudeau added a preface indicating he was wary that his earlier words might have been provocative. He added an "all-purpose disclaimer": "If there are any statements in the book which can be used to prove that the authors are agents of the international Communist conspiracy, or, alternatively, fascist exploiters of the working classes, I am sure that my co-author, Jacques Hébert, who remains a private citizen, will be willing to accept entire responsibility for them." *Two Innocents in Red China*, trans. I.M. Owen (Toronto: Oxford University Press, 1961; repr., Vancouver: Douglas and McIntye, 2007), ix.

Finally, Trudeau's travels in Asia, Africa, and Latin America had left their mark on him. In his first major speech on foreign policy, in May 1968, he had spoken eloquently about the "Third World." Eventually, he declared, "the overwhelming threat to Canada will not come from foreign interests or foreign ideologies or even—with good fortune—foreign nuclear weapons." It would come from the "two-thirds of the people of the world who are steadily falling farther and farther behind in their search for a decent standard of living." Canada, he thought, should now turn to that neglected majority.[30]

Ivan Head, who had now begun to serve as Trudeau's principal foreign policy adviser, wrote that May foreign policy speech. Although formal appointment did not occur until 1970, Head's close presence to Trudeau immediately and correctly confirmed fears in the Department of External Affairs that its historic pre-eminence was threatened. Trudeau liked Head, who was also small of stature but physically robust, eager to debate, and quick to dissent. During the campaign he had written speeches and notes on foreign policy subjects for Trudeau that were often scathing. In the case of development assistance, for example, he bluntly claimed that earlier governments had "never set forth a clear-cut statement of policy on Canadian economic assistance programmes." As a result, Canadians were completely "confused."[31]

To complicate matters, Trudeau did not like Under-secretary of State Marcel Cadieux, the principal civil servant responsible for Canadian foreign policy, although their acquaintance was long, their backgrounds were similar, and they had worked together effectively in dealing with French interference in Canadian politics during the late Pearson years. The fiery Cadieux, however, had offended Trudeau when he told him in the late forties that he was completely unsuited for External Affairs and should not apply. A staunch Catholic with conservative beliefs, he had also angered Trudeau by his objection to one of Trudeau's homosexual friends and by his stern anti-Communism, which girded his fervent support of the Vietnam War and the NATO alliance. Despite their differences, Cadieux initially welcomed Trudeau's victory simply because he despaired of Paul Martin's indecisiveness and his ambiguity toward de Gaulle's policies in Canada. Gordon Robertson, whom he did admire, told him that Trudeau was "much to be preferred" to Pearson in Canada-France relations. The truce between the two old acquaintances was brief, however, and it broke once Trudeau appointed Head as an adviser, expanded Cabinet scrutiny of foreign policy, and announced that there would be a full review of that policy—despite a recent one conducted by the dean of Canadian diplomats, Norman Robertson. This review had generally approved of the current policies (ones that Cadieux had directed).[32]

Unexpectedly, foreign policy, a subject Trudeau claimed was not his primary interest, became the major topic of public debate during his first year in office. When Charles Ritchie, the Canadian high commissioner to Britain, returned to Ottawa in late summer, he found the "Establishment" uneasy and clucking "nervously." The worldly, reed-like Ritchie was the model for an enigmatic British double agent in a novel by his lover Elizabeth Bowen, *In the Heat of the Day*, and he was an anglophile with profound doubts about Canada's criticism of Britain during the Suez Crisis. Ritchie epitomized so much of what Trudeau disliked about External Affairs. When the seasoned diplomat saw Trudeau for the first time on August 29, he recorded the moment in this memorable way: "I turned, and it was Trudeau, looking like a modern version of the Scholar Gypsy in sandals and open-necked shirt, as if he had just blown in from Haunts of Coot and Hern. He is physically altogether slighter, lighter, smaller than his photographs suggest. His air of youth—or is it agelessness?—is preternatural in a man of forty-eight [sic]. . . . The manner is unaffected and instantly attractive; the light blue eyes ironical and amused, but they can change expression, and almost colour, to a chillier, cooler tone."

At that first meeting, Ritchie found Trudeau puzzling. The following day, however, ambiguities vanished as Trudeau began his meeting by asking whether Ritchie thought External Affairs was "really necessary." Ritchie justified the department but left believing that Trudeau "has got it into his head the Department is divorced from the real interests of Canada and is embarking on international projects which have no firm basis in Canadian needs." According to Ritchie, when External Affairs Minister Mitchell Sharp asked Cadieux about the "Swedish" option of neutrality, a favourite of Trudeau, Cadieux acidly replied that the department had "no expert on neutrality." Anti-NATO sentiment was strong, and the "British connection" was unpopular with the new crowd.[33]

Ritchie's shrewd and accurate observations proved the value of diplomacy, and his concern about NATO reflected his understanding of the difficulties of extracting Canada from the alliance, given the nation's centrality in East-West relations. Not surprisingly, the Departments of Defence and External Affairs responded negatively to Trudeau's demand for another full review. They presented papers for Cabinet that generally called for the status quo to remain, with a few minor changes in troop deployments and policy. Trudeau rejected the studies and told the departments to try again. They foolishly underestimated Trudeau's will and the extent to which outside criticism was affecting the government. Even Escott Reid, a former senior External Affairs official and principal architect of NATO, shared Trudeau's view that Canadian forces should be withdrawn from Europe and that military expenditure should be greatly reduced.[34] Trudeau later said that his opinions were affected by the rise of Europe, his antipathy to mindless anti-Communism, his concern for North-South questions, and not least, his friends, who tended to be intellectuals hostile to the Vietnam War and wary of the military. Even within the department, some shared those views.

Cadieux was probably unaware that the brilliant young foreign service officer Allan Gotlieb, with whom Trudeau and he had worked closely and well on the Canada-France issue, was deeply influencing Trudeau's questioning of the status quo. After Trudeau became prime minister, Gotlieb met with him often, warning him that Canada was overextended internationally, with peacekeepers scattered widely and its true interests poorly defined. The realistic Gotlieb struck a chord with Trudeau, who had spent some unhappy time at the United Nations in 1966, when he and another young MP, Donald Macdonald, openly dissented from the policies of Paul Martin on the Chinese admission issue. For too long, Trudeau declared, Canada had been the "helpful fixer," busily attending to quarrels in Cyprus, the Middle East, and elsewhere while ignoring the dangerous French-English crisis at home. Rather, Trudeau decided, interests (the promotion of Canadian trade and the involvement of Canadians in international activities) and values (the representation of a bilingual and bicultural liberal democratic society) must coincide. Under Pearson, they had not.[35]

Once Trudeau had rejected the first "review papers" by the departments, he asked Head to produce a "counter review." Head promptly created a "non-group" of young officers he favoured to carry out the task. Conflict between the two sides was inevitable. When External Affairs Minister Mitchell Sharp and National Defence Minister Léo Cadieux arrived for the meeting of the Cabinet committee on defence and foreign policy on March 26, 1969, they were startled to see not only their own departmental briefs but also a totally unanticipated "Canadian Defence Policy— A Study." This study, produced under Head's direction, proposed a drastic cut of 50 percent in the armed forces, greatly reduced commitments to NATO, an end to a nuclear role, and more emphasis on North America and peacekeeping. The meeting promptly adjourned, and an angry Cadieux called Trudeau and said he and Sharp would resign if the paper went forward to Cabinet. Trudeau withdrew the study, but in permitting Head to circulate it, he had clearly indicated the direction he sought.

The argument began in Cabinet, with two of its most articulate members, Donald Macdonald and Eric Kierans, ferociously supporting complete withdrawal from NATO. On the other side were Sharp and Cadieux, who were increasingly outraged by Trudeau's attitude. Far from stepping aside from foreign and defence policy, he had become directly involved. He startled both ministers at a December 9 meeting when he dismissed the notion of NATO as a deterrent and refused to accept that the Soviet Union, when it crushed the "Prague Spring" in August, represented a threat to Canada that required a Canadian military presence in Europe. A frustrated Sharp told Cadieux more than once that he was considering resigning.[36]

Sharp did not resign, but neither did Trudeau back down. Faced with a critical NATO meeting on future defence planning in April 1969, the government issued a statement on April 3 indicating that Canadian policy was under review. Trudeau told Léo Cadieux that the task force considering Canada's NATO contribution should provide "various options to the government on . . . the phased reduction of the size of the forces in Europe." Sharp, Cadieux, and Canadian representatives abroad no longer talked about the possibility of reduction but about its certainty while NATO's Canadian critics, such as Macdonald and Kierans, continued to urge complete withdrawal. Allies quickly reacted — the Germans with understandable annoyance, the British with little understanding, and the Americans critically, though with some appreciation of Canadian attitudes. The Americans were also dealing with economic pressures that made their own senior officials reconsider the extent of their country's commitment to prosperous Europe — particularly as they were also facing tremendous demands on their military in Southeast Asia. These reactions appear to have had little influence on Canadian policy, but when Maurice Couve de Murville, the French foreign minister in a government that had withdrawn from military participation in NATO, told Trudeau that he should be cautious in withdrawing from Europe too quickly, he apparently had some impact. Not surprisingly, Marcel Cadieux was appalled that a French minister had greater influence on Trudeau than Canada's senior official in foreign affairs. In the end, Canadian troops in Europe were reduced from ten thousand to five thousand, with the armed forces as a whole falling from ninety-eight thousand to eighty-two thousand. And Canada's nuclear role came to an end, though not immediately.[37]

The foreign policy review followed the defence review, but the debate became dispirited as events overtook the process. The discussions about NATO represented an attempt to establish the primacy of politicians over the public service, as Head and Trudeau admitted much later, and these debates did nothing to dispel their critical attitudes toward the Department of External Affairs. Their memoir, *The Canadian Way* (which they wrote in the early nineties), proves this very clearly. It bristles with anger as they recall a meeting they had in Europe with a group of senior Canadian diplomats in January 1969, at a moment when the debate about the civil war in Nigeria was raging in Canada: "Yet to the ill-concealed astonishment of Trudeau and Head [curiously, they wrote in the third person], the Canadian ambassadors in Europe expressed their opinion that this major African drama was of little more than passing importance to Canada and of inconsequential influence in the web of Canada's external relations. East-West should be the focal point, they argued, the driving force of foreign policy, the primary contender for financial and human resources. Each of us, in contrast, was concerned about the demonstrable needs of the developing countries and the inexorable influence that they would bring to bear upon future generations of Canadians."[38]

Head, in particular, held these opinions, and he was a significant influence on the prime minister. Trudeau acted immediately to create the Canadian International Development Agency (CIDA), pledged to increase funding for development assistance, and appointed the energetic businessman Maurice Strong as its first president. Strong also gave form to the International Development Research Centre, whose mandate it was to apply science and technology to international development. At the same time, Trudeau expanded Canada's assistance to francophone developing countries to match the aid given, since the inauguration of the Colombo Plan, to Commonwealth nations.

Yet Head's account in *The Canadian Way* must surely have puzzled many readers who recalled that in 1968, Trudeau had been widely criticized for his attitude toward the Biafra-Nigeria crisis. When a journalist demanded that Canada supply humanitarian assistance to the war victims, Trudeau replied, "Where's Biafra?" Trudeau's apparent indifference to the Nigerian civil war, which historian Jack Granatstein described in the *Canadian Annual Review* as "unquestionably . . . the major foreign policy issue" of 1968, baffled and even embarrassed many of his own supporters. In a decade when African liberation and decolonization had captured the hearts of progressives in the West, Trudeau struck a discordant note and set off vigorous denunciations.

At least the prime minister was consistent. During the election campaign, a CBC interviewer had asked him about aid to the secessionist Ibos of western Nigeria, and Trudeau had responded that he asked "the funniest questions," adding that his government had not even considered the issue. Few noticed the comment. But by mid-August the press, with the devoutly Liberal *Toronto Star* in the lead, wrote scathing attacks on the government, particularly for its refusal to fly medical supplies directly to Biafra. "Up to this point," historian Robert Bothwell writes,

"Trudeau had enjoyed a favourable rating from the press: Biafra proved to be the first occasion on which his reason did not appeal to their passion." The opposition parties quickly recognized this issue, the first to tarnish his "progressive" credentials, and they launched relentless attacks in the House. On September 27, 1968, Trudeau responded in anger: "We cannot intervene, short of committing an act of war against Nigeria and intervening in the affairs of that country."

Yet others were sending aid directly, and Canadian churches sent Conservative member of Parliament David MacDonald and NDP member Andrew Brewin to Biafra, where they reported in early October that aid was meagre, aircraft were needed, the Canadian response lacked basic humanity, and they had witnessed starvation.* Churches and Oxfam organized relief flights to Biafra—"Canairelief"—that began in January 1969, but official Canadian government assistance was withheld because the Nigerian central government would not give permission for direct flights, even though Head himself travelled to Africa to seek it. But as Trudeau critic Walter Stewart wrote, "Nothing happened — except that Biafrans starved, pictures of their starvation flashed around the world, and Canada took the official stance that it was all very sad." Finally, on January 9, 1970, the government allocated funds for relief, including $1 million for "Canairelief." The war ended four days later.[39]

---

* This trip infuriated Trudeau, who also believed that the support for separatist Biafra was profoundly dangerous. In his papers there is a rough note written in 1971: "This govt never supported Portugal in Africa. . . . But NDP & Conservatives were *on the side* [underlining in original] of Portugal in Africa, in its attempt to break up territorial integrity of Nigeria." TP MG 26 020, vol. 22, file 14, LAC.

Trudeau's apparent indifference to the suffering of the Biafrans tarnished his liberal credentials, as did his lack of leadership in the struggle against South African apartheid. There is only one brief reference to South Africa in his memoirs: to a journey to a "shebeen," a popular drinking place in Soweto in 1992. "Why was Trudeau blind to Africa?" Robert Fowler, a Canadian diplomat, African expert, and Trudeau admirer later asked. In an award-winning academic study of Canada and South Africa, Linda Freeman echoes Fowler's question and compares Trudeau unfavourably in this regard to his Progressive Conservative successor Brian Mulroney. She concludes that Canada's economic interests and the advice the Trudeau government received from its advisers were reflected in the country's unwillingness to end Commonwealth preferences for South African goods until 1979, even though the foreign policy review of 1970 had declared that social justice in southern Africa was in Canada's "interest." These policies created an apparent gap between rhetoric—in the lofty expressions of support for international development in Trudeau's 1968 Alberta speech—and the reality of continued trade with the apartheid regime. They also reflected the failure throughout the seventies to reach the levels of development assistance promised at the end of the 1960s.[40]

Trudeau had warned in his first interview after the convention that he was a "pragmatist." He would fight for his positions, as with NATO, but he was willing to compromise. With regard to South Africa, he displayed "irritation" with those who pushed hard for sanctions; he believed sanctions were "unrealistic" and that "his energies would be better used in other areas." Allan Gotlieb, "the realist," found Trudeau a willing listener when he urged him to avoid those areas where Canada's direct interests were minimal, to avoid multilateral forums where rhetoric ruled, and to concentrate on tasks where Canadians derived the most benefit and could have some impact.[41] Yet Trudeau would walk

only so far on the realist path: he also listened to others, notably
Head, who was a self-declared idealist, and to Marchand and
Pelletier, whose views echoed the sympathy for the Third World
that was often expressed in *Le Devoir* and *Le Monde*. They pro-
vided the countervailing force that Trudeau so much valued.
From these differences, policy finally emerged.

Not surprisingly, Trudeau's approach to foreign policy baffled
foreign service officers and caused them to lose confidence in their
minister, Mitchell Sharp, who constantly seemed upstaged by Ivan
Head. The Americans agreed with Sharp's complaints: a mid-
seventies briefing for a state visit by the prime minister describes
Head as "the chief architect of Canada's foreign policy."[42] While
publicly declaring that he lacked Pearson's interest in foreign
affairs, Trudeau did not lack opinions or, more accurately, sentiments, which he expressed often. They deeply influenced policy,
just as they perplexed and often irritated the Canadian officials
who were trying to write the foreign policy review.

In June 1970 the Department of External Affairs published
this long-awaited review: six illustrated pamphlets that featured
"ordinary" Canadians with the sideburns and miniskirts of the
time, all spouting the "trendy jargon of systems analysis." These
odd, colourful little books shared two common positions that
generally repudiated "Pearsonian diplomacy": henceforth "external activities should be directly related to national policies
pursued within Canada," and Canada would no longer be a
"helpful fixer" for the world. Oddly, there was no pamphlet on
the United States.[43]

While Trudeau disdained the past and professed to leave the
formation of policy to public participation and rational debate, he
imprinted his own mark deeply on Canadian foreign policy. In
doing so, he carried forward his beliefs, assumptions, and experiences, which, he correctly argued, differed markedly from those of
the traditional Canadian foreign policy elite. A decade after the

"innocent" Trudeau visited Mao's China, his government formally recognized the People's Republic in October 1970. Trudeau's views also directed Canadian participation in NATO, where membership had previously meant acceptance of the use of nuclear weapons in the event of a Soviet attack. Now, however, Canadian fighter aircraft and missiles would no longer be armed with nuclear weapons. Finally, Trudeau's critical notions about the "English" domination of Canadian foreign policy were reflected in his insistence on bilingualism in the department, support for the concept of the Francophonie, greater recruitment of francophones in the service, and even the appointment of a Canadian representative to the Vatican.

Although economic restraints had led the government to lay off employees and close down consulates, Trudeau insisted on going ahead with the appointment of a Canadian ambassador to the Vatican. Faced with thundering denunciation from fundamentalist Protestants, the government responded that the Holy See was an excellent "listening post" for a diplomat—even though Trudeau had once said that he learned more from reading a good newspaper than from the diplomatic dispatches on his desk. As expected, Trudeau learned little from the Vatican, but he had made his point.[44]

—

Trudeau also made a point when he refused to attend his first Commonwealth Conference in January 1969. He had loathed the British Empire and its Canadian enthusiasts when he was young, and the thought of travelling to London, participating in an imperial gathering chaired by a British prime minister, and sharing the table with other colonials rankled him in the fall of 1968. Biafra would be an issue, and Canada would become entangled in the increasingly bitter dispute between Britain and its former colonies

over Rhodesia and South Africa, where a rich white minority dominated a poor black majority. Let Sharp go, he told his staff, "it's a
waste of my time." Horrified, Gordon Robertson and other senior
officials advised him he would pay a huge price as the first Canadian
prime minister to boycott a Commonwealth Conference. In the
end he went—resentfully.

Because of a death threat, Trudeau received extra police protection on his arrival in London, and the whole situation made
him especially impish. *Time* magazine captured the setting well:
"There in London last week were the Daimler sedans, each with
a Special Branch man riding shotgun in the front, whisking delegates from their suites in Claridges, Grosvenor House or the
Dorchester to the Regency-style Marlborough House. There at
the meeting itself was Harold Wilson, impatiently tapping his
outsize Tanzanian meerschaum on the mahogany conference
table when a speaker droned on. There, too, were Malawi's
Hastings Banda, waving his fly whisk imperiously, and Canada's
Pierre Elliott Trudeau, impetuously sliding down a banister after
one tiresome session."[45]

The Queen was not amused, particularly when she saw
photographs of Trudeau in mid-slide dominating press coverage
of the conference. In regal understatement she told the socialist
aristocrat Tony Benn that she had found Trudeau "rather disappointing." But the British tabloids did not agree with Her
Majesty, and their photographers and journalists swarmed Trudeau.
One day they lurked nearby as he lunched with a glamorous
blonde, Eva Rittinghausen, who told them soon after the encounter
that she was madly in love with Trudeau. He is "the No. 1 catch of
the international set," she declared, and "they had fallen in love at
first sight." She did, for sure, but for Trudeau she was only another
date. The next day her charms and comments appeared on the
front pages. This time Trudeau was furious, and at a press conference he declared the journalists' behaviour "crummy." His

contempt for the press, which his playfulness had often concealed in his first months of office, was now obvious to all.⁴⁶

Pierre O'Neill, who later became Trudeau's press secretary, correctly observed in *Le Devoir* that if Trudeau wanted privacy, he should not boast about his exploits with young women as he so frequently did. Charles Ritchie, now back in London, reported in his diary that the press concentrated mainly on Trudeau's love life, not on the conference itself. He, too, held Trudeau "largely responsible" for this unfortunate outcome. "He trails his coat, he goes to conspicuous places with conspicuous women. If he really wants an affair, he could easily manage it discreetly." Ritchie, the soul of discretion about his own numerous affairs, concluded, "This is a kind of double bluff." Others were reaching the same conclusion in early 1969. The swinging bachelor who publicly celebrated Gandhi and Louis Riel as martyrs and who charmed a gathering of Canadian students at Westminster with his erudition, candour, and wit attracted attention in London as no Canadian prime minister ever had before.⁴⁷ But at home things were going badly.

Within a year of Trudeau's taking office, many were baffled and quite a few were disenchanted. The honeymoon had ended for the new prime minister. When he told a group of students that an intellectual could opt for the best solution, but politicians must settle for the second or third best, the *Montreal Star* firmly rebuked him: "If the country had wanted that man, Mr. Stanfield was available. It was essentially the dreamer of dreams who was chosen, the intellectual for whom the second best was intolerable." Although he had begun boldly with his move to recognize China, to shake up External Affairs, to reject nuclear weapons, to make francophones full participants in Canada's external presentation, and even to recognize the Vatican, Trudeau disappointed some of his most fervent admirers. Bob Rae, now a Rhodes Scholar at Oxford's Balliol College and no longer a Liberal, told his godfather, Charles Ritchie, in December that he disliked Trudeau because he was "much too conservative." Many young leftists like Rae were finding a home in the New Democratic Party after Tommy Douglas prepared to step down, and in Quebec the left regarded Trudeau's caution as a validation of their earlier reservations.[48]

Trudeau's rhetoric raised expectations, his style encouraged hopes, and his background offered reasons for new departures in Canada's relationships with the world. Yet, as Tom Axworthy later pointed out, Trudeau's idealism, which was reflected in his support for international development, was balanced by realism about Canada's role as a large small power in a divided world. Trudeau found truth in Allan Gotlieb's argument that Pearson and his generation had not explained to Canadians that "the foundation of our foreign policy must be our own national self-interest and that, like other states that have always recognized this fact, we should have no illusions about the very purposes which a country's foreign policy is meant to serve." Although he had ambitions to build a better world, he accepted Gotlieb's argument that Canada's own national self-interest must be paramount—and in the late 1960s there was no greater concern than the threat to Canadian unity from Quebec separatism.[49] In 1970 that threat became a crisis— with huge ramifications for Canada.

Taking power: James Richardson, Trudeau, John Turner, Jean Marchand, and Gérard Pelletier on their way to Government House for the swearing-in of Trudeau's first Cabinet, July 6, 1968.

After a rallying speech in North York during the 1968 campaign, Trudeau introduced the star candidate as Barney Dawson, then as Barry Danson, before Barney Danson gave him a card so he could get it right.

Saint-Jean-Baptiste Day, 1968. On the eve of the election, Trudeau's cool, defiant courage in refusing to leave the reviewing stand when angry protesters rioted below him and most in the stand soon fled from the scene impressed many Canadians.

After an extended conversation with Trudeau on December 23, 1969, John Lennon and Yoko Ono declared they were "enthralled." Trudeau wrote later: "He was kind enough to say . . . 'If all politicians were like Mr. Trudeau, there would be world peace.' I must say that 'Give Peace a Chance' has always seemed to me to be sensible advice." Trudeau, *Memoirs*.

Trudeau escapes visiting schoolgirls on Parliament Hill. "He's got me dizzy. He's got all Canada dizzy": Newfoundland premier Joey Smallwood.

Madeleine Gobeil, brilliant, literary, and forthright, was Trudeau's frequent companion for over a decade until his marriage to Margaret, and they ultimately reconnected as friends.
She taught at Carleton University in the late sixties, attracted international attention for an interview she did with Jean-Paul Sartre in *Playboy* in 1966, and introduced Trudeau to both Sartre and Simone de Beauvoir in Paris.

Barbra Streisand accompanies Trudeau to the National Arts Centre, January 1970. "He was the greatest prime minister," she said in October 2006.

CHAPTER THREE

—

THE OCTOBER CRISIS

uring the 1960s Trudeau became convinced that Quebec
would enjoy a better future inside Canada than separate
from it, and his chief motivation for coming to Ottawa
had been to achieve that goal. In terms of foreign relations, he
always insisted that he be personally involved in those areas where
the federal government's policies toward Quebec coincided with
Canada's international policy. Even before he became prime minister, he had worked with Michael Pitfield, Marc Lalonde, and
Marcel Cadieux to stiffen Ottawa's resistance to French support for
a distinct Quebec international presence and to Quebec's assault
on the federal monopoly over external relations.

Early in 1968, for instance, Trudeau took a direct role in
cutting off relations with Gabon, which had invited Quebec to an
educational conference in defiance of Canadian objections. This
aggressive response angered the Union nationale government and
found little support in Quebec's francophone universities.
Between 1967 and 1970, Trudeau deplored the willingness of
Premier Daniel Johnson and his successor, Jean-Jacques Bertrand,
to deepen ties with de Gaulle's France beyond what was acceptable for a component of a sovereign state. Knowing that France's
former African colonies could be pawns in the game France and

Quebec might play, Trudeau quickly expanded Canadian representation in, and aid to, those countries and to the Francophonie as a whole. De Gaulle's encouragement of Biafra's independence only strengthened Trudeau's opposition to it. As the prime minister told journalist Peter C. Newman: "To ask, 'Where's Biafra?' is tantamount to asking, 'Where is Laurentia?' the name Quebec nationalists give to the independent state of their dreams."[1]

Those dreams increasingly became Trudeau's nightmare after René Lévesque broke with the Quebec Liberal Party in October 1967 and created the Mouvement souveraineté-association. In April 1968, the same week that Trudeau won the Liberal leadership, the *"mouvement"* retitled itself the Parti Québécois. Trudeau knew that Lévesque was a formidable opponent, but the PQ was only one of five parties in the province (the NDP and the Créditistes also had support) and initially seemed far from power. There was even some satisfaction among the federal Liberals, including Trudeau, that the ambiguity that had previously cloaked separatism had disappeared. However, economic dislocation, a nasty quarrel over immigrant language rights in the Montreal suburb of Saint-Léonard, a weakening Union nationale government, and a divided Quebec Liberal Party served to intensify nationalist feelings and civil dissent. Jean-Jacques Bertrand's government's attempt to solve the language problem with Bill 63 in 1969 literally drove protesters into the streets. In February a bomb exploded in the Montreal Stock Exchange just before closing time, injuring twenty-seven people. A shocked city and increasingly alarmed country registered the turbulence but reacted in different ways: Claude Ryan deplored the attack on ordinary citizens and warned, in *Le Devoir*, that these tactics would lead to disaster; the *Globe and Mail* reported that murders had increased by 50 percent in Montreal over the previous year and that some two thousand armed holdups had occurred. Ryan's suggestion that this growing "climate of violence" found its source in the grave injustices in Quebec's past found no echo in the *Globe* editorial.[2]

As tensions rose, friends and families divided. Premier Johnson's two sons, Daniel and Pierre-Marc, for example, began to walk different paths at the end of the sixties: "Up to then, their paths had been almost identical. The same education, same apprenticeship for a public life, same group of friends, same holidays, even the same legal studies." Then Daniel entered the world of finance and supported federalism, while Pierre-Marc chose medicine, social activism, and separatism. Both went on to become premiers representing their respective causes. Trudeau's oldest friends similarly took sides, and many parted from him. With others there was a new uneasiness. The economist Jacques Parizeau, whose brilliant wife, Alice, was a particular favourite of Trudeau and had often invited the middle-aged bachelor to dinners in the sixties, announced in the fall of 1969 that he now supported Quebec independence. Labour leader Michel Chartrand, who with Trudeau had fought against conscription in 1942, demonstrated in support of the Asbestos strikers in the late forties, and worked in union politics in the fifties, now called for a socialist revolution in an independent Quebec. Pierre Vallières, who had collaborated with Trudeau as the young editor of *Cité libre* in the early sixties, currently dwelt in a jail cell, where he faced charges of manslaughter for his role in radical separatist violence in the mid-sixties. Trudeau knew his enemies well — many had formerly been his friends.[3]

As the sixties ended, Trudeau was angry. Those who knew him best noticed his mood. Thérèse Gouin Décarie, the psychology student he had loved passionately in the mid-forties and wished to marry, left him a note one day: "Pierre, our Pierre, what has happened to you? You always seem so angry. Your eyes are spiteful, and you appear mean." Gently, she concluded: "We think so often of you."[4] Others less personally attached worried too. He had behaved badly with the press at the Commonwealth Conference in London in January 1969, he'd railed against news coverage on the Official Languages Act, and he'd walked out of meetings in western Canada (where bilingualism and economic difficulties made Liberals unpopular) when protesters confronted him with signs reading "Trudeau is a pig" and "He hustles women."

In August 1969, as Trudeau entered the Seaforth Armoury in Vancouver through a sea of protesters, one wearing an "NDP ski cap" came menacingly close and shouted: "You're a motherfucking creep." Suddenly, the young man's head snapped back, and the next day he charged Trudeau with assault. RCMP officer Victor Irving knew what had happened but testified that he "did not see the PM throw the punch." Fortunately, his interrogator asked a narrow question that allowed him to treat the truth economically. In fact, although he did not see Trudeau lunge, he later admitted that he thought Trudeau had hit "the guy." Still, in his view, the protester "got what he deserved."[5]

Trudeau's shyness and reticence fitted politics awkwardly. The result was these sudden eruptions of anger that reflected his private fury with the demands that politics made on his privacy.

—

Trudeau may have resorted to violence, but he deplored others who accepted it as a means to promote social change or revolution. Long before, when he was young, he too had dreamed of blood and revolution, but he had changed profoundly, even if his mentor of those days, Father Rudolphe Dubé, known better as François Hertel, still mused about violence as a force for change in Quebec. Trudeau would have none of it. He later told journalist Jean Lépine that the frequent bombings in Montreal, the increasing labour violence in Quebec, and the open support for revolution by the Front de libération du Québec (FLQ) caused him to ask the police to investigate the links among terrorists within Canada, their international connections, the role French officials played in promoting terrorism, and more controversially, the infiltration of the PQ by those who wanted revolution, not democratic change.[6] He also worried about the troubling absence of leadership in the province, and as an election loomed, he urged Liberals to revitalize the party in Quebec.

The surprising resignation of Charles de Gaulle in April 1969 did not alter French policy toward Quebec and Canada. The provocative, meddlesome attitude already displayed was deeply ingrained within the French bureaucracy, and the new president, Georges Pompidou, hesitated to break any ties with his eminent predecessor.* Having concluded that the Union nationale was too fond of the French and too willing to play their games, Trudeau sought alternatives. He needed a new Liberal leader in Quebec to work with him against French interference and the increasing turbulence within the province. Once Jean Lesage resigned as Liberal leader in September 1969, three candidates quickly emerged to replace him: thirty-six-year-old economist Robert Bourassa, conservative lawyer Claude Wagner, and veteran

---

* Trudeau had France and "foreign" influence on his mind when he wrote to Solicitor General George McIlraith on February 18, 1969, saying he was "somewhat disturbed . . . at the recent events at Sir George Williams University in Montreal [a major student riot], and particularly at suggestions that agents from foreign countries may be coming to Canada with the deliberate intention of fomenting unrest and disorder." While admitting that the administration of justice was a provincial responsibility, he thought it "prudent to have the R.C.M. Police examine the security aspects of these developments." Such a report should indicate "such federal responsibilities as the government may have in this respect." Ironically, one of the riot's leaders, Anne Cools, was later a Trudeau Liberal candidate who, after defeat, received a Senate appointment. Always a renegade, she later became a Conservative. TP MG26 020, vol. 22, file 12, LAC.

journalist Pierre Laporte. Wagner was the angry hardliner, invariably pointing out in his campaign addresses that fifty bombs had exploded in the province in 1969, including one in Mayor Jean Drapeau's home. In response to Wagner, Bourassa emphasized an open economy, economic modernization, and "political realism"—a platform most congenial to federal Liberals. Bourassa won the leadership decisively in January 1970, and on March 12 an increasingly frustrated Premier Jean-Jacques Bertrand called an election. He showed poor political judgment, as polls soon revealed that his own party had fallen to third place behind the Liberals and the PQ.[7] The federal Liberals quietly threw their resources behind their provincial counterparts; the French apparently offered the PQ $300,000—which Lévesque wisely refused.[8]

The election campaign did not go as well as Trudeau and Bourassa had hoped it would. The PQ rose steadily in the polls, with one poll the week before the election showing the Liberals at 32 percent, the PQ at 23 percent, and the UN trailing at only 16 percent. Lévesque had momentum. One investment firm urged clients to move their money out of Quebec, and on April 26, three days before the election, Royal Trust hired nine Brinks trucks to ship securities from the province. In the end Bourassa prevailed, winning 72 of 108 seats. The UN formed the official Opposition, with 17 seats but only 19.6 percent of the vote, while the PQ won just 7 seats with 23 percent of the vote. "In giving you their support," Trudeau wrote to Bourassa after the election, "it is clear the people of Quebec have accepted your option: the path of work, of reason, and of confidence."[9] As the English-language press celebrated and federal Liberals breathed more easily, Jacques Parizeau, a defeated PQ candidate himself, cautioned that the jubilation was premature and tantamount to waving "a red flag in front of a fuming bull." He warned ominously that the PQ's virtual exclusion from the National Assembly, despite its strong vote, represented "the defeat of our arguments in favour of the parliamentary system."[10]

As Parizeau had warned, the election brought no peace. Bombs punctuated the Montreal summer of 1970, and FLQ calls for revolutionary action appeared on signposts, vacant buildings, and broadsheets scattered around the universities and the student bistros. Rumours of kidnappings, thefts of weapons and dynamite, and declarations of revolutionary solidarity abounded. The Confederation of National Trade Unions (CNTU), which Marchand had led and for which Trudeau had served as legal counsel, regularly paid the bail for the release of FLQ members, including Pierre Vallières, who used the occasion to issue a call for a Cuban-style revolution. A strike by Montreal taxi drivers in mid-summer brought the army to the outskirts of the city.

The Bourassa government could not find its footing on this dangerous terrain. It seemed divided within, as some of its own officials told their counterparts in France that the centralization policies of the Trudeau government were undermining the "last chance for accommodation." On October 5, two days after these comments were made, a pair of gunmen grabbed British trade commissioner James Cross at his home on Montreal's prestigious Redpath Avenue and pushed him into a waiting car.[11]

Trudeau was "stunned." Despite the summer of bombs and violence, he and his government were not prepared for this dramatic kidnapping of a senior diplomat in the prosperous heart of English Montreal. Still, his reaction was immediate: the government must not give in to terrorists. As he later explained: "The reason is simple: if we had agreed, as the FLQ demanded, to release from prison FLQ criminals who had been convicted of murder, armed robbery, and bombings, we would have been putting our finger into a gearbox from which we could never get it out. Puffed up by the success of their tactic, they would have no reason to hesitate to murder, rob, and bomb again, since if they were caught, all their pals would have to do is kidnap someone else to have them released from prison—and on and on indefinitely."[12]

The FLQ immediately announced that it would kill Cross if the government did not stop the searches, free twenty-three "political prisoners," broadcast the FLQ manifesto, give the kidnappers $500,000 in gold bullion, and arrange sanctuary in Algeria or Cuba. Because Cross was a diplomat, External Affairs Minister Mitchell Sharp took responsibility for the "negotiations." He told the House of Commons on October 6 that the government, after consultation with the British and Quebec governments, had rejected the FLQ demands.[13]

Two days later Sharp relented and permitted the reading of the FLQ manifesto on Radio-Canada. It declared that the election defeat on April 29 had ended the revolutionaries' hopes that they could "channel [their] energy and [their] impatience" into the PQ. Never again would they be "fooled by the pseudo-elections that the Anglo-Saxon capitalists toss to the people of Quebec every four years."[14] No more would they listen to the lies of the "fairy" Trudeau and the "dog" Drapeau. Trudeau was angry that Sharp gave in to the FLQ's demand for the broadcast. While outrageous in its rhetoric and claims, the manifesto appears to have stirred the militants and influenced other sympathizers. As Gérard Pelletier wrote in the early seventies, "Who does not long, when he receives a summons from the police or compares his gross pay with the net total of his cheque, to give the authorities a good going over or address a few suitable insults to some minister or other? There, insolence of taunts addressed to public figures encouraged thoughts of this kind to come to the surface in the listener or viewer, who said to himself, thinking of Mr. Trudeau or Mayor Drapeau, 'They got it right in the eye.'"[15]

Opinions divided quickly. Ryan called for negotiations; Jean-Paul Desbiens in *La Presse* supported the government's hard line. The French government shared Ryan's view; the British, hardened by Irish experience, accepted the Canadian government's reasons. René Lévesque sided with Ryan while simultaneously condemning the "sewer rats" who had kidnapped Cross. Michel Chartrand of the CNTU, however, said he had no more sympathy for Mrs. Cross than he did for the thousands of Quebec workers without jobs, while other militants mocked the federal government's hard position. Bitterness swelled.

Then, on Saturday, October 10, the Chenier cell of the FLQ kidnapped Pierre Laporte, the Quebec minister of labour and immigration, as he was playing football at dusk on a field across from his Saint-Lambert home. The stakes were suddenly much higher. Trudeau knew Laporte well: their fathers had attended the same college, and they themselves had shared school benches at Brébeuf, debated nationalism and Quebec politics in the fifties when Laporte was a prominent journalist, and quarrelled about Liberal politics in the sixties, particularly when Laporte had stood for the provincial Liberal leadership just a few months before.

The day after the kidnapping, Laporte wrote a letter to "*Mon cher Robert,*" in which he begged Bourassa to agree to his captors' demands. His life, he said, was in the premier's hands. In Ottawa the government began to believe "that perhaps the FLQ was not just a bunch of pamphlet-waving, bomb-planting zealots after all," to use Trudeau's own words; "perhaps they were in fact members of a powerful network capable of endangering public safety, and of bringing other fringe groups—of which there were a large number at the time—into the picture, which would lead to untold violence." In this climate the fog of misunderstanding became a cloak.[16]

On Thanksgiving weekend, Bourassa moved into the heavily guarded Queen Elizabeth Hotel above the train station in central Montreal. In Toronto, Ontario premier John Robarts called for immediate and harsh action—even a "war" against the FLQ. At the Université de Montréal and the new Université du Québec à Montréal, students rallied behind calls for revolutionary action. The line between political legitimacy and revolution blurred: for instance, Carole de Vault, the mistress of PQ luminary

Jacques Parizeau, was secretly organizing, without his knowledge, an FLQ robbery of a business where Parizeau had got her a job. As rumours billowed and tensions rose, the Quebec government seemed confused. On that surreal weekend, Bourassa and Justice Minister Jérôme Choquette appeared at times willing to compromise, while in other moments they reflected the harder federal line. In Ottawa Trudeau ordered the Canadian military to defend public officials in the capital, and troops soon appeared around Rockcliffe embassies and private homes throughout the city. Nervous soldiers with menacing machine guns protected ministers and sometimes frightened neighbours, who were brusquely questioned by uniformed guards holding raised guns. The first casualty was the assistant to Mitchell Sharp, who was wounded when an inexperienced guard accidentally fired his weapon.[17]

Trudeau and Marc Lalonde, his agent throughout the crisis, began to lose confidence in Bourassa as the crisis deepened, and they feared the impact the revolutionary rhetoric uttered by radical unionists and students might have in Quebec. On Tuesday afternoon, October 13, as Trudeau left his limousine to enter the House of Commons, Tim Ralfe of the CBC thrust a microphone in front of him.

"Sir, what is it with all these men with guns around here?"

Smiling, Trudeau responded sharply and defiantly: "Haven't you noticed?"

"Yes, I've noticed them," Ralfe responded. "I wondered why you people decided to have them."

"What's your worry?" Trudeau asked.

"I'm not worried, but you seem to be —"

"So if you're not worried, what's your . . ." Trudeau began, then snapped: "I'm not worried."

"I'm worried about living in a town that's full of people with guns running around," Ralfe complained.

"Why, have they done anything to you? Have they pushed you around or anything?"

The banter, ever more sarcastic, continued as the cameras recorded Trudeau's cool contempt for his questioner. He responded at length when Ralfe suggested that the troops were there to prevent leaders like Trudeau from being kidnapped.

"Sure, but this isn't my choice, obviously. You know, I think it is more important to get rid of those who are committing violence against the total society and those who are trying to run the government through a parallel power by establishing their authority by kidnapping and blackmail. And I think it is our duty as a government to protect government officials and important people in our society against being used as tools in this blackmail. Now, you don't agree to this, but I am sure that, once again with hindsight, you would probably have found it preferable if Mr. Cross and Mr. Laporte had been protected from kidnapping, which they weren't because these steps we're taking now weren't taken. But even with your hindsight, I don't see how you can deny that."

"No," said Ralfe. "I still go back to the choice that you have to make in the kind of society you live in."

"Yes . . . Well, there are a lot of bleeding hearts around who just don't like to see people with helmets and guns," Trudeau exclaimed. "All I can say is, go on and bleed, but it is more important to keep law and order in the society than to be worried about weak-kneed people who don't like the looks—"

"At any cost?" Ralfe interrupted. "How far would you go with that?"

"Well, just watch me." His smile replaced by an icy stare, Trudeau continued: "I think society must take every means at its disposal to defend itself against the emergence of a parallel power which defies the elected power in this country, and I think that goes to any distance. So long as there is a power in here which is challenging the elected representatives of the people, I think that power must be stopped, and I think it's only, I repeat, weak-kneed bleeding hearts who are afraid to take these measures."[18]

Two days earlier, Claude Ryan, who had urged negotiations from the beginning of the crisis, had called his editorial staff together and mused about the possibility that the weak Bourassa government would crumble from within in the face of the crisis. Ryan told his staff that the time had come to add strength to the government from outside or even to form a provisional, parallel government. He spoke to Lucien Saulnier, head of the Montreal Executive Committee, a body representing the Montreal region, about the possibility of an alternative government that would replace the Bourassa government as it crumbled. Very quickly the news reached Ottawa that Ryan had been discussing the creation of a committee to replace "the elected representatives of the people."

Confusion was constant, and ministers could take radically different positions from one day to the next. The journal of William Tetley, a Quebec Cabinet minister, reveals the wild swings of opinion in Quebec City. On October 13 he wrote: "Bourassa is wavering still. I am hawkish and want to call in the troops, impose martial law. I have completely changed in two days. Bourassa kindly reminds me that two days before I was for releasing all 23 prisoners."[19]

On October 15 *Le Devoir* published a petition calling on the government to support Bourassa's earlier willingness to negotiate with the kidnappers to bring about "an exchange of the two hostages for the political prisoners." It condemned "certain attitudes outside Quebec, the last and most unbelievable of which . . . [were those] of Premier Robarts of Ontario, plus the rigid—almost military—atmosphere we see in Ottawa." This document, which Trudeau thought "incredible," was prompted by a telephone call from Lévesque to Ryan the previous day and bore the signatures of Ryan, Lévesque, Parizeau, several labour leaders, and the psychiatrist Camille Laurin—an old friend whom Trudeau had often walked with in Outremont in the early sixties when they both deplored the separatist option. Three of Trudeau's former academic colleagues and friends—sociologists Marcel Rioux, Fernand Dumont, and Guy Rocher—were also among the sixteen who signed. "I might have understood the man in the street holding such opinions," Trudeau later wrote. "But when university professors, leaders of a democratic party, and labour union leaders displayed such twisted logic, such willingness to capitulate to the demands of the FLQ, it suggested an extremely disordered state."[20]

October 15 continued disorderly in other ways as well. FLQ lawyer Robert Lemieux, Michel Chartrand, Pierre Vallières, and Charles Gagnon (an FLQ activist recently released from prison) gave fiery addresses to students as strikes began at the Université de Montréal, where over a thousand students signed a copy of the FLQ manifesto. Sympathizers at the Université du Québec campus occupied the administrative offices and threatened to stay until the "political prisoners" were freed. Bomb threats had police scurrying through the city as crowds gathered for a mass rally in support of the FLQ scheduled to take place in the Paul Sauvé Arena that evening.

In Ottawa, meanwhile, the Cabinet met to consider the deteriorating situation. The RCMP said they had no leads on the hostages but continued to report ever more stories of plots and nefarious deeds. Justice Minister John Turner, who had returned from abroad just four days earlier, found the capital in turmoil: "The FLQ had tapped into a uniquely Canadian paranoia," his biographer writes, "triggering dark imaginings of revolution afoot in a vast terrorist underground in Quebec." Marchand, who felt personally betrayed by his former colleagues in the labour movement, simmered with anger and despair. Lalonde grew increasingly worried about the apparent weakness of the Bourassa government—a concern that Tetley's journal suggests was overstated. Nevertheless, in times of crisis, perception trumps reality. And personality and memories are also a factor.[21]

The Cabinet made a fateful decision that mid-October day. With the apparent disintegration of resolve and public order in Montreal and a series of warnings from Drapeau, Choquette, Bourassa, and Saulnier that the police would not be able to cope with the challenges ahead, the federal ministers agreed to move troops into Quebec to preserve order in the province and to protect individuals and public places from attack. The record of the meeting betrays the tension, despite its stilted and bureaucratic tone. Marchand, who was Quebec leader in the government, began the meeting with a dire account of the turmoil; Marc Lalonde, who remained constantly in touch with Quebec City, gave updates on the situation throughout the day. Indeed, in his memoirs, Eric Kierans claims that Lalonde was "the dominating figure" at the meeting. He would return from phone calls reporting each time that "things . . . [looked] very bad, bad indeed."[22]

The effect was dramatic. At the previous meeting of the Cabinet, on October 10, Trudeau had reported that Bourassa had asked for special powers, and Sharp had replied that the War Measures Act might be appropriate in the circumstance, rather than special legislation. Turner now appeared to support this suggestion, saying that "special legislation" required parliamentary debate—and that would alert the terrorists to their plans. To pass the War Measures Act, a relic of the opening months of the First World War, debate was not required. Moreover, when Drapeau had announced earlier on October 15 that he had asked for assistance from the Canadian military, he'd spoken of an "apprehended insurrection"—the very term employed in the act to justify its invocation.[23]

Marchand saw conspiracies everywhere and claimed during the Cabinet meeting that the FLQ had "two tons of dynamite" in Montreal, "the detonation of which was controlled by radio equipment." When questioned where he'd obtained his information, he said, simply, police sources. More troubling, he said, was an indication that the FLQ was finding support beyond its own ranks.

In that respect he referred "to the statement made public" by "Mr. Levesque [sic] and a number of other prominent people" (the petition published in Le Devoir calling for negotiations leading to the exchange of the two hostages for the "political prisoners"). Marchand urged the government not only to take swift action in the present crisis but also to break up the FLQ, which had become "a state within the state."[24]

Cabinet debated throughout the morning, took a break, and then resumed in the afternoon as the demonstrations in Montreal mounted and the pressure for action from Quebec officials increased. Trudeau was blunt. Bourassa did not want his "back-benchers to sit around too long. They were falling apart." Some ministers suggested a one-day delay; others, such as Allan MacEachen, favoured consulting first with Parliament; and a few, notably Ron Basford (Consumer and Corporate Affairs) and Joe Greene (Energy, Mines, and Resources), supported special legislation rather than the War Measures Act. None, however, doubted the need for action. Although Eric Kierans later claimed to have had his doubts, the record shows that his only intervention was to remark that "people in his [Montreal] riding were terrorized, and the sooner the government acted, the better it would be."[25]

When Basford and Greene pointed out, correctly, that the security panel had not indicated that the grounds for action— "apprehended insurrection"—were present, their arguments were brushed aside by Marchand. The situation had changed and had become perilous, he argued: Bourassa was in a "weak position," the people were "frightened," and there was a "risk of losing Quebec." Trudeau backed his Quebec leader, stating that the new uncertainties required a strong stand. The police, he said, did not know whether the FLQ "hard core" was two hundred or one thousand strong. If there were a thousand members and the Cabinet "did not react and there were an insurrection, where would the government stand?" Moreover, Bourassa must not be allowed to make "the deal demanded by the FLQ"—granting parole to convicted criminals and allowing them to fly to Cuba. Although later writers have argued that Turner had reservations, he was, in fact, the minister who said that Marchand had made his "case": the raid against perceived FLQ supporters and sympathizers had to occur that night, before word got out of the government's plans, and this decision meant that consultation of Parliament was impossible. "One way out of the dilemma," Turner advised, "was to proclaim the War Measures Act." Legislation could be introduced later, and "we would be regarded as having used the . . . Act as a protective and temporary measure. If, on the other hand, what was apprehended in Quebec really was insurrection," the act could remain in place.[26] Bourassa and Drapeau would make a formal request to invoke the act, and in the early morning of October 16, now only a few hours away, it would take effect.

The raids began at 4 a.m. Tipped off by a sympathetic police officer, PQ leaders raced to their party headquarters and grabbed papers they feared would be seized. Sirens blared and cruiser lights flashed in the darkness as officers clumsily swooped down on suspects chosen hastily from lists assembled by the Quebec and Montreal police forces and vetted quickly by Jean Marchand and Gérard Pelletier. While PQ leaders remained free, many of their supporters were arrested, including such notables as the singer Pauline Julien and the poet Gérald Godin, whose cell adjoined that of celebrated Montreal boulevardier Nick Auf der Maur—a most improbable terrorist.* That night police arrested 397 people,

---

* The outrageously comic Auf der Maur said that he had joined the left to meet women and that in those lively, radical times, "all it took . . . to arrange a full-scale riot in Montreal was a suggestion, and a lot of beer." He edited the radical *Last Post*, which took up the cause of Montreal's taxi drivers against

disrupted many more, and created a climate of anger and fear among radicals.[27]

That fury exploded in the Chenier cell: they took their prisoner Pierre Laporte, strangled him with the crucifix he wore on a chain around his neck, stuffed his body into the trunk of a green Chevrolet, and abandoned the vehicle in the parking lot at St. Hubert Airport. Police discovered it just before midnight on Saturday, October 17.

—

The horror of the murder appalled all but the most militant. Trudeau went immediately to the Parliament Buildings in the early hours of Sunday morning. His face was ashen, his eyes cold, his anger palpable. At 3 a.m. he gave a brief statement on television denouncing the "cowardly" assassination "by a band of murderers." "I can't help feeling as a Canadian," he said, "a deep sense of shame that this cruel and senseless act should have been conceived in cold blood and executed in like manner."[28]

While *Quebec-Presse*, the militant's media voice, blamed the invocation of the War Measures Act for Laporte's death and bitterly attacked Trudeau, most critics firmly rejected this view in the days following the assassination. Carole de Vault, Parizeau's lover, for instance, who had begun to have doubts about the FLQ cause, told Parizeau's wife in his absence about the plot to stage robberies in order to fill FLQ coffers, and at Alice Parizeau's insistence,

---

the airport monopoly by Murray Hill limousines. Some FLQ activists were associated with the movement. Auf der Maur became a civic politician and a supporter of Progressive Conservative prime minister Brian Mulroney, who had been a drinking friend in the seventies. *Montreal Gazette*, April 8, 1998.

became an agent for the antiterror forces. Lévesque sat transfixed before a television screen in the PQ office in Montreal, unwilling to believe what had transpired and deaf to the clamour of party activists about him. He called for harsh action against the murderers, though he continued to criticize the government's actions. In the House of Commons, Conservative leader Robert Stanfield's earlier hesitations about the use of the act disappeared, and when NDP leader Tommy Douglas expressed his opposition to it, four of his MPs broke with him. Invocation of the War Measures Act passed 190 to 16, and several polls revealed overwhelming support for the measure across Canada, including Quebec. To Douglas's charge that the prime minister had used a sledgehammer to crack a peanut, Trudeau replied: "This criticism doesn't take the facts into account. First, peanuts don't make bombs, don't take hostages, and don't assassinate prisoners. And as for the sledgehammer, it was the only tool at our disposal."[29]

After Laporte's brutal murder, the FLQ continued to hold James Cross hostage in an apartment. Disgusted and angry, Cross now refused even to speak with his kidnappers. "I hated the lot of them," he said later, "and would cheerfully have killed them if the opportunity arose." He described them as primitive ideologues fired by the revolutionary sentiments of the sixties. He passed the time watching television, reading the literature scattered around—the writings of Pierre Vallieres, the Algerian revolutionary Frantz Fanon's *The Wretched of the Earth*, and, bizarrely, Agatha Christie mysteries—until December 2. That evening the kidnappers put handcuffs on him, told him the police knew where he was and that they expected an attack. The next morning, however, a federal government negotiator appeared at the door, and they reached an agreement: the Chenier cell members would release Cross in exchange for sanctuary in Cuba. With Cross squashed between them, and accompanied by a lawyer, the kidnappers left the apartment in the battered car in which they had seized him on October 5. At the

Expo 67 site on St. Helen's Island, which had temporarily been declared a Cuban consulate, he was finally released, and from there the kidnappers were flown to Cuba. (In the late seventies, they returned to Montreal and were given very light prison sentences, most of which were then suspended.)[30]

In crises, few people remain consistent, but the negotiation was arguably not a capitulation: it reflected the offer made by the federal government at the beginning of Cross's ordeal. Trudeau always criticized governments such as Brazil and West Germany for negotiating with terrorists for the release of diplomatic or political hostages — in both those countries, he asserted, kidnappings and violence continued regardless. In Quebec at least, after October 1970, kidnappings ended. And Trudeau never deviated from his line. When Gordon Robertson asked him whether he stood firm against ransom and the release of prisoners accused of criminal offences, Trudeau promptly said yes. If Robertson himself were kidnapped, he added for emphasis, there would be no ransom. He would bargain for time, but "law and order in Canada . . . [would come] first."[31]

There is no doubt that Trudeau's steely will dominated the direction the government took, although Marchand and Lalonde sometimes steered the ship. Kierans, no later admirer, wrote in 2001 about Trudeau's Cabinet presence: "Trudeau, as usual, was calm, fully in control. Very, very impressive."[32] Turner reminisced that "[those days were] the closest I ever felt to [Trudeau]. We were like buddies in combat. I mean, when you stand beside a guy who's eyeball-to-eyeball with danger and he doesn't blink, you can't help but feel admiration." Otto Lang claimed that Trudeau's leadership made the final decision to invoke the War Measures Act as strongly supported as any Cabinet decision he could recall. Even Gordon Robertson, whose memoir is highly critical of Trudeau's later career, argues that "Trudeau's firm leadership, putting the preservation of law and order above any other consideration, was probably the most important single contribution he made to the preservation of peace and democracy in Canada during his time as prime minister."[33]

A CTV poll released on November 15, 1970, revealed that only 5 percent of Canadians disapproved of Trudeau's actions, while 87 percent supported the invocation of the War Measures Act. Jacques Parizeau, while dissenting strongly from Trudeau's position, told his biographer in 1999 that, objectively, he admired Trudeau: he was the first French Canadian in a century who said, "I am not weak, and will never be judged by what I have said or not said because I act on things. I admire this approach, and Trudeau is not weak."

Power, as Parizeau recognized, was central to the drama that October. For Trudeau, democratic legitimacy rested with elected officials. The petition published in *Le Devoir* on October 15, which had infuriated Trudeau, Lalonde, Marchand, and Pelletier, was based on the argument that the elected government in Quebec City was weak—an opinion shared in Ottawa. However, the conclusions reached in Ottawa and by Ryan, Lévesque, and their co-signatories in Quebec were fundamentally different. Trudeau rejected the notion that there were "political prisoners"— the term employed in the petition—and deplored the signatories' claim to speak for the broader population. Not least, his anger stemmed from the fact that fourteen of the sixteen signatories had supported the PQ in the earlier provincial election. When Ryan, who had not supported the PQ, continued to advocate negotiation even after Laporte's death and urged that elected officials turn to others to reinforce their weakened state, Trudeau and Lalonde leaked the story about the meeting of *Le Devoir*'s editorial staff and Ryan's musing about a provisional government. Peter C. Newman persuaded the *Toronto Star* to publish the account of that staff meeting. Trudeau, turning Lord Acton's phrase around, famously said of Ryan: "Lack of power corrupts, but absolute lack of power corrupts absolutely."[34]

Ryan initially denied the story when it appeared, but then, in two articles at the end of October, he confirmed that on October 11, before they published the petition, he had spoken with four *Le Devoir* journalists about the possibility of a parallel government or a government of public safety incorporating outsiders. One of those present, the eminent journalist Michel Roy, later said that he was flabbergasted by Ryan's comments. While admitting the meeting and the notion of an alternative, if not a provisional, government, Ryan himself said that it was "no plot, perhaps, but an idea." Lévesque was not present at the meeting at *Le Devoir*, and he ridiculed the notion that there was a plan for a "provisional government." Yet in his own 1986 memoirs, he states that Ryan and others were "even ready, it appears, to envisage the perspective of a coalition government to strengthen backbones" in Quebec City.[35] In the view of Ryan and his co-petitioners, the strengthening of backbones did not mean that the provincial government should take harsh action against the FLQ. Rather, it meant that it should "defy" Trudeau and carry out its own negotiations with the FLQ.[36]

The differences between the petitioners and Trudeau's group were intellectual, political, and personal. Their bitter exchanges illustrate what Freud called the fierceness of narrow differences. Later Pelletier indicated that "Trudeau jumped too quickly on the story of the parallel Cabinet" and Lalonde was of the same mind, but while accepting the influence of "the story" on events, Lalonde emphasized the great uncertainty of the moment and the clear evidence of "deterioration." In his excellent biography of Jacques Parizeau, then the recent PQ convert who was serving as president of the executive council of the party, Pierre Duchesne describes the mood of PQ leaders after the assassination of Laporte. Parizeau was trying to explain to those around him, especially younger party members, what was happening: "First, he explained that the crisis divided contemporaries within the Quebec society. The Marchands, Pelletiers, and Trudeaus would visit the Parizeaus, Laurins, and

Lévesques. 'We would dine together as couples. Sometimes, our wives knew each other and shopped together. We went out together socially.'" Trudeau echoed Parizeau's comments in giving his own reaction to the October Crisis in a later interview: when MPs asked him who those "guys" were in Montreal, he replied: "They aren't Maoists, anarchists, or Trotskyists: they're people we know. But do you even recognize them? They probably drink their coffee in the same establishments, walk in the same streets, and attend the same shows we do. Yet we didn't have a clue." People like us — "notre milieu," as he said: his students at the university, Marchand's "brothers" in the unions, his colleagues at Cité libre, their taxi drivers, and sometimes their oldest friends. Long before, Trudeau himself had believed that Canada took political prisoners — Montreal mayor Camillien Houde, his father's friend, had been locked up for speaking out against the war, and Trudeau had used language similar to the wording of the FLQ manifesto in 1942, when he'd denounced Mackenzie King in an angry public speech for his abuse of powers under the War Measures Act. He, too, had then spouted rhetoric that dripped with contempt and the promise of violence. In the sixties, however, he was on the other side of the barricades, denouncing his youthful and controversial mentor François Hertel for suggesting the use of violence, breaking with his oldest friend Pierre Vadeboncoeur for consorting too closely with the revolutionary left, and publicly ridiculing those who gave the violent separatists comfort. "Notre milieu" had shattered into fragments.[37]

Parizeau agreed: October 1970 was a turning point. Before the crisis, "we could completely disagree on our positions, while maintaining the greatest respect for each other. We realize that we hold incompatible views, but we are well-mannered and good companions. . . . Trudeau has destroyed this." In Trudeau's eyes, the decorum disintegrated and civility ended when his former companions spoke of political prisoners, undermined the legitimacy of democratic government, and came close to the murderous flame of the FLQ.* To Parizeau and his colleagues, the break came with the imposition of the War Measures Act, the revelation that many PQ members were on police lists, and the arrest of numerous PQ supporters: "As soon as they begin putting our friends in jail, it's a whole new story. They've become an autocracy." In future decades both sides of the divide would cling to their separate interpretations of those mid-October events with a furious tenacity.[38]

Two major issues were interpreted in fundamentally different ways by the two sides: the invocation of the War Measures Act and the impact of the actions of both the federal and the provincial governments on Quebec and Canadian history. The disputes over these matters were bitter, and the acrimony soon spread beyond Ottawa and Montreal. In the case of the War Measures Act, for example, historian Jack Granatstein addressed five thousand students crowded around the flagpole at Toronto's newly established York University for a mid-October 1970 "rally for Canada." Granatstein was the sole speaker at the gathering who

---

* Jacques Hébert, perhaps Trudeau's closest male friend and key member of La Ligue des droits de l'homme, Quebec's leading civil liberties organization, joined with other Ligue officials in calling on prisoners soon after they were arrested and pointing out their rights. He later recalled that after one long day and night of travelling from home to home, talking to prisoners' friends and families, he called Trudeau and told him: "You're not making my life any easier." In August 2007, when we spoke, he shrugged off the experience, lamented the whole affair, and was personally fiercely loyal to Trudeau. The most recent discussion of the role of such organizations in the October Crisis is found in Dominique Clément, *Canada's Rights Revolution: Social Movements and Social Change 1937–82* (Vancouver: University of British Columbia Press, 2008), chap. 6.

did not endorse the federal government's decision. A supporter of the NDP at the time, he argued, echoing Tommy Douglas, that Trudeau had used "a mallet to kill a flea" and that "this direct attack on civil liberties could be used to lock up not only FLQ activists" but also hippies and troublemakers everywhere. The crowd booed loudly. Never before had Granatstein feared "being torn limb from limb, but that day [he] was frightened." His fellow historians at the ceremony, Ramsay Cook and Jack Saywell, cautiously supported the government. Later, Cook and Granatstein reversed their positions as Cook developed doubts about the government's handling of the crisis and Granatstein came to believe that "Trudeau's bold actions . . . moved the idea of separatism completely out of the conspiracy-charged FLQ cells and into the bright light of public debate." Afterwards, the debate, though nasty, bitter, and long, was fought in democratic forums by elected governments and political actors.[39] That, in Granatstein's view, was Trudeau's big achievement.

Trudeau always criticized governments such as those of Brazil and West Germany that had negotiated with terrorists for the release of diplomatic or political hostages. In both these cases, he asserted, the kidnapping and the violence had continued. After October 1970, however, kidnappings ended in Quebec, and democratic governments of the twenty-first century are more likely to follow the pattern set out by Trudeau and his colleagues than the one recommended by his opponents in the petition of October 15. Nevertheless, the extensive discussion of those times in his memoirs betrays how very troubled Trudeau was by these events, by the alienation from old friends, and by the implications of his actions for civil liberties.

Margaret Sinclair was with Trudeau the night Laporte was killed. Earlier, they had argued about the War Measures Act because Margaret, then a leftist student, "sympathized" with "the 'long-haired radicals' being persecuted." At 1 a.m. the telephone rang. "I heard Pierre say, 'Oh, my God.' Then, 'Where did they find him?' And I knew that Laporte was dead. Pierre put down the receiver," she recalled, and "I heard him crying. . . . He was a shaken man: I watched him grow old before my eyes. It was as if Laporte's death lay on his shoulders alone: *he* was the one who wouldn't negotiate, and *he* was the man who would now have to take responsibility for the murder of an innocent man. It gave him a new bitterness; a hard sadness I had never seen before."[40]

Trudeau was sadder and harder, but he never doubted the decision he, Marchand, Lalonde, and his colleagues took. Laporte's death was a savage blow, but in Trudeau's view the autopsy it provoked broke a cycle of violence that profoundly threatened democracy in Quebec and Canada.

—

CHAPTER FOUR

REASON AND PASSION

The artist Joyce Wieland watched Pierre Trudeau intensely as he took power in 1968: she hoped he would become the critical link to the burgeoning currents of politics, art, and nationalism that she, a patriotic Canadian artist, craved. She began to quilt—an ordinary, women's task—and created *Reason over Passion*, one of the most celebrated Canadian artistic works of the sixties. She was so taken with Trudeau that she and her husband, Michael Snow, decided to organize a reception for him in their New York loft, where they were living at the time. They invited a swarm of celebrities they knew, and when Trudeau arrived with his entourage, he quickly impressed them all with his knowledge of the "various art scenes in New York"—experimental films, avant-garde dance, and jazz. When Snow introduced him to drummer Milford Graves as the "greatest drummer in jazz," Trudeau retorted: "Oh! Well, what about Max Roach?" Snow was astounded and enthralled, as was Wieland—temporarily.

Trudeau, too, was captured by the moment and the artist, and he bought the French version of the quilt—*La Raison avant la Passion*—for 24 Sussex Drive. Bilingual, populist, feminist, and ironic, "reason over passion" became a metaphor for the times.

When the National Gallery later presented an exhibition on the sixties, this iconic piece was at the centre. Curator Denise Leclerc expressed its ambiguity with her comment: "Here you're saying 'reason over passion,' but this is a bed we're talking about." She relished the irony of a quilt symbolizing the rule of reason: "Here's a man who insists on placing reason over passion—and yet, the political passions he created!"[1]

Some of those passions subsided rapidly as Wieland, like others who shared her views, became disillusioned with Trudeau. She later claimed that the quilt and the New York party were a "joke" on Trudeau, a view Snow clearly did not share. She confessed that, initially, she was intensely attracted to Trudeau but that the excitement disappeared as she came to the conclusion that he was cold, with too little passion and too much reason. He was a "psychopath," she said, whose government sucked in power, ruled autocratically, and revealed its brutal core when it invoked the War Measures Act. She went on to direct a film that celebrated the authenticity of the separatist Pierre Vallières.[2]

Wieland's change of mood mirrored, in extreme form, that of others on the nationalist left for whom Trudeau had been the political embodiment of the cultural revolution of that time. He was a vessel into which many poured their political passions, hoping to create an elixir that would cure the ills of a country divided between French and English and threatened by an imperialist America. The problems persisted, and Trudeau provided but a placebo—or, as Claude Ryan wrote, "slogans that barely touched the core of the problems."[3]

—

The October Crisis became the watershed for Trudeau's supporters and opponents, and his words—"just watch me," "bleeding hearts," and "go on and bleed"—became texts for future debates. In 1971 political scientist Denis Smith published a polemic against the federal and Quebec governments' policies during the crisis with the title *Bleeding Hearts, Bleeding Country*. But Trudeau never wavered from his belief that his decisiveness in the midst of the chaos of October 1970 had halted a freefall toward violent anarchy in Quebec. In a revealing interview later in the seventies, he said that René Lévesque and Claude Ryan's demand that he free the "political prisoners," "bargain with the FLQ and give in to them," and their assertion that "democratic support for a democratically elected government was crumbling," had worried him no end. "To my dying day," he predicted, "I'll think that's where the turning point lay." For Trudeau it was "the dying shame of very eminent people in Quebec to . . . [have signed] that manifesto."[4]

Despite this conviction, Trudeau and his advisers were concerned about the effect the October Crisis might have on his popularity. Even as British trade commissioner James Cross remained a hostage, they arranged for the prime minister to attend the great national sports event, the Grey Cup, to be held in Toronto in late November. They also worried that Trudeau's exasperation with leading francophone intellectuals and journalists would spill over to their anglophone counterparts, who had been key to his political success. Inevitably, their affection had begun to wane, but now some of them were angry. At the prime minister's request, PMO staffer Tim Porteous therefore asked historian Ramsay Cook to invite some Toronto intellectuals and opinion leaders to his home after the game so Trudeau could discuss the crisis.

The arrangements carried through according to plan. When Trudeau arrived in the football stadium in the late afternoon on November 28, he startled the Toronto crowd and the millions watching on national television by wearing a sweeping black cape with an exquisitely stylish slouch black hat.* In the morning papers the next day, his carefully staged appearance had captured more headlines than the Grey Cup game itself. After the event, he proceeded on to Ramsay Cook's house just before nine o'clock, accompanied by full security and determined to justify his actions. The twelve guests divided evenly on support or opposition to the government's actions, but there was a peculiar tension in the air. The RCMP officers checked Ken McNaught's parcel of Dinky Toys for Cook's kids as though the eminent historian had brought a bomb. Trudeau stayed into the early morning, jousting with the others, clearly annoyed and disappointed with the conversation. Eli Mandel, the professor-bard from York University, later wrote a poem about the evening that captured some of its ambiguities:

> if the revolution was about to occur
> would the people of Quebec rise up
> the people of Quebec would rise up
> therefore the revolution was about to occur
> wrong again

Cook, too, was ambivalent, trusting Trudeau but listening to his critics' complaints. Yet A.R.M. Lower, a founder of the Canadian Civil Liberties Union who had supervised Cook's M.A. thesis, firmly supported Trudeau's actions. So did the McGill law professor Frank

---

* Trudeau had dined the previous night with Marshall McLuhan, his wife, Corinne, and his daughter Teri. McLuhan called the visit an "incomparable honour" and reported that Teri and Corinne "insist that their lives have an entirely new dimension as a result of that event!" Referring to Trudeau's stylish costuming for the football game next day, he praised the "unveiling of the dramatic hat and cloak, the kick-off and the [Montreal] Alouette win." McLuhan to Trudeau, Dec. 3, 1970, MP, MG31, Series D-156, Microfilm reel H-2069, LAC.

Scott, who had been the foremost advocate of civil liberties before the Supreme Court of Canada. Both men accepted Trudeau's argument that a democratic government must govern, "which means never giving in to chaos or terror." Lower deplored the condemnation flung Trudeau's way by the Toronto branch of the Civil Liberties Union. "I think Trudeau acted rightly," he wrote to a friend. "There is no use in being sentimental in such situations, as so many well-intentioned people are."[5] Trudeau strongly agreed.

Robert Bourassa had also abhorred the Ryan-Lévesque petition, but Trudeau and his closest colleagues thought—perhaps erroneously—that Bourassa had been "weak." Trudeau later wrote that the October Crisis taught him "that it is absolutely essential to have, at the helm of state, a very firm hand, one that sets a course that never alters, that does not attempt to do everything at once out of excitement or confusion, but that moves along slowly, step by step, putting solutions in place."[6] According to that standard, Bourassa earned a mediocre mark.* Cartoonists in Quebec and the rest of Canada increasingly shared these perceptions as they endowed the reed-like, bespectacled Bourassa with ever more

---

* Some senior federal Liberals had thought poorly of the three candidates for the Quebec Liberal leadership in 1969. In a discussion on October 2, Jean Marchand reported that all the candidates were "weak and that the Party was going to have difficulty staying together." Two federal ministers from Quebec, Bryce Mackasey and Eric Kierans, said that "Bourassa was morally weak and would be pushed around." Bourassa, who had initially supported René Lévesque against Kierans in the 1967 provincial debates about autonomy, was thought likely to "accept Lévesque" as part of the Quebec Liberal Party. Marchand had refused to consider taking on the leadership of the Quebec Liberals, although many had urged him to enter the race. Had he done so, history might have been considerably different (Richard Stanbury Diary, Oct. 2, 1969, privately held). Stanbury was president of the Liberal Party of Canada at the time.

mouse-like qualities. Trudeau, in contrast, acquired a strong mas-culinity. Although shorter in height than Bourassa, and older, Trudeau's cartoon image bore the flavour of the young Marlon Brando and Jean-Paul Belmondo, the brilliant French New Wave actor who played the *mec* so memorably in sixties cinema. Like them, Trudeau was the tough guy, cool, laid back, savvy, surly, and hard. It was an image he cultivated expertly and deliberately.

Trudeau is the only politician included in *Mondo Canuck*, a history of Canadian "pop culture." The authors introduce the chapter on the Trudeau phenomenon, "Pierre Trudeau's Rule of Cool," with his defining words, "Just watch me." The "effortlessly charismatic" Trudeau, for whom "sexuality was as important as policy," was celebrated in this tome for the manner in which he "turned the country into spectacle itself, the glamorous movie it had only ever dreamed of becoming, with Pierre elite Trudeau both its director and star." He was, unlike Bourassa, always in control.[7]

In the manifesto read over the airwaves in the early days of the October Crisis, the FLQ had mocked Trudeau's authority and masculinity and called on various forces to overthrow his tottering and feckless rule. The terrorists' aim was to weaken political authority, particularly Trudeau's, but the tactic didn't work. After the crisis radical separatists hurled jeremiads at Trudeau, deeming him a fascist, an authoritarian with a profoundly malignant strength. Bourassa, in contrast, retained the image of timidity that had gathered around him. Quebec Cabinet minister William Tetley, who admired Bourassa for his role in the crisis, wrote in December 1970 that Bourassa was "worrying about being called weak." Tetley believed the premier had been a wise pragmatist, but he was not Trudeau, who was "flexible and strong when nec-essary" and "can take decisions."[8]

Pierre Vallières, the FLQ's most prominent ideologue, reflected the image of Trudeau as a strong and decisive leader in *L'Urgence de choisir*, which he published in 1971.[9] In this book Vallières did not reject the violence of the FLQ past but, in an interesting twist, declared that Trudeau's ruthless state terrorist tactics meant that he and his FLQ colleagues should abandon violence and, instead, support the democratic ambitions of René Lévesque's Parti Québécois. Vallières' comments probably reflected and influenced the thoughts of others — and, indeed, the bombs did give way to ballots. Although Trudeau's actions during the October Crisis lost him support not only among intellectuals but also among the young, the image of the strong, decisive leader became a political asset of lasting value.*

---

* Attacks on Trudeau by radical separatists continued to be virulent, though the mocking took different forms. He was often compared to Hitler, Goering, and Mussolini, but his sexual orientation was no longer questioned as it had been in the notorious manifesto. The poet Gérald Godin, who was locked up during the police raids and who later became a Parti Québécois Cabinet minister, contemptuously attacked Trudeau in 1971 as a pimp who managed his whores (his Quebec MPs) for the benefit of American corporate interests (*Québec-Presse*, Sept. 12, 1971). Vallières, who was gay himself, was surely uncomfortable with the mocking of Trudeau as a "fairy" in the FLQ manifesto, and he became increasingly dissatisfied with his FLQ colleagues while still profoundly suspicious of federalist intentions. He argued in a 1977 book that the entire October Crisis was manufactured by the federal and Quebec governments and that the murder of Pierre Laporte was not carried out by the Chenier cell. The true aim of the invocation of the War Measures Act, he claimed, was to smash the Parti Québécois (Pierre Vallières, *Les Dessous de l'opération* [Montreal: Québec Amérique, 1977]). Although some members of the Chenier cell repudiated Vallières's exoneration of them, the belief that the two governments' goal in invoking the War Measures Act was to destroy the Parti Québécois remains a widely held point of view. However, that view is explicitly denied by Trudeau in interviews and in his memoirs, and the documentation largely supports him. His target was the FLQ, and his anger against Levesque, Parizeau, and others reflected his belief that they were tactically wrong in urging compromise.

Trudeau's popularity in public opinion polls, if not with opinion leaders in general, had soared in the aftermath of Laporte's brutal death. An *Ottawa Citizen* cartoon captured the paradox of Trudeau's political persona: on one side, a jaunty, beret-wearing Trudeau with a red rose in his teeth and a large "flower power" button; on the other, a military-helmet-wearing Trudeau with a bayonet between his teeth and a medal stating "War Measure Power." Trudeau had created this duality himself in the 1968 election campaign, when "puckering" and jackknife dives existed alongside his steely determination before the violent separatists on election eve in Montreal.[10]

The paradox persisted for the rest of Trudeau's life. Although the "hard edge" won him respect, his distinctive style was sometimes careless and politically damaging. Indeed, his popularity began to wane soon after Cross's release as other issues emerged in late 1970, and Trudeau's "tough guy" demeanour increasingly frustrated the press and troubled his own supporters. With young people, personal staff, and Commons visitors from MPs' constituencies, his personal charm won him enduring affection, but more and more, these excellent human qualities were largely concealed from the general public. And in the House of Commons and with the press, Trudeau could be downright contemptuous and dismissive. In his first term, his combative side often gave his critics considerable ammunition—and justifiably so in several cases. On the genocide in Biafra—the first such tragedy to be widely and painfully televised—he was too quickly dismissive of the emotions of those who demanded direct aid. With western farmers, he was simply unable to show empathy. And after meeting with their leaders, he famously told "*les gars de Lapalme*" (450 striking truck drivers who had lost a Canada Post contract) to "eat shit." Accompanying "*les gars*" was Pierre Vadeboncoeur, his closest friend throughout his schooldays. Trudeau never even looked at him, Vadeboncoeur told a reporter: "It was as if, for him, I no longer existed."[11]

Trudeau's anger could explode irresponsibly in the House of Commons, as it did on February 16, 1971, when he sneeringly brushed off Conservative MP John Lundrigan's demand for expanded unemployment insurance. Lundrigan rushed from the House to waiting television cameras. "The prime minister interrupted me by mouthing a four-letter obscenity," he complained earnestly. "I didn't expect this kind of behaviour from my prime minister of Canada." Lundrigan had a reputation as a hothead himself, but Hamilton MP Lincoln Alexander, the first African Canadian elected to Parliament and a man of innate dignity, confirmed Lundrigan's tale. In fact, he said, Trudeau had "mouthed" the "same thing" (two words) to him: "the first started with the letter F, the second with the letter O." Trudeau's behaviour, he solemnly declared, was "unacceptable." When accosted by reporters, Trudeau denied he'd said anything, although he admitted that "he moved his lips and waved his hands in a gesture of derision." He accused Lundrigan and Alexander of "crying to mama and to television." As the reporters persisted and asked what he was thinking when he "moved his lips," he curtly responded: "What is the nature of your thoughts, gentlemen, when you say fuddle duddle or something like that. God . . ."

"Fuddle duddle" eventually took its place in the *Canadian Oxford Dictionary* and became part of the lore surrounding the clever Trudeau, but editorials at the time almost unanimously condemned his behaviour. The whole incident played poorly in Flin Flon and other spots where the cultural revolution of the sixties caused more irritation than amusement. The context of each of Trudeau's offhand remarks provides some explanation but not justification for the remarks.* He knew that television, with

---

* The problem of context was recognized by Anthony Westell, whose 1972 study of Trudeau's first government, aptly entitled *Paradox*, is a model of

its immediacy and hand-held cameras, along with the more aggressive journalism of the sixties, had tightened the space for political expression—and eventually began to act accordingly in most situations.[12]

—

Five issues in particular bedevilled Trudeau's first term in office. In addition to the foreign and defence policy reviews described in chapter 2, four areas are of particular importance: the reform of the Criminal Code of Canada and associated areas of individual rights, the constitutional process, bilingualism and multiculturalism, and the direction of the Canadian economy. It was also during his first three years in office that Trudeau embarked on a completely new route in his personal life. Altogether, this period was more than usually challenging and action-packed for the new prime minister.

---

political journalism. In December 1968 Trudeau responded to the question "How and when are you going to sell the western Canadian farmers' wheat?" with the rhetorical remark "Why should I sell the Canadian farmers' wheat?" These words sparked outrage and became central to the litany of western Canadian complaints about Trudeau's indifference. Westell pointed out, however, that the infamous sentence was part of a five-hundred-word answer that incorporated economic theory, political assessment, and personal thoughts on international development. It might have worked had it appealed to the West's tradition of economic self-sufficiency, but, writes Westell, "it was never seen in that light, probably because the region was looking for comfort from Ottawa but half expecting a rebuff from mistrusted Easterners." Trudeau often fell short, with his cutting clips on the one hand and ponderous academic reflections on the other. *Paradox:Trudeau as Prime Minister* (Scarborough: Prentice-Hall, 1972), 67–68.

The reform of the Criminal Code was, of course, the political issue that first brought Trudeau wide-ranging attention, especially when he declared in December 1967 that the state had no business in the nation's bedrooms. After he became prime minister, he left the task of implementing the reform to his erstwhile leadership opponent John Turner. The justice minister was a brilliant choice. A superb communicator with a fine legal mind, he was also a prominent Catholic, with close ties to leading bishops and lay people—and his youth fitted neatly with the progressive, "sixties" character of the reforms. Turner was therefore able to serve Trudeau admirably as a lawyer with close links to the business community and the Catholic Church. His effectiveness was only enhanced by the fact that he was a young man with Kennedy-like glamour himself—not least because, one May evening in 1959 at Victoria's Government House, Princess Margaret appeared to be clearly enthralled with him as they danced.

The reform of the Criminal Code was part of a broader "rights revolution" at the time, and Canadian support of individual choice became a significant part of a movement that fundamentally transformed Western society and politics. The principal impulse for the transformation was the Western world's reaction to the horrors of collectivism and racism. Trudeau, who had flirted with collectivist and racist theories in his youth—notably, anti-Semitism and francophone nativism—reflected the broader societal change as he abandoned his corporatist and illiberal views during the mid-1940s at Harvard, Paris, and the London School of Economics. The tide turned as the Second World War came to an end, and then support of individual rights swept like a wave through the West after the United Nations Universal Declaration of Human Rights in December 1948. The Canadian government initially responded to this change with surprising reluctance. Prime Minister Louis St. Laurent was wary of treading on the provincial responsibility for "civil rights" set out in the British North America Act. In the previous two decades, notable abuses of these rights had occurred in Canada, most famously through the Quebec "Padlock Law" passed by the government of Maurice Duplessis in 1937 to combat "communist propaganda." Its broad range allowed the government not only to seize "communist" literature but also to "padlock" meeting rooms of groups it found objectionable. Although the law clearly placed limits on the freedoms of speech and association, it was still on the books in 1948.[13]

Ultimately, the St. Laurent government accepted the Universal Declaration. In the aftermath of fascism and the Holocaust, the tide was too strong to resist, and in the 1950s, Canadian judges made tentative attempts at tearing down the fences around Canadian institutions that had practised discrimination. Jews, the principal victims of savage racism, won the first victories in Canadian courts that same decade — particularly in Ontario, where the initial success came as private clubs, public positions, and housing were opened up to Jews. The 1973 appointment of Bora Laskin as chief justice of the Supreme Court reflected the "revolution" that had taken place after the war. In the thirties, the brilliant Laskin had returned from Harvard Law School to find no good positions open to him. "Unfortunately, he is a Jew," the eminent Toronto law professor Cecil Wright wrote to his close friend Sidney Smith, president of the University of Manitoba, on the eve of the war. "This may be fatal regarding his chances with you. I do not know. His race is, of course, proving a difficulty . . . in Toronto," he continued, even though "Laskin is not one of those flashy Jews." Wright said he would have hired Laskin if he could have and he hoped that Smith would oblige. Smith did not. Tolerance still had high limits.[14]

In his magisterial study of race and the law in Canada, James Walker illustrates how the "judicial assault on American segregation laws" and the international move toward decolonization came into conflict with Canada's traditional immigration ideals. In a debate on immigration reform in 1954, the year of the historic U.S.

Supreme Court decision on racial segregation, the Toronto *Star Weekly*, the most liberal and Liberal major daily in Canada, still declared that racial discrimination "is an established (and most would say sensible) feature of our immigration policy."[15] Despite the strong international pressure embodied in the Universal Declaration and the activism of the U.S. Supreme Court in ending segregation, the Liberal government remained reluctant to act on the initiatives that a few Canadian courts had taken. It was not until the election in 1957 of Progressive Conservative John Diefenbaker, a trial lawyer and civil libertarian, that federal government opinion shifted away from its conservative approach to rights. Then, within a decade, the tremendous force of civil rights swept away most of the foundations of racial privilege.[16]

Trudeau had entered the fight against the Duplessis government in the late 1940s. He and Jacques Hébert were leaders in the Quebec civil liberties movement, and lawyer Trudeau represented journalist Hébert as he waged fierce battles for those whose rights had been denied. Trudeau had also written articles for Hébert's journal *Vrai*, which reflected the arguments that their friend, lawyer Frank Scott, was making in defence of individual rights.[17] By 1967, when Trudeau was minister of justice and increasingly wary of the violent and intolerant tendencies of some elements of radical thought, he wrote in a preface to his collected essays that he had "never been able to accept any discipline except that which I imposed upon myself." And, he continued, "in the art of living, as in that of loving, or of governing . . . I found it unacceptable that others should claim to know better than I what was good for me." Yet, more than in *Vrai*, he now recognized that liberty had limits: "How can an individual be reconciled with a society? The need for privacy with the need to live in groups? Love for freedom with the need for order?" The questions were, Trudeau wrote, the oldest in political philosophy, yet ones he confronted directly in his public life.[18]

The state's restrictions on individual behaviour were principally embodied in the Criminal Code, but they rested on societal consensus and fears. Meanwhile, the "rights revolution" had produced many moments of magnificence: John Diefenbaker's flawed but principled Bill of Rights in 1960; King's "I have a dream" speech in 1963; and the freedom march in Selma, Alabama, in 1965. Trudeau celebrated those moments but worried about where the balance should be found. In the mid-sixties he took part in the commission on "hate laws," where freedom of speech was measured against the needs for order and individual respect and where he worked with his future political colleague Mark MacGuigan. He was less certain than MacGuigan, a law professor, about the need for hate laws, yet he agreed with him that in a free society with a diverse population, there should, for instance, be limits on what can be written and said about the denial of the Holocaust. Both men were practising liberal Roman Catholics who viewed the Index and the Inquisition as aberrations of the institution that represented their cherished faith and welcomed Vatican II's liberalization of the Church in the 1960s. Both clearly supported the historic declaration by John F. Kennedy, the first strong Catholic contender for the American presidency, that his private religious opinions were his own affair and that no president should impose his views on the nation. These events, attitudes, and legal precedents all created the setting in which Trudeau's government framed its response to the rights revolution of its time. The Just Society would rest on a rule of law appropriate to contemporary life.[19]

At a moment when the poet Philip Larkin said, with characteristic irony, that sexual intercourse was invented between the Chatterley trial and the Beatles' first LP, Trudeau appeared to embody the several revolutions of the decade. As Richard Gwyn has written: "He not only mirrored the prevailing liberalism of Canadians, he personified it and magnified it." He seemed, Gwyn continues, "a prototypical, secular liberal leader." But he was not.

He attended church far more regularly than nearly all his colleagues in Ottawa or his neighbours in Montreal, and he admired the profound Catholic faith of his friend Gérard Pelletier. Moreover, he personally disapproved of abortion and accepted the Church's strictures on divorce and even on birth control. Nevertheless, he broke with the ecclesiastical hierarchy over the state's right to limit individual behaviour. A sin it may be, he held, but a crime it is not. Sin is to be settled with God; crimes are the concern of Caesar.[20]

The reform of the Criminal Code reflected Trudeau's own understanding of the relationship between the state and the individual. Without Trudeau the changes would have been less sweeping and, therefore, less controversial. They became the core of the Just Society he proposed to create for Canadians after he became prime minister. Trudeau's Bill C-195, first introduced in December 1967, had more than one hundred clauses that covered a broad range of activities, ranging from homosexual sex between consenting adults to gambling to the use of the lash (this last, surprisingly, was still permitted under Canadian law as punishment for certain crimes).* The omnibus bill troubled John Turner

---

* Under the Canadian Constitution (Section 91 of the British North America Act 1867), criminal law is under federal jurisdiction. It was first codified in 1892 by Sir John Thompson and has been revised several times. It was not exclusive, and prosecution continued to be possible for offences at common law under the British system. The Trudeau-Turner revision, the Criminal Law Amendment Act, came into force on August 26, 1969. This broadest revision to date included the decriminalization of homosexual acts between consenting adults, access to contraception and abortion, legalized gambling, controls over gun ownership, and breathalyzer tests for suspected drunken drivers. The code also had many other important clauses, but the "sixties" issues attracted the attention of the press and the public.

when he inherited it in 1968, and he mused about breaking it up into smaller bills. He even suggested that there might be room for free votes on individual items such as homosexuality activities or abortion. The notion of a free vote had been raised by Conservative leader Robert Stanfield during the campaign of 1968, and not surprisingly, free votes appealed to opponents of these controversial changes because they opened up the possibility of "lobbying" MPs to defy government policy. Trudeau and Turner jousted over this idea, but Trudeau quickly asserted control and told Turner a free vote was impossible. As a result of this delay, however, the reform of the Criminal Code fell from the list of government priorities for that first fall session of 1968. When, on September 5, Trudeau briefed the Cabinet concerning the Throne Speech, he said that official languages, reform of Parliament, and the foreign and defence policy reviews would take precedence. And in an early glimmer of environmentalism, he said that the word "pollution" would be used several times in the speech from the throne.[21]

While Trudeau and the Department of Justice considered criminal law reforms, an international commission established by Pope John XXIII was in its final stages of deliberation. With a diverse membership that included married couples, the commission's mandate was to adapt Catholic doctrine to contemporary life. However, after Turner received his copy of the mandate from the commission in spring 1968, Pope Paul VI issued *Humanae Vitae* on July 25, pointing out that the commission was divided, that the Pope had final authority, and that traditional doctrines on birth and the family should be maintained. To "rulers of nations," the encyclical made a direct plea: "We beg of you, never allow the morals of your peoples to be undermined. . . . [D]o not tolerate any legislation which would introduce into the family those practices which are opposed to the natural law of God."

When the Canadian bishops met in September, this document fuelled debate about their role and their relationship with the political process. An intense lobbying effort began, and Catholic Liberal legislators felt the pressure acutely—none more so than John Turner. In response he deftly turned his close ties with Catholic leaders into an advantage. He argued with them privately that the abortion legislation merely "codified" what was already the existing situation in common law jurisdictions. The proposed legislation, which provided for legal abortion on the advice of three doctors when the mother's health was in danger, reflected the fact that in Canada and other common law jurisdictions, the courts, for more than fifty years, had not allowed a single prosecution against a mother or a doctor for an abortion when the mother's survival was in question. Turner and Trudeau found the Quebec Catholic Church more willing to accept the new legislation than the Catholic Church in English Canada. Perhaps the reason lay in the strong support for the reforms by the United Church, the largest Protestant denomination in the country. During the first parliamentary session, the strong support across party lines for the Criminal Code reform began to dissolve as anti-abortion crusaders battled with others who considered the reforms too hesitant.[22]

Faced with intense pressure, Turner asked for a meeting with the executive of the Canadian Conference of Catholic Bishops. Under the leadership of Bishop Alex Carter of North Bay, they met with Turner at the Cercle Universitaire, an old Ottawa mansion that was now an exclusive private club. Turner made his standard argument that the changes were simply "codification" of what currently existed in the law. At that point Bishop Carter interjected to end the meeting with the words: "Gentlemen, I think John has convinced us. Let's have a drink." The issue, however, did not disappear—indeed, concern about the Pope's reaction to the omnibus bill affected Canadian planning for Trudeau's visit to the Vatican in January 1969. Moreover, the longtime secretary of the Conference of Catholic Bishops, Bernard Daly, has a different memory of the understanding arrived at that day, one that disputes the agreement

Turner claimed was reached.[23] Whatever the outcome, Turner left the meeting ready to move forward with legislation ending the threat of life imprisonment for doctors who approved abortions.

Polls generally favoured the change, as they did for divorce, where existing practices seemed ridiculous. Because adultery was the major ground for divorce, lawyers would pay to "set up" male or female clients who wanted divorces, and courts winked at the fraud. However, public opinion was not so accepting of the proposed reform in the laws concerning homosexuality. In the final days of the debate on the Criminal Code amendments in the spring of 1969, the suggested change to allow physical intimacy or other "indecent" acts between any two consenting adults caused lively debates in Parliament. Under the existing law, anyone committing "buggery or bestiality" with another consenting adult— even in private—was liable for imprisonment of fourteen years, while "gross indecency," an undefined act, resulted in a sentence of up to five years. The proposed change would end criminal sanctions for such activities.[24]

A firm in Trudeau's own riding took a poll indicating that the divorce and abortion reforms were popular with Canadians, with 83 percent favouring the former and 73 percent the latter. However, the proposed changes in legislation dealing with homosexual acts were not popular: only 24 percent approved and 76 percent disagreed. Ironically, Trudeau had fewer doubts about this legislative change than he had about the other two major reforms. He had, in the early fifties, tried to help a prominent Quebec literary figure who had been barred from a job because of alleged homosexuality; many of his friends were gay, as were a number of Cabinet members he would appoint, and he thought the prohibition of private behaviour was a flagrant denial of civil rights. As the reform bill neared approval, the parliamentary debate reflected the polling results, and the homosexual legislation became the major focus. The attack became ferocious and thousands of letters and petitions of protest flooded Parliament Hill, even though several ministers, including Trudeau and Turner, consistently minimized the extent of the changes. A resident of Jasper wrote to Turner: "This present Government . . . will go down in history as the Government which made homosexual acts legal within this country. I imagine many homosexuals did not practice this vice because it had been illegal, and they had enough respect for the law to contain their desires." Now they surely would "because of your Bill!" Turner argued passionately that he continued to believe that the acts to be permitted among two consenting adults were "physically and morally repugnant, but they were now considered private conduct beyond the reach of the state." In the final debate, Diefenbaker, who liked Turner, asked why he was "carrying" the issue, and as so often was the case, Diefenbaker answered his own question: "I know why he is carrying it; he has got a dagger in his back, and on the hand of that dagger is the hand of the prime minister." Créditiste leader Réal Caouette offered the most peculiar interpretation of the new legislation: "Being homosexual is now okay, as long as it is in private between consenting Liberals."[25]

Despite the angry words in the House, the exchange attracted surprisingly little public attention. In April-May 1968, the debates over foreign policy and the Official Languages Bill dominated the attention of Parliament and Cabinet. And, of course, the Canadian reforms were responding to changes in other Western democracies. Trudeau, and especially Turner, continued to attest that these legislative changes represented only a minor challenge to traditional religious and moral positions. Their arguments have proved convincing to some historians. Andrew Thompson, for example, entitled his study of the Criminal Code reforms as "Slow to Leave the Bedrooms of the Nation." He refers to a pamphlet issued by NDP member of Parliament Ed Broadbent, which attacked Trudeau's reforms and derisively dismissed the prime minister as a "swinging Mackenzie King who wanted a with-it generation to accept a conservative program with a clear conscience." Yet the long-term results and the passion of both advocates and opponents suggest that the total package represented a sea change in the relationship between a watchful state and the private actions of individuals.* The debate and the legislation planted the seeds for a real public awareness of individual rights. Those sprouts grew quickly, and the culture wars of later decades were fought on those same fields.[26]

The legislation, then, was not simply the product of an alteration in public attitudes. It was also a reflection of Trudeau's commitment to a Just Society and his own view of individual rights and the public interest. His personal experience had

---

* When similar changes transpired in Britain, those whom it most affected recognized that they represented a sea change. In his diary the British society photographer Cecil Beaton, who was bisexual, observed on December 26, 1966: "This week, one of the most important milestones in English law has been reached, and hardly any of my friends, even those most closely involved, have mentioned the fact that, at last, the recommendations of the Wolfenden Report regarding the behaviour of homosexuals have been accepted. . . . No more important event has happened since the declaration of peace. Yet few people seem to have looked back to remember with what anguish their natural inclinations made them law breakers." Beaton expressed regret that the change (very close to the later Canadian reforms) had not come earlier: "It is not that I would have wished to avail myself of further licence, but to feel that one was not a felon and an outcast would have helped enormously during the difficult young years." Many Canadians surely shared these emotions in the spring of 1969. Cecil Beaton, *Beaton in the Sixties: The Cecil Beaton Diaries As They Were Written*, ed. Hugo Vickers (London: Phoenix, 2004), 168–69.

taught him how slowly attitudes change. When he was first being considered for the Liberal leadership, Lester Pearson, that most tolerant of Canadians, had privately asked him for assurance that he was not a homosexual. During the 1968 campaign, rural Quebec commentators had mocked him about his sexual identity, and right-wing newsletters openly claimed that he was gay. The Ottawa gossip even suggested that his close relationship with his bachelor assistant and friend Michael Pitfield was homosexual in character. The FLQ manifesto, which, to Trudeau's great annoyance, millions heard in both official languages, called Trudeau a "fairy." The rumour even spread beyond Canada's boundaries and made an impact. According to Henry Kissinger, Nixon disliked Trudeau from the beginning because he thought he was a "queer"—"all evidence to the contrary," he added, laughing deeply.

—

As the bachelor Trudeau neared mid-century, he began to date with the energy of a sixties teenager, and as Kissinger aptly said, "power is the greatest aphrodisiac."[27] Although some of his interests—classical music, philosophy, and political theory—were not those of most young people, he possessed a youthful flair, a romantic attachment to the wilderness, a chiselled body, a sharp wit, and, of course, power. Not surprisingly, the press was very interested in his personal life, especially when he was outside Canada. Trudeau usually revelled in the attention. When an attractive female reporter in Hawaii asked him what it was like to be "the world's most eligible bachelor," he replied that he didn't benefit from it too much:

"For instance," he speculated, "if I were to ask you for a date tonight—"

"I'd say no," she interrupted, "because I'm married."

"Because you're married . . ." he responded, " . . . well, you shouldn't hide your ring under your notebook."[28]

In the later sixties his mood shifted, and he spoke surprisingly freely about wanting to abandon his bachelorhood. Perhaps it was the commitment to pursuing the leadership that had prompted such thoughts: his hope for a family was certainly an issue that had weighed on his mind when he'd embarked on the leadership quest and even caused him to consider turning down the historic opportunity. Later, after he became prime minister, reporters quizzed Trudeau at the Ottawa airport about rumours that he had been married during his trip to the North in July 1968. He denied the suppositions but then replied, surprisingly: "I'm constantly thinking of marriage." To a CBC reporter in a 1968 year-end interview, he responded that instead of making a resolution to remain a bachelor, he was "rather despondent that leap year should have passed by without my really having had time to make the kind of deal I would have liked. But, never mind," he said. "This year I'll be taking initiatives!"[29] And he did.

Margaret Sinclair remained very much in his mind and was often by his side after Trudeau wooed her following their encounter at the leadership convention. By Christmas 1969, Trudeau and Margaret "were confessing to each other that [they] were unmistakably in love." Certainly, there were doubts: he was too old and she too young and different. They saw each other secretly in the fall of 1969 and spent weekends at Harrington Lake, where they rumpled the beds in the other rooms to deceive the staff into believing that others had been there. There were only two public occasions in 1970: once at the National Gallery, when Margaret dressed for a costume ball as a "hippie" Juliet, and once at a dinner party at the home of Wendy and Tim Porteous. At the gallery, groups froze when they came near, and Margaret, surprised by the coolness of her welcome, sobbed uncontrollably after they left. At the Porteous home, everyone spoke French, which

Margaret did not understand. For a brief time in the winter of 1970 the two broke up. Margaret began dating a divinity student, and Trudeau and Streisand had their fling. But then, at Easter, shortly after Pierre and Barbra had gone their separate ways, Pierre and Jean Marchand spent a ski holiday at Whistler, and Margaret met up with Trudeau there. Romance blossomed again, and Margaret decided to enroll at the University of Ottawa for the fall term in the Department of Psychology. As she warmed to Pierre, he, not surprisingly, pulled back, telling her she was "too young and too romantic." They broke up once more and Margaret returned to British Columbia, but then he called during a visit to Vancouver in early summer 1970 and asked her to go scuba diving with him in the Caribbean. "What for?" she fumed. "More pain? I can't go on playing this sort of life." He begged for patience and asked her to fly back to Ottawa with him.[30]

She then spent a weekend with him at Harrington Lake, and one summer afternoon beside the shimmering water, Trudeau, entranced, murmured that they should talk about marriage. It was not a proposal, he said later, but Margaret thought it was. As one of Trudeau's closest friends remarked, Pierre was playing dangerously in those times. Margaret jumped to her feet, flung her arms around him, and exclaimed, "When? Tomorrow?" A startled Trudeau replied, "Let's take it easy," but Margaret jumped into the lake and swam around in circles "like a frenzied dolphin." When she finally emerged from the water, Pierre set out some conditions: she should be "a good faithful wife to him, give up drugs, and stop being so flighty." He warned her that he was fifty years old and "extremely solitary by nature." Trudeau was troubled. Had he gone too far? As Margaret wrote later: "This period was the closest I ever came to seeing Pierre out of full control in all our time together." While becoming "most attentive and loving," he believed, in Margaret's words, "that he must convince himself that it would work." The year had been rough politically, with language battles in Montreal streets, continual labour strife, and Aboriginal protests throughout the country.

Trudeau decided to take a break in the month of August, in the Caribbean with Margaret and the noted ocean scientist Dr. Joe MacInnis and his wife, Debby. He then vacationed alone that summer at the Aga Khan's home in Sardinia and on a yacht in the Mediterranean. He also decided to speak with his long-time friend Carroll Guérin.[31]

Carroll had spent much of her time in Europe and England in recent years and had been on a spiritual quest, including a period in a monastery.* For these reasons, she had seen Trudeau only intermittently since he had entered politics, although she remained emotionally committed and dated no others until the late sixties. Strikingly beautiful, Catholic, liberal, fluently trilingual, independently wealthy, and knowledgeable about the arts, Carroll was not in awe of Trudeau, and their relationship was full of respect and playfulness. Over the years, he had raised the question of marriage, to the point where he began one conversation with the disclaimer: "Don't worry, I'm not going to ask you to marry me today." Now he told her he was seriously contemplating marriage (to Margaret Sinclair), and referring to their discussions of the past brought the

---

* The previous volume of this biography relied on the correspondence between Guérin and Trudeau and erroneously conveyed the impression that Ms. Guérin borrowed money from Trudeau, suffered a serious illness that forced her to use a wheelchair and made her less than a "full woman," and was "disappointed" by Trudeau when he failed to meet her on one occasion in 1967 as planned. Having now discussed these matters with Ms. Guérin in several conversations, I have learned that she never had need of a loan, that the wheelchair was used only at an airport when she met Trudeau, and that the missed appointment was a misunderstanding, not an angry separation.

topic up one last time, but Carroll quickly turned it away. "No," she replied. She did not think Trudeau could share the spiritual life she was devoted to and told him that, because they "could not meet at that level of togetherness which would come from Grace," marriage was not a good idea. She also knew that he wanted children, and her health might make that difficult. She has a letter thanking her for her thoughtfulness and for considering his proposal.[32]

Trudeau then flew to Nassau with Margaret, Joe and Debby MacInnis, and other friends and booked in at the Small Hope Bay Lodge on the little island of Andros in the Bahamas. Trudeau's aides warned MacInnis that scuba diving was "a hobby, not a passion" for the prime minister. The aides seem to have completely misunderstood their boss's nature. He was never a man of "hobbies" in anything that he undertook—including his lifelong, passionate exploration of the seas with MacInnis. MacInnis would eventually take Trudeau on dives of remarkable depth, including one of 250 feet. He later said that Trudeau was always "curious about the natural world and his place in it." But at the time there were other passions to satisfy. Margaret and Pierre "lived in a derelict shack on the beach and dived all day, spending romantic and exhausted evenings pacing the sand" as Pierre asked endless questions about her past. He claimed he needed to know everything, to prevent blackmail, and he kept saying, "I know you'll leave me one day." She said she would never leave him, but they agreed to test their love by a separation: Margaret would return to Vancouver, not Ottawa. When they were ready, they would marry, but in the meantime, they would tell no one of their intention. Margaret did tell her mother, who initially opposed the match, and then they began to plan for the wedding. Jimmy Sinclair was kept in the dark until late, as were Margaret's friends, most of whom learned about the relationship when they read the wedding notice.

Margaret began to take instruction for conversion to the Roman Catholic Church, and after some debate, she agreed to give up marijuana. She also began French lessons at the Alliance Française in Vancouver. She describes Father Schwinkles, the priest who guided her conversion, as a shy man with little imagination: he presented her with a manual called *What It Is to Become a Good Catholic*, with the relevant parts underlined in black. When Margaret professed concern that the book suggested that only Catholics went to Heaven and asked what would happen to her Protestant friends, he reassured her that Catholicism represented the "jet plane to Heaven." Protestants, presumably, were condemned to turboprops. A disturbed Pierre, who called nightly, gave her a more academic reading list, which included Newman's *Apologia Pro Vita Sua* and St. Augustine's *Confessions*, to complement her mandated reading. It was a practice he continued after they married, as he tried to ensure that Margaret appreciated the intellectual foundations of her new faith.[33]

In November 1970 Trudeau was scheduled to meet Streisand again in New York, but if he did the press learned nothing of it and, presumably, neither did Margaret. She recalls, however, coming upon a pile of photographs of various women in Trudeau's desk drawer, with Streisand's picture on top. "Are you ranking us?" she asked. "Maybe," he replied wryly. By Christmas 1970, however, Streisand had begun an affair with Hollywood star Ryan O'Neal, then at the height of his popularity for his performance in the saccharine *Love Story*. Margaret, as we know, had been with Trudeau the night Pierre Laporte was killed (it was Thanksgiving), and the experience had brought them closer together. The security was a shock, and the lovers, accustomed to secrecy but not heavy security, misbehaved by trekking into the forest one rainy day at Harrington Lake to escape watchful eyes. They got lost, the security forces panicked, and when the pair finally emerged in a clearing, they heard gunshots. There, in the middle of the lake, was an "absolutely bald policeman" holding an umbrella in one hand and shooting a rifle in the air with the other to guide them home. Margaret later wrote that the security bothered her greatly, but she did not heed her doubts about her upcoming marriage to the prime minister. In her dream, she would "turn his cold, lonely life into a warm, happy one." Late that fall she became completely certain of her choice.[34]

Margaret returned to Vancouver in November and began to sew her wedding dress, modelled on a sari Indian prime minister Jawaharlal Nehru had given her mother in 1954. Margaret finally told her father that she and Pierre were to marry in the new year, and the former Liberal Cabinet minister was overjoyed. He wrote to Trudeau just before Christmas: "Margaret told me her good news this weekend. Welcome to the family. My very best wish for the two of you is that you will always be as happy together as Kathleen and I have been since our marriage thirty years ago. Sincerely, James Sinclair." Margaret mischievously asserts in her memoirs that her marriage fulfilled her father's own dream of occupying 24 Sussex Drive. Whatever the reason, the two Liberal politicians quickly bonded, and Sinclair would later stand by Pierre when Margaret did not.

With their decision to marry now firm, Margaret's parents agreed to let her spend Christmas with Pierre. He wanted her to meet his family, and understandably, she dreaded the experience. They quickly selected some presents from the gifts that Trudeau had received in his capacity as prime minister and drove from Ottawa to Montreal. Pierre's brother and sister, Charles and Suzette, were warm and charming and, according to Margaret, knew immediately that the relationship was serious because Trudeau had not brought other girlfriends home for Christmas. His mother, Grace, who was suffering from advanced Parkinson's disease, could only clasp Margaret's hand silently as her future daughter-in-law sat beside her bed. In Margaret's eyes, the past over-whelmed the Trudeau house, in which "not a corner had been altered since Pierre, as a little boy, had fled in terror from a surreal-ist painting of a skeleton holding a skull." The parlour where guests were received was dark and oppressive, "full of browns and lace," with "*petit point* upholstered chairs." Pierre and Margaret escaped the ghosts and gloried in the abundant Christmas cheer of a family devoted to one another.[35] And sometime during those happy days, they set the date for the wedding: March 4, 1971.

Back in Vancouver, as the marriage neared, the wedding dress took shape in the Sinclair house and the cake was baked. One by one the other members of the family learned that Margaret was getting married. Pierre called every night in an increasingly concerned state, asking, "Are you sure you want to go ahead with this?" Margaret no longer had doubts. She still had hippie friends and had had a narrow escape when she joined three of them on a trip to the United States a few weeks before the wedding. They were stopped at the border and ordered out of the car, whereupon the police seized a box containing ashes from India, mistaking it for contraband drugs. A matron subjected Margaret to a total body search while a portrait of Richard Nixon "leered" at her. Fortunately, the incident attracted no attention. Trudeau's friends in Ottawa noticed that he was intense and frustrated, especially in the House of Commons in February, when he mouthed the infamous "fuddle duddle." A week before the wedding, Margaret went to the shy priest Father Schwinkles, told him she was ready for conversion, and confessed quite a few sins, including the fact that she'd lied about the identity of the man she was dating. It was not "Pierre Mercier" but Pierre Trudeau. The priest gasped, then hurriedly commanded: "Go down on your knees and say the Lord's Prayer. Do three Hail Marys for your sins."

As the day for the wedding approached, Pierre became ever more "nervous and jittery." He made it "much harder for himself by telling no one," Margaret says, "locking himself up with a secret and worrying." He arranged to see Madeleine Gobeil in mid-February and told her he had fallen in love with Margaret and that it was a serious relationship. Madeleine had been his close public companion, and most of his friends thought that she would be his choice should he marry. He had already told Carroll Guérin that he intended to marry a much younger woman he was dating, and they had talked together about how important a family was to him. But Trudeau kept the news from everyone else, including those with whom he worked most closely. On March 3 he gave a speech in which he reflected on the Report of the Royal Commission on the Status of Women. "Society," he declared, "cannot become mature without the full participation of women."[36] That speech and other duties kept Trudeau in Ottawa until the last moment—a dangerous decision, given the weather in that region in early March. Not surprisingly, a snowstorm closed the Ottawa airport the morning of Thursday, March 4, but when the skies opened briefly, Trudeau rushed off to fly to Vancouver. Marc Lalonde accompanied him in his limousine, and engulfed in files, they worked all the way through the drive. At the airport, Lalonde asked Trudeau, "What are you doing for the weekend?" "I'm getting married," Trudeau replied without hesitation and sprinted to the plane.[37]*

The wedding day was cool and clear in Vancouver, but the atmosphere in the Sinclair home was feverish. The best-laid plans for a secret ceremony were going awry. Margaret's hairdresser had influenza, and his replacement had styled her hair to look like a

---

* Many stories indicate that the news of the wedding surprised Madame Gobeil and that Trudeau left their mutual friend Gérard Pelletier to break the news to her. Christina Newman, who knew Gobeil well, suggested that a *Toronto Star* reporter awoke Gobeil with the shocking news and that Pelletier acted for Trudeau in dealing with her. Pelletier, then secretary of state, did assist Madame Gobeil in securing a position in Paris with UNESCO, a cultural agency, where she went on to have an outstanding career.

"fuzzy poodle." The cake Margaret and her mother had baked so carefully was not iced plainly as Margaret had instructed but decorated with little figures of bride and groom, surrounded by bees and doves. Margaret ripped them off, knowing how offensive they would be to Pierre. Trudeau's sister, Suzette, who had not told her husband why they were going to Vancouver, finally filled him in as they were stuck in a snowstorm in downtown Montreal, missing their flight. Finally, Pierre arrived a half-hour late at the small church where he would wed. It was bedecked with garlands of spring flowers and sprigs of wheat as a late afternoon sun lit the interior. Father Schwinkles had agreed to preside—rather reluctantly, according to Margaret; Pierre's brother, Charles, was best man; and Lin Sinclair, the maid of honour. Trudeau's assistant Gordon Gibson, who had been fooled to the last minute, was drawn in to make the wedding party an even fourteen. Margaret's wedding dress was white, hooded, and exquisite in its simple elegance, and the ceremony proceeded flawlessly.

Trudeau once again stunned Canadians with this unexpected move, and there were neither crowds nor reporters until the family reached the Sinclair home after 9:30 that evening. The newlyweds lingered long at the reception there, then changed into informal clothes for the drive away on their honeymoon.

Trudeau did tell Gobeil about the seriousness of his relationship with Margaret Sinclair in February, but he did not mention any wedding plans. This misunderstanding accounts for the discrepancy in the stories. Many of the friends of Trudeau and Gobeil believe that Trudeau was unfair in the way he handled this incident. The Trudeau Papers indicate that they became good friends once again in the 1980s. See also Christina Newman, *Grits* (Toronto: McClelland and Stewart, 1982), 330–33. Interview with Madeleine Gobeil, May 2006; confidential interviews.

Margaret's confused father directed Pierre to a separate room to dress—a suggestion he refused. Late in the night, Margaret and Pierre left in a police car for the Sinclairs' mountain log cabin.[38]

At 6:30 the next morning, the telephone rang. A startled Trudeau leapt from the wedding bed and answered. It was Richard Nixon, thinking the newlyweds were in Ottawa and calling to offer congratulations from Pat and the American people. Other unexpected good wishes appeared on Canadian editorial pages, ranging from the chauvinist greetings from the *Vancouver Sun*, which congratulated Trudeau for his good sense in choosing a British Columbia beauty, to *Le Devoir's* whimsical account of how the provinces had all competed with their own candidates. The gorgeous wedding photos that dominated the media on March 5 were followed by breathless stories of Margaret's athleticism, recounting how the happy couple had put in four hours of skiing. But of all the well-wishers, John Diefenbaker captured the most headlines with his brief comment: the prime minister, he sonorously declaimed, had had two choices—to marry her or adopt her. Trudeau, who liked Diefenbaker despite many angry exchanges, took the remark in good humour.[39]

In New Zealand: always the curious, involved traveller.

Trudeau performs on the South Nahanni River, August 1970. "I liked to set myself challenges . . . in my childhood I was considered a rather frail child." Trudeau, *Memoirs*.

The very young and lovely Margaret Sinclair's first public date with Pierre, National Arts Centre, 1969.

Diving in the Virgin Islands with oceanographer Joseph MacInnis, August 1970. MacInnis, a friend for more than thirty years, took Trudeau diving in the Arctic, Pacific, and Atlantic oceans. He wrote: he "had an explorer's awareness of the beauties, blessings, and uncertainties of the natural world." Earlier that year Trudeau had stated in support of his Arctic Waters Pollution Prevention Act: "Canadian action is an assertion of the importance of the environment, of the sanctity of life on the planet, of the need for recognition of the principle of clean seas."

Fashion statements at the Grey Cup, November 28, 1970. Calgary fans wore Stetsons; Montreal's Trudeau wore a cape. Montreal won 23–10.

"In 1970, I fell in love with a very beautiful girl. March 4, 1971, was the date that Margaret Sinclair and I married in Vancouver." Trudeau, *Memoirs*. Margaret later said that the ceremony had nothing about "worshipping each other; just texts to do with love and peace." Signing the marriage register as Father Schwinkles looks on.

In love: Margaret and Pierre at a Government House ball, 1973.

—

CHAPTER FIVE

VICTORIA'S FAILURE

Trudeau's marriage to Margaret was a beacon of sunlight that broke through the bleak political winter of 1971 as criticism rose concerning the government's handling of the economy and, belatedly, the invocation of the War Measures Act. The major item on the agenda for the spring was the Constitution, a subject that had thrust Trudeau into prominence when he first came to Ottawa but which had attracted less attention after his legendary confrontation with Quebec premier Daniel Johnson in February 1968. Johnson's premature death, the weakness of his successor, Jean-Jacques Bertrand, and other political exigencies had since slowed progress on the constitutional file. Moreover, the federal government had chosen to concentrate instead on the Official Languages Act, a statute that dealt with the place of francophones in Confederation and with minority language rights more generally.* Like the Divorce Act, it was a federal statute that had considerable impact on provincial jurisdictions.

---

* This historic act guaranteed the equality of the French language with English within the federal government. Specifically, it guaranteed that

When Trudeau entered public life in 1965, he did not see any advantage in "opening up" the Constitution, with its hoary and traditional problems of the division of powers between the federal and provincial governments. However, the Ontario Confederation of Tomorrow Conference in 1967, the powerful force of Quebec nationalism expressed by Johnson's position of "equality" or "independence," the expansion of the welfare state

---

francophones could have service in their own language from any federal agency in Canada in jurisdictions where they exceeded 10 percent of the population. The same guarantee applied to English Canadians in Quebec. Opposition leaders supported the legislation, although Progressive Conservative leader Robert Stanfield faced a rebellion from some members who charged that the legislation "stuffed French down the throats" of anglophones. The act was very popular in Quebec, but the move by successive Quebec governments to make French the official language of the province and to restrict English-language education and public use caused a reaction among English Canadians.

The Official Languages Act transformed the federal government, where the senior public service now works bilingually and the percentage of franco-phones in the service roughly equals their percentage in the population. In the 1950s, by contrast, francophones constituted less than 10 percent of the Canadian public service, and the language of work was, with few exceptions, English. The Royal Commission on Bilingualism and Biculturalism played an important part in creating public support for the act, although Trudeau himself was skeptical of the commission's work. He closed it down when it began to consider "constitutional questions." In Jack Granatstein's apt assessment, its "contributions in detail were not great; what it did do was to help prepare English Canadians for the necessity of change. That was a major achievement, immeasurable as it might be." J.L. Granatstein, *Canada 1957–1967: The Years of Uncertainty and Innovation* (Toronto: McClelland and Stewart, 1986), 255.

(which caused the federal government to intrude into traditional provincial realms), and the rapid changes in society's view of what individual behaviour the state should prohibit all meant that the Constitution remained an active file in the late 1960s for provincial and federal public servants and an increasing number of academics. In hindsight, most political commentators today believe that Trudeau's reform of the Canadian Constitution fundamentally altered Canada.

The Confederation of Tomorrow Conference began a new era of political consultation, in which federal and provincial officials got together on a continuing basis and their political masters also met far more regularly than ever before. Mackenzie King had loathed gatherings of premiers and the federal government and kept them to a minimum, but Trudeau had laboured long in the area of constitutional law, and his views on federalism had attracted others to his political candidacy. He enjoyed the debates on the balance of powers between provinces and the federal government, which had been at the core of the increasing number of federal-provincial consultations in the sixties. Moreover, while justice minister, he had published under his own name a government statement entitled *A Canadian Charter of Human Rights* and, under Prime Minister Pearson's name, *Federalism for the Future*. His campaign for the leadership caught fire after his confrontation with Quebec premier Daniel Johnson at a February 1968 federal-provincial conference. In another document published a year later, *The Constitution and the People of Canada*, Trudeau set out the federal position on constitutional change. He himself headed the federal-provincial relations committee of the Cabinet, which ensured its pre-eminence within the structure of government. Similarly, provincial governments, Quebec most impressively in the sixties, developed their own agencies to deal with the myriad problems and opportunities their relations with the federal government presented. Political scientist Richard Simeon described this development as the emergence of federal-provincial diplomacy, and a handful of acronyms emerged to describe the various agencies dealing with federal-provincial interaction.[1]

These agencies and committees met continually, although only three provinces — Ontario, New Brunswick, and Quebec — were deeply interested in their work. But two events in 1970 reinvigorated interest in the constitutional file: the March appointment of Bora Laskin to the Supreme Court of Canada and the April election of the Liberals under Robert Bourassa in Quebec. Laskin was the pre-eminent constitutional theorist in English Canada, and his appointment indicated that Trudeau wanted to have a more activist court. Laskin's biographer Philip Girard notes that, despite their very different origins, "the two men were similar in many ways. Both were intellectuals with a strong desire to shape their society, and both were missionaries of legal modernism. . . . Both saw greater protection for individual rights as an antidote to the outmoded claims of ethnic nationalism. . . . Both wanted the federal government to play a greater role in national life than it had previously done. Both rejected Quebec's claim for constitutional recognition." Girard concludes: "If Laskin had not existed in 1970, Trudeau would have had to invent him."[2]

Trudeau also played some role in "inventing" Robert Bourassa, if only because the alternatives as Liberal leader were less preferable. When this newcomer became premier, Trudeau initially "thought he was someone with whom we could make progress. He was a new man, a federalist, an economist with a clear mind, and a politician not particularly noted as a nationalist."[3] He was not ideal, but better than the alternatives. That was enough for fresh dreams to blossom that spring.

Trudeau's own views on the Constitution were complex and are often caricatured as strongly centralist. They were not. When Allan Gotlieb, an astute young lawyer in the Department of External Affairs, had his first lunch with Trudeau in 1965, he was surprised to hear him speak about the need for decentralization and about respect for provincial jurisdiction. He had similarly astonished and even angered many Quebec colleagues in the mid-fifties when he had opposed federal grants to universities, which many of them saw as the solution to their low salaries and their crushing domination by Duplessis and the Roman Catholic Church. Trudeau was not in favour of conditional grants to the provinces because he believed they skewed provincial needs and interfered with the provincial responsibility for education. Nevertheless, like Laskin, he was a progressive, as well as being a legal modernist, and he believed that the law could take the lead in establishing social and economic justice. Those instincts increasingly drew him toward the centre and the importance of federal government leadership.[4]

The rapid expansion of the Canadian welfare state in the sixties, which had resulted from a series of challenges and responses between the federal and provincial governments, profoundly affected the balance of Canadian confederation. Trudeau, a Keynesian and an admirer of Scandinavian social democracy, believed that the federal government had a critical role to play in monetary and fiscal policy and in furthering the policies of equalization that had begun in 1957. He later wrote that he had sided with the provinces when he thought their jurisdictions had been infringed upon and with the federal government when its authority had been greatly diminished. Now, he argued, the provinces had achieved dramatic gains in resources because of equalization and the transfer of income-tax points, but "the feast had only made the provinces hungrier. Having outstripped the federal government in budgetary resources, they began looking for ways to outstrip it in constitutional jurisdictions as well." Most provinces disagreed, of course. As in so many other areas, the sixties shattered the fabric of Canadian federal-provincial relations.[5]

After Bourassa took office, Trudeau sent his senior aide Marc Lalonde and Gordon Robertson, the Cabinet secretary, to Quebec

City to discover what his "bottom line" should be on constitutional reforms, and they had a series of meetings with Julien Chouinard, the Quebec Cabinet secretary, and his staff. Chouinard was a federalist and eager himself to reach an agreement. At a September meeting, the first ministers (as the political leaders now dubbed themselves) agreed that progress could be made, and they accepted Premier W.A.C. "Wacky" Bennett's invitation to meet in Victoria in June 1971 to celebrate British Columbia's entry into confederation. But in Trudeau's words, the real "breakthrough" came in February, when the premiers agreed to patriate the Constitution and proceed "with such other changes as can be agreed upon quickly." Most important was the amending formula, whereby any province "now containing at least 25 per cent of the population of Canada" could block any amendment. Quebec and Ontario had gained a perpetual veto.[6]

Between February and June, officials worked out further details. Trudeau himself received and accepted advice in May that he spend much more time in Quebec and less in his Ottawa office.[7] The negotiations seemed to go well, and provisions were made for representation in the Commons, the Senate, and the Supreme Court. However, social policy and, in particular, the financing and operation of social programs, became the intractable difficulty. Trudeau was willing to "dovetail" federal and provincial social policy, but he insisted that the policies of the federal and provincial governments should not be incompatible and that the federal government had a role to play in ensuring equality of programs across Canada. A particular problem was the general social allowances plan—in effect, a guaranteed annual income. Claude Castonguay, the Quebec minister responsible for social welfare, tenaciously advanced these plans, but in a way that, to federal officials, cut Ottawa off from direct contact with citizens—and, of course, voters.[8] Still, hopes billowed after the February meeting.

John Turner, the minister of justice, flew from capital to capital testing the "bottom line" of each premier and stitching together the draft of a potential agreement. All proceeded well until May 31 in Quebec City, when Castonguay asked for revisions in section 94A of the British North America Act—the responsibility of the federal government for family allowances, unemployment insurance, and labour training. Turner, Robertson, Lalonde, and Trudeau recognized the danger immediately: the revisions threatened the agreement that had been hammered out among the other provinces in the draft charter.

Trudeau was intense and anxious when he and Margaret flew with Gordon and Bea Robertson to Victoria in mid-June for the Victoria Conference. Pierre and Margaret wore T-shirts and jeans with their bare feet in sandals, and to Robertson's amazement, Trudeau became so totally engrossed in his briefing books during the flight that he was oblivious to Margaret's bare feet caressing his own. To their delight, she was already three months pregnant with their first child. His impressive concentration prepared him well for the four long days of discussion in a circus atmosphere presided over by Premier Bennett. The serious meetings were *in camera*, and Bennett contributed little as Trudeau and Bourassa focused on the revised section dealing with social policy, where Quebec insisted on provincial primacy and the right to federal funding for programs administered by the province. Only this issue remained when Trudeau met the press in the early morning of June 17, his eyes lined with fatigue, a yellow daisy drooping in his lapel. All the provinces had agreed to a basic charter of rights, guarantees of three Quebec justices on the Supreme Court, the recognition of French and English as official languages, and most significantly, the amending formula allowing a veto for Quebec. Before the deal could be signed, however, Bourassa asked for leave to consult his Cabinet about the social policy items and promised an answer within two weeks. For Trudeau, this almost unanimous agreement was a major accomplishment, won by "blood, sweat, and tears." It would not satisfy everyone, but the new

Constitution would be, "in the view of all of us, to the benefit of the Canadian people." Once final approval was given by Bourassa and a few others after consulting their Cabinets, Trudeau exulted, "we'll all wear a crown of laurels." His enthusiasm was not contagious.[9]

Laurels became thorns when Bourassa returned to Quebec to face withering attacks on the new Constitution. On June 22 Claude Ryan wrote in *Le Devoir* that acceptance would be, for Quebec, *"une fraude tragique."* Bourassa met his Cabinet that same day and, at two o'clock the following afternoon, announced that Quebec would not sign the Victoria Charter. The province, he stated, demanded more control over the federally funded social programs. He had called Trudeau that morning, saying that he couldn't sell the deal and that Ryan was threatening to write a series of editorials arguing that Bourassa had given up Quebec's "bargaining power." Furious, Trudeau slammed down the phone, and in the years to come, he never forgave Bourassa. Turner told a friend they were "all a little shell shocked." After making his public announcement, Bourassa entered the National Assembly and all the members, federalist and separatist, rose and applauded. Meanwhile, Ryan mocked Trudeau in *Le Devoir*, saying that "the student he thought he had found in Quebec City is less meek than he appeared."[10]

The collapse of the "house of cards" built at Victoria was but the first indication of the unravelling of Trudeau's vision of federalism. The *Globe and Mail* reflected the anger of English Canada in a biting editorial alleging that "Quebec Premiers do not come to the bargaining table to bargain but to demand, to tell the rest of Canada, 'I deliver the pattern of the future and you abide by it.'" In the past, the *Globe* claimed, it had supported decentralization as compensation for past wrongs, but no more.[11]

Trudeau and Bourassa were civil in their public responses to the failure of the Victoria Charter, and privately both leaders tried to determine whether there was any chance of rescuing it. Bourassa certainly had major hurdles in Quebec: the press and the public service were vehement in their demands before and after the conference. Moreover, separatism, federalism, and socialism intersected prominently in the social policy issues. In June, for example, La Corporation des enseignants du Québec linked independence with socialism, arguing with some merit that the goals of a socialist society could be better achieved through an independent Quebec state, freed of the political and judicial restraints imposed by a national government that was not socialist. The Parti Québécois similarly made socialism a fundamental part of its political program. More conservative nationalists rejected this logic but accepted the primacy of the government in Quebec City over the one in Ottawa. During the remainder of the summer, Bourassa tried to deal with individual issues one by one, beginning with family allowances. "If Ottawa rejects this proposition, it means it wants a unitary federalism, a rigid federalism" — and that, he said, Quebec could not accept. "If war is necessary, I will make war."[12]

In Ottawa there were also rumblings of war. Constitutional specialist Jean Beetz, who was close to Trudeau and Lalonde, called for a firmer federalist stand against *"les grands feudataires"* of the provinces — particularly Bennett, who had demanded equal weight for British Columbia against Quebec and Ontario; William Davis, the new Ontario premier, who nervously avoided any constitutional commitment to bilingualism that would affect his province's school system; and Bourassa, who refused to grant the federal government primacy in the field of international affairs while at the same time demanding provincial paramountcy in all areas of social policy. John Munro, the federal minister of health, continued to work with Claude Castonguay on the family allowance question. At times they seemed near an agreement, particularly when, in March 1972, the federal government proposed a compromise permitting the provinces to decide who should receive family allowances within their jurisdictions. Trudeau argued that this would "meet the basic requirements necessary for the government of Quebec to establish the integrated system of family allowances that it wishes to introduce." However, Quebec's anger about a federal pension increase and Ottawa's frustration with Quebec's own decision to break away from the Canada Pension Plan undermined the negotiations. Beetz urged Trudeau to patriate the Constitution unilaterally after the next election and to proclaim his intention during the campaign, "to capture public opinion." Trudeau underlined these words in Beetz's memorandum, though he kept silent during the fall election campaign. The thought lingered, however.[13]

Critics, notably the senior Quebec civil servant Claude Morin, have charged that Trudeau was too rigid in his dealing with Bourassa and that the process which had begun well in the sixties but collapsed in Victoria in 1971 was Trudeau's failure:

> The Quebec choice and membership in the Canadian federal system as we know it are henceforth irreconcilable objectives. The two could co-exist in the past, since federal and Quebec powers were less in contact. Today they overlap; tomorrow they will overlap more. In a country with federal and provincial governments the effective performance of government and the welfare of the citizens require . . . that there be only one political institution with the decisive legislative and administrative power, and that the authority of this power be unchallengeable. Otherwise, if both orders have comparable powers . . . [they cancel] one another out in ceaseless bickering. . . . [I]t would be totally deceptive in such a case . . . to place our faith in consultation and co-ordination.[14]

The logic of this argument led Morin to take the "Quebec choice" in 1972 and join the Parti Québécois. The polarization he has described here occurred rapidly as the Union nationale and the Créditiste parties weakened and the choice for Quebec voters was, starkly, between the Liberals and the Parti Québécois.[15]

Trudeau welcomed the division for the clarity it brought to the separatist/nationalist demands, and recent research has proved that the impact of the family allowance payments on individuals was rarely the major issue in the actual debate in 1971. What mattered, rather, was power—whether the federal or the provincial government had primacy.[16] Fundamentally, in Trudeau's eyes, the debate concerned the nature of federalism and whether Quebec's sociological and historical differences required legal and constitutional expression. As he wrote in his memoirs: "The Castonguay proposal meant that the federal government would become just an institution to raise taxes, but it would never have any direct relations with the citizens of Quebec. If we had agreed, I saw this as the beginning of a trend in which, eventually, other provinces would want to do the same thing and the government of Canada would end up being the tax collector for a confederation of shopping centres."[17]

Stephen Clarkson and Christina McCall claim that "the myth of Trudeau as the national saviour who knew how to deal with Quebec was broken" when Victoria failed. Other critics argue that the compromise over family allowances offered in 1972 might have saved the agreement. Perhaps—but the vehemence of the reaction and Bourassa's divided Cabinet suggest that such hopes were probably illusory. Often, Trudeau and his ministers wistfully dreamed of what might have been if Bourassa had said yes. Turner, who had crossed the country many times speaking with the premiers, believes that the changes that came later—the rise of the West, the demand for Aboriginal rights, and the growing diversity of English Canada—meant that Victoria represented a brief shining moment, a rare opportunity that was missed. Yet acceptance of the Victoria Charter would have created a tumult in Quebec, which was already roiled by political divisions, economic disorder, and recent memories of assassinations and troops in the streets. Testifying before the Senate in March 1971, Léon Dion, the co-director of the Royal Commission on Bilingualism and Biculturalism, warned that "in the case of Quebec francophones, even in the best of contexts, one cannot predict what their final choice will be." For Trudeau, Victoria was a profound disappointment and Bourassa a lost hope. For both men, 1971 was a difficult year.[18]

—

The old problems persisted. In Quebec, bilingualism became a hotly contested issue as the ever stronger Parti Québécois asserted that French must be Quebec's language of work and that immigrants' education should be in French, rather than English. Bourassa tussled with radical unions, fiery nationalists, and immigrant groups, all of which furiously resisted his government's language bill aimed at promoting the use of French in the workplace and in all schools except those in predominantly anglophone areas. Meanwhile, Trudeau's Official Languages Act, which dealt with federal institutions across the country, received only mild approbation in the French-language media as a step forward for francophones. Progress on bilingualism came slowly in Ottawa, where the English language and anglophone officials had dominated for so long. Language classes for senior bureaucrats in their forties were often ineffective, and the public service unions jealously guarded against any extension of bilingually designated positions. As Claude Lemelin wrote in Le Devoir in July 1972, the measures taken since 1968 "barely scratched the surface of English unilingualism in Ottawa; the proportion of francophones holding senior administrator positions in the public service barely increased; the thorny problem of naming functional bilingual districts has not been resolved; and the establishment of francophone work units has barely begun."

Trudeau did not disagree with these complaints, but he pointed out how different Ottawa was now from the "English

Only" environment of the early fifties. He was right. Between 1966 and 1976, the percentage of francophones in the military and the public service doubled, and francophone communities outside Quebec gained dramatically through enhanced education rights, if not official bilingualism at the provincial level. Anglophones were complaining that "French power" in Ottawa denied them and their children jobs, promotions, and favours. Those English Canadians who had expected Trudeau to "put Quebec in its place," and who had contributed to the surge in support for him during the October Crisis, abandoned him quickly once he made it clear that official bilingualism meant a transformation of the workings of the federal government.[19]

Nevertheless, the politics of bilingualism were difficult. The Liberal caucus, especially MPs and senators from western Canada, beseeched Trudeau to stop suggesting that those who were troubled about French on cornflakes boxes should simply turn the box around. The events in Quebec, where the Bourassa government attempted to propitiate anglophone Montrealers by establishing nonconfessional school boards, set off an angry debate between nationalists on the one side and business leaders and anglophones on the other. Not surprisingly, this argument had an impact on the acceptance of bilingualism in other parts of Canada. Caught in the middle were Italian, Greek, and other recently arrived Canadians, who angrily insisted on the right of their children in Quebec to learn either of Canada's two official languages. Unfortunately for Bourassa, most chose English. These debates troubled Trudeau, particularly the row over the role of French in the workplace and in education. Like his friend Frank Scott, who had been a member of the Royal Commission on Bilingualism and Biculturalism, he rejected the commission's strong recommendations concerning the use of French as the working language in larger businesses in Quebec. Moreover, Trudeau had always been troubled by the emphasis on biculturalism, which he believed slipped easily into the concept of two nations. And now, in addition, there was a new complication.

On October 8, 1971, Trudeau responded to the unease felt by groups neither francophone nor anglophone by announcing an official policy of "multiculturalism"—making Canada the first national government in the world to do so. The policy soon sparked a fundamental debate about society, nation, and human difference, a discussion that in the decades since, as Western societies have become increasingly diverse, has become international in scope. Sociologist Fernand Dumont, political commentator Christian Dufour, political scientist Kenneth McRoberts, and Le Devoir have all argued that Trudeau's declaration of multiculturalism undermined biculturalism and Canada's historically important duality. Others, such as American historian Arthur Schlesinger, Canadian novelist Neil Bissoondath, and Dutch-English social critic Ian Buruma, have worried about the impact of multiculturalism on the shared concepts of nationhood and, to some extent, on Western values of justice and human rights. Princeton philosopher Kwame Anthony Appiah has rejected "multiculturalism" as an idea to understand how we might better live together. It is, he writes, "another shape shifter, which so often designates the disease it purports to cure."

Political philosopher Charles Taylor and political scientist Will Kymlicka have placed the concept within broader questions of identity and rights, but they distance themselves from official multiculturalism in Canada. In response to several xenophobic incidents in Quebec, Taylor and historian Gérard Bouchard wrote a report for the Quebec government that embraced "interculturalism," whereby traditional historical claims for the French language and culture take precedence in the increasingly diverse Quebec society. Finally, Harvard political scientist Robert Putnam and University of British Columbia economist John Helliwell suggest that "happiness" is found least in the ethnically diverse and wealthy cities of modern North America and more often in smaller, more uniform cities such as Saint John, New Brunswick, or the Saguenay region of Quebec.[20] These debates are academic, angry, political, unresolved, and profoundly important.

The significance of the debates as they relate to Pierre Trudeau lies in the choices he made in the early seventies that have deeply affected Canadian society and politics. In 1942 Trudeau had declared that the greatest threat to Quebec and Canada was immigration. A quarter-century later, Jean Marchand, who had shared Trudeau's nationalist and nativist sentiments during the war years, convinced the Cabinet to end all racial barriers to immigration. Trudeau and Pelletier backed Marchand, but most Canadians at the time did not, especially in Quebec.[21] Trudeau, like his colleagues and many other Canadians, supported more open immigration because he accepted the fundamental arguments of the United Nations Universal Declaration of Human Rights and came to believe that a liberal society accepted all peoples as equals. The memories of Japanese-Canadian evacuation, Chinese head taxes, segregation by colour, and the exclusion and extermination of Jews were recent and haunting. Moreover, on a personal level, Trudeau was cosmopolitan in his taste, and he believed that the nation-state was obsolete.

Other less theoretical and principled reasons contributed to the new official policy of multiculturalism. The Royal Commission on Bilingualism and Biculturalism had offended those Canadians who argued that the emphasis on French-English duality made them into second-class citizens. In response, Pearson had added two "ethnic" representatives to the commission to "safeguard" the contribution of "other ethnic groups," and one volume of the commission's report specifically dealt with the "contribution" of "other ethnic" groups to the country. It was well known, too, that "ethnic" Canadians were strongly supportive of the

Liberal Party, with the notable exception of Ukrainian Canadians.[22]
In addition, in 1969 Trudeau's government had issued a White Paper
that proposed to abolish the Indian Act and to grant First Nations
people "equal status and responsibility" to those of other Canadians.
The proposal set off a firestorm among Aboriginal groups, who
rejected it as an attempt to assimilate them into mainstream society,
and this bitter reaction raised fundamental questions about citizenship and group rights.* In frustration Trudeau and Jean Chrétien,
the minister responsible, abandoned the White Paper two years later,
but the experience deeply affected both of them, particularly their
views of individual and group rights.[23]

In these ways, various streams, some of them torrents,
merged to create Canadian multiculturalism during Trudeau's first
government. In September 1971 the Cabinet Committee on
Science, Culture, and Information initially proposed a policy of
official multiculturalism. When the full Cabinet discussed the
matter on September 23, Trudeau was especially cautious, saying

---

* Influenced by American Native protests, the demands from Quebec for group
recognition, and the American civil rights movement (as was the White Paper
itself in a different way), Canadian Aboriginal groups quickly organized nationally and effectively to reject the White Paper. One of the most influential attacks
came from Harold Cardinal, whose book *The Unjust Society* (Edmonton: Hurtig,
1969) argued that Canadian "Indians" could find a place in the Canadian
"mosaic" while rejecting assimilation (12). Trudeau ignored the White Paper in
his *Memoirs*. Sally Weaver provides a fine study of the bureaucratic, political,
and Native interactions that caused the withdrawal of the paper in her *Making
Canadian Indian Policy: The Hidden Agenda 1968–1970* (Toronto: University of
Toronto Press, 1981). A more recent assessment of the motives and legacy of this
incident is Alan Cairns, *Citizens Plus: Aboriginal Peoples and the Canadian State*
(Vancouver: University of British Columbia Press, 2000), 65–71.

that the emphasis should be on self-help, not on federal government help, and that support should be given for cultural but not
economic equality. With Cabinet support, Trudeau finally
announced the policy on October 8 in the House. Because of its
significance, his remarks merit close attention:

> It was the view of the royal commission, shared by the gov-
> ernment and, I am sure all Canadians, that there cannot be
> one cultural policy for Canadians of British and French
> origin, another for the original peoples and yet a third for all
> others. For although there are two official languages, there is
> no official culture, nor does any ethnic group take prece-
> dence over any other. No citizen or group of citizens is other
> than Canadian, and all should be treated fairly.
>
> The royal commission was guided by the belief that adher-
> ence to one's ethnic group is influenced not so much by one's
> origin or mother tongue as by one's sense of belonging to the
> group, and by what the commission calls the group's "collec-
> tive will to exist." The government shares that belief.
>
> The individual's freedom would be hampered if he were
> locked for life within a particular cultural compartment by
> the accident of birth or language. It is vital, therefore, that
> every Canadian, whatever his ethnic origin, be given a
> chance to learn at least one of the two languages in which his
> country conducts its official business and its politics.
>
> A policy of multiculturalism within a bilingual framework
> commends itself to the government as the most suitable
> means of assuring the cultural freedom of Canadians. Such
> a policy should help to break down discriminatory attitudes
> and cultural jealousies. National unity, if it is to mean
> anything in the deeply personal sense, must be founded on
> confidence in one's own individual identity; out of this can
> grow respect for that of others and a willingness to share

ideas, attitudes and assumptions. A vigorous policy of multiculturalism will help create this initial confidence.

Far from a declaration of group rights, Trudeau's announcement
reflected his liberal individualism. Initially, it promised little more
than what its critics suggested: money for folk dances, songfests,
and parties.[24]

The critics were many. With some justice, the Opposition
denounced the policy as merely a bribe to potential Liberal voters.
Bourassa had to cope with almost universal criticism in Quebec of
the dilution of biculturalism and, in particular, Trudeau's limited
definition of "culture"—which was fundamentally different from
that of the Quebec government and the nationalist intellectuals.
The critical Quebec press and government joined the federal
Opposition in claiming—again with some justice—that Trudeau's
multiculturalism undermined the concept of the two nations.
English-Canadian nationalists were also upset. The traditionally
Liberal and thoroughly nationalist *Toronto Star* said that "no
immigrant should be encouraged to think that Canada is essentially a chain of ethnic enclaves like the New Iceland Republic
that once flourished on the shores of Lake Winnipeg." In his statement, Trudeau used powerful words and images to emphasize his
meaning. It was no surprise that nationalists cast poisoned arrows
at the document but little wonder, either, that Trudeau, the
"citizen of the world" from his Harvard days on, enjoyed dodging
these barbs and firing back.[25]

Trudeau's statement on multiculturalism reveals both
strengths and weaknesses in his attitude and position. On the one
hand, he agreed to recognize "other" groups as his political advisers insisted he must. He did so eloquently, thoughtfully, and politically, and the policy statement, combined with a speech to a large
Ukrainian-Canadian audience the following day, soothed MPs
concerned about too much emphasis on Canadian bilingualism.

On the other hand, he shaped the statement in such a way that it was consistent with his carefully developed views on the role of an individual within society. In doing so, he could not resist remarks that he surely knew would inflame many in Quebec.

So it was with many of Trudeau's speeches, policy statements, and political gestures in the early years of his government. Unfortunately, commentators and Canadians more generally often missed his subtlety as they concentrated on the insults, innuendoes, and tirades his remarks provoked. His subtlety sometimes devolved into esoteric obscurity. When, for example, a reporter asked whether he had experienced a struggle of conscience as he invoked the War Measures Act, he replied: "In my own mind the importance of democratic movements not fearing to take extraordinary measures to preserve democracy . . . has always been established, both intellectually and emotionally. So I didn't have to weigh back and forth the kind of struggle that goes on between Creon and Antigone, in Sophocles' famous play about what is more important, the State or the individual. Democracy must preserve itself." Few Canadians outside university classics and literature departments had heard of Sophocles, much less Creon and Antigone. The performance was impressive, but the political substance was missing. Trudeau would soon pay a price.*

---

* When Anthony Westell consulted Sophocles' *Antigone*, he found that Creon of Thebes insisted that he was obliged to uphold the law at all costs. He ordered his niece, Antigone, to be entombed when she defied his orders. The gods did not accept that in doing so, he was acting in the best interests of the state, so struck him down. Creon's last speech in the play is a lament: "All that I can touch / Is falling—falling—round me, and o'erhead / Intolerable destiny descends." Westell notes that "it was a curious precedent for Trudeau to cite." Anthony Westell, *Paradox: Trudeau as Prime Minister* (Scarborough: Prentice-Hall, 1972), 261–62.

—

CHAPTER SIX

THE PARTY IS OVER

Trudeau's fourth year, 1972, began with the Liberals barely ahead of the other parties in the December 1971 Gallup poll: they had 37 percent support, compared to the Conservatives at 33 percent, the New Democrats at 21 percent, and the Créditistes and others at 9 percent. The surge in Liberal support to 59 percent after the invocation of the War Measures Act had soon withered away.[1] Trudeau had always known that the feverish euphoria of the summer of '68, that moment everyone called Trudeaumania, would soon burn itself out and that his future success in Canadian politics would depend on his record as prime minister. As it happened, though, the achievements of his first government were mixed.

In his study of the Liberal Party from the sixties to the eighties, political scientist Joseph Wearing shows that many politicians around Trudeau became intoxicated with polling and with the belief that "Keynesian economics" would allow them to manipulate the economy: "An election could be called to coincide with an economic boom and a rising trend in the government's popularity," he said, "while a judicious reallocation of government expenditures could be applied to mop up any persisting areas of discontent." But in the seventies, the economy proved it was not so malleable, and public opinion showed itself to be largely independent. In short, voters had minds of their own, and polls came to be seen as "snap-shots in time." Occasionally, as John Diefenbaker memorably said, those soundings of public opinion were more appropriate for dogs than for politicians.[2]

Within the Prime Minister's Office, however, Trudeau's key advisers were deeply imbued with the belief that there could be a science of politics and public administration. "They created the impression—at least in the eyes of the key volunteers who ran campaigns—that a party organization would not really be neces-sary for fighting the next election" and that "it could all be done with regional desks and computers."[3] Inside the PMO, Jim Davey, an enthusiast of Marshall McLuhan, systems analysis, and cybernetics, and Quebec adviser Pierre Levasseur took major responsibility for political analysis.* Yet the detailed diary of Senator Richard Stanbury, the party president who conscien-tiously tried to link Trudeau with the diverse party membership, reports scarcely any dealings with Davey. A lawyer, Stanbury cared deeply about the party and was enmeshed through personal and business ties with the Young Liberals, who had transformed

---

* Early in the Trudeau government, Davey had sent a memorandum to Trudeau through Marc Lalonde, warning of the "conflict between the Humanist Left and Technocratic or Rational Centre" in government ranks. Using categories developed by futurist Herman Kahn, Davey separated those on the "humanist left," who believed the "revolutionary end of industrial society" was near, and those in the "rational centre," who believed that the Western world was on the "threshold of [a] new technological, affluent, and humanist society." Both views, Davey correctly asserted, were found among Trudeau's ministers and MPs. Trudeau wrote on the memorandum, "Very interesting. Thanks very much." A much cooler Lalonde wrote, "*Pas urgent mais intéres-sant.*" Davey to Trudeau, Nov. 1, 1968., TP, MG 26 03, vol. 290, file 319-14, LAC.

Liberalism in Ontario during the Pearson years by centring the party in Toronto and linking it with media, communications, and business leaders. He recorded numerous meetings with Trudeau, and his comments reveal the gap between the volunteers, elected party officials, and party organizers on the one hand and the PMO and Trudeau's closest advisers on the other.

Fresh with visions of making "participatory democracy" more than just campaign rhetoric, Stanbury, with Trudeau's full encouragement, began a process of consultation with the party in late November 1969, including a major "thinkers'" conference at Harrison Hot Springs in British Columbia, which was to produce a guide for grassroots meetings of party activists and ordinary citizens. Liberals also had recent memories of the historic Kingston Conference of 1960, which had played a major role in establishing the reform agenda for Pearson's governments. The plan was for these meetings to culminate in a policy convention, where the party's "basic policies" would be set. But the effort failed dismally.[4]

Trudeau had ruminated about mass participation and citizen participation in the 1950s, when he played the principal role in the "Rassemblement" in Quebec—an attempt to emulate the mass parties of continental Europe and, more specifically, the citizens' movement that, under Jean Drapeau, took control of Montreal's municipal government in 1954 with the platform of cleaning up corruption.[5] These dreams lingered, but their realization clashed with the systems approach championed by the new men in the PMO and by many Cabinet ministers, who were skeptical too.

After a meeting of the "political Cabinet" (a subgroup charged with giving political advice), Stanbury flew with veteran parliamentarian Allan MacEachen of Nova Scotia and the voluble Don Jamieson of Newfoundland to a political meeting in Nova Scotia. To his "consternation," he discovered that both men felt that "political organization is not particularly important and that, as Don Jamieson . . . [said], 'Give me a few thousand dollars to use on specific projects and I'll get elected for 50 years and elect other people with me." "No wonder," the earnest Stanbury wrote, "the Maritimes is in bad shape organizationally." He was to learn that in much of Canada, patronage remained, as Wilfrid Laurier had earlier complained, the "lifeblood" of the political system— and that lifeblood created the flow of funds for the party in many provinces. Trudeau tried to improve efforts to reform the system of party financing by providing direct grants to constituency organi- zations and encouraging mass fundraising. And in 1974 his government passed the historic Election Expenses Act, which established election spending limits, regulated political broad- casting, required disclosure of funding, and provided for partial public funding, reflecting Trudeau's own belief—but certainly not the views of many Liberal partisans—that a broader political process was essential for Canadian democracy to flourish.[6]

The attempted democratization of the party conflicted with the trend in the modern state toward the centralization of decision making. At the Harrison Hot Springs Conference, Trudeau had used the rhetoric of participatory democracy, comparing the party to "pilots of a supersonic airplane. By the time an airport comes into the pilot's field of vision, it is too late to begin the landing proce- dure. Such planes must be navigated by radar. A political party, in formulating policy, can act as a society's radar." The conference itself, he continued, should be a "supermarket of ideas." Sometimes, however, the supermarket carried unpalatable goods, and when a three-day Liberal Party policy convention began in Ottawa on November 20, 1970, armed guards were everywhere. The memory of Pierre Laporte's death was fresh, and James Cross was still a pris- oner. Under existing party rules, the convention bore responsibil- ity for producing the central party program for the next election. Before it opened, however, Trudeau and Stanbury had reflected on how difficult it was to make participatory democracy work. Stanbury shrewdly observed that there was a tendency among the young and others "to refuse to believe that the Party was effective" and a feeling that "they could be more effective outside parties." It was a perceptive comment: this trend marked the remainder of the century, and for young and old alike, nongovernmental organizations and "civil society" became their preferred focus of commitment.[7]

Despite the attractions of nonpolitical organizations and the threat of chilling temperatures, more than 1,500 party members came to Ottawa, armed with the policy resolutions that had been passed in their constituencies and at regional meetings. The process made political veterans nervous, and Trudeau expressed concern about resolutions passed at a student convention calling for the legalization of marijuana and for abortion on demand. Reflecting his personal views and perhaps his debates with Margaret, he told Stanbury that he was "concerned about both the abortion and the drug questions . . . and that the changes being demanded would affect the moral fibre of the nation." Still, Trudeau sighed, if the people were ready for them, "perhaps we should move forward with them." For his part, Stanbury agreed that some hesitation in these delicate areas was warranted. The convention managed to pass resolutions calling for government sale of marijuana (the way liquor was already sold in provincially operated stores) while defeating a resolution to make possession no longer an offence. Trudeau and others were irritated when many delegates questioned the "authoritarian" response to the FLQ kidnappings, and Trudeau strongly rejected the idea that a board be established to review that response.

In the end, the convention brought forth a cornucopia of resolutions that were cobbled together by Professor Allan Linden, the convention policy co-chair. Ten months later, Stanbury and Linden presented these resolutions to the political Cabinet in a document entitled "Direction for the Seventies." The ministers reacted quickly. As Stanbury put it: "The attack was led by Mitchell Sharp and

John Turner, with Don Jamieson sometimes being helpful, some-times being difficult; but all of the Cabinet Ministers obviously worried to some extent about the policy ammunition which the results of the Convention [would] give to the Opposition." Trudeau did not want to publish the document, but Stanbury and Linden pointed out that the process was part of the Liberal Constitution. There were, Stanbury later wrote, "some high moments of drama—John Turner was terribly intense and hostile; Jean Chrétien and Jean Marchand were by far the best, but we ended up with a consensus that we should go to the Press Conference but then distribute only on request." The proposed "Liberal Charter for the Seventies," an election program created through a democratic process within the party, was, in effect, tabled by the ministers. Linden left the meeting "really shaken," and he soon accepted a judicial appointment. A decade later he said that his dream had died after the October Crisis, when the "centre" asserted its strength and the "Liberal Charter" died.[8]

The "centre" held, as it did in other Western democracies in the last decades of the twentieth century. The challenge of "the streets" from Paris to Chicago to Margaret Trudeau's Simon Fraser University subsided, and politicians returned to the basic questions of how decisions should be made and what role Parliament, the general public, and political leaders should play in making those decisions. Canadian trends reflected international influences. What historian Tony Judt wrote about Europe applies fully to Canada and illustrates why "participatory democracy" never came into its own: "It was not so much the idealism of the sixties that seemed to have dated so very fast as the *innocence* of those days: the feeling that whatever could be imagined could be done. . . . Whereas the sixties were marked by the naïve, self-congratulatory impulse to believe that everything happening was new—and everything new was significant—the seventies were an age of cynicism, of lost illusions and reduced expectations."[9] In many ways, the political Trudeau remained part of the sixties, with its innocence and joy in novelty, and found the seventies an uncongenial time.

The parliamentary reforms introduced by the Trudeau government in its first year were a response to the "continuing demands made on the prime minister for accountability and participation." Power, then, became more concentrated in the prime minister as the scope of government activities increased. All Western democracies experienced this phenomenon. In the United States, Arthur Schlesinger became troubled when Lyndon Johnson and Richard Nixon used "the imperial presidency" to widen the Vietnam War without congressional approval. In Britain, Trudeau's former classmate Robert McKenzie revealed in writings and as a broadcaster how the Labour Party's democratic structure masked strong oligarchic tendencies and how power was concentrated among the few. And in France, Charles de Gaulle proclaimed his belief that France had become much better governed after constitutional reforms enhanced the power of the French president.[10]

We now recognize that the phenomenon of expansion of the "centre" was a response to the greater complexity of government. Political scientist Donald Savoie, for example, claims that Canada and Britain operate "court governments," where effective power resides with the prime minister and his or her court. Journalist Jeffrey Simpson, with resignation and disappointment, writes about "the friendly dictatorship," while former prime ministerial adviser Eddie Goldenberg boldly argues that the "buck will continue to stop on the prime minister's desk and nowhere else." Although, he writes, "Prime Ministers will continue to be accused of exhibiting dictatorial traits when they set government priorities and make unpopular decisions," they will receive even greater criticism if they do not appear to be leaders who make decisions. Goldenberg implicitly dismisses calls by Savoie and other academics for greater "accountability" and new relationships between the governed and their governors. During the early Trudeau years, furious debates raged about what political scientist Tom Hockin, later a Conservative Cabinet minister, termed the "apex of power" — the office of the prime minister. Trudeau became the lightning rod for the many who argued that he had arrogantly expanded his office and had created a dictatorship where he and his court aloofly ruled.[11]

During the October Crisis, Trudeau's strength was publicly heralded in the polls. Indeed, a Liberal public opinion survey taken just before the crisis observed that Trudeau was already perceived as a "strong man," but it warned that "things would be much better off in another election if fewer people felt he was arrogant, dictatorial, and cold." It was, the analysts continued, "as if these people feel Mr. Trudeau is a little contemptuous of people — that he is living in his own private world (and a pretty plush one at that) and arbitrarily deciding what is both good and bad for everyone else." Christina McCall, the best journalist of the age, captured how the party felt sidelined by Trudeau's "private world." "For the most part," she wrote, "he seemed to pay little heed to what the party thought." He brushed aside party loyalists who objected to his cavalier ways with party events and officials. He avoided as much as possible the chicken dinners that party associations relied on for critical campaign funds. Christina Newman recalled his dismissal of opposition MPs as "nobodies" when they were "fifty yards from Parliament Hill," a remark John Diefenbaker righteously denounced as lacking respect for Parliament. Nor did Trudeau, a former journalist and professor, honour his former vocations. In Newman's view:

> He was unimpressed when journalists and political scientists began to write that he had created a presidential office in the East block. After all, he was a liberal democrat, with a philosophical position. He knew how much democracy a democracy could stand.

He neglected the party oldtimers, such as Keith Davey, who had managed Pearson's campaigns; the clever strategist Jim Coutts; and the former Liberal Party president and campaign organizer John Nichol—even though these men had many friends throughout the party. Moreover, he never consulted party icons such as Jack Pickersgill, whose influence remained substantial at the Rideau Club, and Walter Gordon, who continued to have enormous influence over the editorial and news pages of the powerful *Toronto Star*.[12]

The complaints baffled Trudeau. In his view no Canadian political leader had tried so much and with such sincerity to involve not only the party but also the public in the policy process. His correspondence expanded exponentially to meet the flood of letters addressed to the prime minister, and Trudeau read summaries and, occasionally, individual letters.[13] His reforms of the committee system in Cabinet gave ministers more decision-making authority than ever before.* Similarly, the new rules governing procedures in the House of Commons gave greater freedom and responsibility to MPs, particularly in committees,

---

* Trudeau's complex series of Cabinet committees was created to deal with the greater demands on government, but an assistant warned in August 1971 that the Monday to Thursday ministerial committee system meant that it had been "very difficult to find the sort of Ministerial time for politics and communications that is contemplated for the coming year." Senior official Marshall Crowe warned, however, that it would be "dangerous to restrict the types of work that Committees have been doing" because ministers would lose control and, more seriously for Trudeau, his own "information system," which depended on committee reports, would break down. This dilemma remained throughout Trudeau's first term. Gordon Gibson to Trudeau, Aug. 12, 1971, TP, MG 26 03, vol. 121, file 313-05, LAC; interview with Marshall Crowe, Jan. 2009.

and his promises of more staff, funding, and research capacity for private members freed MPs to focus on both their constituency and their parliamentary responsibilities.

Most confusing was the voters' attitude toward his strength. His popularity rose to astonishing heights as he stared down the terrorists during the October Crisis, and memories persisted of Trudeaumania with its excitement, energy, and enthusiasm. Nevertheless, as the prime minister's first mandate neared its end, he and his closest advisers began to realize that even though Trudeau "comes through as an intelligent (and to many, brilliant) man," who is "perceived as a strong leader who is decisive," he had serious political problems. The party pollsters gave dire warnings. "First, he's coming on a little too hard. The words haughty and disdainful come to mind. Mr. Trudeau just doesn't care enough about how others feel. As more come to feel this way, more will surely come to feel there is a growing chasm between the Prime Minister and the people. The second [problem] is really related to the first. He is perceived as travelling too much, being a playboy, as not being sufficiently serious about his job. In a perverse way, the people are saying that they don't like the Prime Minister because he seems to be enjoying himself." To be sure, Trudeau should enjoy "good times," but the pollster warned that "it would surely help if he didn't *seem* to be having so much pleasure." He should become "deadly earnest . . . about serving his country and its people."[14]

Trudeau's brother, Charles, a shy man, offered some consolation in a generous letter on June 20, 1971, in which he told him how much he admired "everything that you have done for the good of the country, since the days where you were Minister of Justice." No praise meant more to him.[15] Very soon, a flood of photographs appeared, showing Trudeau at his desk, tie pulled open, as he "earnestly" pored over papers. Meanwhile, the fickle moods of public opinion frustrated Trudeau, who increasingly ignored the polls and those who delivered them.

—

Perceptions were not the only problem. The federal government faced fresh challenges after 1968. The Pearson government had used high levels of economic growth and increases in productivity in the early sixties to introduce an astonishing range of federal-sponsored programs, which provincial governments then complemented with initiatives of their own. Medicare, the Canada Pension Plan, extended and improved assistance to seniors, student loans, and a sudden increase in general government services all rested on assumptions of increased exports, continued improvements in productivity, and rising fixed investment in business. Reflecting the affluent spirit of the times, Pearson's government, at the urging of former labour leader Jean Marchand and against the advice of former public servants such as Mitchell Sharp and Bud Drury, extended collective bargaining to most public servants in 1966. The crisis over the Canadian dollar in February 1968, when the Pearson government had almost fallen, signalled that the future would not mirror the past. The effervescence of Trudeaumania cloaked a flat economy in which investment was falling and unemployment was rising. Between 1966 and 1971, unemployment increased from 3.6 percent to 6.4 percent of the labour force. Meanwhile, the federal government began to face the bills from the spending binge it had initiated. The result was immediate government restraint, continual tussles with the provinces about shared-cost programs, and general public disappointment in the new government.[16]

Trudeau had sensed the difficulties ahead and, as we've seen, even during the 1968 campaign he had told audiences that the time for new social programs had passed. Trained as an economist in the 1940s, he clung to the assumptions of that decade, popularly termed "Keynesian economics." He was not alone in believing that the government could use taxation and public spending to regulate the economy and ensure growth and stability. In 1971 President

Richard Nixon said, "We are all Keynesians now," but alas, these suppositions, which were loosely based on Keynes' celebrated writings during the Great Depression, did not fit the challenges Western leaders faced in the 1970s. During that decade, the postwar Bretton Woods system, with the American dollar as the reserve currency and the international financial institutions in Washington as the guarantor for Western countries in need, broke down, and dramatic changes occurred in the international economic system. The stability of the postwar years, with their steady growth, rising productivity, and low inflation, disintegrated in the later 1960s as, contrary to the economic wisdom of the time, inflation and unemployment rose together and created a decade of "stagflation." Politicians were frustrated. Alan Greenspan, a supporter and adviser of Richard Nixon, recalls the turmoil as his "friends in Washington lurched from one remedy to another." Unfortunately, few of those schemes worked.[17]

The conclusion of the Kennedy Round of trade talks in 1967 represented a watershed, as tariff barriers fell throughout the non-communist world and the first glimmerings of late-twentieth-century globalization appeared. U.S. commerce secretary Alexander Trowbridge wrote that the talks represented "a very large step toward the thing we've heard so much about in the postwar years: the truly one-world market." It meant that "the American domestic market—the greatest and most lucrative market in the world—is no longer the private preserve of the American businessman"[18]—or the Canadian, for that matter.

This revolution ended with supply-side economics and monetarism in the 1980s, but that outcome was unanticipated by Canadian politicians in the late sixties and early seventies. The monetarists responded to the economic problems of growing unemployment and inflation with new nostrums that emphasized a decreased role for fiscal spending to maintain equilibrium in the economy and less government intervention in the economy more generally. In the long run, their policies would result in a smaller role for government, decentralized economic decision making, and free markets. When they looked south, Canadian politicians saw that the American decision to provide "guns and butter" as the Vietnam War expanded was inflationary, and they knew that the pressures on the American dollar, which was pegged to gold, were difficult to contain. Meanwhile, the European Common Market was using its single agricultural policy as the glue to bind its members together, with the result that the venerable and valuable International Wheat Agreement began to fall apart. On all fronts, Canadians saw themselves shut out from old markets such as Europe and facing fresh competition in new markets from the subsidized wheat of France and the resurgent economies of Germany and Japan.

Trudeau's first instincts in the gathering storm were to go on the defensive. His government began to cut spending and curtail the rapid growth of the public service, a decision that surely contributed not only to the rise in unemployment but also to unrest in the public service. In 1969 a stern Trudeau defended his war against inflation: "We can only get tougher, we can't get weaker. . . . I'm afraid there are a lot of people who are bargaining that the Government can't act tough for too long because it will only get frightened if it sees unemployment go up to 6 percent. But if people think we are going to lose our nerve because of that, they should think again because we're not." These unwise comments and his upturned finger to the striking Lapalme truck drivers in 1970 as he told them to "eat shit" transformed Trudeau's image for many Canadians. No longer the progressive on the Liberal left, the prime minister became the ruthless conservative on the right. The NDP vote began to swell.[19]

The business community applauded the cuts in spending and in the public service, but business raised its own storm when Finance Minister Edgar Benson tabled the government's response to the Royal Commission on Taxation (the Carter Commission) on November 7, 1969. This historic report recommended "fiscal neutrality"—that all sources of income receive equal treatment— a revolutionary recommendation in a country that lacked a capital gains tax. The Benson White Paper proposed that tax burdens be shifted from the poor to the rich and that taxation promote rational investment decisions. Accountants and tax lawyers were under- standably distressed to learn that the system would be simplified, but they were a small group. The most ferocious and politically troubling protests came from small business. John Bulloch, a lec- turer at Toronto's Ryerson Polytechnical Institute, read the White Paper in the bathtub and immediately decided to lead a campaign against it. His father, a tailor, ran a regular and arresting page 2 advertisement in the *Globe and Mail,* which reportedly had higher readership than the editorial page. Bulloch Jr. took over the ad and began an assault on the Trudeau government and its proposed tax- ation policies. With an attached photograph of the critical moment in the tub, he called for opponents of the tax reforms to join him in the newly organized Canadian Council for Fair Taxation.

Bulloch was irritating, but the fierce opposition of Winnipeg tax lawyer Israel "Izzy" Asper was taken much more seriously. The leader of the Manitoba Liberals, he was considered a rising star in the party. Struck down by illness, he penned an angry attack on the reforms while in hospital, entitled *The Benson Iceberg.* It argued that the goal of the tax paper was no less than the "reshap- ing of society." The question was fundamental to Asper: "Should every Canadian be his brother's keeper or just his helper?" The conservative Liberal raised fears that Canada would become a socialist state. Trudeau's Cabinet became troubled. Paul Hellyer, widely regarded as a spokesman for business interests, had left the Cabinet the previous April, and commentators were beginning to remark on the weak representation of business among Trudeau's ministers.[20]

Barney Danson, a highly regarded Toronto MP with excellent connections to the business community, organized a meeting between Trudeau and leading Toronto businesspeople for November 27, 1970. Three days later, he reported: "The apparent lack of understanding of the government's stance and direction was indicative of a general bewilderment in the business community vis-à-vis its relationship with our new style of government. [The meeting] also highlighted the need for new mechanisms of communication with the business community to establish identification and understanding. There is no one person in government with whom they easily identify, or through whom they feel they have a voice."[21]

In response to these criticisms, in August the following year Trudeau appointed the influential Toronto businessman Alastair Gillespie as the minister of state for science and technology. Meanwhile, the withering attacks on the tax proposals caused the bold recommendations of the Carter Commission to shrivel into a mild reform package. Benson's seventy-page bill took over half a year to pass, in December 1971, and it would not have become law without the invocation of closure. Increasingly disillusioned with Parliament, Trudeau had not given a major House of Commons speech in a year. Nevertheless, he recognized the significance of this bill and concluded the debate on the 17th with the words: "For the first time in Canada, a government has invited the population as a whole to participate with it in the formulation of a major policy." Unfortunately, it had not been an edifying experience for the government, and Liberal fortunes sagged that month to 37 percent—the lowest level since Trudeau had come to power.[22]

Although the reforms eliminated taxes for many of the working poor and introduced a capital gains tax at a rate of 50 percent, the NDP under David Lewis relentlessly attacked Benson's bill as a sop to corporate Canada and to wealthy Canadians, who benefited from the elimination of estate taxes as

well as lower marginal rates. NDP support rose on the federal
level, just as its provincial bases expanded dramatically, with election victories by Ed Schreyer in Manitoba on June 25, 1969, and
by Allan Blakeney in Saskatchewan on June 30, 1971. The highly
nationalist "Waffle" movement within the party, which called for
the NDP to be "the parliamentary wing of a movement dedicated
to fundamental social change," shocked conservatives within and
without the party, but its purge in Ontario, led by NDP leader
Stephen Lewis (son of David), probably strengthened the federal
party's electoral appeal by making the elder Lewis appear less radical
as he thundered eloquently against contemporary capitalism.
Trudeau, the erstwhile New Democrat, was now worried about
business support and inflationary pressures, though he was still committed to state action to reduce inequality and unemployment. He
seemed ever more a paradox, a "collection of contradictions," who
in both the press and Parliament was "denounced variously as a
playboy and an inflexible lawyer, as an overgrown hippie and a con-
stipated constitutionalist."

    Anthony Westell argued that there had been two cam-
paigners in 1968—one the rationalist and philosopher who urged
debate and democratic participation; the other the pop star who
embodied adventure, change, and even radicalism. The year 1971
featured a continuation of this paradox with, on the one hand,
the wedding to the flower child Margaret, disco dancing in the
clubs, and the "fuddle duddle" episode in the House of Commons
and, on the other, the long nights in Victoria discussing the
Constitution and the weary debate about tax reform. In policy
terms, there was also a blurred image—one not uncommon in the
Liberal Party, which had always drawn supporters of varied political tastes.[23]

—

For those on the left, Trudeau's foreign policy offered some satisfaction. His government reduced Canada's military presence in Europe and recognized Communist China, despite serious reservations from several allies. That country and its communist experiment had long fascinated Trudeau, who had escaped from the region during his youthful travels just as Mao's troops were entering Beijing. Trudeau had also made a memorable visit to the country in 1960. In Canada, recognition of Communist China had become a major cause for Canadians on the left and even some on the right—notably, grain farmers in the West who had benefited enormously from John Diefenbaker's willingness to maintain trade with "Red China." The *Globe and Mail* was one of the first Western newspapers to have a correspondent in China, and one of its finest journalists, Charles Taylor, had close personal ties with leading members of the Canadian business community. In his campaign for the leadership, Trudeau promised to recognize the communist nation, and he was determined to keep that commitment, even though the Chinese demonstrated little enthusiasm for Canada's approach.

Trudeau also encountered strong opposition to his plans from others. When he visited Australia in May 1970, the government there warned him that his decision to recognize China was unwise, given China's "subversive" activities in the region. Nixon echoed these reservations, even though his own administration was secretly planning its own historic China initiative. Meeting in Stockholm, a neutral location where both countries had embassies, the Canadians and Chinese finally agreed, in October 1970, to exchange diplomats. After some delay, as the diplomats negotiated what paper to use for the agreement—finally settling on Swedish— the Chinese bought a former convent in Ottawa and established their presence there in February 1971.[24]

Trudeau also turned out to be a surprisingly effective mediator at the January 1971 Commonwealth Conference at Singapore.

Members feared a possible breakup of the Commonwealth, as African nations demanded a strong stand against apartheid, and the new British Conservative government under Edward Heath insisted that it must maintain its military base at Simonstown in South Africa. Trudeau's skepticism about the Commonwealth was well known among Canadian diplomats, but encouraged by Singapore's Lee Kuan Yew and others, he worked out a compromise. The Commonwealth endured, and thereafter, Trudeau's affection for the institution developed rapidly.* He and Heath established a fine relationship, and the Oxford-educated modernizer Lee Kuan Yew became a close friend.[25]

More controversial was Trudeau's visit to the Soviet Union in May 1971. The newly wed prime minister justified the trip by referring to mutual Soviet and Canadian interests in the Arctic and the first buds of détente that had begun to blossom. Still, three years after Soviet tanks had entered Prague, with the Vietnam War still raging and with thousands of Canadians seeking exit visas for their relatives from the Soviet Union, Trudeau's visit had political dangers. At his final press conference in Moscow, Trudeau carelessly spoke about the "overwhelming American presence" in Canada, a remark that Canadian ambassador to Russia Robert Ford believed was a slip but one that nevertheless "reflected a deep-seated distrust of the United States and a friendly feeling toward the Soviet Union."[26] Ford's reaction was unfair to Trudeau

---

* Trudeau told the *Times* (London) that his work in Singapore might have averted the possibility of a "general racial war" in Africa. It was not in Canada's interests to have such a war, he stressed, so his leadership at the conference had a specific goal, not "some vague international role." His "helpful fixing" in Singapore therefore synchronized with his emphasis on Canada's national interests, as expressed in his foreign policy review—at least in his own eyes.

because Trudeau's attitude to both superpowers was more complex, but he did not help matters on his return when he declared: "My position in the Soviet Union or in Canada is that anyone who breaks the law in order to assert his nationalism doesn't get much sympathy from me."[27] Canada's Ukrainian-Canadian community and stern anti-communists such as Peter Worthington strongly denounced the prime minister, whose remarks equating Canadian and Soviet federalism were, frankly, wrong and foolish. *Pravda*, the Soviet newspaper, intensified feelings when it praised Trudeau's "handshake across the pole" in an editorial that irritated Canada's Department of External Affairs. Ford was Trudeau's longtime friend and forgave him his flaws, but Washington was not so forgiving.[28]

Trudeau's ascent on Nixon's swelling enemies list was rapid. Although he won Nixon's respect for his strong reaction to FLQ terrorism, the distrust of the American conservative for the northern leftist "swell" soon returned. Trudeau wrote to Nixon about his Soviet visit, and the president initially drafted a curt reply. Nixon appreciated that Trudeau had spoken "in a frank and forthright manner" and agreed that cooperation within the Atlantic alliance would be "a primary factor in building better relations with the Soviet Union on realistic and acceptable terms." However, he stroked out a final conciliatory paragraph thanking Trudeau for his "kind invitation to Mrs. Nixon and me to visit you and Mrs. Trudeau in Ottawa later this year." He wrote an emphatic "No" in the margin. The final version was a bit milder and indicated that he looked forward to visiting Canada. However, his mood varied. His tapes record that on July 6 he said: "About the Canadians. I would not do anything with the Canadians. That Trudeau is a son of a bitch. That's why I cancelled that business there. I'll never go to that country while he's there."[29]

Trudeau's jousting with the United States began during the foreign policy and defence reviews, when the Americans indicated that they were "deeply concerned at the size of the proposed reductions in Canada's force commitments in Europe and by the speed with which the GOC [government of Canada] plans to carry them out." Further troubles came as the United States moved unilaterally to deal with its serious economic problems, most notably its large balance of payments deficit. In August, after a Cabinet meeting where Treasury Secretary John Connally told the president that the country was "broke," Nixon reacted to pressure on the American dollar by announcing what the Japanese called the Nixon *shokku* — trade restrictions he imposed in reaction to foreign manufacturers capturing markets that had traditionally been American preserves. Although the nickname implied that the protectionist measures were directed at Japan, Canada was deeply affected, too, by the surcharge on imports. The Nixon announcement also dramatically ended the ties between the American dollar and gold, which had, in effect, been the foundation of the international economic system since the Second World War. At the last minute, the Texan Connally, who particularly disliked Canada, threw the Canada-U.S. Auto Pact into the mix, thereby threatening about a third of the trade between the two countries. As an added insult, Nixon said that the measures were aimed at Japan, "America's largest trading partner." The error — Canada was the largest by a considerable amount — betrayed the haste of the action and the administration's indifference to and ignorance of Canadian interests.[30]

At the request of his concerned Cabinet colleagues, Trudeau cut short his European vacation on the Adriatic. In the end, the Auto Pact was preserved and subsidiary agreements were reached, but the experience shook Trudeau. It emphasized to him how dependent Canada was on the United States, and it boosted Canadian nationalist arguments that the dependence must be decreased. Minister of National Revenue Herb Gray was labouring on a report on foreign investment, and in November someone leaked it to the leftist *Canadian Forum*, which immediately published it to considerable controversy. Its criticisms of multinationals operating in Canada captured newspaper headlines across the country.[31] Trudeau's skepticism about nationalism made him hesitate when economic policies rested on nationalist justifications, but the Nixon *shokku* created a strong momentum for nationalist economics in Canada and elsewhere.

A troubled Trudeau asked to visit Nixon in Washington, and at Kissinger's insistence, Nixon agreed to a meeting, on December 6. With his hair fashionably long and sideburns well below the ear, Trudeau sat with Nixon in front of the fireplace in the Oval Office and discussed the *shokku*. Prior to the meeting, Nixon asked Connally, "What to say to this son of a bitch Trudeau?" Nevertheless, formality prevailed when the meeting began. Nixon complained that other countries were "ganging up" on the United States. In reply, Trudeau decried protectionism but added, interestingly: "If you're going to be protectionist, let's be in it together." Claiming correctly that he was neither a nationalist nor a protectionist, Trudeau warned Nixon that "if you were going to take a very protectionist trend, our whole economy is so importantly tied to yours, we'd have to make some very fundamental decisions." The United States, he claimed, could "colonize" Canada by building up a huge trade surplus: "If we're always in debt toward you, the only way in which we can pay our debts is by selling you parts of our country."

In reply Nixon said that Canada was "terribly important" to the United States, but that both countries "are inevitably going to pursue their own interests." Seeing that things were not going well, Kissinger intervened and told Trudeau that Canada would be treated more fairly than was stated when the *shokku* was announced. Trudeau responded that Kissinger's remarks were "extremely helpful," adding, "I think we're reassured by everything you've said that this [protectionist policy] is temporary, [that] this is not a philosophical approach that we want to keep you in a state of domination just because we want to protect our society now." Eventually, both Kissinger and Nixon assured the Canadian that they were only temporarily protectionist. After the meeting, Trudeau told the press with some exuberance that he had been reassured by the president, but Nixon became sour again. After Trudeau left, Nixon called him a "pompous egghead" but allowed that the "asshole" was a "clever son of a bitch."* The president followed up by urging his chief of staff, H.R. Haldeman, to plant a negative story about Trudeau with a particularly nasty Washington columnist.[32]

Trudeau was not fully reassured by Kissinger's comment that the United States would later return to free trade, and within the bureaucracy and the Prime Minister's Office, plans began to be drafted for a review agency to scrutinize foreign — overwhelmingly American — investment in Canada.[33] Moreover, energy, always highly flammable as an issue, became central to Canadian-American negotiations at this time. New difficulties seemed to appear almost daily. It was during his first visit to Washington in March 1969 that Trudeau had uttered his famous line: "Living with you is in some ways like sleeping with an elephant: no matter how friendly and even-tempered the beast, one is affected by every twitch and grunt,"[34] and the words were more than apt. Despite Trudeau's statement and Nixon's earlier vow never to set foot in Canada so long as Trudeau was leader, Nixon finally did visit the

––––––––––––––––––––

* When the first Nixon tapes appeared during the Watergate affair, it became known that Nixon had called Trudeau an asshole. Trudeau responded by declaring, "I've been called worse things by better people." An impish John Diefenbaker condemned Nixon's remark but allowed that Nixon demonstrated an excellent knowledge of the human anatomy. An account of the tape and the Trudeau response are found in the *Toronto Star*, Dec. 8, 2008.

Canadian capital in April 1972. The raw irritations resulting from the August *shokku* had healed, but Nixon made it clear that Ottawa no longer had a special relationship with Washington. Canada and the United States, he declared in remarks he wrote himself, "have very separate identities" and "nobody's interests are furthered when these realities are obscured."[35] Nixon was blunt, but Trudeau genuinely appreciated the strong words and the public declaration. The candour brought him some freedom.*

To be fair to Nixon, although he constantly referred to Trudeau as "that son of a bitch" in private, he normally separated his personal dislike from American interests, and he recognized that Canada had its own objectives too. In a December 1971 White House discussion about the Canadian dollar that took place after Trudeau's visit to the Oval Office, Nixon said: "I've never seen that

---

* Nixon was in no better mood about Canada during this visit. A particular target was Trudeau aide Tim Porteous, who was described as an "ugly bastard, probably very left-wing." Again, Nixon told Haldeman to plant a negative story in the press, this time about Porteous. He told Haldeman: "Play it hard. Find a way, goddammit. You've got to put it to these people for kicking the US around after what we did for that lousy son of a bitch," referring, of course, to Trudeau and to the agreement with Canada to eliminate the harsh effects of the economic actions of August 1971. Nixon said, "That trip we needed like a hole in the head." Porteous later told Kissinger the visit did not help Canadian-American relations, although Kissinger reportedly enjoyed his evening at the National Arts Centre with Canadian television host Charlotte Gobeil, sister of Trudeau's friend Madeleine. When asked what Trudeau thought of Nixon's hostility toward him, Porteous said: "It wasn't the kind of thing that really concerned Pierre. I don't think he had any aspirations to be a friend of Nixon's." Alexandra Gill, "Nixon's Bushy-Haired 'Bastard' Bites Back," *Globe and Mail*, March 23, 2002; interview with Tim Porteous, Sept. 2007.

son of a bitch Trudeau say anything good about [the economic crisis] before but he was very good" during their recent meeting. "I mean . . . we're not trying to exploit Canada—even if we were, we would own 90 percent of their oil resources. You know 85 percent of their auto industry is tied to ours . . . we understand Canada has its own right to its destiny and no Canadian politician could survive without that ideology. . . . But . . . we have to look out for our own interests." Though Nixon's and Trudeau's views on international affairs were different, each one, in his own peculiar way, was a realist, and their relationship was functional and efficient in its approach to details. Nevertheless, Jay Walz, the *New York Times'* excellent Canadian correspondent, concluded on June 19, 1972, that "despite three cordial official visits with President Nixon, [Trudeau] has still not found an effective way of dealing with the country with which Canada does most of her trading." Now, he lamented, the resolution of "about a dozen grievances" would have to await elections in both countries.[36]

—

Burglars had struck the Watergate apartments on June 17, two days before Walz wrote his comments, and the fateful re-election of Richard Nixon in November would complicate Trudeau's task even more. His own campaign plans were in disarray. Most party officials had wanted an election in the spring, but neither Trudeau nor his Cabinet was ready. And meanwhile, the rise of the NDP in the polls forced the Liberals to tack to the left in both foreign and domestic policy.

   Although Trudeau had said he would not bestow "goodies" on Canadians of all kinds, he had indicated in the election campaign of 1968 that a Just Society meant that regional economic differences were the proper concern of the federal government.

Building on earlier regional programs, Trudeau established the Department of Regional Economic Expansion (DREE), with a specific mandate to use the finances and authority of the federal government to spur economic development in depressed areas of Canada. With Jean Marchand as minister, the highly creative former Pearson adviser Tom Kent as deputy, and the talented and experienced Pauline Bothwell as executive assistant, DREE was ambitious, powerful, and influential within government. Its enthusiasm has not been questioned, but its effectiveness has. Many economists believe that DREE and major unemployment insurance reforms introduced in 1971 made the economy less flexible and productive, particularly when other initiatives in the fields of competition, taxation, and tariff reduction were limited.

Manpower and Immigration Minister Bryce Mackasey radically expanded unemployment insurance to include temporary workers previously excluded, as well as extended benefits for the long-term unemployed. Economic conservative Gordon Gibson, then a senior official in Trudeau's office, recalled how he exploded as Mackasey's bill went forward. In the words of many ministers, however, this Irish political brawler, who suffered a heart attack at the 1968 convention while boisterously pressing Trudeau's campaign, seemed to charm Trudeau, and he got his expensive way. Moreover, in early 1972 the impact of these policies was less apparent and politically dangerous than the rising unemployment rate, now over 6 percent. Labour critics of the government, closely tied to the NDP, seldom praised the new spending measures but regularly denounced the government's broader economic policies.[37]

The prime minister and his closest advisers knew they were in trouble early in 1972. Their economic policies had misjudged inflation in 1968; they scrambled to recover quickly, but the unemployment rate remained stubbornly high, even as inflation began to rise. The unemployment rate in Ontario in 1971 (5.4 percent) was more than double that of 1966 (2.6 percent), but there were even higher rates in the other large provinces— Quebec (7.3 percent) and British Columbia (7.2 percent). Trudeau tried to woo defectors on the right as well as the left. He travelled to Toronto to meet business leaders, but he told Senator John Godfrey that he did not believe he had "made much headway with some of those present." That was true. He halted foreign travel and energetically wooed the Canadian media, another community where his popularity had waned. In January 1972 the Conservative journalist John Gray wrote: "Although it is accepted among smart circles that Trudeau's government is a disaster, he has delivered pretty well what he promised in 1968. He promised very little, and those who expected more were projecting their own fantasies. But what fantasies they were; what disappointments they created." Visiting British journalist Jerome Caminada found an angry country in February, one that fed, most unhealthily, on "the personality of Mr Pierre Trudeau." He dominated the front pages of Canadian newspapers through his "flair for physical activity" and his unerring sense of drama, Caminada wrote, but he was losing his audience.

A major act in the continuing drama occurred on December 25, 1971, when Margaret gave birth to Justin, and glowing pictures of the new little family appeared in all the newspapers. The photograph of Trudeau's joy and Margaret's love as she held Justin exudes the extraordinary sense of paternity, maternity, and emotional fulfillment that their children brought to their lives. Briefly, a gentler mood surrounded the stories about Trudeau, but the black mood soon returned. At a February 1972 dinner party in Ottawa, the British journalist "listened while Canadians from contrasting ends of the country tore each other's arguments apart like raw meat in the hands of starving men." Canada was in a cranky mood, and Trudeau himself was no exception.* When Caminada travelled with Trudeau on a flight to Montreal, someone told the prime minister he was seeing Bourassa the next day and asked if he had a message for the Quebec premier. "Tell him to make up his mind," he snapped angrily, still smarting from the Victoria constitutional debacle.[38]

Trudeau shuffled the Cabinet in January 1972 and, unexpectedly, made John Turner minister of finance and Donald Macdonald minister of energy, mines, and resources. Turner had become the most popular minister, particularly among the "upper middle-class English Canadians" who were abandoning the prime minister and his group. Trudeau was already uneasy with Turner, partly because of his insistence on staying in the leadership contest in 1968 and partly because he had become a clear rival. He deeply admired Macdonald, who boldly argued with him in Cabinet and won his respect. Turner's immediate task was to prepare a budget that would reassure business while maintaining the progressive credentials the Liberal Party required for the next election. A strong minister, Turner demanded that Trudeau give a more central role to Finance and its minister. Turner followed through: when he announced his first budget, he recognized that unemployment was a greater challenge than inflation, so he added some stimulation to its mix. Corporate taxes were cut and seniors' benefits were indexed. Press reaction was generally favourable, but continuing labour troubles,

---

* Progressive Conservative leader Robert Stanfield, with characteristic fairness, dismissed claims that Trudeau was not serious about life and Parliament. He told the visiting British journalist: "They haven't observed the wear and tear of four years in office, the lines on his face. He's very earnest, serious and tough, but he gets impatient with people and with Parliament." It was a fair and accurate assessment. Jerome Caminada, "Canada's Struggle for Identity," *Times* (London), Feb. 17, 1972.

economic uncertainties, mediocre polls, and party disorganization meant there would be no election in the spring of 1972.

The party began to pay for Trudeau's disregard for the loyalists, and a campaign had to be cobbled together with two Cabinet ministers in charge: Jean Marchand, Trudeau's longtime friend, and Robert Andras, a popular northern Ontario auto dealer, who was minister of state for urban affairs. In the summer the American poll-ster Oliver Quayle arrived to assess what Canadians thought of Trudeau, while Liberal MPs learned in their constituencies that many of their voters now loathed the prime minister. Once again, labour troubles bedevilled Cabinet's summer repose, and in late August a frustrated Trudeau called Parliament together to force B.C. dockworkers to end their strike. As the back-to-work legislation passed rapidly through the House and Senate on September 1, Trudeau met with members of his political Cabinet, informed them he had decided on a fall election, and showed them his strategy and campaign statement. He planned on seeing Governor General Roland Michener late that same afternoon and would announce an election for October 30.

As Trudeau read out his campaign statement, Turner thought it was "too much of a 'you never had it so good'" declaration. Some problems should be mentioned and their solutions suggested. Mitchell Sharp argued that the statement would become a "tool in the hands of the Opposition." Andras and Marchand said the caucus was also unhappy with the optimistic theme of the document. A despairing Trudeau said he "was pre-pared to sign it in its present form and work on it," but "the alter-native was to go into the election without anything in the nature of a campaign document or platform." Party president Richard Stanbury agreed to support it, though he "was tempted" to point out that it was "not related except in the most indirect way with the deci-sions of the Party taken in November /70" about what party policy should be. As Trudeau left this collective indecision for Rideau Hall, the political Cabinet reached a compromise: "The campaign theme 'The Land Is Strong' would not be announced as such but would simply be allowed to develop in the course of speeches."

And develop it did, quickly but disastrously. For Liberals in 1972, the land was weak.[39]

—

CHAPTER SEVEN

THE LAND IS NOT STRONG

Pierre Trudeau did not like politics much—at least not those parts the oldtimers considered to be the heart of the game. Chicken suppers, calls to soothe wavering supporters, working a room, remembering the kids' names, and kowtowing to journalists were tasks he forswore. It had mattered little in the first months in power when Trudeaumania swept the land. In those good times, Trudeau could organize a dinner for the great Swedish economist Gunnar Myrdal, get away to see Ted Kennedy at Ste-Adèle on the weekend, and free up a morning to meet the French publisher Jean-Jacques Servan-Schreiber but respond, "Hell, No" when the Liberal Party national director asked him to "consider having the National Executive for cocktails sometime over the weekend." But things had changed by 1972, and Trudeau and his group were ill prepared for a more critical political world. Too much debate, too little decision, and far-too-complicated policies meant that the Trudeau campaign team had a weak foundation for the fall election. They had no bold new program to present to voters, and so they decided, almost by default, to run on their record.[1]

The Liberals began the campaign breathtakingly over-confident. Their draft platform of August 10—the fourth draft—was smug, condescending, and adrift. The first Trudeau government had many concrete achievements, but the new platform presented them poorly. "The Land Is Strong," the heading of one section on the economy, began: "The Canadian economy is 20% bigger than it was 4 years ago. People have more money to spend than they did 4 years ago (about $815.00 more for every man, woman, and child). No matter how you measure Canada's well-being, we are in good shape: industrial production is up 18%; manufacturing is up 14%; 744,000 houses were built; retail sales are up 25%; labour income is up 45%; and company profits are up 17%; we are exporting 25% more than we did in 1968. They are the *numbers* that indicate steady and sure growth. Behind these statistics is a man with a good job and a steady wage; a man and a woman starting a new family in a new house; another man with a good job because Canadian products sell so well abroad; still another man with a good job because Canadian enterprise has the confidence in itself and in the country to re-invest to create the new jobs our young people want." The statistics were complex and the sexism jarred. Later, the platform claimed that "there are good jobs in Canada for everybody who wants to work."[2] Although the earlier sentences were largely accurate, the final one was visibly untrue, especially in the Maritimes and Quebec, where 8 percent of the workforce was unemployed when the election was called for October 30 on the eve of Labour Day.

Trudeau opened the campaign with a declaration that his government was "closer to the people" than any other in Canadian history. At his nomination in Mount Royal, his hair was stylishly swept back and the baldness at the front more exposed, with Laurier, rather than Caesar, now the model. He wore a conservative blue suit and white shirt, strikingly unlike the casual leather garb that had horrified political organizers when he showed up for the nomination in the same riding in 1965. The trademark red rose endured. Little was casual at the event, as a demurely dressed Margaret stood in her preselected place and aides crowding the aisles handed out autographed photographs of Trudeau. "As I look at the vitality of Canada today," Trudeau told his constituents, "I see a country which has never before believed as much in itself, never shared such a strong sense of self-confidence, never looked forward with such optimism. Never has Canada been itself to this same degree."[3] The speech and the occasion lacked passion; the tone was reasonable and flat.

The campaign kickoff, especially the statement from Liberal Party national director Torrance Wylie that the government would participate in a "dialogue with the people," not an election campaign, horrified Senator Keith Davey. A pin-striped, ebullient backroom legend, Davey, whose buttonholing and berating had guided the Grits to political success in Ontario during the Pearson years, regarded the efforts of Wylie and the other organizers as thoroughly amateur. Davey was on a so-called national campaign committee, but he soon realized it would play no significant role in the election.* Indeed, Trudeau, to Davey's surprise and

---

* Davey and Richard Stanbury were trying to recruit Judy LaMarsh to be a candidate once again. Since leaving politics bitterly in 1968, she had played a major role in the Royal Commission on the Status of Women. The lack of a female Cabinet member had been a glaring weakness in Trudeau's first government, and the two political veterans saw LaMarsh's return as a solution to this problem. With Davey in tow, she met with Trudeau on June 14. Davey opened with praise for her political talent, and Trudeau followed with a generous invitation for her to run as a candidate, but suddenly she rose and ended the visit abruptly, telling Trudeau he simply wanted to "hang her in the window of the butcher shop like a hunk of cold meat." She soon left the Liberal Party, which, ironically, has a regular Judy LaMarsh dinner to raise funds for female candidates. Keith Davey, *The Rainmaker: A Passion for Politics* (Toronto: Stoddart, 1986), 161–62; Richard Stanbury Diary, privately held, May–Aug. 1971.

disapproval, indicated that government business would continue as usual over the next two months, with the Cabinet meeting as it normally did on Wednesdays.[4]

Lacking a specific platform, the Liberals basked in generalities and favourable early polls. At first the approach seemed to work. The government exulted in reflected glory during the Canada-Soviet Hockey Series in late September, when Paul Henderson scored the dramatic winning goal with 34 seconds left in the game—Canadian hockey's greatest triumph. Soon, however, the celebrations stopped, and Canadians became cranky. The Liberal campaign began to sputter. Campaign co-chairs Jean Marchand and Bob Andras rarely communicated with each other, and once Marchand realized he was in trouble in his own constituency, he virtually abandoned his role at headquarters and went home to fight his own battle. Campaign manager Bill Lee was no Keith Davey, but he knew the constituencies well. A seasoned political campaigner who had run Paul Hellyer's campaign for the leadership in 1968, he had the trust of his immediate counterparts and knew that four years of neglect of party workers had taken a toll in the ridings. His role was far less than his title suggested, however, and he became increasingly at odds with Trudeau's Ottawa office. His pleas that Trudeau become more overtly political went unheard.

The campaign slogan soon became the butt of crude jokes. One soothing television advertisement romanticized the Canadian landscape while an earnest voice insisted, "The land is strong." Conservative strategist Dalton Camp mocked it, quipping, "Lalonde is strong." Then, during a rally in southwestern Ontario, a farmer heckled a Liberal candidate: "If you had any sense you'd know it's horse shit, not Liberal shit, that makes the land strong." Davey and his crowd agreed: the Liberal campaign of 1972 lacked the horse shit so essential to politics on the hustings, and he wrote Trudeau a private letter of despair. On many occasions Trudeau accomplished what had seemed impossible in the electric 1968 campaign: he was dull. Charles Lynch of Southam News, one of the more sympathetic journalists, complained that he denied "his audiences a chance to explode while he is speaking: he turns his sentences down at the end, rather than up. . . . What he seeks to convey is controlled excitement and unabashed pride in his accomplishments." By mid-October his pride had created a fall.[5]

Eric Kierans, who had left Trudeau's Cabinet in April 1971 but remained a very disgruntled Liberal MP, now publicly broke with the Liberals. He was a maverick, an economic nationalist who believed that John Turner's 1972 budget reflected the Finance Department's essential conservatism and its blindness to the sale of Canadian resources to foreigners. He wrote a preface to *Louder Voices: Corporate Welfare Bums*, a book sponsored by the NDP to promote David Lewis's campaign. The phrase "corporate welfare bums" had an unexpected but powerful electoral appeal in 1972 as both inflation and unemployment were historically high, and business executives became an easy target. Here was a slogan that worked, and the eloquent Lewis thundered from the podium against corporate privilege. Long an admirer of his fellow Montrealer Lewis, Kierans released an October 16 letter to Trudeau where he said that to vote Liberal would be to "worsen our present problems."

Walter Gordon, the dominant influence on the news and editorial pages at the *Toronto Star*, had supported Trudeau in 1968 after he appeared to agree with statements drafted by Gordon that expressed opposition to the Vietnam War and concern about foreign investment. Now, completely disillusioned with the Trudeau government, Gordon, together with Peter C. Newman, the editor of *Maclean's*, who had also lost his early enthusiasm for the prime minister, and political economist Abe Rotstein, formed the Committee for an Independent Canada (CIC). They were soon joined by Eric Kierans, Claude Ryan, publisher Jack McClelland, prominent Alberta Liberal and publisher Mel Hurtig, and over 170,000 other Canadians—all demanding a halt in the growth of foreign ownership. The United States was the source of most of the purchases, and fuelling the rage among Canadian nationalists was the sense that the country's resources were not only being lost to Canada but contributing to America's unpopular wars. It was no surprise, then, that Gordon wrote an article in the September *Maclean's* condemning the government's inaction and warning that the first party to endorse the CIC's principles would "resolve [his] personal dilemma"—and that of others like him. "If Pierre Trudeau does not announce some major changes in his policies," he warned, "I expect some of us will decide, on the day of the election, that we must put the future of the country first." This new nationalist movement was highly damaging for the Liberals, and on October 30, multimillionaires Kierans and Gordon both voted socialist.[6]

While economic nationalism drew Gordon and Kierans to David Lewis, the NDP leader's effective attack on "corporate welfare bums" also attracted many less affluent progressive voters, particularly university professors and civil servants, who felt that Trudeau had taken an unexpected turn to the right. Simultaneously, Conservative leader Robert Stanfield's attack on the Trudeau government's handling of the economy began to resonate in newspaper columns, television commentary, hair salons, and lunch counters across the country. Kathy Robinson, who was responsible for "first-time voters" in the Liberal cam-paign, recalls that "unemployment" dominated most of the polit-ical meetings.[7] Eighteen-year-olds had acquired the vote in 1970 (previously the age had been twenty-one), and they faced more limited employment prospects than their older siblings had a few years earlier. True, the major revision of the unemployment insurance program in 1971 provided far more generous benefits to the 6.2 percent of Canadians who were now unemployed than the 4.2 percent without jobs had received in 1968, and this support undoubtedly kept some Liberal seats. However, the benefits also cost Liberal support among small businesspeople, retirees, and bankers, who believed that Bryce Mackasey's controversial unemployment reforms had created too many "welfare bums."[8]

As he toured the country with Trudeau, Richard Stanbury, the Liberal Party president, frequently encountered resentment among young people who told him stories about acquaintances who were prospering on the dole. In eastern Ontario, for example, the owner of "a little 5 & 10 Store in Eganville" and his friend complained bitterly about "the lazy welfare bums and all the people who were supposedly unemployed but just wouldn't work." Similarly, in a long letter to Toronto Cabinet minister Alastair Gillespie, a constituent listed five "abuses" of the system by her own "acquaintances"—a university graduate who had toured the world for a year, for instance, then decided on his return to "take off" another year and live on the unemployment insurance he was entitled to because he had worked before his travels. Jobs had become scarce, and unemployment offices had few jobs to offer, so the situation permitted the "abuse" to occur. To the Liberals' considerable embarrassment, the enriched benefits caused a crisis in mid-campaign when it was discovered that their cost was far greater—by as much as $500 million—than the government had predicted in its estimates. Trudeau pointed out correctly that the opposition parties had not only supported the reforms but also initiated some amendments that even increased their generosity. Nevertheless, much damage was done.[9]

A candidate is usually the last to sense trouble, and that is what happened in the 1972 campaign. Crowds remained enthusiastic, and Trudeau's presence still electrified hockey rinks, town halls, and shopping plazas even if his speeches were generally lifeless.* Polls were less frequent than in later years, and politicians relied more on instinct and gossip to judge the political winds. Trudeau himself seemed more relaxed and, initially, more willing to consider advice than he had been in 1968. Margaret was an infrequent but helpful presence, who managed to charm some of her husband's media critics. Although the Liberals knew they were not as strong as in 1968, Trudeau's campaign team remained confident. In a surprisingly complacent address to Liberal candidates, Trudeau said: "Other parties may be running against us, they may be trying to catch up with us—I know they won't—but it's fairly true to say that we are not really running against them."[10] Most early polls had shown a comfortable Liberal margin of 10 percent, and ten days before election day, campaign official Torrance Wylie still thought that the "most pessimistic count" was 140 Liberal seats. Richard Stanbury estimated that the Liberals had a better chance of picking up 10 seats from the Tories than losing them. The major Quebec organizer predicted 67 seats in Quebec, 11 more than the Liberals held going into the election.

------

* Trudeau's book *Federalism and the French Canadians* (New York: St. Martin's Press, 1968) had been a bestseller in the year it was published. In 1972 Ivan Head edited a collection of Trudeau's speeches with the hope that a similar celebration of the prime minister's intellectual range and insight would occur. It did not occur. *Conversation with Canadians* (Toronto: University of Toronto Press, 1972) did clarify some of Trudeau's controversial remarks, such as the comment he made on December 13, 1968, when asked when he was going to sell western Canada's wheat (102). Nevertheless, the book, with such headings as "The Human Instinct," "The Challenge of Democracy," and "The Threshold of Greatness," reveals Trudeau's apparent distance from the concerns of "ordinary" Canadians.

The final Gallup poll shattered this complacency. Taken the last week of the campaign, it reported a closer race, with the Liberals at 39 percent, the Conservatives at 33 percent, and the NDP at 21 percent. Suddenly, Liberal MPs began to tremble. Trudeau worried that it was too late to reverse the tide, which had clearly turned against him. He swallowed his pride and announced that he had some "candies," which he began to drop on constituencies his advisers identified as "close." Shawinigan got a "leisure park," for instance, and Toronto was promised a major renewal of its bleak harbourfront.* Trudeau's speeches became more emotional and political, and he began to celebrate with eloquence and passion the grandeur of the Canadian landscape and the spirit of its people. He later said that, at first, he had been "embarrassed to try and win an election this easy way, appealing to people's feelings." But he quickly lost that inhibition — and, henceforth, that particular appeal became his charmed political wand.[11] The polls also showed that as prime minister, the majority of Canadians had a clear preference for Trudeau over Stanfield, and the Liberal campaign team hoped that this factor would tip the undecided vote in their direction. It didn't.[12]

On election day, Trudeau voted in Mount Royal and then drove with nervous aides to Ottawa. His headquarters were at the

---

* Trudeau's remarks about candies occurred in Jean Chrétien's constituency of Shawinigan. Trudeau, Chrétien claims, became excited about a new parks program Chrétien was promoting and said that when he thought about it, he was reminded of Christmas, when children got "candies." Trudeau used the English word "candies" as French slang in order to seem more colloquial, as Chrétien had been in his introductory speech. But like most Trudeau gaffes in the campaign, the press leapt on it and made Trudeau look bad. Jean Chrétien, *Straight from the Heart* (1985; repr., Toronto: Key Porter, 2007), 80–81.

Skyline Hotel, where his supporters had partied with such exuberance four years before on the night he became Liberal leader. But the mood was different now, and Trudeau himself seemed shaken when the first returns came in from the Maritimes. The Conservatives had taken a solid lead in the popular vote in all the Atlantic provinces, especially in Stanfield's native Nova Scotia. When Trudeau arrived at his suite on the twentieth-fifth floor, Quebec had finally brought good tidings, but in Ontario many Liberal seats had already fallen. A despondent Trudeau turned to Stanbury and said, "We must have had a bad government."[13]

Then came western Canada, where Liberal support collapsed: in Manitoba, the party took only 2 seats; in Saskatchewan, only Otto Lang, a former law dean with considerable prestige in the province, survived; and in British Columbia, Margaret Trudeau's home province, the Liberals won only 4 of the province's 23 seats. As these disappointing numbers came in one after the other, Trudeau turned to Margaret and said, oddly, "You may be a farmer's wife sooner than you thought." She broke into tears, took consolation in a drink, and sat morosely nearby as Pierre thanked his campaign team.

As leaders must, he called ministers and MPs who had lost their seats. While he made these sad calls, bitterness swelled among his supporters. Some Trudeau assistants became "vituperative," perhaps the product of a "little too much to drink but probably . . . even more the traumatic experience of the election results." Finally, wearing a fresh red rose, Trudeau met the press. With a sombre Margaret at his side, he said the results were inconclusive because the Liberals and the Conservatives were tied at 108 seats. Then he ended his brief remarks with a quotation from "Desiderata," an iconic text of the sixties counterculture: "Whether or not it is clear to you / no doubt the universe is unfolding as it should."[14]

Most Liberals strongly disagreed, particularly when Conservative leader Robert Stanfield tried to speed the unfolding with a declaration that Canadians had lost confidence in Trudeau and that the Governor General should call on him, Stanfield, to form a government.* NDP leader David Lewis, whose party had won a record 31 seats, held the balance of power, and he made it clear he would tilt the balance in whatever direction his party's needs dictated. Although the Liberals had won more of the popular vote (38.42 percent versus 35.02 percent for the Conservatives), they had the plurality in only one province — Quebec. The Conservatives led in every other province, giving Stanfield's argument for his residence at 24 Sussex considerable merit. His claim was strengthened early the following day, when the Conservatives temporarily gained an extra seat in the election tally, giving the Conservatives 109 seats, compared with 107 for the Liberals, before the vote reverted once again to a tie.

On Halloween, a shocked Stanbury and other Liberals phoned contacts across the country for reactions to the "trick" Canadians had played on their party. Some despaired: Davey urged immediate resignation, arguing that Stanfield would so botch governing that the Liberals would soon return triumphant.

---

* Trudeau had the right to meet Parliament and seek the confidence of the House. If the Liberals had been defeated in the House, the Governor General could then have called upon Stanfield to try to form a government. There is ambiguity in these close minority situations, caused in part by the controversies surrounding the 1926 election (when Prime Minister Mackenzie King sought a dissolution that Governor General Lord Byng refused) and the 2008 election (when Prime Minister Stephen Harper successfully obtained a prorogation of the House before facing a vote of confidence in which a united opposition had announced its intention to form a government).

Most, however, wanted Trudeau to cling to power. That decision became much easier when a recount in the partly rural riding of Ontario, east of Toronto, reversed the Conservative win there. The Tories' strong standing had surprised them as much as the Liberals: they had forgotten to send a scrutineer to the recount, which the Liberals won by only four votes.[15] Trudeau's place in history may have been preserved by a Tory error and fewer Canadians than the fingers on one hand.

Trudeau always hated losing. He competed fiercely, whether he was shooting rapids, fighting against his fellow student Jean de Grandpré at Brébeuf, debating with René Lévesque at the fabled meetings in Pelletier's home, or jousting with his far more experienced opponents in the 1968 leadership race. In politics he had never known defeat, and he immediately decided he would not act like a loser in November 1972. He moved aggressively to counter early press analysis that blamed the loss on his personal policies, especially bilingualism, and on a poor campaign. In his first press conference, he rejected the suggestion that bilingualism had caused his defeat but suggested, "If I had the campaign to wage over again, I might give more explanation of the act. It was never intended that every Canadian speak both of the two official languages. I thought that was understood, but it seems it wasn't."[16] He admitted "failures," but at no point did he suggest that he step down. Others did. Ross Whicher, a small businessman from Ontario's rural Bruce riding, called for Trudeau to resign and for Finance Minister John Turner to succeed him. Whicher was never forgiven, but he was not alone in his views. Even campaign manager Bill Lee apparently suggested the same course to Bob Andras, the campaign co-chair.[17]

Trudeau acted quickly to stem any momentum for change by telling party officials that he would not resign. At a meeting of the informal political Cabinet (consisting of the ministers responsible for political advice), Stanbury began with a letter indicating that

Trudeau wished to remain and intended to learn from the troubling election results. The Cabinet members were polled, and three of them urged that the government should resign. Two had lost their own seats: Labour Minister Martin O'Connell from Toronto and Industry, Trade, and Commerce Minister Jean-Luc Pepin, with whom Trudeau had a long but distant and distrustful relationship. The third was John Turner.[18]

———

The majority of ministers and MPs held firm for Trudeau, but after the election, the prime minister knew that the threads binding the party to him were badly frayed. When he met his full Cabinet on November 2, he faced criticism from ministers on both the left and the right. Manitoba's James Richardson, scion of the famed Winnipeg financial family, blamed bilingualism for the defeat in the West. To Trudeau's fury, he also argued that the West shared Quebec's view that each region must build its own way in a decentralized Canada. External Affairs Minister Mitchell Sharp criticized the government's immigration and economic policies, while Bryce Mackasey, the minister of manpower and immigration and a target of the conservative wing of the party, ferociously defended his unemployment insurance changes. Trudeau quickly cut off the fractious debate, telling Richardson that official bilingualism was not negotiable, and because the "other parties were not in a position to solve the issue," it was "one good reason for the government to stay in office." He promised better administration, more effective management of the economy, and policies to counter "welfare backlash." A full and ambitious program to deal with the outstanding issues would soon be ready for Parliament and for Canadians, he said.

By the time Trudeau met with the caucus on November 8, he was in full control, and he made sure that any criticisms "were . . . couched in terms of future action rather than past recrimination."

His eyes coldly penetrating, his focus clear, his determination striking, he rallied his forces for the future war. The caution and defensiveness that had marked his first government disappeared, even with regard to the prime minister's residence. Earlier he had prevented Margaret from making much-needed renovations to the rambling old building, but immediately after the election, he gave her a hug and said: "You're off. Now get going with that house decoration." He planned a long stay at 24 Sussex.[19]

It was all a masterful performance. "Surprisingly," Liberal Party historian Joe Wearing writes, "a national executive meeting following the election agreed that anti-Trudeau feelings had not been a significant factor in the results, even though many Liberal candidates thought so and surveys by Gallup and Radio-Canada indicated that an anti-Trudeau vote was the most commonly held reason for Liberal losses."[20] But Trudeau, in his own words, "refused to see himself as a loser," and his determined belief caused most Liberals, if not others, to agree. What he later called his "half-failure" in 1972 began to "take on the aspect of a challenge that had to be met," and he found himself mentally rolling up his sleeves. As he expressed it, "I felt charged with the spirit of combat that had eluded me throughout the election campaign." Wearing an Aboriginal buckskin jacket for his post-election call on Governor General Roland Michener, where he agreed to form the incoming government, Trudeau drove his sleek Mercedes convertible across Sussex Drive to Rideau Hall to emphasize that "we were treating the results not as a defeat but as a challenge, and there was no question in my mind of giving up."[21]

Although the Liberals had lost almost a third of their seats, surprisingly few ministers had fallen on election night. Nevertheless, the outcome required major changes in the Cabinet. The "welfare backlash" meant that Bryce Mackasey had to go, even though the feisty Irish Canadian was a favourite of the prime minister because he, unlike most others, "made

Trudeau laugh."* Small businessman Bob Andras, who wanted to "rid" the party of its "socialism," replaced him as the minister of manpower and immigration. His appointment placated the commentators on the business pages, but the surge of the NDP and the defection of prominent Liberals such as Kierans and Gordon over the economic nationalism issue demanded a response. Trudeau therefore promoted Herb Gray, the author of the report on foreign investment, to be minister of consumer and corporate affairs.[†] Alastair Gillespie became minister of industry, trade and commerce, a post that the defeated Pepin had headed very successfully.[22] It was an excellent appointment, as Gillespie was not only a highly respected Toronto businessman but an economic nationalist as well, one who had successfully managed Walter Gordon's firm, Canadian Corporate Management.

---

* Trudeau reluctantly sent Mackasey to the back bench. Much later he said that "Bryce had a solution [for seasonal and endemic unemployment] and I think [he] should be remembered. . . . He had a feeling for the little guy, and that's what I liked and that's why I brought him into my Cabinet. He corresponded to my own view, as Marchand did, that we should help first those who need help most, and he was prepared to do it." After the 1972 election, Trudeau asked all ministers to express a willingness to change posts. Mackasey refused, and so he was dismissed from Cabinet. "Interview between Mr. Trudeau and Mr. Graham," May 4, 1992, TP, MG 26 03, vol. 23, file 7, LAC. The comment about Mackasey's ability to make Trudeau laugh was made to me by former principal secretary Tom Axworthy. Pierre Trudeau, *Memoirs* (Toronto: McClelland and Stewart, 1993), 160.

† Herb Gray was Canada's first Jewish Cabinet minister. Although his appointment was very popular with the Jewish community, Gray recalls that Trudeau did not speak with him at the time about issues dealing with foreign policy. Most of Gray's own speeches dealt with social justice rather than issues specific to Jewish

In terms of influence, Trudeau more than made up for Pepin's loss in Quebec by appointing Jeanne Sauvé, Trudeau's first female minister, as Gillespie's successor as minister of state for science and technology and Marc Lalonde as minister of national health and welfare. Lalonde would become, as he had been in the Prime Minister's Office, a powerful force in government and one of Trudeau's few political intimates. Trudeau also did as well as possible with the meagre Liberal returns from both the East and the West. In Nova Scotia and Saskatchewan, he scored with the sole Liberal members elected—Allan MacEachen, whose tactical brilliance Trudeau was beginning to recognize, and Otto Lang, who had a sharp legal mind and whom Trudeau liked and respected. MacEachen was an Ottawa veteran whose knowledge of House rules was unrivalled among Liberals. Although unilingual and usually taciturn, he gradually convinced Trudeau that he was a political asset of the highest value. Trudeau did less well in British Columbia and Manitoba: B.C.'s Jack Davis was a brilliant engineer and scientist but an awkward politician, and James Richardson was conservative and critical of his regime, as Trudeau already knew. The prime minister distrusted them both and believed they were

---

interests. Even though he was a federal minister, he believes he spent more time on the provincial issue of support for independent schools than any other item. He did speak out against the Arab boycott of Israel after the 1973 Arab-Israeli War, but neither the press nor the PMO paid much attention to his comments. Later in the decade, the election of Menachem Begin's centre-right Likud Party brought Israeli politics more directly into Canadian affairs, and Gray even delivered a warning "message" from Trudeau to Begin about occupation of the Golan Heights. Interview with Herb Gray, July 2007. On the value of Gray's initial appointment with Jewish support, see Michel Vennat to Gordon Gibson, Oct. 28, 1969, TP, MG 26 07, vol. 121, file 313.05, LAC.

not truly Liberal. As it happened, Davis's defection to Social Credit in 1975 and Richardson's to the Reform Party in 1987 gave substance to Trudeau's original suspicions.[23]

As the composition of Trudeau's second government firmed up, its visage appeared comfortingly familiar and even conservative. The continuing presence of Turner and Sharp in the two most senior positions, Finance and External Affairs, reassured Bay Street and those who worried about the "socialists" surrounding Trudeau. In terms of education and experience, the Cabinet was one of the best ever forged in Canada. Davis, Lang, Turner, and Gillespie were all former Rhodes Scholars, and several others had advanced degrees or had studied abroad, mainly at British universities, including Energy Minister Don Macdonald (Cambridge), Sharp (London School of Economics), Treasury Board president Charles "Bud" Drury (Paris), Senate leader Paul Martin (Cambridge and Harvard), Lalonde (Oxford), and Trudeau himself (London School of Economics, Paris, and Harvard). The small number of American degrees is striking, and perhaps this gap created a resistance among the ministers to the new conservatism staking out its ground in the United States.

No previous Cabinet had ever been so bilingual, although Cabinet meetings normally took place in English, except when Trudeau addressed a francophone minister. Despite the many complaints about "French power" in some of the anglophone media, Trudeau strengthened the Quebec presence by the addition not only of Lalonde and Sauvé but also of André Ouellet (postmaster general) and Jean-Pierre Goyer (minister of supply and services). The weak western representation led Trudeau to appoint the voluble Eugene Whelan from southwestern Ontario as minister of agriculture. He wore a green stetson everywhere except in the Commons chamber, where his joking flamboyance beguiled the press—if not always his colleagues. Like Mackasey, he was a favourite of Trudeau because he made him laugh;

unlike Mackasey, however, the folksy Whelan was a considerable political asset.[24]

—

Although the new government looked familiar and even cautious,
Trudeau decided for several reasons that it should take a populist
and progressive turn. First, he attributed his "half-failure" in the
recent election to the ambivalence of many of the reforms during
his first government. He had removed some but not all of
the Canadian troops from Europe. He had taxed capital gains at
50 percent, not the full rate urged by the report of the Carter
Commission. Several other projects such as the reform of laws on
non-pharmaceutical drugs, the creation of a foreign investment
review agency, and reform of the Indian Act and the Election
Expenses Act had either failed or not been enacted.[25] Sure, he
could shrug off NDP member Ed Broadbent's accusation that
he was the most conservative prime minister of his lifetime, but
defections of young people such as Bob Rae really stung him.
Moreover, his young wife's politics were certainly progressive, and
they had an increasingly significant influence on him. A second
major reason for this turn to the left was that to survive in the
minority Parliament, the Liberals needed the New Democrats'
support. David Lewis had clear demands, mostly related to economic nationalist issues and unemployment policy.

Moreover, the post-election analysis led ministers to believe
that liberal principles had been buried in the campaign rhetoric
and that, if they were to consolidate their leadership, they had better
be progressive during this second government. In the first meeting
of the campaign committee after the election, for instance, Jean
Marchand charged that the party in English Canada had not
defended bilingualism and progressive policies. Party president
Richard Stanbury agreed, saying that English-Canadian MPs and

party people "had run away from the various backlashes"— bilingualism and welfare and so on—and that it was time to attack that kind of thinking, "otherwise political opinion would polarize and we would lose all possibility of continuing a liberal and tolerant society." Stanbury left the meeting with Trudeau, who, when they reached Trudeau's car, thanked Stanbury for "his remarks," saying he "had summed up the situation very accurately." Not all agreed, but crucially, the prime minister did.

The final reason for his second government's turn to the left was that the near electoral defeat caused Liberal Party veterans to rise up against what they believed were the cautious, abstract, politically inexperienced intellectuals who had dominated government for the previous four years. The heaviest protests came from Toronto, where Trudeau had lost the critical endorsement of the *Toronto Star*, whose founder, Joe Atkinson, had stipulated to his heirs that his "paper of the people" should support the Liberals only so long as they truly were liberal. In its place the first Trudeau government had won the support of Bay Street's favourite, the historically Conservative *Globe and Mail*, but that had proved to be an unfortunate endorsement.[26] And so the Ontario party power-brokers, working in the backrooms, now decided that the party must change direction.

Years of infighting lay behind this move, but in the end, the Toronto group emerged on top. After the electoral disaster of 1958, a group of Liberals known as Cell 13 had taken control of the party in the metropolitan area and had made "Tory Toronto" Liberal in the sixties—a decade that transformed the conservative "British" city. The morning after the disaster of the recent election, a few ring-leaders in the Toronto Liberal crowd, which had played hardly any role in the first Trudeau government, began to call each other in an effort to "save our party." The lead was taken by communications lawyer Jerry Grafstein, a man of many infectious enthusiasms, and long-time party treasurer Gordon Dryden, whose rural Ontario dry wit and wisdom contrasted strikingly with Grafstein's mid-city ways. They adhered strongly to a common Liberal opinion, vehemently expressed in the *Toronto Star*, that when out of office the party must lean to the left. Christina McCall describes their mood and beliefs:

> They believed implicitly that whenever the Liberal Party
> turned right—as they thought it had in the first Trudeau
> régime—it lost its way and its natural constituency. Grafstein
> and Dryden decided during that post-election conversation
> that something had to be done to save the party from the
> forces of reaction, and they set about convening a meeting of
> Liberal friends in Grafstein's office on Richmond Street West
> to decide just what that "something" should be.[27]

Not unexpectedly, it turned out to contain far more politics and far less political theory and scientific management than Trudeau's current advisers were likely to expound.

Trudeau needed no prod from Toronto. He had already begun a "housecleaning" of his office. Jim Davey, who had expected to be Lalonde's replacement as chief of staff and who had won the affection of both Margaret and his own personal staff, was moved over to the Department of Transport, far away from the centre of power.* His replacement as program secretary was

---

* The peculiar key in which debates played during the first Trudeau government is captured well in an exchange during a quarrel between Michael Pitfield in the Privy Council Office and Jim Davey in the Prime Minister's Office. For most MPs and certainly the political veterans, the "key" was out of tune. Writing to Trudeau, Davey explained the quarrel and told Trudeau not to worry because the two "have shared too many important experiences together

defeated Toronto MP John Roberts, while another defeated Toronto MP, Martin O'Connell, took over from Marc Lalonde. Both men fit the earlier mould: they were fluently bilingual and had academic doctorates and intellectual interests. However, as politicians, they also knew that successful elections came from endless coffee party chatter, constant knocking on doors in the evening, and early morning handshakes at factory gates. Trudeau realized that the defection of Walter Gordon had hurt his party, and in adding O'Connell to his office and Gillespie to his Cabinet, both of whom had worked closely with Gordon in the past, he hoped to reopen lines of communication not only with Gordon but also with the *Toronto Star*.[28]

The Toronto group's suggestion that Trudeau ask Senator Keith Davey to be campaign manager initially met with resistance from the prime minister—or at least delay. Davey claims that Trudeau called him a few days after the election to thank him for not "going public" with his criticisms and to ask him to meet with Marc Lalonde. In the meantime, Roberts arranged a dinner at 24 Sussex for the Toronto group promoting Davey, which included former Pearson aide Jim Coutts, former MP Bob Kaplan, Jerry Grafstein, Gordon Dryden, lawyer Tony Abbott, and consummate organizer Dorothy Petrie. Trudeau barely knew these longtime party activists, but they did not hold back on criticisms of his record or on their demand that Davey be made campaign chair.

---

for that to be the case. Possibly he is too Jesuitical in his guardianship of the Cabinet faith and his discernment for the spirit of others. On the other hand, while I hold the faith in common with him I have a more Dominican approach to the doctrine of organization, government and otherwise" (Oct. 3, 1969, TP, MG 26 07, vol. 290, file 319.11, LAC). Pitfield was himself moved to a deputy minister post in 1973.

Characteristically, Trudeau struck out at his detractors: "Look, when my friends and I came into politics, we had fire in our bellies—we wanted certain things for Quebec. But I don't understand what motivates you guys. What's in it for you anyway?" His guests became furious, but they respected Trudeau's office and responded cautiously. According to Christina McCall, "Trudeau was skeptical, but he was also desperate." Eventually, he asked Davey to serve as election campaign manager, and politics immediately became their mutual passion.[29]

—

With a plurality of two over the luckless Bob Stanfield Conservatives and with more than half the Liberal seats from Quebec, Trudeau began to woo those who had resisted him on election eve. The *Toronto Star* was easily seduced. It greeted the Liberal program announced in the Throne Speech of January 4 as full penance for Trudeau's earlier sins: "Stripped of his majority and humbled by the Progressive Conservatives, Trudeau and his Cabinet have rallied to produce a program for this session of Parliament—however brief—that promises the kind of legislation that almost certainly would have won him a decisive victory a few months ago." Trudeau now "deserves a chance," the *Star* concluded. Its nationalist editorial board warmed to the government's promise to extend the proposed foreign investment review to cover all new foreign investment, to restrict the sale of land to foreigners, and to scrutinize foreign firms in Canada more carefully. Although the *Star* worried about the government's failure to mention wage and price controls, it welcomed the further consideration of a guaranteed annual income and new grants for the disabled and the visually impaired.

The *Globe and Mail* was less impressed, and its witty political columnist George Bain mocked the laundry list of promises in the Throne Speech:

We've bills relating to field and stream,
Another allowance-for-families scheme,
For corporate immigrants; yet-new terms
(We're putting more natives on boards of firms).
We've plans for improving the IDB
And tightening the rules of the UIP
And still to make sure that we're back in grace,
Oh, see how we've wrapped in a fond embrace,
A threesome which simply ensures our health—
The Mounties, the Queen, and the Commonwealth.

But it might not be enough, he averred. Trudeau needed to win the West, and he remained unprepared. Bain illustrated his point:

Western Liberal: Do you know how the West was lost?
Pierre E. Himself: No, but if you hum a couple of bars,
I can fake it.

Trudeau soon proved Bain's point.[30]

The Throne Speech appeared to be a good program, and it certainly secured the government time, but in the January 1973 debate on it, Trudeau lost his temper and attacked the opposition for pandering to English-Canadian "bigots"—an attack he described much later as "probably the most unpopular thing I ever did in the House." In defence of his outburst, he told an interviewer that his "rational" approach had not worked. He had tried to "fight with a sword when the enemy was fighting with a bludgeon." He vowed in the future not to be so subtle: "If they want blood and guts, I'll give them blood and guts." Although Trudeau, Marchand, Lalonde, and many (but not all) of the francophone press read the election results as a reaction to official bilingualism, they probably exaggerated its impact on the polling results.

Nevertheless, the language policy definitely affected the Ottawa area and, to a lesser degree, western Canada. In his 1980 biography of Trudeau, Richard Gwyn, who himself worked in Eric Kierans' office in the first Trudeau government, makes a strong and succinct case for the clumsy administration of the bilingual policy and for its negative political impact. He understood well its importance for Trudeau: "Bilingualism is the 'Calais' written on Trudeau's heart. This is the passion behind his reason: the man inside the mask." He describes the agony of fortyish anglophone public servants going across the river to Hull, where "they were chattered at by 600 language teachers, sometimes to be reduced to tears by petites Québécoises who were either separatists or feminists or both, and who delighted in their chance for revenge."[31]

Bilingualism was, in Gwyn's witty but politically incorrect phrase, a "frog in the throat" of many Canadians. Moreover, Official Languages Commissioner Keith Spicer himself later pointed out, to Trudeau's irritation, that much of the money for bilingualism was badly or wrongly spent, that the results were disappointing (with only 11 percent of public servants who took courses attaining full fluency), and that the money would have been better spent on training young people who, thanks to declining university standards, were taking French less in the seventies than in the sixties. Spicer's 1976 report coincided not only with the election of the Parti Québécois, which opposed official bilingualism, but also with a nasty dispute about the use of French in air traffic control, which bigots used as an excuse to rant on radio talkshows in many parts of English Canada.[32]

Yet the evidence is weak that official bilingualism substantially hurt the Liberal Party either in 1972 or later. John Meisel, the astute analyst of Canadian voting behaviour, concluded after a careful examination of polling data from the 1972 election that "anti-French sentiments do exist in English-speaking Canada" and such views affected votes, but that "all the available data [on the

1972 election] nevertheless show that there was hardly more than a trace of this influence except in a very few special areas"—such as Leeds, in eastern Ontario, where there was a dispute about the local Customs Office, or Ottawa, where civil servant anger was real. Meisel further argues that the bilingualism policy probably helped the Liberals in many areas—notably, Quebec, New Brunswick, and francophone parts of Ontario.

Moreover, Liberal weakness in western Canada long preceded Trudeau's leadership and official bilingualism. West of the Ontario border, the Liberals had won no seats in 1958, 6 seats in 1962, 6 seats in 1963, and 8 in 1965. The true aberration was 1968, when Trudeau won 27, but even in 1972, his 7 western seats represented, by historical levels, a high tide of support. Furthermore, the Conservative and New Democratic Party leaders both strongly supported official bilingualism when challenged to do so in a parliamentary vote in 1973. When sixteen Conservatives rose to oppose the policy, they were booed from all corners of the House. Never again would the Tories choose a unilingual leader, and both of Stanfield's successors were deeply committed to bilingualism—which by the eighties had transformed Canadian government. Trudeau, Gwyn concludes, "never made the only mistake that really matters: he . . . never lost faith." Others came to share it. Official bilingualism is, for Trudeau, a lasting and magnificent achievement.[33]

Meisel's study of the 1972 election revealed that the major issue in the campaign was, in fact, the economy. He pointed to the poll carried out by the Canadian Institute of Public Opinion, where potential voters identified major issues: the economy, inflation, and high prices stood first, with 37 percent, and unemployment followed, with 33 percent, while "the Government, Trudeau" and "relations with Quebec, Separatism" received only 6 percent and 4 percent, respectively—approximately the level of "pollution"(6 percent). In the Ontario constituency of Kingston and the

Islands, where Progressive Conservative candidate Flora MacDonald carefully tracked campaign "issues" mentioned at the doorstep, only twelve of eight thousand respondents even mentioned "French-English relations," and two of the mentions were favourable![34] After the flurry of attention surrounding Trudeau's remarks about bigots in January 1973, the minority Parliament reflected ever more what the MPs had heard on the hustings the previous fall. The economy became overwhelmingly the preoccupation of Canadian politicians as powerful international currents converged on Canada and swept over its economic and political life.

Earlier chapters have described how these strong currents formed during the 1960s, when the Vietnam War and American economic policies caused inflation to surge. Simultaneously, the European Common Market gained increasing strength as its protectionist agricultural policy roiled world agricultural markets and its common tariff stifled Canadian attempts to penetrate European domestic markets. In the early 1970s, Canada's second-largest investor and trading partner, the United Kingdom, whose entry into the Common Market had been vetoed by France in the sixties, sought once more to join Europe. A clever Soviet purchase of wheat at low prices and a famine in Bangladesh at the beginning of the 1970s then triggered a series of events that led to a world food crisis, with unexpected shortages and threats of starvation. And on the eve of Yom Kippur, October 6, 1973, Egyptian and Syrian troops stormed across the Israeli border. As the Americans rallied to help beleaguered Israel, Saudi Arabia led Middle Eastern states in an oil embargo against the United States through the newly established Organization of Petroleum Exporting Countries (OPEC). As one of the world's leading agricultural exporters and a major producer of petroleum, Canada's economy benefited, but not all Canadians shared in the prosperity. It was not the first time in the century that the world's troubles profoundly changed the Canadian political landscape.

Trudeau, however, now had a world of his own—and he strove valiantly to keep some balance between his public and his personal life.

—

The outside world entered 24 Sussex Drive only in the evenings, when Trudeau's limousine brought him home to Margaret and baby Justin. Since their marriage, Trudeau had jealously guarded his family's privacy, instructing his press secretary, Peter Roberts, to shield Margaret from prying reporters and gossips, and he enforced those rules ferociously. Foreign missions were instructed not to make courtesy calls to Margaret, "since Mrs. Trudeau . . . [would] not be attending official events or taking part in diplomatic activities."[35] Nevertheless, that first Christmas, virtually every Canadian newspaper's front page featured Justin in swaddling clothes, held by his beaming mother while an adoring Pierre fastened his gaze on his child. In those days they clung closely to each other. Margaret nursed Justin until he was six months old, rising throughout the night to respond to his hunger. Cloistered by the gates, guards, and servants who swarmed about the old house and grounds, she took refuge in her newborn and in a room of her own in the third-floor attic, where Pierre's wedding gift, a sewing machine, buzzed as its needle fashioned clothes for her and her child, her friends and family.

Margaret underwent a metamorphosis in those days from a free-spirited "hippie" in jeans and T-shirts to a seventies earth mother who ate brown rice and wore billowing skirts with blouses that flowed. This clothing was mainly for her private time, which in the first years of marriage was considerable. However, Margaret acknowledged some demands from Pierre's office too. A stunningly radiant woman, she learned to dress for the few formal occasions she attended. Norah Michener, the wife of the Governor General, befriended her and guided her through the appropriate garb for formal occasions, such as the Queen's visit in the summer of 1973. Although Margaret thought the ensembles worn by the visiting royal were "dreary," she actually learned a fashion tip from Queen Elizabeth. When Margaret's carefully chosen hat blew off her head at the Vancouver airport, a lady-in-waiting quickly stepped forward with a hat pin, which the Queen, her very blue eyes gleaming with amusement, used to pin the hat back on. It was a touch that charmed the crowd.[36]

Margaret initially loathed the cold, weathered mansion at 24 Sussex with its seven servants, who seemed ill prepared for her and for children. She particularly disliked the manager, Tom MacDonald, a former army valet with a "haphazard and indifferent touch," and the head cook, a bulky woman whose "old-fashioned English" tastes brought "one long round of steak pie, chicken pie, meat loaf and chocolate chip cookies." Pierre, who Margaret and other female friends claim ate with little regard to nutrition, soon witnessed a battle between the cooks and Margaret as she gradually imposed a healthier and more elegant diet for her family and guests at the official residence.[37]

The Victorian mansion bore the charm and faults of its type. It had too many drafty, small rooms but plenty of coves and warrens where kids could hide. It lacked central air conditioning, and the window air conditioners could not cope with Ottawa's midsummer heat waves. The furniture bore the stamp of postwar austerity and Victorian fustiness, and common features of North American prosperity in the seventies, such as a swimming pool, sauna, or fitness centre, were absent. Margaret gradually began bringing the old house to modern life in her attic retreat, but after the election, she took on the challenge of renovation with gusto — and with Pierre's blessing.

Pierre immediately adjusted some of his working ways and all of his playing time to married life. Children had always adored

Pierre's pranks and generosity to them, and his own children experienced his intense affection from birth. Justin was the first child born to a prime minister in office since John A. Macdonald and the first child ever to live at 24 Sussex Drive, which had become the prime minister's residence only in 1951. Life at home revolved around the children—in those days with gurgles, playpens, and discreet turns away from people when Justin needed nourishment. The honeymoon soon vanished, as Margaret recalled, "under a blanket of diapers and small babies." Margaret became pregnant again in the late spring of 1973. Alexandre "Sacha" Trudeau was born, like his brother, on Christmas Day, after "a long and painful night."[38]

Alexander Yakovlev, who had recently become the Soviet ambassador to Ottawa, relates a story in his memoirs that seems to indicate that "Sacha" was named after him. According to his account, the Yakovlevs, who quickly became close friends of the Trudeaus, told Margaret that "Sacha" was a nickname for Alexander. It is a popular French nickname too, and Alexandre was "Sach" in the family throughout his early years. A good nickname can, of course, have many authors—and Alexandre's does.[39] In any event, the astonishing coincidence of the first two Trudeau boys sharing December 25 as a birthday prompted mirth and amazement, but the births meant considerable strain for Margaret. Of her first thirty-four months of marriage, she was pregnant for eighteen, and her condition sometimes had consequences for her mental and physical health.* When the challenges overwhelmed

---

* Margaret's first official trip abroad was to the Soviet Union in 1971, where the intense protocol often separated her from her husband, the heavy helpings of rich food upset her stomach, and her morning sickness took the joy out of sightseeing. She did, however, discover the advantages of Soviet

her, she sometimes broke into tears; at other moments her nerves and anxieties silenced her. Yet whatever the faults of 24 Sussex and the exigencies of public life, after Justin was born Pierre's insistence on privacy made havens of their home and, even more, their retreat at Harrington Lake. Gradually, however, the external world intruded ever more often, and Pierre's well-entrenched habits persisted.[40]

Although children demand highly flexible schedules, Pierre retained the ordered habits of his lifetime. As he always had, he would rise at 8 a.m. in their chilly bedroom—he always insisted on windows open—while Margaret buried herself in the covers and lingered a bit. Pierre read newspapers over a hurried breakfast while Margaret, in her own words, remained a "blob" until the children arrived. At 9 a.m. Pierre entered the waiting limousine and set out for Parliament Hill, where he often ran a gauntlet of well-wishers and ill-wishers before bounding up the two flights of stairs that led to his corner office in the Centre Block. He would immediately check with Cécile Viau, his personal assistant, who somehow kept close track of his activities with extraordinary discretion and ability. He then met with staff before beginning his meetings—which on some mornings meant Cabinet and on Wednesday mornings brought the party caucus.

As with 24 Sussex, Trudeau had his office redecorated by a new friend, the Vancouver architect Arthur Erickson.[41] The result

---

security. Although she refused to believe their hotel room was bugged, she and Pierre realized it was when they returned to the hotel room and Margaret, exhausted, cried out to Pierre. "Oh Pierre, what wouldn't I give for an *orange!* My kingdom for an orange." Within five minutes, a waiter was knocking at the door with an orange on a tray. Margaret Trudeau, *Beyond Reason* (New York and London: Paddington Press, 1979), 107.

was a spacious, elegant room with clean lines, luxury, and comfort. The light oak walls bore only a striking woodcarving of a black loon, but portraits of his family and Sir Wilfrid Laurier on his desk were immediately obvious to guests—as was a box of the chocolates that Trudeau's sweet tooth craved. He often had a light working lunch after which, when the House was sitting, he prepared for the 2 p.m. Question Period. An aide briefed him for that session—it was usually Joyce Fairbairn, with whom he had a close relationship full of banter.* As he entered the House, he made a much-interrupted passage through milling MPs in the Government Lobby before taking his seat. He pored over documents, preparing for the coming assault from opposition MPs. At 2:15 they began, and Trudeau replied, sometimes with professorial dignity and detail, at other times with biting sarcasm and wit. Unlike Diefenbaker or his own colleagues Jean Chrétien and John Turner, Trudeau did not relish these moments in the House, and a few minutes after 3 o'clock he quickly escaped.

More meetings followed—with the constituents of Liberal MPs, with party members seeking favour or position, or with ambassadors presenting credentials or saying farewell. As the day came to an end at 6 p.m., Cécile Viau would give Trudeau messages, personal letters, and a few documents to sign. He would then check with an assistant about his schedule for the next day before walking down to the waiting limousine.

---

* An injury took Fairbairn away from her job in 1973. On March 2 she wrote to her boss: "I have been following events on the Hill with the usual interest, anxiously listening to make sure you didn't put your foot in the glue. You probably have had a soft time of it this week and I look forward to coming back to bark at you again Monday." TP, MG 26 020, vol. 4, file 10, LAC.

As always, Pierre was punctual, arriving home at 6:45 with a briefcase of files. He would quickly greet Margaret; kiss the boys, who would already have eaten; and leave for a jog. Once the swimming pool was installed, a swim replaced the run. As Margaret wrote in her memoir: "He swims forty-four laps, never more, never less, every evening." That would take seventeen minutes. When the boys were old enough, they then joined him for fifteen minutes of training in the pool. At 8 o'clock, precisely, Margaret and Pierre would have dinner. Margaret later recalled those times: "Most evenings there were just the two of us, and that continued throughout our marriage. The other political families would have been annoyed to hear us: we talked about ideas and ideals, never whether Pierre should put more money into the health program. We always thought that once the babies grew up a bit it would change, and we would become sociable, but somehow it never did."

There were a few friends who dropped by: Michael and Nancy Pitfield, Hugh and Jane Faulkner, Tim and Wendy Porteous, the irrepressible Jacques Hébert (whom Margaret adored), and the Yakovlevs—whose intimacy with the Trudeaus, including dinners for four at 24 Sussex, attracted the interest of Canadian security officials.[42] Nevertheless, the gap in age between Margaret and Pierre, their different interests, and Margaret's weak French affected their social life. Some of Trudeau's old friends did not welcome Margaret: she was too young, too free-spirited, and for some, too anglophone. Although Gérard Pelletier remained close to Trudeau, his wife, Alec, a close friend of Madeleine Gobeil's, did not take to Margaret. At one dinner hosted by the Trudeaus, writes Christina McCall-Newman, Pierre responded to a comment that the table guests, who were old Montreal friends, should speak English with the offhand remark that Margaret wouldn't understand them if they did—a report Margaret strongly denies. Nevertheless, Trudeau's circle of friends changed dramatically with the marriage—and so did hers.[43]

Occasionally, Trudeau would take a break, and he and Margaret would watch a movie or go out to a restaurant—often Lebanese, which Pierre much favoured, or Japanese. Normally, though, the four-course dinner at home was, Margaret said, followed by "three-quarters of an hour while, as he puts it, he digests." They would listen to music, hang paintings, or carry out other small tasks. Then, the forty-five minutes past, Trudeau would bring out the briefcase. It was the habit of his adult lifetime. An earlier female friend recalled how surprised she was when they were on a holiday and she discovered him taking books and files with him to the beach each day. He seemed to enter a trance when he worked. Margaret could not interrupt him, and her night suddenly became lonely as he worked until "about midnight." "Occasionally" she rebelled and "went off in a huff to visit friends." Usually she sewed and nursed the babies until he joined her later in bed.[44] The weekends brought freedom, especially at Harrington Lake, where the weekday structures collapsed: meals became casual, kids romped at will, and Margaret and Pierre gambolled in the lake once summer warmed the Gatineau chill.[45]

Come Monday, though, it was back to the routine—and, for Trudeau, the problems of governing Canada in an increasingly troubled world.

CHAPTER EIGHT

—

THE STRANGE REBIRTH
OF PIERRE TRUDEAU

I n the first years of his marriage, Trudeau's aides, ministers, and MPs saw an even more intensely focused and hard-working prime minister than they had known before. His determination after the 1972 election not only to govern strongly but also to lay the foundation for a new Liberal majority had a major impact on his administration: first, he was less cautious and more willing to take chances; and second, he considered the expressly political consequences of his government's decisions and actions far more often than he had before. And those late nights on the files brought rewards every weekday morning when the stream of meetings began: Trudeau often knew briefs better than the relevant ministers.

Two issues dominated the agenda—the economy and international events—and in the early seventies, they forced all politicians to navigate unexpected and unknown rapids. As we saw in chapter 6, the Nixon *shokku* of 1971 suddenly cut the American dollar from the gold standard, signalling the end of the postwar Bretton Woods system and a new era of uncertainty. As with most epochal changes, those living through them were often mystified by what they meant—and Trudeau was no exception. Schooled in the Keynesian approach to the economy, he struggled to understand what "stagflation"—high unemployment combined with high inflation—would mean for democratic governments committed to the welfare state.

In August 1972 Gus Weiss, a leading member of President Nixon's own advisory team on international economics, briefed Canadian officials on the world economy. He was frank: "We have 10 computer models all trying to forecast economic eventualities," he admitted. "We don't really know what's going on." And they didn't. "Externalities," the bugbear of economic prediction, bedevilled policy makers at the time. As Weiss put it, "the greatest problem today is that there are too many problems."[1] Trudeau, whose Jesuit-trained mind sought order and design, puzzled over what implications the sudden world food crisis, the emerging energy crisis, the turbulent currency markets, and the shifting international trade patterns meant for Canada and the world. Harvard economist John Kenneth Galbraith recalled meeting a highly inquisitive Trudeau at dinner parties in New York and Washington, where the prime minister would constantly pose questions to Wall Street and Beltway guests about the future. He, along with Michael Pitfield and Ivan Head in particular, became deeply interested in the futurists clustered around the Club of Rome, which sponsored the bestselling book *The Limits to Growth*. This controversial work, based on computer modelling, forecast a Malthusian world where population growth would overwhelm diminishing resources. Within Canadian government departments, clusters formed to analyze future trends, and they led internationally in promoting discussion of the club's analyses.[2]

Trudeau experimented with the futurists' emphasis on a "horizontal" approach to government and problem solving, one reflected in the new structure he introduced for Cabinet committees, the movement of officials among departments, and interdepartmental committees and working groups. However, the dire predictions set out in the club's book and in its methodology, which ineluctably led to broader state intervention and bureaucracy, soon became less convincing to him. Far more influential was the advice of his old friend Albert Breton, who had returned to Canada in 1970 from Harvard and who wrote incisive analyses of the Canadian and international economies for him. They bantered easily: when Breton asked Trudeau whether he still believed much of the "stuff" he had written before he went into politics, he got a quick response — "Very little." In November Breton warned that in the wake of the drastic actions the Nixon administration had instituted during the summer, the United States would "in all probability . . . between now and November 1972 [adopt] policies that . . . [would] be erratic and half-baked, and these reactions of Washington could trigger erratic and half-baked policies or policy recommendations both outside and inside the Government of Canada." Breton, an independent thinker, remained skeptical about internal government attitudes and forecasts for the future.[3]

The major battle over the economy in Ottawa swirled around the Department of Finance, where John Turner was now minister, with Simon Reisman as his deputy minister. Turner brought considerable political weight to the office, and Reisman, bureaucratic aggressiveness and strong continentalist, and increasingly conservative, beliefs. Given the personalities involved and the known rivalries between Turner and Trudeau, friction was inevitable. Indeed, even as he appointed Turner, Trudeau remarked, "No one will suggest that Turner is a weak minister," and added, "One characteristic of Turner is that he likes to succeed."[4] The potential for conflict was only increased by the minority government's dependence on the New Democratic Party for its survival. Not surprisingly, then, Trudeau and his closest assistants decided right from the outset that they needed independent voices to counter any domination by this exceptionally confident department.

In Turner's view, the poor performance of the Liberals in English Canada stemmed from a significant move of votes to the right. Maintaining financial "credibility" was essential, he insisted, and he wanted "no deals" with the NDP.[5] Turner was also adamant about keeping the commitments made in the 1972 budget to decrease corporate taxes. Realistically, though, it was difficult to implement that pledge after the election because the NDP had denounced "corporate welfare bums" so effectively during the campaign and now held the balance of power.

In the Throne Speech, Trudeau made it clear that his party would shift to the left and maintain power through the support of the NDP. The very first vote following that speech condemned the American bombing of Hanoi. The decision to support that resolution was an important one, which sealed the Liberals' alliance with the NDP while enraging Richard Nixon, who refused to reply to a letter from Trudeau explaining the domestic circumstances that had caused it. So angry was Nixon that he even declined to send a note of condolence to Trudeau on the death of his beloved mother in January 1973. As the debate over the economy developed within both the Cabinet and the government as a whole, the differences between the prime minister and the finance minister became personal and ideological., Trudeau came to be identified with policies on the left, while Turner, who had developed excellent relations with his conservative American counterpart, George Shultz, became the voice of "business" and the "Americans." The perception was unfair—finance ministers are invariably regarded as a conservative force within government—but the minority situation exacerbated the impression.[6]

The debate zeroed in on John Turner's first post-election budget, which everyone knew was critical to the survival of the government. Turner and the Finance Department initially fought to have the promised corporate tax cuts implemented, although he was willing to adjust the budget to meet NDP demands. Breton was strongly opposed, writing to Trudeau on January 19, 1973, that "whatever the politics of the case for a cut in the corporation income tax may be, the economic case is at best non-existent or very weak." A personal tax cut, he argued, would be more efficient and stimulative: American-owned corporations would realize only half the reduction because of their ability to deduct their Canadian taxes in the United States. In the end, the budget tilted toward the left, with extensive social spending and numerous items that satisfied the NDP, such as reduction in the personal tax rate, increased personal exemptions, higher old age pensions, and indexation of the personal tax rate, which would mean that inflation would not create higher taxes by placing individuals in higher tax brackets. More than 750,000 Canadians would no longer pay income taxes, and the predicted deficit was $1.3 billion, compared to a surplus of approximately $100 million the previous year. The budget was highly stimulative, precedent-setting in its deficit, and politically valuable in that it bought time for the NDP-Liberal alliance.

Despite reports that Reisman had devised the indexation system as a way to restrain future government spending, both Trudeau and Turner supported it. Moreover, the Cabinet debate on February 13 suggests that ministers were aware of that potential effect. By 1973 even Trudeau was actively seeking a means to limit the growth of government—which had been remarkably high for well over a decade—both in Ottawa and in the provinces. Breton warned him that exceptional growth at both levels of government, along with the monopolies created by the rapid unionization of public services, were themselves causes of inflation and, therefore, of political trouble. The press, however, ignored these subtleties and preferred to focus on the personalities: the anti-American and leftist Trudeau, and George Shultz's buddy and business favourite Turner.[7]

The caricatures distorted, but they contained kernels of truth. In the struggle over the 1973 budget, Trudeau emerged the victor, and Turner privately fumed that the prime minister had not supported him sufficiently.* Turner did manage to maintain credibility later by implementing the earlier corporate tax cuts, but this success only reinforced his image as the representative of business interests in an economically conservative department. Turner had thought earlier about leaving politics for the private sector, and he knew that after he contributed to Trudeau's political survival, first through championing the Criminal Code reforms and now through a well-received budget, his own chance of succeeding Trudeau in the top spot became ever more distant. Journalist Ron Graham, who knew both men well, later wrote, "[T]heir looks, their intelligence, and their reputations gave them the habit of controlling their surroundings and assured that they would clash once mutual advantage was exhausted."[8]

After the budget, that exhaustion set in. Trudeau recognized that Turner was his rival, his successor should he falter, and he remembered that Turner had wanted the government to resign immediately after the catastrophe of the 1972 election. In response he decided to maintain his personal distance from the Finance Department and to develop an independent system of economic

---

* Evidence that Trudeau tried to conceal the fact that he had prevailed over the Finance Department and Turner is found in Eugene Whelan's memoir. Whelan, who became minister of agriculture in 1972, wrote: "One thing I learned right away was that Trudeau never overruled his finance minister. . . . Time and again I'd lose, no matter how right I was, because Finance was opposed. And Trudeau would usually turn to me and say that familiar line: 'Sorry, Gene, you lost another one.' Sometimes I'd get so mad I'd just slam my books together, stand up and walk out." Whelan particularly disliked Simon Reisman, who served as Turner's deputy minister, and called him "overrated." Eugene Whelan with Rick Archbold, *Whelan: The Man in the Green Stetson* (Toronto: Irwin, 1986), 199–201.

advisers within the Privy Council, in his own office, and at the Treasury Board, where economist Douglas Hartle was especially influential. In turn, these advisers could be blunt in their critiques of the traditional finance giants. Breton, for example, made this comment on the 1973 annual report of the Bank of Canada in April 1973: "It is sad that an institution which is staffed with some of the best minds in the country, which possesses one of the best Research Departments anywhere has, for unfathomable reasons, become capable only of learning at a very slow pace and hence incapable of providing the intellectual and moral leadership that it should be doing in the area of monetary phenomena and that the country needs."[9] Inevitably, there would be a clash between Trudeau's advisers and the Department of Finance. The only question was when and how it would happen.

—

All agreed that, in the early seventies, the country faced fresh challenges. When he came to office in 1968, Trudeau declared he would make no more additions to the recently established welfare state. He pledged, rather, to work on regional disparity and on inequalities among Canadians, and he put considerable emphasis on the creation of the Department of Regional Economic Expansion (DREE). Later evidence indicated that DREE's panoply of schemes, combined with transfers from the federal government, reduced some regional inequalities, but the large DREE projects usually fell flat. Indeed, as early as 1973, Breton astutely warned Trudeau that "the Government cannot easily engage in the continuation of a policy which has not produced many results." Moreover, the "welfare backlash" during the election campaign, combined with the disorderly creation of the Canadian social security system, forced Trudeau to evaluate just how successful the federal government approach had been. At the increasingly regular federal-provincial gatherings, the provinces continued to snipe at Ottawa for its encroachment on their traditional responsibilities for health, welfare, and education, areas where their spending grew rapidly throughout the seventies. Trudeau soon lost patience with them: he appointed his friend Marc Lalonde as minister of national health and welfare, with "the goal of systematizing a little all the aid programs for the poor, seniors, children, the unemployed, etc." Canada's programs had become almost the equal of those in Western Europe, but they were too dispersed, and competing provincial programs made matters even more confusing. Trudeau described his ambitions to journalist Jean Lépine:

> Imagine integrating all of this. We were paying half of all provincial public welfare. So we wanted to find a system. Everyone who was somewhat progressive at the time wanted the guaranteed annual income, so imagine creating a system to integrate all of this. This quest became the Orange Book that Lalonde created with Al Johnson, one of his deputy ministers. The two got along very well and did a fairly extraordinary job in very little time.

The change did not happen quickly enough. Economic conditions deteriorated, and the Finance Department fought furiously against Lalonde's proposal to unify support payments in a guaranteed income. Trudeau backed down. Later he explained to Lépine: "Normally, I prefer to lean to the left, but since I am told here that we will not have sufficient funding to finance our programmes, I would rather be a little bit more cautious." But Lalonde had told Lépine that the decision was made on personalities rather than the issue itself, and Lépine questioned whether "prudency" was the real cause, particularly when the government was tilting to the left at the time. Trudeau sighed and evaded the question by saying it was "a good example of responsible government."[10]

A finance minister is in a special position, and if a prime minister does not accept the advice of that minister, he risks a resignation. Trudeau knew that Lalonde would never resign, but he was not sure about Turner—and the loss of the popular finance minister at this point could mean the government's fall. So it happened that the guaranteed annual income, which the Liberals had mused about since the sixties, became the essential sacrifice. Finance eventually won this quarrel, but it was to lose most of the others during the minority government period.

—

In the 1972 election, the NDP had won over Canadian nationalist votes, most notably those of Eric Kierans and Walter Gordon. David Lewis and his party held the balance of power, and that meant the Liberals could no longer defer their promise to establish an agency to review foreign investment in Canada. Trudeau himself was dubious: he told Alastair Gillespie, his minister of industry, trade, and commerce, who had responsibility for drafting the act: "You know I'm not a nationalist and this is a form of nationalism, which I find suspect." Although a Gordon disciple and a nationalist himself, Gillespie had become exasperated with the particular kind of nationalism espoused by the *Toronto Star*, which he found insatiable, but his own business experience convinced him that a foreign investment review agency was essential in a country where so much industry and so many resources were foreign owned.

In 1973, therefore, he brought forward the "Gillespie Guidelines," which set out conditions to be applied to foreign investment in Canada. They essentially required investors to show "significant benefit" to Canada and, the following year, were incorporated into the mandate of the Foreign Investment Review Agency. FIRA irritated many businesspeople both in Canada and beyond. Gillespie recalls an "obnoxious" German businessman who denounced the agency. When Gillespie asked, "Why does that concern you?" he answered that his company had 25 percent ownership of Algoma Steel and wanted to increase it. Gillespie replied that there would be no problem if he could show "significant benefit." The businessman exploded angrily and sold off the Algoma shares, which, to Gillespie's satisfaction, Canadians quickly bought. In truth few investors reacted as the German did, and the financial newspaper *Barron's*, which initially excoriated FIRA, reported that the only company "that wouldn't be welcomed in Canada is Murder Inc."[11]

FIRA, the Canada Development Corporation (through which the government and Canadians could make strategic investments in Canadian businesses), and talk about an industrial strategy vanished from the front sections of the business pages when the Yom Kippur War of October 1973 in the Middle East caused the first great energy crisis of the postwar period. Although Ontario claims to have created the oil industry in Canada with the first well in the southwestern Ontario town of Petrolia, the industry really developed in Alberta in the mid-twentieth century, largely under the control of foreign owners. The huge Middle Eastern fields emerged at the same time, creating a historically low price for oil during the economic boom in the Western world during the fifties and the sixties. The Alberta Social Credit governments of the period believed, with some justice, that oil in Alberta was less attractive to the giant international oil companies than oil in Saudi Arabia, where the costs of extraction were exceedingly low. Accordingly, the province accepted low royalties and multinational leadership in developing the provincial oil fields. On the home front, however, the Alberta government moved immediately to establish, through legislation, its control of the resource at the wellhead. The federal government similarly moved to assert its control over international and interprovincial trade in energy products, particularly in the building of pipelines. The dominance of the multinational oil companies, American national interests, and Canadian federal-provincial rivalries all played a role in the conflicts that began to develop in the 1950s.*

In 1956 there had been an angry debate in the House of Commons over the TransCanada Pipeline when John Diefenbaker's Conservatives, who were traditionally anti-American, attacked the Liberals (and especially the American-born "minister of everything," C.D. Howe)[12] for permitting 51 percent American ownership of the new national pipeline for natural gas. Diefenbaker thereupon appointed the Royal Commission on Energy to settle the dispute. The commission's solution was simple: it created the "Borden line" (named for its chairman, Henry Borden), which divided Canada at

---

* For example, the oil companies much preferred to import Middle Eastern and Venezuelan oil into eastern Canada because that commerce was highly profitable. When the Venezuelan government began to demand a higher share of income, the multinationals, faced with the possibility of higher prices, chose eastern Canada as the export destination for that oil because they could maintain higher prices in eastern Canada than in the United States, where cheaper Middle Eastern oil was consumed. The U.S. government strongly supported this policy, as it meshed with U.S. foreign policy interests in Venezuela (J.G. Debanné, "Oil and Gas Policy," in *The Energy Question: An International Failure*, ed. E.W. Erickson and Len Waverman, vol. 2 [Toronto: University of Toronto Press, 1974]). Debanné gives several other examples of how broader multinational interests affected the exploitation of Canadian resources. Other writers, however, have argued that the development of Albertan oil depended on deals with the larger multinational companies with great financial resources and oil development skills. Alberta's problem until the 1970s was selling its higher-priced oil in the midst of American quotas and restrictions on exports to the United States, which had its own oil industry.

the Ottawa Valley, with those to the west using Alberta oil and those to the east benefiting from cheaper Middle Eastern crude. This compromise recognized the multinationals' practice and also satisfied Alberta's needs for a market at a time of ample energy supplies and a protected American market. In the early seventies, however, this carefully constructed scheme came apart.

During the previous two decades, a fundamental transformation had occurred as all Western countries turned away from the coal and coke that had, for over a century, stoked their economic growth, in order to embrace the cleaner and much cheaper petroleum and natural gas.* Ontario had imported nearly all its coal from the United States, while western Canada had exported its ample supplies to the American West. That arrangement caused few problems—unlike the sale of petroleum. The Social Credit in Alberta had negotiated generously low royalty arrangements with the multinationals, who by the late 1960s controlled almost four-fifths of the energy sector. Then a growing number of Albertans and Canadian nationalists became increasingly troubled by this situation. The new Conservative leader in the province, Peter Lougheed, a smart Calgary lawyer and former football star, immediately set to work to fashion an effective critique of the old policies. As historian Gerald Friesen put it:

---

* In Canada in 1950, petroleum supplied 29.8 percent and natural gas 2.5 percent of Canadian primary energy consumption, while coal and coke supplied 47.6 percent. In 1970 the comparable figures were 48.1 percent, 16.5 percent, and only 10.7 percent for coal and coke. As a result, city air was cleaner and the dreaded task of stoking the coals at 5 a.m. largely ended. The statistics also reflect the vast rise in automobile ownership and the growth of the suburbs. See G. Bruce Doern and Glen Toner, *The Politics of Energy: The Development and Implementation of the NEP* (Toronto: Methuen, 1985), 86.

[Lougheed's] fundamental argument from 1965, when he took the Conservative leadership, to 1971, when his party took over the government, was that Alberta had squandered its petroleum revenue by failing to invest in local industries. His allies were the urban professionals—the businessmen, lawyers, and resource industry experts in Alberta's new bourgeoisie—who agreed with him that the province must prepare for the day when the multinationals left—and the morning after, when the oil itself was gone.

Lougheed's arguments were similar to those Pierre Trudeau had made about Quebec in the fifties against the rural, religious, and populist Union nationale party, which had dominated that province's politics for a generation. In the seventies, however, Lougheed's stated ambition was "to strengthen the control by Albertans over [their] future and to reduce the dependency for [their] continued quality of life on governments, institutions, or corporations directed from outside the province."[13] This ambition struck Trudeau and his colleagues as a threat akin to the provincial nationalism of Quebec. Confrontation was inevitable.

Lougheed was a formidable opponent. As historian Doug Owram observed, Trudeau and Lougheed "were used to success." They had done exceptionally well academically, athletically, and socially. What was once said of Lougheed applied to both: "He was the golden boy." Neither accepted losing easily and "neither . . . was the sort to yield for the sake of peace."[14] Lougheed's boldness was immediately evident when he raised the royalty rates on the multinationals in 1972 and defied them when they charged that he had breached solemn contracts.

In 1973 his attention turned toward Ottawa, which had already noticed him and his province's more aggressive stance. Even before the Yom Kippur War in the Middle East, oil was becoming a critical resource, and the Organization of Petroleum

Exporting Countries (OPEC) was gaining strength through the voracious demand for its products from the West. The Organisation for Economic Co-operation and Development (OECD) warned in May that the situation was uncertain and that oil demand was so strong that the wealthy members of the OECD would soon run a "substantial current deficit" with OPEC countries. Oil, it seemed, was becoming scarce. But no one was sure.

In July 1973 Trudeau went to Calgary for a Western Economic Opportunities Conference, which he had proposed in January to try to understand why "so many gifted individual Westerners could feel so much discontent with their present and future prospects as Canadians." These, his opening words to the conference, in which the four western provinces participated, were clearly directed at the "gifted" Alberta premier who sat near him. Lougheed would surely have agreed with many of Trudeau's comments, notably his call for a "special role for the West in strengthening Canada" and his concern for the "unevenly spread and narrowly based" economic progress in the western provinces. But Trudeau's call for a new national policy struck a discordant note for westerners, who saw earlier "national policies" as exploitative, colonialist, and beneficial primarily to the interests of central Canada.[15]

Comments like these irritated Donald Macdonald, the federal minister of energy, mines, and resources. Self-confident, an economic nationalist, athletic, and a favourite of Trudeau, the towering Macdonald developed deep suspicions of Lougheed's ambitions and what they meant for a national energy policy after the OPEC crisis in the final months of 1973. He was not alone. In Cabinet he strongly supported fellow Toronto minister Alastair Gillespie's argument that neither Alberta nor the oil companies should be able to grab the windfall from the rapidly escalating oil price, which had risen from approximately $1.20 per barrel in 1970 to $2.20 in September 1973, when the federal government froze it, and then soared to a world price of over $9.00 by the first months of 1974.

Although the Canadian government had begun to consider the implications of a possible energy crisis in the early seventies, the actual crisis found it surprisingly unprepared and even confused—a view the Americans expressed among themselves.[16] The Alberta government, the National Energy Board, the oil companies, and independent observers could not agree on how long Canadian reserves would last, and the government soon began to consider phasing out exports to the United States, the creation of a state-owned oil company, and a two-price policy for oil: one for export and another for domestic consumers. In Lougheed's eyes, Alberta would pay the price for the confusion and for central Canadian nationalism and selfishness.

Initially, there was hope that the sudden "oil shock" would galvanize both governments to work together toward common ends. Such optimism died quickly. After the federal government established an export tax in September 1973, Alberta informed Macdonald in mid-November that it intended to create an Alberta Marketing Commission, which would "purchase and sell with the province . . . approximately 85% of Alberta's crude oil output." This action would, a critical Macdonald reported to Cabinet, "enable Alberta to set the price within its borders, and allow it to refuse to sell beyond those borders, except at its price." Trudeau, and others worried about Alberta's use of its increased royalties, saw this assertion of provincial authority as a challenge to be met. For his part, Trudeau hoped that Alberta would use its windfall for conservation and for development of new reserves (especially of the oil sands), and most ministers hoped that the problem could be resolved in the discussions of November 22 between Alberta and the federal government.

By November 27 there was less assurance. The NDP, which wanted a two-price policy, a lower price, and more government regulation, had a real impact on the talks. In the end, the Cabinet urged Macdonald not to "applaud the rise in royalty rates" on the part of Alberta as a Cabinet document had suggested he should. Reflecting the consensus, Macdonald assured his colleagues that he "would make clear to Alberta that [the federal government] does not concede the right of the Commission to establish domestic prices for oil and that the Federal Government would establish domestic prices at a rate which would guarantee further research and development of oil resources."[17]

Trudeau and others expressed their willingness to "share" the windfall profits with the producing provinces, principally Alberta, but their comments indicate that they worried about the effect of Alberta's sudden wealth on Canada's equalization program and also whether Alberta's expenditures would benefit Canada as a whole. But negotiations about "sharing" went badly, and the NDP pointed to other producing countries that were creating national oil companies and creating special funds to share the windfalls with future generations. Indeed, in British Columbia, in stark contrast to Alberta, NDP premier Dave Barrett urged nationalization of Canadian energy resources, even though British Columbia was a producing province.

Faced with a growing crisis, Trudeau moved quickly to recover the initiative and called a Cabinet meeting for December 12, where he set out a statement he proposed to make on energy. Jack Austin, the deputy minister for energy, mines, and resources, had met the day before with Alberta officials and told them that the federal government would continue its price freeze beyond January 31 and that the government intended "to close the supply gap by the end of the decade." Alberta asked for a delay, but the federal government would not wait. Accordingly, Trudeau said that he would announce a new "national policy" to ensure Canadian self-sufficiency by 1980. This goal meant: the creation of a national market for Canadian oil; a pricing mechanism to ensure exploration and development; a pipeline for Montreal and eastern Canada; intensification of oil-sands research; the development of nuclear power and exploration of the Atlantic Shelf; and most dramatically, the creation of a national oil company. The last recommendation in effect accepted an NDP motion in the House to nationalize an existing energy company, though the Liberals instead created a new entity, the Crown corporation Petro-Canada.[18]

Lougheed was furious when Canada's "first ministers," as the premiers and the prime minister were now known, gathered on January 22–23, 1973, to discuss oil policy. The international price was $9.60, the Canadian price only $3.80. Lougheed regarded the difference as theft; Trudeau and Macdonald, who worried about rising inflation, regarded it as just. After much bargaining, the assembled group agreed on a single national price and a continuation of the freeze until March 31. Trudeau publicly reiterated his view that in reaching this agreement, Canada had achieved much by acting "collectively and effectively to provide better social services, and to reduce poverty, to promote equality among its citizens, to see that disparities between regions are diminished." Now, with energy costs buffeting Canadian society and the economy, Canadians would have to make sure that they did not "let so much of the gigantic new revenues accrue in a single place that equality of opportunity and reduction of disparity [would] become impossible in Canada." That statement, in essence, remained Trudeau's stand on the development of Canadian energy resources. He had an ally: William Davis, the Conservative premier of Ontario, Canada's largest consuming province, enthusiastically supported the federalist side. For his part, Robert Bourassa, the Liberal premier of Quebec, whose province also benefited from the federal policies, painfully constructed an argument that backed the federal policy without actually supporting the federal government.

Lougheed accepted the compromise but resented the hypocrisy in Davis's and Bourassa's arguments. Had not Albertans paid world prices for the iron ore, refrigerators, and automobiles they'd bought from central Canada? Why should there be two prices for oil but one for the gold, copper, iron, and other resources mined from the Canadian Shield? While dissociating himself from the Alberta bumper sticker—"Let the eastern bastards freeze"— Lougheed denounced the federal export tax as "contrary to both the spirit and the intent of confederation" and said that, in the future, Alberta was determined to sell its resources at fair value. For Lougheed the black stuff oozing from Alberta's soil belonged to Albertans.[19]

—

Trudeau's arguments about the Canadian response to the energy crisis carried the day. Press reaction was warm, and the Gallup poll of February 6 revealed that the Liberals stood at 42 percent, the Conservatives at 31 percent, and the NDP at 21 percent, and Trudeau himself had quickly recovered the popularity his feckless 1972 campaign had devastated. As early as January 1973, a poll had indicated that Canadians believed Trudeau was once again the best qualified to "lead" Canada, and, during that difficult year, polls and press comment confirmed that doubts about his leadership had waned. His popularity, which had fallen almost continuously since early 1971, began to climb quickly back toward the levels of the glorious spring of 1968. As it rose, Trudeau paid close attention to those he had ignored before. With the assistance of Toronto MPs and ministers, he met with skeptical business audiences and editorial boards. Keith Davey introduced him to important figures who could influence public opinion, such as Pierre Berton. Trudeau's distance from the world of middle-class English Canada can be gauged by a memorandum from Davey in November 1973 in which he tried to persuade Trudeau to appear on *Front Page Challenge*, the extremely popular CBC program. Trudeau had apparently never watched it and knew little about its panelists. "Three of the four regulars involved in the show," a Trudeau aide explained, "can be considered on [the Liberal side], Betty Kennedy, Fred Davis, and Gordon Sinclair. The fourth, Pierre Berton, is an N.D.P.er." Thanks to the prodding of Davey, Jim Coutts, and his powerful Toronto ministers, Trudeau came to know much better the city where Davey's stride was bold and long.[20]

Trudeau also began to learn the political charms of travel to certain international destinations. In October 1973, he and Margaret visited China on a trip that received international attention. Even though Richard Nixon had famously recognized the communist country in 1972, Canada's earlier recognition had gained Canada credit with Chinese leaders, especially when the Americans delayed in exchanging ambassadors. It was a memorable and wonderful time for the Trudeaus. Margaret was seven months pregnant with her second child, but her health and spirits were good, and she even outran a journalist to the top of the Great Wall. While Margaret was visiting a kindergarten, Pierre was summoned to meet Chairman Mao, who gave him a rare and long audience in a dark room with curtains drawn in the Forbidden City. Mao, as was typical, dominated the conversation, and with the Yom Kippur War raging in the Middle East, he criticized Canada for supporting Israel too strongly. Nevertheless, Canada did sign a trade deal, which, unlike many trade deals with China, appears to have brought genuine benefits.

The most striking moment was Margaret's. On the last day, Premier Chou En Lai hosted a banquet at the Great Hall. Women and men were usually separated at such events, but Chou invited the blooming Canadian to sit beside him. Then, to the astonishment of Pierre, with the Canadian and Chinese officials sitting nearby, Chou spoke in clear and even colloquial English about women's liberation. He said that Margaret was liberated but Chinese women were not. When she tried to cover her protruding abdomen after Chou described how a Chinese woman had turned away from him because she was pregnant, he said: "Oh dear, no, no, you have come to terms with your self as

a woman. You are proud. To watch you walking as proud as a
queen with your big belly is the happiest sight to see because you
are so proud of it. Chinese women are still feudal in their attitudes toward their own femininity, their own bodies, their own
sexuality. They have just become versions of men." Pierre later
declared that Chou En Lai was the most impressive leader he had
ever met.[21]

These were the best of times. Together, the young expectant
mother and the youthful, if not young, father bore grace in their
steps as they walked hand in hand to the Great Wall; giggled to
each other as the tour guide nattered on about birds and fauna
while their boat navigated the astonishing corridor of spiked
mountains of the Li River; and then, finally alone, strolled through
the narrow passages of the old city of Guilin. Back in Canada,
Justin, now speaking and walking, caused even Conservatives to
smile when he, with a beaming Margaret and Pierre, appeared at
events. Then, on Christmas Day 1973, Alexandre "Sacha" arrived
and made the holiday season even more celebratory. Before long,
the two little boys and their radiant young mother were delighting
not only Canadians but an admiring world.

Although minority government was demanding, Trudeau
thrived on the sense of crisis, and Cabinet documentation reveals a
confident, assertive leader willing to take risks he had earlier
shunned. Trudeau had also established an unexpected personal
friendship with British prime minister Edward Heath, based on his
willingness to accept and even encourage Heath's decision to lead
Britain into the European Economic Community (EEC). Although
he was not a monarchist in his heart, his personal encounters with
the Queen in Canada in 1973 also created a warm relationship with
Elizabeth II, whose insistence on speaking French with her
Canadian prime minister charmed him—and her earlier reservations about his behaviour at his first Commonwealth Conference
seem to have disappeared. He had been a most effective mediator at

the Commonwealth Conference in Singapore, and Lee Kuan Yew of that nation became a friend with whom he enjoyed debating international and philosophical issues. And in contrast to the conservative Lee, the charismatic leftist Michael Manley of Jamaica appealed to Trudeau's progressive past. Like Trudeau, the elegant and handsome Manley had attended the London School of Economics in the postwar years, worked for trade unions in the fifties, and refused to follow the formal dress codes that Jamaican public figures traditionally observed. They bonded right from their first meeting. The strength of their affection pervades Manley's last tribute to Trudeau: "By training and instinct, he believes mankind's best hopes lie in reason, persuasion, accommodation, seeing the other fellow's point of view. To these qualities he adds the breadth of vision and sense of history that make the true internationalist."

Richard Nixon would not have agreed. As we have seen, he immediately and intuitively disliked "that son of a bitch," but Nixon's anger against Canada multiplied after the parliamentary vote condemning the bombing of North Vietnam. By 1973, however, the president was diverted from such matters as the Watergate scandal crept closer to the Oval Office. On November 17 Nixon memorably declared, "I am not a crook," but most Americans and Canadians believed he was. Trudeau seemed to Canadians a far superior national leader, and by comparison alone, he gained in stature. Trudeau admired Nixon's intelligence, and in this dark moment, he thought of sending a message to cheer the beleaguered president up—though he didn't follow through. For Trudeau, life was good that year.[22]

—

When things go well, politicians' thoughts turn to elections, and Trudeau was a typical politician in this respect. He had increasing confidence in the sharp political acumen of Keith Davey and, at his insistence, turned to former Pearson aide Jim Coutts for political advice. Although Coutts, who was devoted to Lester Pearson, had suspicions about Trudeau, they unexpectedly struck up a strong political friendship. The diminutive Coutts, of cherubic appearance, was a worldly bachelor with a sharp eye for detail, and his intelligence and attractive female companions impressed Trudeau. From these new colleagues Trudeau learned that polls were signals, sometimes to be followed and often to be ignored. The winds were blowing favourably as winter ended in 1974, but a shift could come quickly.

Darkening economic clouds meant that delaying the election could bring defeat. Despite the government's attempt to cushion the blow of the oil crisis by controlling prices, inflation spiked dramatically in 1973. The consumer price index had risen from 100 in 1971 to a troubling 104.8 in 1972 to an astonishing 112.7 in 1973, with the major increases coming in food (100 to 123.3). At the same time, unemployment remained relatively high at 5.6 percent in 1973, with significant regional variations.[23] Unemployment was a nagging concern; inflation a new fear. In September 1973 the government moved to alleviate some distress by increasing family allowances and making inflation adjustments on payments, but the increased price of energy meant continuous and accelerated inflation in the new year.

On March 27, 1974, the federal government and the provinces, including Alberta, agreed, after an angry and alcohol-free lunch at 24 Sussex Drive, to a wellhead price for oil of $6.50 and a federal export tax that would assist eastern consumers. On the following afternoon, as Trudeau entered the House of Commons, Liberals greeted him with a standing ovation, a reflection of the praise the agreement had received in eastern Canadian editorials. As Trudeau spoke in the House, an angry Alberta government announced, without informing the federal government, that it would impose a new royalty rate effective April 1 that would bring the province $900 million. Trudeau and Donald Macdonald were furious: the prime minister had warned in an earlier letter to Lougheed that the higher incomes of the producing provinces could render equalization impossible and that these provinces should deal with the "depleting and wasting nature" of their resource exploitation and devote funds to energy development. He further noted, with specific reference to corporate income tax, that "the needs of the federal government to be able to share to a reasonably appropriate degree in the various streams of income across the country are self-evident." Historically, Trudeau added, "it has not been difficult to reconcile the interests of the federal and provincial governments in this regard." Alas, the statement was poor history and false prophecy.[24]

As the fracas erupted, Turner was in the midst of budget preparations, and this placed him in a position where he had to respond, simultaneously, to Alberta's tax and to new demands from the NDP. David Lewis had produced what he called a "shopping list" that had to be incorporated into the budget if his party was to continue supporting the government. It included the end of the corporate tax concessions that Turner had cleverly put through some months before, the end of tax concessions to resource industries, a personal income-tax cut, a prices review board, a lower age for pensions, and even the nationalization of the CPR. It was too much for Turner and for the government. Instead, the finance minister presented a budget on May 6 that offended everyone: his own Finance Department bureaucrats because of the introduction of a Registered Home Ownership Savings Plan; the NDP because many items on the shopping list were absent; and Lougheed because Alberta was not permitted to deduct its new royalties. Nevertheless, the budget appealed to central Canadians with its nationalist tone, several tax cuts, and a slight rise in corporation taxes. Lougheed bitterly attacked the decision regarding oil royalties, claiming that the budget "would seriously jeopardize the Canadian petroleum industry and the livelihood of many Canadians." "If the measures are implemented," he wrote to Trudeau on June 27, "we anticipate a significant decline in exploration and hence a reduction in Canadian reserves of both oil and natural gas. The consequence could well be an energy shortage in Canada in about eight years."[25] In Ottawa, no one was listening.

Seven weeks earlier, on May 8, the government had fallen when the New Democrats joined with the other parties to defeat it. The election was called for July 8. Trudeau had already set the tone for the campaign during the budget debate when he'd mocked Lewis as "David, the daisy, plucking his petals one by one: Will we have an election? Will we not have an election?" Then he infuriated Robert Stanfield by painting him as a friend of separatists in Quebec and of oil barons in Alberta. The leaders left the Commons in an angry mood, ready for a bitter campaign. Trudeau feigned fury when the opposition defeated his government, but he later admitted that his party "actually engineered [its] own defeat in the House of Commons." Over lunch at Ottawa's Cercle Universitaire, Turner, Trudeau, and MacEachen had plotted to offend both Tories and socialists in the budget and to make Canadians believe that the opposition had "forced" the election. In less than two years, Trudeau had learned the political game well.[26]

His opponents had not. The Conservatives read the polls and believed, correctly, that Canadians feared inflation. Almost nine out of ten said they believed that inflation was the major issue. From these results, they concluded that a promise to impose wage and price controls would gain public favour and electoral victory. The NDP thought, probably correctly, that such controls would hurt their labour supporters most, and they turned their political fury toward the Tories. Although the Liberals and the Finance Department had considered controls, Trudeau had made no commitments and had opposed the idea publicly. He saw immediately that Stanfield and the Conservatives had given him a large and inviting target. As his campaign manager Keith Davey put it, "I knew we would win the election—we had the numbers."[27]

The numbers were good. The Liberals would win—at least as another minority government. When the writ fell, the Grits stood at 40 percent, the Tories at 33 percent, and the NDP at 21 percent, while 46 percent believed that Trudeau "would make the best prime minister for Canada," compared with only 22 percent for Stanfield. But numbers can change, as Trudeau had learned in the last weeks of the 1972 campaign. This time he would leave no room for error. Trudeau had spent the minority years meeting party supporters whom he had ignored during his first four years, and in 1974 they came to hear and watch a transformed leader, one whose speeches brimmed with emotion, wit, sarcasm, eloquence, and a welcome thirst for power. The insouciant, even lacklustre Trudeau who had feigned disregard for political emotion was buried in the rubble of that previous campaign.[28]

Margaret knew how much her husband wanted to win, and she immediately insisted that she join the campaign, even though she was still nursing Sacha. Initially, Pierre fiercely resisted, and others who knew Margaret's feisty character also had their doubts. In the end, however, she prevailed over the doubters—to the Liberals' great benefit. Meanwhile, Trudeau had amassed a group of principal campaign partners who contrasted sharply with his 1972 entourage of intellectuals, computer nerds, and systems analysts: Keith Davey, the towering, garrulous, gossipy backroom operator, ran the campaign, while Jim Coutts, the effervescent political enthusiast, handled the media. Davey soothed the hurts and inspired the troops; Coutts kept the message clear; and Margaret, unforgettably, softened Pierre.

Margaret wrote the best account of the campaign, which she and Pierre began on an old-fashioned train in New Brunswick. As it whistled its way through small Atlantic towns, she and Pierre emerged from their car, the last on the train, and waved to ever more enthusiastic crowds. The weather was foul that Atlantic spring, but the warmth was enormous when Margaret emerged with Sacha and the crowd cheered: "Hurray for the baby." On Bible Hill in Stanfield's Nova Scotia, Trudeau told the crowd, "I can tell you the secret of my new deal this time. I have a train and I have Margaret." The press loved it. As a *Toronto Star* reporter enthused: "The paparazzi [went] mad. They can't find enough phones at the 15-minute station stops to file their 30-second in-depth reports. They're dashing into houses, tearing the phones apart to attach their tape recorders, while wailing housewives demand to know about the phone bill." The train immediately captured the public imagination, but there was no time to rest. The trip west began after only a short stop in Ottawa to check on Justin.[29]

A former nun, Mary Ann Conlon, accompanied the Trudeaus and converted their hotel rooms into nurseries while senior political assistants carted along Sacha's stuffed bears and baby carriages. In those days reporters smoked and created a foul stench that probably contributed to Pierre's visible contempt for them, but the family scene charmed the most hard-bitten journalists and Trudeau skeptics. Pierre recovered the touch of 1968 as he flirted with women, played with the kids, and gained energy from the crowd. He was spontaneous, taking advantage of every opportunity. If he spied a swimming pool, he dove into it. Margaret enjoyed most of the antics and activities but resented the rough handling she got from security people in large crowds. After one occasion when a security person jostled her, she shouted, "Take your fucking arm off me." After that instruction, security people kept their distance and, fortunately for the Liberal campaign, their silence.

As expected and initially feared, Margaret was unpredictable. She would walk off the platform if she was the only woman there and join the women sitting in the front row—a gesture that appealed to feminists but bothered campaign officials. She battled continually with Ivan Head, whose speeches, written for Trudeau, she found "full of heavy rhetoric and ponderous, interminable paragraphs meaning nothing." In Saskatchewan she listened to Pierre bore a crowd. Then, after faint applause for him, she rose, apologized for not having a prepared speech, and talked spontaneously about Liberal programs for the family. The crowds began to cheer, as they had not for Pierre. The intervention infuriated some politicians, but Pierre supported Margaret—he threw away his own prepared speeches and began to speak from the heart himself.

Margaret revealed her heart and set the tone for the rest of the Liberal campaign on June 4 at a high school auditorium in her native British Columbia. She knew Pierre not as a politician, she said, but "as a person, as a loving human being, who has taught me in the three years we have been married and in the few years before that, a lot about loving, Not just loving each other, which is pretty nice, but love for humanity—a tolerance toward the individual that reaches out very far." Some said he was arrogant, but Margaret did not know that man. To her, Pierre had never been arrogant: "He's shy and he's modest, and very, very kind." What better political reference for a balding fifty-three-year-old? It was not completely convincing, but it thoroughly surprised and charmed the student crowd.

Alberta, however, was hostile the next day: four hundred protesters mobbed Trudeau in Calgary, carrying signs reading "Alberta Oil lubricates Socialist machine" and "Sacha can't find oil." When Trudeau walked down the street, only twelve people shook his hand, including a Quebecer, a Mexican, and an American. But Alberta represented only 7 percent of Canada's voters in 1974. Trudeau could smile and say, "Usually when I land in a city I hope to go away with a few seats. But for a while today I thought I would be lucky to escape with my skin." When Lougheed tried to help the Conservatives by issuing his angry denunciation of the Liberal energy policy in the second-last week of the election, he probably helped the Liberal cause in Ontario. Sensing that advantage, Trudeau did not bother to reply to Lougheed.

The eastern business community was uneasy with Alberta's aggressiveness and with wage and price controls, and the Liberals looked more attractive. In the final week, the highly influential Paul Desmarais of Power Corporation* wrote to Trudeau to "tell [him] that I think you are conducting one hell of a campaign. Margaret's smile is a knockout. Millions of Canadians would rather look at her than any of our odd collection of Canadian politicians."[30]

Trudeau mocked the "NDP circus of slogans" as well as the Tories' proposed wage and price controls, saying his opponents planned to control inflation by waving a wand and declaring, "Zap, you're frozen." He pointed to Liberal budget measures lowering taxes on essential items, raising the duty-free allowance, and eliminating taxes for the poor. He promised that the Liberals would defeat inflation. As the campaign progressed, more Canadians appeared to believe him.

By the end of the campaign, inflation was no longer the major issue. It had been replaced by leadership—Keith Davey's choice of terrain for the election fight. Trudeau shunned the radio talk shows he had favoured in 1972, and Davey effectively controlled his appearances. These tactics worked, although they apparently caused some tension in the campaign itself.[31] Press treatment of Trudeau and the Liberals was good. Seven of Trudeau's ten major policy statements appeared on the front page of the *Globe and Mail* throughout the campaign. Overall, the Liberals had twelve front-page stories in the *Globe*, ten of them

---

* Interestingly, Desmarais added, "You once told me that being prime minister was a lot of fun. I believe you—run like hell, you will win." Paul Desmarais to Trudeau, nd [June 1974], TP, MG 26 020, vol. 17, file 14, LAC.

positive, while the Conservatives appeared only five times, with two stories being negative ones about Leonard Jones, the Conservative mayor of Moncton who denounced Stanfield's support for bilingualism.[32] Stanfield scored well on integrity, but Trudeau dominated the polls on all other items, including handling of the economy. The majority of Canadians told pollsters that he had "changed his attitude" since 1972 and had become "less arrogant; more humble; easier to get along with . . . more human; calmed down."[33] On June 19 he even entertained the press corps at 24 Sussex Drive, an invitation that stunned journalists who had long endured Trudeau's stares of withering contempt. They, too, had calmed down.

The electorate was also calmer than Trudeau and the Liberals had any right to expect. Although inflation had waned as an issue in the campaign, it remained a reality with the shocking news on June 12 that the Consumer Price Index had risen 10.9 percent since May 1973. What would become the "Misery Index," the combination of unemployment and inflation, stood at record highs, but remarkably, it did not move the polls: there the Liberals maintained a solid lead, the Conservatives were stagnant, and the NDP began to lose votes to the Liberals as workers decided to vote against the Tory plan to freeze their wages.

The campaign ended with an astonishing picnic on Toronto Island, organized by the Ontario campaign under the expert leadership of Dorothy Petrie, at which a casually but stylishly clad Pierre and Margaret both spoke to more than a hundred thousand cheering Liberals. They returned to Ottawa on election night, thoroughly exhausted but proud of what they had done. As the returns came in, the Liberal tide rose in the East; swept across Quebec, where the Liberals took 60 of 74 seats; and gained power in Ontario, where Liberals won 55 of 88 seats—an increase of 19 over the previous election. Liberal support ebbed quickly in the West, although there were two more seats in Saskatchewan and four more in British Columbia. Trudeau had his majority with 141 seats, none of them from Alberta. The results in the West were ominous, but forgotten as Trudeau and his campaign celebrated wildly on election night. Davey, the political guru of the day, declared: "I can tell you the secret of this election in three words— Pierre Elliott Trudeau. It was his victory."[34]

Margaret wept late that election night, perhaps from pain, perhaps from pleasure. It had been a brilliant success—and so had she. The next day, however, her phone never rang. She waited; no call came. Still flush with excitement, tired from travel, confused about her future, Margaret knew that something in her "broke that day." She said, "I felt I had been used."[35]

CHAPTER NINE

—

MID-TERM PROMISE

A s a boy, Pierre Trudeau had learned in his Brébeuf classics courses that victories were sometimes pyrrhic, where
the costs to the victor were greater than the gains. On
election night, July 8, 1974, he relished his triumph, but his
unexpected majority came with high costs. Three problems persisted, and the successful campaign probably exacerbated them.
First, the budget that sparked the election had denied Alberta the
right to deduct its new royalty charges from federal taxes. During
the campaign, Premier Peter Lougheed had responded angrily
to the Liberal policy, as did most Alberta voters. A difficult relationship had become worse, and the impact of the quarrel between
Ottawa and the West promised to injure the tender structure of
Canadian federalism. Second, Trudeau had cleverly mocked
Progressive Conservative leader Robert Stanfield's proposal for
wage and price controls, but inflation remained the major issue for
the new government. Moreover, the powerful Finance Department
and John Turner, its popular minister, were unhappy with the
budget and with Trudeau's presentation of economic issues during
the campaign. In a crisis, the flimsy unity within the minority government could shatter in the new majority government, since
there was no longer need for great cooperation between the parties

to prevent the government's fall. Third, for Margaret Trudeau, the campaign's strains broke the fragile bonds that had maintained her mental health and marriage.

Margaret realized much later that she suffered from bipolar disorder, and she became an eloquent advocate of better treatment of the disease, which was earlier known as manic depression. In 2006 she recalled that she had experienced mild depressive moments as an adolescent but had none in her first two years of marriage. However, as one journalist has described it, "after the birth of her second child, Sacha, on Christmas Day in 1973, [Margaret] was struck with an overwhelming depression. People, particularly her husband, kept telling her that she had 'no reason on earth' to be unhappy. She had a gorgeous new-born and she was totally pampered. But she found herself crying all the time and unable to get out of bed."[1] Doctors diagnosed Margaret's problem as postpartum depression and medicated her heavily. Meanwhile, Pierre was planning for the election, and Margaret was worried about its outcome. Against Pierre's wishes, she decided that she must join the campaign: "He insisted that politics was *his* work and the children and the houses *my* work, and to mix them would only confuse our lives." Margaret, however, would not relent, believing that if she "fought the election by his side, demonstrating on every platform and in every convention hall of the country just how happy we were together and what a devoted family man he was, then Pierre would have a better chance to convince people that he was the man to lead them." She was overwhelmingly right.[2]

But the decision to campaign may have been wrong in terms of the personal toll. In Margaret's own words, "my rebellion started in 1974." As she later noted, her "high-spirited" style was present from the moment she met Pierre in Tahiti, and "being bipolar doesn't mean that you're constantly in a state of mental illness." However, bipolarity brought wild swings, which could be "either unusually low or extremely—inappropriately—high." The first "visible explosions" were "directed at the official life," the "grotesquely formal occasions [that] were forced upon us." For Margaret, life at 24 Sussex became, in her words, "a long tunnel of darkness," a profound loneliness "coupled with the pressures of public life while trying on my own to manage the symptoms of bipolar depression."[3] Pierre was baffled, uncertain how to approach her illness, and hopeful that pharmaceuticals could heal her.

A close reading of the period before and after the 1974 election reveals how the "tunnel" opened. By 1973 the Trudeaus had become accustomed to the ways of Ottawa and exhilarated by the foreign travel that became part of Pierre's official life — as when they left to sample the exotic in China. They also began to relish their intimate family settings, particularly at Harrington Lake. In pictures of those happy days, Pierre, Justin, and the pregnant Margaret seem deeply engaged with each other, and their mutual affection is obvious. Yet even in those times, Margaret tussled with staff, resented the security requirements, and fretted about Pierre's work ethic, which so often meant exclusion.* Margaret enjoyed watching television, for instance, but each night Trudeau brought home briefing notes and spent most of the evening reading and annotating them. Duties prevailed even as they tried to be together. The result, in Margaret's words, was that "a visitor peering through

---

* In a 2006 interview, Margaret Trudeau recalled: "When Justin was born, I was told that if he was kidnapped, no ransom would be paid. I wanted to go out for a walk without the police and I was told no, I had to have the police with me. They taught me how to roll to the curb and hold onto my baby under my body and scream at the top of my lungs so they couldn't easily pick me up and put me into a car." And, she commented, "That was an extra small pressure on a new mom." Interview with Anne Kingston, *Maclean's*, May 19, 2006.

the window of the sitting room would have seen Pierre poring intently over the contents of one of his seven brown boxes and me curled up in front of the television with an enormous set of earphones, like a disc jockey watching a silent movie."[4]

The cause of Margaret's depression the morning after election day is clear: she realized that Pierre would now stay in politics for several more years. A majority government guaranteed five years, although most prime ministers call an election in the fourth year. Before the election she had feared a Liberal loss; after the vote she regretted the consequences of the Liberal win. Now no light was visible at the end of "the tunnel of darkness."

—

Margaret Trudeau was not alone in her disappointment after the election victory. John Turner also knew that a Liberal win would reduce his chances of reaching the Prime Minister's Office. Campaign co-chair Keith Davey had bluntly told him that he would become "this generation's Paul Martin" if Trudeau got his majority. Nevertheless, Turner campaigned nationally and effectively, and like Margaret, he apparently felt that his efforts were not appreciated. He joined Trudeau on election night at 24 Sussex, but there were no warm expressions of gratitude, and he felt excluded by Trudeau's campaign team and close friends, who thought of him "as a jock with political charm." The early days when the Turners and Trudeaus vacationed together in the Caribbean had not broken down the barriers between them. Memories of the 1968 leadership convention persisted, and the recent years of minority government made the men ever more distrustful of each other's intentions.[5] Opposition taunts about the "real leader" of the Liberals continued to irritate Trudeau.

Both men were caught up in the tides of inflation and unemployment that swept not only Ottawa but the entire Western world in the early 1970s. The strong currents tossed the Department of Finance toward more conservative terrain. Turner worked effectively with the Americans during this period, particularly Treasury Secretary George Shultz, and in the late Nixon period these finance officials were strongly influenced by Milton Friedman and the monetarist Chicago School, with its pronounced opposition to state intervention. With Shultz's support, Turner became a major international figure in the negotiations following the OPEC crisis. He continued to work closely with another economic conservative, William Simon, Shultz's replacement at Treasury, and at Simon's suggestion he was appointed chair of the International Monetary Fund Interim Committee dealing with the huge imbalances caused by the energy crisis. However, these successes brought little credit in Ottawa, and the associations Turner forged even raised some doubts. Not surprisingly, Turner worried increasingly about his position.

Turner's deputy minister, Simon Reisman, a blunt, cigar-smoking civil servant who swore like a drill sergeant and liked a good fight, did not help matters. Reisman's ego was legendary, and Trudeau's reforms, which permitted senior officials to present to Cabinet committees, gave Reisman the forum he savoured. Mitchell Sharp recalled one meeting of Priorities and Planning at which Reisman lectured the ministers. After a Reisman diatribe, Sharp said, "Mr. Prime Minister, isn't it wonderful to listen to a civil servant who knows his place." All laughed, including Reisman, but "after a short pause, he returned to the attack, undeterred." More troubling was evidence that Reisman had begun to loathe the prime minister and his party. During the 1974 election campaign, as Keith Davey was poring over some newspapers during a flight, the passenger beside him said, "You're obviously interested in politics." Davey nodded, and the passenger asked what he thought the outcome of the election would be. The ebullient Davey said the Liberals would do well in Ontario, and the passenger exploded: "No way! Take it from me. Every Toronto minister has had it! They're gone!" As the plane landed, he introduced himself: "I'm Simon Reisman."[6]

Some doubt the anecdote's accuracy, but it conveys the increasing suspicion surrounding the Finance Department and Reisman's growing anger directed against Trudeau and his office. During the election campaign, Conservative leader Stanfield attacked Reisman and, more particularly, the department, blaming Finance for the rampant inflation of the time. This widespread distrust of Finance and, to a lesser extent, the Bank of Canada had developed during the first Trudeau government, when their policies appeared to have created the economic problems that hurt the government in the 1972 election. Stanfield was not the only one with doubts. Trudeau, too, increasingly relied on outside advisers, most notably Albert Breton, who now, as a University of Toronto economist, was often sharply critical of government economic policy. When he read the draft of the post-election Speech from the Throne in December 1972, for example, he warned Trudeau that it was "so much at variance with what I believe are your own views . . . and certainly with the image that the Government wishes to project" that he recommended some changes—which Trudeau accepted.[7]

Fundamentally, Reisman, once a socialist, now agreed with the monetarist school's arguments against large bureaucracies, regulation, and interventionist governments. Trudeau, however, remained committed to government intervention to deal with regional and individual inequities and believed in the importance of government as a "countervail" against the forces of business and labour. Although Trudeau and Reisman shared a suspicion of economic nationalism and of "the bureaucratic phenomenon," their differences rapidly began to overwhelm their similarities after 1972.

Turner, a pragmatist and, increasingly, the spokesperson for business in the Cabinet, was caught in the middle.

After the election, Trudeau faced pressures to change the personnel at Finance and to strengthen the economic staff close to him. Reisman had created many enemies, notably Davey, who was at the peak of his influence after the electoral triumph. Breton believed that Finance, including Turner, needed a complete overhaul and that Trudeau's own economic staff should be strengthened to counter the dominance of Finance within government operations. The Department of National Health and Welfare, under Marc Lalonde, fought Finance bitterly over the reform of social welfare, and when Trudeau proposed a compromise, Turner replied that in the troubled financial situation developing in the second half of 1974, Lalonde's proposals cost too much.[8] Serious political trouble loomed on the horizon. During the campaign Trudeau had mocked Stanfield's dire warnings about the economy, but soon after the election, inflation rose continuously and economic growth stalled. Now his memorable words—"Zap, you're frozen!"—haunted him as he wrestled with a Consumer Price Index that rose 12.4 percent in 1974 while, in real terms, the economy expanded only 3.7 percent, compared with 6.8 percent in 1973.[9]

Trudeau was befuddled; economists were confused. Even Marshall McLuhan had inflation on his mind, and he sent Trudeau a long document with his "thoughts on inflation and crowd dynamics." As Trudeau read it, he underlined these words: "Today the fact of the increasing prices has little or nothing to do with the old laws of supply and demand, but much to do with the new media." McLuhan suggested that the current economy had a "great increase of scope accompanied by the panic sense of the loss of control and identity" and that "one obvious cause of inflation is the media-made *consciousness* of it." McLuhan, like Trudeau, sensed that inflation was driven by expectations, which were devilishly difficult to manage.* With divided counsels among his advisers and uncertainty in his own mind, Trudeau now grasped anxiously for solutions, particularly one that would maintain his government's credibility after his ferocious denunciation of wage and price controls in the election campaign.[10] Finding it would not be easy.

—

Trudeau's other post-election dilemma was how to handle the West, particularly Alberta, which had spurned Trudeau's Liberals entirely in the July election. In August, when Trudeau finally responded to the letter Lougheed had sent during campaign, complaining that provincial royalty payments could not be deducted from federal corporate taxes, the prime minister was direct and unapologetic: those deductions would not be allowed. It was

---

* The McLuhan letter can be read as a warning about depending on rational expectations to understand the functioning of the economy. When he wrote, the discipline of economics was increasingly moving toward an emphasis on rationality, which led ineluctably to acceptance of the efficiency of the market and away from a role for government intervention. In a sense, McLuhan and, for that matter, Trudeau were unwilling to accept that there was no longer validity in John Maynard Keynes' view that "animal spirits" caused volatility and irrational behaviour requiring state intervention. More recently, Nobel Laureate George Akerhof and prominent Yale economist Robert Schiller have restated Keynes' argument in *Animal Spirits: How Human Psychology Drives the Economy and Why It Matters for Global Capitalism* (Princeton: Princeton University Press, 2009). They trace the movement away from psychology and the importance of "animal spirits" to the seventies and, in particular, the attack on intervention and regulation by economists of those times.

Trudeau's responsibility to protect the country's revenue base, and the royalties threatened to undermine it. Moreover, the two-price system whereby Canadians were shielded from the higher world price for oil was essential to ensure equity among Canadians. In the increasingly angry debate, Trudeau and Lougheed came to symbolize the interests of their respective governments. In Ottawa, Cabinet discussions reveal impatience with Lougheed and particular irritation with the links between American interests and the Alberta government. In January 1974, for example, Lalonde had argued that if the negotiations did not go well, the Cabinet should consider the "take-over of the control of the oil and gas industry on the grounds of the public interest." In the circumstances, it was unfortunate that Alberta lacked representation in both the Cabinet and the Liberal caucus. Lougheed was no pushover, however, and, increasingly, American energy interests looked warily at Trudeau's government as they began to see Alberta as their effective voice in Canada.[11]

It was a trying time for all Western governments as the postwar boom came to an end and no elixirs could be found to renew its vigour. In the United States, the Nixon presidency lurched toward its demise, which came dramatically on August 9 with the president's historic resignation. European governments also struggled with the energy crisis and political discontent. Whatever Trudeau's difficulties, Canada's economic situation in mid-1974 remained among the best in the world. While others shared inflation and faltering economic growth, Canada's unemployment remained relatively low, and its economy seemed relatively strong. The *New York Times* hailed Trudeau's election as "an impressive demonstration of the health and vibrancy of its democratic institutions and practices" and claimed that Canadians had "sharpened their identity as a united people and nation." Few Canadians would have enthusiastically agreed, but, to an outside observer, Canada seemed an oasis of civility and solidity.[12]

Had Trudeau left office in 1974, he would have served longer than the majority of Canadian prime ministers. Although his successor would have faced serious problems, Trudeau could have pointed to major achievements: reform of the Criminal Code; recognition of China; establishment of Arctic sovereignty; a major role in the transformation of the Commonwealth and the Francophonie; reform of parliamentary institutions and election financing; steadfast promotion of official bilingualism; and, ironically, the channelling of separatist radicalism and violence into a democratic political movement—an achievement he shared with René Lévesque. Now he had at least four more years to change Canada and a mountain of challenges to overcome.

—

The seventies witnessed a fundamental shift in societal attitudes as Trudeau's government and the provinces passed legislation to reform the Criminal Code and the Divorce Act. Between 1966 and 1972, for instance, the divorce rate rose from 84.8 per 100,000 people to 222. The impact of the reforms on homosexuality is more difficult to quantify, but it was also profound, as discrimination against homosexuals diminished in the workplace and in society in general. In the case of abortion, the rate rose from 3 per 100 live births in 1969, clearly a reflection of underreporting of an illegal activity, to 14.9 in 1975 and 18.6 in 1978. The last figure reflects the long fight by Dr. Henry Morgentaler to chip away at the restrictions on Canada's abortion laws by establishing private clinics. In 1973, the year the United States Supreme Court ruled in *Roe v. Wade* that abortion was legal until the fetus was viable, Morgentaler announced he had performed more than five thousand illegal abortions. He was charged and acquitted in a jury trial, only to have the Quebec Court of Appeal overturn his acquittal. The angry debates surrounding the Morgentaler trials continued in Parliament and in the courts for many years.

Although Trudeau had profound reservations about many of these social changes—which he shared privately with his priest in confession, his more liberal wife, and fellow Catholics Marshall McLuhan and Justice Minister Otto Lang—he believed that the reforms he began and Turner completed were essential. In his view they provided legal recognition of a diverse and modern society where individuals bore responsibility for their own decisions and the state stayed out of the nation's bedrooms. Because of this belief, Trudeau did not dissent when the courts ruled that Morgentaler should go to jail. As Trudeau saw it, the abortionist knew the law and made the decision to defy it; as a free individual, he was then obliged to accept the penalties the law imposed.[13]

Trudeau may have been in advance of the current on social issues in the sixties, but by the mid-seventies, the powerful forces of social change, particularly in the women's movement, had left his government in their wake. He tried to avoid the rapids when possible, preferring to adjust details such as the inequitable administration of legalized abortion throughout Canada, which meant that women in rural Canada had more difficulty obtaining abortions than did those who dwelt in the cities. Nevertheless, Trudeau's government, in its reform of the Criminal Code, had set in motion powerful and existing forces of social change. In the United States, the courts, rather than the government, led the way and became an early target in the American culture wars. In Canada, the courts remained at the side, while the government followed the liberal path. This leadership not only loosened legal restraints on individual choice, but also moved toward the abolition of capital punishment in July 1976, when the House of Commons passed Bill C-84. Although there was considerable support for capital punishment on Conservative backbenches, much support from rural Quebec Liberals, and rising resistance to its abolition in the United States,

Trudeau, the NDP, and former Tory leader Bob Stanfield—and his successor, Joe Clark—prevailed in their arguments that capital punishment represented vengeance, not justice. In Trudeau's speech on the issue, which columnist Richard Gwyn called his "finest parliamentary hour," the prime minister argued that "to retain [the death penalty] in the Criminal Code of Canada would be to abandon reason in favour of vengeance; to abandon hope and confidence in favour of a despairing acceptance of our inability to cope with violent crime except with violence." Despite an April Gallup poll indicating that 69 percent of Canadians wanted to retain the death penalty, on the final vote 130 voted for abolition and 124 for retention. Executions came to an end in Canada. Trudeau had made a difference.[14]

—

In the crucial area of Canada-U.S. relations, the primary task for any prime minister is to manage the personal relationship with the president as effectively as possible. Here Trudeau faced a particular challenge: "It cannot be said that Nixon and Trudeau were ideally suited for each other," wrote Henry Kissinger, Nixon's major foreign policy adviser. "A scion of an old Quebec family, elegant, brilliant, enigmatic, intellectual, Trudeau was bound to evoke all of Nixon's resentments against 'swells' who, in his view, always looked down on him." Fortunately, Kissinger and Trudeau got on well; each respected the other's "clear enjoyment of social life," which, in Kissinger's definition, meant swarms of beautiful women and entertainment in swank places. Kissinger smiled quietly when the president denounced Trudeau as a "queer," an "asshole," or most often, "a son of a bitch." Privately, Kissinger told others that he found Trudeau "foppish" and "a mother's boy," albeit a highly intelligent one.

Yet for all their differences and suspicions, Kissinger says that the two leaders "worked together without visible strain. They settled the issues before them and did not revert to their less charitable personal comments until each was back in his own capital." In truth, Trudeau respected the realism of Nixon's foreign policy—an approach he deemed lacking in postwar Canadian policy. He admired Nixon's bold opening to China, although he interpreted it, to Nixon's annoyance, as an American response to his own decision to recognize the communist nation. Trudeau was also an enthusiastic proponent of Nixon's willingness to explore détente with the Soviet Union; Nixon, in turn, thought Trudeau too enthusiastic about the communists. Kissinger summed up the peculiar situation well: "United States–Canadian relations demonstrated that the national interest can be made to transcend personal sympathies."[15] Thus, Canada managed to escape the cancellation of the Auto Pact, lessen the effects of a variety of protectionist measures, conciliate the Americans when a strong anti-Americanism demanded a political response (as with the January 1973 condemnation of the bombing of North Vietnam), and play a strong hand well with the Americans when the OPEC crisis roiled North American energy markets.

In their book on Canadian foreign policy, *The Canadian Way*, Trudeau and Head revealed that they were especially proud of their successful response, after the discovery of oil in Alaska, to the challenge to Canadian sovereignty in the Arctic. They described in great detail how they propitiated various interests as they forged a new approach to international trusteeship for coastal waters—one that had profound influence on the multilateral negotiations surrounding the law of the sea:

> At the heart of the proposal, therefore, was the concept of international trusteeship. In the forefront of the development of international law, Canada would assume responsibility for protecting the vast and threatened Arctic ecological resource off its northern coasts, working all the while for appropriate international mechanisms to be designed and set in place.

We would do this by pursuing two simultaneous goals: (i) the passage of protective legislation designed to prevent oil spills and other deleterious activity; and (ii) the negotiation of accepted international standards to embrace and further the Canadian position. We would emphasize that we were not acting in breach of international law, rather, in the special Arctic circumstances, we were acting on behalf of the international community in the absence of applicable law.[16]

Although Americans rejected Canada's assertion of sovereignty over Arctic waters, they lived with it. Too often commentators have taken Nixon's personal contempt for Trudeau and the often angry words expressed in Parliament and Congress as a metaphor for Canadian-American relations in those times, but they are wrong. The interests of both countries were well served by their very different leaders. Nevertheless, things did become easier when Nixon left office, and Trudeau began a warm and enduring friendship with Gerald Ford, his Republican successor.*

---

* Except in private with his staff or with other leaders, Nixon was a poor conversationalist, but Margaret Trudeau felt obliged one evening to be a polite guest. Sitting between Secretary of State William Rogers and Nixon, Margaret told Rogers that she hesitated to initiate the usual dinnertime pleasantries with the president. Rogers immediately leaned over and said, "Hey, Dick. Mrs. Trudeau doesn't know what to say to you." Nixon gave her a baleful look and began a tedious story about how the pandas China had given him refused to mate. Having done his duty, he turned back to Pierre. When Rogers asked how she found Nixon, she replied: "Quite frankly, I'm still in awe. The only conversation that I have had with the president of the United States is on the sex life of pandas." Margaret Trudeau, *Beyond Reason* (New York and London: Paddington Press, 1979), 157.

—

Trudeau's early reforms in the way Parliament operated led to significant changes for its members. Funding for constituency offices for MPs, more office staff, party research bureaus, and travel allowances for members and their families altered the way that MPs worked and lived. In Parliament, committees were restructured and given a role in legislation, and House rules were modernized, especially with the use of time allocation, through which debate times were structured. Most important of all was the public financing of Canadian election campaigns, which became an enduring feature of political life, both federally and provincially. The laws on election financing now provided for limits on donations, tax credits for those donations, and partial direct funding for candidates who acquired a certain percentage of votes. Liberal partisans grumbled loudly because the Conservatives, and particularly the NDP, benefited more from these changes than their own party did, but Trudeau persisted. Although many of these changes mirrored those in other Western democracies, one lasting and unique change Trudeau initiated was the introduction of bilingualism into Parliament, its committees, and, through example rather than legislation, the life of Ottawa. Robert Stanfield, who resigned after his 1974 loss, was the last unilingual leader of the Conservative Party. Parliament was a world transformed.[17]

Although Stanfield's predecessor, John Diefenbaker, was one of seventeen Conservatives who voted against the Official Languages Bill, the Conservative Party leader, to his credit but perhaps to his political detriment, fought hard for official bilingualism despite strong opposition from his caucus and Progressive Conservative voters. In 1974 the popular mayor of Moncton, Leonard Jones, ran for the Conservative nomination on a platform of opposition to bilingualism. He won the nomination, but

Stanfield immediately refused him as a candidate, saying, "I'm fully prepared if necessary to risk my leadership on the prospects of electoral success on this issue." With Stanfield's support, Trudeau laid the lasting foundations for official bilingualism: that policy assured federal bilingual services for all Canadians and supported bilingual education across Canada. To be sure, there were enormous problems of administration, but "through the carrot approach of funding minority-language education and second-language instruction, the federal government helped to make these programs commonplace . . . and official bilingualism became part of Canadian national identity."[18]

Two leading journalists assessed Trudeau's career in June 1975, his tenth year in Parliament. Peter Desbarats reminded *Saturday Night*'s readers that Trudeau

> entered federal politics as an outspoken opponent of separatism and an advocate of establishing a meaningful French presence in federal politics and the federal bureaucracy. . . .
>
> A decade later, the terrorist FLQ seems as faded a political force as the French-Canadian patriots of 1837. Separatism is still a vital element in Québec, but the stability that has prevailed for the past several years achieves one of Trudeau's main objectives. The amount being spent on bilingualism helps to fulfil another. The federal programme is so comprehensive, and such an established part of the Ottawa scene, that Conservatives now feel they can scrutinize it without opening themselves to charges of racism.
>
> . . . if there are Canadians in future, including those who live in Québec, the first Trudeau decade will be remembered as a critical time when one man's vision imprinted itself on the nation, and the man himself matched the challenge.

Desbarats went on to say that Trudeau's "achievement . . . [was] remarkable," but Canadians barely noticed it.[19]

Desbarats was not alone in giving favourable reviews. In *Le Devoir*, Claude Ryan surely surprised many readers—and Trudeau himself—with an uncharacteristic tribute to the prime minister and his colleagues Gérard Pelletier and Jean Marchand. Ryan began by acknowledging the longevity of the three "doves," as they were called in French, or "wise men," as the English dubbed them. He then commented on how the Quiet Revolution had required Quebec leaders to create a strong government in Quebec. The three "doves," however, believed that to avoid an otherwise certain separatist movement, francophones needed influence in Ottawa; they also believed that all provinces must accept "common rules of the game" and that a central government should possess "real power." He continued:

> The wishes of the three doves have been realized beyond all
> expectations as far as participation in the exercise of power . . .
> Not content to merely accept the challenge of power, they
> have used it in these past years in a manner which, far from
> being harmful, has placed Canada among the best-governed,
> most open and most tolerant countries in the world. This is
> no small accomplishment for a trio of Québécois who com-
> mitted themselves ten years ago to the conquest of a veritable
> political Himalaya.
> . . . No other team of French-Canadian politicians meas-
> ures up to them in terms of complementary personalities,
> culture, competence, knowledge of their milieu and the best
> of modern methods.[20]

Three years later, however, in 1978, George Radwanski, a journalist sympathetic to Trudeau, published the first major biography of the prime minister and concluded: "Trudeau has been a disappointment. Despite a creditable over-all performance and a number of significant achievements, he has not accomplished nearly as much as might be expected of a man of his intellect and public appeal."[21] Radwanski's judgments are a measure of the ferocity of the storms that swept away the previous favourable assessments. Ryan had ended his essay with a question: "Have the three doves created a new equilibrium that will finally rout separatism or have they merely held the fort with dignity and intelligence for ten years?" His premonition was fully justified.

—

Trudeau's world fell apart in 1975. The decade in politics had taken its toll on the long partnership of the "doves." Pelletier was tired of politics, eager to escape the partisan bickering he had always detested. Although their relationship remained personally warm—he always signed his letters to Trudeau *"fraternellement, Pelletier"*—he saw less of his old friend after Pierre and Margaret married. In the fall of '75, Trudeau appointed Pelletier as Canada's ambassador to France, where their enduring friendship had begun almost three decades earlier in Parisian cafés as Edith Piaf sang in the background and they engaged each other in debates about communism, Catholicism, Quebec, Canada, and their future. With Pelletier, friendship aged like vintage wine, tasted occasionally but savoured greatly; with Marchand, however, the personal relationship had turned acidic. The fiery former labour leader resented his switch from the Department of Regional Economic Expansion to Transport in 1972, which he correctly viewed as a demotion, and he complained that Trudeau no longer consulted him. In the 1974 election, he had been co-chair with Keith Davey of the Liberal campaign. They did not get along, and Marchand remained bitter when, despite excellent results in Quebec, he received no promotion for his efforts.

Initially a powerful minister with a warmth that won affection from staff and colleagues, Marchand began to falter. He started to drink heavily, and the ascetic Trudeau noticed. They met and talked about hypertension and other potential problems, but Marchand did not change his habits. In January 1975, when an NDP member asked him in Question Period about a long-delayed transport policy, Marchand astonished the House by replying that the government had "no overall policy." The opposition heckled: "It's a mess." Marchand shot back, "Yes, of course it is . . . and more than you think." As the opposition continued to goad him, Marchand claimed that "racism" was the reason for their criticism. It was a poor performance, rumoured to have been caused by alcohol, and Trudeau forced him to apologize to Stanfield and the House of Commons. On February 26 Marchand stepped down as Quebec leader within the federal Liberal Party and was replaced by Lalonde, whom he resented greatly. A few days later, as he left the Ottawa airport, Marchand hit another car and promptly sped away. A Porsche driver who witnessed the accident pursued him to his home, where he wrote down Marchand's licence number and called the police. When Trudeau read the police report, he revealed his anger in his many underlines and exclamation marks. In July Marchand wrote to Trudeau and told him he could not make a planned trip to James Bay because his doctor had told him that his "blood pressure is going back up." He thanked Trudeau for "*ton encouragement.*"

On August 29, one day after Pelletier resigned to become ambassador to France, an Ottawa court convicted Marchand of leaving the scene of an accident. Trudeau visited him in hospital, where he had been admitted because of acute high blood pressure. Reporters besieged Trudeau when he left the hospital room: "Did Marchand resign?" Trudeau indicated that Marchand had offered his resignation but that he had refused to accept: "It was a very loyal thing [for Marchand] to do. He just wanted me to feel free to dispense with him, but I could not dispense with Marchand."[22] A few months later, however, a Cabinet shuffle allowed Trudeau to move Marchand to the fringes of Cabinet, where he served as a minister without portfolio until he angrily stormed out of Ottawa to fight the Quebec provincial election in 1976. The three wise men were now part of history, and Pierre Trudeau, who had initially seemed the most unlikely politician of them all, was the only survivor. He was lonely.

—

After the 1974 election, the gravity shifted in the Trudeau government. The prime minister's new Cabinet and staff reflected Toronto rather than Montreal, as Keith Davey played a major role in choosing the Cabinet. Once Jim Coutts became Trudeau's principal secretary in 1975, these two men brought a more political focus to the Prime Minister's Office. Because of the election results, Trudeau's Cabinet choices were limited. In British Columbia, Minister of the Environment Jack Davis had lost and was replaced by Senator Ray Perrault, an indication of Liberal weakness in the province. There was no Alberta minister, and Otto Lang remained the sole Saskatchewan member and minister. In Ontario, Trudeau dropped Herb Gray and replaced him with Barney Danson, a popular and effervescent Toronto businessman. Jeanne Sauvé became the first woman in Trudeau's government to head a full-fledged ministry when he appointed her minister of the environment (she had been a minister of state since 1972). Paul Martin, an MP since 1935 and three times a leadership candidate, was dropped from the Cabinet and appointed as high commissioner to London, where he kept an excellent diary. Thanks to the propensity of Canadian politicians to visit London, it is one of the finest sources of gossip about the Trudeau government in the late 1970s.[23]

The most striking change was the appointment of Allan MacEachen to the Department of External Affairs to replace Mitchell Sharp. MacEachen had been perhaps the most brilliant House leader in Canadian history and a superb constituency politician in his native Cape Breton, and External Affairs initially seemed an odd choice for him. However, he had studied economics at MIT, and he represented the party's left and internationalist tradition, one that Trudeau was finding increasingly attractive.

Two changes occurred at this time that had a profound influence on Canadian foreign policy over the next few years. First, Trudeau was no longer preoccupied with domestic political matters. The immediate threat of separatism receded after the October Crisis, and following the overwhelming victory of the Bourassa Liberals in the 1973 Quebec election, Trudeau extended his gaze to international affairs and the significance of what he could achieve there for Canada. In this respect Trudeau was similar to many other Canadian political leaders who find foreign affairs especially alluring as their tenure lengthens.[24] Second, the times seemed propitious for Canada to be "a foremost power" with a foreign policy to match. Trudeau now wanted Canada to be at the centre of the swirl of events surrounding the crises of the mid-1970s — and even more significantly, others agreed. The energy shock and its profound impact on the international economic system, the world food crisis and the appalling evidence of its effects, and the stunning resignation of an American president facing impeachment all forced Americans and other Western nations to cooperate as they had not done since the early years of the Cold War. Moreover, for Trudeau, the international world was more congenial now that Charles de Gaulle was dead, Gerald Ford was in the White House, and Harold Wilson had regained office in Britain. He was finally ready to become a "citizen of the world" representing Canada.

Just at this time, however, the weaknesses in Washington presented new challenges for Canada, including the expanding

European Common Market (ECM) and an increasingly wealthy Japan. In response the new government dusted off the vague concept of a "third option" between East and West that it had conceived earlier and, in the fall of 1974, began negotiations for a "contractual link" with the Europeans and the Japanese.[25]

The Common Market had added three new members in 1972, most significantly the United Kingdom. In British eyes, Trudeau, unlike John Diefenbaker a decade earlier, had behaved admirably as Britain took steps to enter the union. Trudeau told Peter Hayman, the British high commissioner in Canada, that "he considered [that] Britain dealt generously with Canadian problems during the negotiations." Some Canadian officials admitted that the British entry into the market was "helpful" to Canada in "making her sit up and take notice about her own world trading position." Certainly it seemed to affect Trudeau that way. With Kissinger declaring 1973 "the year of Europe," Trudeau conferred with Ivan Head and Michel Dupuy, a senior External Affairs official, about the direction Canada should take in its foreign policy. They both urged a direct approach to Europe itself.[26]

If reason and some traditional affection led to Europe, passion attracted Trudeau to the developing world. In his only campaign speech on foreign policy, he expressed his hope that Canada's role in the world would be judged solely by "its humanism, its pursuit of social justice." Earlier, on his 1973 China trip, he had said that "national greatness is measured not in terms of martial grandeur or even economic accomplishment but in terms of individual welfare and human dignity."[27] Trudeau was not alone in this interest. The energy crisis and, in particular, the surprising success of OPEC in creating a cartel combined with the world food crisis to focus international attention on development issues. The developing countries had formed a "G77" caucus within the United Nations, whose voice became significantly louder there and in other gatherings. It called for a New International Economic

Order, which would create a major restructuring of international economic relations.[28] Trudeau shared their concern about inequalities and what came to be called the North-South divide. After appointing MacEachen, he wrote a long letter to his new minister, emphasizing that he should take a leading role in expressing Canadian "concern about the widespread inequalities found in the world." Trudeau had changed his mind since 1968: Canada could no longer act only at the fringes. Its voice must now be heard at the centre, where the major decisions affecting the "widespread inequalities" occurred.[29]

Unfortunately for Trudeau and MacEachen, the Department of External Affairs was not the powerful ministry Lester Pearson had led in the fifties. Time and Trudeau's own antipathy to the department had taken their toll. In the late sixties the department faced budget cuts and the transfer of some of its finest officers, including Allan Gotlieb and Basil Robinson, to other, domestic departments. Then, when the talented Ed Ritchie, the under-secretary of state for external affairs in the early seventies, had a stroke just after the 1974 election, his loss diminished the department's voice even more at the Ottawa table. External Affairs greatly resented the role that Trudeau had given to Ivan Head, who not only carried out special missions for Trudeau, where he dealt with senior officials and politicians abroad, but also requested that departmental officers assist him in his tasks. With Sharp's departure, Trudeau realized that the department must regain its confidence if Canada was to play a larger role on the international stage. He therefore appointed Robinson to replace Ritchie.[30] But when Robinson tried to assert the department's authority in foreign relations, Head resisted and even dismissed an External Affairs representative in his office, fearing he was "a spy" for the department. Obviously, External Affairs was no longer the central agency dominating Canada's relations with the world, and it struggled to keep up with a prime minister who had finally developed a taste for internationalism.[31]

Trudeau realized that he would have to make frequent trips to Europe and Japan before he could negotiate the contractual link he wanted with these countries. He took advantage of these occasions to raise two principal issues with his hosts: the new international economic order and nuclear non-proliferation. He was enraged in 1974 when India exploded an atomic device, made possible by Canadian development assistance in the 1950s and 1960s, and claimed that the bomb was for peaceful purposes and, for that reason, not in breach of the 1970 non-proliferation treaty. Canadian-Indian relations were soured for decades by this nuclear explosion.

Trudeau's visit to Denmark in May 1975 was typical of his discussions at this time. When he met Prime Minister Anker Jørgensen, they talked about Arctic cooperation and the inevitable fisheries disputes. Trudeau then spoke of the rise of the European Economic Community (EEC), which had evolved from the European Common Market, and its impact on Canada: "As the European community develops it is Canada's wish that the countries involved should understand Canada's desire to cooperate with the community and to establish links with it," he said. "Sometimes Canada is regarded as just a part of the United States. This, of course, is not true, and we have our own separate and distinct interests. We have our own nuclear reactor." Trudeau then spoke at greater length on the "new economic order" and Canada's desire "to ensure that the world economic system brings greater economic justice to the developing world."[32] As he did elsewhere, he referred to his experience with the Commonwealth as a model for a broader collaboration between developed and less developed countries. The Commonwealth, to which Trudeau was initially indifferent if not hostile, had captured his interest because of its collaborative approach to North-South interests.[33]

After much discussion, Trudeau turned to nuclear questions, where "the Commonwealth Conference had not been encouraging." There, he said, many nations "see the control of nuclear proliferation as an example of the white races trying to keep secrets from the brown and black peoples." There was even "admiration for India." To Trudeau's surprise, Jørgensen accepted India's claim that the explosion was for peaceful purposes. Trudeau responded sarcastically: "If it had been South Africa, would you believe them?"—and ended by making "it quite clear that the Canadian Government believes in and supports" NATO. There had been divided opinion some years before, he admitted, but opposition had now disappeared.[34] In all these visits, Trudeau gained support for the contractual link, though the discussions did not define what that link might mean or, concretely, what it would grant to Canada beyond any gains realized in the General Agreement on Tariffs and Trade in the Tokyo Round negotiations.

Trudeau's attempts to expand Canada's interest beyond the United States were supported when he was honoured with the freedom of the City of London, and the speech he presented at Mansion House reflected not only his far-ranging education and experience but the influence of his good friends Marshall McLuhan, Lee Kuan Yew of Singapore, and Julius Nyerere of Tanzania. The occasion, he began, bore significance because it occurred in Britain, where "the concept of freedom has been so debated, its meaning so extended, its practice so protected." Now humanity must move on from the established "freedoms of" to the "freedoms from": want, hunger, disease, nuclear holocaust, and environmental degradation.

> And we find that this struggle is more complex, more awkward, and more wide-ranging than we had thought possible. . . . What involves us today is a struggle of far greater proportions yet with far fewer handles for men and women to grasp. It is not the absence from the scene of a Pitt or a Churchill that causes men and women to wonder in what direction humanity is pointed; it is the nature of the adversary. More than

eloquence and more than leadership is required to come
to grips with monetary imbalances, nutritional deficiencies,
and environmental pollution. . . . Yet these struggles are the
essence of life on this planet today. They are not struggles
that can be confined to a law court or a battlefield or a
House of Commons; they require institutions and regimes
of immense dimensions and novel attributes; they call — in
the final analysis — for worldwide cooperation, for they
demand that we struggle not against other human beings
but with other human beings. They demand a common
cause of humanity.

There must be a new balance, Trudeau stated — "nothing less than
an acceptable distribution of the world's wealth." To achieve this
"global ethic" in a "global village," all "are accountable." "None
of us can escape the burden of our responsibility. None of us can
escape the tragedy of any failure. Nor, happily, will anyone escape
the benefit, the joy, the satisfaction — the freedom — which will
accompany the discharge of that responsibility."[35]

Ivan Head, Trudeau's foreign policy adviser, was an idealist;
Henry Kissinger, Ford's foreign policy adviser, was a realist. Trudeau,
pragmatically, could be both, and in 1975 Kissinger's interests and
Trudeau's values and interests converged. Ironically, Canadian
and American bilateral issues, particularly in energy, culture, and
investment, had become more difficult. Kissinger, however, cared
little for the minutiae of Canadian-American relations and focused
instead on Canada's role on the world stage. There he saw a performance of which he approved. Canadian skill could augment
America's strength at a time when the behemoth staggered. When
Kissinger met Canadian officials in Washington in March 1975,
he "found little to cheer about" on the international scene. He
was unusually subdued as he proceeded "from one gloomy prog-
nostication to another." The Middle East was "a god dam mess,"

and the Israelis were to blame for the failure of his latest efforts to achieve a settlement in the aftermath of the 1973 war. He told the Canadians that his officials sometimes became exasperated with the Canadians and recommended strong reactions against Canada, "but he did not do so because he felt that problems would solve themselves and this was almost always right."

Having calmed Canadian fears about bilateral problems, Kissinger asked MacEachen whether he could approach Israel "to urge it to adopt a more flexible attitude."[36] Earlier, a United Nations Congress on the Prevention of Crime and the Treatment of Offenders had been scheduled to be held in Toronto, and Canada was now debating whether to permit it to go ahead. A U.N. vote in 1974 meant that the Palestine Liberation Organization (PLO) could attend the conference, and Canada had consistently expressed strong opposition to the terrorist tactics of the organization. A few days before the meeting with Kissinger, MacEachen had condemned a terrorist attack in Tel Aviv "in the strongest possible terms." There was, he declared, "no possible excuse for sheer terrorism which results in cold-blooded murder of innocents." Regardless, he and his department believed that Canada could not refuse entry to the PLO representatives, but within the Cabinet, Barney Danson spoke for Jewish leaders who called on Canada to deny entry to the PLO. Ontario Premier William Davis, with the support of Liberal leader Robert Nixon and NDP leader Stephen Lewis, publicly called for cancellation of the Toronto conference. However, Senator Ray Perrault, British Columbia's representative in the Cabinet, pointed out that cancellation of the conference would surely mean that a 1976 Vancouver conference on human settlements would face the same fate. The Cabinet thus agreed to condemn the Palestinians, conciliate the Jewish groups, and announce that PLO representatives would be admitted on an individual basis.

Then, at a Cabinet meeting on July 10, Trudeau abruptly

announced that "after much reflection, he . . . had reached the stage where he was not prepared to tolerate future violence." He would "prefer the support of the Canadian people than admiration from certain international quarters," and Canada would deny entry to the PLO. There was an angry discussion on all fronts, with some ministers pointing out that the United States had condemned Palestinian terrorism but had not condemned harsh Israeli retaliation. The Vancouver conference, others warned, would surely be a casualty, and even the 1976 Montreal Olympics could be threatened. Trudeau, who loathed terrorism, stood firm and said he was prepared to "accept the consequences of such a decision." Moreover, the decision should be a wake-up call to the United Nations, "where questions of substance were increasingly being sacrificed to political issues." MacEachen then met with the U.N. Secretary-General to request that the conference be postponed. The U.N. refused — and in short order, the conference took place in Geneva.[37]

In their foreign policy memoir, neither Trudeau nor Head mentions this decision, though it attracted enormous attention, and astonishingly, they make only four brief references to "Israel," three to the "Middle East," and none to the Palestinians. Trudeau had disliked the United Nations ever since he had served as part of the Canadian delegation in 1966. The General Assembly's raucous debates in the seventies and, in particular, its condemnation of Zionism as racism confirmed his low opinion of the organization. His aversion to terrorism intensified during the 1970s after the October Crisis and the rise of urban terrorism in Europe, as exemplified in the Baader-Meinhof gang and in the PLO massacre of Israeli athletes at the 1972 Munich Olympics.

Like the European left, generally, Trudeau admired Israel. He had done so since his visit in the late 1940s, when he saw Israeli desertlands transformed into lush orchards and green fields. He admired Israeli pluck, the egalitarian kibbutz, and the social democratic principles of the Israeli Labour governments of the postwar era. These beliefs were welcomed in his Mount Royal constituency, with its large Jewish population, which voted overwhelmingly Liberal. Trudeau's identification with the struggle for civil rights in the fifties and sixties solidified his ties with the Canadian Jewish community, and his appointment of Bora Laskin, first to the Supreme Court and then, in December 1973, as chief justice of the Supreme Court, thrilled the Jewish community.* Yet there were complications.

---

* Laskin actually owed his appointment to Justice Minister Otto Lang and, indirectly, to Margaret Trudeau. The sudden resignation of Chief Justice Gérald Fauteux before Christmas 1973 meant that a replacement was needed immediately. Margaret was in the advanced stages of pregnancy, and Trudeau asked Lang to deal with the matter. Normally, the position would pass to the most senior justice—at that time, the conservative westerner Ronald Martland—and Trudeau apparently expected precedent to be followed. Lang, however, recommended Laskin, and Trudeau warmed to the idea quickly. Martland was bitterly disappointed and suggested that Laskin's Jewishness was the reason for the appointment. This probably did influence Trudeau, who correctly believed that Jews had for too long been excluded from the bench, the boardroom, and the Cabinet. He appointed the first Jewish Cabinet ministers, the first Jewish Supreme Court judge, the first Jewish chief justice, the first Jewish principal secretary to the prime minister (Jack Austin), and the first Jewish deputy minister of external affairs—Allan Gotlieb—who later became the first Jewish ambassador to Washington. When a Jewish group met with Trudeau and thanked him for all he had done for the community, he expressed surprise. Once presented with the list, he responded, "I guess I did." On the appointment of Laskin, see Philip Girard, *Bora Laskin: Bringing Law to Life* (Toronto: University of Toronto Press for the Osgoode Society, 2005). Martland made his charge in an interview with the Osgoode Society in 1985 (see Girard, 410–11). Lang has confirmed Girard's account. The meeting with the Jewish group was described in a conversation with Berel Rodal, June 2008.

In his Mansion House speech, Trudeau had declared his determination to play a part in creating bridges between the North and the South, and the continuing Israeli occupation of the West Bank and Gaza had become an increasingly bitter issue in the South. The 1977 election of the Likud Party under Menachem Begin, who had been an Irgun terrorist under the British mandate, profoundly disappointed Trudeau. Begin then angered him when he said he would turn Toronto Jewish voters against the Liberals unless Trudeau moved the Canadian Embassy from Tel Aviv to Jerusalem. "You can tell them [Canadian Jews] what you want," he retorted, "but I don't think it would be very courteous—and I don't think it would be very effective." Joe Clark, who was then the Conservative leader, took Begin's bait and endorsed the move—to his eternal regret. Trudeau never forgave Begin. Herb Gray recalled relatively little interest in Israeli issues in the early and mid-seventies within the Liberal Party but said that matters changed quickly: Trudeau's irritation with Begin was so great that when Gray visited Israel, he sent the Israeli prime minister a sharp oral message: Be more constructive.[38]

France, another early love for Trudeau, disappointed him because of its leaders and policies in the early seventies. When Canada had tried to secure the contractual link with Europe, French Finance Minister Valéry Giscard d'Estaing had been among the Europeans who were cool to the idea. He just would not treat Canada as a serious country. Then, in 1974, after the sudden death of Georges Pompidou, he became France's president. Anxious to assert French leadership, particularly during an international economic crisis, Giscard invited the leaders of the world's major economies to meet at a presidential château at Rambouillet in the late fall of 1975. Those invited included the leaders of the four largest economies—the United States, Japan, West Germany, and Britain—as well as Italy, which ranked seventh. Canada, number six, was ignored. Head was incensed, but attempts to secure an invitation failed despite strong support from the Germans, the Japanese, and the Americans. The United Kingdom gave late and lukewarm support. Trudeau told Kissinger that "Canada should not have to use up its credit on this question," nor should the United States.* The North Americans should not approach the Elysée Palace on bended knee.

Trudeau, fortunately, had two friends in Washington who promised that they would retaliate later. Ford and Kissinger kept their promise by inviting Canada to the successor summit scheduled for Puerto Rico in June 1976. Although the French persisted in trying to exclude Canada, Chancellor Helmut Schmidt and Kissinger refused to budge on Canada's inclusion. As a social democrat, Schmidt wanted Trudeau to participate because of his own interest in North-South issues. In the end, Trudeau, MacEachen, and Energy Minister Donald Macdonald attended

---

* External Affairs Minister Allan MacEachen told his department to treat Kissinger like a minor head of state, especially in media coverage. Unfortunately, he got his wish. A head table microphone was not turned off during the liqueurs, and it recorded Kissinger's view that his recent boss, Richard Nixon, was an "odd, artificial, and unpleasant man," though one of the better presidents. One of the worst, he averred, was John Kennedy, whose first two years were disastrous and who died having achieved nothing "substantial." An outraged Tricia Nixon wrote to protest. Kissinger mixed up the daughters and called Julie Nixon to apologize, which he did with some grace. It appears the Kennedys received no apology. National Security Archives, The Kissinger State Department, Telcons, Document 8, Telcon with Secretary of Agriculture Earl Butz, Oct. 16, 1975, and Documents 9a and 9b, Telcons with Julie and Tricia Nixon, Nov. 1 and 4, 1975. There is an account of Kissinger's overheard remarks in the New York Times, Oct. 17, 1975. These documents can be viewed electronically at http://www.gwu.edu/~nsarchiv/NSAEBB/NSAEBB135/index.htm.

the June 27–28 summit, where Trudeau played a modest role in advancing discussion on the North-South issues. Head acted as Trudeau's sherpa, making preparations for the meeting—yet one more rebuke to External Affairs.

No formal summit resolution incorporated Canada. It simply became a member of the G7, which has sometimes acted as the world's *directoire*, and Canada's membership in this elite group (and later the G8) has transformed the role of the prime minister in international affairs. The annual gathering has provided the opportunity for regular meetings with the most powerful Western leaders, occasions where bilateral issues are discussed at the sidelines and where Canada participated in some of the major decisions of the last quarter of the twentieth century. Leaders matter, and so do their meetings. Giscard, knowing that he would now face Trudeau informally every year, moderated his hostility to Canada just at a moment when relations between Canada and France were of critical domestic importance. Moreover, historians have found that, after 1976, the Canadian files in American presidential papers were more complete and personal. Canada, very simply, became harder to ignore after it was admitted to the G7.[39]

—

Valéry Giscard d'Estaing, Helmut Schmidt, and the Americans created the G7 to deal with international economic issues at the leaders' level, but it soon strayed beyond its economic mandate. The Nixon *shokku* of 1971, which removed the dollar from the gold standard, and the oil crisis of 1973 had shattered many of the assumptions of the postwar era about the management of the economy. From the perspective of the twentieth century's end, two prominent Canadian economists remarked on how decisive that change had proved to be. Tom Courchene claimed that "virtually all aspects of the environment that underpinned the 1950s and 1960s explosion of social programs in Canada evaporated in the decade or so following the initial oil price shock." But Canada was not unique. Richard Harris pointed out that "productivity growth declined in virtually all industrial countries at about 1974, the same year as the first oil shock. This is also the date that most economists use to mark the beginning of the transition to the global economy and the decline in the rate of economic growth of the then-prominent industrial countries."[40]

The Canadian debate about what caused the crisis and what response the government should make mirrored discussions that occurred throughout the Western world. In some countries, government intervened to tackle the challenges of the new economic environment. In Canada, the decision to maintain a lower domestic price for oil, to establish a foreign investment review process, to develop a guaranteed annual income, and to maintain and even strengthen the social programs of the sixties, as the Trudeau government did in 1972 and 1973, reflected the views of many in the Prime Minister's Office—ministers such as John Munro, Allan MacEachen, Jean Marchand, and Marc Lalonde, and in most cases, Trudeau himself. Others dissented, most notably John Turner, his deputy minister Simon Reisman, and most Finance officials, along with other economically conservative ministers such as James Richardson, Jean Chrétien, and Bob Andras. Businessman Alastair Gillespie was fiscally conservative but adamantly nationalist, while Don Macdonald was less conservative fiscally but, on the energy issue, strongly nationalist.

The debate emerged around "stagflation" and the fundamental question of whether to deal with inflation or unemployment in an era where both were increasing rapidly. This troubling issue broke down the Keynesian postwar consensus and led to a major reassessment of what governments could do. Milton Friedman's Chicago School presented the greatest challenge to the old ideas, and his monetarist acolytes were found at the highest level of government as well as in the academy. In 1974 the Nobel Prize in Economics was awarded to the social democratic Swede Gunnar Myrdal and the Austrian-British economist Friedrich von Hayek, author of *The Road to Serfdom* (1944), who had called for a "shift back from Keynesian macroeconomics and the world of the multiplier to microeconomics and the world of the firm, where wealth was actually generated." This symbolized the profound debate about the role of the state and the operation of markets. If the sixties rang in what the economist John Kenneth Galbraith sympathetically called "the liberal hour," the seventies brought first its twilight and then the beginnings of a conservative dawn.[41]

Trudeau's education was Keynesian, his economic instincts were eclectic, his politics were egalitarian, and for all his intelligence his vision in this new dawn was often blurred. Tough times lay ahead.

Entering the House of Commons in 1972 with Alastair Gillespie, who was a valued Cabinet minister from 1971 to 1979. Gillespie was the only major businessman in the Cabinet throughout the seventies.

When Trudeau heard that Nixon had called him an "asshole," he replied: "I have been called worse things by better people."

Riding a camel in Benares, India, 1971. In his memoirs, Trudeau noted wryly: "British prime minister Edward Heath, who visited India at the same time, wrote that my 'élan and exuberance captured public attention and press headlines.'"

Premier Chou En-lai helps Pierre handle chopsticks, China, 1973. Trudeau called him "a fascinating person in his own right. A genuinely likable and impressive individual." According to Henry Kissinger, Nixon was particularly irritated that Canada had recognized the People's Republic of China before the United States did.

Fidel Castro and Trudeau are in tune. But despite the warmth and informal friendship of the 1976 visit that included Margaret and baby Michel—skin-diving, smoking cigars together, dancing under the moon at a spartan cabin on a little island—Trudeau formally cut off significant aid to Cuba on his return, after discovering that Fidel had knowingly misled him on the number of troops involved in Cuba's aggressive incursion into Angola. Years later, Castro made the journey to Canada for Trudeau's funeral.

"I didn't know about this marvellous feeling. It makes you eternally grateful for the miracle of life and for the mother that bore those children." Trudeau, *Memoirs*. Swinging Sacha in Vancouver airport, October 19, 1976.

Inscribed to Keith Davey by Trudeau: "Keith, has Team Canada just scored, or have we gained two points in the Gallup? Best Wishes, Pierre E. T., 1976."

Finance Minister John Turner and Trudeau had a difficult but often successful working relationship. In Turner's words, they enjoyed their personal relationship, especially in the early years.

CHAPTER TEN

—

WRONG TURNS

I n Ottawa the Finance Department and John Turner were unhappy about the 1974 budget that had triggered the election and the continuing battle with Marc Lalonde and John Munro about a guaranteed annual income, but the minority position of the Liberals had offered a strong justification for this approach. After the election, however, Trudeau immediately agreed that the nationalist and interventionist policies, such as the proposed foreign investment review agency and the creation of Petro-Canada, would continue, and this collective decision of Cabinet troubled Finance and its minister even more. Turner had hoped that after the election, Finance would again have its way, as in the early Trudeau years. At that time Trudeau and Turner were both believers in the importance of the welfare state. However, Turner now began to fear that Trudeau, in response to the economic crises of the seventies and the rise of monetarism in the making of public policy, had come under the influence of John Kenneth Galbraith—in particular the ideas he expressed in *Economics and the Public Purpose*. Essentially "socialist" in approach, this book responded directly to conservative economists Friedrich von Hayek and Milton Friedman by arguing that the state must respond through positive action, including government ownership, to promote public values and goals. Trudeau saw Galbraith often in these times, and the Harvard professor later recalled Trudeau's insatiable curiosity when they met at New York dinner parties and debated what the crises of the seventies meant for the traditional economics education they shared.[1] Turner was particularly alarmed when the Trudeaus and the Turners met accidentally on a Caribbean vacation and he found the prime minister engrossed in Galbraith's book on the beach.

But Trudeau heard other voices too, and he continued to establish "countervailing" forces within both his office and the Cabinet. The majority opinion supported Galbraith's earlier views about the need for balance between labour and business in postwar American capitalism. Albert Breton probably had the most influence. In the 1960s he had opposed nationalizing Hydro-Québec because it would benefit special interests for the most part, and this view now formed part of Trudeau's own arguments against nationalism. Breton also stated that the policies Finance and the Bank of Canada had followed in Trudeau's first years in office had created higher levels of unemployment in 1972. Accordingly, in a memorandum he wrote to Trudeau—"Do Markets Work?"—he criticized Galbraith's latest theories: "I personally think that as an economist and social analyst he is a lightweight and deserves very little attention." Trudeau had no good answers himself to the economic problems that exploded in 1975, and he found Breton a fresh, yet trusted, voice.[2]

The Canadian economy began to falter badly in the second half of 1974, and its problems persisted throughout 1975. Unemployment rose to 7.1 percent of the labour force (from 5.4 percent in 1974), the highest since the 1960–61 recession, while inflation reached 9.7 percent, the third-highest level in Canadian history (though this was an improvement on the 13.8 percent rate of 1974). Labour productivity declined for the second year in a row, and a record was set with approximately ten million days lost due to labour disruption. The federal public service, which had gained the right to strike largely through the influence of Marchand, Trudeau, and Pelletier a decade earlier, began the year with a series of rotating strikes and a demand for a 42.5 percent wage increase over one year. Dockworkers, steelworkers, and especially workers in Quebec, where preparations for the 1976 Olympics had created an overheated construction sector, made similar demands, and some did so violently. Voluntary restraint, epitomized by the Food Prices Review Board under the impressive Beryl Plumptre, was clearly inadequate to meet these challenges. Plumptre attacked supply marketing in agriculture, which she claimed made prices for agricultural goods high through restriction of production and control of supply. Eugene Whelan, the agriculture minister, flamboyantly countered that attacks on the marketing methods he had created did not help the government's reputation in rural areas.* Economists of all stripes pointed to these marketing arrangements as interference with free markets, which contributed to spiralling food prices—a major cause of inflation. When Whelan suggested in Cabinet in April 1975 that farmers be exempted from the proposed voluntary restraints, Trudeau replied archly that even highly subsidized sectors must participate.[3]

Long debates on economic policy took place in Cabinet in advance of the June 23, 1975, budget. On May 22 Turner warned

---

* Whelan and Plumptre crossed the country denouncing each other. They were once in an elevator in the Château Laurier and, in Whelan's words, "Somebody in the elevator said with a devilish gleam in his eye, 'Mrs. Plumptre, have you met Mr. Whelan?' And 'Mr. Whelan, do you know Mrs. Plumptre?'" Both answered yes and exchanged no other words. It was the only time they ever met. Eugene Whelan with Rick Archbold, *Whelan: The Man in the Green Stetson* (Toronto: Irwin, 1986), 154.

his fellow ministers that Canada faced a "surge of wages and the sagging of profits" over the next year. Moreover, Canada's export surplus was vanishing quickly because, in 1974, labour costs had risen 11.9 percent in Canada compared to only 6.9 percent in the United States, with the result that the dollar had fallen from $1.028 to 97.2 cents since the election of July 1974. Turner presented four options: severe monetary and fiscal restraints; mandatory wage and price controls; confiscatory taxes on wages and salaries, combined with excess profit taxes on business and professional income and a surcharge on investment income; and a neutral "holding" budget with some restraints, continued discussions with labour and business, and alterations in some programs. Bryce Mackasey, who had returned to the Cabinet, questioned Turner's statistics comparing American and Canadian labour costs, but Jean Chrétien, now at the Treasury Board and an economic conservative, was a strong advocate of restraint.

These same patterns prevailed in discussions on June 19, when Turner said that further study convinced him there were only two options: the neutral budget or mandatory controls. Despite the 1974 election pledge to oppose wage and price controls, there was some support for them now. However, the Cabinet and Turner opted for the "neutral budget"—one that created reductions in unemployment insurance and in the federal part of provincial shared-cost programs for medicare and hospitals. The budget also called for reduced growth in the public service, from 4.1 percent to 3.1 percent, with the added provision that public-sector wage increases should not surpass those in the private sector. Turner argued against higher taxes because profits were dropping, and he provided some plans to deal with the specific problems of youth and regional unemployment. But the minister of finance was squeezed. The soaring costs of the energy subsidy would have to be reduced, a move that would raise prices for consumers. This change, combined with the medicare and unemployment reductions, worried the Cabinet's progressive wing. At the end of this inconclusive meeting and with a divided Cabinet, Trudeau said that he would discuss ways of achieving more "balance" in the June 23 budget.[4]

Cabinet meetings had been tense for several months, as the differing opinions among the ministers hardened into simmering anger. In the early winter of 1975, the proposed guaranteed annual income died a slow, painful death, a victim of economic pressures and obstruction from Finance. Simon Reisman, the conservative deputy minister of finance, held to his conviction that the social spending binge of the sixties, what he considered to be the irresponsibility of Mackasey's unemployment plans, and the nationalist and NDP programs of the minority government period were behind the current inflation and economic troubles. He particularly disliked Michael Pitfield, the new clerk of the Privy Council, who was personally close to Trudeau and immune to Reisman's abrasive pressure. He also resented Turner's involvement in the process for voluntary restraints, consulting, as he had, with business, labour, and the provinces. Reisman saw the promotion of restraints as delaying what really had to be done — strong cuts in expenditures, government cutbacks, and taxation changes to increase revenues. Equally galling were Turner's frequent absences as he went about his prestigious work as the head of the International Monetary Fund committee that was recycling oil funds. Still, Turner was essential: a strong minister who could stand up to Trudeau. Before long, rumours began to spread that Turner might leave Canadian politics to become president of the World Bank. The rumours caused Bay Street to tremble and Reisman to fret.[5]

Not surprisingly, given his frustration, Reisman had announced, on December 4, 1974, that he would quit his post. He refused to criticize the government publicly, but he told the *Globe and Mail* that he wanted "a better chance to fly on my own wings. And the style of government today is such that it is very difficult to do anything that fully absorbs [my] talents and abilities." Jim Grandy, a deputy minister at Industry, Trade, and Commerce who shared most of Reisman's views and whose position required the implementation of the Foreign Investment Review Agency, also resigned. He joined Reisman in an Ottawa-based lobbying firm, one of the first of the multitude of companies in which former bureaucrats advised business and other interests on how best to manage ministers and governments. Trudeau replaced Reisman with Thomas "Tommy" Shoyama, who had served previously in the socialist governments of Saskatchewan. For journalists, Reisman and Grandy became useful sources of informed and strong criticism of their former superiors and their policies.* By these means they fuelled the growing forces within the Canadian business community that were turning against the Trudeau government and its policies.[6]

Meanwhile, Turner's prestige continued to grow as journalists looked to him for leadership and speculated on who would be the first to go, Trudeau or Turner. On March 31, 1975, Turner wrote an article paying tribute to Reisman, which hinted, accurately, that Reisman thought government spending was out of control. Coming on the eve of budget preparations, it signalled to his colleagues that he understood Reisman's desire to "fly on his own wings." The voluntary process was frustrating,

---

* Reisman soon became associated with the conservative Fraser Institute, which business strongly supported. Reisman wrote an essay in the fall of 1976 that appeared in a Fraser publication—Michael Walker, ed., *Which Way Ahead? Canada after Wage and Price Control* (Vancouver: The Fraser Institute, 1977). He strongly attacked the "gadfly" Galbraith, blamed government spending and unemployment insurance as the main domestic sources of inflation, and castigated Trudeau for his anti-market sentiments and declared they would not be accepted "as long as Canadians retain their political freedom." Trudeau and his colleagues were understandably outraged.

labour's demands were too great, and Trudeau's help was just not
enough. Turner, an experienced corporate lawyer, was fully
aware of the wiles of business and the demands on labour
leaders. As Ron Graham, Trudeau's later amanuensis, wrote, the
world that Turner knew "usually required the Prime Minister to
invite the labour leaders for a drink at 24 Sussex, say, or to slap
the backs of the chief executive officers while preaching to them
about their duty to the nation." Trudeau, however, "was never
comfortable using the prestige of his office to achieve his goals."
The tortuous process of drawing up the June budget confirmed
the distance between the two men. The rift had already been
demonstrated in January 1975 when Trudeau revealed in
the House of Commons that he had taken advice from a select
group of economists who had never even met with Turner.*

---

* Trudeau admitted that his principal secretary, Jack Austin, had convened a
group of economists to give him independent advice. That advice was frequently critical of Finance, which regarded the group as a threat to its own
position within government in a fashion similar to the attitude of External
Affairs to Ivan Head. The *Montreal Star* (Jan. 28, 1975) observed that "to establish a panel of economic advisers without telling the Minister of Finance is as
baffling as it is typical of the Prime Minister's style. That sort of action does
more than simply reflect Mr. Trudeau's well-known personal insensitivity, the
snub helps weaken the credibility of the Finance Minister, and thus, of the government." The members of the group expressed many different opinions and
were publicly identified as Albert Breton (University of Toronto), Thomas
Wilson (University of Toronto), Carl Beigie (C.D. Howe Institute), Grant
Reuber (University of Western Ontario), John Helliwell (University of British
Columbia), and private sector economist Benjamin Gestrin of the Canadian
Imperial Bank of Commerce. Under pressure from Turner, Trudeau disbanded
formal meetings of the group, although informal discussions continued.

The government's economic leadership seemed in disarray—
dispirited and uncertain.

With the collapse of the voluntary effort and the approval of
the Cabinet, Turner announced the "neutral" budget on June 23.
Business response was generally favourable because of the investment tax credit, housing funds, and the reductions in planned government expenditures. Nevertheless, economist Thomas Wilson
criticized the budget for "its inflationary and deflationary effects";
he warned that "the higher fuel costs would increase the rate of
inflation and also slow down the growth in real economic activity."
Breton shared these views and told Trudeau that the budget was
harmful and "stagflationist," in that it contributed "both to inflation and, given current monetary policy, to deflation." The
problem resulted from faulty analysis by Finance officials. He
feared that the budget would contribute, along with other factors,
"to setting the stage for wage and price controls later in the year."
He was right: all through the summer months the players
rehearsed their scripts and pressure mounted for the drama to
begin. The lead role fell to John Turner—but then he hesitated.
He made a list of "pros and cons" for his staying on in government,
as he had several times before in the seventies, but this time the
cons trumped the pros: Trudeau had not backed him on voluntary controls or restraint in a party that was increasingly and
"dreamily left." He decided that it was time to go, with his head
held high, before he tripped on the snares in the stage before him.[7]

Turner made an appointment to see Trudeau on September
10. They met in the prime minister's historic East Block office, but
there was no real communication between them. Turner offered
his resignation and Trudeau asked about the bench or the Senate,
but he offered no alternative ministry. The conversation fell flat.
Turner left the office and immediately drafted his letter of resignation from the government. In Radwanski's view, he left "because
he had grown bored and frustrated working with a prime minister

who didn't particularly like him, who seldom praised him, and who refused to make him feel special." Turner later told his early biographer Jack Cahill that the meeting illuminated the differences between them: "The guy is a Cartesian logician and I'm an empiric guy. I'm an Anglo Saxon. I'm not for codes and all that. I'm for working it out." In an interview with Radwanski, published in January 1978, Trudeau was surprisingly frank. "I thought . . . the guy has a hell of a lot of qualities and why . . . should he stay in a job . . . when the boss or prime minister isn't his friend and associate. . . . And when John told me, 'I'm getting out because I want to have more time with my family and kids,' to me it meant exactly that."

Journalist Vic Mackie, who had been "tipped off," presented Turner's side of the story in the *Montreal Star* one month later. Turner, he claimed, would have stayed, but Trudeau refused to woo him. He even told him that his resignation would mark the end of his chances to become prime minister. Not so, Mackie wrote: "It may have been the best move . . . to ensure that he eventually moves into the Liberal leadership if he should decide to make a bid for it when the time comes." When Turner arrived at the Ottawa Rough Riders–Edmonton Eskimos football game in Ottawa one week after he quit, he was greeted with thunderous applause from the crowd of twenty-nine thousand—a measure of his personal popularity and the growing unpopularity of the government.[8]

The Prime Minister's Office responded coolly to Turner's resignation letter, assuring him that because he "did not base [his] resignation on any policy disagreement," Trudeau would continue to call on his "good counsel." The *Globe and Mail* thundered its dissent beside a splendid cartoon showing a bedraggled Trudeau handing Turner a steering wheel for a broken-down car. "Thanks a lot. I'll walk," Turner says. The *Globe* declared that Turner was "unable to arouse the Prime Minister and his Cabinet colleagues to the need for decisiveness to ward off the dangers of collapse.

Mr. Turner has taken the only step left to him. He has bolted the either-or-and-on-the-other-hand lethargy of the Trudeau administration."[9]

Turner's resignation was the tipping point for change. On September 5, five days before Turner resigned, Breton wrote to Trudeau: "It is difficult to know why virtually the entire Economic Establishment in Ottawa now favours wage and price controls." Trudeau met with his Cabinet a week after the resignation and decided to follow the economic establishment, thereby reversing the pledge he had made so dramatically a year before. What had been planned as a careful realigning of ministries suddenly became a major Cabinet shuffle as Trudeau moved Donald Macdonald from Energy, where he had clashed bitterly with Peter Lougheed, to Finance. Despite his reputation as a progressive, Macdonald had strong Bay Street ties. In Christina McCall's words, he "had never drawn the distrust from his colleagues that always clung to Turner's glossy ambition like flies to sticky paper."[10] Previously, Macdonald had resisted the powerful urgings of the Ottawa economic establishment, but now he accepted Trudeau's plea that he stay on as the government moved haltingly toward controls.

Macdonald hammered out the details of the program but did not conceal his disdain for what he was doing when he emerged from a long Cabinet meeting on October 9: "The kind of restraints we have in mind are unprecedented in peace time," he said. "We are moving into an era of government intervention in the economy. If you don't find it as frightening as I do, then let me know." Trudeau, who had held out until the end against controls, seemed to place the blame for controls on Canadians: "We assume that the people want the government to take action, and that's what we're doing." He invited the provincial premiers to his home for lunch on Thanksgiving Day, October 13, and that evening, dressed in a banker's blue suit for a special televised speech, told Canadians with earnest demeanour that he would not freeze wages and prices but would "control" the wages and prices for government employees and 1,500 of the largest industries. The goal would be to protect the weakest in society, and above all, to inspire "Canadians in great numbers" to "practise voluntary restraint." It was, the *Globe and Mail* declared, "inflation control if necessary, but not necessarily inflation control." It was neither good public policy nor a good performance.[11]

An Anti-Inflation Board chaired by Jean-Luc Pepin, with Beryl Plumptre retaining and expanding her previous authority, would monitor wages and prices and roll them back where appropriate. Another agency was responsible for enforcement. After three years, the Canadian people would judge the success of these measures at the polls. Early responses were not encouraging. In the House, the Conservatives quickly reminded everyone of Trudeau's assault on Stanfield's similar proposals a year earlier: "Zap, you're frozen!" The New Democrats, who now formed the government in three provinces and held the balance of power in Ontario, reflected the angry response of organized labour to the proposals. According to Keith Davey, labour leader Dennis McDermott had always said that he hated the Liberals but "really loved 'that s.o.b. Trudeau.'" Once the controls were in place, Trudeau became a "turkey"—and any thoughts of McDermott as a potential Liberal candidate died. In a judicious assessment by public service economist Ian Stewart, the decision to invoke controls "seemed to have no support from any quarter. For much of the business community, the prospect of a reduction in cost pressures was tempered by its growing philo-sophical aversion to government intervention. For the labour community, relations with government, which had been charac-terized by growing unease, degenerated into open protests. . . . For the general public, the imposition of controls represented a dra-matic political about-face, the breaking of an election promise that has been thought by many to have had an enduring effect on fun-damental political support for Prime Minister Trudeau."[12]

—

Trudeau was unusually pensive that fall of '75. Margaret was pregnant with Michel, who was born on October 2. Her emotional turmoil, always high during and after pregnancy, weighed on the marriage and on Trudeau's concentration. Aides noticed that their briefing notes lacked the crisp corrections and annotations from the prime minister's hand. The loss of Pelletier and Marchand's estrangement hurt Trudeau deeply. For Pelletier's Hochelaga seat, Trudeau turned to Pierre Juneau, a *Cité libre* colleague who had chaired the Canadian Radio-Television Commission with authority and grace. He became the new minister of communications; but then, unexpectedly, on October 16, three days after the announcement of controls, the voters of Hochelaga rejected him decisively in favour of a Conservative whom Pelletier had trounced twice before. Claude Ryan correctly observed that Trudeau, in choosing Juneau, had harked back to the ideas of the past and that a new generation had emerged in Quebec that he did not know. Soon polls confirmed what Hochelaga suggested: the Liberals were in political trouble. The November Gallup poll revealed that the party stood at 38 percent, the Conservatives at 32 percent, and resurgent New Democrats at 22 percent. That same month, when the Liberals met for their biennial convention, a surprising 19.2 percent voted in favour of a leadership convention—twice the percentage that had voted for review after the disastrous 1972 election. Trudeau was further humiliated when a rebellion among backbenchers and party loyalists forced Keith Davey, Trudeau's apparent choice for party president, to back down when a yet unknown Maritimer, Senator Al Graham, announced that he would stand for the office.

In the House of Commons, a series of scandals provided an unfortunate counterpoint to the calls for restraint. An Air Canada vice-president had purchased a villa from a holiday resort that had just signed a contract with the airline but had made no payments on the mortgage. Even more seriously, Senator Louis Giguère, a well-known Liberal fundraiser, had made $95,000 on a quick sale of stock given him by Sky Shops after it had received a government lease for duty-free operations at Dorval airport. When the RCMP went to Marchand's parliamentary office to interview him about the lease on November 27, the former transport minister angrily ordered them away. He objected to a CBC crew accompanying the police, denounced the Mounties as acting above the law, and seethed, "I don't want another CIA in this country." Even the politically astute Marc Lalonde lost his cool: when questioned by Eric Malling of CTV, he retorted that "saying the French-Canadians are corrupt and the Italians are corrupt, only you, us, Wasps, are pure and honest, frankly, I think that is a lot of BS." Of course it was, but that fall BS stuck.[13]

Trudeau now seemed far away from the celebrations of July 8, 1974, when he, in an exquisitely casual beige summer suit, and Margaret, in a flowered sundress, celebrated his election triumph in a "strong and confident" Canada. He appeared even more distant from that 1968 spring morning when, as Canada's new bachelor prime minister he had taken possession of 24 Sussex, bearing only two suitcases. Times had changed, dramatically so. Trudeau could not escape the general scorn for politics, stained deeply by Watergate in the United States and by Sky Shops and Marchand's sad antics in Canada. The finest American chronicler of the times, the novelist John Updike, recalled the mid-seventies as a middle state between the sixties revolution and something darker, a time when "college kids had already pulled back from revolution and dharma, afraid of finding no place in the slumping economy and of getting shot in futile protest as at Kent State."[14] Two assassins tried to shoot Gerald Ford during his short presidency, but failed. In Quebec, Trudeau avoided large meetings because militant unionists would menacingly confront him at such assemblies. While there was no whiff of financial scandal around the prime minister, he was careless, especially when he called upon Canadians to accept restraint voluntarily. In the House of Commons, Conservative MP Tom Cossitt harassed him continually about his expenses, the private jets that whisked him away on weekends, and above all, the expensive swimming pool that was constructed beside the old mansion on Sussex Drive.

Trudeau had been extremely parsimonious in his first term in office, but in 1972 he told Margaret she could redecorate the residence as she had wanted to do earlier. Then he decided that he needed a swimming pool at Sussex Drive, too. Just before midnight one day in late August 1972, Trudeau's principal secretary, Jack Austin, along with Jim Coutts and Michael Pitfield, knocked on Keith Davey's Ottawa hotel room door. They reported that Trudeau was insisting on a swimming pool, and they believed it would be politically disastrous. Davey must "bell the cat and talk [him] out of the idea." Davey met Trudeau, but the prime minister was adamant: "Keith, you have often told me that I'm the meal ticket for this party. Well, what would you say if I told you that your meal ticket considered the swimming pool a biological necessity?" Faced with Trudeau's obstinacy, the ingenious Davey thought he would secure a prominent medical authority who would declare, as Trudeau had suggested, that a daily swim was essential for the prime minister's good health. In his quest for appropriate authority, Davey began with the eminent Dr. Wilder Penfield, but after numerous consultations on what "biological necessity" entailed, he ended with his own general practitioner, Dr. Henry Fader, who willingly attested to the need for the pool. Donations to cover the cost of purchase and installation were tax-deductible and confidential. Trudeau gave $10,000 himself, but the amount was only a pittance in view of the final cost—$275,000.

As the shovels dug up 24 Sussex, Tom Cossitt's persistent attacks on the prime minister drew blood, not least because the MP had once been the president of the Leeds Federal Liberal

Association and he had led most of its members out of the party just before the 1972 election. Although he denied that official bilingualism triggered this migration to the Conservatives, he was a stern critic of the policy and, not surprisingly, was loathed by Trudeau because of his views. Clearly a maverick, he garnered attention and respect in many quarters when he refused to support a substantial boost in MPs' salaries—the product of an earlier all-party agreement. By the time the bill reached Parliament on April 8, 1975, inflation was rampant and calls for restraint were pervasive. The bill as proposed was less generous than the one initially agreed upon: rather than a 50 percent increase in the basic salary to $27,000, with a tax-free allowance of $12,000, the new bill provided for a still substantial increase to $24,000, with an allowance of $10,600. However, indexing to the industrial wage composite would begin earlier: 1976 rather than 1978. Most of the NDP members quickly defected, pointing out that old age pensions were indexed to the much more modest cost-of-living index and that the increases proposed for MPs far exceeded those of Canadian workers.

Cossitt and three other Tories joined nine NDP members in opposing the bill, voting for a hoist motion moved by House of Commons dean Stanley Knowles, which was defeated 170 to 13. The thirteen became heroes, resisting the temptation, in the *Globe and Mail*'s words, "to seize for themselves a cozy, personal refuge from inflation and leave the country to make whatever sacrifices might be necessary to hold off the deluge." The Liberal *Toronto Star* similarly attacked those who supported the bill as an "earnest band of grabbers concerned to make sure that the central problem facing Canada doesn't erode their comforts." These comments shook loose a few MPs from the coalition supporting the bill, including John Diefenbaker and Liberals Charles Caccia and former minister Bob Stanbury, but it passed on April 30. Immediately, it became a symbol of political excesses and Ottawa's distance from the concerns of ordinary citizens.[15]

Cossitt was a pest, but his relentless attacks wounded Trudeau. "On the one hand," he declaimed, "we have the average Canadian facing the inflationary increase in the price of gasoline, which is a necessary commodity of modern life, and on the other hand we have the unreal world of the Prime Minister as he drives around in a choice of two chauffeur-driven $80,000 six-miles-to-a-gallon Cadillacs, with the taxpayers of Canada, of course, paying all his grandiose bills." Or again, "We have the housewives of Canada continuously struggling with ever-rising food prices while the Prime Minister eats in an elegant style which, according to Government figures, is costing the people of Canada at least $15,000 this year alone. Perhaps he is even dining by candlelight, since in recent years he has purchased dozens of candles and charged them to the public purse." Cossitt discovered that 24 Sussex bought enough rye whiskey the previous year to serve a bottle each day. There were, of course, answers to these complaints: the cost of security for Trudeau's daily swims at the Château Laurier Hotel was exorbitant; the RCMP insisted on the bulletproof limousines; other national leaders spent far more on food and candles; and Trudeau did not drink rye, though other Canadians who came to 24 Sussex did. *Globe and Mail* columnist Scott Young mocked Cossitt's attack. The price of a prime minister, he argued, is "going up like everything else." What did Cossitt expect? "If the time ever comes when [Trudeau] goes to work on a bicycle after spending the morning hosing his Victory garden, tending a new batch of home-made beer and helping his wife freeze zucchini against the hard winter's entertaining ahead, the rest of us will be in so much trouble that we'll never notice."[16] No doubt his son Neil Young would agree.

In his Thanksgiving address, Trudeau said that the benefit of controls was that it would give "people time to understand and adopt the real cure, which is a basic change in our attitudes." Not surprisingly, this call for individual restraint rang hollow amid the furor over the pool, the pay raises, and other Ottawa "excesses." Bob Stanfield charged that "trust and confidence have been injured in our society." That fall Trudeau seemed distracted in the House. The attack on controls was relentless from labour and, increasingly, from business. But the polls indicated that most Canadians shared Trudeau's conclusion that the controls were necessary to shatter the inflationary expectations and, even more, to rein in the power of corporations and unions that served their own interests, not the common good.

—

Christmas 1975 was a difficult time for Trudeau. Margaret was once again caught in the psychological turmoil he simply could not understand. The polls were bad, the country's mood cynical, the prospects for the new year poor. At the Bank of Canada, Governor Gerald Bouey began to follow monetarist approaches, a policy that won support in the increasingly conservative business community. Nevertheless, Trudeau was in an expansive mood when he met CTV reporters Bruce Phillips and Carole Taylor for an interview on December 28. Taylor asked Trudeau, "What kind of new society do you see emerging?" Trudeau answered at surprising and dangerous length.

"Well, it's amusing, but I have been talking like this for five years now anyhow, perhaps seven or eight. The need in the changing times . . . to develop new values and even change our institutions . . . I think the first shock came in '73 with the OPEC crisis, and suddenly the industrialized world realized that it could be held to ransom for its supply of petroleum. It was a shock then and we . . . began to forget about it until we came to this control situation a couple of months ago. And people are realizing it's a different world and that you can't live in a different world with the same institutions and the same values that you had before—"

"When you mention a new society and a new economic order," an intrigued Phillips interrupted, "are you thinking in terms of the possibility of a complete rearrangement of the centres of power and decision making in Canadian society? Something on the Swedish model for example, a syndicalist or corporate state where the government deals directly with the big groups such as the corporations and the labour unions and every year makes a social and economic contract?"

Trudeau took the bait. "Bruce . . . one thing I'd want to make clear at the outset is that there is no master plan in my mind or in some little elite group in the Prime Minister's Office which will tell the world in general and Canada in particular where it must go in the next little while. I think there's a great deal of unease in the society. People are wondering who is in charge of the economy, who is in charge of the society, and they're concerned. They're worried, and they have cause to be, and it's my job as a politician to try and not only see where we've been and where we're at but where we're going, and I'm telling you that in most of the areas we've been discussing, the economy, the society, the international relation aspect, we'll have to take new directions, new and bold directions. The example you took on controls, economic controls, is very significant. Many people still see those controls as . . . a bit of strong medicine we'll have to take in order to get inflation down, but it's really more than that. It's a massive intervention into the decision-making power of the economic groups and it's telling Canadians we haven't been able to make it work, the free-market system. We've ended up with very high unemployment and very high inflation. We can't go back to what was before with the same habits, the same behaviour, and the same institutions, otherwise we'd be back to high unemployment and high inflation. So I have to get all of us to try and think what was wrong. You know, there's obviously no easy answers and there's no specific scapegoats. It's not the unions and it's not the government and it's not a matter of saying, well, if you just would tighten your belt a little bit up in Ottawa, everything would be fine."

"Is it 'bigness'?" Taylor asked.

Trudeau agreed it was: "Therefore our problem is how do you deal with bigness, not how do you do away with it. And some economists say all you've got to do is get back to the free-market system and make this market system work. It won't, you know. We can't destroy the big unions and we can't destroy the multinationals. . . . But who can control them? The government. That means the government is going to take a larger role in running institutions, as we're doing now with our anti-inflation controls—and as we'll presumably be doing even after the controls are ended because, I repeat, we don't want to go back to the same kind of society with high unemployment and high inflation. And this means that you're also going to have big governments. And it's not simply a matter of saying this government is spending too much and if they'd only cut down, things would go better. Things don't go necessarily better because we spend less on health or on welfare and leave the private sector free to spend more on producing baubles or multicoloured gadgets. The state is important, the government is important. It means there's going to be not less authority in our lives but perhaps more."

"I've always thought of you as a sort of small L liberal," Taylor remarked, "a believer in civil rights and the maximum amount of individual decision-making power, yet you seem to be winding up now presiding over a government which in your estimation is going to get bigger and more powerful and more likely to be making interventions in the state."

"Liberalism is not a doctrine, it's not something that you apply," Trudeau responded. "Liberalism is a way of thinking, a way of approaching problems to make sure that the individual gets the maximum of respect and, hopefully, as great an amount of equality of opportunity in Canada, in the world, as possible without being doctrinaire about it." If you need "more control of the big people," only the state can do it in a way that would permit "more flourishing of liberty in all the other areas, whether it be education or the arts or small enterprise." The state must intervene to protect that liberty to make sure that the "strong and powerful don't abuse their strength and power in order to take freedoms away from the little man."

"Aha," Cossitt declared the following day: "The Prime Minister clearly illustrated what many believe to be his real intention all along—namely, to take Canada right down the road to a dictatorial form of socialism or a similar form of plain old fascism, and that he will use just about any means or excuse to get there, even using the obviously necessary fight against inflation for such a purpose."[17]

Cossitt's analysis echoed much chatter at the doughnut shops across Canada, although the latest exploits of hockey greats Bobby Orr and Guy Lafleur probably maintained their dominant position. More serious was the extent to which a similar interpretation took hold in the boardrooms along Bay Street, the ski chalets at Tremblant and Whistler, the dining room of Calgary's Petroleum Club, Simon Reisman's living room, and even the Leeds Federal Liberal Association—which sent a letter to all Liberal associations across the country, claiming that Trudeau was "making statements which violate the very essence of Liberal philosophy and accentuate the differences between the federal Liberals and the true Liberals of Ontario." Earle McLaughlin, the chair of the Royal Bank, demanded an election if Trudeau wanted to change Canada's economic system, and Edgar Burton of Simpsons department store chain denounced Trudeau as a socialist, whose comments were "the most irresponsible thing I ever heard him say."

While Otto Lang assured westerners that Trudeau still believed in free enterprise, Alastair Gillespie persuaded Harold Corrigan, the president of the Canadian Manufacturers' Association (CMA), to call a meeting at the exclusive Toronto

Club for January 4, 1976. Corrigan opened the meeting and came immediately to the central question: "It was not necessarily what the Prime Minister had said (or even indeed what he might have meant) but what a very large majority of [CMA] members perceived him to be saying—that the free enterprise system had failed and that the government was going to have to design something else to take its place." Corrigan then asked Gillespie: "Is he trying to turn Canada into a socialist state using the powers of the anti-inflation legislation?" Gillespie responded in kind, telling the group that they could "react in a way which conveyed the impression to the public that the free enterprise system was designed for their benefit (or should at least be directed by them); that it is a static system for the benefit of vested interests; that it is unchanging and unchangeable," or they could "take the position that the free enterprise system is an evolving system, a resilient and dynamic system which had adjusted to change in the past, and would adjust to change in the future to meet the public interest." He left hoping that the group, which included Turner's future law partner Bill Macdonald, accepted the second interpretation. It did not.[18]

As the fury mounted, Trudeau was silent. The CTV interview had been aired on December 28, one day after it was taped, and Trudeau departed the same day for a vacation in St. Lucia, followed by a skiing holiday in British Columbia. When reporters finally found him on his vacation and asked about the controversy, he said he had "no worries" about the uproar. His comments horrified many colleagues, and he tried to repair the damage with a nationally televised speech to the Canadian Club of Ottawa on January 19, 1976. Trudeau denied that he had questioned "free enterprise." He emphasized that he had spoken about the "free market," which was not working and, indeed, had not worked in pure form since the Great Depression: "I have said that we haven't been able to make even a modified free market system work in Canada to prevent the kinds of problems we are now experiencing; and it will do no good to try to create a pure free market economy to solve our future problems, because that won't work either." Canada would maintain a mixed economy, and "very large sectors of the economy" would remain "where the free market and consumer choice continue to flourish." He attacked his critics for calling him a communist, a fascist dictator, and a radical leftist. "You can understand my hesitation," he remarked, "when my children ask me what I do for a living." He tried to provide reassurance, claiming that the government had no intention of introducing more regulation in small business, for example, "where free enterprise is strong, where individual initiative, independence and risk-taking are present, where self-reliant men and women continue to build a better life for themselves and their communities." The issue was simply "to what extent we will be controlled by government regulations, and to what extent we will be controlled by our own sense of responsibility." Labour and big business faced a choice, as did all Canadians.

When the speech received poor or lukewarm reviews, Trudeau knew much damage had been done.[19] Polls soon confirmed Trudeau's fears, as the Liberals fell dramatically and the Conservatives surged under their new leader, Joe Clark of Alberta.*

----

* The Gallup polls gave these monthly results:

	Liberal	PC	NDP	Other	Undecided
Jan.	39	37	17	7	42
Feb.	38	37	19	6	41
Mar	34	43	17	6	29
Apr.	31	46	17	6	32
May	31	44	21	5	37
June	34	44	16	5	32

Source: John Saywell, ed., *Canadian Annual Review of Politics and Public Affairs 1976* (Toronto: University of Toronto Press, 1977), 138.

What did Trudeau really mean? In truth, largely what he had said in his remarks in the Christmas interview. To be sure, his comments lacked focus and reflected confusion and even uncertainty. He had been reading Galbraith's recent tome, *Economics and the Public Purpose*, and had absorbed its argument for state activism and regulation, its defence of the social welfare state, and its wariness of big business and big labour. Indeed, Trudeau jokingly told Galbraith later that he hoped his remarks had helped his royalty statements, which they surely did in Canada. Yet Trudeau had resisted controls to the very end, until pressure from ministers, caucus, and the business community forced him to agree to impose some controls. And he did not dissent when Breton sharply criticized Galbraith. His wariness of big business was not ideological so much as practical—the attitude of a small businessperson who resented the market power of the large oil companies that boosted the costs of fuel for the apartments his family owned in Montreal. Trudeau had always taken an active part in the management of the small operations that made up the Trudeau family fortune. His attention to detail is clear, as when he opposed the excessive price that his family's amusement park (Parc Belmont) paid the giant Conklin organization for the "Hot Rods," "Silly Lilly," and "Costume Bob" rides. His papers are crammed with the family's financial records, and he paid close attention to the impact of taxes on his decisions.[20]

Although Trudeau understood business well, he did not think of himself as a businessperson, and his remarks in the interview reflect other influences, ranging from the social thought of the Roman Catholic Church through the socialism of his early mentors Emmanuel Mounier and Harold Laski to John Kenneth Galbraith. And his family believes that he blamed the character of business life for his father's early death, a factor whose influence cannot be measured but is surely significant.[21] With characteristic inquisitiveness, Trudeau was taking sides in the emerging debate about the management of the economy. He dissented from those who called for deregulation but knew that traditional Keynesian approaches had become ineffective. He was baffled and not alone: the prominent Ontario economist Ian Macdonald, who was then president of York University, asked in the fall of 1976: "Can we manage the economy any more? . . . Judging from the performance in the [May 1976] budget, the answer must be 'no.' That is not intended to dismiss the Minister's efforts or good intentions, but rather to ask the question whether 'the budget,' as a single instrument, can really do the job today that was assigned to it in the pure world of Keynesian ideals." Macdonald went on to say that, in the past, he "was as guilty as any when teaching monetary and fiscal policy of applying the unitary state of Keynesian economics to the Canadian federal system," but what occurred in the classroom did not reflect the real world of Canadian politics and its many policies. A former senior adviser to Conservative Ontario governments, Macdonald essentially agreed with Trudeau's analysis that "new values and new institutions" were needed and that the academic Keynesian hopes no longer fit the reality Canadian policy makers were likely to encounter.[22]

Trudeau shared these views about the ineffectiveness of applying traditional approaches, usually termed Keynesian, in the seventies. However, in the emerging debate between, on the one hand, monetarists or neo-conservatives and, on the other, the supporters of the postwar welfare state (for which Keynesian policies provided an intellectual foundation), Trudeau strongly took the latter's side. His economic panel had made him well aware of the debate, and in his Christmas interview he had referred to the monetarists, who wanted to "get back to the free-market system and make this market system work." He had a simple answer: "It won't." He did look to European social democracy for models and told Helmut Schmidt, a Social Democrat he admired greatly who shared his own "middle-of-the-road liberalism," that the German system of labour-business cooperation intrigued him. He and Schmidt began to work together on North-South questions in the mid-seventies, and the contemporary debate on a new international economic order also affected his views. He made little attempt to conceal them in private conversations.

In a remarkable "philosophical" conversation on August 6, 1976, with Thomas Enders, the impressive American ambassador to Canada, Trudeau reiterated the essence of what he had said the previous Christmas. He argued "that the economic systems of the industrial democracies are no longer working well and must be reformed fundamentally" and "that the industrial democracies are losing the struggle for the developing world." Trudeau referred "frequently to Club of Rome thinking on the need for new political and moral approaches to economies." Although he dismissed the extreme views of the Club's book *The Limits to Growth*, he did believe that "the great inflation and the 'great wastefulness' of the seventies shows that something is fundamentally wrong. . . . The market system, intended to mediate greed for social benefit, is instead being dominated by it, with each group vying to outgrab the others." A new social contract was needed, Trudeau concluded.[23]

And so, for many reasons, Trudeau took a strong position in this political and socioeconomic debate—because of his social Catholicism; his admiration for European social democracy and the equality of northern European societies; his suspicion of big business and, increasingly, big labour; his belief in the possibility of benevolent state action; his antipathy for the "wastefulness" of North American development bred from his love of the wilderness; and his longtime association with those who drew a lesson from the Depression that the free market could not deliver the public goods essential in a modern society. In taking sides, Trudeau gave greater clarity to what he meant by the "Just Society" than he had when he first used the term in 1968. However, the link he made between the broad questions of the role of the state and the specific Canadian policy of wage and price controls was

strained and unconvincing. Already, by August 1976, he could tell
Enders that most other leaders at the G7 now regarded the surge
in inflation as the product of exceptional circumstances, rather
than a fundamental change in the character of Western
economies, and that they believed state spending had been excessive. Nevertheless, Trudeau's opposition to the rise of monetarism
and its neo-conservative interpretations continued, and he refused
to restrict the state to only limited areas of activity. As he told his
friend Helmut Schmidt, an inveterate sailor, in navigating the
winds of economic change, he would tack to the left.[24]

—

The discussion with Enders revealed Trudeau's views on the
economy, as well as his increasing pessimism about Canadian
domestic politics. After the 1974 election, Trudeau's major difficulty in federal-provincial relations appeared to be with the
western provinces, especially Alberta. In his election night speech,
he regretted the Liberals' poor results in the West and indicated
that he intended to conduct a government for all Canadians. It
represented a peace offering to Peter Lougheed, whose strongly
critical letter to Trudeau published late in the campaign struck
many Liberals as unfair. The bitter dispute over the spoils of the oil
patch cleared up as soon as the big oil companies responded to
Edmonton's and Ottawa's grabs for revenue by pulling out their
drilling rigs. The quarrels continued, of course, because the stakes
remained huge, but the relationship was greatly improved by two
factors: the replacement of Donald Macdonald by Alastair
Gillespie as minister of energy in the fall of 1975 and the Trudeau
government's decision to raise oil prices, necessitated by a large
budgetary deficit incurred, in part, by the energy subsidy.

In 1975 Lougheed and Trudeau also worked together well
when they faced a crisis in the development of the oil sands, already

believed to be the jewel of Alberta's energy resources. Atlantic Richfield, which owned 30 percent of Syncrude, announced that it was withdrawing from the consortium that was poised to develop the sands. In Winnipeg on February 3, 1975, the federal government agreed to take 15 percent of Syncrude's shares, Alberta agreed to take 10 percent, and energy-poor Ontario agreed to take 5 percent. Macdonald, who had called Lougheed "vicious" and his energy minister Don Getty "dripping with venom," described the mood in February as cordial. Lougheed, in turn, told his provincial legislature that the Syncrude settlement and the federal government's willingness to move toward higher prices had created a "sense of stability" in the oil patch. This historic decision ensured that many years later the oil sands would indeed become an economic jewel, although Ottawa's critical intervention was rarely recalled.

The federal energy strategy released in the fall of 1976 pointed out that one of the major problems the federal government faced was the resistance of the "consuming provinces" to the decision to move the Canadian price for oil closer to the world price.[25] Of course, the federal government managed to irritate Albertans as well, and polls indicated that the era of good feelings after the summer of 1975 did not convince Albertans to vote Liberal. The creation of Petro-Canada and the announcement that it would be Canada's "window" on the energy world outraged many in the oil patch, as did the appointment of Justice Thomas Berger, a former leader of the British Columbia NDP, to investigate the building of the proposed Mackenzie Valley natural gas pipeline.* Trudeau's Christmas

---

* Well-informed journalist Peter Foster wrote about the reaction of the oil patch to the creation of Petro-Canada: "The walls of the Petroleum Club resounded with indignation at the thought that a 'window' should be needed on their activities. The oil community's more general regurgitation of its

musings of 1975 also seemed to confirm deep suspicions about the socialist views of the Liberal leader. However, it was Quebec, not Alberta, that presented Trudeau with his greatest political problems.

—

In his election night victory speech in July 1974, Trudeau expressed regret for his poor showing in western Canada but made no references to Quebec, where the Liberals had done very well. Robert Bourassa had won his overwhelming victory in 1973, and the federal Liberals had triumphed in 1974. Central Canada prospered in 1973 and 1974, and the federal government shielded Quebec, which used imported oil, from the OPEC shock by subsidizing imports to the province. Bourassa did irritate Trudeau, particularly in his musings about "cultural sovereignty" and a Canadian "common market," but Trudeau responded gently, knowing that a Quebec premier had distinct political needs. Times seemed good. Trudeau told a Montreal Liberal audience in January 1975 that "at one time there was talk of Quebec having a special status, but, fortunately, that is now a dead issue." And in the winter of 1975, Bourassa said that relations between Ottawa and Quebec City had "never been better." Certainly, he worried about his province and his language, but "today," he said, "with Pierre at Ottawa, we are in no danger."[26] There were serious differences between the two governments, particularly on Bill 22, which made

---

favourite philosophy, free enterprise good, government bad—intoned with about as much critical analysis as the 'four legs good, two legs bad' of the animals on George Orwell's farm—was now given a particular and all-too-close example against which to rail." Peter Foster, *The Blue-Eyed Sheiks: The Canadian Oil Establishment* (Toronto: Collins, 1979), 150.

French the official language of Quebec, limited the right of francophones and allophones to send their children to English schools, and placed restrictions on advertising only in English. However, Trudeau resisted calls to disallow the bill, even though difficulties were created because Bourassa introduced it just as the federal government was "having a lot of trouble selling . . . [its] concept of bilingualism to the rest of the country."

Gradually, however, the old distrust returned. Bourassa, Trudeau concluded, was "politically stupid," and he said so publicly. When school opened in the fall of 1975, the Bourassa government relented as a result of arguments from the fervently Liberal Italian community and gave a few more spaces in the English system to Italian-Canadian students. Then, suddenly, Bourassa's education minister, Jérôme Choquette, resigned in opposition to the decision and formed a new party, the Parti nationale populaire, which was designed to appeal to conservative nationalists.[27]

By this time, the Parti Québécois had reacted to its disastrous defeat in 1973 by stating that, once elected, it would hold a referendum on sovereignty, rather than leading the province immediately into independence. It took "clean government" as its slogan—and this proved effective. Bourassa had rushed development of the gigantic James Bay hydroelectricity project just as Mayor Jean Drapeau won the 1976 Olympic Games for Montreal. The resulting strain on the construction industry caused a breakdown in labour relations throughout Quebec and, not surprisingly, cost overruns and inflated wages among the trades. Soon, tales of corruption, payoffs to get work done, and sweetheart political deals were told everywhere. Bourassa responded in May 1974 by appointing a special commission chaired by Judge Robert Cliche, the former leader of the provincial New Democrats, assisted by labour leader Guy Chevrette and labour lawyer Brian Mulroney. Sensational testimony to the committee outraged the public and fascinated the tabloids. Suddenly, Mulroney was a celebrity in

Quebec—a circumstance that would have lasting consequences for Canada. The final report said that the commissioners "were too often faced with swindlers, crooks, and scoundrels." The head of the public service commission was judged to have shown "a serious breach of ethics," and the government was deeply wounded by the report it had itself commissioned.

Labour troubles continued, Olympic costs soared, and services were intermittent as workers closed down plants and roads throughout Montreal. Bourassa seemed ineffective in response. Claude Forget, a minister in the government at the time, later recalled his own frustration with Bourassa: "There was no corruption on any extensive scale, certainly not at the level of Cabinet members. But innuendoes and half-truths were used very skillfully; they played well in the media and thus created an image problem, which was compounded by Bourassa's personality. Not being confrontational, he would simply decline to answer or . . . say, 'Well, this is not true; why should we bother about that?'"[28]

As both federal and provincial governments stumbled through the recession, Trudeau and Bourassa began to tussle about a range of issues, including the financing of the Olympics, the patriation of the Canadian Constitution, and the visit of Queen Elizabeth II to open the Olympics. On some of the larger issues, progress occurred. The federal government's proposal for the end of conditional grants and the presentation of an Established Programs Financing Proposal pleased Bourassa, although he wanted all funds to come without any conditions. It was, however, the patriation of the Constitution that caused the most mischief. Trudeau had raised the issue in April 1975 when the mood between Ottawa and both East and West was good. The inevitable qualifications, disagreements, and fears soon arose, and Bourassa's opposition hardened in early 1976. He met Trudeau for a disagreeable two-hour lunch at the Quebec federal Liberal convention in early March. When an irritated Trudeau saw reporters there, he declared, in a vengeful spirit, that he had no intention of paying a penny for the Olympics. Then, before the Liberal crowd at the convention, he cut away at Bourassa for his fussing about the royal visit and especially for his refusal to work with him to patriate the Constitution. Did he want Canada and Quebec to be subject to the British Parliament? Did Canadians and Quebecers? Speaking without notes, Trudeau pressed his arguments with slang and invective when necessary. With contempt, he ridiculed his luncheon host: "I brought my lunch. He's coming. Apparently the guy eats nothing but hot dogs." The image stuck: the feckless, hopeless Bourassa ate "hot dogs."[29]

In this troubled climate, the language that airline pilots spoke suddenly became an abrasive issue that shaved away the civility of Canadian public life. English had been the language of air traffic control in Canada, but a 1962 directive allowed the use of French in emergency situations. French was used by pilots in Quebec, but the Official Languages Act led to a Transport study that suggested in 1973 that air traffic controllers in Quebec should be bilingual. Minister Jean Marchand set up a commission the following January to make recommendations on language use, but its appointment provoked the Canadian Association of Air Line Pilots to write to Marchand, declaring that "English must be the exclusive language of Air Traffic Control communications."[30] When Marchand's committee reported, it recommended that the use of French was appropriate in Quebec and the Ottawa area. Tempers flared, and the anglophone pilots and controllers firmly rejected the report.

When Otto Lang replaced Marchand at Transport in September 1975, he tried to achieve conciliation while insisting that there was a place for French in the air. He achieved little, as pilots and controllers began wildcat walkouts in June 1976, and international airlines, egged on by the Canadian pilots and controllers, announced a safety quarantine of Canadian airspace on June 24. The previous day, the government had appointed a commission to look into the safety of French in the air. French pilots organized their own union, Les Gens de l'air, to advance their case. Trudeau appeared on television to beg for reason, as francophones united to defend their language, and anglophone newspapers, with the notable exception of the *Toronto Star* and the English-language Montreal papers, insisted that safety alone should be the relevant issue. He pointed out that bilingual air traffic control worked well in many countries, that there were many unilingual French pilots in Quebec, and that safety would not be compromised. "What [the pilots and controllers] seem to be protesting, therefore, is the very idea of even looking at the possibility of having safe bilingual control at Montreal." Eventually, on June 26, Otto Lang, acting as mediator, hammered out an agreement with the anglophone group, but Les Gens de l'air claimed that it had not been consulted and that the agreement broke earlier promises. Trudeau was away at the time, attending a G7 meeting, but on his return he found his Cabinet divided, with the francophones rejecting the agreement. A furious and emotional Marchand then resigned, claiming that he could not remain a minister in a government that accepted such an accord. Trudeau accepted Marchand's resignation, stating that, "You will continue to make your irreplaceable voice heard and to pit your genuine character as a Québécois and a Canadian against all these false interpretations with which some are trying to subvert Quebec and divert Canada from its calling." He concluded: "With all my undiminished friendship."[31]

But Trudeau's government was not intact, and neither was Bourassa's. With the Olympics over, the air traffic control controversy less bitter, and the economy gradually emerging from recession, Bourassa met Montreal journalist Ian MacDonald for lunch at a private salon at Chez Son Père in September 1976. Over whitefish and Chablis, he told MacDonald that he planned to call an election in order to thwart Trudeau's attempt to patriate the Constitution. Nearly all the other premiers supported him, and the issue would appeal to francophone voters—who were united as never before in recent memory by the outrages of the air traffic controversies. MacDonald had his doubts, not least because the government was only in the third year of its possible five-year term. But Bourassa's triumph of 1973 had come after three years, and the precedent was tempting. Besides, there was always the separatist card to play, and polls indicated that support for separation was low. Bourassa fretted that Trudeau's proposal to patriate the Constitution, as well as a conference on the subject planned for December, would stir dormant separatist and nationalist feeling. So his office arranged for a private meeting between himself and the prime minister at the Hilton in Quebec City on October 5. At the meeting Trudeau remained determined to proceed with the Constitution, even on a unilateral basis if necessary. Despite the risks posed by Trudeau's position, on October 18 Bourassa called an election for November 15. When asked for his comment later that day, Trudeau would only say, cryptically, "everyone expected it."[32]

Bourassa had made a disastrous decision. The Liberal campaign faltered from the start. When Jean Marchand and Bryce Mackasey announced that they were leaving Ottawa to defeat the separatists and to ensure better language policies, the Quebec Liberals initially hesitated to accept what they considered to be damaged goods.* Eventually, they accepted, though, because

---

* Faced with weakness in his Quebec ranks in the fall of 1976, Trudeau asked Jim Coutts to recruit Brian Mulroney, who had recently lost the Conservative leadership contest to Joe Clark. Trudeau, who believed that Mulroney was the most dangerous candidate from the Liberal point of view, had called him after his loss to say that he had performed well at the convention and that he thought the Conservatives had made a decision that might actually help him. Coutts, a friend of Mulroney, offered him a Cabinet position and a seat in

rejection would have caused even more difficulties. The anti-separatist card was no longer a high trump because René Lévesque now had the referendum card to play, thus allaying fears that Quebec would leave confederation immediately after a separatist government was elected. Bill 22, Bourassa's language bill, which in Lévesque's words imposed "tests . . . on little shavers six and seven years old isolated from their parents" in order to determine whether immigrant children had "sufficient knowledge" of English, was "a horror" for anglophones.[33] And true enough, polls soon revealed that anglophones, a traditional bulwark for Liberals, were defecting to the Union nationale, whose new leader, Rodrigue Biron, favoured official bilingualism and a conservative economic program. A week before the election, the polls were dismal, with the PQ leading the Liberals 50 percent to 27 percent. Bourassa knew he would lose personally, and Claude Ryan prepared to endorse the Parti Québécois on the grounds that it would offer better government.[34]

Trudeau was aghast at what was happening. Political analyst Gérard Bergeron later wrote that because of the prime minister's battles with Bourassa, Trudeau "was the partial and involuntary artisan of the Parti Québécois' rise to power." Lévesque's biographer Pierre Godin agrees that the *"passivité"* of Bourassa in the face of Trudeau's insults helped Lévesque's cause.[35] Trudeau

---

Montreal, if he would join the Liberals. Mulroney, whose leadership bid had left him with considerable debts, told Coutts that he would remain with the Iron Ore Company of Canada, where he was now president. He also said that he remained a Progressive Conservative, although Trudeau's offer was "a lot more generous than [he] had received from [his] own party." Brian Mulroney, *Memoirs 1939–1993* (Toronto: McClelland and Stewart, 2007), 173, 187. Jim Coutts confirmed this story in a conversation with me.

would not have agreed, but his well-known contempt for Bourassa surely was a factor. He had concluded that Bourassa was a weak premier whose ambivalence and silences damaged the federal cause in Quebec.

On election night, the first returns reflected the pre-election polls as PQ support surged in every part of the province, even in the English bastion of West Montreal. With a strong majority assured, the Quebec premier-to-be suddenly found himself surrounded by a bunch of "athletic young men," who pushed him forward through an "uncontrollable mob" outside the Paul Sauvé arena in the francophone east end of Montreal. Perspiring profusely, Lévesque finally reached the stage and declared, amid a sea of fleur-de-lys and joyous supporters: "I've never been so proud to be Québécois. We're not a little people, we're closer to something like a great people!" Trudeau went on the air later and grimly told Canadians: "I am confident that Quebecers will continue to reject separatism because they still believe their destiny is linked with an indivisible Canada." Most observers, however, were not so sure.[36] In some ways, Trudeau welcomed Bourassa's departure and the absence of ambiguity. When Trudeau awoke the morning after the election, he was ready to fight René Lévesque: "I said to myself, 'Okay, now here's the adversary out in the open, and we'll be able to argue this thing to a decision. We'll see what kind of separatism they want, and what kind of a support they have' . . . the fat's in the fire—let's see what they've got and let's fight them." And so Trudeau began the battle of his life.[37]

Margaret Trudeau also watched Lévesque on election night as he electrified the chanting crowd at the arena. Her heart sank. Pierre's fight would continue, but she knew their marriage would die.[38]

—

CHAPTER ELEVEN

BEYOND REASON

T he marriage of Pierre and Margaret Trudeau began to disintegrate after the 1974 election, and following the provincial vote in Quebec two years later, it dissolved. Throughout the marriage, public and private had intertwined, sometimes with elegance and effectiveness, but at other moments with awkwardness and embarrassment. The private lives of prime ministers had been shrouded in Canada's past— Laurier's love for Émilie Lavergne, Bennett's frustrated romance with Hazel Colville, King's spiritualist adventures with his married neighbour Joan Patteson, and St. Laurent's depression— and none of these reached the public spotlight to the degree of Margaret and Pierre's estrangement. The new journalism of the seventies, combined with the Trudeaus' celebrity, placed the breakdown of their private relationship on the front pages of newspapers around the world. In 1979 it inspired a very good play, *Maggie and Pierre*, which begins with their first encounter in Tahiti, when Margaret tells Pierre that she has no need to read about Bacchanalian rituals in Gibbon's *Decline and Fall of the Roman Empire*: she has been there.

Pierre: That sounds like a long journey. How much farther
do you want to go?
Maggie: Forever. And you? . . . I want to be world renowned,
to shape destiny, to be deliriously happy. You might say, I
want it all.
Pierre: I want to be world renowned, to shape destiny, to be
deliriously happy. You might say, I want it all.

Linda Griffiths, the author and the first actor of the play, wrote at
the time that "Maggie and Pierre" were "epic characters," heroes
in that they contain "all the elements of humanity, magnified." In
justifying the play about two living people whose marriage disintegrated, she explained: "Their story has already been shared by
the whole country, and actually by a lot of the world as well."
Moreover, "Things are going too fast to have to wait for death to
tell the story." But if their dreams seemed so much alike at the
beginning, it was their differences that eventually drew them apart.
"Curiosity," Griffiths wrote much later, led Pierre to love a young
woman who "seemed his antithesis . . . the kind of person who
operated entirely on her instincts and passions, whose charm was
an openness as different from his own as could be." Trudeau was
at his best when he took a chance on love; it brought the risks
whose excitement drove his life. For Trudeau, public life was a
stage, and his insatiable curiosity made him the most interested
observer of all the players.[1]

Margaret told her side of the story in her books *Beyond Reason*
and *Consequences*, which chronicled the breakdown of the relationship in great detail. As evidence of the troubles began to seep
out, Trudeau maintained an increasingly dignified silence, responding to reporters who asked him about the state of his marriage with
a sharp retort: "Tell me about yours." When the press hammered
Margaret regularly for her riotous party life, he simply said, "She's a
good woman." In his memoirs he maintained discretion while

admitting some responsibility. He wrote about the way he tried to separate his private life from his political activities, allowing that he had doubts about Margaret's active participation in the 1974 election campaign. Despite these efforts, "some of the political life may have spilled over into the family life." He recognized that the blurring might have been unavoidable "because one of the problems of being in politics is that it is not always a good life for the spouse. The man or the woman in it is fighting all the time, with the excitement that goes with the active involvement in any contest; but the one who stays back home with the kids is stuck on the side-lines just hearing about the nasty aspects of it all, and not enjoy-ing the fight. In my case, what's more, I was a neophyte at both politics and family life at the same time. I married late in life, our three boys—Justin, Sacha, and Michel—arrived fairly quickly, and I was learning about marriage and parenthood at the same time as I was learning about the workings of politics. So perhaps it was a little too much for me and, regrettably, I didn't succeed that well." He chose to say no more, except that the five years after the 1974 election were "turbulent" and personally "difficult" times.[2]

Did those personal difficulties affect Trudeau's judgment and, therefore, Canada's political life? Stephen Clarkson and Christina McCall conclude that they did, because Trudeau "became increasingly disengaged as prime minister, appearing to drift away from his task, but then re-engaging abruptly when issues could not be ignored. During his third term in office—when he commanded a secure majority in the House of Commons and ought to have been at the peak of his form as leader—he was too disturbed to devote his full concentration to the challenges of his job, just at the point when his government fell victim to one crisis after another." McCall, a superb and respected journalist, tapped into the gossip of the press club, the Ottawa summer parties, and the House of Commons lobbies, where Margaret's troubles were whispered about and debated. A 1979 compilation of the best

newspaper articles of "the Trudeau decade" observed that the marriage and, especially, its conflicts dominated press coverage in the
mid-seventies, although the editors note, accurately, that many
anglophone journalists showed much less discretion and paid much
more attention than their francophone counterparts. Trudeau's personal troubles had a definite impact on his political life.

Coverage of these troubles began on September 17, 1974, when
Margaret, pale and visibly weary, emerged from Montreal's Royal
Victoria Hospital and told journalists that she was suffering "severe
emotional stress," a condition the prime minister's press office had
carefully concealed. Margaret's photograph and comments appeared
on the front pages of most Canadian and many international newspapers, and rumours quickly spread that she was a victim of postpartum depression. The first accounts were not sensational, although
several of the editorial pages nervously justified their coverage
because of Margaret's key role in the previous election. The
Canadian Annual Review of Politics and Public Affairs for 1974,
however, followed Canadian tradition and ignored the issue entirely.[3]

Margaret's distress after his most satisfying political victory
stunned Trudeau. She had initially retreated to her "freedom
room" in 24 Sussex, but then she took off without a passport on
a "freedom trip" to Paris, where she fruitlessly searched for her
former lover Yves Lewis before fleeing to Greece. There she
backpacked and spent nights in a sleeping bag on Crete. On her
return home, she immediately went off to New York to watch a
celebrity tennis tournament and came under the spell of Senator
Edward Kennedy, who enthralled her completely. Once back in
Ottawa, she began to drink heavily. A troubled Pierre demanded
to know if she had been unfaithful. Angry, she took a kitchen
knife, admitted she had "fallen in love," and threatened suicide.
"You're sick," he snapped, turning away in disgust. It was "all
[Pierre] said at last." Margaret was indeed sick. A hospital stay
followed, then a controversial trip to Japan with her sisters, paid

for by a Hong Kong shipping magnate, and on October 27 a nationally televised interview on the CTV network. Carole Taylor, a skilled interviewer and future politician, drew Margaret out as the interview proceeded.

> Taylor: Are you a flower child at heart?
> Trudeau: Oh more than at heart, in my soul. That's my generation. That's what I blossomed in.
> Taylor: Do you find it something that you have to grow out of or is it something that is compatible with this kind of life?
> Trudeau: I'd really hate to grow out of what I—when I call myself a flower child, I think of myself as someone who cares and who doesn't care about the unimportant things, doesn't put too much value on money and social status— although how can I say that when I'm the Prime Minister's wife, except that I, you know, didn't marry my husband to be the Prime Minister's wife. I long for the day when we will no longer be, I no longer will be the PM's wife, when I can just be Pierre's wife.

The answer abounded with contradictions and confusion, but as Margaret later noted, many Canadians were charmed by the interview, though others were appalled or intrigued, particularly journalists in English Canada and abroad.[4]

The critics noticed the flower child's jetsetting ways: the hotel Georges V in Paris; winters in the Caribbean; weekends in New York; couturier fashion from Holt Renfrew; and trips on private jets with her close friend Queen Alia of Jordan, who gave her expensive cameras as she embarked on a new career as a photographer. Earlier commentators claimed that the exceedingly private Pierre did not share his concerns with others, which is true in the case of his political colleagues. Marc Lalonde can recall only one remark Trudeau made about his marriage breakdown, one very similar to the comment he made in his memoirs. However, he turned to his traditional confidants: his priests and his close female friends. Nancy Pitfield, Michael Pitfield's new wife, selected some "fantastic clothes" for Margaret at the expensive and exclusive Creeds in Toronto, and Wendy Porteous, the wife of Trudeau's assistant Tim Porteous, joined Margaret for a "giggly, happy drive down to Montreal" before she entered the hospital. Pierre's old friend Carroll Guérin was surprised to receive a phone call from Trudeau that fall asking her if he and Margaret could come to see her on the weekend. Margaret had just left the hospital when she and Pierre arrived by helicopter at the quietly elegant former seigneury at Mont-Saint-Hilaire, where Carroll lived. On the grounds, as Margaret rested, Pierre told Carroll: "I don't understand. I don't know what to do." And he didn't.[5]

In 1975, as his political popularity waned, Trudeau tried to take Margaret away from the "old grey mansion" at 24 Sussex, which had become a "prison" for her. They spent more time at Harrington Lake, visited cottages on other weekends, took diversions from official tours, and sometimes the official documents were set aside. Once on a beach, with the briefcase far away, a bored Pierre asked Margaret, "What are you reading?" She passed the book to him and said, "You might like it." He didn't put it down until he finished the last page: Erica Jong's bestselling *Fear of Flying*, a feminist and, to some, pornographic classic about a brilliant woman in an unfulfilled marriage who flees her husband and has anonymous sex. Trudeau's thoughts remain a mystery, but they may be surmised.

Margaret's rebellion, which we now know was the product of bipolar depression, lapsed in 1975 because she became pregnant once again in early winter. Although she accompanied Trudeau on the whirlwind of trips he undertook that year, she shunned the official functions, and on the rare occasions when she attended political gatherings, she departed early.* When, for example, the Canadian Embassy in Copenhagen worked out a detailed itinerary for her during Trudeau's meeting with Danish officials in May, her assistant replied politely but curtly: "Mrs. Trudeau thanks you for your suggestions for a program for her, which she found quite interesting. However, given her present state of health, she would prefer to have no program and to be free to rest and perhaps to do some shopping."[6] Trudeau, who was becoming increasingly angry about Margaret's expenditures, probably shuddered when he read her alternatives.

---

* In May, Margaret went to Montreal with Trudeau, but once the Young Liberal convention began on the 26th, she and Justin left for home. According to William Johnson in the *Globe and Mail* (June 27, 1975), Trudeau then dined with the Liberals on meatballs and shepherd's pie and fielded questions before he began "freestyle dancing to a hard rock beat."

"The hall was hot, girls and women and sharp-eyed men with moustaches formed a close circle around the Prime Minister. He soon doffed his blue suit jacket and decorum and out came swinging Pierre, arms outstretched, fingers snapping, hips swiveling, waist wiggling, legs writhing.

"The sweat stood out on his forehead. A middle-aged woman reached over the shoulder of the younger women crowding around him and wiped Mr. Trudeau's forehead. He grabbed the woman by the waist and soon they were whirling around ballroom style dancing.

"People slapped hands, urging him on. He danced with one partner, then another, as girls and women worked their way to the edge of the circle to be the next one he chose for a few beats.

"Finally he danced his way to the head of the stairs leading out, put on his coat, walked to the big bullet-proof black limousine, bussed five women on the cheek and aides and guards leaped into their car as he set off to return to Ottawa."

And yet they visibly loved each other when they were together. Shortly after the birth of Michel in October 1975, Trudeau planned an official visit to Latin America early in the new year, including stops in Mexico, Cuba, and Latin America. The trip was badly timed from a political point of view, and given his heavy and much criticized travel schedule of the previous months, even his own office opposed it. Although the Americans had begun to break down their ideological barriers with Cuba, as Nixon had earlier with his policy of détente with the Soviets and recognition of China, the Cubans had responded poorly to these tentative approaches. Then, when Cuba expanded its intervention in the Angolan civil war in November, the United States recoiled and expected Canada to follow suit. Trudeau, perhaps because of the strains in his personal life but more likely because of his own interest in Cuba and Latin America, decided to go ahead with the trip anyhow. This visit to the hemisphere's most illustrious communist dictator troubled not only the American leadership but also the Canadian business community, which was already enraged by Trudeau's year-end comments about the precarious future of capitalism. To lessen the damage, External Affairs issued a statement condemning the Angolan intervention just before the prime minister arrived in Havana on January 26. Castro, many of his ministers, and tens of thousands of Cubans all turned out to greet Pierre, Margaret, and Michel at the airport. Castro immediately charmed his visitors with "romantic and flowery English" and his exuberant embrace of the Trudeau baby, whom he dubbed "Miche." He even had an official badge made for him, reading "Miche Trudeau, V.I.P., Official visitor of the Canadian delegation."[7]

In a history of Trudeau's "three nights in Havana," historian Robert Wright argues that the warmth of the Cuban sun, the sambas, Castro's flirtatious Latin charm, the flamboyant generosity of Cuban hospitality, and the gaiety of the people made Margaret and Pierre leave their arguments behind and love each other once again. Canadian ambassador Jim Hyndman, who accompanied the Trudeaus throughout the trip, concluded that Pierre "was still in love with" Margaret. The visual record of their days together confirms his view, with Margaret radiant and exuberant and Pierre solicitous and physically near. Castro's outrageous flirting charmed them both: he surprised them late one evening when, in his "silken English," he told Margaret: "You know my eyes are not very strong, so every day to make them stronger I force myself to look at the sun. I find it very hard. But do you know what I find harder? That is to look into the blue of your eyes."[8] Not surprisingly, Margaret, who had found official and political life formalistic and tedious, thought Cuba (and Castro) thoroughly captivating, so unlike the grey, socialist, workers' state she had expected. She and Pierre had ceased to discuss Canadian politics, but in Cuba she suddenly "felt a resurgence of political consciousness." Here was "the answer to Utopia," she thought. "If this is revolution, it is truly marvellous."[9]

Trudeau, who did not regard Cuba as Utopia but did respect its health care and social systems, initially argued with Castro about Cuban participation in the Angolan civil war. Before long, however, these two Jesuit-educated, highly physical, flirtatious, and charismatic leaders engaged with each other emotionally and intellectually. Castro proposed that, on their last night on the island, he spirit his guests away from officials and the press for an unforgettable stay on Cayo Largo, a small key where they would share a two-bedroom bungalow and a small shed. Margaret begged Trudeau to let her accompany him, a request that Ivan Head, whom Margaret described as "pompous and somewhat self-important," promptly opposed. Enthralled with Margaret, Castro would not hear of her absence, and Pierre finally agreed she could go. It was, Margaret later wrote, "a memorable evening . . ." for which "lights had been strung up in garlands around the table, one long trestle table with benches, at which we all sat down to eat together, everyone from our nanny to the drivers." Castro and

Trudeau spoke Spanish, but the Cuban graciously switched to English when a topic arose that he thought would interest Margaret. On that final evening in Cuba, protocol vanished in a haze of "loud music, good food, bright colors" as they all danced late into the night. When they had to say their farewells next day, Margaret was overcome by joyful tears. Trudeau commented wryly to his wife: "I'm glad you're still with me. I thought you would ask for asylum."[10]

Things began badly at Caracas, the next stop. The Canadian ambassador's wife had planned the normal program for a prime minister's wife, but Margaret would have no part of it. She insisted on seeing a daycare centre sponsored by the wife of the Venezuelan president, Carlos Andrés Pérez—a suggestion that horrified Canadian officials. Nevertheless, Margaret persisted as she had in Cuba, and Señora Pérez agreed to accompany her to the slum where the centre was located. Margaret was so impressed with the work being done there that, after the visit, she wrote a song for Señora Pérez. Pierre, still in a playful mood from his Cuban adventure, urged her to sing it that evening. The occasion, however, was not a small gathering but "possibly the most formal and pretentious dinner" Margaret had ever attended as Pierre's wife. Nevertheless, with Pierre's encouragement, she rose and sang:

> Señora Pérez, I would like to thank you.
> I would like to sing to you
> To sing a song of love.
> For I have watched you
> With my eyes wide open,
> I have watched you with learning eyes.

The song, which undoubtedly would have charmed in a more intimate setting, embarrassed much of the crowd, most notably the Canadian delegation—which "to a man was horrified." The news spread quickly to the top spot in all the Canadian media. "Margaret Trudeau did it again," the *Globe and Mail* reported. In deliberate understatement, it continued that "those who attended said Mrs. Trudeau's voice was strong, though untrained, and carried to all parts of the hall. She sang unaccompanied."[11] Indeed.

Even though Conservative *Globe* columnist Geoffrey Stevens declared the trip useful from the point of view of Canada's foreign policy, talk-show hosts ridiculed the trip and regaled listeners with tales of Margaret's misbehaviour and her charge on the flight back to Ottawa that "officials" had tried to steal her song during the dinner before she could sing it. Next morning, jet-lagged, Margaret woke to hear the clock radio broadcasting comments on her performance, nearly all of them caustic and negative. The host teasingly said, "Margaret Trudeau . . . why don't you give us a call?" She did. It was, of course, a mistake, as was her decision to participate in a "call-in" program the following week.

As 1976 progressed, the Olympics, a royal visit, and even more travel and official dinners all brought further tensions to the marriage. In Japan, Ivan Head, who had become Margaret's detested minder on official trips, told her she could not attend Pierre's final press conference. She "made a scene" and Pierre gave in, but Margaret was, in her own words, "possessed." Once in the official car, she demanded to get out, but the doors were locked. "The horrified Japanese guard hastily unlocked the door and, under the amazed and startled gaze of the officials standing in serried ranks up the stairs bowing, [Margaret] rushed up, three steps at a time, shouting, 'Fuck you' at the top of [her] voice." As she suggests, "it wasn't easy to live that one down."[12]

The incidents multiplied, and Margaret's celebrity—or notoriety—increased. Letters flowed in from all parts of the country and abroad, and full-time staff were hired to answer them, partly to shield Margaret from their vitriol. Trudeau himself sought help, but his interactions with his wife were increasingly argumentative and difficult. When they met Pope Paul VI at his summer retreat at Castel Gandalfo, Pierre irritated Margaret by denying he had any problems when the pontiff asked him if he did. He told Margaret he would not talk about his troubles in front of her—a clear indication of the counsel he was seeking from spiritual leaders and his distance from his wife. He began to seek guidance from others who knew Margaret well, such as Jane Faulkner, the wife of his Cabinet colleague Hugh Faulkner. Increasingly, Margaret's antics attracted press attention, in a decade when the rules of political journalism were being rewritten by Woodward and Bernstein in their coverage of Watergate and by the outrageous political satire of *Saturday Night Live*, which the Canadian Lorne Michaels created in 1975.

Moreover, Margaret's feistiness was not unique; it had a southern counterpart. Before Margaret spoke publicly about her psychiatric problems in the fall of 1974, Betty Ford, the wife of President Gerald Ford, had told the public about her mastectomy. Later, she was similarly candid on other subjects, expressing strong pro-choice views (despite her husband's silence on the abortion issue), support for psychiatric intervention, acceptance of premarital sex, and her own enjoyment of sex. She was, the *New York Times* later wrote, "a product and symbol of the cultural and political times—doing the Bump along the corridors of the White House, donning a mood ring, chatting on her CB radio with the handle First Mama—a housewife who argued passionately for equal rights for women, a mother of four who mused about drugs, abortion and premarital sex aloud and without regret."[13] Conservative Republicans dubbed her "No Lady," rather than "First Lady." Canadian journalists, like their American counterparts, were quick to take advantage of this new openness toward political leaders' wives and adapted to the new candour, particularly in English Canada. Peter C. Newman, whose frank and gossipy books on Diefenbaker and Pearson had transformed political writing in the sixties, now served as the editor of *Maclean's*. Under his direction, that venerable monthly became a lively weekly—and it recognized few boundaries or taboos.

Sexual candour flourished, but the nervousness and uncertainty about mental illness persisted. Public opinion forced Thomas Eagleton, the Democratic candidate for vice-president, to resign in 1972 when the media revealed that he had undergone psychiatric treatment. It was not surprising, then, that Trudeau's office reported in 1974 that Margaret was entering the hospital for "rest" and exhaustion, not that she was undergoing psychiatric treatment. The following year, the film *One Flew over the Cuckoo's Nest* won a record five Academy Awards for its portrayal of a "sane" criminal who acted "insane" to secure entry to an asylum, hoping for a soft life. He found, instead, conditions of totalitarian oppression, where good and evil, sanity and insanity, love and fear were hopelessly inverted. This deeply influential film reflected and strengthened the arguments of French philosopher Michel Foucault that "mental illness" in contemporary psychiatric thought was a method of enforcing bourgeois morality and state authority. As news of Margaret's confinement in the psychiatric ward seeped into the press, the reporting reflected the evolving understanding of what "mental illness" meant—a change clearly evident in an elegant letter Margaret received from the widely admired novelist Gabrielle Roy.

> Dear Mrs. Trudeau:
> I saw you and listened to you last night on television and I was deeply moved by the note of sincerity that rang through all your comments. Television has not accustomed us to such frank and soul-baring remarks.
> I also had the impression that you were not talking for yourself alone but on behalf of all women, that you were speaking for each one of us all more or less enchained. Because the moment we love, do we not fall into a sort of

> slavery? Doubtless men do, too—who is truly free? but less
> perhaps than women for whom love is the center of life and
> who are thus the most vulnerable of creatures.

Roy concluded by wondering "if young women like you, full of
the greatest courage there is, that of telling the truth, did not do
more than governments to change the world."[14]

Margaret's own memoir of her psychiatric treatment and of
the oppressiveness of conventional morality was clearly influenced by this contemporary ambivalent perception of mental
illness. While the tabloids speculated, other publications maintained discreet silence: the *Canadian Annual Review of Politics
and Public Affairs*, for example, never mentioned Margaret's ill-
nesses or even Margaret herself in its thick volume on 1976, and
it made only one reference to her in 1977. Francophone journalists generally turned their eyes away from the prime minister's
private life, even if they mounted strong opposition against him
politically. The Quebec tabloids also showed discretion—a characteristic that was absent from their European counterparts and
the *Toronto Sun*, which frequently placed the Trudeaus' troubles
on the front pages.[15]

Trudeau was baffled. He spoke with Margaret's father,
Jimmy Sinclair, about the problems when they secretly toured
the Northwest Territories and the Arctic in the summer of 1975.
He encouraged Margaret to take up photography, to travel when
she wanted, and even to shop when the urge struck. In the
summer of 1976, despite collapsing polls, he agreed to a trip to
Jordan so he and Margaret could visit their friends King Hussein
and Queen Alia of Jordan. Because of the "tricky" politics of the
region—and of his own Mount Royal constituency with its large
Jewish population—he added a week in Israel, a visit Margaret
loathed because it was an official tour. She fought with the
Canadian ambassador and with Pierre, who called her a

"detestable" travelling companion. Once home, she defiantly smoked marijuana, infuriating Trudeau and taunting the RCMP security staff. In one fight, she tore Joyce Wieland's *La Raison avant la Passion* quilt from the wall, ripped off the letters, and threw them down the stairs at Pierre. They argued constantly, but Trudeau "kept repeating" to Margaret: "You must do exactly what you want to do. You can do anything you want." The trouble, Margaret wrote later, "was that I needed direction, not freedom." Trudeau, as one perceptive commentator wrote at the time, may have had the body of a man in his twenties but not the mind of one. He turned back to where he had been before, getting old answers to new questions. In speaking to an interviewer on September 30, 1975, he said, "People want to be led, but they don't want to be pushed. The distinction is vital. They have to be convinced that you are right in order to follow you willingly, and they have to remain convinced that you are consistently right." Both in politics and in marriage, Trudeau no longer seemed able to convince others he was right.[16]

The Trudeaus spent Christmas 1976 with their architect friend Arthur Erickson in the Caribbean, where the premier of St. Lucia supplied a car, a yacht, and provisions. Nevertheless, despite the luxury and lush tropical ambience, Pierre and Margaret "lived locked in [their] own private nightmares." When they returned on January 9, Margaret enrolled in a photography course at Ottawa's Algonquin College, though she took time off to visit Washington with Jane Faulkner to open an exhibit at the Hirshhorn Gallery. She charmed the crowd and, especially, Canadian ambassador "Jake" Warren, who rhapsodized that "for many Americans, Mrs. Trudeau's vitality, charm and engaging informality personify something special of [the Canadian] character."

Then, in late February, Trudeau made a historic trip to Washington, primarily to counter a reassuring speech René Lévesque had made the previous month to the Economic Club in

New York about Quebec independence. Trudeau and the new American president, Jimmy Carter, immediately warmed to each other, as did Margaret to Rosalynn Carter. When the Trudeaus arrived, the two couples posed on the White House veranda, and Margaret looked stunning in a white fur hat. On the evening of February 21 at the official dinner, however, she wore a short dress with a run in her nylons that gave the appearance of racy stockings. The crowd murmured, but her youthful beauty and exuberance charmed those she met. The guests dined on Alaskan king crab and stuffed saddle of lamb while the band played popular, romantic, and in the circumstances inappropriate music, such as Cole Porter's "I Concentrate on You," and *My Fair Lady*'s "I Could Have Danced All Night," with its image of a young innocent girl falling in love with an older mentor. The White House was crammed with celebrities—John Kenneth Galbraith, Canadian-born *Bonanza* star Lorne Greene, singer Harry Belafonte, Elizabeth Taylor, and two young Carter enthusiasts, Bill Clinton and Hilary Rodham—but Margaret and her ripped stockings captured the most attention. The *Washington Post* featured her in its report, and the *Globe and Mail* found an "official" of a Canadian fashion association who condemned her for embarrassing her country. Why couldn't she behave like a French president's wife and make her nation's fashion industry proud? Many years later President Carter recalled that he and Rosalynn could never understand what the controversy was all about. Even the *Globe*, to its credit, in a later editorial, approved of Margaret's decision to "go short," declaring that "the ability of contrasting hem lines to swirl harmoniously together was encouraging to behold."[17]

On February 23 Carter sent a handwritten letter to "Pierre & Margaret Trudeau," no doubt with the controversy fresh in mind:

> Rosalynn and I really enjoyed your visit with us, and we look forward to seeing you often in the future.

Pierre, your experience & naturally frank discussion were
very helpful to me as a new president. I feel that our countries are being drawn even closer together.

Margaret, you brought a delightful breath of fresh air and
charm to Washington. Thank you. Your friend, Jimmy.

Trudeau received this note just as he was signing his own typed
reply. He picked up his pen and added: "Your handwritten note
has just been handed to me, and I find in it all the warmth and
directness which made meeting and talking with you such an
unforgettable experience. Margaret and I are very grateful for
Rosalyn's [sic] and your friendship, and hope that there will be
many more occasions to renew it in the future."

There were not. A few days later, on March 4, their sixth
anniversary, Margaret decided to leave Pierre for a ninety-
day trial separation. No public announcement was made. Even
Trudeau's aides were unaware of why Margaret was now so
often absent.[18]

Margaret had planned a trip to New York, but instead, she
accepted an invitation to go to Toronto to hear a concert by the
Rolling Stones. They met at the new Harbour Castle hotel on
Lake Ontario in Mick Jagger's suite, where the singer was initially
"polite and charming" over wine. Then they departed for the
El Mocambo, a rock club on Spadina Avenue, where the Stones'
appearance surprised the audience. The next night Margaret
stayed on in Toronto; went to another Stones session, which she
photographed; and then helped to care for Keith Richards' young
son while Richards, already facing a heroin possession charge, was
curled up on the floor. In the early morning hours, she invited the
partying Stones into her room, where they drank, played dice, and
smoked "hash." The next day she flew to New York as headlines
blared that the wife of Canada's prime minister had partied hard
with the baddest boys of rock. Paul Wasserman, the group's agent,

lied to the press, saying that Margaret had flown to New York with the Stones, which she had not. Jagger repudiated this story, telling journalists that he hardly knew Margaret—a "very attractive and nice person"—and that he was in New York with his wife and had not seen Margaret there.[19]

Despite Jagger's reassurance, the separation remained a secret and the tabloid stories ran wild, especially in Europe, where Canadian "off the record" sources were easily found. Trudeau's new press officer, Patrick Gossage, was bewildered as hundreds of calls demanded confirmation of rumours about the Harbour Castle party, of Trudeau's marital state, and of Margaret's whereabouts. Gossage wrote in his diary: "Has lust for personal knowledge of the great become the only common currency, the real edge of competition, which worries even the mighty *Toronto Star*, [and] the esteemed *Globe and Mail?*" Whenever Margaret returned to 24 Sussex, the Trudeaus maintained their discretion, although journalists staking out the house saw her come and go. Gossage's diary records how difficult it was to handle the situation, particularly as Margaret had publicly declared that she had "had enough"—she had "abdicated." Still, the prime minister's official representatives were baffled and reflected their confusion in their comments. When the Trudeaus appeared as a family for the opening of the Canada Games in mid-May, they thoroughly befuddled the press, along with Trudeau's own aides. But then, on May 30, the Prime Minister's Office released a statement:

> Pierre and Margaret Trudeau announce that, because of Margaret's wishes, they shall begin living separate and apart. Margaret relinquishes all privileges as the wife of the prime minister and wishes to leave the marriage and pursue an independent career. Pierre accepts Margaret's decision with regret, and both pray that their separation will lead to a better relationship between themselves.

The marriage ended as it had begun, in Linda Griffith's words, with "all elements of humanity, magnified."[20]

Patrick Gossage recorded in his diary that reporters "rationalized" their coverage of the marriage breakdown by relating it to the question of how it affected Trudeau in his role as prime minister. Did the troubles hurt his performance? Did the end of the marriage cause his popularity to soar, as Margaret alleged? The answer to the first question is probably yes, although the evidence is mainly circumstantial. After the separation, journalists recalled how he was uncharacteristically indecisive after the 1974 election, how frequently he travelled, and how quickly his temper exploded — in particular how, in November 1974, he became enraged in the House when he interpreted an opposition comment as a reference to his marriage breakdown. Still, anyone watching his interviews, reading transcripts of his news conferences, and examining his papers can only be impressed with his knowledge of issues and his quick responses. When, for example, he met the press in Washington after the "short dress" incident, Trudeau was well briefed, witty, and focused. Contemporary commentators were certainly impressed. Dick Beddoes of the *Globe and Mail* wrote sympathetically after Margaret gave an interview to *People* magazine, in which she talked about her intimate lingerie: "Trudeau has been uncommonly graceful about his wife's indiscretions, his domestic pressures appearing not to harm either the country or his skill for government." In an interview in which Quebec journalist Alain Stanké tried to break down Trudeau's personal reserve, the prime minister remained thoroughly in control, except when he talked about his three sons — there his joy was irrepressible. Otherwise, he refused to admit close personal relations with anyone. While admiring Trudeau's reserve, Gossage wondered what lay beneath the cool surface: "If you haven't been through that route, you don't know anything about the ragged ends of unravelled emotion."[21] The ends were indeed ragged.

Trudeau's closest aides, while admiring his reserve in public, recall his private distraction as his marriage passed through its final, agonizing months. Gossage wrote in his diary in May 1977 that one of the prime minister's most senior aides reported that Trudeau had become "unusually and extraordinarily unpredictable." Others recall that his usually incisive comments on memoranda became markedly fewer. In the Commons and whenever he jostled with the press, his edges were sharper, his emotions closer to the surface.* Others remember that the months before Margaret decided to leave were noticeably tense, uncertain, and difficult. Yet he told an interviewer in 1977 that after the separatist win in the 1976 Quebec election, "the fates" had cornered him. He could not leave politics, as Margaret wanted, when the "very execution of the task that I got into politics for" was in doubt.[22]

The second question—whether the divorce caused Trudeau's popularity to soar—can be answered with a definite yes. Ironically, the Lévesque triumph on November 15, 1976, which Margaret and, apparently, Pierre regarded as the final blow to the marriage, was offset by a remarkable outpouring of public and private sympathy for Trudeau when the elegant statement of separation appeared six months later. Although no scientific answer can be provided, and pollsters did not and surely could not frame a question to indicate exactly how much the

---

* One fascinating example of how private and public blended in Trudeau's thoughts occurred on November 26, 1976, when he was asked whether Canada should have a national referendum if Quebec had a provincial referendum on separation. Trudeau said that the question was interesting: "It is like in a marriage. We do not simply ask the husband or the wife: do you want a divorce? We ask both of them whether it is working and try to get an answer from both." *Le Devoir*, Nov. 26, 1976.

impact of the marriage breakdown contributed to Trudeau's increased popularity, the prime minister was never as popular as he was in the summer of 1977, except for that brief surge during the October Crisis. The polls immediately after the Lévesque victory had been disastrous for the federal Liberals. In January 1977 the Conservatives led with a big enough margin to form a majority government. Then, as Trudeau's marriage came apart, a dramatic shift occurred.

	Liberal	PC	NDP	Other	Undecided
January	35	45	16	4	33
February	41	37	17	4	32
March	42	36	17	5	37
April	44	34	18	4	39
May	47	32	17	4	31
June	51	27	18	4	31
July	51	27	18	4	31
August	50	29	17	4	34
September	49	30	18	3	38

At the beginning of 1977, polls indicated that John Turner would be a far more popular Liberal leader, and pundits mused about Trudeau's imminent departure. By June, however, no one doubted that Trudeau would remain and that he and Lévesque were now engaged in the fight of their lives.[23]

—

While Trudeau's personal life probably inflated his poll numbers in 1977, his own response to the separatist victory in Quebec in the early part of that year also played a part. After initially stumbling in his response to Lévesque's win by reacting churlishly and even personally, Trudeau managed to gain strength as Lévesque overplayed his hand early in the new year.* When the new Quebec premier spoke to the prestigious Economic Club of New York on January 25, he sought to reassure Wall Street that the Parti Québécois represented no threat to American equity or bond holders. His task was admittedly difficult, given that the PQ was heavily dependent on union and leftist support and its program was avowedly social democratic. Still, Lévesque had given the key Cabinet positions to ministers whose background and beliefs reassured the business community—notably economist Jacques Parizeau, who became finance minister, and former civil servant Claude Morin, a "gradualist" who became intergovernmental affairs minister. The Quebec business community, traditionally dominated by anglophones, was deeply integrated within the North American context and was fearful of Quebec independence and the socialism of the PQ. According to a contemporary study, eleven head offices had left the province in 1975 and sixty-one in

---

* Since the late 1960s, Trudeau had publicly indicated that he welcomed the formation of a political party incorporating a separatist platform rather than the many groups, some violent, that had promoted the cause. Although he regretted the election of the Parti Québécois in 1976, he welcomed the chance to confront the separatists directly. An unidentified Liberal minister from Ontario told Lévesque biographer Peter Desbarats *before* the 1976 election that a separatist victory "wouldn't be the end of the world. We've had the Sword of Damocles hanging over our heads since 1960. A victory for Lévesque might be the catharsis we all need." The remark reflected the frustration of federal Liberals with Bourassa, but Trudeau was not as optimistic as the Ontario minister that it would now be possible to have a "real negotiation" with Quebec. Peter Desbarats, *René: A Canadian in Search of a Country* (Toronto: McClelland and Stewart, 1976), 205. For Trudeau's pessimism about negotiation, see Pierre Trudeau, *Memoirs* (Toronto: McClelland and Stewart, 1993), 246–47.

1976, and the rate was quickening in 1977, while another study showed that Quebec-based stocks had suffered relatively greater losses than other Canadian or American stocks after the provincial election.

Given this response, Lévesque needed to reassure his audience in New York, and he promised that Quebec would remain in an economic union with Canada and that separation would be implemented only after a referendum. He failed in his task. The next day *New York Times* editor James Reston described Lévesque as an excellent speaker but concluded that "he suggests some scary problems." He had listened to the speech with "admiration" but also "regret," for "the melody of separation, like the longing of the Scots and the Welsh for independence, seems out of date and almost tragic." The business pages seemed to blame a sharp drop in the stock market on the speech, and both Moody's and Standard and Poor announced that they would review Quebec bond ratings. A bitter Lévesque unwisely blamed a "fifth column" in the audience for destroying his positive message.[24]

Lévesque had troubles closer to home as well. When he addressed the Montreal Chamber of Commerce on February 8, he lacked his usual eloquence and power, partly because of a gruesome car accident two days earlier when he had struck a body lying on a Montreal boulevard, but also because the New York speech continued to get bad reviews. He appeared "tired" and "visibly shaken" before the chamber, yet he spoke for one hour and twenty-seven minutes to little applause from a large audience. In contrast, when Trudeau had spoken to the Quebec City Chamber of Commerce on January 28, he had challenged the PQ to hold its referendum soon and had received a standing ovation from a crowd of 1,500 that rose and sang "O Canada." It was a rehearsal for his main political act that winter.[25]

In response to the new crisis, Trudeau accepted the recommendation of the Cabinet's Political Planning Committee that he begin regular press conferences, weekly if possible.[26] Although reluctant, Trudeau agreed with the recommendation and used one of the press conferences to deny that his upcoming address to the United States Congress, the first ever by a Canadian prime minister, would respond to Lévesque's Economic Club speech. He would talk about "Canada," not particular issues, he claimed.[27] But there was only one issue, and Lévesque was at its core. Trudeau delivered the address on February 22, and it was immediately published on high-quality bond paper and circulated widely. He began with eloquent praise for the American experiment and experience. In particular he mentioned the "social revolution" of "recent years," in which the United States had overcome "difficulties of immense complication and obdurateness . . . through the democratic process" and provided "a model for all nations devoted to the dignity of the human condition." At this point Trudeau linked the historic road to freedom of African-Americans with the acquisition of legal, social, and political rights by the conquered French Canadians. Despite many achievements since Confederation, he said, French Canadians had not felt fully equal: "And therein is the source of our central problem today. That is why a minority of the people of Quebec feel they should leave Canada and strike out in a country of their own." Trudeau then moved to reassure his audience: "The newly elected government of that province asserts a policy that reflects that minority view despite the fact that during the election campaign it sought a mandate for good government, and not a mandate for separation from Canada."

Trudeau argued that separation would be disastrous and was contrary to the direction the world must take. In the most memorable passage in the speech, he said: "Most Canadians understand that the rupture of their country would be an aberrant departure from the norms they themselves have set, a crime against the history of mankind; for I am immodest enough to suggest that a failure of this always varied, often illustrious Canadian social experiment would create shock waves of disbelief among those all over the world who are committed to the proposition that among man's noblest endeavours are those communities in which persons of diverse origins live, love, work and find mutual benefit." Then, as promised, Trudeau moved beyond Canada to the challenges faced by the continent and, more eloquently, by the world:

"Even as we have moved away from the cold war era of political and military confrontation, however, there exists another danger: one of rigidity in our response to the current challenges of poverty, hunger, environmental degradation, and nuclear proliferation. Our ability to respond adequately to these issues will in some measure be determined by our willingness to recognize them as the new obstacles to peace. Sadly, however, our pursuit of peace in these respects has all too often been little more imaginative than was our sometime blind grappling with absolutes in the international political sphere. Moreover, we have failed to mobilize adequately the full support of our electorates for the construction of a new world order."

Finally, Trudeau, who long ago in his Harvard dormitory had disdained American patriotism, paid tribute to American leadership and called on Americans to reject George Washington's warning that they beware the "insidious wiles of foreign influence" and steer clear of "permanent alliances with any portion of the foreign world." Now, he said, Canada needed America. "Yet here I stand, a foreigner, endeavouring—whether insidiously or not you will have to judge—to urge America ever more permanently into new alliances." He dared do so because of the bond between Canada and the United States and the spirit America represented. Building on this bold assertion, he concluded: "Thom. Paine's words of two centuries ago are as valid today as when he uttered them: 'my country is the world, and my religion is to do good.' In your continued quest of those ideals, ladies and gentlemen, all

Canadians wish you goodspeed." Ironies abounded—Tom Paine had rebelled against the British Crown to which Trudeau's Elliott forebears had remained loyal, Trudeau's early years had been marked by a conservative Catholic's disdain for the spirit America represented, and his first government had minimized Canada's international significance—but the address adapted belief to the new realities of Canadian nationhood. It hit its mark clearly and effectively.[28]

Press reaction in English Canada was strongly favourable, and Conservative leader Joe Clark, who had been sharply critical of Trudeau's early responses to the PQ election, said he would have applauded the speech had he been there. NDP leader Ed Broadbent was even more generous, deeming it "sensitive and elegant." In Quebec English-language journalists were predictably flattering, but francophones were critical of the soaring rhetoric and vague detail. To Claude Ryan, "the Washington speech will change nothing."[29] The criticism focused on the absence of any specific answers to Quebec grievances, but the overall approach Trudeau took in the speech marked a real difference in the federal government's response to the problem, one that had been stirring ever since the separatist victory.

First, the speech recognized the primacy of the Quebec issue for Canadian politics. The breakup of Canada was a "crime against humanity"—a declaration that raised the stakes enormously and cast the gentle conversation about economic union and consultative referenda to the side. By linking the Quebec issue to the broader international problems and by linking the fates of Canada and the United States together, Trudeau sought to internationalize the issue, as Quebec had done for a decade in its relationship with France. Trudeau knew that, for Quebec, the relationship with the United States was far more significant economically, and that it would ultimately be more influential with individuals as they decided whether to vote *oui* or *non* in any referendum.* There is impressive evidence that Trudeau's speech had the desired effect. Reston wrote in the *New York Times* that Lévesque's appeal to Americans to accept the "dismemberment" of Canada was the "worst proposition put to the U.S. Government since Nikita Khrushchev invited us to accept the emplacement of Soviet nuclear missiles in Cuba"[30]—bad for the United States; fatal for Canada.

Second, Trudeau rejected responses that in his view would lead ineluctably toward significant decentralization within Canada. In the confusion following the Quebec election, to give but one example, Ed Broadbent broke with the NDP's traditional centralist position and urged that decentralization be considered as a response, a view that the Liberal and nationalist *Toronto Star* surprisingly endorsed. Even more significant were the reactions from the provinces. During the Quebec election campaign,

---

* After a series of incidents between Canada and Quebec over international representation, Lévesque visited France in early November 1977, where he became a Grand Officier de la Légion d'Honneur. Canada objected to this recognition because there had been no consultation with the Government of Canada, as was required when a Canadian received a formal honour in a foreign country. Although the French had invited Lévesque to speak before the National Assembly, Canadian pressure forced them to back down. He would have been the first foreign leader to do so since Woodrow Wilson in 1919. Lévesque did speak to the members of the assembly, but in a different location. Jacques Chirac, the Gaullist mayor of Paris, feted Lévesque and endorsed Quebec separation, while French president Valéry Giscard d'Estaing, who hosted the luncheon where Lévesque received the honour, offered support whatever course Quebec chose. Pierre-Louis Mallen, *Vivre le Québec libre* (Paris: Plon, 1978), 11ff, and J.T. Saywell, ed., *Canadian Annual Review of Politics and Public Affairs 1977* (Toronto: University of Toronto Press, 1979), 283.

Alberta premier Peter Lougheed sent a letter on behalf of other anglophone premiers agreeing to discuss patriation if the division of powers in the British North America Act was also put on the table and significant powers passed to the provinces. Although Trudeau had once thought himself that, given the new challenges of government, decentralization and a tighter delineation of responsibilities were appropriate, the actual experience of government had changed his views. The oil crisis, with the subsequent sudden shift of wealth to the Canadian West, and the increasing demands from Quebec for more powers caused Trudeau to reply sharply to Lougheed's badly timed letter, and he told him that any further meetings with the premiers would "prove of little purpose if the provinces merely seek to gain powers."

When the new Conservative leader Joe Clark echoed Lougheed's and Lévesque's demands for greater provincial powers, Trudeau took a clear stand against any such alteration. He replied bluntly to a student from Alberta at Oxford, who suggested that rewriting the British North America Act to give more power to the provinces might strengthen Confederation: "Well, it's hard to understand how you would strengthen Confederation by weakening it." Canada, he continued, "is already one of the most decentralized countries in the world, and you can go further toward decentralization, but then you are losing the notion of a country which can act in unison and you are beginning to work toward a Confederation of semi-independent states." Eventually this long answer was trimmed down to a question: "Who speaks for Canada?" For Trudeau, the answer was obvious: Canada's prime minister.[31]

Third, Trudeau firmly rejected special status for Quebec within the existing federation, and he also refused the possibility of any special relationship after separation. In the first days after the Quebec election, special status seemed to many Canadians a preferable alternative to separation. The Toronto Star, which had firmly opposed special status in the sixties and early seventies, changed its opinion after the shock of the separatist victory. Trudeau had declared that separatism was "dead" many times after the 1973 Liberal victory in the province, the *Star* reminded readers, but November 1976 now proved it was very much alive, and a new response was necessary. The idea of special status won support among some English-Canadian intellectuals, particularly those associated with the New Democratic Party (whose endorsement of some type of special status had caused Trudeau to abandon the party in the early sixties). Within the federal Liberal Party, the notion of compromise was also favoured by some younger Quebec MPs, and immediately after the election, in the Liberal caucus, they expressed an interest in "special status." The most vocal was Serge Joyal, but there were others who argued for an open approach *(une attitude d'ouverture)* toward the PQ. With the polls immediately after the Quebec election showing Joe Clark with a solid lead, a television interviewer asked Trudeau whether he should not listen to the dissenters and find some solution. No, he answered firmly: "In my government I don't hold people by force or blackmail. They work with me if they share my views and my concept of what Canada is. If they don't, they won't have to go to war against me or kick me out. I'll simply say, 'Bye-bye.'" MPs, Trudeau reminded his audience, had known his views when they stood for election. He would discuss "an exchange of powers," he said, "but don't get the idea that I'm moving toward a view that is diametrically opposed to the one I've been preaching for ten years."[32] By Christmas 1976, no one doubted where Trudeau stood.

Trudeau's position had even greater clarity by March, a precious quality in a political world where shock and confusion reigned. Canadians betrayed great uncertainty as they spoke to pollsters, and in Quebec, even as voters supported a separatist party in November 1976, they told pollsters that they did not want separatism. Public opinion seemed like a weathervane, catching the strongest gusts. A Martin Goldfarb poll in May indicated that

33 percent of Quebecers would support "separation," but the Gallup polls throughout the year consistently yielded results around 20 percent. CROP, a Montreal-based polling operation, put the figure at 19 percent in May, but when the question was rephrased to "independence with an economic association," the percentage rose to 38 percent, with 50 percent supporting separation if the referendum simply asked for a mandate to negotiate "sovereignty-association." To confuse matters more, a Radio-Canada poll in November indicated that the preferred choice of Quebecers was "renewed federalism."

Outside Quebec, opposition to Quebec separation was strongest in the provinces bordering Quebec, notably Ontario, and opposition to special status and bilingualism was especially strong in the Prairie provinces. English Canadians told the Gallup poll by a margin of 54.2 percent to 38.3 percent that they opposed negotiating "special political and economic agreements with Quebec to try to prevent separation." Yet francophones supported such negotiations by a margin of 66.9 percent to 23.2 percent. Likewise, when English Canadians were asked whether "the governments of Canada and the provinces [should] promote and finance more extensive bilingualism throughout the country to try to prevent separation," only 27.8 percent agreed, while 64.1 percent opposed such a policy. With francophones, the percentages were almost exactly the reverse: 56 percent yes, 33.1 percent no. On the one hand, the ambiguity of these answers gave Claude Morin in Quebec the freedom to develop his gradualist approach to separation through a carefully worded referendum; on the other, it gave Trudeau freedom to lead rather than follow.[33] That freedom allowed him to capture public imagination—for a while.

In the early winter of 1977, Christina McCall wrote in *Saturday Night*: "Like him or not, much of what happens to Canada in the next few years will depend on Pierre Trudeau." He was "the champion of the federalist cause," she said, "and we are the uneasy bystanders." She agreed that in the words of Conservative senator Grattan O'Leary, "fortune has a way of turning in his favour." McCall, who wrote the best study of the Liberals in the seventies, believed that, like Churchill in 1940, the defeated man had found his moment and his challenge. Individuals, she wrote, determine the course of history as much as ideology.[34] The turn of Trudeau's fortune in early 1977 was an astonishing reversal from what had been a dreadful period for him and his government. His marriage crumbling, his dream threatened, Trudeau now faced his greatest challenge.

CHAPTER TWELVE

—

OFF THE TRACK

Trudeau's determination to tackle the Constitution anew, his marriage breakdown drama, and his nimble response to the Parti Québécois victory in Quebec caused most Canadians to forget that between the fall of 1975, when John Turner resigned, and the sudden Liberal recovery in the polls in the spring of 1977, both the Trudeau government and the Liberal Party itself had stumbled badly. Although many Canadians at the time tended to overlook these messy details as they focused once again on Trudeau as their champion, the problems deserve attention: later they would stir from their dormant state and profoundly affect Canadian political life. His government was not as strong as polls suggested in 1977. There was a rot within that endured.

To begin, wage and price controls appeared to have failed, as Albert Breton, Trudeau's key economic adviser, had predicted in the fall of 1975. Although some economists later gave the controls credit for breaking expectations of inflation, the overall results were damaging to Trudeau. By early 1977 the decision to implement them seemed wrong: inflation had diminished and now appeared to result more from international than domestic factors; moreover, wage controls had proved devilishly difficult to enforce. Trudeau, in his own later words, "paid a heavy price in lost credibility" for that decision. The controls increased Quebec union militancy, caused bitterness toward the Liberal Party, and probably contributed to the separatist win in Quebec in November 1976. Certainly Trudeau's caustic remarks about the "hot dog eater" Bourassa, and his decision that year to push ahead with patriation of the Constitution, hurt the Quebec Liberals, if only because they led Bourassa to call an unnecessary election—which he lost.[1]

After the wage and price controls diminished Trudeau's position and his Christmas 1975 remarks about the future of the capitalist system created distrust and confusion within the business community, the Liberals fell in the polls, and the trend continued throughout the following year. The government, which had been largely free of scandal, suddenly faced several controversies that directly involved ministers. André Ouellet, the minister of corporate and consumer affairs and a rising force in the government, was forced to resign in March when a judge found him in contempt of court for comments he had made about price fixing in the sugar industry.* As the Conservatives pressed the issue in the House,

---

* Security and domestic intelligence matters also boiled over in 1976, when former RCMP constable Robert Samson testified that he had participated in an illegal break-in of L'Agence de presse libre du Québec, a separatist news agency. This March 16 testimony led to a series of shocking revelations about the spying activities of the RCMP and continuing embarrassment for Solicitor General Jean-Pierre Goyer. In October the opposition raised the question of whether there was a "blacklist" of public servants who should be watched because they might aim at "the destruction of the existing political and social structure of Canada." Goyer denied the allegation, and Trudeau ridiculed it, but eventually its existence was confirmed. On the list were several future eminent public servants, including Maureen O'Neil, who became president of the International Development Research Centre, and Robert Rabinovitch, later

Trudeau called them "a bunch of hyenas"—to which came a quick rejoinder from boisterous Conservative MP Patrick Nowlan that members of the Liberal front bench were all "horses' asses."

In fact, several Liberal warhorses were either exhausted or disillusioned. The atmosphere in the House was sulphurous when Jean Marchand resigned angrily from Cabinet on June 30, 1976, to protest the decision favouring the use of English in the air traffic controller dispute. He and Bryce Mackasey later announced that they were leaving federal politics to run in the upcoming Quebec election. Mackasey's departure followed an interview with Trudeau on September 14, where, like Turner, he came prepared to negotiate but found a prime minister unwilling to reassure, barter, or debate options. Furious, Mackasey told reporters: "It was concern about policy. What the hell, how many battles can one guy fight by himself? You may get a little despondent, you get a little tired, and then you're not thinking as clearly and you get a little sensitive." The ebullient Mackasey was popular among the rank and file, and Trudeau himself was fond of the "irascible Irish fighter." When he announced the Cabinet shuffle that resulted, he told the press that he had tried to persuade Mackasey to stay, but the former minister wanted to pursue different interests. Mackasey retorted that he found the interview a peculiar form of persuasion.[2]

The September 1976 Cabinet shuffle occurred with the Liberals at 29 percent in the Gallup poll, their lowest level in thirty-three years. Two more senior ministers left the Cabinet—

---

a senior Trudeau adviser and CBC president. Victor Rabinovitch, who went on to be president of the Canadian Museum of Civilization, claims it was he, rather than his brother Robert, who was the actual RCMP target. Interview with Victor Rabinovitch, June 2008. Canada, *House of Commons Debates* (16 Oct. 1976).

Charles "Bud" Drury and Mitchell Sharp. Trudeau had always called on Drury, a former brigadier-general and successful businessman, to deal with troubled issues or portfolios, and he missed him greatly. The *Toronto Star* concluded that the new Cabinet, with many fresh faces but with so many past giants gone, "confirmed that [Trudeau] alone is the government and the government is him alone." One of the few remaining veterans, Allan MacEachen, almost resigned when Trudeau moved him from External Affairs to House leader: the normally dour Cape Breton Scot left the swearing-in ceremony after he lashed out at Michael Pitfield, whom many blamed for Trudeau's troubles.* Other resignations soon followed: Lloyd Francis of Ottawa stepped down as

---

* Pitfield was often the target for ministers who believed that Trudeau had mistreated them. His appointment as clerk of the Privy Council was controversial because of his long friendship with Trudeau. Highly intelligent, innovative, often late, and sometimes distant, Pitfield became a symbol of the concentration of power in the group around the prime minister. For Trudeau, he was a friend on whom he could fully rely. Their closeness led to rumours that Trudeau and Pitfield had a homosexual relationship, an outrageous story spread by, among others, a former senior civil servant who particularly loathed Pitfield. Later in the early 1980s, Trudeau responded to Conservative MP Otto Jelinek, who had repeated charges about Trudeau's homosexuality in a mailing to constituents. Trudeau boiled over and demanded that Jelinek be called before the bar of the House of Commons to withdraw and be punished. Senator David Smith and others tried to convince him to ignore the remarks. Trudeau insisted, even when Smith and others told him he had to be absolutely sure that no one could come forward who would say that he was a homosexual. "Is there anyone?" they asked. "There might be," Trudeau responded, "but he'd be lying." Finally, Trudeau sensibly agreed to let the matter rest. Interview with David Smith, Sept. 2002. Confidential sources.

parliamentary secretary and attacked federal bilingualism, as did
defence minister James Richardson. On October 18, Trudeau's
birthday, the Liberals lost two by-elections, one of them in John
Turner's Ottawa-Carleton riding, which they had held for ninety-
four years. The margin of Conservative Jean Piggott's victory there
was an astonishing sixteen thousand votes. On November 15,
Quebec's election day, Montreal MP Hal Herbert publicly called
for a leadership review, claiming that there should be "open recognition of the fact that the leadership is being questioned."[3] These
political events profoundly threatened Trudeau's position, which
was very much in doubt before Lévesque took power in late
November 1976.

The remarkable recovery of the Liberals in 1977 derives partly
from the public outpouring of support for Trudeau after Margaret
left the marriage and partly from the sense, identified by Christina
McCall, that Trudeau was the only federal leader able to meet the
separatist challenge. Yet many Liberals privately and publicly disagreed with her, and Quebec MPs Hal Herbert and Serge Joyal
were not alone in their dissent. Many journalists, and probably the
majority of francophones, remained strongly critical of Trudeau's
leadership. Moreover, English-Canadian opinion leaders such as
political scientist Denis Smith, author Margaret Atwood, and a
swarm of businesspeople in Toronto, Calgary, and Montreal argued
that Trudeau was Canada's greatest problem, not its saviour. There
were many reasons for Canadians not to entrust Trudeau with the
fight against separatism, they said. Had he not declared separatism
"dead" many times in 1976? Had he not contributed to the Quebec
Liberals' collapse? Had he not governed indifferently after the 1974
election? Had not many of the best Liberal politicians of the era
walked away from his government? Even Trudeau's supporters
could not strongly disagree with these criticisms.[4]

And yet, despite significant weaknesses, Trudeau managed
to "turn fortune" in the winter of 1976–77. He once again found

his political voice, and it echoed reassuringly among increasing numbers of Canadians. His response to the separatists was constructed on the uncertain bedrock of public opinion, but at a moment when most Canadians needed encouragement, Trudeau's clarity and apparent determination resonated widely. Later critics, such as André Burelle, a speechwriter of the later 1970s, and political scientists Kenneth McRoberts and Guy Laforest all argue that Trudeau's insistence on bilingualism as the central response to the separatist challenge and his refusal to consider either special status for Quebec or appropriate decentralization to the provinces were ultimately wrong and damaging. They assert that a more flexible response would have produced a better outcome.[5] Yet there is strong evidence that had Trudeau considered such an approach in 1976, he would have lost his legitimacy to lead, not simply because he would have abandoned a promise but mainly because Canadians would not have followed him. Joe Clark did countenance decentralization and some accommodation on bilingualism, and the NDP had historically favoured special status. The alternatives to Trudeau were presented, but Canadians did not want them—hence the shift in the polls.

The polls indicate clearly why special status and decentralization lacked political appeal. The Gallup poll published on April 9, 1977, asked: "Should the government of Canada negotiate special political and economic agreements with Quebec to try to prevent separation?" This question summarizes the essence of "special status" without using the term. Anglophones opposed these proposals 54.7 to 38.3 percent, an indication that any political party supporting them would have had huge political difficulties. And when Gallup asked Quebecers about the question of special status in July 1977, only 22 percent favoured it, while 72 percent were opposed, with national figures registering 10 percent and 86 percent, respectively. Special status was clearly understood as tantamount to separation by most Canadians, if not

346 JUST WATCH ME

in university common rooms. As long as Trudeau was able to "frame" his opponents' response to the challenge of the PQ as indicating their willingness to bestow special status, he gained politically.

Trudeau's emphasis on bilingualism within the public service and among francophone and anglophone minorities in Canada was also seen by many critics as an Achilles' heel. Winnipeg's James Richardson, for example, resigned from the Liberal Cabinet because he said the West would not accept Trudeau's focus on bilingualism. After John Turner resigned, the Liberals decisively lost his seat when the Conservatives and the NDP campaigned on a fairer break for anglophone public servants. Joe Clark's first speech after the Quebec election suggested that Trudeau's obsession with bilingualism was a cause of national disunity, and the polls of the day supported his argument. The April 9 Gallup poll, for example, asked: "Should the governments of Canada and the provinces promote and finance more extensive bilingualism throughout the country to try to prevent separation?"* In English Canada, only 27.8 percent said yes, and 64.1 percent said no. Among francophones, however, the answer was very different— 56 percent versus 33 percent, even though the PQ and many

---

* The astonishing popularity of the book *Bilingual Today, French Tomorrow: Trudeau's Master Plan and How It Can Be Stopped* (Richmond Hill, Ontario: BMG Publishing Limited, 1977), by Lieutenant Commander (Retired) J.V. Andrew suggests how intense the hostility was to bilingualism in many areas of Canada. The book had ten printings in 1977 and 1978. Accusing Trudeau of forcing Canada to become an "all-French" nation, he wrote: "We are faced with the problem of getting rid of a totally ruthless man who has sworn to remain in power, regardless of public sentiment, until Canada becomes functionally Bilingual from coast to coast and thus for all intents and purposes a French-speaking country" (129).

separatist opponents such as Claude Ryan claimed that the bilingualism focus was wrong, misguided, or foolish.[6] On the whole, though, the numbers were far more balanced than any one poll would indicate, and in many areas they were a source of political strength for the Trudeau Liberals.

When Joe Clark spoke against renewed and expanded support for bilingualism, he reflected the views held most strongly in the western provinces, where he had won 49 seats in the 1974 election, compared with only 13 for the Liberals, of which 8 were in British Columbia. Conversely, the support for bilingualism was strongest in Quebec, where Clark had won only 3 seats, while Trudeau had taken 60. Clark could not therefore expand his support, as he needed to do to win an election. He merely reinforced those areas where he currently had an overwhelming lead. The Liberals also captured 6 seats in New Brunswick, where the francophone vote appears to have been the deciding factor, and one in Manitoba, where it was definitely the basis of victory. Although Trudeau's support for bilingualism cost him little in the West, it almost certainly solidified his support among francophones outside Quebec—a significant political force in New Brunswick, Ontario, and St. Boniface in Manitoba. For many constituencies, the francophone vote provided a margin of victory. In Quebec itself, moreover, bilingualism was a popular federal cause, even if the PQ and many francophone leaders dismissed it.

The same balance across the country applied to the devolution of greater powers from the central government to the provinces. Trudeau's opposition to both special status and decentralization was unpopular with Quebec francophones, but it appealed very much to Ontario. The 55 seats the Liberals won there in 1974 gave Trudeau his majority. Although Alberta strongly supported decentralization, Clark currently held all of its 19 seats. His hopes for a majority depended on Ontario, where Conservative premier William Davis vigorously attacked any mention of decentralization or special status. By the spring of 1977, therefore, Trudeau had found the personal and policy foundations for solid electoral triumph.

Suddenly, Clark was on the defensive. Jacques Lavoie, the Conservative MP for Hochelaga who had won a stunning victory over the eminent Pierre Juneau in a by-election in October 1975, announced in June 1977 that he was leaving the bickering Tories and joining the Liberals. Even more astonishing was the move across the aisles on April 20 by self-professed Alberta redneck Jack Horner, who declared Joe Clark unequal to the "supreme task" of keeping Canada together. As John Diefenbaker sputtered that the "sheriff [was] joining the cattle rustlers," Trudeau appointed Horner a minister without portfolio in his government. Soon they developed an unexpected warm friendship.[7] The Liberal political team began to prepare for an election after the party won five of six by-elections on May 24, five of them in Quebec. The victories, which saw the Liberal vote rise in comparison with that of the 1974 election, brought credit to Marc Lalonde, who had replaced Marchand as the government's Quebec lieutenant. They came less than a month after the Parti Québécois had introduced Bill 1, which declared that French would be the working language of Quebec, thus going well beyond Bourassa's legislation entrenching French as the sole official language of Quebec. The by-elections seemed to signal that Trudeau had won the first round of the battle with Lévesque.

On the evening of the by-elections, however, Trudeau unexpectedly said, "Tonight's victory doesn't show that we're in need of a new mandate." The *Globe and Mail* did not believe him and remarked in an editorial that "the temptation for Mr. Trudeau to call an early election must be enormous." In another editorial, it accused Joe Clark of having "squandered" his chances "by his indecision, his fear to be seen to take any position because it might help his opponents, [and] his admission to manipulation—almost like a puppet—by his immediate advisers." For many around

Trudeau, the temptation was indeed great—but then, the announcement of Pierre and Margaret's separation three days after the by-election win quickly stopped the speculation.[8]

Before long, however, the conjectures began again. The "politicos," the new media assistant Patrick Gossage wrote, would surely see the "image of Trudeau as single father as a sure vote-getter." And Trudeau was "eligible" once more, eager to seduce and be seduced—or so it seemed to some journalists and a few interested women. His aides began to worry about "hungry women reporters . . . taking advantage of his interest in blatant charms" and Trudeau responding to their hunger too quickly. At a press conference shortly after the separation, they questioned whether he had paid far too much attention to Catherine Bergman, an attractive, highly popular Radio-Canada journalist. Still, the rising polls did prove the truth of Gossage's hunch, and the advisers persuaded Trudeau to spend the summer in a round of political barbecues, shrimp festivals, and church basements. Often one or more of the boys were with him: during a tour of the Gaspé in early July, for instance, a picture of the "natural and photogenic" Sacha walking hand in hand with his father appeared on front pages throughout Canada.

To the public, Trudeau appeared playful once again. His charisma was back. Before the separation announcement, when he showed up in London in early May for the G7 meeting (which was then called the "economic summit"), Trudeau had captured the attention of the *Times* by wearing a "natty tan corduroy suit with an orange rose pinned to his lapel." But he startled everyone at the elegant state dinner when he lingered behind as the Queen was leaving, and then, suddenly, performed an elegant pirouette. It was not a "spontaneously rude and impulsive gesture" but one Trudeau had planned carefully in the hours before the dinner. He resented the British protocol of separating heads of state such as Valéry Giscard d'Estaing, whom he disliked, from mere politicians who were not heads of state, such as himself and German Chancellor Helmut Schmidt.* The summit is long forgotten, yet the photograph of the poised yet bizarre gesture endures as perhaps the most famous Trudeau photograph of all.[9]

Trudeau returned to London in June for the Commonwealth Conference, so he had ample opportunity to talk about the situation back home with veteran Canadian politician Paul Martin, who was serving as Canadian high commissioner there. He made it clear in May that his thoughts about leaving politics "a few

---

* It was not only at state dinners that the British offended Trudeau's more republican sensibilities. When he arrived for the G7 in 1977 at Heathrow, High Commissioner Paul Martin noted that Trudeau was not given a formal welcome like the ones presidents of smaller states received. As noted in volume 1 of this biography, Trudeau's opposition to the British Empire was a strongly held belief, one that brought him his lowest university mark when he wrote a scathing essay on the empire for anglophile Harvard professor William Yandell Elliott. By 1977 Trudeau's bristling attitude had moderated considerably, not least because he had come to value the Commonwealth meetings but even more because he had developed an admiration, and eventually a fondness, for the Queen. He told interviewer Ron Graham that she did a "first-rate job" and that she impressed him. She was so easy to talk to that Trudeau became bold at a "rubber chicken" dinner in Alberta. He asked her if he could pose a question that had long bothered him. His maiden aunt, he continued, "was a rather refined lady and once, when we were eating chicken together, she picked up a drumstick." Someone frowned at the gesture and Trudeau's aunt said, "The Queen does it." Trudeau looked at the Queen and she looked at him and said, "Hmm." Trudeau concluded: "I imagine she wouldn't do it." Paul Martin, *The London Diaries 1975–1979* (Ottawa: University of Ottawa Press, 1988), 249. Interview between Ron Graham and Pierre Trudeau, May 12, 1992, TP, MG 26 02, vol. 23, file 2, LAC.

months" before had disappeared. He was now sure he would win an electoral campaign, though he had been making no plans for one despite pressure from various Liberals. By June, however, after the by-election victories and the announcement of his separation, he seemed much more inclined to call an election. He asked Martin, an extraordinarily shrewd observer of politics, when the election should be called. Martin said it could be a good "weapon against Lévesque" and implicitly endorsed an early vote.

In Ottawa the election fever built, stoked by poll results even higher than in the heady days of Trudeaumania. Wage and price controls were a political problem, but Judith Maxwell of the C.D. Howe Research Institute had pointed out in early 1977 that, despite considerable Canadian grumbling about Trudeau's economic policies, real personal disposable income per capita had risen in Canada between 1969 and 1975—the Trudeau years—by 5.1 percent annually, compared to only 3.3 percent in Britain and 2.2 percent in the United States. Moreover, 1976 was the best year of the decade with a 5.9 percent growth of real GNP.[10] In midsummer, after "fighting it off," Trudeau agreed to consider an election, after he took a three-week holiday. Trudeau aide Colin Kenny said that "everything that happens is turned into an argument for an early election" by Trudeau's closest political advisers, although the Liberal ministers and caucus were much less enthusiastic at their own gathering. Jim Coutts, the closest Trudeau aide, was particularly adamant in his support of an election, and in mid-August, Trudeau began to meet with his advisers, who, when polled, all strongly favoured a fall vote.

There were, of course, some doubts and problems. There was the example of Ontario, where the Conservatives had recently called an election following favourable polls but had ended up with a minority. Moreover, Trudeau had appointed a task force on Canadian unity chaired by former Ontario premier John Robarts and Jean-Luc Pepin, who had stepped down from the largely irrelevant Anti-Inflation Board, and an election could easily appear as undermining its work. In early July Trudeau had also appointed the Royal Commission into Certain Activities of the RCMP (the McDonald Commission) and, again, an election could complicate its task. Then, on July 8, energy minister Alastair Gillespie fired the president of Atomic Energy of Canada for disastrous overruns on the Candu reactors sold to Argentina. Obviously, many potential landmines might explode during an election campaign.[11]

Yet Clark seemed very weak; Trudeau was warmly welcomed in Jack Horner's Camrose, Alberta; and the economy continued to improve. On August 2, when Coutts was spending a holiday at the farm of Paul Martin Jr., he told his host, who was contemplating entering politics, his reasons for wanting an election: "(1) The economy might not be good next year; (2) The Tories may select a new leader this November; (3) Inflation and unemployment will be up; and (4) National unity may not be the prime issue."[12] When he pressed these arguments on the prime minister, Trudeau promised he would decide by the end of August. On Friday, August 26, his office was hectic with preparations for a possible election, and the gossip mill was in full swing. Gossage captured the frenzy in his diary:

> "Bullshit!" Perhaps the loudest I have ever said it on the phone. This to counter another Gallery rumour that Friday was the day for an election call. Our office has been at a rolling boil all week.
>
> We know the thumbscrews Coutts and Davey applied on Monday, Tuesday, and again on Thursday. Jim [Coutts] has been looking frantic for the first time this year. It almost is like a plot—the promised jobs, the elaborate ruses to keep things hushed. Monday is to be the decision.

Trudeau did not wait until Monday to make up his mind. At day's end on Friday, a downcast Colin Kenny called Gossage: "Well, that's the way the cookie crumbles." There would be no election.

It was Trudeau's worst political decision. Later, there were stories that Jean Marchand had urged him to hold off, but that is most unlikely, given that Trudeau no longer had faith in Marchand's judgment. Others have argued that the federal Liberals faced danger because the essence of their election program would be official bilingualism in response to Lévesque's Charter of the French Language—yet that is precisely the battle Trudeau longed to fight. In his memoirs Keith Davey, who favoured an election, claimed that Trudeau listened to caucus, but that suggestion is also unconvincing because the debates in August took place long after the summer caucus had ended. For Trudeau, backbenchers might no longer be the "nobodies" he had once declared they were, but they were definitely not a major influence on his decision.

Patrick Gossage, who was "close to the charisma" of Trudeau in these months, has a simpler and more convincing explanation: "I think of the PM facing this lonely decision pushed on him by advisers who know little of his inner life." He was reading the transcript of Alain Stanké's *"portrait intime"* of Trudeau, and he pondered Trudeau's comments during the interview: "I think of Trudeau, who seeks the peace . . . to know the name of every tree and flower, to count the blades of grass and 'planter des radis.'"[13] Even though Trudeau went through the motions of campaigning that summer in the Gaspé, in Camrose, and in Vancouver's downtown, his heart and mind were elsewhere. In these short bursts, he performed brilliantly because, as always, he knew his lines well, but he was not ready to perform a play of several acts, which an election would inevitably be. Trudeau's hesitations are understandable, even as he accepted Coutts's reasons as to why he was wrong.[14]

Reasons of the heart, sad ones, explain Trudeau's lack of will for an election in the late summer of 1977. His private and public comments at the time betray his mood. He wrote to Marshall McLuhan in late July: "You continue to fascinate us with your treatises on the interaction and interrelation between technology and man. Your recent thoughts on the effects of the media on private morality present provocative though frightening observations of our society. One begins to wonder if our age of rapid communication leaves room for anything private—not just morality but thoughts and even creativity." He needed some time for himself, away from the madding crowds of politics and photographers. In the summer he finally began to answer with brief notes the surprisingly numerous expressions of regret that friends had sent after the announcement of his separation from Margaret. To one letter from an old friend in the foreign service who said he knew it was "a hard blow, especially for a man like you, who attaches so much value to family life and the happiness of others," Pierre answered simply: "Your note of May 30 touched me deeply. I would just like to say thank you."[15] He said little more to anyone about personal matters in those days.

Coutts, of course, was disappointed, especially because he and some others in the Prime Minister's Office had wanted to run in the election, but he accepted the decision, whatever its motives. Trudeau puzzled Coutts. Writing about him eighteen years later, he recalled that politics is normally a profession for the gregarious, but that, for Trudeau, the power to concentrate, one of his greatest assets, "was honed in hours spent alone. He enjoyed and required solitude to read, think, and write. More surprisingly, he also used his time alone to rehearse—for he was an actor"—as Trudeau so elegantly demonstrated with his pirouette in London. Margaret's books and interviews are replete with examples of Trudeau's powers of concentration and its corollary—the need to be alone and to keep personal distance. The prerequisite for these habits was discipline, a quality that Trudeau often extolled in the mid-seventies as disorder marked his public life and, for that matter, the decade. That essential discipline, the careful rehearsals, and the intense focus were simply not possible for him in 1977. He maintained an impressive silence about his private life, resisted those who called him to the political stage for his greatest perform- ance, and gathered his resources to fight another day.[16]

—

As Coutts and Davey feared, the polls started to turn soon after Trudeau decided against an election. By October, the Conservatives had gained five points from their July low, and the twenty-four-point lead the Liberals had enjoyed was only eight points by December. Bad news came early after Labour Day when Donald Macdonald, considered by Trudeau and many others as the leading anglophone minister, announced he was leaving politics. Earlier, Jean Chrétien had considered a move to contest the Quebec leadership, but, now he eagerly accepted Trudeau's request that he replace Macdonald and become the first French-Canadian finance minister. The press in Quebec and elsewhere applauded his appointment, but, on the whole, the shuffle that brought only one new face to the Cabinet table (Norm Cafik of Ontario) was branded as unimaginative. Warren Allmand, who had been popular in the portfolio of Indian Affairs and Northern Development, publicly said he had been "shafted" when Trudeau moved him to Consumer and Corporate Affairs. Two other appointments attracted attention: Marc Lalonde went from Health and Welfare, where he had promoted a guaran- teed annual income without success, to become minister of state for federal-provincial relations, and Monique Bégin, who had earlier refused the Ministry of State for the Status of Women because she thought it a token appointment, accepted the same portfolio because it was now attached to Health and Welfare. She became an outstanding minister.[17] All told, however, the Cabinet shuffle did not represent the fresh start that a government in the third year of its mandate so badly needed.

Trudeau had confided to Paul Martin in the summer that Macdonald was his finest Ontario minister. Why, he asked, were there not more able candidates, as in the days of St. Laurent and Pearson? Macdonald's departure reinforced the impression that Trudeau could not work with other strong ministers, especially ones from English Canada. As Liberal fortunes fell in the autumn, journalists and some Liberals began to talk about John Turner again and to ask, often hopefully, "Will Trudeau go?" Then, after a brief respite, the economic problems returned to the front page. On the same day that Trudeau shuffled the Cabinet, Gerald Bouey, the governor of the Bank of Canada, warned that inflation, which had dropped in 1976, was rising again in 1977, while unemployment had reached 8.2 percent. "Stagflation" had settled in with a vengeance—and it affected workers and those on fixed incomes in particular. The rise in inflation was due partly to the continual fall in the value of the Canadian dollar, which the election of the Parti Québécois appeared to have stimulated. By October 14, 1977, it had fallen to just over 90 cents, the lowest level since the outbreak of the Second World War, and ten days later, it stood at 89.88 cents, a level previously seen only in 1932 at the height of the Great Depression. Although Bouey could correctly note that the adjustment in the currency rate would enhance Canadian competitiveness and create Canadian jobs, Bay Street and Main Street were increasingly nervous.[18]

Queen Elizabeth opened the fall session of Parliament on October 18 with grace and dignity, qualities that soon disappeared in the House as television coverage was introduced, with predictable results. It was a raucous session as the government dealt with a faltering economy, controversies over bilingualism and the Quebec language bill, and continuing scandals related to the RCMP and its irresponsible reaction to the rise of separatism. Trudeau and Solicitor General Francis Fox trod clumsily on the fine line that separates a security force from political interference.

As revelations accumulated of break-ins at news agencies and offices of the Parti Québécois, and of long lists of individuals regarded as security risks, including even NDP leader Ed Broadbent, their defences crumbled. Monique Bégin broke Cabinet solidarity when she told a group of Carleton University students that "Francis Fox should clearly state . . . that he . . . disagrees with what the police did, more than defending them or explaining that they might have had good reasons." Increasingly, the beleaguered Fox agreed with Bégin as his anger with the RCMP mounted, but he tried to halt the Quebec-appointed Keable Commission from extending its investigations into areas of national security. To the federal government's considerable embarrassment, on December 9 Judge James Hugessen of the Quebec Superior Court ruled against Fox and the federal government, stating that "the law should encourage frankness and openness in everything dealing with public matters."[19] Not surprisingly, the press dubbed it the Canadian Watergate.

These problems had little impact on the government's position, even though they received justifiable press attention. The focus was on the challenge of Quebec separatism, and other issues faded into the background. Trudeau had scored well in his first encounters with Lévesque and had strengthened his position within the Liberal Party and the country. Indeed, in that round he probably saved his own political life. By the end of 1977, however, the scandals surrounding the RCMP, the intractable problems of the economy, and the ongoing quarrels between the provinces and the federal government had eroded Canadians' confidence in Trudeau. In fact, he had lost confidence himself. When he met the esteemed novelist Mordecai Richler for lunch in September, Dick O'Hagan, his press secretary, urged him to reassure the cynical author, who planned to write a highly critical article about the separatist movement and Quebec for the *Atlantic Monthly*. Trudeau said he could not because "he was less than sanguine himself about the country's future." He looked "worn," Patrick Gossage observed on September 21, and his government was losing its way: "At the nexus of a nation in considerable agony, I can see many failed opportunities and little teamwork or exercise of common sense. There has been a 'study' of the PM's use of time and 90 percent is 'operational.' Now more time is to be devoted to long-range thinking and planning, and the Cabinet shuffle reflects this. Fine, but who will look after nuts and bolts?" In Gossage's view, the Cabinet system paralyzed, rather than facilitated, decision making, and a new framework was imperative.[20]

At O'Hagan's prompting, Trudeau had begun regular press conferences after the PQ victory and, reluctantly, met with reporters more frequently. He even agreed to cooperate with journalist George Radwanski on a proposed biography. He gave him eight one-hour interviews in the winter and spring of 1977 and told aides and his sister, Suzette, to cooperate. This extraordinary access provided Radwanski with insights into Trudeau long denied to others. When published in 1978, the book, simply entitled *Trudeau*, revealed details that had long been shielded from the public. In the opening chapter, "A Day in the Life," Radwanski follows Trudeau from 9:07 a.m., when the limousine departs from 24 Sussex, until 6:16 p.m., when it bears him home. On that early July day, Radwanski saw a disciplined and hard-working prime minister who relied heavily on some very talented people, notably a core group of four who met with him each morning when Parliament sat: Michael Pitfield (the clerk of the Privy Council), Jim Coutts, Dick O'Hagan, and de Montigny Marchand (a member of Pitfield's Privy Council team). There were occasional "wisecracks," Radwanski wrote, but even though Parliament would soon rise and there were no outstanding issues, "the demands on Trudeau's time [were] too many to allow anything but a brisk pace." The same pressure continued throughout the day. At the end of the chapter, Radwanski reports on the study that the PMO had done of Trudeau's time: the prime minister worked 250 hours per month, far more than most Canadians.* On the day Radwanski "trailed" him, he had worked eleven hours, but he was "publicly visible" for only eighty-eight minutes of it.[21]

The quotidian details of Trudeau's life—the telephone system that allowed him to reach senior aides simply by pressing a button, and the box of chocolates for his sweet tooth—are interesting, but it is the comments about Trudeau made by close colleagues that fascinate. Mitchell Sharp, for example, had served as a senior minister until 1976 and remained a major figure in Ottawa. Nevertheless, he was astonishingly frank in his assessment of Trudeau's current difficulties: "One of [his] serious faults is his lack of sensitivity to human relations. He has never been able to generate a feeling amongst his followers that any individual follower is important to him except for close personal friends like Marchand and Pelletier. He told me once: 'I find the most difficult part of this job is dealing with people.' He's a man who inspires, but who seems to lack warmth in his personal relations. I've heard this from so many people. They're here, they're gone, with never any appreciation expressed. He never says, 'I'd like you to help me.' It has had an understandable effect."

Radwanski indicates that Trudeau particularly admired Donald Macdonald because he was frank, direct, and extremely competent. Yet Macdonald, who had left the Cabinet only in the late summer of 1977, was also critical of Trudeau: "There's one area where he does have weakness, and that's dealing with people.

---

* Of the 250 hours, about 90 were spent on government business, 50 on political activities, 12.5 on contact with the news media, 30 with PMO and PCO staff, and 67.5 on "paperwork, correspondence, and telephone calls." George Radwanski, *Trudeau* (Toronto: Macmillan, 1978), 20–21.

You know, he's a very private person himself and he doesn't, I think, have a great deal of empathy for other people, and he can fail to comprehend or sympathize with other people's situations." While he believed Trudeau was not "deliberately callous," he had difficulties being "warm and sympathetic," and it had caused difficulties in his relationships with colleagues.[22]

These comments betray a *fin de régime* mood of reminiscence and remembrance, not a tone of expectation or enthusiasm.*

---

* Trudeau's correspondence has abundant examples of sensitivity and thoughtfulness, but he expressed such emotions with a reserve that surely reflected his mother's example. For example, Robert Ford, Canada's ambassador to the Soviet Union, profoundly disagreed with much of Trudeau's policy, but they remained warm friends. After his retirement Ford's wife, Thereza, wrote to Trudeau, thanking him for his understanding about Ford's physical disabilities, which limited his mobility. He had written to her, asking if he could help when they retired. She replied: "Like to go on record that the Government owes us absolutely nothing and assure you of what an enriching, passionate work it was to try to follow on your footsteps through all those years. . . . I must touch on another subject very close to my heart and that is the utter elegance, the understanding, the minimization of Robert's disability. Never once did I feel patronized but at the greatest of ease with you on what at times must have been very difficult circumstances. For that I shall always be intensely and eternally grateful. Yours, most fondly, Thereza." Ford to Trudeau, nd, TP, MG 26 o20, vol. 4, file 26, LAC.

Interviews with Trudeau's secretarial staff are filled with instances of personal kindnesses, although there is no doubt that such examples are much rarer in the case of his political colleagues. And there is a significant gender gap. Trudeau found it difficult to be close and warm with men. While Patrick Gossage's diary regularly notes Trudeau's distance from himself and other male colleagues, Trudeau aide Joyce Fairbairn, who briefed Trudeau for Question Period, was highly personal in her communications, as for example on his

Trudeau's own remarks are retrospective and lead directly to Radwanski's conclusion—that as a prime minister, he was "unfulfilled," that he had not attained greatness even though no alternative leader could have done more, and incongruously, that his career was entering its "decisive phase" on a terrain he had so carefully tilled. The book, admirable in its research and thoughtful in its analysis, reflects its times, and for that reason it offers insights into the curious rise and fall of Trudeau as a champion of "English Canada" against the challenge of René Lévesque's PQ government. Historian Ramsay Cook has argued that such a "casting" reduces "the debates of the 1970s to mere personality clashes" and thereby "banishes confusion at the risk of introducing obfuscation." Yet the times framed the debates as a stand-off between Lévesque and Trudeau. The issue that divided the two defined the Canadian political scene in the late 1970s, and the extent to which politicians responded cogently and convincingly to that question defined their success: Was it best for French-speaking Canadians to be a majority in a pluralist Quebec state or a minority in a pluralist Canadian state? As a result, so much of the Trudeau government's broader record became obscured in the dark clouds and thunder that accompanied the contest between the governments of Quebec and Canada. Radwanski wrote his book as Lévesque's referendum loomed and as Trudeau's increasingly unpopular government was framing its own answers to this challenge.[23]

---

birthday: "Happy birthday Laddie. Here are some homemade chocolate-nut cookies for you and the boys. If you return the tin I will refill it." She knew his sweet tooth for chocolate well. Fairbairn to Trudeau, Oct. 18, 1978, TP, MG 26 020, vol. 4, file 10, LAC. Trudeau also treated old school chums, several of whom worked in the government, with particular friendliness, often asking senior officials if they could have an appointment when the old friend requested one.

—

Trudeau's speech to the American Congress and his interventions in Commons debates in early 1977 set out three possible choices for Canada: Would it be a pluralist, bilingual country with individual rights as its centrepiece, or two separate countries, or two linguistically distinct entities bound together loosely by an as yet undefined understanding? The clarity of this vision was increasingly appealing to many francophone and anglophone Canadians in the spring and early summer, as a referendum loomed and the PQ concept of an "association" seemed confusing. But then the vision became blurred. Trudeau's parliamentary opponents attacked him for rigidity and inflexibility—and, indeed, his strong opposition to special status and to decentralization did seem adamant. In the late summer and fall, as his policies developed, they were much more ambiguous than they had been before. Trudeau responded to this change when he wrote in his memoirs that in terms of the distribution of powers, "I was determined to show that I could be as generous as the next guy, and perhaps even more."[24] And generous he was in the "deal" he offered the provinces in 1979, as we shall see. He was flexible, but as he later complained, his flexibility was misunderstood.

One of Trudeau's first responses to the separatist challenge had been markedly decentralist, although its full impact was not recognized at the time except by political economists and Finance Department bureaucrats. At the first ministers' conference of December 1976, Trudeau agreed to remove the conditions attached to the major cost-sharing programs—a move that responded to Quebec's demands after the Quiet Revolution and, as Trudeau pointed out later, to his own early writings on the Canadian Constitution. The agreement affected Quebec less than the other provinces because it had already opted out of many cost-sharing programs, and Lévesque was quick to assert that the federal government's true aim was to reduce its own costs. There was truth in the charge, but the agreement remains a major source of growth in provincial autonomy. In the House of Commons in February, when Donald Macdonald introduced the new Established Programs Financing Act, Ed Broadbent denounced the agreement as "the first major step toward the balkanization of our country . . . The inevitable result of these proposals is to downgrade the national government's role in ensuring minimum standards in health services and in post-secondary education."

Later, when Trudeau attacked Brian Mulroney's constitutional innovations, some of the Meech Lake defenders, including Liberal elder statesman Jack Pickersgill, pointed to the 1976–77 agreement as the most radically decentralizing decision of the postwar era. The criticism was unfair because it lacked the context of the times: the cost of social programs was rising rapidly while federal government revenues stagnated, and the federal government needed the provinces who administered the programs to take more responsibility for them. Still, both spending and the political influence that derives from direct contact with citizens were shifting to the provinces.[25]

Most Canadians did not notice these federal-provincial agreements, which seemed like another tedious act in a long and boring drama. However, they did pay attention in July 1977 to the appointment of the Task Force on Canadian Unity, chaired by John Robarts and Jean-Luc Pepin. The creation of this task force seemed puzzling at the time and remains so today. Robarts, the former Ontario premier, was a spent force, and Pepin was much more open to special status and nationalist views than were his former Cabinet colleagues. Gordon Robertson, the deputy minister of federal-provincial relations, later wrote: "I think Trudeau never believed that the result of the task force's work would be something he could accept as a solution to the constitutional problem. His thinking and that of Pepin were miles apart." The only reason for the appointment, he suspected, was that Trudeau "believed . . . something had to be done to respond to the PQ victory." But for most Canadians, the resulting report was one further blow to the clarity of Trudeau's message about national unity. When Pepin visited Quebec City, he reportedly asked Lévesque whether sovereignty-association was different from renewed federalism, and Lévesque responded, not surprisingly, that sovereignty-association was renewed federalism in a hurry. This exchange did not help Trudeau's cause. Nor did the task force win support for the government elsewhere. Five days after the Quebec City encounter, several groups walked out of the meeting organized in Toronto because the task force had allotted only two days for its stay in that city — the same as in Charlottetown. Despite this tight agenda, Premier William Davis insisted on speaking for over an hour. In Edmonton, however, Premier Lougheed chose not to speak at all and sent no Cabinet member to the task force hearings. It was not a good start.[26]

Simultaneously, the federal response to the Lévesque government's Bill 1, which later became Bill 101, also perplexed Canadians. When Trudeau's old friend Camille Laurin, now one of the most militant PQ ministers, first brought forward this bill delineating the language of education in the province, the federalist and English-Canadian response was strong and hostile. Yet as the year progressed, Ottawa made it clear that despite the bill's objectionable features, the federal government would not disallow the legislation, as many anglophone groups in Quebec were demanding. Disallowance, though legally possible, was politically unthinkable. More surprising was Ottawa's decision not to refer the legislation to the Supreme Court. After all, had not Trudeau said that the legislation was retrograde and a return to the "Dark Ages"?

Events over the summer of 1977 confused matters further. At their meeting in St. Andrews, New Brunswick, the premiers approved a statement in which they agreed "that they . . . [would]

make their best efforts to provide instruction in English and French wherever numbers warrant." Lévesque would not accept this pledge but offered, instead, to work out bilateral or multilateral agreements with the provinces—an offer the anglophone provinces understandably believed would represent their de facto acceptance of Bill 101. Yet on September 2, Trudeau released a long public letter to Lévesque in which he acknowledged the latter's disappointment with the other premiers' statement "because there is nothing in it to provide any certainty of implementation or any guarantee of permanence." However, Trudeau went on, this deficiency could be met "by appropriate constitutional provision," although he was willing to discuss "other less desirable alternatives." Lévesque replied a week later that he was pleased that the Government of Canada was "now willing to accept, as the criterion for admission to Quebec's English-language schools, the Charter of the French Language's main teaching criterion, namely the parents' language of education. We take this to recognize our law's constitutionality." He also noted that Trudeau's letter implicitly recognized that Quebec's situation differed from that of the other provinces. Nevertheless, he rejected embedding educational rights within the Constitution because they would then be subject to interpretation by the Supreme Court—which would always have an anglophone majority.

On October 6, Trudeau released his reply to Lévesque's letter—and this time he took a much harder line. He began with a statement that "the position and policy of the federal Government are for full freedom for all Canadians to be educated in the official language of their choice, wherever numbers justify it. Regrettably, in our view, your government has a different perception of future prospects for the French language in Quebec and of the conditions needed to assure its continued development than that held by the federal Government. You do not accept freedom of choice." He then took issue with Lévesque's dismissal of a constitutional guarantee of language rights: "It is my personal and deep conviction that the citizen in a democracy should enjoy certain fundamental rights and freedoms which take precedence over the laws promulgated by any legislature and the regulations decreed by any government, because they are so fundamental to the very existence of such a democratic society that they should be beyond the reach of its governmental institutions." He taunted Lévesque for the restrictions being placed on the English language in Quebec and hoped that, in time, they could be loosened to "enlarge somewhat" what sociologist Fernand Dumont "once called '*l'aire de la liberté au Québec.*'" It was a subtle reminder of past battles that Lévesque, Trudeau, and the prominent academic Dumont, now a separatist, had fought together. Trudeau ended with a defence of the Constitution, the Supreme Court, and the need for a constitutional guarantee that would preserve minority rights. But he also announced that the federal government would not refer Bill 101 to the Supreme Court.[27]

Journalist Geoffrey Stevens fastened on the decision not to refer the bill: "If the Trudeau government really believes all the things it said about Quebec's Bill 101, the course it proposes to take is woefully inadequate, an unsatisfactory compromise between action and inaction. It's trying to talk loudly and carry a small stick." Stevens recognized that the government was trapped by a game of political cat and mouse, one where the Quebec government had the longest string because Trudeau would face an election first.

In the maelstrom of events, Trudeau wanted to maintain focus on the central issue: the threat of Quebec separation. To that end, in September 1977 he appointed Marc Lalonde to coordinate the federal response as the minister of state for federal-provincial relations. Lalonde, who had proved himself as Quebec lieutenant after he succeeded Marchand, now brought that same intensity and loyalty to the task of orchestrating the federalist response to Lévesque. He consulted with the provinces, issued a call to arms in a booklet titled *A Time for Action*, and introduced Bill 60, which provided for the patriation of the Constitution and the framework of a charter of rights, including minority education.

As the government entered the fourth year of its mandate, election thoughts stirred once again. On the same page where Geoffrey Stevens discussed the government's decision not to challenge Bill 101, the *Globe and Mail* reported that several branches of the federal civil service were moving out of Ottawa—thirteen of them to Liberal ridings across the country. The most notable was to Camrose, Alberta, the home of Jack Horner, the recent Tory defector to Liberal ranks.[28]

The Prime Minister's Office was "again indeed on a war footing; on twenty-four-hour alert for yet another election decision," Gossage wrote in his diary. "Entrails of all kinds are being examined. . . . It is all hanging out. Seats are being opened up so that favoured candidates can be run." Rumours swirled: Jean Chrétien was leaving federal politics to go to Quebec; Radio-Canada was a nest of separatists who would not give Trudeau or other federalists fair coverage; a minister's personal foibles would soon be exposed. On January 30, 1978, the last rumour proved true, when one of the most promising young ministers, Solicitor General Francis Fox, a favourite of Lalonde and Trudeau and brother of the popular Trudeau aide Marie-Hélène Fox, rose in the House and admitted that he had signed as a husband to permit a married woman, pregnant with his child, to have an abortion. Trudeau wept in his office. Throughout the week, he "remained moody, affected as he hasn't been since the split with Margaret." The press ruthlessly pursued their quarry; feminists asked why women needed a husband's signature; and pro-life activists used the incident to denounce the existing legislation and what they saw as the hypocrisy of the Trudeau government.

Preparations continued for a federal-provincial meeting in late February, at which the constitutional plans were presented in an attempt to seize the momentum. Instead, in Gossage's words, "the real moment of the conference came when a determined wedge of Péquistes left the hall and drove through the Delegates' Lounge for their spoil-sport 3:00 p.m. press conference, a full hour or so before the conference closed. The federal officials blanched. Their months of preparation, of tilling the difficult provincial soil, seemed to evaporate in seconds. Lévesque pulled off the most diabolically effective upstaging of a national forum that could be imagined. It was brilliant." It was the tenth anniversary of the upstaging of Quebec's Daniel Johnson by the new federal justice minister, Pierre Trudeau, from which his quest for the Prime Minister's Office followed. The path ahead in 1978 was not nearly so clear.[29]

Lévesque and his government had gained assurance and credibility throughout their first year in power. The process of "francization" of Quebec, which had begun with Bourassa's Bill 22, proceeded quickly as restaurant menus, shop signs, traffic tickets, and the directions for daily life all appeared only in French. The departure of anglophones sped up, but the acceptance of the new reality in Quebec by those who remained was greater. Polls released by the Quebec government indicated that the language bills had overwhelming support in the French-speaking community, and by 1978, a surprising degree of acceptance among anglophones and allophones, many of whom were studying at the numerous language schools springing up in Montreal and other English-speaking enclaves. Moreover, Lévesque's energy and candour impressed not only journalists but also the general public. Pierre O'Neill, who had earlier worked in Trudeau's press office but had returned to Quebec to work with Radio-Canada, commented later on the attractiveness of Lévesque's political personality. When the premier returned from vacation in 1977 to learn that one of his ministers, Bernard Landry, had blamed a sudden surge in unemployment solely on the federal government, for example, he did not hesitate to show his anger and call a press conference to clarify matters. Ottawa, he said, "naturally shared some responsibility, but Quebec could have better anticipated the situation and done more to stimulate employment."

In earlier days Trudeau had dreamed of a mass party in Quebec led by an elite that would sweep away the corruption and rot of Duplessis. Lévesque's government—with its strong base among workers; its coterie of intellectuals, poets, and thinkers; and its willingness to drastically reform Quebec's electoral system to root out old-fashioned patronage—harked back to the image Trudeau had held when he was organizing the "*rassemblement*," a mass party, in the fifties. There was much for Trudeau to admire in Lévesque's movement—but, given its purpose, even more to fear.[30]

For Trudeau, the challenge from Lévesque was personal: indeed, when they met in December 1977, Lévesque reportedly raised his glass of Vosne-Romanée to Trudeau and said, "To your misfortunes." Without hesitation, Trudeau raised his own glass: "Likewise."[31] Trudeau's focus on the challenge from Quebec became ever more intense, and he showed a Churchillian willingness to make pacts with enemies to defeat the greater evil of separatism. As Chrétien toyed with leaving the federal scene for Quebec, Claude Ryan began to emerge as a potential provincial Liberal leader. Ryan and Trudeau had clashed bitterly for over a generation, but the editor of *Le Devoir* now began to write more favourably about Trudeau in the fall of 1977, praising his letters to Lévesque for their eloquence and for raising the level of the debate. Still, there were many wounds to heal. As the federal Liberals began to dip in the polls, the recruitment of a major public figure of unimpeachable personal integrity and great intelligence to lead the provincial party became essential. The wounds did heal fast, even if distrust abided. From his diplomatic post in London, a puzzled Paul Martin pored over Ryan's "views on constitutional change," particularly his support for "two nations or special status," and asked himself rhetorically, "How will Trudeau get around this last one?" That evening, March 7, 1978, a troubled Martin called Trudeau and found him "in good form and confident of his political future." He was awaiting the next poll, he told the old political veteran, and then, if the results were the same the following month, he would probably call an election.[32]

After so many delays, it seemed the writ would finally be dropped. Trudeau's office again became frenzied as it cast about for ways to make the prime minister popular. The most successful initiative, a CTV "portrait" produced by Trudeau's friend Stephanie McLuhan, Marshall McLuhan's daughter, included an endearing piano duet played by Justin and his adoring father at 24 Sussex, along with displays of diving prowess in the pool. Trudeau was constantly in motion that spring, flying to Quebec for an overnight trip to honour MP Raynald Guay's fifteen years of service, visiting his Mount Royal constituency to thank volunteers, and throwing out the first pitch at the Blue Jays game at Exhibition Stadium in Toronto. Justin and Sacha appeared on the *Globe*'s front page with their Blue Jays caps and Canadian flags, but their father failed to charm the fans. As he wound up to throw the first pitch, the crowd, unexpectedly but spontaneously, began to boo. The next week the board of Sun Life confirmed that the major insurance firm would move from Montreal to Toronto, and the Gallup poll showed Joe Clark's Conservatives tied with the Liberals. Once again, the election was off the agenda. [33]

—

On the international stage, the jostling between Ottawa and Quebec City continued. Trudeau, like so many prime ministers, turned to the arena outside Canada for personal satisfaction and domestic political gain. In March 1978 he spoke to the prestigious Council of Foreign Relations in New York and also to the Economic Club, where only fourteen months previously Lévesque had done so poorly. Trudeau was impressive. At the Council, 300 of New York's business and academic elite crowded into a room that normally seated only a third of that number. After an introduction by David Rockefeller, Trudeau spoke extemporaneously for ten minutes. As the consul general wrote, "Again and again" he emphasized that "things really were changing in [Canada] with respect to the place of French Cdns," not only in government but also in the "upper and middle strata of public organizations and private corporations." The audience at the Economic Club — some 2,100 — was the largest since its creation in 1908. The consul general's report claimed that the "audience saw in PM the embodiment of Cdn will to preserve unity of the country," and, in that respect, it fully supported him. There were, it continued, some who grumbled about Canada's third option (Trudeau's proposal to shift trade away from the United States), the Foreign Investment Review Agency, and Trudeau's questioning of the free market, but those critics were mainly Canadians living in New York or visiting to hear the speech. The *New York Times* was generous in both the space it allocated to the speech and the comments it made about Trudeau's efforts, quoting his claim that there was "a growing realization among all Canadians that we would be a foolishly self-destructive society if we allowed our country to be fractured because of our inability to imagine with generosity a solution to the problem of a federal state composed of different regions and founded on the recognition of two languages."[34]

The *Times* noted that Canada was nervously floating a $750 million bond issue and that Trudeau "conceded" that the separatist challenge had "been a major factor depressing the Canadian economy." The Canadian economy was indeed troubled, with the dollar reaching a postwar low a week after Trudeau's speech. The *Times* warned that "the state of the Canadian economy, with the rate of inflation at nearly 9 percent and more than one million persons looking for work in record unemployment of 8.3 percent of the labor force of ten million, is certain to be the principal issue to be raised by the opposition parties in the federal elections that Mr. Trudeau is expected to call in June or in the fall at the latest." For Trudeau and his close colleagues, however, any certainty about the primacy of the economy was increasingly difficult to accept, particularly when the breakup of the country was the principal issue for them—though no longer for most Canadians. A divide developed among Trudeau's advisers, with Keith Davey, who agreed with the *Times'* analysis, on one side and Lalonde, his co–campaign manager, on the other. To make his point, Davey liked to quote Jean Marchand's story of the shipyard labourer coming home from the yards and telling his wife, "I just couldn't get anything done today because I worried so much about the Constitution." Trudeau and Lalonde failed to see the humour, though they admitted that the Canadian economy was in increasingly bad shape.

Trudeau shared his concerns with German chancellor Helmut Schmidt, who continued to be a close friend, and just before he spoke in New York he wrote to Schmidt, saying that he believed "the economic difficulties" the West was facing should be the central concern of the upcoming G7 summit in Bonn. He also accepted an invitation to stay on in Germany for talks with Schmidt after the summit ended in mid-July.[35] In their analysis of G7 summits, Robert Putnam and Sir Nicholas Bayne rank the Bonn Summit as one of the most significant. Trudeau, by his own admission, was preoccupied with national unity, but as he concentrated on the challenges facing the Western economies, his concern mounted. Although Carter and Trudeau joked about Schmidt's and Giscard d'Estaing's habits of opening the summits with long-winded discourses on the economy—a tendency shared by all former finance ministers, Carter later observed—Trudeau had developed a profound respect for the intelligent, self-confident

Schmidt, who had fought the battle against Giscard d'Estaing for Canada's inclusion in the elite summit. The Bonn meeting resulted in a remarkable degree of agreement on the need to reinvigorate the Tokyo Round of global trade negotiations, fiscal discipline, and a "comprehensive global growth package."[36]

After the meeting ended, Trudeau accepted an invitation to join Schmidt on his sailboat on the North Sea, but first he spoke warmly of him at a private dinner. He praised Schmidt's economic leadership, which had "managed to keep popular expectations within the bounds of realism"; Germany's "system of management and labour relations, [which] has maintained stability and pro-ductivity in your industry"; and Germany's "constitutional practises [sic], [which] have avoided the pitfalls of unnecessary duplication while ensuring a strong voice for Germany in international affairs." This success, Trudeau went on, had enabled Schmidt to place his "political imagination" at the disposal of the international com-munity, particularly in the policy of détente and integration within the European Community. Schmidt had done what Trudeau dreamed he himself might do. When he left Schmidt, Trudeau determined to steel Canada for the economic and international challenges it had to face.[37] Gossage, who accompanied Trudeau, was struck by the close friendship between the two leaders. He saw "the real Trudeau, relaxed in a way possible only when you are with a friend who stimulates and respects you, who wants nothing, and with whom you know you are accepted."

Trudeau returned home intent on fulfilling the commit-ments he had made in Bonn. He called in his aides, quickly drafted a speech in both French and English, booked television time for 8 p.m., August 1, and sternly lectured his listeners. He told Canadians he was "fed up" with events in this country and was determined to turn the post office into a Crown corporation, cut government spending by over $2 billion, and freeze the size of the public service. He was also considering moving some government services to the private sector. He acted so quickly that neither he nor his principal secretary, Jim Coutts, informed Finance Minister Jean Chrétien, who was holidaying at his Shawinigan home, about the speech or its message. Chrétien's able assistant Eddie Goldenberg had spoken to his chief several times that day, but no forthcoming speech had been mentioned. He was astonished to hear on his car radio at 7:45 p.m. that Trudeau was addressing the nation on the economy. He called Chrétien but could not reach him for two hours, long after the speech had ended. When he finally spoke to the finance minister, he learned that Chrétien knew nothing about Trudeau's comments or actions. He had been, in Goldenberg's words, "publicly humiliated by the prime minister and the PMO." Chrétien thought of resignation, considered its potential impact on the impending election, and decided to be a "good soldier." His answers when the press quizzed him about Trudeau's actions revealed him to be, in journalist Allan Fotheringham's words, "fumbling and naked." Again, the election was postponed.[38]

As Bill 60 proceeded through the inevitable consultations on patriation of the Constitution and a new charter of rights, and as election planning moved forward by fits and starts, Trudeau increasingly turned to the international arena, partly because domestic politics frustrated him and partly because his status as an "international statesman" contrasted sharply with Conservative leader Joe Clark's inexperience. Clark's foreign ventures brought forth ribald jokes about how his luggage was always one country behind him and how foreign leaders found him wanting. Trudeau had come to enjoy international gatherings and, as David Rockefeller said in his introduction at the Economic Club, he had become the "senior statesman" of the Western world. He had survived the fall of Charles de Gaulle, the impeachment of Richard Nixon, and the disappearance of Edward Heath, Harold Wilson, and many other national leaders. He was also the sole Western leader who had emerged from the tumult of 1968. On the tenth anniversary of his becoming prime minister, the prestigious British newspaper the *Observer* gave Trudeau poor marks on the economy but added that "the one achievement no one can deny him is in foreign affairs."

In truth, many people were critical of his role in international relations, especially in the Department of External Affairs, where Trudeau's disdain for the department was blamed for its low morale. The astute journalist Sandra Gwyn reflected this view in an April 1978 article entitled "Where Are You, Mike Pearson, Now That We Need You?" She lamented that Canadians simply did not care about foreign policy. This ambivalence, along with Trudeau's indifference to the department and the very personal nature of his international interventions, contributed to the malaise. And yet, Gwyn wrote, "the whole of all of this is smaller than the sum of its parts. . . . When you shatter a nation's myths, something Trudeau should have realized, you weaken its will to endure. More than ever, these bleak days, we're in need of a new externalized myth to keep us going."

Trudeau seems to have realized the need for such a myth after 1976, and the impact of his address to Congress and of the Carter administration's opposition to separatism provided evidence of the important influence of Canada's external relationships on domestic politics. As Gwyn recognized, the appointment of Don Jamieson, a popular and highly influential Newfoundlander, as minister of external affairs and the return of the influential Allan Gotlieb to the position of under-secretary of state significantly strengthened the department's voice within government circles. Ivan Head, who had been the dominant force in Canada's foreign policy, moved on to become the president of the International Development Research Centre, although his critical attitude toward the department endured and deeply influenced the book that he and Trudeau later wrote about Canadian foreign policy.* Nevertheless, Canadian membership in the G7, the activity of first Quebec and then Alberta in the international arena, and the need for an "externalized myth" all caused Trudeau to turn to professional diplomats to guide his way as he ventured more often into their world.[39]

One particularly treacherous path was Canada's relationship with India, the largest recipient of Canadian aid in the mid-1970s. This aid included the development of nuclear power, and Canada insistently tried to secure a commitment from India that it would not produce an atomic bomb. In 1973 Trudeau and Indira Gandhi, whom the Canadian prime minister disliked, met in Ottawa, but no commitment was forthcoming. The following year when, during the Canadian election campaign, India exploded its atomic device, which it claimed was for "peaceful purposes," Trudeau was furious: he immediately cut off nuclear assistance and induced a general chill in Canadian-Indian relations. However, Commonwealth meetings meant that Trudeau had to meet annually with the Indian leaders, and on the margins of those occasions they quarrelled about nuclear questions. When Trudeau met Carter in February

---

* Thomas Enders, the U.S. ambassador, held this view—as did others. Patrick Gossage wrote in his diary on January 25, 1978: "Joyce Fairbairn, the PM's loyal legislative assistant, and Ivan Head, his foreign policy adviser, have the insider track in this PMO; the one has genuine warmth, the other has cool analysis. A general in the PCO tells Dick [O'Hagan] that this isn't the White House. Ivan sometimes acts as if it were." Head's role set a precedent for later prime ministers who sought to have independent advice on foreign policy—in the way that American presidents have national security advisers who almost inevitably quarrel with the secretary of state. Patrick Gossage, *Close to the Charisma: My Years between the Press and Pierre Elliott Trudeau* (Halifax: Goodread Biographies, 1987; original, 1986), 109.

1977, he found a sympathetic ear. Carter, according to the Canadian government report, "directed discussion toward non-proliferation by saying that he was grateful to Cda 'for your almost lonely stand' which had been developed after the Indian explosion 'which was *not* your fault.'" Carter said he was "really worried about non-proliferation" and encouraged Trudeau to advance those purposes. Trudeau confided that Schmidt had told him he did not want to increase safeguards because "he felt that there was *no* way of controlling Americans." However, Trudeau added, Schmidt was "a very intelligent man" who was resigned to the view that "everybody would have explosive capability" within a decade. His sense of "hopelessness" came from a belief that the "USA and France would never accept controls." Trudeau, an antinuclear activist from the sixties who was committed to ending Canada's nuclear role, did not share this pessimism.[40]

In the spring of 1978, Trudeau asked members of the Canadian foreign service to help him with a major speech at the United Nations on the nuclear issue. Klaus Goldschlag, an outstanding diplomat and student of international affairs, assisted Trudeau in drafting a speech that called for nuclear "suffocation." The strategy "consisted of a coherent set of measures, including the elusive comprehensive test-ban treaty, an agreement to stop the flight testing of all new strategic delivery vehicles, an agreement to prohibit all production of fissionable material for weapons purposes, and an agreement to limit and reduce military spending on new strategic nuclear weapons systems."[41] Later academic critics wrongly dismissed Trudeau's May 26 speech as a typical "solitary international mission," one that could offend allies for minimal effect. In fact, Trudeau's speech accurately reflected not only the views of Carter, the leader of Canada's most important ally, but also the spirit of 1970s détente. That spirit died when Soviet tanks crossed the Afghan border the next year. Nevertheless, the speech won support from Canadian antinuclear voters, who tended to stray easily to the NDP. The strongly anti-nuclear *Toronto Star* and *Le Devoir* liked the speech, although the *Globe and Mail* deemed it "pretentious," self-congratulatory, and not particularly "original." *Globe* columnist Geoffrey Stevens agreed that, though the issue was important, the real problem was that Trudeau, Parliament, and Canadians had no "sustained interest in foreign affairs."[42]

Attacks such as the *Globe*'s infuriated Trudeau and Head, and their 1995 book, *The Canadian Way*, is an exhaustive attack on the charge that Trudeau paid only intermittent attention to foreign policy and, more particularly, chose lofty thoughts over concerted action. Interestingly, Trudeau's contemporaries in the seventies also disagreed with the *Globe*. Jimmy Carter and his vice-president, Walter Mondale; Helmut Schmidt; and numerous others testify to Trudeau's effectiveness in certain international areas, although Mondale's suggestion that he was an "indispensable force" there is excessive. In G7 meetings, Trudeau did take the lead many times on North-South issues, and he also played a creditable role in sorting out the divisions between rich and poor—as we shall later see. When a Carleton University academic attacked the broken promises of Canadian aid policy and the sporadic attention Trudeau gave to foreign affairs, Head replied with ferocity, pointing to the fact that Canadian development assistance quintupled between 1968 and 1975, that Canadian media did not report on Trudeau's foreign activities fully, and that the "officials" who criticized Trudeau were unfair. Yet even he had to admit that Canadian development assistance, which had risen to 0.54 percent of GDP in 1975, had begun to fall as the Canadian economy weakened. Indeed, by 1981 it stood at only 0.37 percent, far below the 0.7 percent advocated in the historic Pearson Commission on International Development in 1969 and by subsequent Liberal Party conventions.[43]

Many critics of Trudeau's foreign policy were unfair, partly because they had expected too much from the multilingual,

cosmopolitan, and articulate prime minister, but even more
because Canada's domestic problems had to be the major priority
in the late seventies. Although Coutts and Davey accepted that
Trudeau's international celebrity was a political asset, they privately
lamented his taste for the bright lights of Broadway and the Rive
gauche of Paris over the Calgary Stampede or the South Shore of
Nova Scotia. Yet because of the fundamental challenge of Quebec
separation, he travelled far less than his successors or most of his
G7 counterparts did. He even missed a large part of his first G7
summit meeting as a result of domestic affairs. The ongoing process
of remaking Canada's Constitution occupied much of his time
during his early years in office and, again, after the PQ's election.
Trudeau's passionate opposition to nuclear weapons had preceded
his political involvement, but even the speech on nuclear suffocation bore too much of the weight of Canadian domestic politics
and the interests of Atomic Energy of Canada. His speeches to the
United Nations and to Congress also had too much cheerleading
about Canada, which surely detracted from the universality of his
arguments. However, the insistent demand that he keep his focus
firmly on domestic troubles frustrated Trudeau, especially once
he realized that Canada's problems were largely the product of a
troubled international economy.

Trudeau himself was challenged at a Quebec City press conference a few days before he spoke at the United Nations, by a
reporter who complained: "This is the first time in some time that
you have expressed any interest in the United Nations and spoken
there, and, secondly, it is the first time I've heard in a long time
that you are planning to speak on disarmament, and it appears,
and especially now since you don't want to scoop yourself, that
there is a certain amount of cynical stage managing with regard to
your speech in New York—that in fact you are doing this to try to
get both national and international attention, to the detriment of
the Canadian public, who would like to find out what your policy

is." A furious Trudeau replied: "If I were looking for publicity abroad, I take it I would have made the speech at some other occasion—one of the ten General Assemblies in the past years. It so happens that I feel that on this particular occasion I do have something to say, and I want to say it there and not here to you." When he faced the opposition in Question Period on his return from New York, he heard the same complaint from its leaders.[44]

Politics mattered more than ever in the fall of 1978. The polls were bad; an election was unthinkable. As Trudeau hesitated to call an election, MPs resigned and others sought the sanctuary of the bench or an appointment, opening up their seats as they left. When times were good in 1977, the Liberals had appointed Conservative MPs to some positions, notably the excellent Gordon Fairweather as the first chief commissioner of the Canadian Human Rights Commission. As things started to go badly wrong, few vacancies were filled, and the empty seats in Parliament loomed as serious hurdles to be overcome before a general election. Keith Davey recommended that Trudeau call by-elections for half the fifteen empty seats; Trudeau defied him and called by-elections in all the constituencies they represented for October 16. It was a disastrous decision, particularly when party pollster Martin Goldfarb warned him that Liberal chances in the scattered ridings "ranged from slim to dreadful." The Liberals had recruited several "star" candidates, notably University of Toronto president John Evans and leading feminist journalist Doris Anderson. They were among the thirteen Liberals who lost on election day: only two Quebec candidates won their seats.

As the results came in, an official in the PMO phoned Trudeau at 24 Sussex Drive. Trudeau claimed he was not watching the results but agreed to come to the Parliament Buildings to make a comment. The next morning, as the staff pondered the results and set about revising their own résumés, they read two different interpretations in the morning papers: first, "the knives were out" for Trudeau because he was a "star" who focused "discontent with the government on himself in a dramatic way," and second, the voters were trying to "teach Trudeau a lesson." Both of these views pointed to a difficult winter—and an inevitable election in the spring of 1979.[45]

The results illuminated the three fundamental problems the government was facing as an election neared: the government was tired, the economy was poor, and the separatists were now less menacing to English Canadians than they had been two years before. As Trudeau marked his tenth anniversary in office, commentators invariably noted who had left his side: the other two wise men, Gérard Pelletier and Jean Marchand; the expected successor, John Turner; the best anglophone minister, Don Macdonald; the wise elders Mitchell Sharp and Bud Drury; the brilliant Eric Kierans; the popular Bryce Mackasey; and the promising Francis Fox. Scarcely a week passed without reference to Turner's critical views of the government, which were allegedly circulated in a private newsletter published by his Toronto law firm. Attempts to renew the party were unconvincing (as with Jack Horner in Alberta) or proved to be futile (as with Evans, Anderson, and the celebrated environmentalist-businessman Maurice Strong, who withdrew as a candidate not long after his nomination). Trudeau's ties with the business community had not been repaired, and only Alastair Gillespie and, to a lesser extent, Barney Danson maintained strong connections with Bay Street.

As minister of energy, Gillespie had worked with some success to improve the relationship with the oil patch and even the government of Alberta, but the cost of allowing oil to rise to the world price irritated the Ontario government, whose consumers and manufacturers believed that they bore the bulk of the pain. And there was real pain. When Trudeau called the by-elections in August 1978, the twelve-month inflation rate was 9.8 percent— almost three years after the imposition of wage and price controls.

Unemployment stood at 8.4 percent, and pessimism was pervasive in the manufacturing and mining sector. *Canada Has a Future*, a bestselling book sponsored by the American Hudson Institute in 1978 and paid for by leading Canadian businesses, recognized that Canada had "a widespread lack of confidence in leadership — economic and intellectual, as well as political." There was a crisis of identity, compounded by the serious economic problem of stagflation. The book's principal authors, Marie-Josée Drouin and B. Bruce-Biggs, noted that, while American neo-conservatism had not yet established a base in Canada, there was a decided turning to the right in response to the economic problems. They agreed that Canada's problems were shared by much of the Western world, and they made the point that "historically, the privileged classes have had approximately a U.S. income, while workers and farmers had lower incomes, which was a major impetus to the massive emigration to the U.S. Over the past generation this has changed — the middling Canadians have achieved near parity with their peers in the U.S., so the prosperous (except high civil servants) have suffered and are getting restless."

Indeed, they were. Evans lost in Toronto's rich Rosedale riding, and Anderson in the upper-middle-class Eglinton riding. Reflecting their readers, the upper-crust *Globe and Mail* and *Financial Post* were grumpy; the liberal *Toronto Star* complained about Trudeau's indifference to the plight of workers; and the sassy new tabloid, the *Toronto Sun*, echoed redneck complaints about welfare bums, Chardonnay-sipping bureaucrats, and fraudulent immigrants. It seemed that the Liberal hour had finally passed.[46] Few denied that the economy would be the central issue in English Canada during the next election.

When the Quebec issue dominated the political scene immediately after the election of René Lévesque's separatists, Trudeau had emerged as the effective voice of Canadian unity. Fears gradually abated, however, as the expected referendum did not occur

and as Lévesque's government impressed even its federalist opponents with its competence and probity. Although the Quebec
economy was suffering serious blows at the time, Lévesque's
popularity grew: "After two years in power, René Lévesque has
delivered on practically all his electoral promises. Columnists
unanimously praise his overall performance, his innovative reforms,
and his responsible management while opinion polls show very high
public satisfaction." Yet his success did not bring greater support for
separatism, even when it was cloaked in the more comforting notion
of sovereignty-association. Once Claude Ryan became Quebec's
Liberal leader in 1978, Trudeau's position as the sole powerful
spokesperson for federalism was weakened. Ryan's leadership probably reduced support for Trudeau more in English Canada than in
Quebec because it reassured English Canadians, especially in
Ontario and the Maritimes. Indeed, Daniel Latouche, then a
member of Lévesque's team, claims that Ryan's reputation, particularly in the constitutional field, had the effect of freezing support
for sovereignty and preventing a referendum in 1978 and early 1979.
So, as Canada did not quickly disintegrate or face a referendum, the
significance of the "national unity" issue waned, though resentment
of Quebec's language policies rose. It was a deadly combination for
the federal Liberals.[47]

By the late fall of 1978, Trudeau was exasperated. Lalonde
told a November party executive meeting that English-Canadian
Liberals had let the party down. The Pepin-Robarts report
appeared on January 25, 1979, and recommended a decentralized
Canada with a degree of special status for Quebec. Cleverly
turning the report to his own advantage, Lévesque predicted that
acceptance of its "sort of semi-special status" would lead Quebec
to demand greater powers. Recognizing the implications, Trudeau
acknowledged the report in the House of Commons but refused
to endorse it. Pepin told his wife that a prime ministerial aide had
confided to him that, when Trudeau was handed the report, he

tossed it immediately in the waste basket without reading it. Apocryphal or not, the story reflected Trudeau's dismissive attitude. But what were the alternatives? Before the federal-provincial meeting of February 1979, Trudeau himself agreed to many proposals that favoured decentralization and the provinces in a desperate effort to salvage an agreement. The constitutional plate was overloaded; neither Alberta nor Quebec would accept that "compelling national interest" could override their provincial interests, and political posturing abounded. Liberal senator Eugene Forsey, once a passionate supporter of Trudeau, now turned against the patriation proposals because, as a "Red Tory," he believed that Bill 60 threatened the monarchy. He wildly suggested that the constitutional proposals were "a nightmare" that "could be interpreted as a bid for a Canadian republic," while Forsey's friend John Diefenbaker denounced the proposals as "more dangerous to the future of Canada than anything else that has taken place since Confederation."[48]

The bill died when the Supreme Court said that some of its provisions went beyond the powers of the federal government. So ended too any hopes for a constitutional triumph that would sweep Trudeau into power—a reflection of that first conference on the Canadian Constitution eleven years before. The times had changed, and the looming election was nearer than ever.[49]

—

On March 26, 1979, Trudeau finally called the election for May 22. The Gallup poll taken the month of the election announcement showed the Liberals and Conservatives tied at 41 percent each, but the national figures masked an enormous Liberal lead in Quebec and considerable Conservative strength in Ontario. Still, on a personal level, Canadians far preferred Trudeau to Clark as prime minister, and on that foundation the Liberals built their campaign. Trudeau, as Keith Davey feared, insisted on talking about the

Constitution and defending bilingualism, but there were some hopeful signs. Margaret's book *Beyond Reason* appeared in early April, and, as before, her candid remarks caused a wave of sympathy for Trudeau. Keith Davey sent a memorandum to "all Liberal candidates" instructing them to echo Trudeau's statement that his personal life was "not an election issue." Alas, the surge in support was brief, and the Conservative support grew.[50]

Sensing defeat, Trudeau campaigned energetically. He spoke without notes, jacketless, with his fingers curled in his belt loops and his body thrusting forward. At a Kitchener, Ontario, high school he faced hecklers bearing placards declaring that "Maggie dumped him, you should too." While his supporters swarmed around, he moved forward gingerly, smiling wanly, saying little, almost ethereal in the milling crowd. Then, on a scuffed hardwood stage, he spoke in a staccato cadence about his Canada, scowled at the Radio-Canada technician whose camera bore a PQ sticker, and explained why Joe Clark's vision of a Canada of communities would keep Canadians apart. The mood of the crowd became electric, but it was just one small group, as accompanying journalists rightly observed.

In his largest rally, at Maple Leaf Gardens on May 9, with banners proclaiming "a leader must be a leader," Trudeau spoke angrily about the failure of the last federal-provincial conference and the long, unsuccessful attempt to patriate the Canadian Constitution. He declared that, if elected, he would give the provinces one last chance. If they failed to grasp it, the federal government would act unilaterally to bring the Constitution home and bestow a charter of rights on Canadians. Otherwise, the Liberals made no startling promises. The Conservatives made many—too many, considering that they had a good chance to gain power. They would dismantle Petro-Canada, move the Canadian embassy from Tel Aviv to Jerusalem, and cut taxes by $2 billion while showering new benefits on individuals and groups. The promises had the desired effect: the Conservatives gained in strength during the campaign. Liberals hoped that a debate among the leaders on May 13 would allow Trudeau to "knock out" Clark or, alternatively, cause him to lose credibility, as had happened to Gerald Ford in the 1976 American presidential debate when he claimed that Poland was a "free" country. Clark, however, made no errors and, in the view of most observers, exceeded expectations. Ed Broadbent, whose party was also assisted greatly by the new regulations governing election expenses, probably gained most simply by being there with the major party leaders.

As the campaign progressed, the Liberal weaknesses became apparent, particularly in Ontario and urban centres, where for close to two decades the Pearson and Trudeau brand of Liberalism had thrived. As the Hudson Institute report of 1978 indicated, the "prosperous" were troubled. Later research showed that whereas 60 percent of university-educated Canadians had supported Trudeau in 1968, only 36 percent did so in 1979. The Conservatives received 38 percent of these votes in 1979, compared to only 30 percent in 1968, with the New Democrats rising from 8 percent to 19 percent in the same period.* Davey, Coutts, and others who read the private polls could not believe it. They kept hoping that something would "turn up," as had so often happened before with Canada's most dramatic prime minister. But the telephones, the

---

* Interestingly, Trudeau's support among those with only elementary education rose from 44 percent in 1968 to 47 percent in 1979, while the Conservatives remained roughly even (30 percent to 29 percent) and the New Democrats also rose slightly (15 percent to 18 percent). The additional Liberal support came mainly from Quebec, where the Créditistes had disappeared. "The Gallup Report," June 16, 1979, Keith Davey Fonds, box 11, file 12, Victoria University Archives.

best indicator of a politician's fortunes, stayed quiet in most Liberal campaign offices. As election day came near, the leading journalists left Trudeau's campaign and joined Joe Clark's entourage. As for Trudeau, he knew the political end was near, and his private life was in turmoil. He later told a friend, who said that a recent separation had left him disconnected, with a sense that his body and mouth were "somewhere else," that he understood: "I lost an entire election in that state of mind."[51]

Trudeau invited Keith Davey and his wife, Dorothy; Jim Coutts; and his old comrade Jean Marchand to join him and his sons at Stornoway for election night. The first results from the East were good, with the Liberals losing only one seat in Atlantic Canada. Then Quebec proved loyal as before, with the Liberals virtually sweeping the province with 67 of the 75 seats, six more than before, while taking an astonishing 61.7 percent of the votes. But Trudeau's world fell apart at the Ontario border: the Tories took 57 seats, and the Liberals only 32. Then the West threw its support overwhelmingly behind Alberta's Joe Clark. When Trudeau knew he had lost, he went to meet his workers at the Château Laurier. Many were in tears, most were stunned, and a lot were soon to be unemployed. Trudeau reassured them:

> The important thing is that we haven't given up an inch on our principles as Liberals. We stood for minority rights as the Liberal Party always has and always will stand for minority rights in every part of this country. We've fought for equality of opportunity, we've put forth programs while we were the government and during the election campaign to ensure that equality would be even greater. . . . We've fought also for something which I think extraordinarily important at this time in our history, that is a strong national government, and I believe we were right in that, and I still believe that that's the kind of government that not only this country deserves

but that it needs at this time. And I want to say for those of you
who were perhaps surprised to see me talk in the last weeks of
the campaign about having a Canadian Constitution made by
Canadians, in Canada, for Canadians. I still think, I believe
this was the right course, I knew that when I took that course
we took the risk of failing greatly and perhaps we did in the
short run, but I'm absolutely certain, that in the medium and
longer term, this is the course that Canada will have to follow.

The crowd shuffled, but then Trudeau leaned forward, looked
directly at them, and smiled: "With all its sham, drudgery and
broken dreams, it's still a beautiful world—strive to be happy."
With that, he waved goodbye and went home to his boys.[52]

The best of times. Throwing Sacha in the air while an excited Michel waits his turn.

Trudeau meets Elizabeth Taylor at the White House, where celebrities swarmed the Trudeaus, February 1977.

"He magicked us." Peter C. Newman. Trudeau was famously irreverent—but he was also a consummate showman and practised in advance his famous pirouette at Buckingham Palace behind the Queen, 1977.

"Can I come out of the rain, Your Majesty?" October 15, 1977.

The Gunslinger, January 1978. The party needed a tough guy to fix the bad polls. The famous *Weekend Magazine* photograph, used in the 1979 campaign, was staged by Trudeau's director of communications, Jim McDonald, and the photographer David Montgomery. However, it was a pose Trudeau had taken on years earlier.

Trudeau and a young Jean Chrétien. In the early 1970s, Chrétien was Trudeau's chore boy, landed with all the difficult jobs, until he was appointed minister of justice. Trudeau relished the battles he "fought side by side" with the man he called "a good soldier and a happy warrior." Trudeau, *Memoirs*.

The Gunslinger, as seen by Duncan Macpherson, *Toronto Star*, March 21, 1978.

Pierre and the boys, photographed by Margaret Trudeau. "The things that were true to him and real to him were us." Sacha Trudeau, as told by Jane O'Hara, *Maclean's*.

—

CHAPTER THIRTEEN

THE FALL OF PIERRE TRUDEAU

For Pierre Trudeau, the world was not unfolding as it should. When, on election night, he spoke of a beautiful world despite all its cynicism and grief, he again drew upon "Desiderata," the poem often found hanging in college dorms and hippie hangouts in the sixties—a reminder of halcyon times when it seemed that a new political age had dawned. That vision of change crumbled on May 22, 1979, as English Canadians decisively tore up the remnants of Trudeaumania. The next morning, melancholy mingled with sadness when newspapers throughout the world featured a photograph of Margaret Trudeau dancing wildly in the early morning at New York's fashionably notorious Studio 54. The newspaper coverage that followed was not kind. According to the *Los Angeles Times*, which published a large photograph and a detailed story of the event, Margaret thought Pierre's defeat was "a shame because [she] loves Canada." The conservative *Chicago Tribune*, which also featured the photograph, mocked her claim that Pierre would be good in opposition because he would fight "boringness." She told reporters amid the din of the disco that the defeat had upset her greatly and that she planned to fly home soon to be with Pierre. "I've never left him," she declared. "He's the most wonderful man I know. We're always together even though we're apart."

The marriage had been irremediably broken for some time, but the erstwhile fairy-tale couple came together again as they prepared to move their possessions out of 24 Sussex Drive. Apart from his mother's home, it had been the only house in which Trudeau had lived as an adult. The eleven years he had spent there changed his way of life dramatically—initially, because of the large retinue that served him and, later, through the presence of a wife and three children. When Pierre and Margaret legally separated in 1977, he gained custody of the children, but Margaret remained very much a part of their lives and had visiting rights for her sons, which she exercised fully. She spent five days every two weeks with them when she was in Ottawa, and sometimes Pierre joined the group. On one visit in 1978, for instance, they took the boys on a day's canoeing trip. According to Margaret, "we packed a picnic of their favorite food [and] joked all day long." But then it was time to depart. "Mommy, don't go," Michel, the youngest, pleaded when Margaret told him she had to leave to finish her latest film. Justin, the oldest, explained: "She has to go. She's working." Sacha, the bluntest, rejected this justification: "Why doesn't she work at being a mother then?"[1] But as we shall see, she did, very hard.

Anger drove Pierre and Margaret apart, but as Margaret said on election night, her love—let's use her word—for him endured. Pierre's feelings for her seem to have been an unusual blend of frustration, occasional bitterness, a sense of failure, and lingering affection. The children were a continuing bond, and, to their mutual credit, as parents they avoided the bitter encounters that frequently mark separated couples in their interactions with their children. There were problems, of course, particularly in the first months, when Margaret lived in borrowed New York apartments, travelled constantly seeking work, dated celebrities, wrote *Beyond Reason*, and became an actor in the film *Kings and Desperate Men*. Always parsimonious, Pierre was foolish in that he refused to give her any financial support, which would have made his own situation, and

hers, much easier. To be sure, Margaret initially craved the excitement of Park Avenue accommodation and the fever of New York
discos, but her strong sense of motherhood compelled her to return
to Ottawa often to be with her children. Lacking funds, however, she
had no Ottawa home. As she later wrote, Pierre was "loath to aid me
to live a life apart from him and our sons." Answering Sacha's plea,
she replied, "Mummy *has* to work." And that was true.

Sometimes on her visits, "Mummy" stayed at 24 Sussex; at
other times she stayed with friends. The situation troubled Pierre,
whose own youth had been marked by regularity and discipline, and
he felt uneasy about Margaret's extended visits with her Ottawa
friends, many of whom he also knew. Opening the hard shell that
normally encased his emotions when dealing with colleagues, he
even asked Hugh Faulkner, the minister of Indian affairs and northern development, whose wife, Jane, was perhaps Margaret's closest
friend, whether he minded that Margaret was staying with them.
Faulkner was unsure what Trudeau meant by the question, and the
conversation soon loped into generalities. The situation remained
messy until Trudeau finally lent sufficient money to Margaret for a
down payment for a home. After she settled in a house not far from
24 Sussex, the boys' life gained a welcome pattern, and Trudeau
campaigned in 1979 knowing that their mother would be there for
his children. He came to realize he could count on her love for
them, and that was an exceptional blessing. In Jane Faulkner's retrospective view, Margaret was a wonderful mother, whose children
became her world.[2]

For her part, Margaret admired Trudeau's own devotion to
their boys, who increasingly became the centre of his world now
that he was a single father. As we have seen, the breakdown of the
marriage occurred during a period of intense political turmoil in
Canada, one where Trudeau needed to make critical decisions.
His extraordinary ability to compartmentalize, born of the intense
self-discipline developed in his youth, served him well as he coped

with the emotional demands of single fatherhood in his late fifties. When Trudeau's aides later responded to a question about how Trudeau coped with his personal problems, the term most often used was "discipline," a quality he never lost whatever the external events.[3] While the responsibilities were enormous because of his role as prime minister, he was fortunate in having a strong support system around him. He was able to count on highly skilled and compassionate help to care for the children and, not incidentally, to keep his tight schedule working. When he was at 24 Sussex, the routine was clear. Trudeau would wake up at 8, have breakfast, and kiss each child before he got into the limousine that sped him to Parliament Hill. On her first day in 1978, household coordinator Heidi Bennet discovered quickly how much precision mattered to Trudeau. Shortly after he greeted his nervous new employee, Trudeau asked, "Where's Michel?" The little one was missing when Justin and Sacha lined up for the morning hug as Trudeau departed for the office. Annoyed, he told Bennet curtly that he expected to see all three boys before he left each morning. They both began to search for him, without success. Then, just as Trudeau reluctantly got into the car to leave, Michel toddled out the front door calling, "Dad, Dad, Dad." A beaming Trudeau leapt out of the back seat of the limousine, grabbed his son, and carried him back into the house. Bennet concluded that despite his initial bark, "a man who so obviously loved his children couldn't be all that bad."[4]

Other staff came to the same conclusion, even if Trudeau was a demanding "boss"—a term well known in the home, where young Justin referred to his father as "the boss of Canada." Leslie Kimberley-Kemper and Vicki Kimberley-Naish were responsible for the evening drill at 24 Sussex, which began with dinner for the boys at 5 p.m. and Trudeau's return just after 6, as they were finishing the meal. The boys would rush to embrace him as he greeted them heartily with "*Salut, les enfants.*" While Trudeau changed into his swimming trunks and began his fifty laps, the boys went upstairs to put on their suits, too, and according to an exactly timed schedule, arrived at the pool as Pierre was swimming his final lap. If they were a minute late, Trudeau, "a very precise man," would querulously ask, "Was there a *problem* getting the children down here on time?" A "*problem?*" Kimberley-Kemper later wrote with gentle sarcasm. "Three preschoolers finishing dinner, upstairs into robes, and downstairs at a precise time! Why would there be a *problem?*"[5]

Each night, Trudeau would read to the boys, first from the Bible and then something secular and literary—children's stories in the early years, the classics later. They would laugh, ask questions, wonder as children always do, and then, just before they went to sleep, they would pray together—following the pattern Trudeau had known since he first heard his own mother's voice.[6]

Although the staff was superb, Trudeau sometimes faced challenges alone as single parents must. There was the Labrador puppy, for instance, that Farley and Claire Mowat had given the Trudeaus. He had soon been named "Farley," and like his namesake, the Lab delighted children but could be most unpredictable. Once Trudeau was awaiting the arrival of Pakistani prime minister Ali Bhutto, and he had asked Energy Minister Alastair Gillespie to come earlier to brief him on a lively debate Gillespie had had with Bhutto on nuclear proliferation. Trudeau met Gillespie at the door and showed him into the living room, where Bhutto and other guests would soon arrive. The prime minister and his most elegant Cabinet minister immediately became aware of a large pile that Farley had left in the middle of the carpet. Trudeau quickly found a dustpan and cleaned up the mess. No sooner was that done than he noticed a photograph on a table of India's Indira Gandhi, which he quickly stuffed into a drawer. Then, as he scurried about the room, trying to make certain that everything was in its proper place, he discovered clusters of nuts that Sacha, the rascal of the three boys, had hidden in and around the sofa.

Finally, the prime minister and his minister were able to turn to their discussion of nuclear non-proliferation.[7]

Despite the careful schedule that surrounded Trudeau, when he was with his children, "he gave the impression of having all the time in the world." He participated in their games with tremendous enthusiasm, and the children adored him for his childlike and childish ways. Often they played "Monster," where Trudeau would hide and the boys would try to find him in the many hideaways in the old mansion. When they approached his lair, the fearsome beast would leap out, roar, and chase the squealing boys back to bed. During weekends at Harrington Lake, the formal routine broke down, although Trudeau continued to schedule work every day, as well as playing, canoeing, swimming, and hiking with the boys. Despite the informality of these interludes, Trudeau rarely gave compliments or "words of thanks" to staff directly, preferring to have any expression of gratitude passed on through the appropriate hierarchy. In this respect and several others (tipping, for example), he reflected earlier times. Yet the staff felt they were "part of the family" as 24 Sussex became, in Heidi Bennet's words, not so much the Official Residence of the Prime Minister of Canada but "first and *foremost* the home of a very busy dad and his three sons," all of whom sought "as normal a life as possible."

Bennet believes that Trudeau also thought of their group as part of his family. Media aide Patrick Gossage recalls that neither his senior political staff nor his ministers were invited to Christmas celebrations at 24 Sussex: the guest list included his chauffeur, his private secretary, the housekeepers, the RCMP officers who guarded him, and the ordinary folks who were truly his family. Bennet tells of an instance when she found the cleaning maid Gertie weeping: her son was dying of cancer. When Bennet gave Trudeau the sad news, he exclaimed, "On no, poor Gertie," and went off to search for her before Bennet could say another word. The sixty-year-old single father needed a family.[8]

Leaving 24 Sussex so Joe Clark and Maureen McTeer and their daughter, Catherine, could move in was difficult. The Trudeaus had transformed the old mansion, with the swimming pool, the sauna, and the children's rooms all reflecting those changes. Stornoway, the official residence of the Opposition leader, is in some ways more attractive than 24 Sussex. Unlike the prime minister's residence, which stands isolated on a cliff overlooking the Ottawa River, it is deep in the heart of the prime Rockcliffe residential area, and its interior design appears more comfortable and functional, especially after much-needed renovations were made in the summer of 1979. To the Trudeaus, however, 24 Sussex remained home, and Stornoway was a disappointment.

June 4 was the day designated for Trudeau to submit his resignation to Governor General Ed Schreyer, one of the prime minister's most controversial appointments. It was a clear, sunny morning, and Trudeau astonished waiting reporters when he drove his vintage white Mercedes 300SL* across the road and into the spacious grounds surrounding Rideau Hall, the Governor

---

* Trudeau's well-known penchant for keeping older objects had once again paid off. A car fancier wrote to him on February 16, 1979, saying that the Mercedes had tripled in value. This increase was, the auto enthusiast wrote tongue in cheek, "in the National Interest for the following reasons:

"1. The convertible constantly emits a large cloud of blue smoke both denoting its lineage and allowing the R.C.M.P. to always know where you are.

"2. Its top speed diminishes yearly, effectively eliminating any temptation on your part to exceed 55 MPH. When Justin reaches driving age, you will be able to jog faster than the automobile. What could be safer than that?" Douglas Cohen to Trudeau, Feb. 16, 1979, TP, MG 26 O20, vol. 3, file 3-14, LAC. When Justin married, he drove away from the church in the Mercedes with his bride. He still drives it occasionally today.

General's residence. As soon as he emerged, they were ready with their questions:

"What are you going to do?" they wanted to know.

"I'm going to think about it," he replied.

"But how do you feel?"

"I'm free."

Then he drove off, halting briefly on the driveway to greet a surprised Heward Grafftey, who would soon become a minister in the new Clark government. "Congratulations and God bless," he said.[9]

—

Defeat did bring freedom: there were no guards at the gate, no security people close at hand, and fewer obnoxious reporters and cameras. But freedom tasted bittersweet to Trudeau—who had come to relish the diverse choices facilitated by political power. Normally reticent, Trudeau found political life a theatre where his reserve evaporated as he met heads of state, mixed with celebrities, and flew off on weekends to New York on the Challenger, the government jet, to meet new friends like Barbra Streisand, Arthur Schlesinger, and Anthony Quinn (who became a good friend). Through architect Arthur Erickson and his partner, Francisco Kripacz, Trudeau was drawn into Hollywood and to wealthy retreats on the Mediterranean and in the Hamptons—a world of yachts, long parties, late night swimming, and, in the words of the day, beautiful people.*

---

* Erickson and Kripacz were noted for their parties and regularly invited Trudeau to them. Sometimes they even arranged them around Trudeau's presence in New York. On April 3, 1981, Trudeau had gone to New York with

Not least among the charms of political power was its appeal to interesting men and enchanting women. As his traditional family came undone in the mid-seventies, Trudeau eagerly sought out brilliant minds, great artists, and striking women. He would invite leading writers and thinkers to dinner at 24 Sussex, and rarely were the invitations declined. Trudeau was congenitally flirtatious, and as he and Margaret grew apart emotionally, he reached out for the assurance and intimacy that other women could give him. In 1976, before they had separated, he had become entranced with the classical guitarist Liona Boyd, then at the height of her fame. According to her account, she first met Trudeau in June 1975, when Liberal MP Bob Kaplan, a family friend, asked if she would like to entertain the prime minister. She eagerly accepted and, to her surprise, joined the Trudeaus with Kaplan at Harrington Lake.

Jim Coutts and other members of his staff to attend a performance of the Canadian Opera Company. Trudeau stayed at the Pierre, his usual hotel in New York and, ironically, Richard Nixon's New York home. Taking advantage of the occasion, Erickson and Kripacz held a dinner party two days later and invited the socialite conservative Pat Buckley, fashion guru Diana Vreeland, presidential chronicler Theodore White and his wife, Beatrice, *New York Review of Books* editor Robert Silvers and Lady Grace Dudley, actor Shirley MacLaine, singer Diana Ross, the chairman of Tiffany's, and Canadians Stephanie McLuhan and Paul Desmarais. The rich and the famous mingled easily, and Trudeau was drawn especially to the spirited and unpredictable Shirley MacLaine. Another Trudeau lover told me that MacLaine, along with Margaret and herself, was one of the three women Trudeau said he adored. MacLaine shared the same birthday, April 24, with this woman and also with Trudeau's close friend Barbra Streisand—a fact that intrigues astrologers. The Erickson guest list is found in TP, MG 26 020, vol. 17, file 13, LAC. Interview with Arthur Erickson, Sept. 2007; confidential interview.

After an afternoon in the water, where Pierre did water-piggybacks with the delighted Sacha and Justin, she brought out her guitar and elegantly and expertly played a classical selection for Margaret and Pierre, Kaplan, and the children, who were gathered before her in the spacious living room. In February 1976, when Trudeau was in Kamloops, British Columbia, a local newspaper editor invited Boyd, who was also in the city, to bring her guitar to Trudeau's suite to entertain the weary prime minister and his staff. She played for half an hour. Then she and Trudeau swapped stories about her time in France and his youthful wanderings there. She claimed in her memoir that "Cupid had caught me completely by surprise."[10]

Trudeau had just returned home from his trip with Margaret to Latin America, where they had often jousted over the arrangements and Castro had flirted gallantly with his wife. They had been close and loving certainly during their magic spell in Cuba, but as Margaret noted, when they returned home, their problems quickly resurfaced. Boyd accepted Trudeau's invitation to visit them in Ottawa, and she did so one evening after an Ottawa concert. At Trudeau's request, she also performed for British prime minister James Callaghan in mid-September 1976. Trudeau was attentive to her, but a letter he wrote to her on November 17 indicates that their relationship, if warm, was not intimate: "Margaret and I were disappointed to miss your concert with Gordon Lightfoot at the Arts Centre. We do hope to be in your audience the next time you are in Ottawa and, meanwhile, we do wish to thank you for your latest recording which we are enjoying greatly. Sincerely—and a big hug! Pierre."[11]

In her memoirs, Boyd described the growing affection between her and the prime minister as simmering while his marriage was failing. Trudeau intimates, including members of his family, believe the closeness of the relationship was exaggerated in this book. According to Boyd, it reached a sudden intensity in 1977 when Margaret and Pierre parted and Boyd brought, in her words, a "lightness" to Pierre's life.* By mutual agreement, the lovers cloaked their relationship in secrecy, depending on Trudeau's competent and discreet assistant Cécile Viau to work out the liaisons and on his driver Jack Deschambault to ensure their privacy. Because Margaret returned regularly to 24 Sussex until she was finally able to buy her own nearby home, there was always potential for embarrassment, and one day it happened. Margaret appeared at Easter, and the boys began, in Boyd's words, "an animated account of my activities with them and their father at Harrington Lake during the preceding days." On another occasion, when Margaret arrived home unexpectedly, Boyd was whisked away to the Château Laurier, where, she claimed, Pierre used fire escape stairs to reach her later for their tryst.

By this point, Trudeau and Margaret were publicly separated, although still legally married. Their public appearances often seemed affectionate but the marriage had clearly collapsed. Trudeau was understandably sensitive about keeping up "appearances in front of the boys." And Boyd was not Trudeau's sole romantic interest. There were many others, and they, too, conducted relationships that Trudeau concealed behind the shades. But, according to Boyd, she and Trudeau enjoyed being drawn into the web of celebrities spun by Erickson and Kripacz, who in her words "cultivated" the international set "like Mikimoto pearls."[12]

---

* Alexandre Trudeau perceptively commented: "I know my father opened up to women in a way he did not to others, and I also know he found refuge with them from the deadly serious matters which occupied him during his day job. In this sense, I don't believe he sought to discuss political matters with them and, when he happened to, he took a didactic or poetic position (much as he sometimes did with us)—a reduction of his actual thoughts. Especially in later years, he chose women for their energy and unpredictability because they dazzled him and gave him an escape."

Although secrecy was paramount, Trudeau could be reckless. Boyd recalls how they later attended a "Rosedale pool party where everyone nonchalantly disrobed." Trudeau, she writes, "was definitely a risk-taker. How easy it would have been for gossip to travel." But the Canadian press in those times did not gossip, at least not about the prime minister. Margaret Trudeau, however, was not off limits, partly because the foreign reporting of her controversial ways gave Canadian newspapers a pretext to describe her apparent misdeeds, usually with a tone of fifties sanctimony, rather than sixties liberation. Trudeau, though a modest international celebrity, largely escaped scrutiny of his private life. That double standard was unfair—and Margaret, with considerable justification, resented it.[13]

When Keith Davey invited the prime minister to dinner after the Grey Cup Game in Toronto in November 1976, his staffers told him that Trudeau would be bringing Iona Campagnolo, the glamorous MP from British Columbia, but then said it would be Kristin Bennett, the attractive daughter of Bill Bennett, who had worked as an assistant for former Cabinet minister C.D. Howe. Trudeau had met Kristin in 1968, and they would date regularly in the late 1970s.[14] Trudeau, it seemed, needed beautiful women beside him, and his correspondence with women resumed in 1976. In the fashion of many public figures, such as Franklin and Eleanor Roosevelt, Harold and Dorothy Macmillan, Harold Nicolson and Vita Sackville-West, Trudeau seemed prepared to stay with Margaret in a public relationship while each of them had other private relationships. His Roman Catholic faith made separation difficult and divorce a major challenge. Margaret later said that Pierre was willing to allow her to live in his house but not to let her pursue her career and dating life publicly. Yet the strong emotions they both felt overwhelmed the possibility of discretion, and, in Margaret's words, "Pierre's position became intolerable." His anger exploded into a clash in the spring of 1977 that left Margaret with a black eye, which was remarked on when they appeared together at the National Arts Centre. When they finally parted, his resentment expressed itself in the demanding separation agreement in which Margaret was given neither custody of the children nor financial support.* Margaret also gave her wedding and engagement rings back to her former husband.[15]

Yet Margaret and Pierre remained close. Evidence supports Margaret's claim that their separation improved their relationship. She and Jane Faulkner, for example, helped Trudeau look for a house in Montreal after his defeat in 1979. He did not, however, take their advice—they detested the one he chose, the art deco masterpiece designed by Ernest Cormier high on the slopes of Mount Royal. At times Margaret also chose clothing for him, as in 1981, when she purchased a beautifully tailored suit by the Italian designer Zegna at Toronto's stylish Studio 267. Of course, the children caused them to interact continually—and as time went by, more happily. In this respect Margaret fits into the broader pattern

---

* Trudeau and Margaret had a marriage contract, which had been signed after their wedding. Trudeau's brother, Charles, contacted Don Johnston, later a Trudeau Cabinet minister, about legal advice for "someone from Ontario" who was getting married. Johnston, who was Trudeau's lawyer, gave the advice before the marriage, indicating that, under recent Quebec law, a marriage contract could be signed following the marriage. After they were married, Pierre and Margaret, accompanied by RCMP guards, showed up at Johnston's home, to the astonishment of the Johnston neighbours, and signed the agreement. By its terms Margaret essentially had no claim on the assets of Trudeau-Elliott, the holding company for the Trudeau assets, which appears to have had a value of approximately $3 million in the early 1970s. Conversation with Don Johnston, June 2009. The marriage contract, signed in June 1971, is found in TP, MG 26 020, vol. 6, file 6-39, LAC. See also Don Johnston to Trudeau, June 29, 1971, ibid.; interview with Michel Jasmin, Dec.16, 1981, ibid., MG 26 013.

of Trudeau's ongoing connections with women he had dated or
with whom he had developed deep friendships.

For Margot Kidder, a later companion, it was Trudeau's sensitivity to women that created the lasting bond, one that endured
sometimes careless behaviour or long absence. He maintained lifelong warm relationships with the greatest love of his youth, Thérèse
Gouin, and with Carroll Guérin, the most important woman in
his life in the early sixties. With Madeleine Gobeil, there was a sev-
erance after the abrupt break-up when he married Margaret—but
then they got in touch after the marriage collapsed and he shared
his deepest feelings with her. With Kidder and with some others,
the attraction was Trudeau's "unconscious ability to make women
see the little boy who lives trapped under the layers of defences,
because once a woman has seen that essence in a man she'll never
get over him." Trudeau, Kidder believes, had once been hurt, and
the wound never healed—and intrigued each new woman he
allowed into his life. He also exuded "the air of a protective and
adored father," which made some women "want to crumple up
into [his] chest like some furry pet." These qualities, Kidder
believes, are a common trait of men who are "truly successful with
women," and Trudeau had them both. He also focused intensely
on each woman for the full time she was with him, making her feel
very special. Kidder, like Margaret, "fell head over heels in love
with him, and just plain stayed that way."[16]

And yet the loss of power in 1979 affected Trudeau's personal,
as well as his public, life. The dinners at 24 Sussex, the swimming
pool, the sauna, and the celebrity cast a certain spell on Trudeau's
relationships, as Kidder, Boyd, and others openly attest. There was
no question, Kidder wrote, "that it tickled the ego to be ushered into
Sussex Drive as if you belonged there and have your suitcases taken
up to your room (minutes, no doubt, after another lady had been
ushered out, but you didn't know that until years later when you
began comparing notes)." And celebrity attracted the same response

from Trudeau, a truth that Gale Zoë Garnett, one of Trudeau's most clear-eyed lovers, claims is important in understanding him. After Margaret left, Trudeau usually invited particularly captivating female celebrities, such as the classical pianist Monica Gaylord, actress Kim Cattrall,* and Liona Boyd, to public events in Ottawa or elsewhere. In Boyd's case, she often provided the entertainment herself—as when she appeared at the state dinner for Mexican president José López Portillo. As she entered the room, she was greeted with ebullient Mexican "wolf-whistles and loud calls of "'*guapa*,' '*rubia*,' '*que linda*.'" Trudeau also invited singer Buffy Sainte-Marie to a dinner in November 1977. She replied: "Just to thank you personally for the invitation to dine . . . with 1600 people? It would have been lovely I'm sure, [but] perhaps there'll be another chance sometime to dine, with about 1598 fewer folks." And there were—for many.[17]

—

After the disappointing Liberal defeat, however, Trudeau had a lot to think about beyond his personal life. Amid the tears on election night, there was considerable grumbling about his leadership.

---

* Cattrall, of *Sex and the City*, met Trudeau at a premiere of a movie in 1982, at which he asked for her phone number. Later, she got a message on her answering machine, requesting that she call him. She invited him to the Genie Awards in Toronto. In her words, "I was completely enraptured by him. He was so incredibly sexy." When asked why he was sexy, she responded, "He was very soft-spoken, incredibly smart, sensitive and truly an extraordinary Renaissance man—we'd talk about yoga, and he meditated. . . . He had so much class, from the way he dressed to the car he drove." To her, he represented "the best" of what it meant to be Canadian. Line Abrahamian, "Taking Chances, Making Choices: Face to Face with Kim Cattrall," in *Reader's Digest* (April 2005), 70–71.

John Turner's name came quickly to the lips of many, especially as polls during the campaign seemed to demonstrate that the former finance minister could have crushed Joe Clark. Others, angry with what they believed was Turner's disloyalty, looked instead to Donald Macdonald as the next potential leader. Trudeau, however, continued to inspire many Liberals, particularly among ethnic groups in English Canada and, more broadly, in Quebec, which had given him 67 of 75 seats and a remarkable 64 percent of the vote. That strength provided insurance against an early caucus revolt. Yet even Trudeau's closest supporters wondered about his future, and the precarious Clark minority government made such musings imperative. Although the Liberals remained strong in Quebec and respectable in Atlantic Canada, west of the Ottawa River the party's future seemed in doubt. In none of the four western provinces did it receive more than 24 percent of the popular vote, and in Ontario it stood at only 37 percent, compared with 42 percent for the Conservatives.

Moreover, the loss of many Cabinet ministers closely identified with Trudeau in both Ontario and the West represented a real personal defeat for him: Iona Campagnolo and Len Marchand in British Columbia; the Tory turncoat but Trudeau friend Jack Horner in Alberta;* Otto Lang in Saskatchewan; and in Ontario, Tony Abbott, Norm Cafik, Bud Cullen, Barney Danson, Hugh Faulkner, Alastair Gillespie, Martin O'Connell, and John Roberts.

---

* Despite Horner's electoral loss and much denunciation of him as a traitor in Alberta, he had no doubts about his decision. He wrote to Trudeau in 1984: "Having been born into a conservative family in western Canada, I, like a lot of conservatives, was skeptical of the direction you seem [sic] to be taking Canada. As time went on I realized you were a leader of men; you did really care about the one Canada concept and all parts of Canada." He regretted nothing. Horner to Trudeau, TP, MG 26 020, vol. 6, file 6-19, LAC.

Ironically, Jean-Luc Pepin, whose report on Canadian unity Trudeau had reportedly dumped in the waste basket, won a Liberal seat in Ottawa, though some critics suggested that Trudeau's well-known antagonism toward him may have played a role in his victory. Trudeau stayed silent behind his mask, seemingly indifferent to the disappointments accumulating around him. Not surprisingly, when Ontario constituency associations met in the spring of 1979, many grassroots Liberals asked when Trudeau would finally leave office. His closest aides did not know—and, in truth, neither did Trudeau.

First, however, there was housekeeping to do. Trudeau had to reduce his political staff—drastically. He kept Jim Coutts and Tom Axworthy but not Colin Kenny. Gone, too, was the private plane and the seamless delivery of luggage to elegant hotel suites. Now the rooms were of normal size, and Pierre was responsible for his own room-service charges. Trudeau was notorious among his staff for never carrying a wallet, but now he had to pay for his own taxis. According to Richard Gwyn, when Trudeau took a six-dollar ride in a Toronto taxi one day, he offered the driver an extra 25 cents. Plaintively, he asked, "Is this enough?" The driver, who recognized him, said nothing and declined the modest tip.

Despite many complaints, the Liberal caucus suppressed the grumbling, and in mid-June endorsed Trudeau's leadership, although it was Allan MacEachen who met the press after the meeting, not Trudeau. Then, on July 19, Trudeau called a press conference and announced that he intended to remain as leader. Why? reporters wanted to know. "My judgment as of now is that I'm best," he responded. Perhaps he sensed that Joe Clark's Conservatives lacked "the discipline of power," the title of journalist Jeffrey Simpson's fine analysis of Clark's victory and its aftermath. More likely, Trudeau knew that Lévesque's referendum was now imminent, and that as Opposition leader he would gain far more listeners than he would as a mere former politician. In any event, summer had come to Canada. Decisions could wait, but his boys could not.[18]

With school out, Trudeau first took the boys on a holiday, and then he joined a motley group of canoeists on a trip down the Arctic Hanbury-Thelon Rivers. All the canoeists had duties, three as chefs and five, including Trudeau, as rotating dishwashers. The meals in the rugged wilderness were worthy of a prime ministerial residence, with baked stuffed fish, lamb kabobs, cheese fondue, and Mouton Cadet Bordeaux. Trudeau was a newcomer to the group, which included future MP John Godfrey, current Liberal MP Peter Stollery, Craig Oliver of CTV, Gérard Pelletier's son Jean of *La Presse*, Tim Cotchet of CTV News, public servant and art connoisseur David Silcox, and adventurer John Gow, who, though he had survived an air crash in which he lost half a leg and half a foot, was physically strong and full of energy. Trudeau canoed with Jean Pelletier, but he did not know many of the others. He called Gow "Don" for three days until Godfrey finally summoned the nerve to correct him.

According to Godfrey, Trudeau's special talent was "making fireplaces out of flat rocks every evening as we set up camp. He was painstaking, meticulous, even Cartesian in this time-consuming activity." He also specialized in over-proof martinis, which dominated happy hour on this most elegant of wilderness excursions. Trudeau was convivial, no doubt partly because of the libations. On the final night, he and Godfrey had a lively discussion about personalism, Trudeau's particular approach to Roman Catholicism, which unfortunately remains lost to history because Godfrey cannot remember any of it. David Silcox does recall Trudeau correcting him on a classical reference, which revealed Trudeau's capacious memory and fine classical education. He was good company, but sometimes he would leave the group and wander along the lake by himself, lost in contemplation. He was reserved, and his eminence brought respect. However, John Gow dared the confident Trudeau to take on some hazardous rapids in his canoe, rather than walking around them in an easy portage. Godfrey tells the tale:

Pierre could not have resisted a challenge like that from a young buck. In a canoe we are all sixteen years old again. But Pierre was also the master of the calculated risk: *voir, juger, agir*. I don't know how many times he walked up and down that bloody rapid, looking and judging. John Gowe *[sic]*, in his early thirties, was the first to go. A mountain guy, he . . . shot down that S [rapid] as if nothing was involved. As Pierre prepared to go, most of the others, especially the journalists, rushed to the top of the bluff, telephoto lenses at the ready, prepared to document the death of the former prime minister. Since my camera was not that good, I decided it might be more helpful to be at the foot of the bluff to lend a hand if anything went wrong. Pierre came shooting down. It was not going well, and he was coming straight at the wall of the cliff. Since I was level with him I could see what the others could not: his eyes. At one moment I saw a look of horror as he thought he was going to crash, and then he took a mighty swipe with his paddle and in a raggedy fashion saved himself. . . . At the bottom of the rapid, as we reloaded the canoes, everyone congratulated him on his successful run. Afterward I said to him, aside, "That was pretty good, but I was watching you and there was a moment." He turned to me and said simply, "There is always a moment."[19]

—

Trudeau's canoeing partners had observed that his physical strength remained remarkable, his intellectual agility impressive. But in the fall of 1979 it seemed that his political moment had passed. He returned to Ottawa refreshed and appreciative of the joys of life without helicopters hovering above and security personnel all around. Then, at Erickson's invitation, he went off to Tibet, very much a forbidden kingdom but one whose mystery intrigued Westerners. It was his first long trip away from the boys since his separation, and they waited anxiously for his return. When he came back, in Sacha's words, "he looked and seemed different." He had a beard and a tan but also "a strange energy." He was "more aggressive and alive than usual." Sacha still beams when he recalls his father then: "It was as if his eyes still reflected the sights that he had seen, as if his body was still poised to meet them head on. This was a new father, not the patient and adoring father but the free spirit who had wandered the world. The lone traveler. The observer of things. The holder of secret knowledge." He brought back wooden swords used in Chinese operas and papier mâché masks for the delighted kids.[20]

When Trudeau left Ottawa, he had been grumpy, blaming his aides for the bad election result. He had always treated junior staff graciously, but most uncharacteristically he had refused to come out to say goodbye to the switchboard operators at the final party at 24 Sussex. In the fall, after his holiday, his mood was better. One of his surviving staff members, press secretary Patrick Gossage, wrote in November that Trudeau had become "more adaptable, but his convictions have not changed. He is asking as much as answering questions now, and he enjoys the turnabout. He is closer and more open with those around them." On a political trip to Calgary, Trudeau's "delight" was "infectious," especially when a Turkish-born taxi driver "bowed and scraped" and refused to accept the fare from his eminent and gregarious passenger. Sometimes, however, he missed the intrusive bodyguards: at a Liberal dinner and dance, Trudeau, "caught in the ample arms of a huge blond . . . made it crystal clear as he swirled by [Gossage] that he wanted to be saved." The gallant PR man "cut in" — and Trudeau escaped.[21]

Still, there were limits on his freedom. When he returned from Tibet, sporting his grey and, frankly, scraggly beard, he asked Jim Coutts what he thought of it. Coutts replied, "If you're staying in politics, shave it immediately." And he did. He was not ready to leave yet. Although there were troubles in the Quebec wing when younger MPs rebelled against the appointment of Trudeau's old friend Jean Marchand as caucus chair, the impending referendum imposed unity on the party.[22] In late September the energized Trudeau impressed the late summer caucus, though he had angered them all when he decided to fly to China and Tibet on the eve of the recall of Parliament. The respite was temporary, as dissatisfaction emerged again during a gathering of Liberals in Winnipeg in mid-October, where whispers about leadership change were frequent. But when Parliament finally opened on October 9, Trudeau was very much in control. The shadow Cabinet was decidedly to the left of his earlier Cabinets, with Herb Gray, who was then considered a leftist and a nationalist, named as the Liberal's finance critic.

When Trudeau asked Clark his first question in the House, he spoke in restrained and "mock humble" tones about Clark's failure to reach agreement on energy prices—a reminder of how often the Conservatives had attacked him for his government's failure to handle Premier Lougheed properly. Clark did not know what to do with the "cuddly boa constrictor" appearing across from him, but he responded, as did his ministers, with strong answers. Then, as the debate began, Trudeau's restraint vanished. He attacked the Clark government's proposed sale of Petro-Canada, mocked its inability to find an energy price despite its kowtowing to the provinces, ridiculed its backing down on its election pledge to move the Canadian Embassy in Israel to Jerusalem, and exco-riated Clark's notion of Canada as a "community of communities." The Liberal backbenchers cheered him on with cries of "resign, resign," hurled not at Trudeau but at the Tory ranks.[23]

Canadians agreed with the Liberal backbenchers. The Clark government had fumbled badly. It had delayed much too long in recalling Parliament, and the promise to move the embassy revealed a troubling naiveté in foreign affairs. Clark appointed Robert Stanfield to investigate what should be done, and, predictably and wisely, the former Conservative leader recommended "Nothing." The pledge seemed like cheap politics to win Jewish votes, made worse by Israeli prime minister Menachem Begin's threat that he would turn Jewish voters against Trudeau if he did not support Clark in making the embassy move happen. In this unfortunate episode, Begin, a rightist whom Trudeau despised because of the threat, bestowed considerable credibility on Trudeau as a wise international figure.

Domestically, Clark found his fellow Conservative and Albertan Peter Lougheed as difficult to deal with as Trudeau had. While Premier William Davis decried Alberta's insistence on moving quickly to the world price for oil and made the point that there were far more Conservative MPs from Ontario than from Alberta, Lougheed continued to insist that Canada pay that price, even as it rose rapidly because of the crisis in Iran. Clark's advisers also came to believe that Lougheed, a former football star, moved the goalposts farther away each time Alberta thought it had scored a deal. By the end of October, Clark was sufficiently angry to inform the House of Commons that he would use federal legal powers to make certain that Alberta oil continued to flow east. Trudeau revelled in this public spat among Tories and took every opportunity he could in Parliament to proclaim a plague on the houses of Clark and Lougheed, although not on those of Conservative premiers William Davis in Ontario and Richard Hatfield in New Brunswick. That distinction would become important later. The beneficiary of the Tory feuds and Clark's stumbles was the Liberal Party, which moved up sharply in the Gallup poll from a five-point lead (42% to 37%) in October to a nineteen-point lead (47% to 28%) in November—a margin that, if maintained in an election campaign, would bring a strong majority government.[24]

An exultant Trudeau lashed out at Conservative incompetence and called on Liberals to "throw out" the Tories. He did not follow through on his challenge, however, nor did he repeat the charge in the House. When Keith Davey told him that the November polls would be very good for the Liberal Party, he replied that House leader Allan MacEachen had told him the NDP intended to give the Tories a year to govern. With no election on the horizon, Trudeau then seemed to lose his ardour for politics, becoming ever more listless both in Question Period and in his leadership. In early November he told British Columbia Liberals that he could not attend a weekend policy seminar because he had a dreadful cold. Unfortunately, a photographer outside New York's elite Club Ibis caught him that same weekend squiring a glamorous woman into the disco. Art Phillips, a new and highly promising Vancouver MP, reported that the people back home were very upset, while Trudeau's intended host, Liberal activist Shirley McLaughlin, said that Trudeau's "fib" "really made her mad." In the House of Commons, NDP leader Ed Broadbent moved a motion declaring that disco dancing be made tax-deductible for curing colds. On the CBC news report, the Trudeau story followed an item about seniors and bingo. Host Knowlton Nash could not resist providing a transition: not all sixty-year -olds played bingo, he intoned, and some loved disco dancing. CBC political analyst and future Conservative senator Mike Duffy suggested that Trudeau's insouciant reaction to the publicity — "Why no, I can't imagine they're upset" — meant that Trudeau had "little interest in rebuilding" the Liberal Party.[25]

Since his marriage breakdown, Trudeau had often found excuses to skip party events in favour of weekend dates, but this time he'd been caught. Chastened, even though he had just had painful root-canal surgery, he agreed to attend an Ontario Liberal convention at Toronto's Harbour Castle hotel the next weekend, November 14–16, and to face the feisty student Liberals in a question and answer session. In a hot, sweaty room, with TV lights glaring, Trudeau talked about Liberalism with deep feeling, "picking up cues from the entranced young audience." Gossage was impressed: "Somehow he was not in that sweaty room; he was not being fried by four TV lights right under his nose; he was not barely balanced on a rickety chair; he had not just had oral surgery that left one side of his face swollen. He was as if in a big hall; cool, rested, and preoccupied solely with what he was saying." Watching the performance, Mike Duffy changed his mind: Trudeau was staying, he reckoned, and ready to fight new wars.[26]

In the corridors, however, the chatter about leadership continued. A party convention was scheduled for the late winter, where members would vote on whether there should be a leadership convention. At a reception for constituency presidents, Trudeau seemed bored and tired. His face was swollen, the pock marks were surprisingly evident, and he did seem to be recovering from a cold. To add a personal aside, my wife and I had our first conversation with him during that reception, and he initially appeared inattentive. Then he spied, on a nearby table, *Between Friends / Entre Amis*, the book of photographs the Canadian government gave as a curious bicentenary gift to the United States in 1976. "Could you bring it here?" he asked. "Look at page 232." We opened the book to the page where M. and Mme René Deschenes of Ste-Anne-de-Madawaska, two seniors, sat on a well-stuffed couch. An earnest M. Deschenes has his arm around his smiling, stouter wife in a room with two television sets, a dominating painting of the Nativity, a bejewelled cross, one portrait of the Virgin Mary, another of Christ, and between them, a small portrait of Pierre, Margaret, Justin, and Sacha. Trudeau's eyes suddenly lit up and the familiar smile radiated as his finger jabbed at the page: "There we are."*

* Beneath the photograph of M. and Mme Deschenes was a quotation from Louis-Olivier Letourneux, a Canadian jurist of the 1840s: "Nationality, in our opinion, does not merely concern the distinctiveness of ways and customs,

Four days later, on November 20, before the regular
Wednesday morning caucus, Trudeau unexpectedly called
senior staff to his office and, one by one, Cécile Viau led them
in to meet Trudeau. When they left, their faces were downcast
and some were weeping. Then he walked into the caucus
meeting at ten o'clock and said, simply, "It's all over." He had
decided to resign as party leader. Now tears welled in Trudeau's
eyes, too, as he began to read his statement: "You've always
known I'm an old softie," he declared, a remark that softened
others and brought the handkerchiefs out. Clad in a tan corduroy
suit and wearing a yellow rose, Trudeau next walked across
Wellington Street to the National Press Club. He read a brief
statement blandly, rarely looking up, and gave few hints about

---

language, or religion; it is much more connected with the history of a people,
its myths, its traditions, and its memories." It was curiously appropriate for 1979,
though written in 1845 (*Between Friends / Entre Amis* [Toronto: McClelland and
Stewart, 1976]). The constituency I represented as a delegate at the convention,
Kitchener, reflected most of Ontario at the time. The majority of constituency
executives wanted Trudeau to leave gracefully. Most—but not all—were
willing to give him time. Leading Toronto Liberals who later played a
prominent part in the Trudeau government and former Ontario Cabinet ministers were calling grassroots Liberals, urging them to prepare for the turnover.
Later, they publicly denied making such calls. When I wrote about this activity
in Robert Bothwell, Ian Drummond, and John English, *Canada since 1945:
Power, Politics, and Provincialism* (Toronto: University of Toronto Press, 1981),
Drummond, an eminent economist who knew the individuals much better
than I, received angry calls attacking the comments. I told Drummond,
who asked for my source, that the Toronto-based complainant had personally
called me. He reported my reply, and the request for a retraction was
quickly dropped.

his future except to say that he would fight for Canada. When he ended, he crumpled his notes, smiled, and, paraphrasing Richard Nixon's famous outburst, said to the journalists: "I'm kinda sorry I won't have you to kick around anymore." Spontaneously, they applauded.[27]

Later that afternoon, the House passed a resolution, moved by Prime Minister Joe Clark and seconded by Stanley Knowles, the dean of the House and NDP member for Winnipeg North Centre, thanking Trudeau for his enormous contributions to Canada. Knowles was warm in his praise, though he acknowledged that Trudeau was controversial. Nevertheless, he added, "one way not to receive criticism is to do nothing at all," and no one could deny that Trudeau had done something. In response Trudeau was once again restrained, perhaps because he feared tears would appear once more. He spoke briefly, his elbow held by one hand as his finger moved about his chin: he paid tribute to the importance of public life, of the commitment of all the members to Canada. The only slightly partisan note was sounded by Allan MacEachen, who said he regretted the resignation because he had believed that Trudeau would soon lead the party into office once again. Although many had expected his departure, his decision caused a flurry of comment as Canadian journalists and others rushed to judgment on his long political career—a prime-ministerial tenure exceeded only by Macdonald, Laurier, and King, the giants of Canadian political history. Did Trudeau belong in their ranks? they asked.[28]

—

In the first major biography of Trudeau written after he resigned, *The Northern Magus*, Richard Gwyn said that, "except for Quebec commentators who were kind to their own, the editorialists and pundits, in a rough preview of what the history books would say, gave Trudeau more minuses than pluses," although he correctly claimed that "ordinary Canadians" were not nearly as negative in their assessment.[29] Whatever the actual view of main-street Canada (and Gwyn suggests that, based on the surge in Liberal support in the fall of 1979, "ordinary Canadians missed Trudeau"), his description of the "editorialists and pundits" is largely correct. They were, on the whole, negative and surprisingly unreflective. The *Globe and Mail*, astonishingly, did not write an editorial on Trudeau's departure, although several columnists expressed their diverse and generally critical opinions. Geoffrey Stevens wrote the longest piece, entitled "The Singer Who Couldn't Sing Any More," while the increasingly conservative Richard Needham declared: "I'll say of Pierre Trudeau's resignation what I said of Harold Wilson's resignation in the U.K.: when a man's done all the damage he possibly can, it's time for him to step down and let someone else take a bang at it."

As with his Liberal predecessors Lester Pearson and William Lyon Mackenzie King, the political obituaries mirrored recent controversies rather than mature reflection. Some commentators did try to place Trudeau's career within a broader historical context, while recognizing that Clio, the muse of history, has notoriously fickle opinions. Trudeau himself refrained from reflecting on his contributions in his generally restrained and not at all eloquent farewells. In an interview with Michel Roy of *Le Devoir*, he was forceful when speaking of the impending referendum but refused to discuss his own place in history. Gossage, who accompanied Trudeau, was puzzled but impressed: "A man who keeps no diary, he is like a thirty-year-old whose past weighs little against the challenge of the present. He was writing, with his ideas and actions, a new chapter in his life. His age meant nothing. He was taking his space with him."[30]

The trait persisted—Trudeau refused to look back. But others did, believing that his impact on Canada should be understood by all who contemplated the nation's future.* Two of the most thoughtful appraisals came from opponents. On the right, Allan Gregg, a young adviser to Conservative leader Joe Clark, wrote a

---

* Trudeau received many letters from young Canadians after his resignation. One of the most interesting came from future Power Corporation president André Desmarais. Then twenty-three, Desmarais wrote to Trudeau on December 2, 1979:

> Last week, when I heard of your decision to resign as head of the liberal party [sic], I was deeply saddened. Although it goes without saying that I fully respect your decision, I feel compelled to write to you.
>
> I wish to let you know to which [sic] extent as a young Canadian, I feel extremely privileged to have had several occasions to spend some time with you.
>
> Your years as prime minister of Canada will always be something I will look back to as a great source of pride. I believe all Canadians will in retrospect, realize that the foresight and wisdom with which you led our nation is what made Canada and Canadians what they are today.
>
> Your enormous contribution to all parts of our vast land, your complete devotion to the principles of liberty and justice as well as your determination and relentless efforts to preserve Canadian unity will never be forgotten.
>
> There are no words to express my thanks to you Mr. Trudeau, for all you have done for Canada.

Desmarais, who wrote in both French and English to Trudeau, later married Jean Chrétien's daughter, France. Trudeau gave them a journal as a wedding gift. Writing from Cap d'Antibes on his honeymoon, Desmarais thanked Trudeau for the gift and noted that there was "a striking resemblance between LaFayette and you." Desmarais to Trudeau, Dec 2, 1979, and May 26, 1981, TP, MG 26 O20, vol. 2, file 3-58, LAC.

memorandum nine days after Trudeau's electoral defeat. Although Trudeau had lost, he mused, his presence still dominated: "Unlike Trudeau, Clark has never been able to engender unanimous concurrence as to his leadership qualities on any dimension, be it honesty, toughness, competence etc. This in itself is not that uncommon in as much as 'style' over the last ten years had been defined by Trudeau himself and notions of what 'Trudeau is' have taken root over ten years." Rarely, if ever, had a Canadian politician so dominated his times as Pierre Trudeau had during the seventies.

On the left, political scientist Reg Whitaker, who had written the definitive history of the Liberal Party under King, published a thoughtful article, in which he deprecated the tendency to dismiss Trudeau as "an anachronism, passed over by the rush of events." Trudeau might be out of office and favour, he wrote, but remained "close to the heart of our central dilemmas." Although he was critical of many of Trudeau's actions and contradictions, he questioned whether there were better ideas than Trudeau's to confront two major challenges: the threat posed by neo-conservatism to North American liberalism, and the ultimatum presented by a francophone population in Quebec tempted by notions of political freedom:

> Are there any among us who could remain entirely unmoved by [Trudeau's] appeal after the PQ victory, that Levesque [sic] had surrounded himself with blood brothers, but that he, Trudeau, wished to speak to us of a loyalty higher than to blood alone? Which critic of his mechanistic liberalism could tell us, in good conscience, of a community Good which could replace individual pursuit of goods, without entailing the kind of civil conflict which Trudeau has always sought to avoid? . . . Coming to terms with both the strengths and the failures of Pierre Trudeau in his extraordinary passage across our intellectual and political life means

coming to terms with some of the central values and central conundrums in the present crisis.[31]

In terms of style, Trudeau had electrified the Canadian political stage since his first dramatic appearances in 1968. On substance, however, disagreements abound. How much did Trudeau change Canada and how beneficial were those changes? If Trudeau had left politics forever in November 1979, would he have been, as George Radwanski suggests in his biography published the year before, an "unfulfilled" prime minister, whose promise was largely unrealized? In some respects, Trudeau would have agreed with Radwanski's assessment when he stepped aside. His hopes for a charter of rights and the patriation of the Canadian Constitution had not been achieved. Moreover, the election of René Lévesque in November 1976, which destroyed those hopes, represented a significant defeat for Trudeau, who had minimized the possibility of separatism in the mid-seventies. Trudeau's critics rightly pointed to his bad relationship with Robert Bourassa as a factor in Lévesque's victory. Without doubt, his dismissive approach to others who were federalists but did not share his views was unhelpful.

Many Trudeau supporters, and even Cabinet colleagues who shared his animosity toward separatism, were troubled by the tactics he employed to confront separatists, particularly the role of the police. Trudeau's reputation as a civil libertarian, forged in the heated encounters with Duplessis and Quebec authorities in the fifties and sixties, seemed at odds with the harsh use of authority during the October Crisis in 1970 and the illegal activities of the RCMP in countering separatism. Trudeau supporters pointed to the unusual nature of the challenge from Quebec, the advice he received from his brawling labour union friend Jean Marchand, and the incompetence and independence of the RCMP Security Service. And yet, even when these factors are taken into account,

Trudeau's positions and actions while prime minister reflect a hardened view of the rights of the individual vis-à-vis the claims of the state.

Although the presence of separatist "spies" was a serious security issue, the federal response to RCMP illegal activities, which occurred throughout Canada and not simply in Quebec, was ineffective and sometimes careless. Trudeau's anger, combined with the many inadequacies of the RCMP Security Service, was a factor, but so was his emphasis on the proper balance between security and individual rights—a balance he now saw differently than he had in the fifties and sixties, when he'd railed against the possibility of identity cards. Despite his mission to enshrine individual rights in a charter, Trudeau believed those rights possessed limits when the collective security of citizens was threatened. When socialist Ken McNaught, who had supported Trudeau during the October Crisis, sent the prime minister a commentary on a document from the McDonald Commission (which had investigated the excesses of the RCMP in confronting violence), Trudeau wrote this fascinating response: "The [document] represents a refreshing (but—from you—not unexpected!) change from the usual muddled thinking on the subject of freedom and order. Lawyers and judges properly define law as 'those wise restraints that make men free'; but they are nearly always concerned with individual freedom, not collective, not the freedom which calls for 'social engineering.'"[32]

For Trudeau, the balance had tipped. He had adjusted to the "new reality," where he believed Canadian democracy faced threats from extra-parliamentary groups that in some cases openly espoused violence. Further, well before the October Crisis, he had expressed his strong opposition to violent acts in support of Quebec independence, notably in his break with his early mentor François Hertel and his successor as editor of *Cité libre*, Pierre Vallières. After the October Crisis, he worried about the penetration of federal institutions by separatist forces, believing, correctly, that separatists not only used spies to discover what Ottawa intended, but on occasion continued to think of violence as a means to achieve their goals.*

---

* The profound distrust between separatists and federalists after October 1970 was revealed in the testimony to the McDonald Commission and the Lévesque-appointed Keable Commission and in later publications. The principal source of both fear and resentment was the alleged creation of the supposed "Parizeau network" (*réseau Parizeau*), which PQ activist Jacques Parizeau had created in the fall of 1970 to spy on Ottawa. There were, it was alleged, three principal agents: Louise Beaudoin, director of the office of prominent civil servant Claude Morin and a future senior PQ minister; Loraine Lagacé, who served in the Quebec government's office in Ottawa; and Jocelyne Ouellette, also a future PQ minister. The RCMP was extremely suspicious, particularly of Beaudoin's close relationship to Jean Marchand, and of Ouellette, who was frequently seen with senior federal ministers. Morin himself was later revealed to have given the RCMP information—a revelation that profoundly affected the way Quebec separatists viewed the prominent PQ minister. Parizeau admitted to the National Assembly in 1977 that he had organized an information network "to see from where the next shot would come." The suspicions and enmity no doubt were deeper because the spies and those spied upon had close personal relationships—in many cases of several decades. Marchand's relationship with Beaudoin troubled those who knew about it, including Trudeau. RCMP allegations of separatist "prostitutes" were ludicrous, although Ottawa, with its abundant ambiguities during the seventies, did have a surprising affinity with spy novels like those of John Le Carré. Confidential interviews. On the network, see Pierre Godin, *René Lévesque: L'Homme brisé (1980–1987)* (Montréal: Boréal, 2005), 108–9 and 199ff., the chapter entitled "Entre fiction et réalité," a reflection of the confused story of double loyalties. This was particularly relevant to the case of Loraine Lagacé, whose close relationship with Liberal MP Pierre de Bané caused her to be distrusted on both sides. On Morin, see ibid., chap. 18.

While Trudeau had his own doubts about the RCMP Security Service, which lacked both a civilian presence and proper civilian oversight, he believed that the ends of maintaining democratic order and law justified sometimes clumsy means. All the same, the McDonald Commission rightly concluded that Trudeau had tolerated RCMP wrongdoing too long and, in particular, that his government's instructions to the RCMP to investigate separatist groups were too broad.

In Trudeau's defence, it should be said that when he came to office, he faced distinct threats of violence unlike those any other Canadian prime minister had confronted in peacetime. His responsibility was great, and his tools were inadequate. Other democratic leaders who later faced similar threats of violence from domestic or external terrorism reacted similarly and, in many cases, more harshly. Spain, Germany, and Italy faced domestic terrorism in the seventies after the FLQ crisis, and each reacted with extra-judicial and restrictive legislation. There was, European historian Tony Judt writes, "a spontaneous response to the threat terror posed" to society and the legitimate left "because the 'lead years' of the 1970s served to remind everyone of just how fragile liberal democracies might actually be."[33] Later, when dealing with Irish and Islamic terrorism, for example, the British Labour Party under Tony Blair placed far greater restrictions on individual liberties than Trudeau ever contemplated. Indeed, Trudeau's approach of responding quickly with overwhelming force and greatly enhanced intelligence systems became a model for other Western leaders, such as the social democrats James Callaghan of Britain and Helmut Schmidt of Germany.

Trudeau himself would argue that he welcomed the creation of a democratic separatist party in Quebec, where the decision on the province's future would be made by Quebec voters, not by an undemocratic fringe. Again Whitaker, who was also a leading and critical authority on RCMP security work, disagrees with critics who argue that Trudeau's actions in October 1970 created a polar-ization between armed federalism and armed separatism. More support for this interpretation appears in the 1972 book written by former armed revolutionary Pierre Vallières, who "tacitly admitted" that Trudeau's actions had a pacifying influence and who, in 1972, rejected violence in favour of the democratic path to independence. Once on that road, the separatists moderated their program, organ-ized a democratic party, and played the political game. They did achieve power peacefully, but not separation. When Trudeau was defeated in the spring of 1979, the PQ had not held its promised referendum, in large part because Lévesque believed it would fail as long as Trudeau was prime minister. As Martine Tremblay, a leading Lévesque government official of the time, wrote much later: "The population is clearly unwilling to accept the second half of the bargain struck with the PQ in 1976. Substantive argu-ments on the issue have failed to win over disappointed federalists and undecided voters."

Immediately after Trudeau resigned, preparations for a refer-endum began in Quebec. Without doubt, his presence had made a supreme difference in separatist planning. Had his chief political challenger in 1968, the unilingual Bob Winters, or the Conservative leader, the unilingual Robert Stanfield, succeeded Pearson as prime minister or won the election of 1972, it is doubtful that the federal government would have responded to the challenge of separatism as effectively.[34] Characteristically frank, Lévesque publicly declared after Trudeau's defeat that the course ahead for separatism had become much easier. While denouncing Trudeau's many flaws, Lévesque never failed to acknowledge the strength of his opponent and his major achievement in creating "French power" in Ottawa. The transformation of the public service, the rapid spread of bilin-gualism in its higher ranks, and the recruitment of brilliant young francophones to the federal public service to counter the highly effective Quebec bureaucracy were major accomplishments of

Trudeau's first decade in office. They became a major plank in the platform with which he confronted separatism.[35]

Still, Trudeau was frequently criticized both during the 1970s and later on for his "obsession" with the separatist challenge. The price of that intense focus was a strained relationship with western Canada and a lack of attention paid to the economy. Western grievances against Trudeau have become the stuff of legend. Although the greatest wrong—the National Energy Program—occurred in the eighties, commentators in November 1979 frequently listed the "West" as an area where Trudeau had "failed." The election returns in May 1979 certainly seemed to confirm those arguments, as Trudeau won only three seats and less than a quarter of the vote west of Ontario. Even though he had pledged, when re-elected in 1974, that he would pay close attention to the West, those plans were disrupted by the election of the PQ and the continuing spats with Premier Lougheed, who demanded that Canada move quickly toward a world price for oil despite strong resistance from eastern Canada. Although the relationship between the federal Liberals and the Alberta Conservative government actually improved in the later 1970s as Canada moved inexorably toward the world price, the Iranian Revolution then spiked oil prices, and the issue became even more inflamed.

However, Western alienation from Ottawa and the Liberals had not begun with Trudeau: as Joe Clark discovered soon after his election, there was a fundamental incompatibility between eastern and western opinion. Lester Pearson, for instance, had won only 8 seats and less than one-quarter of the vote in Alberta and Saskatchewan in 1965. But Trudeau's governments augmented the differences, with their emphasis on the Quebec issue, bilingualism, and regional development, all of which became increasingly unacceptable in western Canada. From the first years, there was an acute awareness that the focus on Quebec and the Constitution would cause problems in western Canada. Hugh Faulkner, who was first elected MP for Peterborough in Ontario in 1965, noticed the rift. He developed a great interest in national unity, and, during the Pearson years, he met with Trudeau and Pelletier to express his views on the issue and to learn theirs. After Trudeau's election, however, he warned Pelletier that all the attention focused on Quebec was creating a sense of abandonment in the West. In response, Pelletier was blunt: francophones and anglophones must feel equal within the country, and other priorities must wait. Trudeau largely shared these views.

As Trudeau looked westward in the mid-seventies, he saw personal income rising considerably more rapidly in Alberta and Saskatchewan than in eastern Canada, and unemployment rates strikingly lower. In 1976, for example, the unemployment rates in Saskatchewan and Alberta were, respectively, 4 and 3.9 percent, whereas those in New Brunswick, Quebec, and Ontario were, respectively, 11.1, 8.7, and 6.2 percent. A government committed to smoothing regional and linguistic differences had a clear choice, and Trudeau took it.[36]

On the economy, later judgments on the Trudeau government's work in the seventies have been much less harsh than those of contemporaries. Thus, a standard economic history summarizes the problem much as Trudeau did at the time: "Canadian policy officials were as uncertain of how to deal with the stagflation in the [early 1970s] as were their counterparts elsewhere." Mistakes were certainly made, as economist Albert Breton told Trudeau regularly in the mid-1970s: the Bank of Canada should not have manipulated the exchange rate to protect Canada's floating dollar; Bryce Mackasey's unemployment reforms were wildly overgenerous; and government grants under regional development programs were too often based on local political whims. As for the wage and price controls, there is evidence that they did cause wage restraint, but the social costs were probably too high.

Yet Canada's failures were hardly unique: inflation levels in

Western Europe exceeded Canada's in the mid-1970s, and the German economic miracle became a nightmare for many of its industrial workers. Government deficits were common throughout the Western world as governments found that their social security systems, constructed in times of full employment, faced new strains. It was also a bad decade for the Americans as they adjusted to the sudden challenge of Japan and energy shortages, and their presidents paid the price: one was impeached and two were defeated. Critics of Trudeau frequently overlook the rise of the Canadian standard of living relative to the United States through-out the 1970s. The purchasing power of total real national income per adult rose from 72 percent of the American level in 1970 to 84 percent at the decade's end—the highest it has ever been. In counterbalance to the complaints from the Canadian West, the most effective government intervention of the 1970s was probably Ottawa's support of oil-sands development. A recent study argues that without the considerable subsidies and direct support by Ottawa and, to a lesser extent, Alberta and Ontario, the oil sands would not have become an economic dynamo thirty years later. Ironically, the province that liked Trudeau least was the main ben-eficiary of a policy on which he personally insisted.[37]

In the turmoil of the seventies, it is true that Trudeau focused on the problem of Quebec separatism to the detriment of policy development for the Canadian West, the economy, and, to a lesser extent, international affairs. Yet it is in foreign policy that Trudeau had some of his most significant success. He came to office calling for Canada to concentrate on its domestic troubles and worry less about being "helpful fixers" for the world. Later, he developed the reputation of having been whimsical and inconsistent in his approach to international affairs—an argument that neatly began with his proclaimed indifference in 1968, passed through his grand speeches on international development in the mid-seventies, and ended with a seemingly quixotic peace initiative in 1983–84 just as his public life was ending.[38] Trudeau's position on the international scene was also undermined by the fact that he got along poorly with Reagan administration officials and especially with Margaret Thatcher, and Canadian ambassador Allan Gotlieb's assessment of Trudeau's foreign policy in his 1980s Washington diaries is harsh.[39]

However, it is inappropriate to impose such judgments on the 1970s because Trudeau was widely admired by nearly all his counterparts in that decade. Nixon did not like him, but Kissinger did, and Trudeau and his officials worked well with Gerald Ford and Jimmy Carter to protect Canadian interests during the extraordinary turmoil of the early seventies. Ford and Carter both admired and liked Trudeau. All British leaders of the period respected him, including the Conservative Edward Heath, who came to value Trudeau's contribution to Commonwealth Conferences. At those meetings, Trudeau won the affection of the major African leaders of the day, especially Julius Nyerere and Kenneth Kaunda, permitting him to serve as a valuable conduit between the West and the developing nations. Singapore's Lee Kuan Yew, an extraordinarily talented leader, developed a warm friendship with Trudeau. And the closeness and respect of his relationship with Helmut Schmidt is reflected in their frequent letters. At Schmidt's request, he became the leading figure within the G7, dealing with the difficult issue of the demand of developing nations for a new international economic order, and his work in those areas garners considerable praise from those who witnessed his efforts. The seventies were, in so many ways, a disappointing decade, but for Trudeau they were a better fit than the decade that followed.[40]

Had Trudeau's political life ended in 1979, he would probably not have ranked among the "great" Canadian prime ministers— Macdonald, Laurier, and King. However, Canadians would have acknowledged his extraordinary impact on his times and his many major contributions to Canadian public policy. Like John F.

Kennedy, he was fond of quoting Robert Frost's memorable phrase that there were miles to go before he slept—and they became kilometres in Canada thanks to Trudeau's insistence in the seventies on a change to the metric system. The generation of the seventies would forever be, in filmmaker Catherine Annau's words, Trudeau's children.[41] However, as winter's chill fell upon Canada in 1979, Trudeau's often difficult, unpredictable, but radiant path seemed to have reached its end.

CHAPTER FOURTEEN

—

TRUDEAU REDUX

The new government led by Prime Minister Joe Clark stumbled into the autumn, and, as Jeffrey Simpson argues in his book about its troubles, "the Government seemed determined to drive away the disaffected Liberals and New Democrats." On the international front, the proposed move of the Canadian Embassy in Israel proved politically impossible, the expected accord with Alberta on energy pricing failed to materialize, and mediocre relations with Bill Davis, the Conservative premier of Ontario, worsened. Already, there was an urgent need for additional government revenues to make up for the disappointing gains from energy production in the West, and to pay for the election promises of property tax relief and the deduction of mortgage interest payments from taxable income.

To this end, Finance Minister John Crosbie, who had personally opposed the mortgage interest plan, now proposed an excise tax on gasoline. Though he initially met stiff resistance from Cabinet colleagues, they finally agreed after heated skirmishes on an eighteen-cent tax. They knew it would be politically controversial, but Trudeau's resignation made Crosbie and others believe that the budget would face no serious opposition in the House. Journalists confidently predicted after Trudeau's departure that the

Conservatives were safe "at least into the spring of next year, because the last thing the leaderless Liberals want to force is an election." Candidates for the Liberal succession were jostling for position: Donald Macdonald made it clear he was interested, and John Turner refused to reveal his intentions.[1]

Trudeau met with Macdonald in Toronto during the Liberal convention—a favour that was correctly interpreted as a bestowal of his support. There were rumours of other candidates too: Quebec maverick Pierre de Bané openly declared his interest, and defeated British Columbia MP Iona Campagnolo had many supporters. When she wrote to Trudeau in late November, she expressed her sense that the Liberals were not ready for a female leader, that Turner and Macdonald had crowded out the field, and that the party would never see another leader like Trudeau. She revealed, incidentally, how uniquely jocular and warm their relationship was:

My dear General (dispatches from a fascist raincoast),

I sent you an official letter (for your files) on your decision to leave the leadership of our party.

Now that I've had a week to think about it—this note is for you.

First of all, you are definitely *not* dead! (I thought I was for a full two months after my defeat) but discovered finally a new role in life. With all the hypocritical eulogies, you, too, must have wondered at your mortality—Be assured the overwhelming number of words in your praise were utterly sincere.

Typical was a sweet old woman who phoned me in tears last Wednesday night—she would not give me her name as she voted NDP provincially, but she said "Who will look after us old ones now that Trudeau's gone? Clark's gang only work for business." You had a huge emotional effect on people and no matter what you do now you'll always be P.M. to a huge number of Canadians. . . .

So now, to the rumour mill of the leadership race. Tonight I watched Laurier LaPierre for the "bleeding hearts" and Doug Collins for the "red necks" dissect my very modest publicity bubble for leadership (I'm not running but have not said so—Collins, fulminating at my loss of $13 m of the "taxpayers money"; Laurier, blessing me because I worked at learning French. Then "man in the street" comments from women saying they could never support a woman etc. (praise Islam & Pope J.-P.!)

Anyway, I will fatten my trading stock and support Don MacD [sic] for better or worse and stick with the C.B.C.

Campagnolo went on to explain why she felt a woman could not yet win the Liberal prize:

Humiliating a woman candidate will be injurious to the party in the same way humiliating a Francophone will be (jean c?). Be assured you have been an outstanding feminist and it is the reactionary times and not your policies which have called forth the Chauvinist Liberal Caucus in such numbers, cynically, casting about for a good kid to make the party look equality-minded . (Swift polarization to Turner and Don has killed off any attempt at policy evolution). We could well end up with a single ballot convention and Turner not even running.

She concluded with a wry reference to Crosbie's mockery of Liberal elitists: "Well, as one of Crosbie's middle-class 'trendies' to an upper-class one, my real candidate for *leader* is still you. This country is almost ungovernable and an aberration in today's world—You did the job so well."

Another defeated minister, Barney Danson, summed up the mood of late November among Liberal veterans: "I can only say that I was proud to serve under you and grateful to you for the fun, experiences and challenges we enjoyed together—even when I thought you did some dumb things, and especially when you tolerated my dumb things."[2]

With vivid memories, billowing hopes, and growing confusion, Liberals gathered in Ottawa on December 12, 1979, for their Christmas party in the West Block on Parliament Hill. Turner had announced on December 10 that he would not stand for the leadership, and the following day Crosbie had delivered his budget, which included not only the gasoline tax but also several other new ones on the increasingly popular Canadian sins of smoking and drinking. As the smoke billowed and glasses clinked at the Christmas party, Trudeau entered the room at 9:15. He accepted a curious retirement gift (a chainsaw "to cut down the government"), greeted friends, and quickly left. Earlier that day he had told the Liberal caucus that they should vote against the regressive Conservative budget but added that he would not stay on if, as a result, the government fell. MPs and hangers-on mulled over the meaning of Trudeau's words, speculated on possible reactions by the Conservatives, and, fuelled by the spirits of the season, vowed to attack the Tories in the morrow.[3]

The Conservatives knew that the Liberals would vote against the budget—that they had decided to support NDP finance critic Bob Rae's sub-amendment to the Liberal non-confidence motion. But the combined Liberal and NDP vote amounted to 140 votes, one shy of the total number of Conservatives and Social Credit. The latter group had generally voted with the Conservatives, although the government House leader had been cavalier in his treatment of Social Credit leader Fabien Roy—a careless attitude, given Roy's tribute to the retiring Trudeau as "one of the most brilliant political minds Canada has ever known." As evening fell on Ottawa, nearly all the political journalists expected that the government would survive—though barely. Throughout the day, however, Allan MacEachen and Jim Coutts quietly rallied Liberals, still fortified by the convivial spirits of their Christmas party and even more by the November Gallup poll and Martin Goldfarb's private party polls. The Conservatives, in contrast, were insouciant, confident as they entered the chamber after dinner on December 13 that the Liberals—"disco Daddy and the Has-Beens," as Crosbie wittily dubbed them—would not actually bring down the government. External Affairs Minister Flora MacDonald had not hustled back from Europe, another minister was in Australia, and no one had made any effort either to woo Social Credit members or to delay the vote. On the other side of the House, Liberal ranks were thin, and the government MPs began taunting and jousting with the Tories. Then, as voting began, the Liberal benches suddenly filled with members who the Tories believed were absent and others they thought near death.

And so, at 10:20 p.m., to the shock of almost everyone, the Clark government fell: it was defeated on the vote, 139 to 133.* Canadians now faced a winter campaign, with the election set for February 18, 1980.

---

* In his memoirs, Crosbie deplores the Conservative strategy: "I didn't know it at the time, but the Conservative party had done no polling of its own since August. The responsibility for this omission lay with the leader and his political advisers—Lowell Murray, now a senator, and Bill Neville, then chief of staff in the PMO. Worse, we'd made no effort to snuggle up to the Créditistes, believing we could wipe them out in the next election and elect some Tories in Quebec. Looking back, if I'd been the leader of a minority government, I would have put a higher premium on survival. I would have counted carefully, cuddled up to the Créditistes and kept them very happy, but Joe mistakenly assumed that the Liberals wouldn't risk another election. He insisted that we act as though we had a majority." Crosbie admits that he never told Clark he was making a mistake. Moreover, Stephen Harper successfully employed

The next morning, journalist Robert Sheppard reported: "If last night's mood [among Liberal MPs] was any indication, the almost unanimous choice will be Pierre Trudeau" to lead the party into the election. Jim Coutts buzzed about the parliamentary corridors, feeding the lively conversations with hints that Trudeau would stay. The following day, Friday, the Liberals gathered in caucus, first in regional groupings and then in a national caucus at noon. Soon it became obvious that Liberals beyond Parliament Hill were not at all unanimous in their support of Trudeau as leader for the next election. In late night and early morning telephone calls, riding association presidents told MPs that there was considerable opposition to Trudeau and much support for another leader, particularly Donald Macdonald. The Ontario and western Liberal caucuses reflected this sentiment and favoured a quick leadership convention. The large Quebec caucus, however, stood behind Trudeau, as did the Maritimes.

Trudeau, who shortly after the government fell had told some Liberal MPs he would return only if the "Emperor" asked him "three times on bended knees," was less categorical when he opened the national caucus meeting, but his reluctance was evident as, in a low monotone, he read out a list of reasons why he should not return. He insisted on near unanimous support and already knew that many were opposed to him. However, as the caucus reassembled from the regional meetings, it became clear that the majority favoured Trudeau, though a significant minority opposed him. The Quebec caucus expressed its support for Trudeau but added,

---

Clark's strategy in similar circumstances in 2007–8, although the Liberals were less willing to risk an election despite having a leader. John Crosbie with Geoffrey Stevens, *No Holds Barred: My Life in Politics* (Toronto: McClelland and Stewart, 1997), 177.

crucially, that it would support an alternative if English-Canadian Liberals clearly wanted one. This position derived from Marc Lalonde's view that Trudeau should be pressured into accepting the leadership and should not seek it openly. The voice of the West was faint, but Ontario's was powerful. Nevertheless, several leading Ontario Liberals, notably former ministers Judd Buchanan and Robert Andras, who had not supported bringing down the government, were known to oppose Trudeau's return firmly.[4]

The dominant presence in the corridors was Jim Coutts, but in the caucus it was Allan MacEachen, who had brilliantly engineered the defeat of the Conservatives. After he listened to doubts, contrary arguments, and confused positions, he rose to argue the case for Trudeau. Beginning slowly, almost hesitantly, he turned to Liberal principles and Tory dangers and cast the Tory budget as a fundamental assault on everything the party represented. Then his powerful voice, careful cadences, and Scottish eloquence overwhelmed the room as he moved on to the argument for Trudeau. One MP told Stephen Clarkson and Christina McCall that "for the first time in many years, Liberals seemed to know what they stood for, and the idealism Allan expressed was like a shot of helium gas that pumped us up for the campaign that followed." For the Liberals present at that meeting, there was suddenly no other but Trudeau. When they finally ended the caucus early Friday evening, the press announced that caucus had unanimously agreed that Trudeau should return—or so it seemed. The truth was far more complex: Liberal phones rang endlessly throughout the weekend. Judd Buchanan, for instance, made many calls, urging that a leadership convention be called, and in Toronto the campaign team organized to support Don Macdonald fretted about what it should do. Meanwhile, the Liberal Party's national executive gathered in Ottawa to approve the recommendation of the caucus.[5]

Many of the executive members were angry. Neither Coutts nor MacEachen had consulted them about the plan to bring down the government. As so often, they resented the unelected influence of Jim Coutts and Keith Davey, but Allan MacEachen was more trusted because he had the advantage of his long and loyal service to Liberal leaders since Louis St. Laurent. He berated the executive, arguing that Liberals had had no choice but to oppose the reactionary Tory budget, that the polls showed the Liberals could regain power, and that a divisive convention would only help the hated Conservatives. His arguments carried the day. On Sunday, when Trudeau returned to Ottawa from Montreal, he phoned Macdonald—the man who had been his personal choice to succeed him. Macdonald told Trudeau he was ready to step forward. Trudeau replied that he had not yet decided whether he would refuse the call to stay, but he asked whether Macdonald would run as an MP if Trudeau remained as leader. "No," Macdonald replied. Later that Sunday evening, Trudeau met with MacEachen, party president Al Graham, and representatives of the national executive. Over the weekend, Goldfarb had polled six critical ridings, and the results showed that the Liberals' solid numbers increased still further with the assumption that Trudeau would be leader. But Trudeau also learned that he faced strong opposition in Ontario, and he knew that there were others who sought his position.

On Monday Judd Buchanan reported that his conversations with leading Liberals in Ontario swing ridings indicated a preference for a convention and a new leader. He, along with Bob Andras and John Reid, urged Trudeau to resign. Surprisingly, Jean Marchand and Marc Lalonde also told him he would lose the election and advised him not to "come back." However, Gérard Pelletier, whom Trudeau trusted most, strongly urged him to stay to fight the referendum battle, while Coutts and MacEachen warned that Turner might now return to politics and defeat Macdonald in a convention. All the while, Davey and MacEachen appealed to Trudeau's sense of duty and his distrust of Turner.

With tensions mounting, Coutts, MacEachen, and Davey met in the Château Laurier Grill at lunch on Monday and spied Trudeau dining nearby with Gordon Robertson. After lunch Trudeau joined the three and tried to clear up "his concerns." Would it be fair to Macdonald if he stayed? What would he do with the new home in Montreal, where he planned to retire and raise his boys? Had he worn out his welcome? The last question was quickly answered with the new polls, but the other two lingered and bothered Trudeau. In the end, all agreed that there would be a press conference on Tuesday at 11 a.m. Coutts, MacEachen, and Davey were uncertain what Trudeau would decide, so Coutts agreed to draft two speeches for the occasion. That night Trudeau again called Macdonald, who reiterated his desire to run but refrained from advising Trudeau on the course he should take. Trudeau then phoned Coutts and told him he was going for a walk to think about his future. On that cold winter evening, he reviewed all his options before he returned to Stornoway and went to bed.

What thoughts flowed through his mind as he trod the empty, snow-covered streets of Rockcliffe that night? Surely, he reflected deeply on the implications for his boys. Margaret had settled in Ottawa, but if he retired, he would take the boys with him to Montreal, where they could grow up, as he had, in the world he knew and cherished — one without security details, near to his family, and close to the cottage, Jean-de-Brébeuf college, and the French language, which the youngsters too often resisted in Ottawa's more English atmosphere. Even though Andras and Buchanan simply irritated him, Trudeau's mind must also have dwelt on the warnings of Marchand and Lalonde, friends with whom he had shared so many battles in the past. Then there was Macdonald, who had been loyal when others were not and whom he had assured of his support only a few weeks earlier.

But different thoughts also crowded in: a scowling René Lévesque and the separatist banners and hecklers who confronted him regularly on Montreal streets. He could hear Pelletier's voice telling him that he could not walk away from the challenge: Lévesque had publicly declared that the chances of the *"Oui"* group had vastly improved with Trudeau's retirement. Other friends, such as Michael Pitfield, whom Clark had fired as clerk of the Privy Council, wanted him back for the great battle: "Look," they said, "you can be there at the time of the referendum. You can fight a hell of a lot more effectively if you're the prime minister."[6] But Trudeau was not yet convinced. When he went to sleep in the early morning hours of December 18, resignation still seemed the best course. But at about 8 a.m., he woke abruptly and said to himself: "My God, I made the wrong decision last night." According to his *Memoirs*, Trudeau then called Coutts in the morning to come to 24 Sussex, where they debated the issue, before he finally told his excited aide: "Okay, we're going to do it." Coutts believes now that he had already made up his mind but enjoyed the game of discussing the decision.[7]

Once Trudeau had made up his mind, his doubts vanished. As Jeffrey Simpson remarks, Trudeau "had read the press notices after his resignation and had not liked what he had seen: the general impression was of a man and a Prime Minister who had failed to fulfill the promise expected of him when he took office in 1968." Now a political miracle had occurred, a second act, and a chance to perform as never before. He had loathed opposition and had missed the perquisites and habits of power. At the press conference at 11 a.m. on December 18, Trudeau announced his return in the slow monotone he favoured for such occasions: "I decided last night, after two days of long consultation with friends and colleagues in the caucus and the party, that because Canada faces most serious problems, because the Government has been defeated, and because our party faces an election, my duty is to accept the draft of my party—that duty was stronger even than my desire to continue with my plan to re-enter private life." He added that the Liberal Party had "a vision of Canada which I feel is the correct and just vision of Canada." It was, of course, very much his own. Facing press questions about the announcement, he was insouciant and, in the view of the *Globe and Mail* editorialist, "lifeless" and "uninterested." When asked how long he would stay as Liberal leader, Trudeau answered: "If [Canadians] love me so much that they want me forever, the answer is I'm sorry, they can't have me. But if they want me and the party for a few years, well, we're here." He seemed impatient, even walking out in the midst of a question from the respected CBC correspondent David Halton. The journalists winced — Trudeau was back to kick them around once more.[8]

—

Thus began Trudeau's most unusual election campaign — and one of the strangest in Canadian history. Joe Clark, confident that Trudeau's return would quickly cause a drop in Liberal support, began his campaign with enthusiasm, a clear policy, and a vastly improved organization. Trudeau's election meetings across the country were brief, just long enough to capture notice on the front pages, and after his December 18 announcement he refused to hold any press conferences. The Liberal campaign was, as Trudeau admitted, tightly controlled. Influenced by hockey fanatic Keith Davey's belief that he should simply "rag the puck" while taking occasional but devastating shots at Clark, Trudeau appeared rarely in public and shunned the press wherever possible. Davey, Coutts, and campaign co-chair Marc Lalonde advised Trudeau to refuse to debate Clark and Ed Broadbent, the feisty NDP leader. As it happened, Trudeau gradually came to enjoy electioneering in this style. He abandoned the corduroy suit he had favoured for the 1979 campaign and joined Toronto advertising executive Jerry Grafstein on a trip to the stylish Harry Rosen store in Toronto, where he gathered together new garb that made him appear a senior level executive rather than a common-room philosopher.[9]

In St. John's, for instance, the press corps sent him a bilingual petition requesting a news conference late in the campaign. When Gossage handed him the petition with twenty-nine signatures, Trudeau put on his reading glasses, scrutinized it, and scrawled on the document: *"fiat medial conferenciam."* Gossage checked the Latin, scheduled the first press conference, and watched Trudeau deftly fend off all attempts to get information from him. Late in the campaign, he quoted the French poet Léon Bloy, which inspired radio journalist Jim Maclean to thank Trudeau for "raising the level" of the campaign. Maclean then challenged Trudeau to identify the source for a parody he proceeded to read over the public address system of Trudeau's DC-9. He received no immediate answer, but the next day in Winnipeg, Trudeau himself did a parody of *The Tempest* and remarked: "That's to get even with the press who suspected I didn't even know some parody from *The Merchant of Venice.*" For the remainder of the campaign, journalists were treated to "Poetry Wars," in which Trudeau did parodies of poems in his speeches, and Maclean, a poetry lover himself, tried to identify them. Looking back, press secretary Patrick Gossage recalls these moments as startling. To have a francophone prime minister identify, without error, numerous poems in English testified not only to Trudeau's remarkable memory but to a romantic nature that the harsh political storms most often concealed. Near the end of the campaign, as the Liberal lead in the Gallup poll reached 20 percent, Trudeau inserted into his speech: "Things fall apart, the centre cannot hold, and mere anarchy is loosed upon the Tory Party." Maclean recognized the cleverly chosen source: "The Second Coming," by William Butler Yeats.[10]

As Trudeau's own "second coming" neared, the confident Liberal campaign team scheduled a Saturday night party with members of the press, who had been so deftly rebuffed during the campaign. The mood was uproarious, Trudeau was engaged, and laughter filled the room at Toronto's Royal York Hotel. The Liberal leader ended the night with an impressive impromptu recitation of the extended poem "Les Conquérants de l'or," by Cuban-French poet José-María Heredia, which describes the Spanish conquest of Peru. The journalists, with one exception, were stunned by Trudeau's capacious memory. The exception was George Radwanski, a *Toronto Star* editor who had written the best-selling biography that assessed Trudeau as an "unfulfilled" prime minister. Throughout the dinner, the Liberal leader referred to him as "Peter," even though Trudeau had spent more time with him than with any other journalist in recent times. Radwanski thought the error was intentional, an insult both to him and to Peter C. Newman, who had declared that the Liberals could never win again with Trudeau.[11]

Trudeau enjoyed taunting and teasing the press during the campaign, especially as it became clear in early February that his hopes would be fulfilled. He later wrote that the "whole theme" of the campaign was straightforward: "If you're the government, you've got to govern, and that means making decisions—and we can do it." There was no leaders' debate because, in 1979, in Trudeau's contemptuous words, the debate "was being run by the journalists rather than by the participants in the election." He resisted public appearances: they brought out the hecklers, and he realized that his quick temper might provoke him to say something stupid or, even worse, obscene. Yet the Liberal campaign had clearer policy direction than any of his previous campaigns, partly because the Clark Conservative campaign, with its budget, decentralist, and mortgage interest deductibility proclamations, defined the major issues not just for themselves but also for the Liberals. Moreover, members of the Liberals' national executive at its meeting on December 15 had insisted on a role for the party in writing the platform. Lorna Marsden, a sociologist at the University of Toronto, with substantial assistance from Trudeau's aide and speechwriter Tom Axworthy, took the lead in creating a nationalist platform that stressed government intervention to maintain and expand Canadian industry while protecting the disadvantaged in society. MacEachen, whose political views had been formed both by the hard times of Cape Breton coalfields and by the Catholic social thinking of Moses Coady and his famed Antigonish movement, brought a passion for social and economic equality to the drafting table. Axworthy flew with Trudeau throughout the campaign and fed him "Gainesburgers" — meaty program chunks, like a well-known dog food, that entered Trudeau's speeches in "short snappy lines."

Gossage became convinced that "however much TV reporters talked over a Trudeau clip, however they served it up and carved it up, and however the pundits (many of whom had become entranced with Clark and his Cabinet) ranted, Trudeau's words, and the carefully nuanced nationalist Liberal program, got out to the public." Most important, Trudeau was comfortable with this platform. Clark's assertion that Canada was a "community of communities," for instance, soon overcame Trudeau's own wariness of nationalism and gave a strong focus to his attacks on Clark and other "enemies" of "the spirit of Canada." He bitterly opposed provincial autonomists such as Peter Lougheed in Alberta, who had resisted negotiations with Clark as much as he had previously with Trudeau, and he despised Brian Peckford, the new Conservative premier of Newfoundland, whose claims for offshore oil were garlanded with assertions of provincial rights and autonomy similar to those of Alberta. In the words of Stephen Clarkson and Christina McCall, "Axworthy had deliberately used his knowledge of Trudeau's intellectual roots to find ways to persuade him that the proposed energy and industrial-strategy policies did not reflect the old negative nationalism but were portents of a new positive Canadianization."[12]

—

On election night, February 18, Trudeau invited Keith and Dorothy Davey to Stornoway to watch the results with the boys. Davey recalled that "Trudeau seemed far more interested in the overall numbers than in the individual candidates. At five or ten minutes to the hour, when the political commentator would hold forth on television, he would listen most intently. Years later Trudeau would no doubt be able to remind certain commentators of some outrageous comment made on election night 1980." The early returns from Atlantic Canada were good, even from Newfoundland, where the Liberals' stand on offshore resources ran counter to Peckford's rhetoric. They took 5 of 7 seats there, and 19 of 32 overall in Atlantic Canada. Then came the decisive moments as polls closed in Quebec and Ontario. In his native province, Trudeau won the greatest victory of any prime minister in Canadian history—an astonishing 74 of 75 seats, with 68.2 percent of the votes.* With

---

* Trudeau's popularity in Quebec was remarkably high, according to the Canadian Institute of Public Opinion. In December 1979, Trudeau's "approval" rating in Quebec stood at 87 percent, with only 10 percent disapproving when the question was asked: "Do you think Pierre Trudeau is or is not a good leader of the Liberal party?" The answers to the equivalent question for Clark were 20 percent yes and 59 percent no. Trudeau's ratings on the questions were higher than Clark's in all regions, even though the results in the Prairies were a dismal 22.2 percent of the vote. The Liberal Party also scored better than the Conservatives in January 1980 on the issues of unemployment, national unity, energy, and astonishingly, inflation. Polls also indicated that "inflation" was the major issue in the view of Canadians in January and February 1980. William Irvine, "Epilogue: The 1980 Election," in *Canada at the Polls, 1979 and 1980*, ed. Howard Penniman (Washington, D.C.: American Enterprise Institute, 1981), 374–76.

the referendum looming, those results stood as a stark warning to separatists that they were facing a serious battle. In Ontario the Liberals took 52 of 95 seats, regaining urban fortresses that had fallen to the Tories in 1979. Trudeau already had his majority, but it swelled little as the results came in from the West, where the Liberals won only 2 of the 90 seats beyond the Ontario border. The Liberals had conquered—but they had also divided.[13]

Joe Clark graciously conceded the election in Spruce Grove, Alberta, where he paid tribute to the democratic process and, amid chants of "No, no," wished Trudeau and the Liberals well. After Clark spoke, Trudeau worked his way through the exultant Liberal throng gathered at Ottawa's Château Laurier. Wearing a dark suit, a thin crimson tie, but, surprisingly, no rose, Trudeau revelled in the moment as he kissed many women and greeted old friends. As the crowd burst forth in what the CBC announcer called the "shrill sound of victory," Trudeau cast his glance about the crowd and began, memorably: "Welcome to the eighties." The decade would be "full of problems and opportunities" for Canada, but the country would now be able to confront the difficulties and seize the opportunities because the 1980 election showed decisively that "Canada is more than the sum of its parts." Trudeau was surprisingly serious and far more aggressive and energetic than on the day when he announced his return to politics. "It was exciting," he later wrote. "Like Seneca, who wrote, 'Live every day as though it is your last,' I was resolved that I would govern in this next term as though it was going to be my last." He did—and as things turned out, it would be his final and his most significant government.[14]

—

After the May election the previous year, when the Liberals left the prime-ministerial "bunker," the Langevin Block opposite Parliament Hill, they scrawled in lipstick on the washroom mirrors: "We'll be back." In that spirit, they quickly moved to reoccupy the premises after the election. There was no time for delay, with the Quebec referendum looming and the Parti Québécois's intensified preparations for the vote in the spring of 1979. Then, on November 1, the government of Quebec released its lengthy platform for the referendum, entitled *Québec-Canada: A New Deal*. Following the carefully crafted strategy of Minister of Intergovernmental Affairs Claude Morin, the document argued the case for "sovereignty-association" with Canada. The concept was admittedly vague, but early polls taken during the Clark government indicated that Quebec voters tended to approve of it. These results, of course, were not lost on Trudeau and his closest colleagues, who despaired because, in their view, Clark seemed indifferent to the gathering forces of separatism. Quebec Liberal leader Claude Ryan was organizing the "no" side in the referendum, and Clark's overwhelmingly anglophone government had not been well equipped in knowledge or in skills to participate in those organizational activities. Besides, Ryan neither wanted nor needed him.[15]

Trudeau presented Ryan with a more difficult choice. When Trudeau resigned, Ryan's tribute had been generous, despite their bitter differences in the seventies. But during the election campaign in May 1979, they had disagreed publicly when Trudeau said that, if re-elected, he would hold a national referendum to patriate the Constitution—a course Ryan strongly opposed. When Trudeau won his overwhelming victory in Quebec in February 1980, Ryan's leadership of the "no" side in the Quebec referendum debate was obviously affected. Unlike Clark, Trudeau was a francophone with strong views on the nature of constitutional reform. Ryan had responded to Lévesque's promise of a referendum by creating a commission to bring forward a report not simply on Quebec's constitutional position but also on the broader question of Canadian constitutional reform. The result of this process, the *livre beige*, the name the press gave to the document Ryan issued for the referendum, "owed obvious intellectual debts to the Pépin-Robarts [sic] report published twelve months before," according to legal scholar Edward McWhinney. "A number of the Pépin-Robarts [sic] research staff spilled over into . . . [Ryan's] Liberal commission, and the wider ranks of research staff spilled over into the Liberal commission and the wider ranks of its specialist consultants." Trudeau, as we know, had purportedly thrown the Pepin-Robarts report into his waste basket soon after it landed on his desk, and the *livre beige* may well have encountered the same fate.

But perhaps not. Trudeau's long political tenure had taught him the value of ambiguity, particularly when the question announced by Lévesque in December was, for federalists, maddeningly ambiguous.* Carefully crafted to reflect Quebecers' opposition to "separation," it responded to polls that indicated they would support "equality." The ambiguity lured "tired federalists," such as Léon Dion, the eminent Laval academic and father of future Liberal leader Stéphane Dion. He declared that Trudeau's federalism was too rigid and Ryan's too complex. While refusing

---

* The question read:

The government of Quebec has made public its proposal to negotiate a new agreement with the rest of Canada, based on the equality of nations.

This agreement would enable Quebec to acquire the exclusive power to make its laws, administer its taxes and establish relations abroad—in other words, sovereignty—and at the same time, to maintain with Canada an economic association including a common currency.

Any change in political status resulting from these negotiations will be submitted to the people through a referendum.

On these terms, do you agree to give the government the mandate to negotiate the proposed agreement between Quebec and Canada?

"separatism," Dion indicated that he was compelled to vote *oui*. Trudeau's own speechwriter for the referendum campaign, André Burelle, later claimed that he was deceived into thinking that Trudeau would accept more radical change: "I did lend my pen to Mr. Trudeau during the May 1980 referendum to sell to Quebecers a Canada of 'several smaller nations under one,' in the vision of [Emmanuel] Mounier [the French personalist who became Trudeau's mentor]. However, after appearing to buy my ideas (which many other federalists shared) to cajole Quebec, Mr. Trudeau discarded them immediately after the referendum battle." Burelle's complaints have some merit. Just as Lévesque employed an unclear question to broaden his support, so Trudeau cloaked his views in ambiguity and, for a while, set aside old feuds. For Trudeau, it was the battle of his lifetime against a brilliant foe. He could not afford to lose supporters because of a wayward phrase or a careless comment.[16]

When the new Trudeau government took office, the referendum campaign was well advanced, but Trudeau moved quickly to enhance the federal presence and create a stronger national government. First he attempted to strengthen his majority in its weakest area: western Canada. Shortly after the election, he called NDP leader Ed Broadbent and asked whether he would join the government. The NDP had won 22 seats in western Canada, while the Liberals held only 2, both in Manitoba. Despite winning 32 seats, their highest total ever, the New Democrats had been gloomy on election night. There had been no breakthrough in Ontario, Broadbent's own province, and Trudeau had won by staking out the nationalist and leftist turf that the NDP regarded as its own. NDP finance critic Bob Rae later recalled that, when Broadbent appeared at the first post-election caucus meeting, he expressed frustration at how the Liberals and Trudeau had undercut the NDP, robbing the party of its hopes of power. Not surprisingly, then, Trudeau's offer astonished Broadbent, particularly when the prime minister responded to Broadbent's joking comment, "Let's see, I'll take five or six Cabinet portfolios," with quick agreement: "You've got them."

There had been coalitions before in Canadian politics, most frequently on the right, but the NDP and its predecessor, the CCF, had vivid memories of the history of the British Labour Party and its "betrayal" by Ramsay MacDonald in 1931, when he and a group of Labour MPs joined with a Conservative majority in a coalition government to fight the Depression. Broadbent and Rae, with whom Broadbent consulted in the washroom during Rae's wedding at Toronto's Primrose Club, had both studied in Britain and knew the history of the "betrayal" well. Rae believed at the time that "it was an old left-Liberal strategy" to do in the socialists and it "was never on."* Ironically, five years later, as Ontario NDP leader, he made such an accord with the provincial Liberals to displace the provincial Conservatives. And in 2008–2009 Rae, as a leading Liberal MP, urged his party to embrace a coalition with the NDP.[17]

Broadbent rejected Trudeau's offer—an important turning point in Canadian political history. Acceptance might have transformed Canadian party politics by "uniting the left" and ensuring a decade or more of government for the liberal-left coalition; on the other hand, it might have led to a split within the Liberal camp and a strengthening of the Conservatives in increasingly conservative times. But no matter what the outcome might have been, the rejection of the coalition offer created a dilemma for Trudeau. Should he proceed with his plans for major constitutional reform

---

* Rae was correct; Dorothy Davey, a prominent Liberal organizer and wife of Keith Davey, later said that it had always been Keith's ambition to "unite the left" by bringing in the NDP to a coalition. Conversation with Dorothy Davey, May 2009.

and nationalist economic programs, both of which would meet with strong opposition in the West? With the referendum imminent, there was little time to ponder, and his plans soon crystallized. Although constitutional patriation had not been an issue in the 1980 campaign, he had promised in the 1979 campaign that if re-elected, he would "bring home" the Constitution, even if he had to act without provincial consent. His distrust of Ryan had grown during the course of the debates about reform in 1979–80, and the Quebec Liberal Party, he later wrote, "was drowning in a swamp of its own verbiage, while the Parti Québécois was speaking out with pride in firmness."

Trudeau is unfair: the *livre beige* was an impressively detailed and carefully worded document, drafted mainly by Ryan himself, but it was a mistake. Ryan later admitted to journalist Ian MacDonald that the time spent drafting and discussing the document in the winter and early spring meant that the Liberals "had not really prepared for the debate in House"—and the document was an easy target for the skilled PQ front bench. The polls confirmed how badly Ryan and his party had done in the Assembly debates in March 1980. Whereas the "no" side led by a comfortable margin of 52 percent to 41 percent during the first two weeks of February, a poll taken in the second week of March showed the "no" side leading only 47 percent to 44 percent. Moreover, Lévesque was 8 percent more popular than his party, while Ryan was 18 percent less popular.

Horrified by these figures, the federal government abandoned its hesitations completely. Trudeau immediately made Justice Minister Jean Chrétien the federal representative on the "no" side with this instruction: "Get in there a bit more vigorously. Play whatever role you want. . . ." The appointment, in the words of political analyst Gérard Bergeron, would offset Ryan's political style: "This populist street-fighter would stand apart from Claude Ryan's authoritarian and dialectical leadership." Moreover, Trudeau told

Ryan on April 4 that he would take a direct role himself and do whatever was necessary to win the campaign.[18]

The campaign was angry and all-consuming, and it went down in history as "the battle of the champions"—a struggle between two remarkable politicians who had first confronted each other in the Montreal Radio-Canada cafeteria when Trudeau, then co-editor of *Cité libre*, taunted TV celebrity Lévesque, who had promised an article, with the words: "Hey, Lévesque, you're a hell of a good speaker, but I'm starting to wonder whether you can write." Their contests continued in the early sixties in Gérard Pelletier's modest home when Lévesque, then a minister in Bourassa's government, called on Trudeau, Pelletier, and others to help him interpret the convulsions of the Quiet Revolution. Their common quest ended as Lévesque chose a separatist path in the mid-1960s and Trudeau emerged as the most eloquent voice for an altered Canadian federalism. Then, in the later 1970s, they faced each other on opposite sides of a profound divide as Lévesque brilliantly marshalled the diverse separatist forces behind a common banner while Trudeau, with increasing difficulty, sought to band federalist troops together for a battle in which many Canadians outside Quebec had lost interest.[19] "The champions" (as they were described in a National Film Board documentary) were not heavyweights slugging away at each other but middleweights like Sugar Ray Robinson and Sugar Ray Leonard—artists who deftly jabbed, dodged, bobbed, and weaved as they jousted with each other. Long before, Lévesque had said that Trudeau had an "inborn talent for making you want to slap his face." The feeling had become mutual.[20]

The debate went poorly for the federalists in the Quebec National Assembly, but Trudeau entered the fray in the new Parliament on April 15, 1980—the very day Lévesque announced that the referendum would be held on May 20. Rarely referring to his notes and speaking in an effective monotone, Trudeau told a strangely silent House that he would not negotiate sovereignty-association with Quebec if there was a "yes" vote. The question was too vague, the separatist arguments too dishonest, and the constitutional ability to undertake such negotiations uncertain. But a "no" vote would not mean that political change in Canada would be frozen. Rather, it would be "the first step" in reforming the federal system, one where Parliament would become more effective in representing the interests of all Canadians, as it must: "When there is a conflict, the country must be convinced that there will be a national government that will speak for the national interest and that it will prevail." Parliament would work to guarantee the civil and political rights of all Canadians, and a national referendum could affirm that the federal Parliament brought together "the only group that can speak for every Canadian and for the whole nation." In this way Trudeau cleverly used the impending referendum in Quebec to advance the cause of constitutional reform that had stalled in the seventies and to add the new cause of the reform of Parliament itself. This potential referendum had become a clarion call to stir tired political bodies and to alert those, like Joe Clark, who had turned away from the battle for Quebec. Though he appeared confident in the Commons, Trudeau's nervousness emerged as he left the chamber: he stopped to shake hands with a woman, and when her ring pinched his finger, an expression of pain passed over his face. Photographers caught the moment, and as he started down the stairs, he tripped.[21]

But he stumbled seldom in the critical weeks ahead. Gradually, the "yes" side lost ground in the polls, particularly when Lise Payette, a Lévesque Cabinet minister, attacked women who supported federalists as "Yvettes"—a name widely identified in Quebec with docile, taciturn, and traditional women. In response, Claude Ryan's wife, Madeleine, whom Payette had foolishly attacked personally, set out to organize women to advance the federalist side, and on March 30 in Quebec City, she held a *"brunch des Yvettes,"* which attracted enormous attention. It was followed by many other rallies, including one with over fourteen thousand "Yvettes" in the Montreal Forum.[22] Yet the polls were volatile—a reflection of the uncertainty and the intensity of the campaign. Trudeau's speech in the House, promising that a "no" vote would not mean the end of change but, rather, a renewed attempt to alter the federal system, provoked considerable criticism, not only in Quebec but also in other provinces, where there was little appetite for such challenges. As the campaign neared its end, the tone became bitter, particularly as the "yes" lead diminished.* Lévesque became careless and, in the fashion of earlier Trudeau foes, reportedly mocked Trudeau's middle name, "Elliott." When Trudeau heard the allegation, it fired his anger just before his final speech of the campaign, on May 14 at the Paul Sauvé arena.

There, in November 1976, the PQ had celebrated its electoral victory with historic brio. Now the red Maple Leaf flag waved beside the Quebec flag, and chants of Canada-Québec rocked the hall in a spirit as intense as that of the proudest separatist moment in that space. Trudeau began by saying that the other parties and leaders in Ottawa were united against separatism and shared his commitment to a renewal of federalism. Then he became personal.

---

* One bizarre nationalist commitment was made by Bernard Landry, a PQ minister and future leader, who, along with *"son équipe,"* swore off wines, which he normally drank, in favour of Quebec cider. The apparent result: "Some of them ended the campaign with stomach ulcers." Michel Vastel, *Landry: Le Grand Dérangeant* (Montréal: Les Éditions de l'homme, 2001), 170.

Mr. Lévesque has asked me what my attitude would be if the majority of Quebecers voted YES.

I have already answered this question. I did so in Parliament. I did so in Montréal and in Québec City. And I say it again this evening: if the answer to the referendum is YES—I have said it clearly in the House of Commons—Mr. Lévesque will be welcome to come to Ottawa, where I will receive him politely, as he has always received me in Québec City, and I will tell him that there are two doors. If you knock on the sovereignty-association door, there is no negotiation possible.

(Applause)

Mr. Lévesque continues to repeat, "But what about democracy—what would you do if a majority of the Québec people voted YES? Would you not be obliged, by the principle of democracy, to negotiate?"

No indeed!

It is like saying to Mr. Lévesque, "The people of Newfoundland have just voted 100 percent in favour of renegotiating the electricity contract with Québec. You are obliged, in the name of democracy, to respect the will of Newfoundland, are you not?"

It is obvious that this sort of logic does not work.

The wishes of Quebecers may be expressed through democratic process, but that cannot bind others—those in other provinces who did not vote to act as Québec decides.

So by that reasoning, Mr. Lévesque, there will be no association. Now, if you want to speak, if you want to speak of sovereignty, let me say that you have no mandate to negotiate that, because you did not ask Quebecers if they wanted sovereignty pure and simple.

You said: Do you want sovereignty on the condition that there is also association?

So, with no association, you have no mandate to negotiate sovereignty; you do not have the key to open that door, and neither do I.

(Applause)

I do not have that mandate either, because we were elected on February 18, scarcely a couple of months ago — for the specific purpose of making laws for the province of Québec.

So don't ask me not to make any, don't ask me to give full powers to Québec.

(Applause)

On the other hand, if Mr. Lévesque, by some miracle, and it truly would be a miracle, knocked on the other door, saying: I have a mandate to negotiate, and would like to negotiate renewed federalism, then the door would be wide open to him, and I would say: you did not have to go to the trouble of holding a referendum for that; if it is renewed federalism you want, if that is what you wish to negotiate, then you are welcome.

But is it really possible that Mr. Lévesque would say that, because what are the YES supporters saying?

The YES supporters are saying — and I asked Mr. Lévesque this a couple of weeks ago: What will you do if the majority votes NO? What will you say then? Will you respect the will of the people, or will you claim that a NO vote does not mean as much as a YES vote, and that a NO does not count for the moment, but that another referendum needs to be held?

I asked Mr. Lévesque that, and this was his answer: We will not refuse a few crumbs of autonomy for Québec, but we will still be going around in circles.

Mr. Lévesque, if the people of Québec vote NO, as I believe they will . . .

(Applause)

. . . won't you say that since the people have rejected sovereignty-association, it is your duty to be a good government and put an end to the status quo on which you place so much blame, and to join us in changing the Constitution?

Mr. Lévesque told us: We will still be going around in circles.

Well, that should enlighten all those who intend to vote YES in order to increase Québec's bargaining power, all those who intend to vote YES out of pride, and all those who intend to vote YES because they are fed up.

If Mr. Lévesque does not want renewed federalism even if the people vote NO, then, clearly, if the people vote YES, he is going to say: "Renewed federalism is out of the question."

For my part, I will say: Sovereignty-Association is out of the question.

(Applause)

Which means that we have reached an impasse, and those who vote YES must realize right now that a YES vote will result in either independence, pure and simple, or the status quo—that is what the YES option boils down to: the independence of Québec, the separation of Québec, or else the status quo, no change, because Mr. Lévesque refuses to negotiate.

That's what we have to say to the YES side: if you want independence, if you vote YES, you won't get independence because you made it conditional on there being an Association, an Association being achieved along with independence.

If you want Association, your YES vote doesn't mean anything because it is not binding on the other provinces, which refuse to join in an association with you. And if you vote YES for a renewed federalism, your vote will be lost as well, because Mr. Lévesque will still be going around in circles.

So you see, that is the impasse that this ambiguous, equivocal question has led us into, and that is what the people who are going to vote YES out of pride, that is what they should think about.

Voting YES out of pride means that we are putting our fate in the hands of the other provinces, which are going to say NO, no association, and then we will have to swallow our pride and our YES vote.

And those who are saying YES in order to get it over with, YES to break away, Yes to get negotiations started, they read in the question itself that there will be a second referendum, and then maybe a third, and then maybe a fourth. And that, my friends, that is precisely what we are criticizing the Parti Québécois government for; not for having wanted independence—that is an option we reject and we're fighting it openly.

But what we are criticizing the Parti Québécois for is for not having the courage to ask: INDEPENDENCE, YES or NO?

(Applause)

YES or NO?

(Applause)

Next, Trudeau talked about how the referendum had divided families, created bitterness among old friends, and drained the energy from other purposes. His brother, Charles; his sister, Suzette; and other family members were in the audience when, for the first time, his voice broke with emotion, as he responded to Lévesque's reported taunt about his mother's name:

I was told that no more than two days ago Mr. Lévesque was saying that part of my name was Elliott and, since Elliott was an English name, it was perfectly understandable that

I was for the NO side, because, really, you see, I was not as much of a Quebecer as those who are going to vote YES.

That, my dear friends, is what contempt is. It means saying that there are different kinds of Quebecers. It means saying that the Quebecers on the NO side are not as good Quebecers as the others and perhaps they have a drop or two of foreign blood, while the people on the YES side have pure blood in their veins. That is what contempt is, and that is the kind of division which builds up within a people, and that is what we are saying NO to.

Of course my name is Pierre Elliott Trudeau. Yes, Elliott was my mother's name. It was the name borne by the Elliotts who came to Canada more than two hundred years ago. It is the name of the Elliotts who, more than one hundred years ago, settled in Saint-Gabriel-de-Brandon, where you can still see their graves in the cemetery. That is what the Elliotts are.

My name is a Québec name, but my name is a Canadian name also, and that's the story of my name.

Trudeau then reminded Lévesque that Pierre Marc Johnson was one of his ministers, the son of Premier Daniel Johnson. So was "Louis O'Neill," that fine francophone. And, Trudeau asked, what about the leader of Quebec's Inuit, Charlie Watt? His people had lived on the land long before Cartier met them over four hundred years earlier. Would he deny Watt's right to call himself a Quebecer? This question and the Elliott history became the story of the speech, which endured as perhaps Trudeau's most memorable address, even though he considered it not one of his best. His opinion is understandable: the first paragraphs were familiar rhetoric, and the last part, for Trudeau, was surely too personal— too close to his own memories of his struggles with identity and his relationship with his past. Journalist Ian MacDonald, a strong critic of Trudeau, was overcome at the meeting and later wrote that the speech was "the emotional and intellectual coup de grâce of the referendum campaign." It exposed how deeply he engaged with his own identity. Long ago, in his essay on canoeing in the wilderness, he had written that individuals acquire "nationalism" when they "feel in [their] bones the vastness of the land and the greatness of its founders." In those wartime days, Trudeau's nationalism had no feeling for the country beyond the Ottawa River and Quebec's eastern boundaries. By 1980 his patriotism spanned the nation, embracing the North and all Canada's people.[23]

Trudeau left Montreal quickly that night and took no further part in the campaign. Meanwhile, after some initial jousting, Jean Chrétien (as federal representative on the "no" side) and Claude Ryan had developed a solid working relationship, and Ryan now accepted the help of his federal "cousins" graciously. Yet troubles were brewing. As political analyst Gérard Bergeron and Globe and Mail columnist Geoffrey Stevens pointed out, Trudeau's presence in the debate and his assertive program for the post-referendum period pushed Ryan and the official campaign into the shadows, and the questions of "yes" and "no" became a duel between Lévesque and Trudeau, one that changed the terrain and assured future battles. On referendum day, Quebec voted as never before as young and old, the athletic and the infirm, anglophone, allophone, and francophone all crammed into the polling stations.[24]

On the morning of the referendum, Trudeau went to Ryan's modest duplex at 425 St. Joseph Boulevard in Outremont. On the street he had known since childhood, in a house where he had long ago met with colleagues from the Université de Montréal, and where Marc Lalonde had lived upstairs when Ryan moved in, the two warriors of modern Quebec politics stirred their coffees together. Ryan had already voted; Trudeau would later. Both were confident of victory as they spoke of the uncertain future. Trudeau troubled Ryan when he stated that he wanted to move ahead and patriate the Constitution after the referendum, but Ryan said nothing directly that day; it was not the time for debate or disagreement.

After Trudeau left Outremont, he voted in his riding of Mount Royal and returned to Ottawa to watch the results at 24 Sussex. Ryan remained in Montreal, preparing for his speech that night in his working-class Verdun constituency. Trudeau invited a small crowd to join him, including House speaker Jeanne Sauvé; Jim Coutts; Michael Pitfield; de Montigny Marchand, a member of the key referendum group in Trudeau's office; and André Burelle, his principal speechwriter for the campaign.[25]

As they milled about the two television sets, Trudeau was transfixed by the results. The "no" side triumphed immediately and ended the evening with 58.6 percent of the vote. An astonishing 85.61 percent of eligible voters had cast their ballots, and the federalists had a majority in all parts of the province and, most important, among both anglophones and francophones. Just after 7:30 p.m., Lévesque entered the Paul Sauvé arena, where less than a week earlier Trudeau had electrified the federalist crowd. Now separatists filled its seats and aisles as a weary Lévesque prepared to speak, his wife, Corinne, at his side and, oddly, Lise Payette, the minister who had created the Yvette fury, nearby. Otherwise, he was alone in a grey spring suit with a few notes. The crowd chanted almost deferentially as he approached the microphone. When he finally stilled his supporters, he said that if he understood their cheers correctly, it meant *"à la prochaine fois"*—until next time. Lévesque conceded, but he reminded the crowd that Trudeau had said that a no victory would not mean staying with the status quo. And he told his listeners that federalists had "immorally and scandalously" abused the electoral process by flooding the province with advertisements, contracts, and other inducements, but nevertheless, he would respect this last expression of "old Quebec." Make no mistake, however, he warned: he and his followers would rise again to fight another day. Many thought his comments bitter, but

Trudeau, unlike others at 24 Sussex, was emotionally moved by Lévesque's defeat and his words. He knew him better than the others did, and perhaps he cared more.

Meanwhile, Ryan was preparing his remarks at the Verdun Auditorium, furious that an ebullient Chrétien had appeared earlier that day on television and was planning to introduce him that evening. Wearing a black suit with a dark tie, Ryan made remarks that were unexpectedly harsh toward the separatists, perhaps the result of his quarrel with Chrétien, but more likely the product of his decision to demand an election. He called for healing while telling Lévesque that this great defeat compelled an election in the fall. The mood in the cavernous auditorium was strangely lacking in celebration and festivity. Finally, late in the evening, Trudeau had his chance to speak. Perhaps the crowd's mood, combined with the sudden surge of empathy for Lévesque in defeat, made Trudeau reflective: "I wish to say simply that we have lost a little in this referendum. If you take account of the broken friendships, the strained family relationships, the hurt pride, there is no one among us who has not suffered some wound which we must try to heal in the days and weeks to come." He would keep his promise, he said, that "no" meant going forward to a renewed federalism and not a return to the status quo. It was not a night to gloat, he told his listeners, but still, there was a tremor of pride and satisfaction in his voice when he declared: "Never have I felt so proud to be a Quebecer and Canadian." He slept soundly that night.[26]

Trudeau's aide Patrick Gossage stayed awake, however, thinking about what the day had meant. "That night," he felt, "was really the end of Trudeau's single-minded crusade for Canada. The constitutional battles to come, however much tenacity they required, could only ever be the legal ribbons on a package that had been delivered with all his mind and heart to waiting Quebecers in his remarkable referendum interventions."

Trudeau, however, was in no mood to look at the past. The next morning he called Chrétien into his office and told him: "Get on a plane and go sell our package to the provinces." Another day had dawned.[27]

Trudeau shelters Michel from the Arctic chill, Melville Island, 1980. Michel would grow up with his father's love of adventure and the outdoors.

Trudeau admired classical guitarist Liona Boyd's artistry and femininity.

Osgoode Hall law student Deborah Coyne gives Trudeau a hockey sweater, February 23, 1979. Just over a decade later they would have a daughter together, Sarah Coyne.

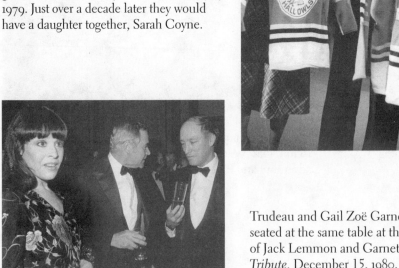

Trudeau and Gail Zoë Garnett were seated at the same table at the premiere of Jack Lemmon and Garnett's film, *Tribute*, December 15, 1980. They began a relationship soon after and would remain close friends until his death.

In a richly decorated desert tent on November 18, 1980, Saudi oil minister Sheik Yamani dances, with Sacha watching.

"A dumb thing" to do, Peter Lougheed—sometimes called the blue-eyed sheik—later said of this photograph taken with Trudeau as they toasted the National Energy Program, 1981. Trudeau's own comment in his 1993 memoirs: "A fair compromise—good for Alberta, good for Canada, and good for a celebratory glass of champagne."

Two very different personalities in a titanic struggle: René Lévesque and Trudeau at the First Ministers Conference in 1980. Lévesque refused to join the other premiers and Trudeau in reaching agreement on a new Canadian Constitution with a Charter of Rights and Freedoms in 1981.

It moved: after the referendum, 1980.

CHAPTER FIFTEEN

—

CLOSING THE DEAL

The pugnacious, colloquial Jean Chrétien and the austere, precise Claude Ryan, the leader of the "no" campaign in Quebec, had clashed often during the referendum campaign, but their partnership had been highly effective—until the campaign ended. It was Chrétien, not Ryan, with whom Trudeau consulted immediately about his plans to shatter the status quo in federal-provincial relations following a "no" vote. He told Chrétien that he was now determined about two goals: to patriate the Canadian Constitution and to create a Canadian charter of rights. But that was not what "reform" meant to Ryan and many others, including Trudeau's major speechwriter for the referendum campaign, André Brunelle. They believed that another course—a radical redistribution of power by which many current federal powers would devolve to the provinces—was the appealing notion that had won the soft nationalists over to the "no" side. In their view, the proposed charter, which would strengthen the authority of the federally appointed Supreme Court of Canada to determine political, economic, and cultural rights, would counter any movement toward decentralization or special status for Quebec. Chrétien realized that Trudeau's plan meant a battle—and he was delighted.[1]

Chrétien knew instinctively that he was facing the fight of his life. He and Ryan had parted on bad terms on referendum night, when Ryan, angered by an interview Chrétien had given earlier in the day, clung tightly to the microphone at the Verdun Auditorium and refused to let Chrétien speak to the crowd celebrating the victory. Their differences were not simply personal but also tactical, political, and intellectual. Neither Trudeau nor Chrétien accepted the argument that decentralization and the transfer of powers to the provinces and, especially, to Quebec were the essential promises made during the referendum campaign, and both had come to believe that Canada's decentralization had gone much too far in the seventies. Trudeau had mocked Joe Clark's claim that Canada was "a community of communities" and had begun to ask the key question, "Who speaks for Canada?" During the election campaign of 1980, Trudeau complained about Clark's attitude and his "provincialism," though he did not talk about constitutional change. He spoke often and passionately about the need for a more activist federal government to face the energy crisis, to deal with the economic challenges, and to realize, at last, a "just society." These broader commitments profoundly affected the constitutional process, and they reflected Trudeau's determination to act when he returned to office. He knew the bitter taste of losing power, and that knowledge made his victory in 1980 and his unexpected fourth term in government particularly sweet.

Tom Axworthy, who became Trudeau's senior policy adviser after the election and his principal secretary in 1981, recalls the different mood in Cabinet meetings that summer and fall: "We had a group of tigers. In field after field they wanted to get things done. The cautious and the naysayers were remarkably few. The sense of reborn liberalism affected virtually everyone." For Trudeau the time in opposition had caused him to reflect on the things he had not done, as well as on how quickly the accomplishments he cherished had been reversed by the Clark government. And so he became "the *raw demon* of our government system." The size of the PMO was reduced, as were the number of meetings and briefing books. On Trudeau's orders his staff "pushed as much as possible out and kept as little as possible in." The prime minister became even more disciplined, rigorously scheduling time for Justin, Sacha, and Michel and leaving most weekends free for his lively dating life with a variety of often talented and always attractive women. During the week his attention fastened with burning intensity on the issues that mattered most to him and, in particular, his legacy. He left to others the things that mattered less.[2]

The areas where Trudeau concentrated his attention were the Constitution, the economy (in particular, the energy sector as part of an overall "industrial strategy"), and international affairs. His Cabinet reflected his personal commitments. As minister of justice, Chrétien held the constitutional file tightly to his chest, and his folksy candour and political common sense turned arid legalisms into matters of human concern. Chrétien's political gifts were supplemented by the shrewd advice he received from his politically brilliant and perpetually ingenious young assistant Eddie Goldenberg, the son of Carl Goldenberg, who had advised Trudeau in 1968 on constitutional matters.

In the aftermath of the second energy crisis, caused in 1979 by the seizure of American hostages in Iran, energy and economic policy were intimately linked. The Liberal platform for the 1980 election had trumpeted a new and fairer energy policy, and to lead on that file Trudeau turned to his most trusted colleague, Marc Lalonde, for Energy, Mines, and Resources. During the opposition period and the election campaign, Lalonde and the platform committee had created an ambitious energy policy. Lalonde drew on his long experience in Ottawa, beginning as an assistant to Conservative justice minister Davey Fulton in 1959 through service as Trudeau's principal secretary in his first government to ministerial service in health, justice, and federal-provincial relations.

464   JUST WATCH ME

A powerful presence who had delivered Trudeau's smashing political victories in Quebec in 1979 and 1980, Lalonde, like Trudeau, had experienced too much equivocation in the past and was now eager for ambitious action.

For the key role in Finance, Trudeau chose another political veteran, Allan MacEachen, who had first come to Ottawa in 1953 and had served in many ministries. His skills were mainly and exquisitely political, and in December 1979 they had saved Trudeau's political life. MacEachen and Lalonde had developed a deep respect for each other's abilities, and they, in turn, had Trudeau's complete trust and considerable freedom to act independently.

The same was not true of Mark MacGuigan, Trudeau's surprising choice as minister of external affairs. A former dean of law, the earnest MacGuigan had known Trudeau since the sixties but had never held a Cabinet post since first being elected in 1968. A conservative in foreign relations with deep suspicions of Soviet communism, MacGuigan was, however, a liberal Catholic who shared Trudeau's growing interest in international development issues— or what was then termed the Third World. Still, MacGuigan's memoir of his tenure in foreign affairs makes clear the main reason for his appointment: Trudeau wanted to become deeply involved in foreign affairs himself. Whenever things got interesting, MacGuigan later recalled, "Trudeau pushed me out of his way."[3]

Few other ministers had that problem, as Trudeau focused intensely on the issues of deepest interest to him. John Roberts, the minister of the environment, for example, could not recall a single instance when Trudeau intervened or even spoke to him in any detail about his ministerial work. Roberts was one of several ministers in the new Cabinet who had considerable Ottawa experience—in his case as an MP between 1968 and 1972, a Trudeau aide between 1972 and 1974, and then as a minister in Trudeau's third government. Others in the 1980 Cabinet who had worked closely with Trudeau in the past included Roméo Leblanc, the minister of fisheries, and Don Johnston, the secretary of the Treasury, who had been Trudeau's personal lawyer. Showing his disregard for personal foibles, Trudeau appointed John Munro, who had resigned from the Cabinet because of an inappropriate call to a judge in 1978, as minister of Indian affairs and northern development; and Quebec MP Francis Fox, who had resigned after admitting that he had forged another man's signature on an abortion permission document, as secretary of state and minister of communications. If Trudeau regarded such sins as venial, he made it very clear that disloyalty had become a cardinal infraction. John Reid and Judd Buchanan, two talented young former Ontario ministers who had opposed Trudeau's return as leader, were not reappointed to the Cabinet table. The articulate and engaging Jean-Luc Pepin, who had annoyed Trudeau with his report on the Canadian federation, was too useful and popular to omit, however, and he was appointed as minister of transport—far away from the vital negotiations on the Constitution but close at hand for the important negotiations to end the archaic 1897 Crow's Nest Pass Agreement, which had guaranteed lower prices for grain shipments and thereby caused the railways to spend less on equipment.

Two able women, Monique Bégin and Judy Erola, became, respectively, minister of health and welfare and minister of state (mines). The West once again was weakly represented, with British Columbia, Alberta, and Saskatchewan each having a senator in Cabinet. Manitoba had stronger representation, with the highly promising newcomer Lloyd Axworthy, who became minister of employment and immigration. Although Axworthy had strong ties with John Turner, he was perceived, correctly, as a powerful voice on the Liberal left. He and his brother, Tom, were articulate western voices supporting the centralist and interventionist approaches of the new government. For most people, however, Axworthy was still an unknown. Those troubled about the leftward drift of the new government fastened on Herb Gray, the new minister of industry, trade and commerce, who had been dropped from Cabinet in 1974 but who was identified with such nationalist policies as the Foreign Investment Review Agency and the earlier "Gray Report," which encouraged restrictions on foreign investment. His appointment upset the increasingly conservative *Globe and Mail.* Gray was, its editors declared, a politician of "admirable perseverance and tunnel vision," who saw only economic nationalist nostrums. Gray would, as before, do his "discouraging best."[4]

The comment was unfair, and the Cabinet's membership much stronger than the *Globe and Mail* would admit, as the future stellar careers of many of its members, including Herb Gray, confirm. The *Globe,* however, reflected the increasingly conservative mood of Bay Street, which was highly uncomfortable with Trudeau's tilt toward the left. Although some informed commentators and Liberals, such as Don Johnston and Trudeau confidant journalist Ron Graham, minimize the "leftist" direction of the government, Trudeau's private papers strongly argue the contrary case.[5] Moreover, Johnston recalls how Gray, Axworthy, Bégin, Munro, and others fought regularly in Cabinet with the more conservative and business-oriented ministers such as himself, Judy Erola, Ed Lumley, and surprisingly and only occasionally, Allan MacEachen—and that the conservatives lost most of the fights.[6] As Margaret Thatcher's Tories began their assault on British trade unionism, entrenched state bureaucracies, and market regulation, and as Ronald Reagan's Republicans stoked the embers of the Cold War and began an aggressive rebuilding of the American military, Canada under Trudeau stubbornly resisted this new Anglo-American consensus.

Trudeau rejected the Reagan-Thatcher argument that government was part of the problem, not part of the solution. He was surrounded by young activists such as Tom Axworthy, who had played a key role in writing the Liberal nationalist and interventionist platform for the 1980 election, and he was deeply influenced by his leading campaign strategist, Keith Davey, who constantly repeated the mantra that Liberals lose when they don't lean left, and his principal secretary, Jim Coutts, who had become deeply involved in community organization in downtown Toronto as a prelude, he hoped, to running for office soon. Indeed, *Towards a Just Society*, a 1990 collection of essays written by many of the principal actors in this government and edited by Trudeau and Tom Axworthy, is a detailed defence of how they "fought for a fairer, more humane Canada, in which the power of government was a necessary instrument in the quest for a more just society."[7] In 1980 Trudeau stayed on his course and quickened his step, even as Reagan campaigned for a new "morning in America" where the federal government would withdraw from economic intervention and New Deal welfare policies, transfer many social responsibilities to the states, and reject policies of détente, disarmament, and interventionist international development.

The "Reagan revolution" gained strength from its internal consistency and the powerful intellectual framework erected to support it by market-oriented economists Milton Friedman and Allan Greenspan, for example, and social analysts James Coleman and Diane Ravitch. But Trudeau's rejection of Reagan's declaration that government was the problem also possessed an internal unity, one that linked constitutional reform with the National Energy Program and the commitment to a fairer distribution of the world's wealth between the rich and the poor. Don Johnston is correct in pointing to Trudeau's conservative quirks where financial matters were concerned and his acceptance of "a strong and vigorous private sector," but the intellectual climate of the 1980s and what Stephen Clarkson termed "the Reagan challenge" provoked Trudeau toward a strong response, partly because of his innate contrarianism but mainly because he believed deeply in the importance of medicare, economic equity, and what European socialists earlier and later came

to term a "middle way," somewhere between massive state intervention and unregulated market freedom.* Trudeau did have
doubts about the effectiveness of many of the social and educational
programs that had been developed in haste in the 1960s. We have
seen how, as early as his leadership campaign of 1968, he declared
that the days of Santa Claus were over, and how, once in power, he
introduced a series of austerity measures. Nevertheless, in the eighties, Trudeau usually stood firm as Thatcher, Reagan, and much of
the media pushed the pendulum dramatically to the right. He identified with the moderate German Social Democrat Helmut Schmidt
and, in the international arena, with European socialist premiers
Olof Palme of Sweden and Andreas Papandreou of Greece, whom
he regarded as his personal friends.[8]

---

* Johnston's invaluable memoir contains an exchange about the character of
Liberalism in the spring of 1981 between him and Trudeau, when Bay Street,
if not yet Main Street, was becoming angry with the Trudeau government.
Trudeau responded to Johnston's call for closer attention to these complaints
with a statement that the Liberal Party had succeeded best when it was
"a moderate voice of reform between the conservative and socialistic camps,"
a tradition he believed "must be continued" (65). A later anecdote summarizes
well Johnston's bafflement with Trudeau's attitude toward money issues. In the
early 1980s, an angry Johnston stormed into Trudeau's office to complain about
the transfer of domestic flights from Dorval to Mirabel airport, the costly
mistake of the seventies built far outside Montreal's city centre. Trudeau was
steely in resisting the complaints until Johnston, who as Trudeau's personal
lawyer knew well his miserly ways, said that the taxi fare to Mirabel would be
one hundred dollars return. Trudeau removed his glasses, asked, "Are you
serious?" and quickly decided in favour of Dorval. Don Johnston, *Up the Hill*
(Montreal and Toronto: Optimum, 1986), 88. Mr. Johnston confirmed the
details to me during a conversation.

The American presidential campaign of 1980 coincided with a high-pressure ridge that settled over the centre of the continent that summer, bringing sweltering heat from late spring to early fall. For Jimmy Carter, the summer brought bad times, which Canadians increasingly shared. The so-called Canadian caper, which enabled some American hostages to escape from Iran, earned general applause from America for its northern neighbour. But this did not end the drama in Teheran, where the new Islamic theocracy continued to hold some American diplomats hostage, along with President Carter's chances for re-election. Détente seemed dead as Soviet tanks and warplanes pounded Afghan cities and villages and the CIA began its fatal attraction to the Islamic fundamentalists who were fighting Soviet aggression.

The normal summer celebrations that accompanied the Olympics did not occur as Canada, with considerable reluctance on Trudeau's part, joined the American boycott of the Moscow Olympic Games. Although Trudeau much preferred Carter to Reagan in the presidential race, Carter's increasingly hard stance against the Soviet Union irritated and disillusioned him, and on some items such as the embargo of wheat sales he refused to join fully in the boycott— to Carter's surprise and disappointment.[9] For their part, the Soviet leaders noticed Trudeau's dissent. Their ambassador in Ottawa, Alexander Yakovlev, welcomed his friend's re-election to office in the Soviet journal *Novy Mir* in May 1980, claiming that Trudeau "returned to his old hunting grounds more enriched in charisma, enjoying the backing of both the whole of his party and the whole of his nation." To Trudeau's good fortune at a time when the Cold War was chilling, Yakovlev wrote anonymously.[10]

—

In his confidential reports to Moscow, Yakovlev noted with some regret that Trudeau had little time for international politics because domestic matters, particularly the Constitution, absorbed nearly all his attention. Separatism had not died with its referendum defeat on May 20. Indeed, Lévesque had exclaimed to his wife in English, when he finally sprang out of bed at eleven o'clock the following morning, "It's a new ball game."[11] But most of the players were the same as before, and the two stars, Lévesque and Trudeau, still dominated the field. Despite his central role in the "no" campaign, Ryan became increasingly ineffective, and Lévesque more central, as Trudeau advanced his constitutional plans. When the premiers met Trudeau in Ottawa on June 9, Lévesque quickly realized that the prime minister wanted to change the rules of the constitutional game and was delighted when the other premiers baulked at them. Lévesque and his close adviser Claude Morin recognized the value of Quebec forming alliances with the other premiers. He therefore appeared whimsical, detached, and even helpful as others tore into Trudeau's proposals. The federal government presented a sweeping program for change, which included not only patriation but also a "People's List" and a "Government's List" of changes. The People's List, later to be called the "People's Package," consisted of a statement of general principles, a charter of rights, equalization (which would ensure that wealth was shared with the poorer provinces), and lofty sentiments, while the Government's List included gritty detail about communications, the Senate, broadcasting, fisheries, and other items that had bedevilled courts and constitutional change for generations.[12]

When Trudeau and the premiers emerged from 24 Sussex Drive, where steel barriers had physically and symbolically shielded the deliberations from the press and the public, there were a few shreds of optimism. Trudeau told the media that the group had agreed to reconvene after Labour Day to seal the constitutional deal. But when detailed questions came, Trudeau admitted that the premiers had produced their own lists, with such items as the ownership of fisheries or the right to self-determination. When asked whether a new Constitution would be the crowning achievement he had long sought, a tired Trudeau answered: "If we do reach agreement on all these items, I would be very, very anxious to retire. That might be an incentive to a lot of people." Of the premiers, only Richard Hatfield of New Brunswick (who had presented a baffled Trudeau with a plastic bag full of fiddleheads at the opening of the conference) and William Davis of Ontario shared Trudeau's enthusiasm for the new constitutional adventure. Davis's Progressive Conservative colleague, Peter Lougheed of Alberta, described Davis with derision as Trudeau's "lap dog"—a comment Davis dismissed while faintly praising Lévesque's willingness to "see" the process through and "participate in it."[13]

Chrétien's Challenger jet took off once more for provincial capitals, where he found that the federal lists had inspired premiers to extend their own predictable shopping lists. The process unfolded through the Continuing Committee of the Ministers on the Constitution (CCMC), which Chrétien co-chaired with Saskatchewan attorney general Roy Romanow. In Ottawa, Trudeau's advisers followed the process and consulted constantly but worked on their own plans. Expecting resistance to his constitutional proposals, Trudeau had brought in a new team to deal with the premiers. Gordon Robertson, who had been Trudeau's superior in the fifties when the young civil servant first encountered the peculiar world of federal-provincial relations and who had supervised the constitutional file since the sixties, was now shoved aside in favour of Michael Kirby. Recruited by Michael Pitfield, who had returned from Harvard to the Privy Council, the diminutive and boyish Kirby was bright, ingenious, energetic, and a mathematician by training, but largely uninformed about Canadian constitutional history and practice. Called Machiavellian by his enemies, Kirby revelled in the description, quoting his "mentor" in documents he wrote and devilishly adorning his 1981 Christmas card with a paraphrase of a quotation from Machiavelli that he had first noticed in the office of the Saskatchewan deputy minister of intergovernmental affairs: "It should be borne in mind that there is nothing more difficult to arrange, more doubtful of success, and more dangerous to carry through than initiating changes in a state's Constitution." His lack of experience was itself a qualification for his work. "I didn't need advice," Trudeau later said. "At that point I knew exactly what I wanted"—"a deal-maker and a negotiation-closer, not a thinker and discussant." Kirby proudly became "Trudeau's son of a bitch."[14]

And soon enough, things did indeed become bitchy. As Chrétien reported the premiers' views and officials recounted the difficulties they were experiencing in negotiations with their counterparts, Kirby, with Pitfield's encouragement, prepared a strategy that would force the premiers to come to an agreement. If they failed, he directed, the federal government would act unilaterally—it would divide in order to conquer. But the divisions were already deep, even within the Privy Council and the Prime Minister's Office. Trudeau's principal speechwriters, Jim Moore and André Burelle, quarrelled in the summer over Trudeau's public statements to Canadians and, in particular, to francophones. Sharp differences emerged over the concepts of the "nation" and federalism, with Burelle believing that contemporary Quebec nationalism, being civic in nature, was best embraced in a linguistic and federal system similar to that of Switzerland. With the eyes of a lynx, Trudeau regularly corrected any drafts produced by Burelle that expressed this concept, stroking out every "nation" related to Quebec he could find. Moore, meanwhile, sharply dissented from Burelle's declaration to the Canadian people for Canada Day 1980, drafted in French:

> Your latest version of the statement of principles is, in my opinion, so profoundly different from the earlier versions as to raise the serious question of whether the new version will

be seen in English Canada as a provocation rather than an attempt to bring Canadians closer together.

The changes which cause concern are:

1. In the first paragraph, the PM would be seen as abandoning, in the face of nationalist criticism, the idea that Canadians are one people. The retention of "un peuple" on the fourth line would not suffice to overcome that impression.

2. Anglo editorialists in the Bible Belt of western Canada are going to have a field day when they compare the old and new versions of the statement, and see that the PM is willing to drop God.

3. By reversing the order of French and English on the fifth line, you have eliminated the equal balance of the earlier version. Now the statement seems to say that, while French and English are equal, the Constitution will consistently place French first.

As Trudeau and Burelle jousted over the summer months, the francophone speechwriter pondered his future in Ottawa.[15]

Gordon Robertson, meanwhile, had suddenly become a man of the past. But he was still an influential presence at the endless *"cinq à sept"* receptions in the city, the luncheons where retired "eminents" met at the elite Rideau Club, and summer gatherings in the Gatineaus. He was clearly uneasy with the new ways and the confrontations. The long relationship between Robertson and Trudeau began to disintegrate as differences became strong disagreements and, eventually, bitter disillusionment. But Robertson was old school, careful, respectful of Cabinet secrecy, and wary of paper trails or, as Trudeau himself said, "a mandarin, concerned with the common weal, afraid of irreparable damage to the fabric of society." He was "too much of a gentleman" for the tough times ahead. His brash and brawling successors irritated not only Robertson but others who felt excluded from the inner circle, or who believed that the confrontational style or even the constitutional process itself was wrong. Not surprisingly, leaks soon appeared, first in quiet asides at dinner parties or lunches, but then in the deliberate passing of documents to reporters or, more seriously, to the government of Quebec. Diplomat Robert Fowler, who was seconded to the Privy Council to assist in the constitutional wars, later recalled with some anger how, at a closed meeting, he looked about the table, studied his colleagues' eyes, and saw some avoid his gaze. Secrets mattered, especially when they were not kept.[16]

When the premiers returned to Ottawa on September 7 for another meeting on the constitutional reforms, they got together first in the hotel room of Sterling Lyon, Manitoba's Conservative premier, to discuss their own strategy. Quebec intergovernmental affairs minister Claude Morin passed around a memorandum on the federal strategy signed by Michael Kirby. This document, reportedly leaked by a separatist mole, argued for an aggressive strategy that contemplated unilateral patriation of the Constitution and suggested that the federal government approach the meeting with the expectation that there would be no agreement. That same evening, Governor General Ed Schreyer, a former premier of Manitoba, invited the premiers and the prime minister to Rideau Hall for an opening dinner, where the atmosphere was immediately electric with suspicion and anger. Formalities melted into biting jabs, caused initially by the request that one of the premiers co-chair the meeting with Trudeau—a proposal that infuriated Trudeau. The food was poor and, by the time a cake for Saskatchewan premier Allan Blakeney's fifty-fifth birthday appeared, the mood was so foul that Trudeau turned away during the tribute. He urged Schreyer to speed the service so he could leave quickly, allegedly dismissing the RCMP bodyguard with the comment, "Fuck off, and don't follow me home."[17]

It was a wretched start to a dreadful week. The Kirby memorandum probably made little difference; indeed, an earlier leaked

"Pitfield memorandum" had broached the distinct possibility of unilateral patriation, and in late August, at a ministerial meeting, Claude Morin had told the press unequivocally that the federal government intended to act unilaterally. Even Romanow, despite his warm relationship with Chrétien,* openly argued with him over the federal insistence on a charter of rights and its policy on natural resources. Months before, lines had been drawn, alliances forged and tested, and personal grudges created. As soon as the leaders gathered at the conference table the next morning, all these bad memories surfaced.

Lévesque sat back, cigarette smoke swirling about him, while he responded indifferently with a toss of the head and a flick of the ash as the premiers and Trudeau spoke. Hatfield of New Brunswick tried, a bit too eagerly, to be the jokester, seeking consensus through weak humour. Lyon of Manitoba, sternly conservative and as British as Winnipeg's Manitoba Club in the days of empire, expressed those values with a blustery defence of parliamentary supremacy over the courts. Much less conservative but equally tied to the British parliamentary tradition, Blakeney combined a Prairie socialist's suspicion of Liberals with a sharp legal mind that, paradoxically, also trusted politicians more than judges. The law was a distant realm for British Columbia's Bill Bennett, who lacked his father's outrageous style but not his strong commitment to his province's natural resource interests. He shared those interests with other premiers, including Newfoundland's Brian Peckford, who came to the table with dreams of offshore oil lodes dancing feverishly in his mind. Ontario's riches, in contrast,

---

* They joked that Chrétien would translate French questions to his unilingual co-chair of the Continuing Committee of the Ministers on the Constitution if Romanow translated the Ukrainian questions.

no longer resided in the minerals of the Canadian Shield but in its manufacturing plants, whose operators craved cheap energy. This pressing need fuelled the intense clash between bland "Brampton Billy" Davis, Ontario's deceptively shrewd premier, and Alberta's Peter Lougheed, whose opposition to such claims was eloquent, adamant, and longstanding.

In retrospect, it was a strange and inappropriate group that gathered at Ottawa's conference centre. Only Trudeau and Lévesque were bilingual at a conference where the entrenchment of language rights in the proposed charter of rights was a fundamental issue. They were also the only Catholics, the faith of 46 percent of the population, and the only participants not of British origin—a trait 56 percent of Canadians shared. All the participants were middle-aged men, again a minority demographic, and, except for Trudeau, none was a Liberal. These characteristics were hardly auspicious for concerted action.

Yet profound differences also lay beneath the surface similarities among the premiers. Lougheed and Davis had both become premiers in 1971, Davis before the historic Victoria Conference and Lougheed shortly after the conference failed. They were initially friendly, with the articulate and engaging Lougheed presented as a "star" in Davis's October 21 election campaign.* But their ways began to part when OPEC shattered the energy world, and Lougheed wanted to pick up Alberta's exploding share. By 1981 they

---

* Davis had become premier after Premier John Robarts resigned. He won a leadership contest despite considerable concern about his lifeless speaking style and boyish appearance. As minister of education in Ontario, he had acquired a reputation as the "reddest" of Tories, notably for his promotion of the Hall-Dennis Report, which recommended fashionable "sixties" nostrums to "modernize" Ontario's traditional educational system.

had harsh words for each other as their provincial and political interests trumped their Tory fraternity. While Lougheed often found himself arguing on the side of Quebec for provincial rights, Davis began the September conference firmly in support of the federal government. The traditional Quebec-Ontario alliance gave way to an odd Alberta-Quebec entente. Davis's alliance with Trudeau, however, had some political dangers, and he was accused of trying to introduce official bilingualism into Ontario. He quickly denied such a possibility—and earned strong criticism in Quebec. Even the *Globe and Mail* contrasted this manoeuvring with the courage Hatfield had shown when he called for entrenchment of bilingualism in the charter.[18]

Although Lougheed generally agreed with Lévesque, he was oblique in expressing that support. Peckford, in contrast, enraged the federalists when he stated that he was closer to Lévesque's view of Canada than to Trudeau's. Lougheed was the big player, however, and Trudeau confronted him continually. When Lougheed said that the federal response to provincial demands was "nominal and relatively insignificant," Trudeau snapped back that the government should withdraw its offer to negotiate resource ownership in exchange for a Canadian common market. He firmly rejected Lougheed's complaints about centralization: "We know that, in Canada, we're living in the most decentralized federation in the world," he said. "The provinces have enormous power, more power under our Constitution than any component parts of any other government in the world." But his arguments were all to no avail. The conference confirmed Canada's many differences, and, in Trudeau's mind, it demonstrated the futility of the painful search for consensus and the need to push forward firmly toward his goals. Finally, he closed down the conference, slammed his books shut, and warned the "gentlemen" that it was not over. Sterling Lyon proclaimed that Trudeau could not possibly go forward in the face of the provincial dissent, but Romanow, who had worked closely with Chrétien, told the press as he left, "They're going."[19]

And they were. Trudeau met with his caucus on September 27. The MPs still bore the enthusiasm of recent triumphs in the election and the referendum. Even those who had doubted Trudeau in 1979 and those who would later urge his departure were firmly behind their leader as he rose and informed them that he did not have time to wait. He explained that the nine "English-speaking premiers had accepted a completely new list of demands" drafted by Lévesque and Morin, and that some premiers were so drenched in their understanding of the British parliamentary tradition that they would join Lévesque in resisting a full charter where the courts upheld the basic rights of citizens. He concluded with the prediction that they would have an epic battle ahead of them if they wanted a full charter. The caucus sensed the moment: a Quebec member rose and declared, "*Allons-y en Cadillac.*" A full-size North American model it would be, one where the Constitution would no longer rest in London, where Canadian courts and legislatures were completely sovereign, where a charter enshrining basic rights would prevail over legislative fiats, and where the Supreme Court would make historic decisions that would profoundly affect the way Canadians lived their lives—just as the controversial American Supreme Court had done in the postwar era with its historic rulings on school segregation and the rights of prisoners.

The following day, Trudeau met his Cabinet. Although records of the meeting are not yet available, few, if any, secrets remain. Trudeau had warned the Cabinet before his September meeting with the premiers that they faced a tough fight over the Constitution and the charter: the provincial leaders would oppose them strenuously, the British would waver, and opponents of the entrenchment of minority language rights for the English in Quebec and for the French elsewhere in the country would resist bitterly. In short, he concluded, "We could tear up the goddam country by this action, but we're going to do it anyway."[20] Time had run out for him and the country. Buttressed by the dual mandate of the overwhelming victory in Quebec in the 1980 election and the referendum, Trudeau now set out with determination to remake his country.* Some in the Cabinet hesitated: Pepin, as expected; franco-Ontarian Jean-Jacques Blais, who feared a backlash; Senator Ray Perrault, who was always unpredictable; and Charles Lapointe, a young Quebec minister who was part of a group of Quebec MPs uneasy with the challenge to the *nationalistes*. The notion of a pan-Canadian referendum as an alternative to unilateralism was briefly mooted, but the Cabinet rejected the idea. Doubts soon disappeared in the face of Trudeau's determination and the exuberance of the caucus. With

---

* In a satirical column entitled "Too Many Traitors," political columnist Geoffrey Stevens anticipated the impending conflict with a mock report on how the Americans might cover the Canadian political war: "In an exclusive interview with NBC News at his command headquarters at the Banff Springs Hotel, Peter Lougheed, leader of the breakaway Alberta sect, vowed to 'establish provincial paramountcy in interprovincial trade if the blasphemous child-molesters from Ottawa lay their heinous, lice-encrusted hands on a single drop of sacred Alberta oil.' Meanwhile, in Ottawa, Assistant War Minister John Roberts said he will dispatch the entire fleet of Jet Star executive aircraft to bomb the Diefenbaker Library in Saskatchewan unless 'that foul infidel Allan Blakeney and his goat-eating cohorts stop levying indirect taxes by noon tomorrow.' Finally, from Harrington Lake, where he has fled to escape the intermittent strafing of the capital by the PEI Air Force, Prime Minister Trudeau announced that any provincial quislings who survive 'interrogation' will be tried for 'crimes against national unity' when the Fifty-Three Years' War ends." *Globe and Mail*, Sept. 27, 1980.

the Liberals in agreement, Trudeau tried to find allies to bolster
those areas where his government was weak. And so he invited
NDP leader Ed Broadbent in for a chat on October 1, 1980.[21]

Broadbent, as we know, had turned down Trudeau's earlier
attempt to form a coalition with the NDP. Besides, the party faced
a major internal challenge, divided as it was between western MPs
suspicious of the Liberals, Quebec, bilingualism, and central
Canada and eastern MPs supportive of patriation, resource taxes,
a charter of rights, and official bilingualism. During the summer,
MPs such as Ontario's fluently bilingual Bob Rae had expressed
support for Trudeau's initiative, while westerners were far more
reluctant.[22] Trudeau and Broadbent had an uneasy relationship,
perhaps because of Trudeau's own NDP past but more likely
because the NDP and the Liberals fought for the same voters.
Trudeau now told Broadbent that he intended to go forward with
patriation and an entrenched charter, regardless of the provincial
opposition. Broadbent agreed to support the initiative, subject to
a few amendments seeking greater control of resources to assuage
Saskatchewan socialists.

But Broadbent had not consulted his MPs widely enough.
His decision caused a tempest in his party, with Blakeney leading
his critics and accusing him of betrayal and ignorance. One of his
own aides told his biographer Judy Steed that Broadbent "failed to
massage the party's egos at the critical moment. He forgot about
playing politics. And for that he got the shit kicked out of him."
David Lewis, who backed Broadbent, disagreed deeply with his
son, Stephen, who took Blakeney's side, and four western MPs
openly opposed their leader. But the commitment held.[23]

Fortified by the enthusiasm of his caucus and armed
with Broadbent's support, Trudeau appeared on television on
October 2, 1980, and announced his plan to patriate the
Constitution unilaterally. It was the night when Larry Holmes
fought Muhammad Ali in Ali's fourth comeback. That fight brought

a quicker and clearer outcome—Ali's only defeat by a technical knockout—than the battle that had begun in Canada's political forums. Trudeau's speech had three distinct parts: patriation of the Constitution; a charter of rights and freedoms enshrining minority language and education rights, which would be binding on all governments; and a method for arriving at an amending formula for the Constitution. Trudeau said that any group that opposed the plan "would look foolish in the eyes of the world." Conservative leader Joe Clark immediately registered a strong dissent, one echoed not only by Quebec Liberal leader Claude Ryan but also by Premier René Lévesque. Their greatest objections were to Trudeau's refusal to offer new powers to the provinces or "special status" in exchange for the bargain. Broadbent offered support as expected, though he expressed disappointment at the limited provisions for provincial control of natural resources. The following morning Ontario's William Davis broke with Clark and announced that he would back Trudeau's plan. Peter Lougheed, after consultation with Bill Bennett, announced furiously: "We will fight back any way we can devise." The gloves were off.[24]

Trudeau's proposals did offer some conciliatory gestures to the provinces. Ontario would not be required to become officially bilingual, land sale restrictions in Saskatchewan and Prince Edward Island were exempted, and the provisions for free trade among the provinces were dropped—an omission the Canadian Chamber of Commerce protested and one Trudeau and many others later regretted. These concessions were quickly brushed aside by his opponents, who focused on the "centralization" implicit in the charter. Joe Clark's virulent attacks on Trudeau and the constitutional changes resulted from his party's strong support in the West, his hopes for a Tory breakthrough in Quebec, and, not least, the growing threats to his own leadership within his party. In September 1980, as Clark was readying his response, Brian Mulroney, his leadership opponent in 1976, gave a public address calling for a reinvigorated party with a strong Quebec base. Mulroney, in common with nearly all Quebec anglophones, supported the proposed charter. Thus, while looking forward, Clark also had to look behind. Lougheed, too, had jousted with him when the Tories were in office, but now the Alberta premier expected much from Clark in the duel against constitutional reforms.[25]

—

Before long, a second front opened in the federal-provincial war. On October 28, 1980, Finance Minister Allan MacEachen rose in the House and, in his slow, deep voice, unveiled the National Energy Program (NEP)—a plan that caused perhaps the greatest economic controversy since John A. Macdonald's National Policy a century earlier. The NEP quickly turned the West against the East and manufacturers against natural energy suppliers while simultaneously enriching the coffers of the central government.

Like the National Policy, the NEP is best understood through its politics rather than its economics, although both elements are central to its origins and its effects. Marc Lalonde, the minister of energy when MacEachen introduced the policy, points to the economic and political arguments in his later defence of the NEP. Clark, he says, had also experienced difficult negotiations with Alberta—his finance minister, John Crosbie, even called Lougheed by the name of Bokassa II, a reference to the mad emperor of the Central African Republic—and on their return to power the Liberals were determined to end the "image of fuzziness and aimlessness" they had projected before their 1979 defeat. The NEP built squarely on one of Trudeau's campaign speeches of January 1980, which had promised a "made-in-Canada" price for oil, the expansion of Petro-Canada, energy security through the development of Arctic and offshore oil, increased Canadian ownership of the energy sector, and the incorporation of energy into Canada's industrial policy. It "detonated like a bomb over Alberta, stunning the petro-leum province momentarily, while its fall-out spread slowly across the continent."[26]

For Lougheed, the NEP, following on the threat of unilateral patriation in late September, was the final straw. Angered, brittle, and deeply suspicious of the federal government, he linked the con-stitutional proposals with what he now believed was a fundamental assault on the provinces' ownership of resources. Even before his Conservatives came to power in Alberta in 1971, Lougheed had asserted that Alberta's sole control over energy resources was essen-tial, and he had criticized his Social Credit predecessor for failing to stand up for Alberta's interests at the Victoria Conference on the Constitution. The NEP, though it did not question Alberta's own-ership, still asserted Ottawa's right to control pricing, taxation, and international trade in the resource. Economists called the struggle a debate over economic rents, but journalists in the various media personalized that abstruse concept as Ottawa versus Edmonton, Toronto versus Calgary, Lougheed versus Trudeau, Galbraith versus Friedman, and rich versus poor. And crude as they often were on the front page and the cartoon page, these images were a rough approx-imation of reality. Fundamentally, the NEP was about politics: who gets what, when, and how.[27]

On November 4, exactly one week after MacEachen and Lalonde presented the NEP, Ronald Reagan swept to victory in the American presidential election and in his inaugural address referred to his "intention to curb the size and influence of the federal establishment and to demand recognition of the distinc-tion between the powers granted to the federal government and those reserved to the states or to the people."[28] The NEP, with its interventionism, its nationalist promise to regain Canadian own-ership of its energy sector, and its favouring of Canadian firms over multinationals, suddenly became a direct affront to the new American administration. Lougheed, of course, noticed, but so did his socialist neighbour Allan Blakeney, whose strong opposition to Trudeau's constitutional reforms now intensified with the aggressive federal stand on energy policy. Although much of the Ontario business community and the press vigorously opposed the NEP, essentially because they preferred the new conservatism, Premier Davis recognized that the lower oil prices and the focus on Canadian nationalism were popular among his constituents. He therefore made only muffled noises about the NEP while continuing to back the federal Liberals on the Constitution.

In Quebec, as always, the political issue was more complicated, with Lévesque's social democratic government opposed to Reagan's antigovernment stance and favourable to the economic equalization aspects of the NEP, particularly the Canadian-controlled oil price and the higher taxes on producers. Yet Lévesque and Lougheed found common ground on decentralization and provincial rights. Indeed, Ted Byfield's *Alberta Report*, the influential conservative journal, claimed that provincial government officials had concluded just before the referendum that a "yes" vote would be best for Alberta because it would undermine Trudeau's "centralization" ambitions and weaken the province of Ontario. No provincial politician, the magazine added, dared make such views public, but they were widely held.[29] To muddle things even more, the economy was sputtering into the worst recession since the Great Depression, with unemployment averaging 7.5 percent and rising every month; by 1982 it would be over 12 percent. The five-year mortgage rate stood at 18.38 percent, and inflation at 12.4 percent. With the so-called "Misery Index" at its highest point in Canadian history, it was not an easy time to remake a country.*

---

* The underlying forces behind these political differences are revealed by a comparison of the Canadian average gross domestic product per capita and

Trudeau knew that it never would be easy. Unlike the confusion following the collapse of Keynesian approaches in the seventies, however, the eighties appeared to offer clearer choices. There were, on the one hand, the monetarist and supply-side economists, who were increasingly linked with neo-conservatives and who regarded excessive welfare as debilitating and demoralizing for any society; on the other were the social democrats and liberal interventionists, who continued to look to the state for leadership in the creation of a more equitable and just society while recognizing the failures of specific welfare policies. The NEP, then, was a broader response to the economic challenges the government faced. Believing that energy prices would continue to rise dramatically throughout the decade, the federal government wanted more revenue to sustain its programs, from the increasingly expensive medicare to support for the poorer regions of the country. Energy seemed the key to unlocking the engine that would secure a stable financial future for the western provinces, especially Alberta and Saskatchewan, and, simultaneously, release abundant new revenues for the federal government, where expenses were growing rapidly and the budgetary deficit had ballooned. Conflict was inevitable.

---

the provincial equivalent: in 1971 Ontario stood at 117.8 percent of the Canadian average; Quebec, at 90.1%; Alberta, at 107.%; and Saskatchewan, at 83.3%. In 1981 the comparable figures were Ontario, 102.7%; Quebec, 86%; Alberta, 157.2%; and Saskatchewan, 103%. Not surprisingly, Trudeau insisted that the constitutional reform include equalization among the provinces. *Canada Year Book 1994* (Ottawa: Statistics Canada, 1993), 614. The "Misery Index," created by American economist Arthur Okun, combines inflation and unemployment rates. It was highest in the period 1979–81, according to a study reported by columnist Ellen Roseman. *Toronto Star*, March 24, 2008.

Lalonde and MacEachen surrounded themselves with brilliant young analysts who had been attracted to Ottawa in the early Trudeau years, when so much had seemed possible, and the art and science of government intriguing. Ed Clark, the son of Canada's most eminent sociologist, S.D. Clark, was a development economist who had written his Harvard doctoral thesis on Tanzanian socialism. He gave leadership in drafting the NEP. Mickey Cohen, a tax lawyer who had been deputy minister of energy, mines, and resources in Joe Clark's government, guided the NEP through the thicket of his bureaucratic colleagues. He also secured the cooperation of Ian Stewart, a former Rhodes Scholar who, as deputy minister of finance, sought a middle way between the Keynesians and economic liberals in Trudeau's circle and the many monetarists and a few supply-siders in the Bank of Canada and the Finance Department. At Lalonde's side throughout this period was his executive assistant, Michael Phelps, a young Manitoban with an LLM from the London School of Economics.* Possessing

---

* Ed Clark was a particular focus of journalist Peter Foster, who attributed the overreach of the NEP to a "bureaucratic elite," who "if they had actually worked . . . were likely to have been lawyers or academics." They had not put in time in the civil service trenches as earlier mandarins had done. Foster rightly says that "there was enormous competitive spirit among these people. The game was to get to the key policy areas and come up with the bright ideas." Clark, according to Foster, came to be seen, "particularly in Alberta, as the epitome of Ottawa's anti-business, interventionist bias, and as a key force in the resurgence of the fiercely nationalist sentiment." In Calgary he assumed "a notoriety never before accorded any public servant." His thesis on Tanzanian socialism was "photocopied and passed around Calgary's Petroleum Club, with 'selected quotations' highlighted in an angry yellow, felt-tip pen." Peter Foster, *The Sorcerer's Apprentices: Canada's Super-Bureaucrats and the Energy Mess* (Toronto: Collins, 1982), 52, 74–75.

the energy of youth and the debating skills to skewer their opponents, the young economists and lawyers on the energy file were
a parallel regiment to the one assembled around Michael Kirby on
the constitutional file. Together they marched toward their greatest challenge as the economy teetered and constitutional reform
seemed in doubt in the first months of 1981.

—

On New Year's Day, 1981, *Globe and Mail* political columnist
Jeffrey Simpson bade farewell to 1980 in a column entitled "PM's
Free Hand Gives Canada Its Bitterest Year." The coming twelve
months, he argued, promised more of the same. Simpson linked
together the heavy resistance from the energy provinces and from
Quebec to Trudeau's attempt "to reassert the primacy of the
federal government." Faced with continuing and growing budget
deficits, which had reached $11 billion in 1980, a shortage of
revenue, and increasing inequalities, Ottawa demanded a proper

---

Interestingly the backroom "socialists" of Ottawa became very successful in
corporate boardrooms. Clark later became the chair and CEO of the TD
Bank; Phelps became the CEO of Westcoast Transmission and chair of Duke
Energy in the United States (after he engineered the sale of the Canadian
company to the American energy giant); and Cohen became CEO of Molson
and a director of many other companies, including the TD Bank. Their
obvious skills transferred easily out of government and are testimony to the outstanding young people drawn to Ottawa in the early years of Trudeau's government. While Trudeau and Pitfield's fascination with academic theories and
system designs may not have translated well into the practice of government,
it attracted many young intellectuals who shared the contemporary belief that
government could be made better.

share of the expanding energy pie. Trudeau's position was relatively strong: "He still has a freer hand to pursue his vision of the
country through the exercise of political power than a prime minister could reasonably expect." And more than before, Trudeau
understood the uses of power.

But so did the provinces and his opponents. Soon after the
announcement of the NEP, Lougheed fired three effective salvos:
a constitutional challenge to the natural gas tax; a staged reduction
in shipments of oil to other provinces; and a freeze on the oil
sands, whose development the NEP encouraged. Although the
Petroleum Club and the radio talk-shows in Alberta cheered
the premier, and bumper stickers declared "Let the Eastern
Bastards Freeze," Lalonde had included provisions in the NEP
that attracted key Albertan players. These entrepreneurs and their
lawyers rightly saw the provision that there must be 50 percent
Canadian ownership on the Canada Lands—those potentially rich
areas under government control—as highly beneficial. Dome
Petroleum, Nova, and Petro-Canada therefore complained about
the new taxes on gas and oil but did not join Lougheed's general
denunciation of the NEP. The influential Bob Blair of Nova, a
major figure in the oil patch, openly declared his Liberal allegiance and remained in close touch with both Trudeau and
Lalonde. "Smiling Jack" Gallagher of Dome most enthusiastically
embarked on the acquisition of foreign oil companies, which were
eager to abandon Canada in the wake of the NEP. Ensconced in
a new tower in the heart of Calgary, dubbed "Red Square" by its
critics, Petro-Canada was the creation of the Trudeau government,
and it welcomed its enhanced role under the NEP.

All these companies would eagerly pursue the new Petroleum
Incentive Payments, which encouraged a shift away from conventional resources in Alberta toward exploration on the Canada Lands.
What the NEP sought to force was an end to Alberta's dominance
over the oil and gas market through the creation of offshore

resources and the development of the northern frontier. To that end "new" oil received more generous treatment than "old" oil.[30]

The rhetoric was bitter and personal, and it worried Lougheed, whose Canadian patriotism was never in doubt, even if his anger with Ottawa was profound. He quietly told his energy minister, Merv Leitch, that it would be better to negotiate an agreement with Ottawa on sharing the revenues. After the Iranian hostage incident and the fresh evidence of the power of OPEC to set world prices, neither Ottawa nor Edmonton doubted that energy prices would rise continuously through the decade and that the "new" oil and gas would begin to flow. In short, there would be ample funds to share. Moreover, British Columbia and Saskatchewan, though much less significant in the energy field, were firm allies of Lougheed. In the case of Saskatchewan, the situation was complicated by the growing closeness between Roy Romanow and Jean Chrétien in sorting out constitutional details. While Chrétien tugged at Romanow to join in the patriation exercise, Blakeney stuck firmly with Lougheed — so much so that Chrétien, who respected Lougheed, believed that the socialist from Saskatchewan "seemed afraid to cross" the Conservative Albertan. Inevitably, the two tracks continued to intersect as energy and the Constitution dominated Canada's political life in the winter and spring of 1981.[31]

Trudeau cared more about the Constitution than the NEP, and he urged Lalonde to reach an agreement with the producing provinces. For his part, Lougheed was also anxious to make a deal on the NEP, to achieve some stability. Nevertheless, things threatened to get out of control. The reliable Don Braid of the *Edmonton Journal* reported on January 16, 1981, that several Tory MPs from the West had spoken openly about separation in caucus. No separatist, Lougheed realized that Alberta's new Heritage Fund, the disproportionate wealth of his province, and the serious troubles in Ontario's large manufacturing centres could turn the rest of the country against Alberta, and Albertans against Canada itself. The results of such isolation could take the form of a provision in the Constitution that would be harmful to Alberta's interests. In short, both parties faced pressures to compromise, particularly when the Alberta Court of Appeal ruled in March that the new federal excise tax on natural gas was not within federal jurisdiction. Ottawa immediately appealed, but the decision was a blow to the NEP. Then, in April, Alberta cut production, reducing the flow of Alberta oil to the rest of Canada, and the federal government responded with a "Lougheed levy" (a special tax of half a cent per litre on gasoline and other petroleum products, to make up for the cost of buying foreign oil). That same month, Lalonde and Merv Leitch met, and they soon settled down to reconcile the 150 items of difference between the federal government and Alberta.[32]

That summer the federal government continued both to taunt and to woo Albertans. As the House of Commons sat late into the summer, tempers flared regularly, including Trudeau's. Crisis piled upon crisis, calamity upon calamity. On July 9 Imperial Oil suspended work on its Cold Lake project (which had been sustained by a $40 million federal loan since January) because it had no agreement on a price for oil recovered from the oil sands. Lalonde, with Trudeau's backing, told the Commons that the government would "not be blackmailed" by an oil company. A northern Alberta MP responded: "What the hell justice is that to the people of northern Alberta? Are they not Canadians?" Lalonde was less adamant when complaints came from Jack Gallagher of Dome that the grants to encourage frontier exploration were inadequate. He revised them promptly and consulted regularly with Gallagher and Nova's Blair to make certain that Ottawa had allies. In their company, Lalonde even wore a stetson, drank Alberta rye, and courted other, smaller Canadian firms. But nothing seemed to help: the polls consistently indicated that Albertans stood firmly behind their premier in opposing both the NEP and the constitutional reforms and, of course, Liberals.[33]

When Alberta cut production for the second time, in June, the federal government again responded, with a 1.6 cent per litre tax. With the third cut looming on September 1, 1981, the pressures were too intense, and both sides gave in. The federal agreement allowed Alberta to administer the Petroleum Incentive Payments, thereby keeping federal fingers out of many Alberta business arrangements. The federal government also gave up its right to tax the export of natural gas and accepted a complicated formula that divided "old" oil from "new" oil derived from the oil sands, offshore, and the Arctic frontier. As a result Canadian oil moved closer to the world price, but the federal government would also get the revenue it wanted and badly needed from the expected energy bonanza.

For Canadian consumers, the deal meant that the price of oil would triple and the price of natural gas would double over the next five years, with the first increase of 0.4 cents per litre taking effect on October 1 as the "Lougheed levy" came to an end. In addition, it meant that a two-tiered system would persist, with "old" oil remaining below the world price while "new" oil rose to the world level. There would be a division of tax revenue whereby "industry," more of which would be Canadian-owned because of the NEP, would receive 44.2 percent, Alberta 30.3 percent, and the federal government 25.5 percent—up from roughly 10 percent allotted to the federal government in the period before the fateful October 1980 budget. After the bitter arguments and salvos, the most welcome part of the agreement was the federal government's commitment to make no tax changes during its term. With the patriation fight still festering, Trudeau said that "in keeping with the long tradition of Canadian federalism, we've bargained hard and we've reached a compromise—a good Canadian term—a compromise which is to the advantage of both the people of Alberta and generally the people of Canada." On the front pages of Canadian newspapers, a beaming Trudeau clasped Lougheed's firm hands as their eyes met warmly. In yet another photograph that appeared later, Lougheed and Trudeau were toasting each other with champagne just after the deal was sealed. But the romance was brief.

Lougheed later regretted that photograph, which captured a moment when the deep rift between Alberta and Ottawa appeared to have ended. The celebration faded quickly from memory as the NEP came apart. The assumptions about energy prices, so carefully crafted by a gaggle of econometricians, proved badly wrong. Even at the time there were doubts, as analysts pored over the voluminous detail of the agreement. Jeff Sallot declared in the *Globe and Mail* on September 2 that a number of points remained "fuzzy," but more troubling still was the price of oil itself: "The Alberta Government is gambling that world oil prices will continue to escalate at or near the same rates as they have in the past while the federal Government is tacitly acknowledging that there is indeed some kind of relationship between domestic and foreign prices for crude." Although on that same day the *Globe* printed a detailed chart showing that consumer oil would increase from $27.30 on September 1, 1981, to $68.70 on July 1, 1986, that assumption rested mainly on the uncertain ways of OPEC, where Islamic fundamentalists and erratic Libyan dictators played a major part.

On this wobbly foundation, Finance Department officials began to produce the fall budget, believing that the great uncertainties surrounding the energy sector had been sorted out.[34] The agreement with the producing provinces appeared to have guaranteed future revenues for the federal government. As a contemporary analysis demonstrated, a rising oil price meant that the federal government would be the greatest beneficiary under the agreement.[35] The converse was also true: a falling price would mean that the federal coffers would suffer most. In the fall of 1981, however, no serious commentator believed that the price would fall. Finance officials therefore continued with their preparations for a budget that would propose a revolution in the Canadian taxation system, believing that revenues were solid. As so often occurs with economic assumptions, the future confounded the prophets and the politicians.

—

Almost exactly a year before, in October 1980, Trudeau had made his television announcement that he would patriate the Constitution. This declaration, and the turbulence it caused, intersected with Canada's energy struggles and passed directly through the western provinces. There, Lougheed led the opposition to unilateral patriation of the Constitution and simultaneously demanded that provincial ownership of natural resources be enshrined in the revised Constitution.

Lougheed had further roiled the federal plans with an almost inadvertent proposal that he had made during the September 1980 federal-provincial conference on patriation. In 1971, while preparing a provincial bill of rights in the fashion of John Diefenbaker's federal statute, Lougheed, as new premier of Alberta, had met with Merv Leitch, then his attorney general, who told him that the proposed bill should have a "notwithstanding clause." "What the hell is a notwithstanding clause?" Lougheed asked. Leitch explained that such a clause would be necessary if the government wanted to propose legislation contrary to the rights contained in the proposed Alberta Bill of Rights. Nine years later, when the premiers and the prime minister gathered in Ottawa for their first ministers' conference, and Premiers Lyon and Blakeney voiced their opposition to Trudeau's charter on the grounds of the supremacy of Parliament within the British tradition, Leitch again engaged

Lougheed in a private discussion, suggesting that he "intervene by proposing a 'notwithstanding clause' along the lines of section 2 of the *Alberta Bill of Rights*." It was a crucial intervention, even though Lougheed discovered that most of his fellow premiers had no idea what he was talking about at the time.[36]

Despite the confusion, the idea of a notwithstanding clause whereby legislatures could ignore the provisions of the charter rapidly gained support. It combined with other forces that fundamentally changed the process begun in October 1980. Trudeau's announcement of patriation immediately set off a fierce debate in the Commons with Joe Clark, one of the most effective parliamentary speakers of his time, who led the opposition to the proposal. The issue was complex, but the debate centred on the Charter of Rights and Freedom, which comprised sections 1 to 30 of the proposed new Canada Act. For Trudeau the major concern lay in sections 16 to 23, relating to the language question, which were cleverly drawn from the educational provisions of the so-called Canada Clause proposed by Lévesque in 1977. These sections stipulated that Canadian citizens whose first language was English or French could demand to have their children educated in that language during their pre-university years, so long as the numbers in the school warranted it. Another contested issue was the amending formula, which allowed for an interim period where unanimity would be required. If agreement was not reached in that time, a national referendum would be held, following the formula accepted at Victoria in 1971 by all provinces except Quebec.*

---

* The complicated formula required approval by the Senate and the House, the legislature of every province with 25 percent of the population, two of the western provinces with half the population of the four in the West, and two of

There were other points of contention and unanswered questions too. Before long, Aboriginals, women, academics, business
representatives, constitutional experts, and ordinary citizens all
rushed forward to give their point of view to the joint parliamentary committee that had been established to hear Canadians'
response to the proposal. The committee, under Senator Harry
Hayes of Calgary and Quebec MP Serge Joyal, planned to end its
hearings in early December, to expedite the passing of the resolution for the British Parliament. Their plans soon went awry, probably because they decided to televise the hearings in an age when,
according to Andy Warhol's famous quip, everyone would have
their fifteen minutes of fame. Observers are widely divided in their
opinions of the results of the consultation. Edward McWhinney,
a specialist in constitutional law, is harshly critical: "On looking
through the committee's list [of witnesses], it is difficult to avoid
the conclusion that it was heavily weighted in favour of the more
aggressive, vocal, and unrestrained, and also the best financed, of
our burgeoning army of national pressure groups and special interests lobbies. There was an observable absence of balance—ethnic
and cultural, religious, political and ideological, and above all
linguistic and regional—in the list. Various interest groups and
governments, in Quebec and in the West, decided to boycott or at
least stay away from the committee's hearings."

the Atlantic provinces with half the population of the four in the East. An alternative would be a referendum, with the overall approval of the population and
a majority in each of the provinces with 25 percent of the population, and
again of two of four provinces in both the West and the East. There were
further details, but the provinces were fearful of the referendum option, and
the federal government was concerned about the complications in the system.

Yet feminist and Aboriginal groups celebrated the process as one that corrected some of the profound weaknesses in the earlier drafts of the new Constitution. Initially, however, the patriation package changed little. When the government tabled the resolution in the House on February 13, 1981, the only change was a preamble that included the addition of "God" (the product of intense lobbying by Conservative members) and the "rule of law," although the meanings of that distinguished concept and of "God" were undefined. This lack of definition caused confused Conservative MPs on the committee to oppose a Liberal motion that included the word "God" because it seemed too vague. It was all good sport for Trudeau, who declared that the Conservative shenanigans were "inspired more by fear of the electorate than of God, and that is not very flattering to God." While he himself did not think the word "God" was necessary in a secular document such as the Constitution, he solemnly declared that, personally, he had always favoured God.[37]

In truth, Trudeau paid relatively little attention to the hearings, although he was pleased at the intervention of New Brunswick premier Richard Hatfield, who asked that his province be declared officially bilingual. Instead, the prime minister was focused on the struggle with the opposing premiers, who raised the stakes by declaring, first, that they would oppose patriation by lobbying in London, where the British Parliament had to pass a bill to permit patriation to occur, and, second, that they would try to overturn the legislation in Canadian courts. The Manitoba Supreme Court was the first to hear the case, as proceedings began in Winnipeg in December 1980. There were three central questions. First, if the patriation resolution was accepted, would "federal-provincial relationships or the powers, rights or privileges granted or secured by the Constitution of Canada to the provinces, their legislatures or governments be affected, and if so, in what respect or respects?" Second, did a constitutional convention exist that allowed the federal government to request an amendment to the Constitution affecting federal-provincial relations without provincial consent? And third, was provincial agreement "constitutionally required" for amendments affecting federal-provincial relations and the rights of the provinces?[38]

The Manitoba court rejected its own province's arguments on February 3, 1981, by a 3 to 2 margin, although Chief Justice Samuel Freedman, who wrote the decision, declined to rule on the first question. It was a narrow win that caused little celebration in Ottawa's Langevin Block. Worse news came on March 31, when three justices of the Newfoundland Supreme Court unanimously supported the province's position on the same three questions that had been asked in Manitoba. Trudeau had argued that there was no legal question, but the courts' divided decision now meant that there was. He was angry. He told the *New York Times*: "I still think it's a political process and I'm determined to pursue it politically. And I feel so strongly about that, that I'm amazed that there hasn't been an uprising in the country, at least amongst the thinking people." He added, bitterly, "In a sense I'd rather lose the whole effort than go on record as saying that legislatures cannot legislate until they got permission from the Supreme Court."[39]

By this time Trudeau's frustrations were evident to all. On March 23 he responded at length to criticisms of both the patriation package and his own view of Canada. There was, he argued, no "permanent equilibrium in the political affairs of any nation" but, rather, a "moving equilibrium," particularly in a federation. His government was seeking an equilibrium for its times: "In sloughing off the last vestiges of colonialism, in entrenching those values Canadians hold in common, we are merely setting the stage with a contest about the kind of Canada we will have in the future. The contest about the two kinds of Canada, perhaps, will be laid out. Will we be highly centralized? Will we be a loose confederation of shopping centres, as some wag said about Los Angeles? Will we be something in between? I don't know." But he did know his own choice. He wanted his successors to have the freedom "to choose Canada's destiny," to be able to have "that debate about the equilibrium, about the kind of Canada they want." In ending, he quoted a favourite poet, Charles Péguy, that "it is easy to keep one's hands clean when one has no hands." Casting his gaze around the Commons chamber, he declared: "We have hands, we set them to the plough, and we are not afraid to get them dirty for the simple reason that it is for a cause about which everybody is agreed that this is what the people want."[40]

But not all the people wanted what he proposed. Unlike the top courts in Manitoba and Newfoundland, the Quebec Supreme Court agreed with Trudeau on all three questions, four justices against one. And so, on April 28, 1981, the federal government took the case to the Supreme Court of Canada. This court had long been a backwater of the Canadian government: its justices were unknown, its judgments were rarely cited in other jurisdictions, and its presence in public discussion was almost invisible. Trudeau's appointment of Bora Laskin to the court in 1970 and as chief justice in 1973 had jolted the legal community and the court's own somnolence. Jewish, Harvard-educated, an academic rather than a practitioner, and a civil libertarian, Laskin had already shaken the tradition-encrusted foundations of Canada's Supreme Court.

Laskin, in the words of his biographer Philip Girard, hoped "that the *Patriation Reference* would finally give some shape to fundamentals of the Canadian Constitution that had long remained obscure." He shared Trudeau's frustration that Canada was alone among developed nations in lacking the ability to amend its own Constitution. He also agreed with Trudeau that patriation should occur quickly—that the British MPs should "hold their nose" and speed passage of the bill at Westminster so that Canadians could mark Canada Day 1981 with their new Constitution. Many of Canada's most eminent lawyers gathered in the Supreme Court building, designed in the thirties by Ernest Cormier (who was also the architect of the art deco home in Montreal that Trudeau had recently bought), and their arguments ranged widely for five days over the broken terrain of Canadian constitutional history. Those who knew the court well realized immediately that the justices were divided and that Laskin would not be able to lead them to a consensus. The court duly adjourned, but no judgment came. Trudeau was furious.[41]

April was an exceptionally cruel month that year. On April 13, 1981, Lévesque had trounced Claude Ryan's Liberals in the Quebec election. A bitter Ryan, and much of the Quebec press, blamed Trudeau for his loss, and during the summer he announced that his party would take a nationalist approach and oppose Trudeau's patriation plan. Then, on April 16, when the "gang of eight" opposing premiers gathered in Ottawa, they signed an accord calling for a "simple" patriation of the Constitution — without a charter, equalization among the provinces, or protection for language rights, but including provisions for the provinces to "opt out" of constitutional amendments that they believed diminished their power. Lévesque was a major player in the plan, and his enthusiasm made him agree to an amending formula that would prevent Quebec from having a veto over any constitutional amendment. His agreement attracted little notice immediately but came to be of historic importance later. Trudeau declared bluntly that the accord was "a victory for those who want to move Canada toward disintegration." What the premiers proposed, he reiterated, was "a confederation of shopping centres . . . and that's not the kind of Canada I want." When asked whether he would negotiate, he pointed out that the premiers had sent him their accord by messenger and then fled the capital without even contacting him.

Meanwhile, the appeal made by the provinces and by Aboriginal groups to the British Parliament had surprising success. Despite Prime Minister Margaret Thatcher's firm commitment that it would "only receive a request . . . from the Federal Parliament of Canada," a British parliamentary committee under Sir Anthony Kershaw heard provincial grievances, welcomed Aboriginal delegations, and advanced "legal claims over Canada and its Constitution in language that seemed better suited to the era of General Gordon of Khartoum."[42] The foes of the empire had beheaded Gordon almost a century earlier, and Trudeau may have wished he could administer the same fate to Kershaw. However, he realized that Scottish nationalists, old-fashioned imperialists, and publicity-seeking politicians in Westminster did not matter as much as the British prime minister's commitment to pass the patriation bill.* Unfortunately, Thatcher was increasingly less amused by the troubles Trudeau had caused her, and her own position with her caucus was weak.

In Ottawa, Britain's high commissioner, the remarkably maladroit Sir John Ford, indicated that he believed the British would and should not pass the patriation bill. An astonished Mark MacGuigan, the minister for external affairs, told the Commons that such conduct was "completely unacceptable to the Canadian government." Sir John then held his own press conference and,

---

* Trudeau sent MP David Smith, a descendant of British Prime Minister Sir Henry Campbell-Bannerman, to lobby the British parliamentarians. Once arrived in London, Smith learned that the work would have to be completed with the Lords by August 12, when the grouse season began. Interview with Trudeau ministers, Dec. 2, 2002, LAC.

incredibly, warned that "it would be a very great mistake to assume the British Parliament would immediately do exactly what they were asked to do." An enraged Jean Chrétien declared in the House: "The age of being taught from England is passed." For its part, the British government quickly replaced Sir John, who took early retirement in May. Trudeau's dormant anti-British sentiments were stirred once more. Watching an aide enraptured with visiting royalty, he said bluntly, as they looked out the parliamentary window: "Always remember, they shit too."[43]

That populist note marked Trudeau's approach in the House during the warm summer months while the NEP simmered, the Constitution festered, and the economy got worse. Chief Justice Laskin and his closest friend at the Supreme Court, W.Z. "Bud" Estey, attended a large gathering of Canadian lawyers at Queen's College, Cambridge, in late July, attracted by the wedding of Charles and Diana, generous tax deductions for their travel and "education," and the presence of the major players in the constitutional struggle—Jean Chrétien and provincial attorneys general Roy Romanow of Saskatchewan and Roy McMurtry of Ontario. Laskin seemed weary, while the ebullient Estey reflected the fierce debate occurring among the justices as the court faced its greatest challenge and opportunity. A ruling against the federal government would destroy the patriation plan and, almost surely, Trudeau's political career.[44]

Trudeau himself was anxious and temperamental as he awaited the court decision. He and his speechwriter André Burelle jousted over the language questions at the core of the charter. In particular, Burelle objected to the provisions in the proposed charter that countered Quebec's Bill 101 restrictions on school choice while accepting Premier Davis's demand that Ontario escape official bilingualism. Burelle shared his views with Gérard Pelletier, who indicated that he agreed. When Pelletier returned from his ambassadorial post in Paris on a brief visit to Ottawa, he called on Trudeau and expressed his views. Trudeau exploded in fury, blamed Burelle for influencing Pelletier, and rejected the criticisms so bluntly that Burelle told his mentor he would no longer pass on his complaints lest they undermine the relationship of the two old friends. The incident reveals how deeply and personally Trudeau became involved in the constitutional project and how sensitive he was to criticism. The lonely heights of 24 Sussex became even more elevated that summer.[45]

On September 28 Laskin appeared before the cameras for the first televised decision of the court. Unfortunately, the audio did not work, and thousands of lawyers, students, and others across the country watched as Laskin mouthed the words of the historic decision. Even if they had heard him speak, the audience would have been confused; the court, like the country, was divided. On the first question, whether the charter imposed restrictions on federal and provincial power, all justices agreed that it did. On the second question, whether the patriation of the Constitution, including the charter, was "legal," the decision was yes, 7 to 2. The two dissenters were Diefenbaker-appointed justices Ronald Martland and Roland Ritchie. On the third question, whether there was a "convention" that provincial agreement was needed for major constitutional changes, six judges held that there was one such convention that required "substantial" provincial agreement for a major constitutional change, while three—Laskin, Estey, and William McIntyre—disagreed. Laskin had indeed not been able to lead his court. Ironically, Trudeau's appointee and former academic colleague Jean Beetz, who had mooted the possibility of unilateral patriation in the wake of the failure of the Victoria Conference, now voted with the majority and wrote some of the majority judgment. Trudeau learned of the decision on a stopover in Seoul, South Korea, on his way to the Commonwealth Conference in Melbourne, Australia. He was disappointed, enraged, and, even more, perplexed.[46]

Trudeau had counted on Laskin and had sincerely thought that the legal issue was clear. He knew now that the eight premiers who were against patriation represented "substantial" opposition, and he realized that his plan was imperilled. He called Chrétien, and they agreed on a ploy: they would declare a victory, rather than complaining about this complex decision. Trudeau also indicated that he would make one further attempt to acquire more provincial support by having a final federal-provincial conference. As his mind wandered through the possibilities during the long flight over the Pacific, he remained fastened on his goal. He would make one last effort with the premiers, but if it failed, he would then seek unilateral patriation. If that request was rejected by the British Parliament, he would put it to the public in a referendum as a declaration of independence for a sovereign Canada. An alternative would be an election in 1982. He would not give up.*

Chrétien continued to meet with McMurtry and Romanow, who had bet Chrétien a good bottle of scotch that the Supreme Court would side with the provinces. Bill Davis and Richard Hatfield still supported the government, but the court decisions

---

* Election rumours were rampant in the fall as unilateral patriation seemed possible. Governor General Ed Schreyer was one source of the musings. He told the press in January 1982 that he would have called an election "if all the provinces were strongly opposed to patriation and Trudeau went ahead and asked London to pass the bill." Trudeau and his staff were incensed. Trudeau's aide Ted Johnson wrote "intolerable" on a copy of the interview and added the note for Trudeau that Schreyer was "1. Wrong 2. Shouldn't talk. 3. Would have been breaking a confidence." They considered asking for his resignation, even though he had been a Trudeau appointee. After a phone call on the matter, Schreyer agreed to a "complete withdrawal" of his remarks. These pencilled notes are in TP, MG 26 019, vol. 165, file 35, LAC.

and the strident opposition of their federal Conservative colleagues made their position difficult. In Quebec, Ryan was as strong as Lévesque in his opposition and joined with him in supporting a joint resolution of the National Assembly condemning unilateral patriation. Nine anglophone Liberals defected, however, and Ryan's already fragile leadership was weakened. On October 13 Trudeau told the CBC that he had promised to meet with the premiers in early November for one last try to reach an accord.[47] If none was reached, his government would do what the people wanted. Private and public polls indicated that the charter and patriation were popular throughout the country, and the hint of a referendum was intended to stir the opposing premiers from their constitutional bunkers.

The premiers came to Ottawa on November 2, 1981, hoping that their meeting could prevent unilateral patriation. Trudeau was intimately involved in the details. As Michael Kirby and his team laboured long into the evenings, Trudeau pored over documents at 24 Sussex. Kirby would sometimes call Trudeau, exchange some wording, and then return with or without a change. There were uncertainties: Trudeau and the Liberal caucus were willing and, in some cases, eager to consider a referendum; Chrétien strongly disagreed. In his own words, "I had seen too well the splits the Quebec referendum had made in families and friendships: I never wanted to go through another one." But Kirby and Trudeau believed it an essential weapon for the federal side, one that could weaken the gang of eight opposing premiers, with their populist appeal.

Intrigues flourished as the premiers gathered in the cavern of the old railway station across from the Château Laurier. Lévesque was already suspicious of his fellow gang members: Blakeney, he thought wrongly, was Trudeau's "joker." He worried about Davis's ties with other Conservative premiers and fretted about his own delegation and its idiosyncrasies. His minister of intergovernmental affairs, Claude Morin, was indispensable, but his ties with federal officials were suspiciously close—a fact confirmed after the conference by Loraine Lagacé, a Lévesque staffer who was soon supplying him with federal "documents" that confused rather than clarified.

Several among the Quebec delegation had already concluded correctly that she was a "double agent," and many were suspicious of Morin himself, again with good grounds. Old animosities persisted: Claude Ryan, who had joined with Lévesque to condemn Trudeau's action, received no reply when he begged the premier not to abandon Quebec's "historic" veto. In spite of the divisions, the gang held together through the first day, but the nervousness of many of its members was obvious. Brian Peckford, who had outraged Trudeau by siding, earlier, with Lévesque, now openly expressed a willingness to compromise, declaring that Canada could not "afford the luxury of a winner-take-all attitude."[48]

By the third day of the conference, it appeared that there would be no winners. Sterling Lyon, the most conservative premier, had to return to an election campaign in Manitoba, and Lévesque was threatening to leave. Trudeau had met with his Cabinet on the previous evening and, with them, debated the referendum option and the response he should make to the proposals that Davis, after consultation with the gang of eight, would produce. Many ministers supported the referendum, but Chrétien, the major negotiator, remained strongly opposed. Faced with division, the Cabinet gave Trudeau a free hand. The following day, the meeting went badly. Over breakfast, Blakeney proposed changes to the premiers, but Lévesque peremptorily rejected them. By mid-morning Trudeau's frustration was visible, and Lévesque's fatigue rimmed his eyes. Trudeau focused assertively on his plan and proposed that a referendum should resolve what the premiers could not. As old arguments were repeated, Trudeau turned to Lévesque and, speaking in French, challenged him, as a democrat, to "face the people." Lévesque jumped at the idea, and

Trudeau immediately adjourned for lunch, telling waiting reporters, "The cat is among the pigeons." Quebec and Ottawa had a deal. There would be a referendum.

But the referendum was a dead cat. That night Trudeau's own closest advisers, notably Lalonde and Chrétien, argued against it. Moreover, the opposing premiers were quickly coming to terms with a proposed deal, first presented by Davis: it allowed opting out of federal programs, but without compensation; language rights, but with a notwithstanding clause; and the "seven provinces / 50 percent of the population" amending formula proposed by the premiers in April that, with Lévesque's agreement, gave no veto to Quebec over constitutional change. Trudeau was unhappy, reluctant to give in on the referendum, and willing to have the conference collapse. He would then go to London with his own version of the Constitution, not this watered-down one. At 10 p.m. Davis called 24 Sussex, where Trudeau and his ministers were meeting. He said that neither he nor Hatfield would support Trudeau if he did not agree to the deal the premiers were drafting that night. While Trudeau was talking with Davis, Chrétien also argued against a referendum with his colleagues. When Trudeau returned to the room, the mood was different. He listened but said little, and when the ministers left, most were unsure what the morning would bring. As Chrétien prepared to go, Trudeau drew him aside and said, "Jean, if you can get the majority of the provinces with a majority of the population to accept your solution, I think I'll be able to accept it." Then he added, "But let me sleep on it," thus ensuring a sleepless night for Chrétien.[49]

Earlier that day Chrétien had met Roy McMurtry and Roy Romanow for breakfast, first at the Château Laurier and later at the kitchen of the convention centre. They had sketched out a proposed settlement on a piece of paper: a charter in exchange for the provincial amending formula; opting out without compensation; and the inclusion of a notwithstanding clause. During the day the three "peddled" the proposed agreement among ministers, officials, and others. Then, throughout that night, as Chrétien tossed in his bed, the premiers' officials and ministers met—but with no participation by Quebec. At 6:30 in the morning, Romanow told Chrétien that Lougheed, the most powerful player, would buy in but that Quebec did not yet know anything of the plan. A worried Chrétien told Romanow that Lyon should not sign, so that Quebec was not the only holdout, but Lougheed proved his power once more by convincing Lyon, who loathed both the charter and Trudeau, to sign. At 7:30 Chrétien told Trudeau he had a deal.

That morning it was Brian Peckford, an odd choice, who presented the deal. Trudeau, always the actor, grimaced as the Newfoundland premier read it; Lévesque noticed and grinned, expecting a curt rejection by Trudeau. But then Trudeau raised his eyes and declared: "It makes a lot of sense." Lévesque was isolated and frustrated and became, in the words of his biographer, "a shattered man." The Quebec premier asked plaintively for the veto, but that had disappeared in April, when he had joined the gang. Just as Lévesque had compromised then, so Trudeau did now. As the other premiers celebrated with the prime minister, Lévesque stormed out of the convention centre. For him, patriation of the Constitution, facilitated by the "night of the long knives," had become a "dagger" in his heart.

Trudeau knew the victory was not sweet. But in the words of Lévesque's favourite adviser, Claude Charron, it was Trudeau's. The struggle between "the champions," Lévesque and Trudeau, had ended. The former, Charron said, was what the Québécois are; the latter, what they hoped to be—a comment Lévesque himself often made, and in Charron's view it was a compliment to both leaders. The populist Lévesque, the patrician Trudeau; the crusading journalist, the engaged intellectual; the fiery nationalist, the passionate antinationalist; the charming *roué*, the disciplined actor; the crumpled suits and cigarette ash, the perfect cut with the rose in the lapel—these two leaders had shaped their times, their province, and their country. November 5, 1981, marked one of Trudeau's greatest triumphs, but it would also be his last.[50]

Celebrating, at the weekly caucus meeting, the first anniversary of their return to power, February 1981: Allan MacEachen (left) and Gilbert Parent (right).

Margaret Thatcher and Pierre Trudeau were often painfully out of step. He called her his "ideological sparring partner." She refused to extend good wishes to him at his final G7 summit in June 1984.

Trudeau chairing a working dinner at the Montebello Economic Summit, July 28, 1981. Counter-clockwise from top left: Ronald Reagan, Helmut Schmidt, Zenko Suzuki, Giovanni Spadolini, Roy Jenkins, Margaret Thatcher, and François Mitterrand.

"We won." Allan MacEachen on Trudeau's right; Jean Chrétien on his left, November 5, 1981.

The Constitution comes home. Trudeau called it "a proud moment for all Canadians." From the right, Michael Kirby and Michael Pitfield assisting as Gerald Regan looks on, April 17, 1982. Trudeau said in his memoirs: "The Queen favoured my attempt to reform the constitution. I was always impressed not only by the grace she displayed in public at all times, but by the wisdom she showed in private conversation."

With Margot Kidder at the
Canadian Embassy in
Washington, April 1983.
Ambassador Allan Gotlieb noted:
"The Vancouver lady will add
glamour and a dose of Hollywood
radical chic." She also helped
hold him to the peace initiative.

Kim Cattrall, the Vancouver-raised actress,
reputedly asked Trudeau to escort her to the
Genie Awards. "I don't have a boyfriend;
would you take me?" He did. She later said: "I
was completely enraptured by him. He was so
incredibly sexy." *Reader's Digest*, April 2005,
70–71. Gale Zoë Garnett, who was in a relationship with him at the time, was seated on
his other side at the dinner table that evening.

With eminent portrait artist Eva Prager:
"The most interesting conversation I ever
had until an aide pulled him away."

—

CHAPTER SIXTEEN

HARD TIMES

On the evening of November 5, while the anglophone premiers celebrated in Ottawa and René Lévesque returned, bitter and rejected, to Quebec City, Pierre Trudeau flew to New York to accept the "Family of Man" award for "international excellence." This award had first been won by John F. Kennedy in 1960, and then by Lester B. Pearson in 1965 — the only other Canadian to be so honoured. Trudeau's departure marked the end of his intense focus on the Constitution and the beginning of his concentration on international issues, just as the Cold War was entering a new chill. Foreign policy and the economy dominated Trudeau's final years in office, and the context in which he approached those challenges was for him less certain than the constitutional terrain he knew so well.[1]

In spite of Trudeau's new emphasis, the constitutional wars did not end with the champagne and the tears spilled that evening in early November 1981. Trudeau basked in praise from English Canadians, particularly in Quebec, where his adamant defence of minority language rights won plaudits from journalist L. Ian MacDonald, a future senior aide to Brian Mulroney. Writing on November 7 in the *Montreal Gazette*, MacDonald said that Trudeau's success in protecting minority rights was "the crowning achievement of his career, the end of an unwavering path he has followed since he began writing in *Cité libre* that his people were confining themselves to Quebec when all of Canada was their rightful home." At the end of the first ministers' conference, Ontario's William Davis, a frequent critic, praised Trudeau's willingness to compromise: "You have demonstrated what is essential in this country: the ability to compromise and to accept the diversity and the views of so many others," he said. Concession was not a quality often associated with Trudeau, but it had marked his recent constitutional course. The result of his flexibility, he declared as he left for New York, was "a charter of which Canadians can be proud and of which, I hope, we will still be able to say it is, probably, the best charter in the world."[2]

Yet the first major academic study of the events of November 1981 opted for the title *And No One Cheered*. It reflects the second thoughts that came quickly after the champagne ran out. Conservative leader Joe Clark initially withheld his support because of the Quebec government's strong opposition, though pressure from the Conservative premiers—the midwives of the "deal"—quickly caused him to end his hesitation. But many others were unhappy. Constitutional historian and former Liberal senator Eugene Forsey, who had left the NDP to follow Trudeau in the sixties, fulminated against the accord in one of his characteristically angry letters to a newspaper editor:

> The amended Charter of Rights and Freedoms just won't do.
>
> The provinces have shot it full of holes: great, big, gaping holes.
>
> First, what the charter rightly calls "Fundamental Freedoms"—freedom of conscience, freedom of thought, freedom of speech, freedom of peaceful assembly, freedom of association—are put at the mercy of 10 provincial legislatures, which can override them at will.

The same applies to "Legal Rights"—such as the right
to *habeas corpus*, the right to public trial, the right to
counsel, the right to be secure against unreasonable
search and seizure, the right not to be arbitrarily detained
or imprisoned.

Forsey went on to argue that the rights "will vary from province to
province in a legal crazy-quilt." He pointed to two groups particularly harmed by the accord: women and Aboriginal peoples. In
the case of women, the equality rights that had been accepted by
the premiers in April had been "disembowelled" by the notwithstanding clause. Moreover, the two clauses that had protected
Aboriginal rights in the proposed constitution were now missing—
in particular, the proposed section 34, which had included "Métis"
within the definition of Aboriginal peoples. Like Forsey, women
and Aboriginals had already noticed their losses, and their outrage
quickly swept away virtually all other discussion of the Constitution
and ended the premiers' celebrations.[3]

The Women's Ad Hoc Committee on the Constitution, with
the full support of Judy Erola, the secretary of state responsible
for the status of women, soon made an impact on MPs throughout the land. Erola, a feisty and independent minister, organized
the opposition from her own office. After the November 5 agreement, she told her colleagues and the prime minister that there
was "not much point in being minister for the status of women
when women have no status in the country." Trudeau seemed
stunned by the reaction, claiming in the House that he did not
know whether the override clause would affect section 28, where
equality of the sexes was guaranteed. But feminists pointed out that
ignorance was not an excuse, and his reply betrayed at best an
inattention to the political force of the women's movement in the
eighties. The premiers were also astonished by the strength and
spontaneity of the protest, and they quickly fell in line, with

Saskatchewan's cautious socialist, Allan Blakeney, being the last to agree. Chrétien recalls that he warned Roy Romanow, the Saskatchewan attorney general: "I'm about to make a speech in the House of Commons. If you give in [on women's rights], I'll say your boss is a great guy. If you don't, I'm going to sock it to him." The women, however, already had. In the words of Penney Kome, the historian of the feminist challenge to the November 5 draft of the charter, the women "took over" section 28 and made it Canada's equal rights amendment. And their efforts made a difference. Conservative critics of the court such as Calgary's Ted Morton point to the strengthened section 28 as the reason why women's lobby groups won not only many charter cases but also profound changes in the "policy status quo." In short, their efforts changed Canadian policy in areas such as abortion, pornography, and job discrimination.[4] Their successful protest taught women that men in suits had made the "flawed" Constitution and that, in future, Constitution making must not leave them at the sidelines.

In contrast to Canadian women, Canadian Aboriginals had focused their lobbying in London, where their colourful, traditional costumes captured the attention of British politicians and journalists. While romantic and sometimes moving in their appeal for the Queen's protection, based on the lofty promises of British monarchs more than a century before, the protest accomplished little, simply because London no longer mattered. Indeed, the Kershaw committee's embrace of their cause in the British Parliament probably hurt their protest in Ottawa or, more accurately, in the provincial capitals, where the call for "Aboriginal rights" became a target for politicians worried about what such rights actually implied. On this issue the three western premiers, despite their political differences, fretted in unison about what these rights meant for land claims, treaty rights, and taxation, although Blakeney did call for attention to Aboriginal rights during the process.* Since the failure of the White Paper dealing with the Indian Act in his first government, Trudeau had largely ignored the Aboriginal question, not so much from lack of interest as because other items took priority.

The meaning of collective "rights" always troubled Trudeau because of its implications for Quebec and, in addition, his own carefully constructed notions of the primacy of individual rights. Meanwhile, Ed Broadbent faced his own opposition to the charter on traditional grounds from Allan Blakeney and others within the New Democratic Party, including British Columbia MP Svend Robinson and the party's left, who demanded greater recognition of "rights." He therefore approached Trudeau personally to urge him to consider that Aboriginal rights be included in the charter. Trudeau asked him, in Socratic fashion, what "Aboriginal rights" meant, and Broadbent replied with a history lesson about democratic rights in general. At the end of the interview, the two products of the London School of Economics, thoroughly irritated with each other, parted with the issue unresolved.[5]

The strongest objection to the extension of Aboriginal rights came from Alberta's Peter Lougheed, although an exchange

---

*In his memoirs, Mr. Blakeney points out his support for recognition of Aboriginal rights in the constitutional meetings but also indicates that Aboriginal leaders did not necessarily support the clause he had advanced in Ottawa. He thinks Premier Lougheed's addition of the word "existing" to the final accord was correct in that it did not recognize historical rights. In the case of women and Aboriginals, Blakeney blames the CBC for misreporting his comments. He is a target of both the federal and the Quebec politicians in their memoirs, who accuse him of legalism and ambiguity. Allan Blakeney, An Honourable Calling: Political Memoirs (Toronto: University of Toronto Press, 2008), chaps. 17 & 18.

between Chrétien and Roy McMurtry, Ontario's attorney general, leaked on November 19, revealed that disquiet extended beyond the West. Ontario, the letter declared, was worried about the impact that recognition of Aboriginal rights would have on property rights and the "unfairness, disruption, uncertainty and divisions" that such recognition would bring to Canadian society. Premier Davis, ever cautious, quickly dissociated himself from these sentiments, although they seemingly reflected earlier private conversations. But Aboriginal leaders would not be put off. In British Columbia, Premier Bennett's Social Credit convention was disrupted by militant Aboriginals demanding justice, while thousands of Aboriginals marched on the Alberta legislature, seeking an audience with the premier. Lougheed resisted tenaciously but, isolated in his opposition, he finally gave in. The Canadian press, astonishingly, missed the irony in his opposition to the extension of Aboriginal status to the Métis people: Lougheed's great-grandmother, Mary Allen Hardisty, was Métis, and his great-uncle, Senator Richard Hardisty, had nobly fought for the rights of the Métis in the Northwest a century before. In the end, the Constitution Act was revised, so that section 35 (2) of the final draft included the "Indians, Inuit, and Métis peoples of Canada" among the "aboriginal peoples of Canada" whose "existing aboriginal and treaty rights" were "recognized and affirmed."[6]

Women and Aboriginals gained new clout in the patriated Constitution but, René Lévesque complained, the province of Quebec lost power. There can be no doubt that Lévesque's anger was genuine. He believed that Lougheed had become his friend and ally,* that the "gang of eight" had reached an agreement to

---

* Lévesque's identification with Lougheed is strongly expressed in his memoirs: "This Albertan, by far the most remarkable man on the Prairies in his time, is so passionately concerned about sovereignty in his own way that, even though

hold together against Trudeau's centralizing reforms, and that the patriation plan was fundamentally illegitimate. The cascade of losses and disappointments that followed during those early days in November shattered his sang-froid and confidence. His wife, Corinne Côté, remembered that, when he called her that terrible night of November 5, "I had never encountered him in such a state. . . . He had never been so cheated, and in a way that was thoroughly Machiavellian. He was broken. I believe that René died for the first time after the night of the long knives." When Lévesque left Ottawa that evening, he had declared that three aspects of the accord were unacceptable: the refusal of fiscal compensation for provinces that "opted out" of constitutional amendments; the section on mobility rights, which, in his view, placed limits on the powers of the Quebec legislature; and minority education rights, which, he thought, also diminished the power of the legislature. Over the weekend the rhetoric of meetings in Quebec City added new ingredients to the mix as he poured out his anger to his Cabinet, and this made any changes even more unpalatable to the other provinces and the federal government. The well-informed Claude Charron recalled that Lévesque's fury against the "English" was so great that he said he wanted to "kill" them. That was pure bluster, but he could not forgive the "manipulative and treacherous" Trudeau, who had told Lévesque bluntly when he plaintively asked for a referendum after the other premiers accepted the accord: "The people have spoken; you have lost."[7]

---

opposing us, he can understand our position." Trudeau's response to Alberta's initiatives reflected his understanding of this implicit alliance of opposites. René Lévesque, *Memoirs*, trans. Philip Stratford (Toronto: McClelland and Stewart, 1986), 42.

And lost he had. Lévesque soon learned through a quickly commissioned poll that the "people" of Quebec would not oppose the proposed patriation and chartering side in a referendum on the Constitution and, moreover, would defeat the PQ if an election was held on the issue of sovereignty. The support for separatism in the aftermath of the Ottawa conference had risen, but not enough. This unwelcome news surely fuelled Lévesque's frustration: it exploded in his address to Quebec's National Assembly on November 9, in which he condemned the new Constitution, concocted in "a night of deceit" during which the English provinces and the federal government had betrayed Quebec. He accused them of treating Quebec solely as "a force to contain," not as a partner in the negotiations. In this speech Lévesque also focused on Quebec's loss of its veto, and on November 13, he embodied his rapidly increasing objections to the revised Constitution in a resolution he placed before the National Assembly.

When the resolution came to a vote on December 1, the Liberals did not support the motion. Ryan stated that there could still be an agreement, and in any case, the Constitution was an improvement on what had existed before. The following day, the House of Commons in Ottawa voted on the constitutional resolution that included the changes relating to Aboriginal and women's rights and two changes affecting Quebec, which the federal government had inserted after discussions with Ryan. One of these changes related to section 23 1(a), which would have limited Quebec's ability to stream immigrant children into French schools. The other permitted opting out with compensation in the areas of culture and education. The House approved the resolution by a vote of 246 to 24, with the MPs singing "O Canada" bilingually as they cast their votes. The French voices reportedly drowned out the English words as the anthem rang throughout the chamber. The overwhelming level of support, notably from

Quebec MPs, gave Trudeau confidence that the Charter would endure the challenges it would face in the future as the courts gave it meaning.[8]

Lévesque was livid, and his fury only increased as he and Trudeau exchanged a series of letters on these developments. Their personal anger and mutual suspicion burst through the letters they wrote. Trudeau taunted Lévesque about the loss of the veto, and in a long public letter on December 1, claimed that Lévesque had already given up the veto when the gang of eight was formed in April 1981. He traced the recent legal history and concluded with sarcastic familiarity:

> This, then, my dear Premier, is my understanding of the constitutional law and history respecting the claim for a provincial veto. Whether we are talking of patriation or of the amending formula, it is hard to understand how—by Order in Council or otherwise—you can maintain that a Quebec veto exists by law or custom.

Lévesque replied immediately by telex:

> It was with sorrow, though little surprise, that I acknowledge your letter dated December 1, 1981, where you explicitly deny to Quebec what generations of Québécois have considered absolutely necessary to their survival in this polity, the veto that the Québécois have previously used in several instances. The letter strongly indicates the extent of the uprooting generated by the federal system.

Trudeau responded bluntly:

> . . . let me remind you that it was you who signed the Premiers' Accord of April 16, 1981 and, in so doing, *you*

abandoned a veto for Quebec in the constitutional amending formula. . . .

That a Premier of Quebec subscribed to such an affirma-
tion will seem aberrant and, indeed, irresponsible, especially
when one remembers that the federal formula I posed to you
contained a right of veto for Quebec.

Let us be clear, then. On April 16th, your government
subscribed to the notion of the equality of the province and
there was no question then of Canadian duality or even of
a special status for Quebec! If Quebec, then were to have
a veto, one would also have to say that each of the other
provinces had a veto too and the amending formula would
have to be unanimity to respect the equality of the
provinces. But the Supreme Court in its decision on the
Patriation Reference stated that unanimity is *not* required
for constitutional amendments. Therefore, if the provinces
are equal and unanimity is not required, there is no veto
either for Quebec or for any other province. This is precisely the position you agreed to on April 16th. [Emphasis
in original]

With these defiant exchanges, the long debate between Trudeau
and Lévesque on a series of significant issues drew to an end. They
would encounter each other in the future, but in much less meaningful ways.[9]

Without doubt, the future of Quebec and of Canada was
determined to a large degree in those final weeks of 1981. Their
fate rested in part on the reactions of Lévesque and Trudeau
to the events that suddenly unfolded. The question lingers:
Was there an alternative outcome? Both men later reflected on
this question.

In his memoirs Lévesque denounces the "cruel deception"
that he and his colleagues faced in Ottawa during that November

meeting with the other premiers and Trudeau. In reflecting on events that followed the referendum defeat in Quebec in May 1980, Lévesque takes deserved pride in his party's quick recovery from that setback. For their success in the election campaign less than a year later, on April 13, 1981, he takes only partial credit: "Claude Ryan could do nothing but improve our chances," he wrote, "and he didn't miss a trick." Immediately after the victory, Lévesque met with the seven other premiers who had developed their counterproposal for patriation of the Constitution without a charter, for an amendment process based on seven provinces with 50 percent of the population, and with provision for a province to opt out of an amendment if two-thirds of its legislature approved. Lévesque was intrigued but troubled, especially by the two-thirds requirement. He is candid about his objective: if a simple majority were required, he wrote, "this way, I speculated, might we not, little by little, be able to build the associate state we had been refused?" Lévesque admits he did not share his thoughts about an "associate state" with the other premiers, but neither did they share their private musings with him. After a late night and early morning meeting, the other premiers agreed to drop the two-thirds requirement in return for Lévesque's promise "to solemnly affix my signature in the right place on an historic document headed up by the maple leaf flag!"[10] At the time the plan seemed like a splendid stroke to cut down Trudeau.

As we have seen, April was a month of disasters for Trudeau, with Ryan's defeat in the Quebec election, the Newfoundland Court of Appeal decision against his patriation plan, and the creation of the gang of eight with its own plan for patriation without a charter. Lévesque, understandably, was ebullient, if not overconfident. In his memoirs, he argues strongly that "opting out" with compensation, as was agreed by the gang, was of tremendous value to Quebec: "From state to state . . . we could create something very like a country in that fashion." Admittedly, Quebec would lose its veto, but, Lévesque writes, "this old obsession has never turned me on." The veto, he argues, was "an obstacle to development as much as an instrument of defence."[11] To him, the "opting out" path obviously possessed much more political weight.

Lévesque's characteristically frank comments in his memoirs explain why he did not speak of the veto as an issue when he departed furiously from Ottawa on November 5. Nevertheless, the storm came quickly when he returned to Quebec, where the nationalists denounced the loss of the veto as a catastrophe. And Trudeau, as we have seen, taunted him for giving up the jewel when he joined the gang of eight in April. Moreover, the other premiers blamed Lévesque for breaking their April agreement when he carelessly accepted Trudeau's challenge to test patriation and the charter in a referendum during the fateful meetings of early November. Claude Morin's account of the incident essentially confirms this interpretation, although it also suggests that, for Lévesque, the accord of April was already dead. In Morin's opinion the purpose of creating the gang of eight was to destroy Trudeau's plans for a charter when he patriated the Constitution. When the premiers, notably the distrusted Allan Blakeney, toyed with compromise, Lévesque's hopes turned first to frustration, then to anger. The gains of April were lost; the harvest of November was betrayal.[12]

Consumed with bitterness, Lévesque then went too far. "I continued to rage and storm," he writes. "From 'the night of the long knives' to 'the most despicable betrayal,' I couldn't find words strong enough to express my burning resentment." He even considered making Quebec anglophones take the "school medicine" francophones received in the rest of Canada, where many could not receive education in their official language. This "rage" brought "a release," but Lévesque himself admits, "it became excessive." It contributed to a sour mood of revenge at the Parti Québécois congress in December, one that split the party between hard-line sovereignists and those who favoured "association."* Faced with a divided party, Lévesque threatened to resign. After he pushed back the radicals, he stayed, but Morin, the author of *"étapisme"* (separation by steps), gave up and left. Lévesque's adviser Claude Charron followed in February 1982 after he was arrested for stealing a $125 jacket from an Eaton's department store. Lévesque, his party split and dispirited and the economy collapsing, stumbled in his last term in office. Then, on June 20, 1985, after the party declared, against his wishes, that the next election would be fought on the issue of sovereignty, Lévesque resigned as leader of the PQ. Believing that commitment to run on sovereignty foolish, on October 3, he stepped down as premier.

Two years later, on November 1, 1987, Lévesque died of a heart attack. He was only sixty-five. Despite widespread knowledge of his deteriorating health, his death was a shock, and many wept openly on Quebec streets when they learned that Quebec would

---

* Lévesque's rage against the "English" was not reflected in his policy of sovereignty-association, which strongly implies close association with Canada's other official linguistic group. Graham Fraser, who knew Quebec well as a journalist during the seventies and eighties, later said: "Even though very few members of the Parti Québécois really shared his passion for this formula of sovereignty-association, he managed to keep their loyalty. And he kept their loyalty because nobody in the Parti Québécois really believed he was as fervently attached to this formula as he turned out to be." His "rage" in November thus excited the militants to believe—wrongly—that he might go beyond his stated political position. Fraser, quoted in Robert Bothwell, *Canada and Quebec: One Country, Two Histories*, rev. ed. (Vancouver: University of British Columbia Press, 1998), 157. Fraser's own book, *René Lévesque and the Parti Québécois in Power*, 2nd ed. (Montreal and Kingston: McGill–Queen's University Press, 2003), gives a fine, detailed account of Lévesque's relationship with his province and his party.

no longer be pervaded by his enormous presence. The Friday night before Lévesque died, Trudeau had seen Lévesque at a festival for Canadian authors, where Trudeau was launching a book of his speeches on international affairs. Wearing a tuxedo, a beaming Trudeau stared at Lévesque, who was gingerly holding the new book with Trudeau on the cover. A grinning Lévesque then reportedly turned toward Trudeau and said, "So you're dramatizing again." On hearing of his rival's death, Trudeau mused, "When we were not talking about politics, we agreed." He paid his respects on the Tuesday night as Lévesque rested in state in the old Montreal court house. As he entered the room, a young man shouted, "You have no business here." Although Gérard Pelletier and Jean Marchand attended the funeral mass, Trudeau did not.[13]

Death did not end the debate, particularly about the loss of the veto. In Lévesque's words, his province stood alone after November 1981. The image lingered, threading itself through future political visions of what Canada and Quebec actually were and what they should be. Like Lévesque, in his *Memoirs* and in later interviews, Trudeau confronted the issue of whether Quebec chose, or was forced, to stand alone. In the *Memoirs*, he claims that Lévesque would never have agreed to the compromise on patriation because he was a separatist who did not want Canada to succeed. More revealing, however, is an extended 1992 interview with journalist Jean Lépine. Again and again Lépine returned to November 5 and asked why Trudeau did not make one final grand effort to bring Quebec into the agreement. Did he truly think Lévesque would never sign? At first Trudeau was brisk and brief, but as Lépine kept repeating the question, Trudeau expatiated on the point at length, arguing that Lévesque had left Ottawa demanding three changes—relating to language, mobility rights, and the lack of compensation for provinces when they "opted out." He admitted that he had not been sure what Quebec would do, but he claimed that, within the following week, Lévesque had asked for three new items, including the veto. That request made negotiation impossible and even farcical. At that point Lépine returned to the question once more:

> Now that you are in shape, I ask you once again the question I posed at the outset. My question was: today, when one recalls those events, one asks: Why did Trudeau, at the last minute on the 5th, seeing that Quebec would not sign, not make a supreme effort to bring Quebec onside? . . . Do you recall that you were sure at that moment that Quebec absolutely would not sign?
>
> Yes I was sure. . . . I just proved to you that [Lévesque] did not know what he wanted. He gave three pretexts, three reasons not to sign the accord and then, one week later, he said that the accord was unacceptable for three other reasons. Put yourself in my skin!

Clearly, the persistent questioning troubled Trudeau.

The accord was not perfect, but it was essential, as Trudeau told his dissenting aide, André Brunelle. Lesage had denied Pearson patriation in 1964, and Bourassa had undermined the Victoria Charter in 1971. By November 1981 the sentiment at the table among federalists was strong—time had run out—and that sentiment extended far beyond the table. Two of Trudeau's closest confidants on the constitutional file sent their thoughts to him soon after the deal was sealed. Ramsay Cook wrote on November 8: "I guess it is not quite the constitutional package you would have liked, but it is a pretty good one. . . . At any rate, congratulations for your great steadfastness in seeing this through." Trudeau replied: "As you know, it is not quite the constitutional package I would have liked, but I respect the spirit of compromise that allowed us to find common ground." F.R. (Frank) Scott, who had fretted about Canada's constitutional woes for decades, reacted in a similar way: "Unhappy as I was at some parts of the package — and no doubt you were — I was delighted that you called a halt to further negotiations." Time had indeed run out. The process was "a mess," as Trudeau told an interviewer, but it was a new mess with richer ingredients.[14]

It was not the constitutional package that Trudeau would have liked, but it was far better than the alternative of continuing constitutional deadlock and a country without individual rights entrenched in a charter. On November 5 Trudeau noted "with much regret" the absence of a provision for a referendum in the case of constitutional deadlock. The image of middle-aged men in suits deciding such fundamental issues by themselves denied what Trudeau called "the ultimate sovereignty of the people." Moreover, the notwithstanding clause bothered Trudeau, as did the limitations on mobility rights. And there was also that lack of a veto for Quebec.

Trudeau countered the Quebec claim that the denial of the veto was a historic wrong because, as he so often pointed out, Lévesque had ceded the veto in April 1981 when he had joined the gang of eight. But Jean Chrétien in his memoirs says that Lévesque's request for a veto at the November meeting was proper, "not for Quebec as a province but for a minority population with unique concerns in linguistic and cultural matters." He regrets that Lévesque's belated plea was not granted but points out, correctly, that the opposition of even one province to the request was enough to deny it, and there were many ready to join those ranks. Oddly, Trudeau is silent in his memoirs on the subject. However, in 1983 he told Ramsay Cook, who had criticized the amending formula, that he "hoped that historians would record [Trudeau's] reservations" about Quebec's loss of the veto and "the fact that [he] had favoured one which included a Quebec veto."

Historians, especially in Quebec, have not reflected Trudeau's hopes, but the fundamental truth remains. Until 1981,

Trudeau's governments had always supported the Quebec veto.
Could a Herculean effort by the federal leaders have persuaded
nine provinces to change the amending formula? Probably not,
but the blurred historical memory of those times may suggest that
Trudeau should have taunted Lévesque less about his compromise with the gang of eight and emphasized more his personal
regret that his own province, with its "linguistic and cultural" differences, lost a significant power within the Canadian federation.
Moreover, the later attempts to deal with the veto through the
Meech Lake and Charlottetown accords revealed how much
this loss affected Quebec and Canadian constitutional history.
Meech Lake and Charlottetown had a huge impact on the views
about the events of November 1981 held by most Quebec intellectuals and politicians—not only separatists but also federalists
such as Brian Mulroney and Daniel Johnson Jr.[15]

But hindsight obscures political and personal considerations.
In April 1981 Trudeau was stunned by the Newfoundland court
decision, irritated by hesitations among British parliamentarians,
politically wounded by Lévesque's re-election, and challenged by
the creation of the gang of eight. His constitutional project, his
"magnificent obsession," seemed about to collapse. That it did not
was the result of his deft manoeuvres, Lévesque's carelessness, and,
as he said to Cook, the spirit of compromise that suddenly swept
through the Ottawa conference centre during those fraught days
in early November. Trudeau's disappointments with the final
agreement were the product of those compromises. He negotiated;
Lévesque, suspicious and increasingly angry, missed his chances.
Perhaps the two did agree when they did not speak of politics, but
politics was so central to their lives that discord normally prevailed.
Asked by Lépine to sum up his views of Lévesque, Trudeau said
that he never really knew what Lévesque wanted—he did not
know whether he was an "indépendantiste" or whether he truly
believed in "la souveraineté-association" or whether, "like Claude

Morin," he saw sovereignty-association as a series of "steps to be taken to reach complete independence."

"What did you respect about Lévesque?" Lépine asked.

"Well, I respected that he was . . . I respected that he . . . Well, an interesting sort, he was lively, he was obstinate, he . . . I don't have anything to say about Mr. Lévesque."[16]

Lévesque's biographer Pierre Godin correctly observes that Lévesque and Trudeau "had contributed to a complete redefinition of Canada." In a Canada on the edge of breakup, they dominated their times. Both had, through their jousting, sarcasm, and struggle, "forced English Canada to look at Quebec's place in the federation in a new light." It was a shared accomplishment and, for Canadians and for Québécois, one of enormous significance. For Trudeau, patriation of the Constitution, with the addition of the charter, reversed the course of constitutional history, which had derailed in the seventies, with defeat at Victoria leading to a desperation that ended in utter failure in 1979. His reach was long when he returned to power in 1980, but his grasp almost equalled it. The dissenting premiers, perhaps fearful of their electorates' condemnation if they killed the charter, with Lévesque as their fellow executioner, went far beyond the meagre crumbs they had offered Trudeau in April 1981 when his position had seemed so weak. In the end, the charter was changed little, opting out was limited, equalization of the provinces was entrenched, individual rights were guaranteed, and the role of the federal presence in the lives of Canadians was assured. Ironically, Claude Ryan, with his commitment to special status for Quebec and decentralization in favour of the provinces—a position close to Conservative leader Joe Clark's vision of "a community of communities"—would probably have been a more effective opponent of Trudeau than Lévesque. As Romanow said when he left the conference, "in a bizarre way," Lévesque's arguments meant that "we have a stronger Canada now." If that was so, Trudeau's determination to counter those arguments had made it so.[17]

Trudeau's public reward came on a chilly April 17, 1982, when in an outdoor ceremony in front of the Parliament Buildings in Ottawa, Queen Elizabeth II, wearing a turquoise coat with matching hat, formally signed the Royal Proclamation of the Constitution. As the strong wind blew Trudeau's sprinkling of hair, thirty-two thousand loyal and drenched spectators applauded. Nine premiers sat nearby, but the absent Lévesque was in Montreal, leading a protest march. Trudeau began by declaring that at long last Canada had complete national sovereignty. Then, as he began to talk about Quebec, the clouds darkened, rumbles of thunder began, and heavy rain followed. The Queen's words intermittently broke through the storm, as when she called the achievement "a defiant challenge to history." After a state dinner on the Saturday night, where the architects of the new Constitution were honoured, the Queen departed from the capital. Trudeau accompanied her to the airport, and once she entered the plane, he surprised the onlookers with a sudden, elegant pirouette. On the historic day of the signing ceremony, Trudeau had ended his remarks with the words: "Let us celebrate the renewal and patriation of our Constitution, but let us put our faith, first and foremost, in the people of Canada who will give it life." It remains, rightly or wrongly, Trudeau's lasting challenge to the people and their history.[18]

The immediate popularity of the charter, recorded in many polls, did not pass directly to the Trudeau government, whose ratings fell steadily throughout 1981 and even more in 1982. The Liberals began 1981 with a ten-point lead over the Tories, but despite much internal dissent directed toward Joe Clark, the Tories were leading 42 percent to 28 percent by the end of the year. Although the charter was received well in much of English Canada, Liberal support fell there while remaining stable in

Quebec, where the government and much of the press strongly opposed the constitutional reform, although not the charter.

One of the casualties of collapsing Liberal support was Jim Coutts, who had left Trudeau's office to run in a by-election in Toronto's Spadina riding. Trudeau had appointed Peter Stollery, a canoeing pal of his, to the Senate, thereby opening the riding for his principal secretary. But the device seemed too clever, and Stollery much too young for the Senate — and the constituency, Liberal for thirty-six years, rejected Coutts and elected Dan Heap, a radical Toronto NDP councillor. Trudeau missed Coutts. Although they were not friends, they instinctively understood and trusted each other. Coutts had devilishly helped secure Trudeau's return in 1979 and had managed the first months of power effectively. He retained the "lean and mean" staff of opposition days, and in the view of press secretary Patrick Gossage, he kept Trudeau's focus on the things that mattered most politically — the constitutional file above all. Coutts's departure brought a new mood, one that was more open but less disciplined. It meant, in Gossage's words, that an "end of an era" agenda began to take shape.[19]

—

Jim Coutts, like Trudeau, jealously guarded his personal life, and, as a bachelor, he was particularly understanding of Trudeau's insistence on privacy. One of the conditions of Trudeau's return to politics, which he had set out clearly to his staff in early 1980, was sufficient time for his children and his own life. For the kids — Justin, Sacha, and Michel — the move back to 24 Sussex Drive was a belated 1979 Christmas present. They splashed about daily in the swimming pool, and their dad became boyish when he came home in the evening, swinging them about as they rushed to greet him and relating a few of the day's events. Pierre was an enthusiastic father. After visiting him at home, a female friend wrote to him: "You are one of the most attentive, conscientious fathers I have ever met. It's wonderful."[20] And it was, for both Pierre and the kids. Justin recalls the early eighties as a precious time, when his parents, despite their many preoccupations, played the central part in the boys' lives. Not yet teenagers, and at that wonderfully curious stage when the world is particularly fresh, the children were encouraged to become individuals, to question, and to know that their parents wanted them to express their talents and their real selves as fully as possible. A young friend of Justin's from their pre-teen years recalls that "time spent in the company of Justin's dad was almost always defined by physical and mental challenges: show me what you have learned. Show me what you can do. Show me how you live." And Pierre would readily show them what he could do, as on the summer day at Harrington Lake when none of the assembled kids could meet his challenge to stand on a surfboard in the water. The boys' father showed it could be done as the "excited voices of children [counted] off second after unbelievable second" until he finally and elegantly disappeared into the depths.[21]

Family life became easier after the return to Sussex Drive because Margaret, by then, had a home just three blocks away. During the election campaign of 1979–80, she cared for the boys while Pierre was away. The purchase of the house, made possible by some funds from Trudeau and revenues from *Beyond Reason*, ended the arrangement whereby Margaret occasionally lived in her own room on the top floor of 24 Sussex or, when Trudeau was in opposition, at Stornoway. Although they tried to make the boys' lives as normal as possible in the circumstances, they were not. Margaret and Pierre had sometimes fought furiously after the children went to bed.

One night at Stornoway, after Margaret had asked for money and Pierre had offered her only fifty dollars, she exploded in frustration, and in the scuffle that followed, tried to scratch out his eyes. A brown belt in judo, Pierre quickly pinned her down, but the children heard her screams and came running. They pleaded with their father not to hurt her. Finally Micha, who was only four, asked Pierre to come to his room. In Margaret's words, "they were gone half an hour, talking things over, and Pierre always says that Micha put a lot of sense into him. Then he left." The incident shook both parents, and they took counselling from a family therapist, undoubtedly a wise move under the complicated circumstances because, however much Margaret sometimes irritated Pierre, such occasional violence was a troubling sign of the anger and concealed furies within Trudeau's closed self. With the therapist, they discussed their marriage and discovered, again in Margaret's words, that they "had thought all along that we were really communicating with one another, [but] we were not." Margaret claims that she became aware that Pierre was essentially a loner—though he used the term "solitary"—and that he had erected "an immense barrier between himself and the outside world," which made intimate and trusting relationships difficult. But she also learned of, and was touched by, his "appreciation" of her as a mother. He liked the way she "handled" the boys, and she realized that she did love Pierre as a parent for her sons. For Trudeau, the children were a way for him to penetrate that barrier, perhaps for the first time. And despite the turmoil and the emotion, Margaret and Pierre gave the boys a good foundation on which to build the rest of their lives.[22]

And so Margaret settled into her small house nearby, with its porch and bunk beds. The boys came to her after classes were over at Rockcliffe Park Public School and had their snacks and their playtime before the waiting police car escorted them to 24 Sussex Drive, where they waited for their father to return at approximately 6:45. Having told the boys in the fall of 1979 that they were separating permanently, Margaret and Pierre worked out what was, in effect, joint custody. When they had first split in 1977, Pierre had retained sole custody of the boys but had agreed to "generous" access to the children.* His anger swelled after the publication of *Beyond Reason* and Margaret's escapades in the late seventies, but he recognized that the boys loved their mother and wanted to be with her. The new circumstances offered an ideal situation. They agreed that each would "have the boys" a week each, with the weekends negotiated. Pierre wanted them to go with him to Harrington Lake on alternate weekends, but Saturday morning TV cartoons at Margaret's were too popular. The boys' tastes triumphed, and Harrington Lake weekends began at noon. Their parents developed, Margaret writes, a "mutual agreement about values such as honesty and loyalty, education (that it should be bilingual) and behaviour (at least when it comes to manners and regular meals). Out of these strengths has come a way of life."[23]

Trudeau cherished his time with the boys, and he frequently arranged for them to accompany him on his travels. On one memorable occasion in 1980, he took six-year-old Sacha with him on a trip to Saudi Arabia, where Sheik Ahmed Zaki Yamani, the legendary Saudi minister of oil, invited the Canadian party to spend

---

* As a practising Catholic, Trudeau would not divorce. He told Margaret, according to her account, "You are my wife, you will always be my wife, and errant as you may be, nothing will ever change that." Under Canadian law at that point, a divorce after three years was possible if both parties agreed, but Trudeau would not. Without such agreement, five years "separate and apart" were required, and Margaret later learned that her days in the attic at 24 Sussex did not count as "separation." In 1984 Margaret filed for divorce and soon married Ottawa businessperson Fried Kemper, with whom she had two children. Trudeau did discuss the possibility of remarriage with his children, but he never indicated that he gave it serious consideration. Quotation from Margaret Trudeau, *Consequences* (Toronto: McClelland and Stewart, 1982), 77. Interview with Alexandre Trudeau, June 2009.

two nights in the desert. Trudeau, always an adventurer, accepted and, with Sacha in tow, stayed in a Bedouin tent. One evening the Arab music began and Trudeau, in desert garb, began to sway to the rhythms with Sacha. Then Trudeau and Yamani danced together in the desert night in an encounter that enthralled the Canadian reporters—and, of course, Sacha. But the memorable moment came when Sacha, clad in Arab dress, eagerly mounted a white camel and rode off. "Sacha of Arabia," his father joked, "off into the desert. See you tomorrow."

The boys, like their father, came to love the Canadian North and the frontier. And they were often present when the most eminent visitors arrived in Ottawa. One they particularly liked was President Ronald Reagan, who, like Trudeau, charmed children with his undivided attention and actor's wiles. On one occasion, former U.N. Secretary-General Boutros Boutros-Ghali, an Egyptian, had to act as a translator for a meeting between Trudeau and President Sadat of Egypt at the presidential palace. Trudeau solemnly introduced Sacha to the president and to another guest, President Senghor of Senegal. Sacha, who had just returned from the zoo, commented: "At the zoo, earlier today, I saw four giraffes, three elephants, and now I'm meeting two presidents." Senghor, who understood English, burst out laughing; Sadat, who did not— and Boutros-Ghali did not translate—accepted the words as the praise a president was owed. Even when the kids didn't travel with their father, they had access to the best tickets for Sesame Street and other shows, and the chance to meet the stars backstage after the performance. And there were their dad's new friends—the many women who came to call at Sussex Drive.[24]

The women began to appear soon after Pierre and Margaret separated, but Margaret's intermittent presence at 24 Sussex made matters difficult. Margaret describes the nervous atmosphere one Friday, when she arrived home just as Pierre was preparing to welcome Liona Boyd. Trudeau quickly changed his plans, and he and Boyd spent an unexpected weekend at Harrington Lake. After Margaret found her own house, Trudeau had more freedom, which he grasped with alacrity. He had told his staff when he returned to office that he must have privacy when he was not working, and he scrupulously separated his private life from public concerns, in a way he could not do when he and Margaret were married. His personal secretary, Cécile Viau, carefully maintained the separation and, on Trudeau's behalf, expressed outrage when private correspondence was opened in his political office. Trudeau's closest friends, usually but not always female (architect Arthur Erickson was a constant correspondent), were told to stamp "confidential/personal" on their letters, postcards, or notes, and Viau gave them to Trudeau at the end of the day. The friends knew Mme Viau, and she regulated the various degrees of access they had to Trudeau and enforced the restrictions. She was, Marc Lalonde observes with a wry smile, the "soul of discretion."[25]

Trudeau himself was obsessively discreet. To be sure, he regularly squired attractive women on his arm at public events, but he set out clear rules for the numerous women with whom he developed more intimate friendships in the eighties. They were not to speak publicly about the relationship, and their times in Ottawa were normally cloak-and-dagger affairs. Sometimes they would get a flight on the government Challenger when it was nearby. At the airport Trudeau's chauffeur, who shared Mme Viau's passionate confidentiality, would whisk them away through private exits and entrances to their meeting with Pierre. The women themselves were generally young, often in the arts or theatre, usually intelligent, frequently extroverted and witty, and invariably beautiful. His personal papers are replete with letters, notes, postcards, and Christmas greetings from women he met on beaches, in airplanes, at diplomatic gatherings, or on the Hill. He flirted continually and outrageously, and despite his concern for privacy, he seemed to enjoy flaunting his attractiveness in the presence of women.

Margaret, for example, recalls one night when she was in her room on the top floor at 24 Sussex while a group gathered downstairs after a reception at Rideau Hall. Trudeau came up to her room, said she would know everyone, and asked her to join them. She discovered Liona Boyd, who had played at the Governor General's reception, among the group and said "wickedly" to Trudeau, "so you had a mistress play." Trudeau quickly replied, "Not one, but two"—a *chanteuse* had also performed that evening. In a similar vein, Allan Gotlieb, Trudeau's ambassador to Washington, complains in his wonderful diary about a dinner he hosted in honour of Trudeau, which "turned out to be one big pain in the ass," not least because there were three Trudeau "girl-friends" among the fifty guests.[26]

Margot Kidder, then at the height of her celebrity, was accustomed to Trudeau's multiple dates. On March 30, 1983, after a dinner in Toronto with Greek prime minister Andreas Papandreou, she thanked Trudeau "for the evening with the Greeks," but, she added, "why didn't you tell me you had a date? How do you expect a girl to flirt over dinner when the man she wants to make eyes at has another girlfriend on his right?" Playing in *Pygmalion* at the time, she drew Trudeau's attention to a Shaw quotation: "Are you a man of good character where women are concerned?"

The "girlfriend" on Trudeau's right that evening was probably Gale Zoë Garnett, a warm, talented writer, actress, singer, and wit who thoroughly charmed Trudeau after they met in the early eighties. Orphaned at fifteen, Garnett had moved from Toronto to New York, where she appeared in plays and wrote, as a teenager, the words and music for the song "We'll Sing in the Sunshine," which reached the top of the popular music charts in the United States and endures as a sixties classic. Provocative in its content for the time—a young woman saying she'll live with a man for a while and then move on—the tune brought royalties and freedom to the young Garnett. When she returned to Toronto, she appeared in the first production of *Hair* and began a career as a journalist. Her first encounter with Trudeau occurred when she asked him for an interview, and he responded with an invitation for dinner. She replied, "Interviews I can get—good company for dinner is a far greater rarity." They went out for a Japanese meal in Ottawa sometime in the spring of 1981. Garnett had already learned about Trudeau's zeal for privacy and wrote: "I could kick myself for not ringing you sooner! What a silly business! I just didn't think you'd be up for anything that public."[27]

The friendship, marked immediately by "naturalness and ease," blossomed quickly, and Garnett's frequent letters give a clear idea of what they spoke about. She wrote on June 12, soon after a visit to Ottawa: "God. I keep meaning to ask you about this—it's been on my mind since I visited 24 Sussex. You told me about Sacha's 3-question ritual with you. You said that one of his questions that night was 'Who made God?' You went on to say 'and I answered that.' You were on your way to making a point and I did not wish to interrupt you. But I keep asking, 'Who made God?'"

Two days later, she reacted to the latest news, knowing that Trudeau himself was angry about the policies of Likud, the leading Israeli right-wing party: "The news is full of Israel. I think I hate Menachem Begin. I hate everything about the way he thinks. Sometimes would you, could you talk to me about this. It is hard to talk about because of the guilt button that gets pressed whenever anyone mentions Israel critically."

About other aspects of Canadian foreign policy she had doubts—but not about Trudeau's constitutional success. On November 9 she sent Trudeau "a massive, multiple BRAVO! My God, what an incredible reversal! Yours is a sparely-occupied pantheon—others include Muhammad Ali, Frank Sinatra, & Olmec Jaguar of the Aztec. Maybe Houdini." An amusing grouping, but Trudeau took flattery well—and, like most men, especially from women.[28]

They met the next summer, when the parliamentary furies were at their height. Afterwards, she told him that she had enjoyed a "super visit." Then she added: "I am always rather skittish about paying you (honest) compliments as I know the Spartan part of you is discomfited by them. I sort of sneak 'em in sideways." She offered "a whole collection of them" that he could "have upon request." That Christmas she gave him "the book of nonsense," and Trudeau thanked her and told her he was already enjoying it. Garnett granted Trudeau respectful admiration for the demands imposed on him by public life. She urged him to take "silliness breaks" often, which she correctly advised were important "when one leads a 'big life.'"

Now in his sixties, Trudeau was troubled by aches and pains, particularly in his back and shoulder. In September 1982, after he and Garnett had enjoyed a swim in the pool and she had joined him in the sauna, she massaged his creaking joints. He especially liked the massage oil she used. So she sent him a bottle of the oil, and in his note of thanks, he referred to it as "half a loaf." She responded poetically:

> In order for this half-loaf to be bred
> Into pleasure
> You must *have* a *masseuse*
> Fortunately,
> The *masseuse*
> Can be
> *Had*.

It was, she added affectionately, a very "silly note," written early in the morning. She thanked him for "a lovely time—and it was, as always, wonderful to see you."

Garnett, not surprisingly, charmed Prime Minister Andreas Papandreou when Trudeau asked her to sit with him and the

Greek leader at that Toronto dinner.* The timing was perfect: Garnett hoped to spend the spring and summer in the Greek islands, and Papandreou asked her to stay in touch—which she did. Her next visit was at the invitation of Papandreou and his wife. On her arrival a presidential car met her, and Papandreou, well known for his attraction to engaging women, invited her to dinner and, in Garnett's words, "talked with me all evening, on all subjects." She reported to Trudeau on May 30, 1983, "he *genuinely* liked *you*, politically and personally, and would deeply welcome a state visit. He suggested October or November (Mrs Gandhi, whom *nobody* likes very much, is coming in September). He says the Greek people like you very much and that a visit would probably be pleasurable for you. Considering all the things he's giving *me*, he'd probably give you *Crete!*" Encouraging her to sample the Greek islands, Papandreou lent Garnett a seventy-four-foot private yacht, and she embarked on her personal odyssey in early June.[29]

On June 22 a telegram arrived at the Department of External Affairs from a puzzled Canadian Embassy in Athens: a "Gale

---

* Papandreou, the charismatic leader of the Panhellenic Socialist Movement, had become prime minister on October 21, 1981, after an election in which he attacked Greece's membership in NATO, called for dramatic restructuring of Greek democracy, and denounced the presence of American military bases in Greece. After a coup by the Greek military in 1967, Papandreou had been briefly incarcerated but then freed when the U.S. government exerted pressure on the generals. Papandreou, "a world-class academic economist" with a Harvard doctorate, had taught at York University in Toronto from 1969 to 1974. During that time he rallied Greek exile forces and played a major role in the Canadian Greek community, which strongly supported the Trudeau Liberals. On Papandreou's academic reputation and career, see Richard Clogg, "From Academy to Acropolis," *Times Higher Education Supplement*, Dec. 22, 1995, 16.

Garnette *[sic]* hospitalized . . . Subj requested that Prime Minister [be told] that she is presently being treated in infectious disease hospital Aghia . . . for meningitis. . . . Subj told us she lives in Toronto, no/no family in Canada and has refused twice to show us a [passport]." An official, accustomed to whimsical demands for prime-ministerial intervention, sent it, with a dismissive note, to Cécile Viau in the Prime Minister's Office. Immediately, a message came from Mme Viau to Athens and External: "PM Trudeau, who knows Ms Garnett well, is dismayed by the news in your telegram and wishes her quick recovery. Are you able to send flowers in his own name. . . . For your own information, Ms Garnett was at the table of honour at the Toronto reception in honour of Prime Minister Papandreou." The flowers, Ms Garnett wrote in a letter that reflects her very serious illness, were "elegant, graceful and a *bit* exotic — rather like the sender." Papandreou, on learning of Garnett's illness, flooded the room with flowers and sent his own personal physician. With such care, Garnett recovered from the meningitis. Her main nurse, "a gutsy delightful creature named Despina," told the orphan Garnett: "Others have mothers & fathers, *you* have Prime Ministers."[30] Indeed.

—

Garnett, at Trudeau's invitation, had sat in the gallery of the House of Commons when Finance Minister Allan MacEachen presented his budget on June 28, 1982. It was, she told Trudeau, a "petulant, injustice-collecting time," an opinion the prime minister shared.[31] His economic programs unravelled that year as labour, business, and voters ferociously attacked the government's economic policies. The June budget responded to the failure of the one presented on November 12, 1981, two months after Lougheed and Trudeau had toasted a new energy agreement with champagne. The celebration had been premature: as the rise in oil prices stalled, drilling rigs quickly left Canada, and the flow of funds both Trudeau and Lougheed had anticipated for their treasuries became a trickle. With the revenue underpinnings of his 1981 budget gone, MacEachen confronted an economic storm that blew from unexpected directions with devastating impact.

The winds from the south blew coldest. After the election of Ronald Reagan, Paul Volcker, the chairman of the Federal Reserve Bank of the United States, adopted monetary policies that raised interest rates to unprecedented heights in a successful effort to end the rampant inflation. Simultaneously, the Republicans began to cut taxes, a reflection of their commitment to supply-side economics—a belief that the benefits of tax cuts would create rapid economic growth that would "raise all boats." The close integration of the Canadian and American economies quickly transferred the impact of these policies to Canada, with catastrophic results for the Canadian economy and federal government policy. The Bank of Canada followed Volcker's path and also restricted the money supply drastically. Later, Volcker said, "Whoever expected twenty percent interest rates? But you get caught up in the process, and you can't let go. You don't want to let go. Letting up, giving up—that was not in my psychology." And so unemployment soared into double digits, housing prices dropped, car lots were crammed with unsold vehicles, mortgage interest rates stood at an incredible 22 percent in August 1981 — and Canadian politicians ran for cover.[32]

The 1981 budget had supported the Bank of Canada's policy of wringing inflation out of the system with severe restrictions on money supply. In MacEachen's words, the bank's policy "has to be supported by greater fiscal restraint." He promised to cut back on spending, counting on revenues from the NEP, rather than imposing new taxes, to produce additional income. But the NEP revenues did not come through. Meanwhile, the social programs of the sixties and seventies continued to create extra costs for the

federal treasury as unemployment rose, resulting in a projected
budget deficit of $13.3 billion. However, MacEachen estimated that
this deficit would fall to $10.5 billion in 1982–83 and $9.6 billion the
following year, so these parts of the budget, including the projections, were not highly controversial. Almost everyone believed that
the NEP would flood the government's coffers. Nevertheless, troubles came when MacEachen, whose social Catholicism gave him
a passion for equality and an abhorrence of poverty, unexpectedly
attacked tax breaks—the panoply of special deductions, political
payoffs to insurance companies, income averaging, pension
income deductibility, and "writeoffs" for mining, property, and
financial firms that had accumulated in the postwar era.* The
budget created an accountant's nightmare: an end to the complex
architecture of special privileges that the Carter Commission had
tried to break down more than a decade earlier—though admittedly Trudeau's own governments had added some buttresses to it
in the seventies. In the view of MacEachen and his advisers, the

---

* MacEachen's timing was bad. J.H. Perry, the leading historian of Canadian
fiscal policy, wrote amusingly about the "taxpayer onslaught" in the 1981
budget: "Seldom has the aplomb of taxpayers, by now inured with the
conviction of the age that taxes were an evil to be avoided at all cost, been
more outraged." He concluded that future governments should avoid appointing economists like MacEachen or accountants like Edgar Benson to the post
of finance minister and should favour lawyers, who tend to be "much more
reasonable chaps" when taking on taxpayers. The real problem, Perry rightly
points out, was that "this sort of shock should be spared a country on the eve of
a serious recession." Of course, when MacEachen introduced his budget in
1981, he was unaware of the ferocious economic downturn Canada was facing.
J.H. Perry, A Fiscal History of Canada: The Postwar Years (Toronto: Canadian
Tax Foundation, 1989), 91–92.

changes would bring in new revenue that could then be spent on
the small businesses, homeowners, and others struck down by high
inflation and the recession.[33] But those affected—special interests
such as insurance companies, accounting firms, property develop-
ers, and law firms—were not pleased. They crowded Ottawa-bound
airplanes with their representatives as winter set in.

The 1981 budget quickly came undone as lobbying combined with the stunning impact of high interest rates to undermine the drive for equity. The assumptions underpinning the
NEP also fell apart as oil prices began to collapse with the end of
economic growth and the beginning of a serious recession.
Canada had a terrible year in 1982. Its real GNP, which grew
3 percent, second only to that of Japan, in 1981, dropped 4.8
percent in 1982, by far the worst among the G7 nations and a
number unequalled in the postwar era. Its unemployment rate
(12.6 percent) was exceeded only by that in the United Kingdom
(12.8 percent) and was much higher than that in the United States
(9.7 percent). Volcker's stringent actions caused inflation to drop
to 6.2 percent in the United States, but it remained at 10.8 percent
in Canada. More troubling was productivity growth, ultimately
the source of economic growth, which declined 1.6 percent in
1982, again, worse than in any other G7 nation. In June the
Canadian dollar reached a historic low of 76.8 cents U.S. before
recovering to 81.4 cents at the end of the year. Ian Stewart,
MacEachen's deputy minister of finance, wrote later that "the
federal budget of 1981 pursued tax reform and reductions in
the rate of growth of federal transfer to the provinces in continued
pursuit of deficit control, just as the bottom was about to fall out
of economic activity and the automatic stabilizers were to drive
deficits up rapidly." The public blamed the government, and
Trudeau tumbled in the polls.[34]

"Quite frankly," Trudeau wrote in his memoirs, "neither I
nor MacEachen nor anyone else in the Cabinet had realized the

extent to which [the 1981] budget would upset so many private interests in so many sectors of the population." He had paid close attention to economic matters in the seventies, but in the early eighties he seemed less interested and made almost no meaningful statements on the subject. Monique Bégin, one of his leading ministers, found him puzzlingly indifferent to economics at the time.[35] There were several reasons for this behaviour. First, his two finance ministers, Allan MacEachen and Marc Lalonde, were his strongest and most trusted colleagues. A prominent public servant later recalled Trudeau saying that he "owed" MacEachen his ambitious 1981 budget—MacEachen had, after all, played a pivotal role in rescuing his political career in 1979.[36] Lalonde, a dominating figure in Trudeau's last government, was not only highly competent but also completely loyal, a quality Trudeau prized. Second, monetarism and supply-side economics, which had become the new dogma in Washington and among many Canadian economists, including those at the Bank of Canada in the case of monetarism, did not coincide with the economics Trudeau had learned at Harvard and debated with others in the seventies. He was too old to learn new ways, but too intelligent not to recognize their importance.* Third, economic events of the early eighties fundamentally undermined the policy mix that the Liberals had brought to office in 1980—the interventionist NEP, a robust Foreign Investment Review Agency, and an activist industrial strategy. Falling energy prices undermined the first, strong opposition

---

* Trudeau's uncertainties were mirrored among economists more generally. The eminent Canadian economist Richard Lipsey, who served as president of the Canadian Economics Association in 1981, reflected the general confusion among economists in the early 1980s in his presidential address, in which he questioned whether the claims of monetarists were justified.

on Bay Street and in Washington and declining direct investment defeated the second, and the third became impossible as soaring deficits limited the freedom of Trudeau's government to intervene to secure its ambitious goals.[37]

And then there was the constitutional war: its battles ranked first in importance for Trudeau, as his instructions in the fall of 1981 that Lalonde come to terms with Alberta clearly indicate. Moreover, even though Trudeau was often absent from economic discussions, his philosophy suffused them all. And that approach was exemplified during a discussion in December 1980, when Alberta businessman Jack Gallagher pushed Trudeau for a quicker move to the world price for oil and the prime minister responded, "Is it fair?" Would going to the world price not penalize too many people? Similarly, in August 1981, when Trudeau and Lalonde attended a U.N.-sponsored conference on new and renewable sources of energy in Nairobi, Kenya, Trudeau declared that the rising costs of energy were the "enemy of freedom." He announced the creation of Petro-Canada International to assist developing countries in achieving their own self-sufficiency. Lalonde followed the same path and argued that Canada was assisting developing nations by becoming self-sufficient itself, thereby freeing scarce energy resources for others.[38]

Self-sufficiency, programs to achieve social and economic equity, and the use of state power to rebalance the tilt of the market toward "fairness" met with stiff opposition in the eighties as Reagan's comprehensive neo-conservatism took hold throughout much of the Western world. Initially, strong opposition came not only from Ottawa but also from France, where the new socialist government of François Mitterrand nationalized banks and strengthened the state, but gradually, the new faith won converts and Mitterrand's resistance faded. A few outposts remained in Scandinavia and elsewhere, where there was successful resistance, but the attack on the interventionist state and the celebration of the market became an increasingly dominant outlook within the Anglo-American democracies. It included a retreat from government regulation, massive tax reductions, and a deep faith in the rightness of the market in moral as well as economic terms. The blend of neo-conservatism and market economics profoundly challenged the platform on which Trudeau had been re-elected in 1980. Already by 1981, the government was retreating on its pledges to strengthen FIRA and to extend the interventionist policies represented by the NEP into other sectors of the economy. Reeling from the worst economic downturn of the G7 since the Depression, the Trudeau government seemed on the defensive, reacting too late to the unexpected and watching in disbelief as its carefully crafted programs quickly came undone.[39]

In their accounts of what happened, Trudeau, Lalonde, and others attribute their problems to the unexpected decline of the price of oil. "Had prices moved within a reasonable range of the projections [$79.65 by January 1990]," Lalonde argues, "the Canadian consumer would be paying a lot more today for petroleum products, but the oil and gas industry would be very prosperous, the governments of producing provinces would have large Heritage funds and the federal government would probably have no deficit." He points out that the Alberta Heritage Fund reached its peak, at $12.7 billion, in 1987, when resource royalties ceased to be transferred to it and the federal government deficit under Brian Mulroney, Trudeau's Conservative successor, stood at $34.96 billion. In the Canadian fashion, blame was placed across the board. Lalonde reminds his readers of a late eighties Calgary bumper sticker—"Oh God, give me another oil boom: I promise I will not piss it away." The Albertans, he and others implied, had botched things, failing to take advantage of their rich resources when times were good. After all, 4.5 million Norwegians had hoarded a treasure trove from their energy resources that was twenty times the size of the fund for 3.3 million Albertans. Recriminations abounded among Albertans, with Lougheed's successor Don Getty receiving much of the blame, but they directed most of their rancour toward Ottawa and, in particular, the NEP.[40]

Like the constitutional initiative, the NEP must be placed within the context of Trudeau's understanding of his times and his belief that a weakened federal government had to reassert itself, particularly amid the economic nostrums proclaimed by Ronald Reagan and Margaret Thatcher. The federal government had been pulling back since the late sixties, as the provinces extended their reach in spending money, keeping in direct contact with citizens, and asserting their authority over language (Quebec) and resources (Alberta). Trudeau and his colleagues saw their policies in the last half of the 1970s as a series of retreats before relentless provincial assaults: the decision not to use the courts or special powers to challenge Lougheed's claims that the resources "belonged" to Alberta; the untying of grants for established programs to the provinces in 1977; the Cullen-Couture immigration accord in 1978, which permitted Quebec to play a direct role in selecting immigrants; the constitutional proposals of 1978 and 1979, which envisaged a significant decentralization of Canada; and the move to the world price for oil, which began after Trudeau replaced the aggressive Donald Macdonald as minister of energy with the more accommodating Alastair Gillespie.

The 1979 election defeat and Lougheed's subsequent failure to reach an energy accord with the Conservative Clark government left a mark both on the Trudeau Liberals and on the officials within the Department of Energy, Mines, and Resources, who had become exasperated with what they believed were truculent provincial governments. As political scientist Bruce Doern wrote in 1983: "Revenue was a genuine issue, but it was also a surrogate for many of the normative concerns that are inherent not only in energy policy but in Canadian politics in general: different views of federalism, the role of western Canada, the control of resources, regional disparities, growing budgetary deficits, and Canadian ownership of the economy." Trudeau, on his return to politics in 1980, vowed that he would retreat no more.[41]

The NEP was not simply about revenue but also about the Trudeau government's sense that it must seize the agenda it had lost in the seventies. The federal government's spending had soared in that decade, but its authority, Trudeau believed (and most agreed), had weakened.[42] It was imperative now for the federal government to confirm its relevance and effectiveness to Canadians, wherever they lived. Most, of course, lived in central Canada, and the tensions between the claims of Alberta in energy and those of Quebec in provincial rights ran counter to the interests of Ontario, as they were defined by the Conservative government there. Premier William Davis supported Trudeau against René Lévesque and Joe Clark, and he and Frank Miller, the Ontario finance minister, backed the NEP, even though central Canadian business interests were generally not supportive. Ontario even bought a 25 percent share in oil sands producer Suncor in 1981—an action that implicitly endorsed the Canadianization approach of the NEP. "Fairness" in regard to energy meant different things in Edmonton and in Toronto.

Faced with rising costs caused by the high unemployment of the early eighties, the tax expenditures of the seventies (such as indexing of payments and of taxation), and the rising payments on the national debt stemming from record high interest rates, Trudeau's government fought hard to maintain a coherent economic focus. In the seventies Canada had pursued two approaches. The first approach, trade liberalization through international negotiations such as GATT, meant that the historic protectionism of Canada's National Policy dissolved and Canadian manufacturers now faced challenges from Toyota automobiles and Sony electronics and, increasingly, from textiles imported from many developing countries. Political considerations—particularly the concentration of textile manufacturers in Quebec—caused much delay in freeing some of the trade, but the trend was clear. These liberalization policies had strong support from trade and finance officials, the government-appointed Economic Council of Canada, and a few ministers such as Jean-Luc Pepin,* as well as from Bay Street, the conservative and business-supported Fraser and C.D. Howe Institutes, and, most vocally, Simon Reisman.

The second economic approach—that Canada would thrive through an interventionist government that supported critical new industries—was advanced by the government-appointed Science Council of Canada. The November 1981 budget's economic statement, in the words of Kenneth Norrie and Doug Owram, "was based on [the] view that Canada's economic future lay in its rich natural-resource base. These sectors would be the leading ones around which manufacturing and services would evolve to serve them." The result would be "resource mega-projects such as oil-sands plants, offshore exploration and development, pipelines, and hydro-electric developments." This statement was a deliberate slap

---

* The divisions or, rather, the duality of approach remained within the Trudeau government. The energetic Pepin, an economic liberal, tried to end the historic Crow's Nest Pass grain rates, which had been established in 1897, through an agreement with the Canadian Pacific Railway, as a subsidy both for eastbound grain and agricultural products and for westbound settlers' goods. Pepin proposed in the Western Grains Transportation Bill (1983) that the Crow rate be replaced by a rising price for grain shipments in return for an infusion into the railways, which were underservicing the grain trade because of the low rates. After angry debate, the bill passed in the fall. The Conservative government of Saskatchewan opposed this attempt to move to market prices, and the federal government and Trudeau made neo-liberal arguments against subsidies. R.B. Byers, ed., *Canadian Annual Review of Politics and Public Affairs 1983* (Toronto: University of Toronto Press, 1985), 83–85.

at Reagan's famous declaration that government was the problem; for Lalonde and Trudeau, it remained a solution and a source of future Canadian opportunities.[43]

But increasing numbers of critics believed that government was not the solution, and the Reagan tax cuts attracted many Canadians who were distressed that their country was recovering more slowly than the United States from the recession. In June 1982 MacEachen's new budget reflected the confusion about how to proceed amid the most dramatic economic slowdown since the Great Depression. The budget limited wage increases for public servants to 6 percent for one year and 5 percent the following year. Government agencies and firms with rates needing government approval were also limited to price increases of 6 and 5 percent over the two-year period. The solution harked back to the seventies, when Trudeau broke his 1974 election promise and imposed wage and price controls on the country. But the choices now seemed very limited.

Two economists on the left, Clarence Barber and John McCallum (a future Liberal minister), set out the government's dilemma in a 1982 study written just before the June budget: "There is no simple solution to this general problem. On the one hand, Canada lacks the institutions and the underlying social consensus that have helped to contain inflation in Japan and certain European countries. On the other hand, the Canadian economy seems to be less flexible, more regulated, and less competitive than the American economy, and this may be one reason why inflation appears to be less downwardly mobile in Canada than in the United States." In their view, Canada, unlike many European countries, did not have the voluntary consensus, the close collaboration among labour, business, and government, that limited inflation's gains. Conversely, the United States had a more flexible market, which also acted to limit inflation. The result was a need for wage and price controls in Canada. For Trudeau, the

European option was the best—a view he increasingly expressed throughout the eighties and nineties—but Canada was not Europe. Pragmatically, he chose controls.[44]

In September 1982, with criticism mounting and the economy collapsing, Trudeau moved MacEachen from Finance to External Affairs and appointed Marc Lalonde in his place. Although the press reaction was mixed, everyone respected Lalonde's strength and influence on the government process. The classical pianist, political progressive, and frequent Trudeau date Monica Gaylord welcomed Lalonde's appointment in a letter to Trudeau: "I heard of your Cabinet shuffle today & with a toughy like Lalonde in Finance, I know our economic recovery is inevitable. I really like him. Would you consider making me your Minister of Meditation and Peace?" Like many Trudeau supporters, she wanted a balance. That balance was reflected in Lalonde's first budget on April 19, 1983: he offered some stimulus and a few tax incentives that pleased the business community, but he refused to join the Reagan-Thatcher revolution. In the words of Timothy Lewis, the author of the major academic study of "deficit fighting" in Canada, Lalonde was "perhaps Canada's most Keynesian finance minister." With Trudeau's open support, he indicated that he would "not tighten the screws on the economy, cut billions from government spending, or seek to eliminate inflation by brute force." In short, he confirmed that the government would continue "to ensure that the strong and affluent helped the weak and vulnerable."[45]

Trudeau reinforced the message in a national address on June 28, which echoed the defence of equity in Lalonde's budget and the rejection of Reaganomics. He pointed to improvements in the Canadian economy, where sixty-three thousand new jobs had been created in May, most of them for younger Canadians, and claimed that his 6/5 program had cut the rate of inflation in half. Although he thanked the business community for its cooperation on the wage and price policy, his words echoed Stockholm and

Paris more than Washington and London, social democracy rather than Reagan and Thatcher:

> But there are those who would lead us from this crossroads back to conflict, back to discord, back to fragmentation as a nation. Such leaders are the few who think that now is their chance to grab a bigger share. . . .
>
> The Canadian government is not prepared to let a few impose a return to conflict and inflation on the vast majority of Canadians. . . .
>
> We will seek ways in which the combined weight of federal and provincial spending can be used to prevent a few cases of unjustified price increases, and excessive executive salary increases and wage settlements, from becoming a pattern for our future.
>
> The government is particularly concerned that the money set aside in the budget for Special Recovery Capital Projects to create jobs not be used simply to pay higher salaries for executives, or higher wages for fewer workers. We will examine these projects in light of these settlements.
>
> We will not spend public money to allow any group of Canadians to take a bigger share at the expense of other Canadians, not when a million and a half people are still without work.

Trudeau concluded with a call for the nation to work together as it went forward. But it would be a different direction from the one taken by the Republican administration south of the border.[46]

—

At the time that Trudeau made this speech, the Conservatives stood at 50 percent in the Gallup poll and were in the process of replacing Joe Clark with Brian Mulroney. Clark had refused to accept 66.9 percent as adequate support in a leadership review vote in January and had called for a leadership convention. Most expected either William Davis or Peter Lougheed to step up, but both declined, and Clark seemed on the way to a victory. Then Brian Mulroney's well-oiled machine overcame Clark's early lead. Mulroney, who had never sat in Parliament and had lost to Clark in the leadership convention in 1976, was fluently bilingual and, as a leading Canadian businessman, appealed to those conservatives who found Clark weak and too liberal for these conservative times.* In August 1983 Mulroney won a by-election

---

* Mulroney's own political views were secondary to the opposition to Clark. A firm supporter of bilingualism and, unlike Joe Clark, a proponent of the charter and patriation after Trudeau's announcement of his constitutional initiative, Mulroney had strong Liberal ties. In the 1980s he became the president of Iron Ore Company of Canada, principally because of the support of William Bennett, the former assistant to the legendary Liberal C.D. Howe. Bennett's daughter Kristin had dated Trudeau and, in the 1980s, married Liberal MP Doug Frith. Jim Coutts had approached Mulroney about joining the Trudeau government in 1976, an offer he declined. Mulroney claimed that conservative Conservatives were attracted to him because, as he told Peter C. Newman, "I make a point of including people. Clark always excluded all people like Dan McKenzie [a right-wing MP from Manitoba]—he let the press paint them all as crazy right wingers. You disagree with Clark, you get excluded." He told caucus after he was elected: "Do you want to form a government or spend the rest of your time writing letters to the editor?" It was the right question. Mulroney was the most successful Conservative leader since Macdonald. Interview with Jim Coutts, Feb. 2008; confidential interviews; Peter C. Newman, *The Secret Mulroney Tapes: Unguarded Confessions of a Prime Minister* (Toronto: Random House, 2005), 63–64. On the offer from

in Nova Scotia, and in September the Tories stood at an astonishing 62 percent in the Gallup poll. Whispers about Trudeau's resignation became murmurs and then, in the late fall, loud declarations from Liberal riding presidents, Turner loyalists, and even some Liberal parliamentarians.

In the Commons and in the constituencies, Trudeau and other Liberals accused the Tories of shifting to the right and embarking on the neo-conservative path. Mulroney, however, refused to be specific, while reassuring Conservatives during the leadership race that "all of the candidates have good policies but all of these policies aren't worth the powder to blow them across the street if we don't get elected." Not surprisingly, the Liberals sought to force Mulroney out of his political hiding places, but he was elusive, and in some cases his policy stances were congenial. Like Trudeau, but unlike Stanfield and Clark, he openly opposed "special status" for Quebec and spoke publicly against opting out with financial compensation.[47] These stances were popular with English Canadians, but the Liberals thought they had the winning issue with medicare—Canada's most popular social program.

Since the 1970s spending on medical care, the costs of which were shared between federal and provincial governments, had soared. In 1977 the federal government had freed the provinces from the obligation to spend transfer funds specifically on health care, and the result seems to have been an increase not only in health costs (from 5.2 percent of Gross National Expenditure in 1977 to 6.1 percent in 1982) but also in extra billing by doctors.

Coutts, see Brian Mulroney, *Memoirs 1939–1993* (Toronto: McClelland and Stewart, 2007), 187. Mulroney says that Trudeau told him after he lost the 1976 Conservative leadership contest: "Your election would not have been a pleasure for me" (173).

Mr. Justice Emmett Hall, a well-known Conservative, had condemned such charges in a report in 1981. The issue seemed
perfect: the provinces where extra billing was an issue were the
Conservative Alberta and Ontario. The practice was unpopular
with citizens but much praised by Conservative think tanks such
as the Fraser Institute and by conservative medical associations.
Health Minister Monique Bégin was popular, articulate in both
languages, and ready to fight the conservative establishments. On
July 25, 1983, just after Clark's defeat but before Mulroney's entry
into the House of Commons, Bégin announced that she would
introduce a Canada Health Act that would prevent extra billing.
The plan was to withhold one dollar from the provinces for each
dollar of user fee or extra billing. The New Democrats immediately backed the proposed bill; medical associations and several
provinces denounced it; and Mulroney's Conservatives hesitated.[48]

With the National Energy Program in tatters, the strengthening of FIRA a casualty of the recession, and debt costs soaring,
the Liberal government took refuge in the popular social programs
their party had established in the sixties. In response to the recommendations of the women's movement, it strengthened the
child tax credit and promised improved funding for child-oriented
policies. Tom Axworthy, Trudeau's principal secretary, emerged
from the Prime Minister's Office and publicly presented the case
for progressive policies—and, of course, for the continuing presence
of Pierre Trudeau. His eloquent arguments, backed by polls that
indicated Canadians' continued support for those policies, rallied
the Liberal legions that had fought the hard battles for Trudeau.
Bégin's proposed Canada Health bill got immediate endorsement
from major seniors' groups, and polls indicated overwhelming
support for the bill and opposition to the extra billing. But Liberal
ranks were thinner than in 1980, and many were exhausted. Then,
in December, when the Canada Health bill finally came forward,
Mulroney rallied the Conservatives to support it unanimously. It

was a deft blow that deflated the Trudeau Liberals' hopes for a fight—and a resurgence of progressive passion.[49]

Within the Cabinet, some ministers mused about contesting the leadership while others glanced toward Toronto, to detect signs that John Turner, a favourite of the business community, might come forward to revive the Liberal Party's flagging fortunes. Although Trudeau's defence of equity, medicare, and social programs remained popular with most Canadians, many younger Liberals complained that he was out of step with the times, a throwback to the sixties when all things seemed possible, budgets were in surplus, and unemployment was a distant memory.[50] They were correct: Trudeau's last years in office represented strong dissent from the conservative forces unleashed internationally by Reagan and Thatcher. Spurred on by close friends such as Kidder, Gaylord, Garnett, Pelletier, Marchand, and Hébert, a troubled Trudeau turned outwards and decided to challenge the superpowers. In the words of his sixties visitors John Lennon and Yoko Ono, it was finally time to give peace a chance.

CHAPTER SEVENTEEN

—

PEACE AT LAST

The Cold War was middle-aged when Pierre Trudeau became prime minister. The fears and ferocious enthusiasms of its early years had largely passed, and Trudeau well suited the new spirit, where people worried less about external threats than their immediate surroundings. The challenge of Quebec separation, the provision of social security, and the assurance of economic and political stability emerged as the dominant themes of the later sixties, and Trudeau consistently emphasized that these issues would take precedence in his new government. His attitude reflected a general mood. The halcyon days had ended, when Canada could play its best game on the narrow international playing field on which its youthful exuberance and diplomatic skills had shone among older, rougher, but mostly congenial colleagues in their common battle against menacing and awkward foes.

Even Lester Pearson, Canada's greatest player, had developed strong doubts in the sixties about the North Atlantic Treaty Organization (NATO), of which he had been a founder, and the United Nations, in whose corridors he had won the Nobel Peace Prize. The presidency of Lyndon Johnson and the expanding Vietnam War shattered his confidence in American leadership of the West, the foundation on which Canadian diplomacy had rested. Robert Bothwell, the leading historian of Canadian foreign policy, notes that this "sense of an unsatisfactory present" meant that "it was time for a change, to find someone or something that would cross the political and social crevasse that had opened up under Canada's national institutions." This sense caused Pearson to look to Trudeau as his successor, the contender who promised a sharp turn away from those institutions that Canada and Pearson himself had helped to build.[1]

When Pearson told Paul Martin, his external affairs minister, that his time to lead the Liberal Party had passed, the bell tolled for Canada's activist internationalism focused on the United Nations, close alliance with the United States, military commitment to the defence of Europe, and a key role in building the Commonwealth from the ashes of the British Empire. Trudeau had always stood outside the mainstream of Canadian foreign policy. He had opposed the Second World War and, later, the American-led United Nations intervention in Korea, and he had attacked Canada's alliance politics and Pearson's acceptance of nuclear weapons for Canadian forces in 1963. By the time he came to power, however, the standards had become muddied, and clear direction was no longer apparent. For Trudeau, the neutralism of his fellow "wise men" Gérard Pelletier and Jean Marchand, or of his valuable Toronto supporters Walter Gordon and Donald Macdonald, was not an option. The forces of Liberal tradition remained too strong. Knowing that he could represent a search for new direction while forswearing a clear break with the past, Trudeau found agreement with Pearson on a central proposition: the crisis of national unity must take precedence. It was time to search within, not to project to the world a confident face that concealed a confused soul.[2]

In his campaign for the Liberal leadership, as in the election campaign of 1968, Trudeau refused to speak out against Vietnam (as he had earlier urged Pearson to do), hesitated to renounce NATO and NORAD with their nuclear weapons (as he had angrily demanded in 1963), and stayed clear of any hints of a Scandinavian neutralism (which had intrigued him earlier). Instead, he satisfied his critics by promising defence and foreign policy reviews, recognition of Communist China, and more attention to international development. These policies represented no break with Pearson's tradition, but the difference came in Trudeau's frequent declaration that Canada should concentrate on its own interests and not be driven in its international activities by multilateral institutions and commitments. Canada should no longer be a "helpful fixer" for the world; it was now time to heal itself.

Thus Trudeau—the cosmopolitan who spoke several languages and fancied himself a "citizen of the world," the advocate who had lectured earnest audiences in the fifties on the importance of international policy—now told Canadians that their country and its economic and political interests must come first. Defence of the continent was the proper role for the military; advancement of trade and the economy was the principal task of Canada's foreign service officers; and strengthening Canada's internal institutions was the major concern of government. Like Mackenzie King before him, Trudeau took refuge in ambiguity and evasion. In summarizing Trudeau's approach in 1968, historian J.L. Granatstein, who at the time supported withdrawal from NATO and greater independence from the United States, wrote: "The only charitable solution to unravelling the tangle of Trudeauvian statements on defence policy seemed to be that he was deliberately taking all sides of all questions so that, when the review was completed, he could find support for its decisions somewhere in his past remarks."[3] There is some truth in the charge.*

---

* Although Lester Pearson would agree with Granatstein's vigorous defence of peacekeeping and even of unification as laying "the groundwork for a military

The primacy of domestic over foreign politics is clear in the Cabinet records of Trudeau's early years—and it brought a certain consistency to his first government. When, for example, Paul Martin vigorously defended a continuing Canadian role in NATO, Trudeau responded that one-sixth of the total budget was spent on defence, and as the Cabinet members tried to reduce that expenditure, they were hampered by the inflexibility of this NATO commitment. In a remark that surely irritated not only Martin but also External Affairs Minister Mitchell Sharp and Defence Minister Léo Cadieux, Trudeau mused: "Could the forces be used to build highways, to solve problems of pollution as cadres for social development?" He wanted to retain "freedom for spending," especially as the demands of Canada's social security system, where transfers to the provinces had risen dramatically since 1965, were already challenging budgetary planning. In the end, Trudeau compromised and accepted a significantly reduced presence in

---

force capable of carrying out coherent, realizable roles," he did not share the belief that Canada should pull out of NATO and NORAD, whatever their faults, and strongly opposed the emphasis on the "national interest" in the foreign policy review. In his own copy of the document, Pearson wrote: "Surely a far better foreign policy is that which is based on a national interest which expresses itself in co-operation with others; in the building of international institutions and the development of international policies and agreements, leading to a world order which promotes freedom, well-being and security for all." The copy with Pearson's handwriting was in the possession of Geoffrey Pearson, Lester's son, who shared it with me. Granatstein's later criticisms of the focus on peacekeeping and unification are found in his *Canada's Army: Waging War and Keeping the Peace* (Toronto: University of Toronto Press, 2002), 353–61, in which he presents an excellent summary of Trudeau's defence review and its impact.

PEACE AT LAST 559

Europe for the Canadian military, along with a new focus on Arctic sovereignty and Canada's borders. Just as the Germans defended their homeland, Canada would protect the "peculiar ecological balance that now exists so precariously in the water, ice and land areas of the Arctic archipelago." "We do not doubt for a moment," he presciently told the House of Commons in October 1969, "that the rest of the world would find us at fault, and hold us liable, should we fail to ensure adequate protection of that environment from pollution or artificial deterioration."[4]

In his first years, Trudeau said little at Commonwealth gatherings, avoided pronouncements on foreign policy, and allowed the foreign and defence policy reviews to end with a whimper in Cabinet, thus preventing explosions in the land. Although he developed a taste for political foreign travel and even conversation with foreign leaders, he avoided commitments. During his trip to the Soviet Union in 1971, for example, he recoiled when the Soviets asked him to sign a protocol calling for yearly meetings. Like his extremely cautious Liberal predecessor Mackenzie King, he rejected any notion that Canada was a "great power," adding that he—and Canada—could only "react to those things which are essential to us." To punctuate his point, he added: "We're not, in other words, trying to determine external events; we're just trying to make sure that our foreign policy helps our national policy." Where challenged, Canada would respond ferociously, notably to intrusions by French diplomats, politicians, and agents in Canadian affairs. Here foreign policy did become an important tool in helping "our national policy." But in the whirlwind of multilateral diplomacy, the preferred action appeared to be a tentative withdrawal from world affairs.[5]

The Soviets, who brushed over domestic concerns while pursuing global ambitions, were surprised to see a national leader reject "greatness" when it was thrust upon him. With Trudeau, it reflected his willingness to compromise on his own beliefs in order to advance what he correctly believed was his prime political interest. Those policies he would have favoured had he been writing articles for *Le Devoir* in the late sixties—opposition to Vietnam, withdrawal from military alliances, rejection of nuclear weapons for Canadian forces, and radical reduction of the Canadian military—were politically impossible for the leader of a party that carefully balanced strong Quebec support with generous contributions from Bay Street and votes from urban and middle-class suburbs of English Canada. Sometimes the ambiguity did slip away, as when he taunted diplomat Charles Ritchie that Canada no longer needed the Department of External Affairs, suggested that reading the *New York Times* was more useful than diplomatic dispatches, or directed Ivan Head and a group of younger officers to rewrite the initial defence and foreign policy reviews, which largely supported existing policy.

It was not only the Constitution and Quebec but also the difficult economic challenges of the seventies that kept Trudeau's governments fastened mainly on domestic affairs. Canadian nationalism was a wild beast in those times, one whose protectionist and anti-American directions Trudeau feared. With Richard Nixon as president, most Canadian prime ministers would have kept a wary distance because of his unpopularity in Canada and his unpredictable behaviour. Trudeau was sufficiently shrewd to realize that Canada's relationship with the United States was the principal foreign policy concern, and he trod diffidently as a result. Canada under Trudeau chose its initiatives carefully: the law of the sea; protection of Arctic waters; advancement of détente and human migration through the Helsinki agreements; mediation within the Commonwealth; and development of a "third option" to the close economic embrace of the United States. In these initiatives, described well by Trudeau and Head in their memoir *The Canadian Way*, Trudeau's intelligence, linguistic abilities, and personal charm usually advanced Canadian interests.

Those qualities became more widely visible when Canada joined the G7 in 1976 and Trudeau developed, for the first time, close personal ties with major Western leaders, most notably President Jimmy Carter and German chancellor Helmut Schmidt. With the election of René Lévesque, Trudeau took advantage of his ties with Carter to ensure American support for a united Canada, and he capitalized on his long tenure in office to contrast his international experience and reputation with those of the new Conservative leader, Joe Clark. In a series of initiatives, he called for general nuclear "suffocation" in all countries and acted as a mediator between the wealthy Western democracies and the developing world. He clearly revelled in his much greater exposure on the world stage, particularly his role within the G7. For a while it seemed that the hesitant internationalist might become a major figure on a global stage where actors from the developing world were not fringe players. But it was too late; Clark's triumph in the spring 1979 election ended those dreams.[6]

Writing in 1981, three Canadian academics praised Trudeau's recent international activities and his accomplished style but concluded that "the image which persisted among many [is] still that of Trudeau the new prime minister, sliding down the banister at an early meeting." In support of their argument, they pointed to a 1978 special issue of the *International Journal* in which the various authors expressed their sharp disappointment with Trudeau's foreign policy. In the lead article, Harald Von Riekhoff, a political scientist at Carleton University, summarized the general opinion: "In assessing Trudeau's impact on Canadian foreign policy, we are . . . dealing with a residual function of his over-all political activity and hardly the one which will determine his place in Canadian history."[7]

The analysis was unfair. In the 1970s Canada had achieved significant advances in specific areas, although the glamour of the golden age of Canadian diplomacy was admittedly lacking in this workmanlike approach to international issues.* In the eighties the international scene looked less promising for Canada. When Trudeau returned to office in the winter of 1980, a Quebec referendum was in the offing, the Canadian economy was perched on the edge of the worst recession since the Great Depression, and the Liberal Party platform had promised a radical restructuring of the Canadian energy sector which would surely cause domestic disruption. Nevertheless, Trudeau signalled immediately that he would embark on an ambitious international agenda, one that would concentrate on the gap between rich and poor—and the urgent need to close it.[8]

—

Even before his election loss in 1979, Trudeau had committed himself to a new direction. In the G7 meetings of 1977 and 1978, with the strong support of Helmut Schmidt and Jimmy Carter, he

---

* There is evidence that some departmental officers found the workmanlike approach preferable to the glitter and pinstripes of the golden age, whose reputed glories caused considerable resentment among the successors of Pearson, Norman Robertson, and Charles Ritchie. In reviewing the memoirs of the tough-minded and blunt Derek Burney, one of the finest diplomats of the later period, the equally frank Paul Heinbecker, who served as ambassador to both the United Nations and Germany, said that Burney's group was a "made-in-Canada generation, tough-minded, self-confident and savvy, even a little ruthless, neither to the manor nor to the manse born, contemptuous of the fake Oxford accents and Ivy League preciousness that many predecessors had cultivated." There are echoes of Trudeau's 1968 attitudes in Heinbecker's remarks. Paul Heinbecker, "Burney's Prescription Is Not a Good Fit for Today's Washington," *Diplomat and International Canada Magazine*, May–June 2005.

had vigorously urged consideration of the interests of developing countries. When Carter first met Trudeau in 1977, Zbigniew Brzezinski, the president's national security adviser, urged him to "recognize Canada's special access and credibility among third world countries, particularly the poorest, and bear in mind that Canadian policy toward China and Cuba has evolved more rapidly than ours." In his reply to Carter's toast on that February 1977 visit, Trudeau thanked the president for his comments about Canada and the "Third World" and pointed out that Canada had become one of the "top four or five nations" giving assistance to developing countries, even though, he concluded, "we in Canada today tend to be a little bit cynical toward the role of Canada in the world and toward its generosity." The "modest" Canada minding its own knitting, which Trudeau had evoked in the late sixties, was becoming outdated.[9]

Canadian money followed where Trudeau's speeches pointed: Canadian development assistance rose after 1974, and the Canadian International Development Agency (CIDA) was reorganized and expanded. By 1980, when Trudeau returned to office, his determination to advance the development agenda was met with skepticism by a new member of the G7 club, Margaret Thatcher, who had become prime minister of Britain in May that year. Formidable, opinionated, wedded to market economics, and suspicious of the Soviet Union and of socialists generally, the "Iron Lady" reacted strongly to the report on North-South differences issued by a commission chaired by Willy Brandt, the Social Democrat former German chancellor: "The whole concept of 'North-South' dialogue, which the Brandt Commission had made the fashionable talk of the international community, was in my view wrong-headed," she later wrote. And she had little use for the multiracial Commonwealth either, which she regarded as "another conspiracy of the unscrupulous and the profligate, given to ideal-istic schemes which had to be tempered by a dose of British realism."[10] Never one to conceal her opinions, Thatcher let Trudeau know quickly that she thought poorly of the proposal by the Mexicans, strongly supported by Canada, that a summit on the North-South divide take place in Mexico to discuss urgent topics such as technology transfer, energy, and food reserves. Trudeau and Ivan Head, now the president of the International Development Research Centre but still close to Trudeau, were already enthusiastic proponents of Mexico's plan. And with Canada due to chair the G7 in 1981, Trudeau used his convening power to place development at the centre of the agenda for the summit and to set the stage for the Mexican event at Cancún later that year.[11]

Before the G7 summit convened at the Quebec resort of Château Montebello in July 1981, Thatcher found a sympathetic companion when Ronald Reagan soundly defeated Jimmy Carter in the U.S. election of November 1980. This Anglo-American conservative romance provoked Trudeau's strong contrarian spirit and stirred him occasionally to tweak the beak of the American eagle; to resist ever more strongly the conservative tides that were sweeping through the Canadian media, economics departments, think tanks, Bay Street, and some government departments; and to become a countervailing force against the strong currents looking to limit the role of the state. Because of his determination to advance his development agenda and his concern about Reagan's and Thatcher's impact on both international affairs and Canadian domestic politics, Trudeau regularly eclipsed Mark MacGuigan, the external affairs minister, and placed himself at the centre of Canada's international activities. MacGuigan, who had served without Cabinet position since 1968, quietly resented Trudeau's interventions and grimly endured his secondary status.[12]

In some respects, MacGuigan fit the times better than Trudeau. Carter, with whom Trudeau had established fine personal relations, gave up on détente soon after the Liberal government fell in December 1979, particularly after the Soviets

invaded Afghanistan on Christmas Day and the Cold War began
anew. "Détente," historian John Gaddis writes, "had failed . . . to
halt the nuclear arms race, or to end superpower rivalries in the
'third world,' or even to prevent the Soviet Union from using military force again to save 'socialism.'" In January 1980 an angry and
humiliated Carter withdrew the SALT II treaty from the American
Senate, placed sanctions on the Soviet Union, and announced an
increase in defence spending, which he, Ford, and Nixon had cut
by almost half during the years of détente.[13] MacGuigan, who was
deeply suspicious of Soviet communism, was not surprised, but
Trudeau was very disappointed in Carter's actions. Under the
tutelage of his friend Helmut Schmidt, Trudeau in the late 1970s
had embraced NATO as an instrument of détente: he decided that
Canadian forces should remain in Europe, that defence spending
should rise, that the armed forces should receive new equipment
(notably Leopard tanks bought from West Germany in 1976), and
that NATO should continue its commitment to détente even
as the Soviet arsenal grew rapidly throughout the seventies.[14]
Together, Trudeau and Schmidt disputed Thatcher's caustic
dismissal of Third World interests and regarded the assertive Anglo-
American celebration of the free market as dangerous.[15]

　　When Trudeau returned to office for his fourth, unexpected
term, he determined to focus his attention on two issues of special
importance to him, which he had left unfinished in 1979: the patriation of the Constitution at home and, abroad, the divide between
North and South. Both the left and the burgeoning nongovernmental agencies were denouncing Canada for its failure to achieve
the 0.7 percent of Canadian GDP he had promised for international aid in the 1968 election campaign. Indeed, tough economic
times had reduced the percentage to 0.47 percent of GDP in
1979–80, from a high of 0.53 percent in 1975–76. Aid advocates
also complained that Canada clung to punitive tariffs against
developing nations' products, subsidized agriculture in a manner

that undermined poor countries, and tied too much of its assistance to the purchase of Canadian materials and services.[16]

The North-South Institute, an Ottawa-based think tank created in 1976, assessed Trudeau's legacy in a "report card" issued in 1980 and gave him failing marks on nine out of twenty-one commitments, "unsatisfactory" marks on four, "good" on two, and "excellent" on only one.[17] The young and often strident "new political economy" groups in Canadian universities also castigated the government's record: they used the fashionable dependency theories of international economic development to challenge free-market theorists, as Trudeau did, but also employed Marxist analysis to explain the economic weakness of the South, as Trudeau did not. He therefore became a familiar target for his "hypocrisy," and many condemned his energetic advocacy of development issues in international gatherings as no more than opportunism and cheap politics. Trudeau responded with disdain for his critics and for the Canadian public's seeming indifference to the issue, as he initiated a flurry of activity designed to restore North-South issues to the forefront of the international agenda. MacGuigan later recalled that in dealing with these issues, Trudeau "was filled with youthful vigour and idealism" and, in 1981, was "totally consumed" by the North-South agenda. A critical Margaret Thatcher shared MacGuigan's opinion.[18]

Despite opposition from the Anglo-American conservatives abroad and criticism at home, Trudeau believed that circumstances now gave him some advantages—particularly in the several international conferences scheduled for 1981. First came the G7 summit at Montebello in July, followed by the International Meeting on Cooperation and Development in the Mexican resort city of Cancún in October. All along he had supported the Brandt Commission's call for an international summit to advance "global negotiations," and now it took concrete political form as Mexican president José López Portillo and Austrian chancellor Bruno Kreisky organized the Cancún meeting. As host of the earlier G7 summit, he knew he would have the opportunity to try to steer the West's major leaders to support the goals of this second get-together. The third international gathering was the Commonwealth Heads of Government Meeting, scheduled for September 20 to October 7 in Australia, where Prime Minister Malcolm Fraser shared Trudeau's North-South concerns and where the large majority from developing states would be certain to isolate Thatcher and Reagan's hostility to international economic reform. Perhaps there was a chance.

It was a frenzied year for Trudeau: constitutional battles captured the front pages of most newspapers, the National Energy Program dominated the business pages, and the recession's rapid progress meant that human interest stories, almost always sad, were featured on the evening news. Trudeau missed few steps in the path toward Cancún, even though the constitutional drama and the economic crisis were periodic and unpredictable diversions. He travelled frequently and, his detractors claimed, frantically and expensively. The year began badly, when a planned trip to Austria both to visit Chancellor Kreisky and to enjoy a ski holiday had to be cancelled after a snowstorm stranded him in the resort town of Lech. When he finally emerged, he skipped a visit to Algeria and flew directly to Nigeria and Senegal, where he doled out generous aid and announced his commitment to international economic justice. He later visited many other African countries, where he opposed apartheid, committed Canada to increased aid—0.7 percent of GDP by 1990—and supported a "new international economic order," although he always accompanied his enthusiasm with a caution about the dangers of rapid change.[19]

With his Western partners, however, Trudeau was deliberate and forceful: he insisted that a full half-day would be devoted to North-South issues at the meetings at Château Montebello. By mid-June Trudeau had visited over twenty capitals to prepare for the G7 summit and the North-South discussions. In Ottawa, even international development critic Bernard Wood praised Trudeau's efforts as Canadian "interest in North-South relations reached a high water mark in this country in mid-1981, and the world community looked to Canada as never before."[20] A special parliamentary task force report had called for a new level of Canadian commitment and, unusually, the government responded to the report by permitting a two-day House of Commons debate on development in mid-June as a prelude to the G7 summit. In the debate Trudeau clearly set out his understanding of the problem: "The South is not a myth; it is a group of countries, most of them former colonies, held together by a shared perception of their status in relation to the rest of the world. In their view," he said, "solidarity among themselves is the way to exert countervailing power against the weight of the industrial North. Their vision of a new international economic order proceeds from their common view that the old rules have not permitted equal opportunity or an equitable sharing of the fruits of effort. They are right [that] justice is on their side."[21] Still, the interaction between North and South could be a win-win situation: Trudeau acknowledged that the North benefited from the new markets in the South, and that the new international economic order could contribute to international peace and security.

Despite this nod to the North's self-interest, Trudeau's views were anathema to Thatcher and probably to Reagan too, although the president was temporarily waylaid by an unsuccessful assassination attempt on March 30. The new American administration made it clear that rather than engaging in a vague discussion of aid levels and needs, it wanted to focus on the corruption and economic weaknesses of developing countries themselves. However, as an American official said later: "Canada said no; Pierre Trudeau would not sponsor a summit that would address the domestic policies of developing countries in any significant ways. These policies," he stated, "were not our business."[22] Better known and more intellectually congenial was German chancellor Helmut Schmidt, who on Trudeau's personal invitation spent the pre-conference weekend of

July 18–19 secluded with him at Harrington Lake. In Schmidt's recollection, "the reflective and outwardly almost always cheerful Canadian prime minister was a clever host; he had called the meeting in a large log cabin–style hotel in an almost untouched landscape. None of us could help but feel well here—most especially Reagan." Trudeau had indeed chosen Montebello because he wanted to keep the meetings informal and to encourage direct interaction among the leaders, even though its distance from the capital meant that he had to return by helicopter each night for a press briefing while the other leaders frolicked and hiked. With its river views and rustic style, Montebello echoed a romantic past where the folksy U.S. president felt supremely comfortable.*

---

* When Reagan visited Ottawa on March 10, he had what he termed a "warm welcome" from Canadians lining the street. Curiously, he and his wife, Nancy, were given separate bedrooms—the first time they had slept apart in their married life. On meeting Trudeau, he wrote in his diary: "Discovered I liked him. Our meetings were very successful. We have some problems to be worked out . . . but I believe we've convinced them we really want to find answers." He impressed Trudeau less, particularly when he told a joke about two Israeli soldiers on a patrol looking for Egyptian soldiers, for which they had been promised a reward of fifty thousand dollars for each one captured. They fell asleep, woke up, and found themselves surrounded by the entire Egyptian army. One Israeli soldier turned to the other and said, "We're rich." J.L. Granatstein and Robert Bothwell, *Pirouette: Pierre Trudeau and Canadian Foreign Policy* (Toronto: University of Toronto Press, 1990), 321.

Trudeau met Reagan in Washington on July 10 for discussions about the summit. Reagan concluded correctly that the summit would "discuss ec. Issues, N.-S relationships & some East-West trade matters." They also discussed pipelines and economic policies. Reagan concluded ominously: "I think our problem is that he leans toward outright nationalization of industry." He had

In Ottawa, some two thousand reporters were crammed into hotels, and the social whirl was intense as minor celebrities passed in and out. By Sunday, when most of the leaders arrived, the city was an "armed camp," and Schmidt and Trudeau drove down the river to Montebello together from Harrington Lake. They knew the balance had shifted from the progressive and reformist mood of summits during the seventies. En route to the conference, Thatcher visited Washington, where she and Reagan swore fealty to their common conservative faith on the White House lawn. Mitterrand, the "consummate opportunist," was the wild card at the summit. Many of the leaders had not met him before, and Thatcher even mistook him for a doorman when she arrived at Montebello. His socialist domestic policies, which included nationalization of the banks and reduction of the work week, gave some evidence of his views, but his stand on international matters was still a mystery. In his recent writings he had spoken, as Trudeau had in the fifties, about moral equivalency between the Soviet bloc and the West, but during the brief period since his election in May, he had begun to express concern about the Soviet armaments and their new nuclear rockets pointed at Western Europe. The ingredients were present for a lively and interesting summit.[23]

As it turned out, it was an interesting but unsuccessful summit: when Sir Nicholas Bayne, a distinguished British diplomat, and Robert Putnam, an eminent Harvard academic, ranked

dined with the Reverend Billy Graham on the Friday before he left for the Monday conference, and they had talked about international affairs and the many world leaders Graham knew "thru personal acquaintance." He said little about the summit in the diary but was, as Schmidt reported, enthralled with Montebello, "a marvelous piece of engineering." Ronald Reagan, *The Reagan Diaries*, ed. Douglas Brinkley (New York: HarperCollins, 2007), 7, 31.

the G7 summits, they gave it a "C." Of the previous summits, only Puerto Rico, Trudeau's first summit, held in 1976, received a lower grade (D). Trudeau's hopes for informal, thoughtful discussion leading to serious commitments on North-South issues and the major trade issues quickly dissolved. Things started off badly when Reagan expressed shock on his arrival that most of the staff spoke a foreign language to each other. Then, at the first meeting, he stunned the others when he pulled out note cards for the discussion and read from them. Frustrated, Trudeau insisted on informality, and Reagan switched to telling his favourite stories — during which the Japanese prime minister Zenko Suzuki dozed off and Trudeau played studiously with his rose. When East-West issues came up, for instance, Reagan, in Trudeau's recollection, "launched into one of his anecdotes about his time as president of Actors Equity in Hollywood in the 1940s." He claimed that the KGB sent a priest to "spread discord among the actors in the union." In a private conversation about the Middle East that had occurred when Reagan visited Ottawa in March, Reagan had mused that religion was the answer. Puzzled, Trudeau tried to draw him out. Reagan explained that religion was the key to driving out communist influence from the Middle East because everyone there was religious—Muslims, Christians, and Jews—but the communists were atheists. Everyone else therefore had a common interest in fighting the communists. As Reagan spun out his tale, Trudeau humoured him, slyly eyeing Reagan's embarrassed assistants as he focused his full attention on the president. Reagan's anecdotes amused and troubled Trudeau simultaneously.[24]

Trudeau, however, was less troubled by Reagan than by Mitterrand, who at the Sunday night dinner "made everyone at the table realize that a formidable, and staunchly anti-Communistic, statesman was in charge of the world's third nuclear power." Although Schmidt was cautious about the hard line toward the Soviets taken around the table, he too welcomed evidence that

Mitterrand's statements about the Soviets and the Americans being morally equivalent were abandoned. Moreover, Schmidt had met with Reagan before the G7, and while disturbed by his ignorance of issues, found him much preferable to Carter, whom he saw as unpredictable and emotional. As Schmidt left Reagan on May 22, he concluded: "After four years of insecurity I was once again dealing with a consistent and therefore reliable American president." Trudeau, who liked Carter, yearned for the earlier days of détente, distrusted Reagan's "obsession with communism" and the free market, and wanted the summit to focus on North-South issues, found himself increasingly isolated as the summit began.[25]

The North-South issue received relatively long but truly perfunctory attention. The summit's importance lay in the forceful coalition established between Thatcher and Reagan, whom she protected carefully and whose positions she effectively advanced. Unlike Reagan, whom he treated in a patronizing fashion, Trudeau took Thatcher seriously. He needed her support badly for his constitutional initiative, and she obliged. When Trudeau was asked to give a generous speech after the November 1981 resolution to the first ministers' conference on the Constitution, he told aides that if they forced him to do so, he would say that Premier Allan Blakeney was hopeless and René Lévesque evil but that he owed a debt to Thatcher, who had "balls."[26] The aides agreed he should not give that speech. Moreover, Thatcher's debating style also impressed Trudeau. She was not anecdotal but, rather, very well informed; she drew her arguments for the free market from the writings of Sir Keith Joseph and the Nobel Prize–winning economist Friedrich Hayek, and her arguments against current approaches to development assistance from the development economist Peter Bauer, whose dismissal of central planning and protectionism in the South eventually became conventional wisdom. With Reagan's inarticulate backing, she effectively made the case for freer trade and market solutions while arguing, with help from Mitterrand and even Schmidt, that the Soviet SS-20 missiles required a strong response from NATO.[27]

On the Tuesday afternoon, Trudeau and his colleagues returned to the National Arts Centre in Ottawa, where he presented a positive spin on the conference in his official host's statement. He acknowledged that before the summit, the presence of four new summit participants and the differences among the nations made many commentators predict it would be a "very difficult summit." Trudeau declared that the prediction was wrong: the summit had created confidence and produced agreements. On trade there was an agreement for more structure and the need for a new trade agenda; on economic policy, particularly the high interest rates in the United States, the leaders agreed that the fight against inflation could not be accomplished solely through monetary policy; on the East-West divide, the current situation with "the Soviet military build-up and Soviet actions in the Third World" required increased "defence capability," although Trudeau emphasized the continuing importance of "dialogue and negotiation." Finally, Trudeau said that the Cancún process, with its emphasis on "global negotiations" to improve the lot of the developing countries, received support: this "openness to the process of global negotiations represents a consensus which did not exist before our Summit and seemed very remote not too many months ago."[28]

Trudeau was right. The Carter administration had refused to consider a Cancún meeting unless a precise agenda with specific goals was prepared. The Reagan administration, however, believed that the meeting could be a useful forum where the demand for "global negotiations" might be defused rather than advanced. In public speeches Reagan and other officials diminished expectations for the conference, while in private meetings they strongly asserted their positions. In a meeting with Ambassador Andrés Rozental, the Mexican official responsible for summit planning, and other officials from Mexico and Austria, Richard Allen, the assistant to the president for national security affairs, said that Cancún could be an occasion for dialogue but not for the beginning of "global negotiations"—a term he claimed the United States did not understand. Rozental assured him that there would be no link between "global negotiations and Cancún," but Allen retorted that Trudeau had said that "global negotiations must replace the dialogue since the latter means nothing more than talk, talk, talk." The discussion ended with Allen suggesting that "Latins have a greater appreciation for imprecision than we do in the US."[29]

As the planning for Cancún continued, Trudeau emerged as a probable replacement for the conference co-chair, Austrian chancellor Bruno Kreisky, whose health problems made his participation doubtful. Trudeau intensified his focus on the process, and in late July and early August, when he visited Africa for a U.N. Conference on New and Renewable Sources of Energy, he rallied "South" support for the meeting. He reported to the conference that the "summit participants in Ottawa demonstrated a readiness to respond more effectively to the needs of Third World countries." The current economic crisis, he averred, should not drive poor and rich nations apart but should bring them together to satisfy their mutual "craving for national and international stability."[30] But that craving had already created different tastes.

Alexander Haig, Reagan's secretary of state, advised the president to take advantage of the occasion to establish strong bilateral relationships with other leaders, to reassure the twenty-two countries in attendance that the United States continued to be "sensitive to the concerns" of developing countries, and to promote free market solutions to global problems. Although Mitterrand had impressed the Americans with his unexpectedly stern anti-communism in Ottawa, he was equally strong in his demand for "global negotiations" and a World Bank energy facility, which the United States opposed. Cancún, then, offered an opportunity to derail such a plan through a bilateral deal with

Mitterrand. Bilaterals, Haig advised Reagan, could be used to promote the American proposal for later subministerial meetings. The proposal was completely insincere: "Publicly," Haig added, "we should say we desire this so the momentum of Cancún is not lost. Privately we see it as a check on the dialogue." In truth, Reagan agreed to attend for only one reason: Thatcher had persuaded him to go "because she thought it important that they should be there to argue the free-market case" and to block plans to put the International Monetary Fund and the World Bank under United Nations control.

Trudeau met Thatcher just before the Cancún conference, at the Commonwealth Heads of Government Meeting in the first week of October in Melbourne, Australia. There he began his remarks by indicating that "Mrs. Thatcher had said, almost wistfully, that the world had not achieved greater stability even though the number of nations in the UN had increased from 50 to more than 150 in the post-war years." The remark probably did not amuse Thatcher, but Trudeau redeemed himself by reminding the non-aligned Commonwealth leaders that Canada was aligned with the West, and that non-aligned countries "should use their influence to make sure that they were even-handed in their arguments." She was surely not so pleased when he declared publicly that 1981 was a historic year in which the world must decide either to fight global inequalities or to miss a great opportunity. With winter descending on the North, twenty-two world leaders then arrived on Cancún's warm sands on October 21, 1981, to face history's judgment.[31]

Trudeau had a remarkable ability to create mental compartments that he crammed with the detail required for the moment— a facility he used to the full when it became clear that Kreisky's illness would prevent him from acting as co-chair and that Trudeau would have to take over. Even though the historic meeting in Ottawa on patriating the Constitution was only two weeks away, he was superbly prepared for the Cancún sessions.

Fluently moving from French to English and then, unexpectedly, to Spanish, Trudeau stood out among leaders not simply because of his commitment, preparation, and linguistic ability but also because of his casual elegance in white suits, silk shirts, and informal clothes that emphasized his lean, well-muscled body among quite a few flabby ones. In the group photograph, which he reproduced in his memoirs, he wears sandals and a stylish, partially unbuttoned shirt as he smiles directly into the camera. Most of the other leaders are wearing suits, with Thatcher in a dark business ensemble with pearls. Reagan sports no jacket and black leather shoes, but he stares curiously away from the camera. Trudeau's experience as chair of many meetings and his strong relationships with some of the participants, particularly several from Africa, helped him to steer the debate. Reagan was, as promised, jolly and cooperative. Thatcher cleverly blocked attempts to create new commitments and, at the final press conference, declared the conference a "success." For her it was successful because, as she wrote later in her memoirs, it had ensured that the "intractable problems of Third World poverty, hunger and debt would not be solved by misdirected international intervention, but rather by liberating enterprise, promoting trade — and defeating socialism in all its forms."[32]

Trudeau and Head were bitter in their disappointment: "The profound ignorance of Reagan about circumstances in the developing countries, and his naïve belief in the ability of free-market mechanisms to solve all problems everywhere, was a depressant." Still, there was a chance of compromise and even success, but the Austrians, seeking an impossible perfection, encouraged several developing nations to scuttle it. The result, Trudeau and Head wrote, was that "a golden opportunity for real North-South progress was lost, cascading the relationship into the depths of Northern indifference for years thereafter."[33] The "historic" opportunity was missed, Trudeau's chance to make a clear mark on the North-South divide disappeared, and Canada and its prime minister turned to other issues and interests.

—

Trudeau's failure at Cancún was followed less than two weeks later by his triumph at the conference of November 5, 1981, when he persuaded all the premiers except René Lévesque to support both the patriation of the Constitution and a charter of rights and freedoms. He had only a brief moment for celebration, however, as the economic crisis caused by high interest rates and unemployment, and a political crisis caused by angry American attacks on Canada's energy and foreign investment policies, required immediate attention. So angry were the Americans that fall that high-level officials considered expelling the Canadians from the exclusive club of the G7. Their presence there, after all, was the result of American pressure on the Europeans in happier times. The interventionist policies of the Liberal government offended Reagan's economic conservatives, and its energy policies, particularly the provision for government "backing in" on previously established American claims, seemed punitive to other Americans who were ordinarily sympathetic to Canadian interests. Partly in response to these problems, in 1981 Trudeau sent Allan Gotlieb, who had been an adviser to him since his days as justice minister, as the Canadian ambassador to Washington. His major purpose was to soothe American anger.* In departing, Gotlieb warned

---

* Gotlieb soon found that Trudeau had another purpose for him: to supervise the building of a new Canadian Embassy. The Departments of Public Works and External Affairs had held a competition, which Trudeau's close friend Arthur Erickson lost badly. Furious, Erickson demanded that Trudeau

Trudeau that there were some within the Privy Council who were anti-American: "Every time you express exasperation with the Americans or utter some criticism, these scribes immediately

---

intervene because he suspected, correctly, that officials at Public Works did not like him. They had accused Erickson, one of Canada's most respected architects, of sloppy presentations that would lead to excessive costs and complications. Trudeau did intervene, Erickson's design was selected, and Gotlieb was now charged with supervising the construction of the new building, even as other Canadian officials in Ottawa made constant difficulties for him. Trudeau, Cabinet colleagues said, always had a strong interest in architecture and would carefully examine models brought before him, as with the model for Vancouver's Canada Place designed by Toronto architect Eb Zeidler.

Trudeau had thought Ottawa a pathetic national capital when he lived there in the fifties because it lacked the architectural grandeur of other national capitals. Facing his last term in office, he was determined to leave his physical mark on the city. His government commissioned the two major museums in Ottawa: the National Gallery, designed by Moishe Safdie, and the Canadian Museum of Civilization, designed by Douglas Cardinal. As the museum was still in the planning stage as Trudeau's political life came to the end, he told his ministers and aides: "I want the biggest hole you can possibly dig." By the time the Conservatives came to office, the hole for the Canadian Museum of Civilization was so big, it was impossible to stop. Gotlieb's frustrations are described throughout *The Washington Diaries: 1981–1989* (Toronto: McClelland and Stewart, 2006). Trudeau's interest in architecture and the plan for the "hole" are described in detail in my interviews with many of the principals at Library and Archives Canada, December 2, 2002 (tape now at LAC). On December 14, 1981, Erickson asked Trudeau to intervene and told him: "Your name frightens" the bureaucrats. Erickson to Trudeau, Dec. 14, 1981. TP, MG 26 020, vol. 2 contains this note and many other letters, including one of April 16, 1984, telling Trudeau that there must be rapid work in Washington or the Conservatives may come into office and halt the project.

telephone around town, intimidating people, telling them that Trudeau was in a terrible snit about the Yanks and so we officials better be as tough as nails in dealing with them." Yet Gotlieb, in reflecting on his final conversation with the prime minister before he departed, said that "Trudeau believes the Soviets can do no wrong" and that the "United States seems alien to him."[34]

These diary reflections were written for the moment and are not a mature consideration of Trudeau's complex policy or of his attitudes toward democracy and dictatorship in the early 1980s. Of course, Trudeau was angry with the Americans, loathed Reagan's approach to international affairs, and believed that the Soviet Union's interests were lost in the "obsessive" anti-communism in Washington and, more recently, in London. And yet, as Gotlieb pointed out in the same diary entry, Trudeau had increased defence spending steadily since 1975, despite economic pressure, and had provided the forces with the new equipment they needed for the defence of Europe against possible Soviet aggression. Moreover, Gotlieb noticed that Trudeau's rhetoric about the Third World was not matched by the realpolitik that marked many of his policies, as, for example, in South Africa.

Despite these efforts, Gotlieb knew that he faced distrust in Washington. With characteristic energy, he placed himself in the whirlwind of official Washington, where he found cold, angry winds blowing northward. He tried to still them, but Ottawa, particularly Trudeau, often frustrated his efforts. Trudeau's apparent indifference to the remarkable rise of the anti-communist labour movement in Poland—an expression of his realpolitik if not his own early support for Catholic trade unionism—irritated American conservatives and, of course, Polish Canadians. When the Polish government, under pressure from the Soviets, imposed martial law, Trudeau's statement in the House of Commons on December 18, 1981—that "if martial law is a way to avoid civil war and Soviet intervention, then I can say it is not all bad"—was even used by the

Polish communists to justify their move.[35] Inevitably, there were consequences.

In July 1982 Helmut Schmidt called on Trudeau in Ottawa, his last visit as chancellor, and told him how "negative" Americans had become toward both Canada and him as the country's leader.* Canada's diplomats had long ago conveyed that message, but Trudeau's animosity toward American foreign policy had become much more pronounced in the early eighties with the renewal of the Cold War. At the Montebello summit, Trudeau was the sole voice questioning the harsh analysis of Soviet motives, and his press conference after the summit did not reflect his genuine differences with the others. In Australia, at the Commonwealth Conference, in the presence of an irritated Margaret Thatcher, he made a plea for a return to the policies of nuclear suffocation in all countries, a stance he had advocated vigorously in the seventies. At that time the Soviets had achieved a strategic balance with NATO through the Strategic Arms Limitation Talks and the SALT I treaty, but in recent years the sclerotic Brezhnev regime had become arrogant and was challenging Western interests in the Third World, installing SS-20 missiles to intimidate Western Europe,

---

* When Allan Gotlieb met Helmut Schmidt in Austria in August 1986, Schmidt remarked, "How nice a man Trudeau was." Gotlieb questioned the statement, agreeing that he was a "great man," but then quoted Lord Acton: "Great men are almost inevitably bad men." Gotlieb, who had been close to Trudeau, Michael Pitfield, Albert Breton, and others, became increasingly critical of Trudeau in the 1980s. His diary suggests that Trudeau's sharp criticisms of the United States and, to a lesser extent, Israel were a factor. When Schmidt was critical of the United States, Gotlieb replied: "I am very pro-American. That is why we must understand how their system works and therefore what is realistic to expect from them." Gotlieb, *Washington Diaries*, 399–400.

and invading Afghanistan. While Western military spending had fallen considerably during the period of détente, Soviet spending had grown rapidly—as was obvious from the endless parade of tanks, rockets, and goose-stepping soldiers in Moscow on May Day.

Carter's response to Afghanistan had surprised Trudeau, but he understood it to be the product of anger and fear. But Reagan was different. On May 17, 1981, at Notre Dame University, Reagan had declared that the future would be great both for America and for the cause of freedom: "The West won't contain communism, it will transcend communism . . . it will dismiss it as some bizarre chapter in human history whose last pages are now being written."[36] The next year it was Trudeau's turn to receive an honorary degree from Notre Dame, but his message was very different. Gotlieb, who accompanied Trudeau to South Bend, said that the speech on East-West relations was "exactly the speech he should *not* have given because it was anti-hardline on dealing with the Soviets." Gotlieb agreed that expression of that view was not "deplorable" in itself, but felt that Trudeau had injected the "moral equivalence" theme into the discussion, in which both the Soviets and the Americans were "bad boys," jeopardizing world security.[37]

A close reading of the speech does not justify the charge that Trudeau suggested moral equivalence between the United States and the Soviet Union, but there is a subtlety and ambiguity to Trudeau's argument that Canada is a part of the Western alliance and that the United States should "take bold initiatives" and "pledge" that "we will not be the ones to start a war." Gotlieb's reaction, which MacGuigan and senior Reagan administration officials shared, reflects the intensity of belief in Reagan's Washington that fruitless and dishonest negotiation with the Soviet Union was counterproductive and that firmness was needed to counter Carter's "spineless" approach to Afghanistan.[38] Trudeau profoundly disagreed, and in the spring of 1982, with arms control in a shambles and the Reagan administration bitterly attacking his government's National Energy Program, the Foreign Investment Review Agency, and the NATO "two-track policy" of rearmament, Trudeau only irritated American wounds. MacGuigan arrived in Washington on June 11 and told Gotlieb that at the NATO and G7 summits in Europe, "our leader constantly contradicted, refuted, and needled Reagan." Moreover, "he was the only one to do it." In Alexander Haig's opinion, Trudeau had behaved "mischievously." MacGuigan, who was present at the summit, agreed. Trudeau's "inner impulse" compelled him to "support the underdog Mitterrand and harass the powerful Reagan."[39] Mitterrand, who had ended the French government's flirtation with Quebec, was increasingly in harmony with Trudeau on international matters.

Rumours, almost certainly untrue, swirled that Trudeau had called Reagan an imbecile. It was true, however, that when Reagan was fumbling questions at a press conference in May 1982, Trudeau quipped: "Ask Al [Haig]. He knows." Such behaviour confirmed suspicions that Trudeau was a dangerous socialist who threatened American economic interests and did not respect Reagan. Even though Canada's November 1981 budget signalled that FIRA would be reined in and that the NEP would never be a precedent for other areas, it was not enough. Canadian conservative columnist Lubor Zink published a scathing article on June 25 in William Buckley's *National Review*, a favourite of Reagan's court. A menacing photograph of Trudeau dominated the cover, and the inside story painted the Canadian prime minister, in lurid prose, as a communist dupe. Shortly afterwards, when senior White House adviser Michael Deaver confronted Gotlieb at a dinner party, he told him that "things went poorly between our two guys at the recent [G7 and NATO] summits" and added that Zink's article "made an impression on the president." "You mean the president read that garbage?" an incredulous Gotlieb asked. The answer was yes. Fortunately, Reagan's own diary suggests that he thought little about Trudeau or Canada in a late spring that saw the British invade the Falklands, Haig resign over policy differences, and the president worry whether his agnostic father-in-law would die without accepting Christ. Reagan's neo-conservative courtiers, however, cared very much, and Gotlieb worked quickly with Michael Pitfield and MacGuigan to try to make amends. Canada, they agreed, could not afford to anger a highly national-ist American administration when the Canadian economy was faltering badly, the president was unpredictable, and the Canadian business community was organizing as never before to counter the Trudeau government's policies.[40]

Their efforts, which included a grovelling letter to Reagan, the replacement of MacGuigan with Allan MacEachen (who knew the new American secretary of state George Shultz well), and more significantly, a commitment by Canada to test the cruise missile within its borders, calmed the storm, but the dislike and distrust of Trudeau abided at senior levels in Washington. The cruise missile and the advanced version of the Pershing missile were the core of the NATO response to the Soviet's SS-20 missiles, which destabilized the balance in Europe.[41] Trudeau had agreed to the "two-track" strategy of confronting the Soviet Union with these weapons while at the same time negotiating arms reductions. He was profoundly reluctant to accept both rearmament and Canadian testing for the cruise missile—a view that reflected the swelling antinuclear movement in Canada and the West. These activists, spurred by the nuclear plant disaster at Three Mile Island in Pennsylvania, stoked by the end to the SALT II negotiations, and fired to a new level by Reagan's harsh rhetoric against the "evil empire" of Soviet communism,[42] promptly took to the streets. Among their targets was Pierre Trudeau—the man who had proudly worn the symbol of peace in the sixties, ferociously denounced Lester Pearson's decision to accept nuclear weapons in 1963, embraced peaceniks John Lennon and Yoko Ono in 1969, cut off nuclear assistance to India when it exploded a nuclear bomb in 1974, emotionally urged the United Nations to suffocate nuclear weapons in 1978, and irritated Thatcher and Reagan at NATO summits with his pleas for negotiation with the Soviet Union. But all was forgotten and nothing forgiven when Trudeau's government agreed to consider American testing of the cruise missile in northern Canada.

Trudeau's doubts about the decision were profound, but Helmut Schmidt was insistent: "Pierre, you're part of NATO and you're part of the club. You have reduced your troops and your budget, but . . . NATO has made a decision to deploy new missiles. I'm going to catch hell for that from my peace movement. You're being asked to test an unarmed Cruise missile over your North." It was, Schmidt said, "the least you can do."[43] For Trudeau, the least was a lot, and the American charge that Canada was not fulfilling its defence responsibilities was exaggerated. During the early seventies, when the U.S. defence budget shrank, Canada's grew steadily. From 1972 through 1978, by which time Trudeau had committed to long-term regular increases in the defence budget, the Canadian expenditure had more than doubled, from $2,238 billion to $4,597 billion, while the United States, taking advantage of the détente dividend, had risen only from $112,934 to $178,189 billion. While it is true that Canada's defence budget dropped from approximately 2 percent of GDP in 1970 to approximately 1.7 percent between 1970 and 1979, it began to rise again under Trudeau in the 1980s and had reached 2 percent when he left office in 1984.* Moreover, the Canadians had significantly

---

* These figures were included in a report produced by the Parliamentary Information and Research Service of the Library of Parliament at the request of Liberal senator Colin Kenny, a former Trudeau aide. When the report was

improved their equipment, with Leopard tanks, Orion patrol aircraft, CF-18 aircraft, and six shiny new frigates.

"Typical sleazy Liberal tactics," NDP defence critic Pauline
Jewett thundered on July 15, 1983, to hundreds of peace demonstrators gathered on Parliament Hill with banners denouncing
Trudeau. His defence and external affairs ministers had just
announced that Canada would allow the testing of the cruise
missile in the North.[44] MacEachen wrote that same day to his

---

released, Kenny compared Trudeau favourably to Brian Mulroney, under whom
defence spending fell almost continuously, reaching 1.6 percent, even though,
in defence specialist David Pugliese's words, Mulroney "brought in a hawkish
defence policy in the late 1980s." He pointed out that Prime Minister Stephen
Harper had increased defence spending to only 1.2 percent of GDP, far lower
than the 2.1 percent average of the Trudeau years. "They talk the talk but when it
comes time to walk the walk they're just not there," Kenny charged. "They don't
even come close to the so-called pinko days of Mr. Trudeau." (Pugliese's story,
with Kenny's statement, appeared in the National Post, Dec. 4, 2007.)

The Conference of Defence Associations (CDA) responded by pointing out
that defence spending under Liberal prime minister Louis St. Laurent had aver-
aged 6.5 percent; under Conservative John Diefenbaker, 5.4 percent; and under
Lester Pearson, 3.8 percent. Citing J.L. Granatstein's Who Killed the Canadian
Military? (Toronto: HarperCollins, 2004), which called Trudeau "indifferent" to
defence needs, with an "anti-military attitude"(116–17), the CDA stressed that
Trudeau's record should be compared to that of his predecessors, not his successors, and that spending under Trudeau, in terms of the percentage of GDP
among Canada's NATO allies, fell short. Although sharply critical of Trudeau,
Granatstein does admit that Trudeau reflected the views of Canadians at the
time. A research report produced for this book by Tavis Harris, a military historian, assembled articles from the 1970s which reflect the strong anti-military sentiment present at the time, even in such unexpected locations as the editorial

586   JUST WATCH ME

friend George Shultz, telling him that the cruise missile decision had been a "serious concern" for the Canadian government. Now that it was made, the government must be able "to assure the Canadian public that the arms control aspect of the negotiations in Geneva is being pursued as vigorously and as earnestly as is the deployment of new missiles." He concluded in a surprisingly personal note: "As you may be aware, George, one of our major long-standing preoccupations in Canada has been and continues to be our firm belief that the problem of verification is at the core of the disarmament and arms control issues."[45] For many Canadians it was not truly a "preoccupation," though it increasingly was one for Trudeau and some of his closest friends.

---

board of the *Globe and Mail*. There were strong forces urging greater defence expenditures in the business community, particularly on equipment spending, and in the Maritimes, where in many areas the economy was dependent on defence expenditure. Col. Alain Pellerin of the Conference of Defence Associations and the office of Senator Kenny assisted Harris in his work.

Trudeau's greatest impact on the Canadian military was his insistence on bilingualism in the armed services, a part of Canada's government where francophones were very much underrepresented and where the use of French was rare. By 1993 the percentage of francophones in the military was 27 percent, higher than that in the general population, and functional bilingualism was a requirement for promotion above the rank of lieutenant-colonel. Despite much bitterness and complaint, the result, Granatstein writes approvingly, was an army that "was a better reflection of the country's duality than almost any federal institution — indeed, better than any Canadian institution of any kind." Granatstein, *Canada's Army*, 372.

Trudeau's son Alexandre joined the Canadian Reserves when he was a student at McGill University in the mid-1990s, trained at Camp Gagetown in New Brunswick, and was commissioned as a second lieutenant.

—

Trudeau paid little attention to Jewett, a former Liberal MP, but protests by students against his defence policy stung him sharply. For the first time in his life, on defence and nuclear issues, he found himself on the wrong side of the barricades—as some of his friends regularly reminded him. In 1983 Gale Zoë Garnett, who remained close to Andreas Papandreou, expressed the Greek prime minister's profound doubts about American leadership— views that Trudeau knew well from NATO meetings, where Papandreou railed against the policies of Reagan and Thatcher.

Even more virulent was Margot Kidder, ever the peace activist, as she had been when she first met Trudeau and wrote a letter to her prime minister asking that Canada oppose nuclear weapons. Trudeau told her, correctly, that Canada, as a NATO member, had no choice but to lend support for these weapons— the key component in the NATO arsenal. Nevertheless, he asked to meet her to discuss the question. Not for the first time, "peace" was hardly the real purpose for his invitation—but it became important in 1983 as their relationship flourished.

Trudeau asked Ambassador Allan Gotlieb to invite Kidder to a dinner when he visited Washington on April 26–27, and Gotlieb agreed, noting that "the Vancouver lady will add glamour and a dose of Hollywood radical chic" to the occasion. At the black-tie event, held under a tent in the embassy garden, celebrities, including Christopher Plummer, Donald Sutherland, and Norman Jewison, enjoyed "Newfoundland halibut, Quebec maple surprise, Manitoba whitefish caviar," and other delicacies. Kidder, sitting beside Trudeau, argued vehemently with senior Reagan administration officials while he urged her on by squeezing her thigh each time she scored a point. There was "much gossiping throughout the evening about the fact" that the National Film Board production celebrating Australian antinuclear activist Helen Caldicott had won the Academy Award. Later, Trudeau danced slowly and sometimes frenetically, but always exquisitely, with Kidder. In Gotlieb's view, the prime minister's "mysterious magnetism" and the flavour of Hollywood stole the evening.[46] At his most charismatic, Trudeau even charmed the leading Washington socialite Susan Mary Alsop to the point where she asked if she could write an article for *Architectural Digest* on the extensive renovations he had recently made to his art deco house in Montreal.*

The next morning, Gotlieb found Trudeau exhausted when he picked him up for his meeting with Reagan and senior officials, and he blamed Kidder. During the discussions, Trudeau pressed the arms issue, but to Gotlieb's delight he also praised the president's speech from the previous night and warmly acknowledged the United States' role as the true leader of the West.

Fortunately, Kidder did not hear the remarks. Encouraged by their wildly successful date, she sent Trudeau a formal letter on

---

* Alsop, the wife of prominent columnist Joseph Alsop and a descendant of John Jay, the first chief justice of the United States, had once declared that she saw "no future in being an ordinary person." She did write the article, "Architectural Digest Visits: Pierre Trudeau," which describes the remarkable renovations of the Cormier art deco house (*Architectural Digest* 1, 1986, 106–13). Trudeau's pride in the house was evident in an exchange with Barbra Streisand. He sent her photographs of the house in 1983, to which she replied: "I'll show you mine . . . if you show me yours! My deco house, that is!" Streisand had developed a strong interest in art deco and believes that she may have been responsible for Trudeau's choice of home. They often discussed architecture when they met. Unfortunately, she was not able to tour Trudeau's Montreal home until after his death, when Justin Trudeau showed her around it. Interview with Barbra Streisand, July 2009. Streisand to Trudeau, nd, TP, MG 26 020, vol. 11, file 11-57, LAC. The description of Alsop comes from her obituary in the *New York Times*, Aug. 20, 2004.

May 17, arguing for a nuclear "freeze" and urging him to meet peace activists Randy Forsberg and Helen Caldicott. She was troubled by the "premises" in a letter he had sent to peace activists in Canada. Still, he was her best hope: if the "Conservatives get in, we in the Peace Movement are up shit creek without a paddle," she said. "We have a vested interest, to say the least, in keeping you in power. You're a potential ally. (I'll get you on our side if it kills me.)" She promised to see him in July, when he would have to listen to her arguments against the cruise missile and respond to them, "if you're to have any credibility at all regarding your present position on it." She urged him to speak to liberal American senators who opposed cruise testing and suggested that she would join the Liberal Party to stir up enough "shit to make sure the issue of nuclear arms gets on the party platform." In conclusion, she summarized her confusion:

> This is weird. I've never mixed politics & romance before. At least not when I'm dealing with someone who appears to be on the "other side."
>
> I think of you often with confusion, with fondness, with many questions about what it is you might want from me. But I do think of you often, so I hope you're flattered. (Isn't it the *man* who's supposed to say this stuff?) I'm too spoiled. I'm too used to being courted. Oh well, fuck it. Love, Margot.[47]

Slowly, Pierre began to shift to her side.

The Williamsburg G7 summit took place shortly after this exchange with Kidder. Trudeau arrived in the historic American town fresh from two days of meetings in Ottawa with Mikhail Gorbachev, the impressive Soviet agriculture minister. In the foul Cold War climate of 1983, a session with Gorbachev had political costs for Trudeau, and he initially hesitated to see him just before the summit. However, he trusted Soviet ambassador Alexander

Yakovlev, who told him he simply must meet Gorbachev. "Why?" Trudeau asked. "Gorbachev is the future leader of our country," Yakovlev replied.[48] The meeting took place, and to Yakovlev's surprise, Trudeau confronted Gorbachev immediately and directly, asking why the Soviets were escalating global tensions by mounting the SS-20s. "I am speaking to you frankly, Mr. Gorbachev," he said bluntly, "so you will know there is a lot of criticism [in Canada] of the United States. But on the need for a reduction in the SS-20s we are in agreement." While both men concurred that the Reagan administration's rhetoric was overblown and that the world was increasingly dangerous, they disagreed on Soviet policy since the invasion of Afghanistan. Despite their differences, Gorbachev and Trudeau impressed each other enormously, and Trudeau was encouraged by their discussions to speak out more forcefully at Williamsburg.[49]

Trudeau determined to moderate the hard line he expected Thatcher and Reagan to take there. What he had read about Reagan's recent views troubled him greatly. In a speech to evangelical Christians on March 8, Reagan had intensified the rhetoric, declaring that the Cold War was a "struggle between right and wrong and good and evil." Americans, he declared, were "enjoined by Scripture and the Lord Jesus to oppose it with all our might." The Strategic Defense Initiative, or "Star Wars," soon followed, with its promise to build a shield over America that would end the "mutual assured destruction" on which deterrence was based.[50] The words and the action astonished and puzzled Trudeau, as well as advisers such as his principal secretary, Tom Axworthy, whose brother, Lloyd, both inside and outside Cabinet, was angrily opposing cruise testing. The plan for Williamsburg was to have no draft communiqué from bureaucrats but a discussion and then a statement, in the hope of encouraging an informal exchange of views. Welcoming this informality, Trudeau arrived prepared to talk, wearing a "snappy brim-down straw hat, a well-tailored brown suit, and a long-collared yellow shirt."[51] A much more conservatively dressed and very determined Thatcher came with a draft committing the meeting to installation of the cruise and the Pershing. For his part Reagan didn't bother about his briefing book, and watched *The Sound of Music* with his wife, Nancy, before the meetings opened on May 27.[52]

When Thatcher produced her draft, and Trudeau and Mitterrand objected, even the jovial Reagan lost his temper. During the debate, Thatcher icily mocked Trudeau's fears of nuclear weapons, and with Schmidt replaced by the conservative Helmut Kohl, Trudeau had only Mitterrand as an ally. Annoying Thatcher intensely by speaking to each other in French, they tried to thwart acceptance of her draft but without success. Reagan watched in admiration as Thatcher thundered and dominated the discussion. "I thought at one point," he wrote in his diary, that "Margaret was going to order Pierre to go stand in a corner." Gotlieb sympathized with Thatcher in his diary: "Our prime minister, true to form, is playing the bad boy." While conceding that Trudeau was "probably sincere in his peace-loving role," he could not understand his "lack of acknowledgement of the limitations on Canada's interests in all this." There were many angry moments and denunciations of Trudeau to Gotlieb by American hardliners, but in the end Trudeau did manage to ensure that a short paragraph was added, in which the leaders stated that they had "a vision of a world in which the shadow of war has been lifted from all mankind, and we are determined to pursue that vision." Trudeau smoothed matters by praising Reagan's hosting of the summit both privately and publicly, but, devilishly, he taunted Gotlieb, whom he regarded as too fearful of American conservatives. As they flew back from Williamsburg on a helicopter, Trudeau quipped: "I wouldn't be upset if they were upset with me . . . but I acknowledge it would have been a lot more difficult for you." It was, Gotlieb commented, a "deft twist of the Trudeauvian stiletto."[53]

Trudeau knew he had lost. He left Williamsburg quite shaken, and soon after, the stationing of the missiles began. As Margot Kidder had urged, he called and met with Helen Caldicott, who impressed him. Principal Secretary Tom Axworthy and diplomat Robert Fowler also set up a meeting with Robert McNamara, the former secretary of defence under Presidents John Kennedy and Lyndon Johnson, who had become a strong critic of NATO's policy and the nuclear arms race. McNamara told Trudeau that with East and West now arming rapidly and fears billowing, it was imperative to act immediately. Old politicians simply became "ghosts," he told the wistful and pensive prime minister, and he should act while he still had a political life. Axworthy and Fowler informed him that nuclear dangers were mounting monthly, and he listened to Kidder's taunts about her lover being on "the other side," watched the Caldicott film *If You Love This Planet*, dodged angry protesters chanting on Parliament Hill, and thought about "all the retired generals, admirals, and politicians . . . who had spoken out about peace after they had left office." Finally, he said to himself in late August 1983, "Well, I'm not going to do that. I was for peace before I entered politics, and I'm not going to wait until I'm out before speaking out and trying to get things changed."[54] His time to act had come.*

—

---

* Marie Choquet, a friend of Trudeau and a political activist, wrote to him after an evening at Sussex Drive, two days before the cruise missile announcement on July 15, 1983. She told him to "get moving!" He now had "international stature" while "the whole world is going berserk, largely because of the vacuum or, if you prefer, the complete breakdown of foreign policy in the U.S." In a blunt conclusion, she talked about his sons and then told him:

Trudeau's peace initiative drew on his personal ambitions, and was fired by his friendships and his sense that time was running out, but it also reflected his belief that the world had reached a dangerous crossroads, where a wrong turn could lead to nuclear catastrophe. He was not alone in his fears in the fall of 1983. Yuri Andropov, Brezhnev's successor as general secretary of the Communist Party, and his colleagues in Moscow interpreted the NATO manoeuvres as possible preparations for a "first strike," and the Soviet military was put on high alert. Word of the Soviet fears and action came back to the United States from their leading spy, Oleg Gordievsky, and against the wishes of administration hardliners, Reagan learned about the Soviet suspicions and the high alert from some of his officials. He, like Trudeau, became terrified about the possibility of a nuclear war, but their positions were very different after Soviet fighters shot down a Korean Airlines plane with 269 passengers, 10 of them Canadians, which had strayed into Soviet territory on August 30.

Time is running out and now, more than ever, there is an opportunity for you to do what you are best at: long-term world vision strategy.

Get away from the shackles you let yourself in for by being too docile vis-à-vis your staff and your cry-baby Cabinet & do what you were given the capacity to do.

Otherwise, as a great admirer of yours said to me recently: "I'm so afraid that history will see him as the man of missed opportunities."

Choquet to Trudeau, July 13, 1982, TP, MG 26 020, vol., 3, file 3-3, LAC. Another close female companion of that period spoke to me about Trudeau's mood at the time. Choquet's comments about the "cry-baby Cabinet" were reflected in her memories of the period as well. Confidential interview.

The Canadian Embassy in Washington reported that Senate "doves" had had the "ground cut out from under them," while the conservative response bore a "distinctly anti-Russian flavour" that bordered on the demagogic. The "minority" view was that the incident confirmed the need for "even more strenuous attempt[s] by both superpowers for viable arms control agreement," but the vast majority now favoured Reagan's massive increase in spending on arms to intimidate the bellicose Soviet Union. Reports from the Canadian Embassy in Moscow, where Lester Pearson's son, Geoffrey, constantly counselled against provoking the Russians, found a sympathetic ear in Trudeau's office, though not at External Affairs, where fear of offending the Americans was strong. The minister, Allan MacEachen, favoured a strong reaction, though he had few sanctions left to implement against the Soviets because most of the cultural and economic agreements had been suspended after the Afghan invasion. The Soviet response, at first denying responsibility for the deadly attack and then turning on the accusers, was nasty, brutish, and stupid.[55]

While favouring a more cautious route, Trudeau let MacEachen impose sanctions on an Aeroflot flight into Montreal—an action welcomed by the Americans but ferociously denounced by the Soviet Union. Privately, Trudeau expressed doubts, saying that the harsh response from the Americans had put the Soviet regime off balance and created their foolish response of initially denying the clear evidence of an attack. By October he was expressing his beliefs publicly. He called the Korean aircraft incident an "accident" and later told investigative journalist Seymour Hersh that "it was obvious to me very early in the game that the Reagan people were trying to create another bone of contention with the Soviets when they didn't have a leg to stand on." Both sides "were talking past each other." Tom Axworthy recalled that "a whiff of Sarajevo was in the air." In this tense atmosphere, Trudeau ordered his assistants to begin making plans for an international initiative to start the superpowers talking.[56]

External Affairs grumbled, but Ivan Head, still at the International Development Research Centre, prepared a memorandum arguing for a comprehensive initiative from the two superpowers to eliminate "the fear of pre-emptive strike systems." Canada's position and Trudeau's reputation and seniority among world leaders, he declared, placed "an inescapable burden" on him to act. Robert Fowler, the foreign affairs officer seconded to the Privy Council, wondered whether his diplomatic colleagues were up to the task, and he warned Trudeau that there would be bureaucratic opposition and tangles. Nevertheless, Trudeau persisted, debating intricacies of arms control strategies and listening carefully to an array of experts that Head, Fowler, and Axworthy had arranged for him to meet. On September 21, Trudeau listened to their ideas, doubts, and plans while he rocked back and forth with his head in his hands. At the end of the day, he established a task force to turn the abundant ideas he had heard into concrete proposals.[57]

At this meeting one External Affairs official warned that the initiative could be seen as "political." An irritated Trudeau snapped that officials should leave politics to the politicians. But, of course, the initiative did have a political purpose, as Trudeau himself freely admitted to the task force on October 7. Ever since April 17, 1982, when Trudeau had joined the Queen to sign the Constitution, the Quebec issue—the propeller of his political success—had faded. Lévesque had lost his way, his party divided, and separatism seemed a spent force in Quebec and in Canada. With the economy in dire straits, the only area where Trudeau scored well against Brian Mulroney, the bilingual, youthful new Progressive Conservative leader, was international affairs. Pollster Martin Goldfarb, Tom Axworthy, and Keith Davey all saw potential rejuvenation for the sagging party in the peace initiative—and a powerful argument for Trudeau remaining at the helm of power. Gotlieb, increasingly critical of Trudeau, concluded that the initiative was the "culmination of a lot of planning in the PMO and PCO to get Trudeau back on centre stage and combat his decline in the polls." It was certainly that, but it was also much more for Trudeau. It reflected the challenging and encouraging voices of Kidder, Garnett, and many other personal friends, his desire to make an international mark before he left office, and, not least, a genuine fear as a father of the terrifying confrontation between East and West.[58]

Significantly, Trudeau chose a university, Guelph, to launch his peace initiative on October 27, 1983. There, standing before a row of Maple Leaf flags, he delivered a sharply worded, often eloquent speech, in which he announced that he would meet with the heads of the five nuclear states and other foreign leaders to go beyond the "two-track" NATO approach. He suggested that he would add a third rail "of high-level political energy to speed the course of agreement—a third rail through which might run the current of our broader political purposes" in the interests of peace. He was deeply critical of superpower rhetoric and behaviour, deplored the breakdown of arms negotiations, called for the five nuclear powers to negotiate reductions in their strategic arsenals, yearned for the days of détente, urged the "imposition of a political dynamic upon the static" Mutual and Balanced Force Reduction talks in Vienna, and called on the superpowers to accept "a sense of responsibility commensurate with their power." He pointedly concluded that "you can not make a desert and call it peace."[59]

The crowd, made up largely of students and peace activists, thunderously applauded his conclusion, even though many of them had read columnist Michael Valpy's warning that morning in the *Globe and Mail* that Trudeau had "charmed us eloquently before in the role of world statesman, and failed to deliver." The morning after, Valpy, clearly affected by Trudeau's obvious

passion, saw ironic echoes of Pearson's commitment to active internationalism but claimed that Trudeau's engagement this time was
complete and impressive.[60] But could he rise to the challenge he
had set for himself? The Americans had just invaded the small
Caribbean island of Grenada without informing Canada. Would
they pay attention to Trudeau? Did Canada matter?

Wisely, Trudeau began his travels in Europe, where,
Granatstein and Bothwell write, "the stays were short, the conversations slightly tepid, the press coverage . . . insipid." He had omitted
Britain from his schedule because he had debated the issues of
war and peace with Thatcher in late September in Ottawa. But
Thatcher noticed that the foreign offices were buzzing about
Trudeau's intervention, even though the European press was ignoring him, and she observed that Mitterrand had surprisingly and
disappointingly expressed an interest in five-power negotiations on
nuclear weapons. So the annoyed British prime minister invited
Trudeau to meet her in London, where, at lunch, the "Iron Lady"
memorably told him that "one had to remember that things were
growing again one year after Hiroshima."[61] Trudeau was shocked.

Despite Thatcher's opposition, Trudeau's European trip
encouraged him, and he made plans to raise the issue at the
Commonwealth Conference in India in late November. He
angered Indian prime minister Indira Gandhi by calling for an
expanded Non-Proliferation Treaty, but he did get an endorsement
of the initiative from other Commonwealth leaders, many of whom
had become friends during his long tenure. Then he received more
good news: China, one of the five critical nuclear powers, accepted
his request for a visit, and he flew on to Beijing from Goa. He
managed to see China's most powerful figure, Chairman Deng
Xiaoping. It was a bizarre meeting where Deng, regarded as a
heroic reformer, smoked incessantly, spat into a spittoon, and
refused to be interrupted. He raged on about the superpowers and
told Trudeau that even though a nuclear war would leave two

billion dead, "China would survive." Trudeau cut the meeting short and flew home, arriving on December 5.[62]

He was disheartened with his progress, but Patrick Gossage, recalled from the Washington Embassy to become a press officer on the peace initiative, reported, in early December, that the press was generally supportive. Older journalists remembered the halcyon days of Mike Pearson—a memory the government jogged by renaming the Toronto International Airport in his honour. Within the Liberal caucus, long depressed by bad polls, the initiative sparked new hopes. Toronto MP Roy MacLaren, no peacenik but a businessman with close ties to the military, wrote in his diary on December 7: "International relations given pride of place in today's speech from the throne. And rightly so. Trudeau's 'peace initiative' has evoked a notable response. At a time when many Canadians have concluded—for the nth time— that they don't like him, the support for his four-part peace initiative is overwhelming." A few days later, the NATO ministerial meeting gave Trudeau his first tangible gains: an agreement that ministers would attend an important disarmament meeting in January 1984 in Stockholm and would support, despite British and American opposition, a declaration calling for "genuine détente." Now Reagan noticed, and he invited Trudeau to meet with him on December 15.[63]

Trudeau arrived in Washington just as Andropov had pulled the Soviet Union out of disarmament talks in Geneva and denounced the Americans for duplicity. U.S. intelligence had learned that the Soviets saw NATO manoeuvres as preparations for war, and Reagan, to the despair of his officials, was increasingly anxious to depend less on nuclear weapons. Along with tens of millions of Americans, he had watched the "made for TV movie" *The Day After*, a powerful depiction of a devastated America following a nuclear attack, and he was deeply moved. Hardliners in his administration were angry with George Shultz and others whom they feared were drawing Reagan away from his rigid anti-Soviet stand. A statement Reagan made in the Japanese Diet in November against nuclear weapons and war troubled this group—Richard Burt, Richard Pipes, Dick Cheney, and Lawrence Eagleburger. They were right to worry. What one American journalist has called "The Rebellion of Ronald Reagan" against "hardline" advisers had begun—and eventually it would lead to the remarkable meeting of Gorbachev and Reagan in Iceland in 1986, where both essentially agreed that nuclear terror must end. The eminent Marxist historian Eric Hobsbawm pays tribute to Gorbachev for the initiative, but he rightly adds: "Let us not underestimate the contribution of President Reagan, whose simple-minded idealism broke through the unusually dense screen of ideologists, fanatics, careerists, desperados and professional warriors around him to let himself be convinced" of Gorbachev's arguments.[64]

Reagan's internal thoughts, far distant even to those nearest to him, were unknown to Trudeau when they sat down to speak for a tightly scheduled hour in the White House that December day. With hindsight, it is clear that Reagan was far more receptive to Trudeau's message than either the Canadians or the president's advisers had expected. Trudeau had noticed Reagan's speech in the Japanese Diet, but on Gotlieb's advice, he was "soft" in his approach to his host. For his part, the genial Reagan talked freely about the dangers of nuclear war and the media's distortion of his message. When the two leaders emerged on the White House lawn, both men said that their discussions had been useful, and Reagan bade Trudeau "Godspeed" on his peace mission. Canadian officials sighed with relief.

But even before Trudeau arrived, negative leaks had appeared in the press from American officials demanding that he stay away from Soviet-American relations: great powers did not work through intermediaries, they claimed. Trudeau attacked the source of the leaks as "pipsqueaks," but Richard Burt, a frequent guest at the Canadian Embassy and an influential American official, confronted Gossage, insulted Trudeau, and coarsely attacked the peace initiative with four-letter words. Then, after the generally good press following the meeting and Reagan's comment that the talks were useful, a "senior [American] official" reportedly said off the record, but to a large audience: "Whoever thinks we would agree to [Trudeau's proposals] must have been smoking something pretty funny." Reporters soon exposed his identity — Lawrence Eagleburger, the State Department official responsible for Canada, and Gotlieb's most senior and best contact in the administration. Eagleburger apologized, said his words were spoken in jest, but tauntingly told Gotlieb that some large Canadian corporations had offered him a job. Gotlieb wrote, "I'm not sure he was joking."[65]

Trudeau never met Andropov, who died in January 1984, and his peace initiative flagged after the Reagan meeting. When a reporter asked what impact Andropov's death would have on his initiative, Trudeau continued walking, looked straight ahead, and said, "I won't be seeing him." He and MacEachen fought over whether he should visit Eastern Europe and challenge NATO's tactics there, but he did go, en route to Andropov's funeral, where he met the Soviet president's successor, Konstantin Chernenko. The January disarmament meeting in Stockholm took place with ministerial representation, and Andropov's death brought a pause in the angry rhetoric. However, the peace initiative was clearly losing steam as Canadian officials quarrelled and the international climate changed. In response to press criticisms that little had been accomplished in Washington and that he had been too soft on Reagan, Trudeau noted that his "tactic was essentially to nail Reagan down publicly to the newer and more positive aspects of his Diet statement, and — even more important — to commit him publicly & personally to the progressive statement made by NATO in Brussels." That progressive statement owed much to

Canadian pressure. Moreover, "if [Reagan] should flinch in pursuit of this new course, he can be held to account."[66]

In the end Reagan did not flinch, and Margaret Thatcher, after discussions with Trudeau about his meeting with Gorbachev, decided that the new Soviet leader was a man "to do business with." Trudeau's impact on the end of the Cold War was marginal: perhaps a small push on Reagan to follow the direction toward which his instincts were already leading him, maybe an encouragement to other smaller nations to speak up against nuclear madness, and more likely an influence on Mikhail Gorbachev, whose Canadian visit deeply affected the path of perestroika. However, if Trudeau won powerful friends in Moscow, he offended and upset others closer to home, notably External Affairs, the defence establishments, conservative think tanks, and, more troublingly, some of his old supporters. This disillusioned group included Allan Gotlieb, who increasingly saw the merits of the American complaints about the Canadian prime minister; Mitchell Sharp, without whose backing he would not have become leader in 1968; and Allan MacEachen, who was the key to his return to politics in 1979. And then, of course, there was Margaret Thatcher, who never forgave him for the peace initiative. Years later, MacEachen recalled that at Trudeau's final G7 summit in Britain, Thatcher "could not have been more disregarding toward Mr. Trudeau." There was no reference to his imminent departure from power, and "when he tried to intervene, she would never give him the floor." Geoffrey Howe, Thatcher's foreign secretary at the time, told him that she simply would not mention Trudeau's name. On Thatcher at least, Trudeau had left his mark.[67]

By contrast, the peace initiative brought an outpouring of personal accolades for Trudeau. Margot Kidder forgot the decision to test cruise missiles in the North and celebrated the fact that her close friend was no longer "on the other side." Gale Zoë Garnett, Barbra Streisand, and many others joined the chorus.

Jimmy and Kathleen Sinclair, Margaret's parents, told him, "We are so proud to follow your crusade for a sensible approach to peace and clarity among the nations." Olof Palme, the Swedish prime minister, to whom Trudeau had dedicated his book of speeches on nuclear issues and the peace initiative, praised him warmly. So did many who had travelled the path of peace with him. Patrick Gossage and Robert Fowler remained loyal to the end, and became angry with colleagues who mocked the initiative and questioned Trudeau's sincerity. Thousands of letters poured into his office. Pascale Hébert, the daughter of his closest male friend, Jacques, praised him because he took "the most beautiful path on earth, the path of peace—it is very moving." Sometimes, she went on, when she lost hope, "seeing a man like you, one of the only ones who could appease, subdue, and lead the great powers to dialogue, I am reassured." Her father wrote separately, telling Trudeau that the initiative had a wonderful effect on Canadians, "especially young people!"[68]

Nothing mattered more than young people to Trudeau, but they were not enough. Time had run out for him: the peace initiative petered out in February 1984, and the brief surge in the polls had retreated late the previous fall. The caucus became openly rebellious, the press sharply critical, and future leaders jostled in the wings. There can be no doubt that Trudeau wanted to stay: Tom Axworthy juggled the polling numbers to prove to the prime minister that he remained the most popular leader and that his international stature carried Canadian votes; his female friends worried about the emptiness of his life after politics, which had filled his world so completely; he remembered the frustrations and disappointments he had felt when he briefly lost power in 1979; and he knew that he still had work to do and dreams to fulfill. His physical vigour, his intellectual quickness, and his capacity for work remained at their exceptional peak. But there comes a time in political life when choices narrow quickly, and they did for

Trudeau in February 1984, the beginning of his fourth year in office in this, his fourth government. An election had to be called before long, and most believed that another Liberal leader would triumph again. He, most surely, would not.

Four years before, he had taken a walk on a snowy winter's night and decided the following morning that he had many more miles to go before his political sleep began. Now, on February 28, he left 24 Sussex Drive and walked again into the snow, thinking about the boys, the house in Montreal, and the fights with Reagan and Thatcher, but surely too about the power, the people, and the access that would vanish when the "ghost of power" finally descended. Later, he wrote that George Santayana had defined happiness as taking the "measure of your powers." That night he measured his own and knew that it was finally time to go.[69]

At a fundraising dinner at Toronto's Royal York Hotel, known as "The Last Supper," December 1983. Trudeau's passion for Canada's interests was still clear.

He did it his way. With his boys, after the Liberal Party tribute, June 1984.

The kissing never stopped. Staff and visitors gathered along the halls of the Centre Block, Parliament Hill, to say goodbye on his last day in office, June 1984.

Leaving 24 Sussex for the last time, in his beloved Mercedes, June 1984.

"I spy a Tory!" Trudeau declares to Catherine Clark at a children's Christmas party. "The Trudeau boys," he said of this picture, "also seem to be having a good time." Trudeau, *Memoirs*.

Trudeau was reticent and subdued at this Peace Rally in Toronto in the winter of 1994. Then he met a nine-year-old lad, Jonathan English (my son), and I saw his face light up.

Trudeau, Gérard Pelletier, and Jean Marchand—"the three wise men"—reminisce in September 1986.

Trudeau angrily and eloquently protesting Meech Lake in a remarkable six hours of testimony before a joint parliamentary committee of the Senate and the House of Commons on August 27, 1987.

"The Mess that Deserves a Big No." Trudeau's challenging speech against the Charlottetown Accord, at an event sponsored by *Cité libre*, reversed public opinion. This meeting at the Montreal restaurant Maison du Egg Roll captures Trudeau surrounded by Liberal critics of the accord: Concordia University academic Brooke Jeffrey, Trudeau loyalist Charles Caccia, and Senator Anne Cools, whom Trudeau appointed to the Senate.

—

CHAPTER EIGHTEEN

HIS WAY

Margaret Thatcher humiliated Pierre Trudeau at his last G7 summit in London in early June 1984, refusing to recognize him when he tried to speak, failing to note his upcoming retirement, and neglecting to wish him well for the future. His peace initiative had infuriated her, particularly in the early winter, when he had urged Western leaders to speed negotiations with the Soviet Union at a time when she believed, perhaps correctly, that a demonstration of strength was their immediate need. Ronald Reagan wrote in his diary that Trudeau and socialist French president François Mitterrand usually had a "different viewpoint" but "we overcame them." Still, he continued, "There was blood on the floor—and not ours." As Trudeau, dejected and isolated, gathered his papers at the summit's end, Reagan suddenly sat down beside him and, as others watched and heard, amicably expressed his affection for "Pierre," as he always called him, and offered his "good wishes" for the future. "Reagan didn't have to do that," Trudeau told Don Jamieson, his former minister who was now Canadian high commissioner to the United Kingdom. "Whatever else he may be, he's a good man."[1] But Thatcher's disdain raised Trudeau's fears that he was tumbling into the dustbin of history—and his alarm was justified.

As he drove to Heathrow Airport with Jamieson after the meeting, Trudeau's mood changed abruptly from celebration of the past and reflection on the troubled international present to concern about the future of the Liberal Party after the leadership convention in Ottawa the following weekend. Some months before, he and Jamieson had talked at the high commissioner's residence in London about the next election. Jamieson, a shrewd political analyst, thought the polls were bad and that Trudeau should step down lest he suffer a disastrous defeat. Trudeau, instinctively the contrarian, responded: "Politics is still fun. I enjoy what I'm doing and can't think of anything I want to do more." Now, as the limousine neared Heathrow's VIP compound and officials gathered to escort Trudeau for the last time as Canada's prime minister, Jamieson realized that his companion truly was not "happy about calling it a day." He liked his job and took great pride in it, and resignation was inevitably a loss for a man who hated to lose. Years later his son Alexandre said that part of his father had died that February night in Ottawa, when he walked through the blizzard and discovered no signs of destiny, nothing but driving snow. Never again would he find so fully the challenges he craved and the energy to face them.[2]

Perhaps Trudeau had stayed in power too long. Unlike King, St. Laurent, and Pearson, who guided the choice of their successors, he stood at the sidelines as the next leader emerged. Within hours of his resignation, it was clear that John Turner was now ready to leave Bay Street and would almost certainly win the leadership. The Toronto stock market soared when the news broke at 12:30 p.m. on February 29 that Trudeau was going, and wild applause greeted the announcement at a gathering of oil men in Calgary. Margaret Thatcher was respectful, if a bit oblique, in her remarks, stating that "none of us who worked with the Prime Minister over the years ever had reason to question his commitment to his personal vision for Canada or the ideals he held with such tenacity." Meanwhile, the American government issued a reserved statement in which it wished Trudeau well in his "future endeavors." But an assistant for Republican senator Jesse Helms revealed a wider disregard when he asked, "What country is that?" after he heard of Trudeau's departure.

The provincial premiers also varied widely in their response. Alberta's Peter Lougheed, whom Trudeau had grown to admire, was typically generous and offered "sincere appreciation" for Trudeau's "long career in the public service of the country." Bill Bennett, the Social Credit premier of British Columbia, said only that he would leave it to "historians to measure Mr. Trudeau's stewardship," while Sterling Lyon, the former Conservative premier of Manitoba, freely gave his assessment: Trudeau had been "an absolute disaster." René Lévesque, who was still premier in Quebec, largely agreed with Lyon but tempered his criticism with the words that "in some ways," he was sorry to see him go. Trudeau's vision of a bilingual Canada was unrealistic, but he grudgingly allowed that it was a "potentially generous" dream.[3]

On the long flight home from London, Trudeau surely must have thought about the events of the next few days, when he would hand the leadership to Turner and receive a tribute at the convention. Two decades earlier, he had embraced the Liberal Party only hesitantly, but in the years since, he had stirred its heart and troubled its soul while leading it to four election victories and almost fifteen years of power. His inquisitive mind, trained in the Brébeuf classrooms decades before to present both sides of an argument effectively, pondered what that long tenure had meant for him, for Quebec, and for Canada. Quebec remained within Canada, its citizens' rights embodied within a charter, and both francophones and anglophones could, for the first time, work in and with the national government in either French or English. Canada had become a different country because of his years as prime minister. Yet the federal government was more distant from

Canadians than it had been before, new fissures had opened within the Canadian confederation, and the nation's mood was churlish — very different from that unforgettable summer of 1968, when he, as the Liberals' new leader, made his historic electoral progress across the land into a shining moment of Trudeaumania. And he would be returning home to Montreal, where he would find much hostility in his old haunts of university common rooms and intellectual soirées. Wistful he no doubt was as he thought of what he had done—and, perhaps even more, of what he might have done.

As he remembered things past, he likely turned, as he always had, to what mattered right now. He clung to the remaining fragments of his peace initiative and took heart from Reagan's unexpected declaration that Moscow and Washington must begin to negotiate to end the nuclear standoff. Margot Kidder, the close friend who became his stern critic after he allowed cruise missile testing in Canada's North, had enthusiastically cheered his pilgrimage for peace. Together they shared a new sense of accomplishment when she came to 24 Sussex for the last time on May 4, and later sent him a postcard saying, "And woman's best friend is man (don't tell the feminists I said that)." Among the thousands of letters he received after February 29, many mentioned his last months when he travelled the world for peace. The image lingered as Liberals gathered in Ottawa on June 15, 1984, for their leadership convention, and a few days previously, the respected political writers Sandra and Richard Gwyn had published a surprisingly favourable assessment in "The Politics of Peace." "It roused Canadians and marked Canada's re-entry into the world," they claimed. Geoffrey Pearson, who like his colleagues in the Department of External Affairs had long been critical of Trudeau's idiosyncratic approach to diplomacy, wrote a private letter to the departing prime minister in which he praised the peace initiative: it created a better international climate, he said, and galvanized "the good will of the Canadian people."[4]

Just before the Liberal convention, however, External Affairs ungraciously published critical accounts in its journal, *International Perspectives*, one on Trudeau's peace initiative and the other on his foreign policy generally. Fortunately, only a handful of the thousands of Liberals and hundreds of journalists who gathered at Ottawa's Civic Centre had read it.[5] The leadership race had become more interesting than anyone had expected, as John Turner stumbled at the starting gate. Although a group had formed in Toronto to plan his campaign in 1983, little had been accomplished because Turner did not want to appear to be grasping at power. One of his anxious young supporters, lawyer Alf Apps, told the press that he had supported Turner because he would "clean house" in Ottawa. He complained that he and his group knew Trudeau was "going to resign and all January and February we were trying to get out and organize, but couldn't get the go-ahead. It was like being in a pressure cooker with the lid about to blow off." Turner quickly attracted some of Trudeau's strongest allies in Cabinet to his side and, very cleverly, made the left-leaning Lloyd Axworthy his honorary campaign chair. Still, his Bay Street base positioned him as the conservative candidate — and, implicitly, the opponent of Trudeau's legacy.

The shrewd and popular Jean Chrétien initially believed that because Turner's support was exceptionally strong, he should not contest the race. However, when he heard Turner distancing himself from Trudeau in his March 16 press conference, he decided he would throw his hat into the ring, and he quickly emerged as the populist and progressive candidate who reflected the Trudeau tradition. "Turner," he later claimed, "wanted to create three fundamental impressions. One, that he had nothing to do with Trudeau. Two, that he was to bring the Liberal Party to the right, closer to the business community. Three, that he was to be soft on the language issue in order to attract votes in the West." As the convention neared, he daily gained strength even as Turner became the object of sharp media attack. Through it all, Trudeau remained silent and increasingly grumpy, but he was preparing to steal the show.[6]

In "cleaning house," Turner was expected to toss out, in Apps's words, the "Coutts, Davey, Axworthy, Goldfarb crowd," which many of his supporters, with some justice, blamed for the leftist tilt of the party in recent years. But Trudeau's crowd still controlled the present, if not the future. Davey wrote to Ottawa's favourite son Paul Anka on April 2, telling him that he had "always believed that 'My Way' is the greatest exit song of all time. Indeed," he continued, "your words appropriately describe our Prime Minister." Davey told Anka that with the help of his "friend and classmate" director Norman Jewison, he had arranged for the first evening of the convention to be a tribute to Trudeau. Earlier, newspaper baron I.H. "Izzy" Asper had agreed with Davey that "My Way" was the ideal theme song, but he warned, as he envisioned the scene, "You are going to have a big orchestra because it must go off with a blast and be repeated several times because there will be a long-standing, cheering ovation, and the music has to go all through that part." It should be Trudeau's "exit music, with all the house lights down and a single white spot light on him as he walks out alone, preferably with the three boys, with a single wave to the audience when he reaches the exit curtain." He strongly urged Davey to "have a young man from Ottawa [Anka] sing the song he wrote . . . with a portable mike . . . with a single spot light on him singing it, ending it when he reaches the Prime Minister, where he hands him the autographed original manuscript for the song."[7]

Davey, an American pop culture addict, also tried to persuade Barbra Streisand to attend, offering a private plane to whisk her in and out, but her son's graduation created an impossible conflict. Nevertheless, she did send best wishes to be broadcast across Canada. Anka accepted the invitation to sing in tribute to Trudeau, and he asked Davey how he could "personalize" the song for the occasion. Davey emphasized the peace initiative, the National Energy Program ("the Canadianization of the Oil Industry"), the referendum, the four election victories, and Trudeau's "remarkable style and intellect."[8] And the charisma held: when Trudeau arrived at the convention to pick up his credentials package at 9 a.m. on the Thursday morning, an "uncontrollable mob scene" ensued: the media knocked over tables to get near the departing prime minister, and delegates thrust their programs before a bemused Trudeau, who willingly autographed them.[9] It seemed like Trudeaumania all over again—except that the key player would receive his old age pension the following year.

The sun was still shining when the tribute began in the early evening of June 14. Surrounded by family and friends, Trudeau took his central spot for the spectacle, entitled "Pierre Elliott Trudeau: We Were There." First, there was a twenty-minute film, produced entirely without comment but with many images, including video clips and photographs, and documenting Trudeau's life as the anthems of the age played in the background: "Every Breath You Take" from The Police, "I'll Take You There" from the Staple Singers, and many more. It was, cultural critic Ian Brown wrote, a "political rock video" that its creators privately dubbed "Trudeau's Last Supper." The tributes were warm, generous, often amusing, and brimming with hyperbole. Trudeau wept openly. Finally, he took the stage at 9:07 in the darkened arena, without notes and with the spotlights only on him. As always, he began softly, talking about values, Liberalism, philosopher John Locke, and, inevitably, the historian Lord Acton. The Canada he had discovered in 1968 was an adolescent country, Trudeau said, but during his time it had reached a "certain maturity."

Then, suddenly, he became the gunslinger, his fingers in his belt loop, defiant in his gaze, spitting out his words as he attacked those who had tried to stare him down: "And I have found that in any of the reforms, the difficult reforms that we have tried to bring in my years, whenever the going was tough and we were opposed by the multinationals or by the provincial premiers or by the super-powers, I realized that if our cause was right, all we had to do to win was to talk over the heads of the premiers, over the heads of the multinationals, over the heads of the superpowers to the people of this country, to the people of Canada." That was how "we" had won the referendum, brought home the Constitution, and given Canadians the "people's package."[10] Trudeau had reached the final curtain but, he declared: "Our hopes are high. Our faith in the people is great. Our courage is strong. And our dreams for this beautiful country will never die."

Then, as Davey and Asper had scripted, Anka began to sing "His Way." Of one thing Canadians were certain, through all those fifteen years Trudeau had done things his way. As the crowd cheered ever louder, many were crying and others joined in the music until the end. At that point, Justin, Sacha, and Michel emerged on the stage with "Trudeau" inscribed on their caps, their love for their father abounding, even if they did not understand what he meant when he said: "I want my kids to see that the line of business their dad was in had some importance in the country."[11]

The applause had been deafening when Trudeau described how he had stood up to the Goliaths in Washington, yet the evening throbbed with the vitality of American political and pop culture—from Streisand's breathless words to Anka's celebration, first written for Frank Sinatra: "old blue eyes, the chairman of the board, the leader of the pack." Preceded by comedian Rich Little's mocking imitations of Republicans Richard Nixon and Ronald Reagan, Trudeau's speech eerily echoed Ted Kennedy's farewell on behalf of his fabled family after he gave up the fight for the Democratic nomination in 1980—a tribute to Trudeau's memory and his desire to link himself with the progressive path from which he had often deviated but to which he adamantly returned during his last months in office. There, he had been joined not only by Margot Kidder but also by peace activist June Callwood and nationalist hero Walter Gordon, Pearson's political mentor, who had denounced Trudeau in 1972 because he had failed to challenge the Americans and their Canadian collaborators on almost all issues of concern to them. Trudeau's way had become their way once again.[12]

But it was not the way of most Canadians, who had begun to follow the Americans in their shift to the right.* The next day, Turner, in his speech at the convention, avoided the past while pointing to a future with a more responsible economic policy, less conflict with the provinces, and accommodation toward those who had stood outside the Liberal Party during the Trudeau years. About Trudeau, he said only that he was the "most remarkable Canadian of his generation"—a remark that produced thunderous applause and general agreement, even from Trudeau's critics. On Saturday night, when Turner won on the second ballot, Liberal Party president Iona Campagnolo declared him first in the vote, with Chrétien first in their hearts. Trudeau joined Turner on the stage but said nothing.

—

* There were many tributes to Trudeau. The *Globe and Mail*, a frequent critic, praised him for his vision of Canada and the clarity of that belief: whatever his faults, it allowed, "he stood for something." It also published a tribute by York University historian Paul Axelrod, declaring that historians would rank Trudeau among the "great" prime ministers—with Macdonald, Laurier, and King. However, editor Richard Doyle, later a Conservative senator, ridiculed the tribute, citing the editor of the *Ottawa Citizen*, who called it "third-rate schlock." He added: "He did it his way and, in truth, that is what the convention was about—any way but his." *Globe and Mail*, June 16 and 18, 1984.

When the celebrations ended, Trudeau told the staff at the National Archives in Ottawa that he would begin working on his papers once he was bored. In London he had told reporters that he had no plans for the future apart from being with "the boys." He met with Turner after the victory, requested that some of his favourite colleagues receive positions, and agreed to leave office on June 30. Before he drove away from Sussex Drive in his Mercedes 300SL, he made numerous patronage appointments. Turner announced seventeen others on July 9, when, urged on by caucus hawks and encouraged by polls, he called an election. The new prime minister explained that the appointment of these Liberal MPs to the bench, the diplomatic service, and other agencies had been delayed because he needed to maintain a majority in the House. But the excuse was not convincing. Although Trudeau remained largely absent from the actual campaign, canvassing for only a few old allies, this rash of appointments became a central election issue. In Canada's most decisive televised political debate, Brian Mulroney suddenly turned and lashed out at Turner about them:

"I had no option," Turner replied defiantly.

"You had an option, sir," Mulroney immediately countered. "You could have said, 'I'm not going to do it.'"

On the way home from the studio, Mila Mulroney told her husband, "The earth just moved."

Conservative pollster Allan Gregg told the Tory team that Canadians disliked the Liberals but liked their liberal policies. "These findings," wrote Clarkson and McCall, "persuaded Mulroney to work hard at assuring Canadians that his government would not undermine Pierre Trudeau's legacy and [would] come out four-square for universal social programs, bilingualism in Manitoba, and peace in our time." Privately in Washington, however, he criticized Trudeau to Canadian ambassador Allan Gotlieb, who, fed up with the former prime minister himself, welcomed Mulroney to his embassy in late June. But during the campaign, Mulroney was careful "never to knock Trudeau in public, only Turner." And Trudeau kept silent, although he suggested that Mulroney was preferable to Clark because he spoke directly to the people. On September 4 Mulroney won an astonishing 211 seats and the Liberals only 40. In Quebec, where they had won 74 seats in 1980 with Trudeau, they now had 17. [13]

Trudeau moved into his Montreal home, the art deco masterpiece that was, as Margaret had warned, scarcely suitable for raising three rambunctious children under the age of fourteen, with its marble floors, multiple levels, and original Cormier furniture. Gone, too, were the drivers, nannies, and cooks who had eased life at Sussex Drive.[14] But he managed well. That summer he promised the boys that they would see the places he had visited when he was young, and they were thrilled to know that over the following years they would visit the Soviet Union (where family friend Alexander Yakovlev was making a considerable mark on the reformist Soviet leader Mikhail Gorbachev), China (where the Communist regime seemed to be opening and was perhaps unravelling), Britain (where Trudeau had studied with the great socialist Harold Laski so long ago), and of course Paris (where he showed them a little hotel near Notre Dame where he had lived and debated about God, love, and poetry long into the night).[15]

And there were honours, too. Just after Trudeau retired, the Queen awarded the former rebel against the Crown the Order of the Companions of Honour, which never expanded beyond sixty-five living members, chosen for their exceptional service. And in November he accepted a peace prize from the Albert Einstein Peace Prize Foundation in Washington. Invitations flooded the mailbox at Trudeau's Avenue des Pins home in Montreal, tourists gawked from their buses, and motorists slowed as they passed. The RCMP offered security personnel to watch the house, and he surprised RCMP Commissioner Robert Simmonds when he asked whether he should consider carrying a pistol. Soon after he left politics, he accepted the position of senior counsel at Heenan Blaikie, an enterprising, smaller law firm founded by his former personal lawyer and, later, Liberal Cabinet member Don Johnston, the eminent labour lawyer Roy Heenan, and the prominent Conservative Peter Blaikie. When he spoke to Jim Coutts about the position, Coutts suggested that he could bargain for a high salary. Trudeau replied, "But I can walk to work." And he did just that on most working days when he was in Montreal, sometimes wearing a beret but inevitably dapper and noticed. Taunts were rare, respectful nods many. Trudeau had come home.[16]

His return and his silence were not an exile like de Gaulle's at Colombey-les-Deux-Églises, though there were some similarities in that the times no longer seemed a fit for his large ambitions. The Liberals under Turner were in disarray, while the Mulroney Conservatives were also stumbling badly. Neither side attacked his legacy directly, although the business press increasingly blamed Trudeau for the government's deficit, which continued to rise. Women remained a large part of his life, and he craved their company, especially when they were young.* On November 1, 1985, he met twenty-three-year-old Brooke Johnson, an aspiring

---

* In the early eighties, Trudeau took a particular interest one summer in a parliamentary guide. When he met her on the Hill, he asked if she was free that evening. She said she was going to a party at the home of another guide whose name was Neatby. "Neatby!" Trudeau exclaimed. "I know Blair and Jacquie Neatby well." It was true—he had met them in the early fifties when they were both young historians in Ottawa. That night the eminent biographer of Mackenzie King, Dr. Neatby, was surprised when security officers and a limousine appeared at his home. The prime minister had come to his daughter's party. Conversation with Dr. H.B. Neatby.

616 JUST WATCH ME

actor, at a fundraiser for the National Theatre School, and he first asked her to dance and then invited her to go with him for a walk in the country. Johnson later created a record of their platonic but close friendship in the play *Trudeau Stories*, which gently exposes his thoughts, strengths, and weaknesses. He told her that he no longer read very much, a fact his family verifies. As he always did with women, he wondered what she thought and what the future held. Through Tom Axworthy and Helmut Schmidt, Trudeau had become involved in InterAction, a new organization of former leaders committed to progressive international policies. In her play Johnson asks what the group did. Trudeau replies:

"Oh, we talk about current issues in the world, a variety of things, and try to come up with solutions. . . ."

"That's kind of comforting, that you get together that way, to talk, I mean outside the pressure of the political . . . *hullabaloo*. . . ."

"Well, it's interesting. I hope we accomplish some things."

But he isn't sure. Still, he adds, "It's always nice to travel."[17]

InterAction did bring travel, which Trudeau certainly enjoyed. He told Johnson that he had been in every country except Albania. But belonging to this group also allowed him to reflect on the major topics of the day, along with other retired leaders and a few thinkers such as the eminent but unorthodox Catholic theologian Hans Küng, and his former aide Tom Axworthy. He chaired two "high-level experts" projects, far fewer than Helmut Schmidt and former Australian prime minister Malcolm Fraser, but the results were interesting. The first group studied "Ecology and Energy Options" and met in Montreal on April 29–30, 1989. Its report opens with startling prescience: "Global warming is with us. If present trends continue unchecked, rapid and continuous shifts in climate—including possible droughts in mid-continents and increases in frequency and intensity of tropical hurricanes—accompanied by increases in sea-level, will occur over the next decades." These changes, the report continues, are "bound to endanger the well-being, perhaps the survival, of humanity." His other report, the product of a London meeting on April 6–7, 1991, considered "economic transformation" in the former Warsaw Pact nations. Although supportive of the need to introduce trade liberalization and a market economy into Eastern Europe, Trudeau hesitated to recommend rapid change: "The failure of the socialist model should not be taken as a pretext to advance a 'theological' solution of pure capitalism as the only possible alternative," he said. Rather, the report urged that "time sequencing is essential" and that, in making reforms, the former Warsaw Pact must "make haste slowly."

Trudeau's concerns about making haste too quickly, with potentially disastrous results for the health of any society, were apparent in the mid-nineties, when Castro's Cuba, reeling from the impact of the abrupt end of financial support from the Soviet Union, considered opening up its rigid state socialist system. Because of its historic economic ties with Cuba, Canada became involved in discussions with the Cuban government. James Bartleman, then the chief foreign policy adviser to Prime Minister Jean Chrétien, later indicated that Castro abandoned his plan to loosen socialist restraints after a conversation with Trudeau, who cautioned him about its impact on the social health of his country. No record of Trudeau's conversation is available, but Bartleman's account rings true because of Trudeau's friendship with Castro and his respect for the gains achieved by Cuba in the areas of health and education. In far wealthier Eastern Europe, the rapid end of communism had brought social disruption and sharp declines in life expectancy. Trudeau's report for InterAction reflects these cautions, although it expresses the consistent view that a democratic state with a market economy and a strong system of social support is the best guarantee of Aristotle's ideal of the good life.[18]

Trudeau's conversations with Castro and with other authoritarian leaders are marked by an absence of discussion of human rights. Indeed, Trudeau seems to have been intrigued by strong leaders, even dictators, and especially those on the left, although Singapore's authoritarian conservative prime minister Lee Kuan Yew was a particular favourite. While it is easy to point to Trudeau's Jesuit training, with its emphasis on the role of an elite, and his own early flirtations with anti-democratic movements, as the causes for this attraction, the reasons were likely more diverse: a sense of history drawn principally from the classics, in which leadership plays a dominant role in interpretation; his intellectual approach to Roman Catholicism, with its traditions of hierarchy and obedience, and its historical ambiguity toward the modern nation-state; and, finally, a traveller's sense that different countries develop different systems, all with their own validity. When Trudeau took his sons to visit China in 1990, shortly after the Tiananmen Square attack on students and demonstrators, the Chinese treated them to a series of banquets. In Sacha's memory, "When called to speak, my father would invariably refer very delicately to the sad difficulties that China had recently faced." China, he stressed, "is an ancient land with its own internal imperatives . . . outsiders simply cannot know what is best for China or how it needs to travel down its chosen paths." Missteps in such an immense land, Trudeau later told the boys in explanation, "lead to death and suffering on a gargantuan scale." It was best, then, to make haste slowly toward the spring, when thousands of flowers—liberty, freedom, and democracy—would flourish.[19]

—

The world at the time was much more interesting than Canada, as China and Russia reformed, Reagan and Gorbachev met and talked nuclear disarmament, and the Cold War began its final thaw. Yet the Western world had become conservative, with Reagan and Thatcher bestriding their group like a mighty colossus and Mulroney following in their wake. With liberals and the left on the retreat, there would be no meaningful international appointments for Trudeau, as many had suspected when he undertook his peace initiative in his last months in office. In Quebec, Robert Bourassa made a comeback, sweeping to victory on December 2, 1985. The Liberal win seemed to confirm Trudeau's declaration that separatism was dead, but the aging fighter did not trust Bourassa. People who knew Trudeau best invariably confirm that Bourassa was near the top of the list of people he disliked. Meanwhile, in Ottawa, during his first years in power, the new Conservative prime minister kept a respectful distance—though Mulroney's later animosity toward Trudeau brims over in his memoirs. He called Trudeau on appropriate occasions, as when he received the Order of the Companions of Honour, and he appointed him in March 1986 as Canada's representative at the funeral of Trudeau's assassinated friend, the Swedish socialist premier Olof Palme. Yet Bourassa and Mulroney had a personal friendship, enhanced greatly by Bourassa's quiet support from the provincial Liberals for Mulroney's Tories in his first campaign. They were ready to make a deal.

The deal came together on April 30, 1987, at Meech Lake in the Gatineau Hills north of Ottawa, when after a long day of bargaining, Mulroney and the premiers announced that they had reached agreement on five key items: a provincial role in appointments to the Senate and the Supreme Court; entrenchment in the Constitution of the Cullen-Couture agreement, through which Quebec essentially gained control of the choice of immigrants to the province; limitations on federal spending power in areas of provincial jurisdiction, with provision for both opting out and compensation; an amending formula that gave a veto to Quebec; and recognition of Quebec as a distinct society, along with constitutional recognition of French and English minorities throughout the country. Trudeau had known that the constitutional negotiations were proceeding, and Bourassa had even told him about his five "conditions." Although Mulroney had spoken publicly about the need for Quebec to find an honourable place in Confederation, when he met with Trudeau in the late summer of 1984 he agreed that, if needed, the former prime minister could advise him on constitutional matters.* Like nearly all Canadians, including the participants, Trudeau had been skeptical that the retreat at Meech Lake would produce an agreement.[20]

Knowing that approval from Trudeau would matter, both the federal and the Quebec governments sent representatives to test his reaction. They dutifully pointed out that he had, in the past, supported many elements of the accord, either at Victoria in 1971 or in his constitutional proposals later in the decade. They failed, however, to sway his doubts about the distinct society, the spending power, and the provincial role in the Supreme Court and the Senate. He told Gérard Pelletier that he must speak out to Canadians, and his old friend put him in touch with the editor of *La Presse*. On May 27 Trudeau published his angry denunciation of the accord in its columns. There he called Mulroney a "weakling," an unworthy successor to all previous Canadian prime ministers. Two days later he appeared on the CBC program *The Journal*, where a critical Barbara Frum consistently emphasized that

---

* Mulroney did ask Trudeau if he would advise him on "foreign affairs," and Trudeau agreed. He told him that he should be "friends with the United States" but not "subservient to the American government." Mulroney then irritated Trudeau by calling a press conference immediately after the meeting and making "a big production out of the announcement that Trudeau was going to advise him on international affairs." The Liberals, of course, were not amused. Trudeau, *Memoirs* (Toronto: McClelland and Stewart, 1993), 358.

he stood alone against all the premiers and the three major political parties. Trudeau was not intimidated. In a grey suit with a rose completely open on his lapel, a slouching Trudeau initially showed his sixty-six years. But he soon came alive as he explained that although he had been "remarkably silent" since leaving politics, the Meech Lake proposal put the nation's future at stake, and he would be silent no more. The strength of his passion and the simplicity of his argument—there could not be "two Canadas" in the Constitution—animated and increasingly drove the angry debate that consumed Canadian political life for the next three years.

Once Quebec formally ratified the accord on June 23, the other provinces had to follow suit within a strict three-year limit. Trudeau's attack became a catalyst for others to speak out against Meech: Aboriginal groups had been ignored in the terms of the agreement, women had been excluded from participation in the discussions, and many others worried about a weaker federal government. Historian Michael Bliss has described the problems caused by the lengthy ratification period and the contradictory position of its advocates: "[Meech] was fundamentally a contradictory set of propositions, and as people talked about it the contradictions became very apparent. Bourassa and the Quebecers were saying this was the greatest gain since the Quebec Act, and people like [Ontario Premier] David Peterson and the other premiers were saying, 'Oh, this is just symbolism; it doesn't mean anything at all.'" Trudeau rejected Peterson's arguments directly and most notably when he testified on March 30, 1988, before the Senate committee of the whole, which was considering the Meech Lake Accord.

In a remarkable six hours of testimony, Trudeau began eloquently by discussing why the ancient Greek Thucydides had proved to be so great a historian: he wrote, Trudeau said, knowing that Athens, like all things human, would not last forever. The time would come when Canada, too, would no longer exist, but when it disappeared, "let it go with a bang and not a whimper." As feisty as he was in his conversation with Barbara Frum, Trudeau now called on the Senate, as the chamber of sober second thought, to strike down the agreement. He refused to discuss Liberal leader John Turner's support of the accord; it was governments that made decisions, he countered, not opposition leaders. To assertions that the accord merely corrected what had been left out of the 1982 constitutional agreement, Trudeau replied: "There was no point in winning a referendum if we were going to give to those who lost it everything we got by winning it." When the journalist Michel Vastel began shouting from the gallery, "En français," Trudeau turned on him, as Vastel was being ejected, and said, ominously: "Last time, as far as I know, I spoke in French, and what I said was not widely reported by the French media." Several times sympathetic senators broke into applause, while Trudeau's energy and passion never wavered.[21]

In three years the strings binding Meech together came undone, first in October 1987 in New Brunswick, where Frank McKenna, the newly elected Liberal premier, said he would not ratify Meech without amendment; then in Manitoba, where a minority government depended on Liberal leader Sharon Carstairs, a vocal opponent of Meech; and, fatefully, in Newfoundland in April 1989, when Liberal leader Clyde Wells promised in his successful election campaign that he would reopen Meech. Brian Mulroney wrote in his memoirs that Wells turned for advice to Trudeau, "whom he admired greatly and whose rigid, almost messianic views he worshipped. Trudeau now had his camel's nose inside the tent."[22]

Opposition to Meech in English Canada had intensified in December 1988, when the Bourassa government introduced Bill 178. It used the notwithstanding clause to nullify a Supreme Court decision against French-only public advertising. Turner's defeat in the federal election that year and the ensuing Liberal leadership campaign also made Meech an issue within the

Liberal Party. Chrétien, who had left federal politics in 1985, emerged as the favourite and the heir to the Trudeau tradition, although he remained ambiguous about his opposition to Meech. His leading opponent, Montreal businessman Paul Martin, supported Meech openly and arranged to meet Trudeau for lunch at Montreal's private Mount Royal Club. As they sat in the dining room, recognized by all around them, Martin asked Trudeau why he opposed Meech. "Do you support it?" Trudeau asked, before their food arrived. Martin no sooner began to answer than Trudeau threw his napkin on the table and walked out. Meech trumped manners in the spring of 1990.

At another luncheon in Ottawa, Trudeau agreed to speak about Meech to an elite gathering at the Rideau Club. The invitation came from the eminent former civil servant Gordon Robertson, who frequently joked that he was Pierre Trudeau's first and last boss when he supervised him at the Privy Council in the early 1950s. Trudeau began, as he had in an earlier Senate presentation, by saying that two clear visions of Canada were being presented, one that envisaged a decentralized and unbalanced federation and another that emphasized the equality of citizens and its parts. Jack Pickersgill—the principal aide to Mackenzie King and St. Laurent, a minister under St. Laurent and Pearson, and the best parliamentary performer of his time with the exception of John Diefenbaker—sat formidably at Trudeau's immediate right, hostile to the core. The debate was bitter and direct, and the long partnership and friendship between Robertson and Trudeau ended that day. Trudeau may have been making his mark, but he was also making new enemies.[23]

The Liberal leadership convention coincided with the fateful day of the Meech Lake Accord, June 23, 1990. Just as Chrétien became leader of the party on the first ballot, Meech came apart as an Aboriginal member of the Manitoba legislature, Elijah Harper, refused to participate in the unanimous consent necessary for

Meech's passage. Meanwhile, in Newfoundland, Clyde Wells allowed time to run out on the accord. Meech was dead, and in the eyes of many, Trudeau had been the assassin.

But Brian Mulroney was not ready to give up on his ambitions to succeed in Quebec where, in his view, Trudeau had failed. He returned to the bargaining table, took into account the opposition to the Meech accord, and pointed to what he regarded as the consequences of its failure—the emergence of a new Reform Party in western Canada, which gave articulate voice to its grievances, and even more troublingly, the creation of the Bloc Québécois under the leadership of Mulroney's former Quebec lieutenant, Lucien Bouchard. Arguing that there was one last chance to keep Canada together, Joe Clark, now Mulroney's point man on the constitutional file, used his considerable negotiating skill to bring Wells, McKenna, and other leaders together, including Aboriginal chiefs and the heads of a variety of prominent interest groups. Another accord was reached, similar to Meech Lake but with a "Canada Clause," which was intended to dilute the attacks on a "distinct society" for Quebec. In late August 1992, this Charlottetown Accord received approval from the premiers, Aboriginal leaders, territorial leaders, the NDP, and the Liberals under their new leader, Jean Chrétien. But unlike the Meech Lake Accord, Charlottetown would not be decided by the various leaders alone; rather, it would face a referendum where "the people" would affirm their support in both English Canada and Quebec. The date was set for October 26, 1992—less than two months after its ratification.

Trudeau despised both the accord and the historical interpretation it represented. At the University of Toronto's Convocation Hall on March 21, 1991, with Chief Justice Brian Dickson sitting before him, he attacked the justices of the Supreme Court, including Dickson himself, who had made up the majority in the 1981 decision on patriation of the Constitution. By this decision they had promoted political compromise rather than legality, he argued, and the federal government had been weakened vis-à-vis the provinces as it moved forward on patriation. What the future might bring was uncertain, but, he declaimed, "it is not too early to observe that, with the passage of time, the fading of memoires, the growth of a guilt complex at Queen's Park, plus much falsifying of history in Ottawa, the subsequent allegation—fabricated by many of Quebec's opinion leaders—that their province was humiliated in 1982, gradually took on the appearance of historical fact." As a result the "stage was set for an unprecedented abdication of sovereign powers by the federal government, undertaken in order to placate those very politicians who had merely played the game of 'loser takes all,' and who modestly asked for nothing more than to have their cake and eat it too." Dickson was enraged by this accusation and confronted Trudeau personally, telling him that he rejected everything he said. Trudeau quipped, "Well, I did appoint you chief justice." Dickson was not appeased and said later that "Trudeau would have been better advised to have maintained his self-imposed vow of silence."[24]

Trudeau broke the vow frequently as he challenged the Charlottetown agreement, first in an article for *Maclean's* and *L'Actualité* on September 28, and then in a presentation at the Montreal restaurant Maison du Egg Roll, which was published and widely distributed under the title "A Mess That Deserves a Big No." His impact was immediate and significant: the polls suddenly began to shift from approval to disapproval as Mulroney, whose popularity now lingered below 20 percent, became an issue. In the referendum Charlottetown was defeated nationally 54.3 to 45.7 percent. Trudeau was soon identified as the major influence, and commentators pointed out that within forty-eight hours of his Egg Roll declaration, the polls had reversed from 43 to 29 percent in favour to 46 to 34 percent against. After the defeat, Bernard Ostry, a former Trudeau-appointed public servant, called Mulroney and was, in the prime minister's words, "pretty profane." He had "a few choice words for Trudeau and his henchmen Keith Davey, Jim Coutts, and Jerry Grafstein, who, among other things, 'spend all their fucking time either screwing Jean Chrétien or Canada'— they want," he claimed, "to make certain that no one succeeds where their guy failed." A furious Bob Rae, the New Democratic Ontario premier, blamed Trudeau for making "anti-French feeling respectable." He would "never forgive him" for becoming a source for angry Ontarians who used "Trudeau's words to justify their anti-French sentiments."[25]

Trudeau shrugged off such attacks. The blame rested, he claimed, with those "unscrupulous politicians" who, like Mulroney, gave in to blackmail: "French Canadians will be rid of this kind of politician if the blackmail ceases, and the blackmail will cease only if Canada refuses to dance to that tune. Impartial history has shown that it was exactly this attitude that pushed separatism to the brink of the grave between 1980 and 1984." Mulroney, Bourassa, and, later, Peterson and others, he claimed, had raised separatism from the grave and, in the process, threatened to destroy Canada. It is fair to ask: Was Trudeau's bitter opposition to the Meech and Charlottetown accords driven by personal resentment at being excluded by his successors, by principled opposition to constitutional change, or by a desire to return to the battlefields where he had found past glory? Probably each element played its part, though his closest colleagues and his family members all testify to the fierce passion both these accords aroused in him. Gérard Pelletier confessed to others that Trudeau's ferocity surprised him. For Trudeau, however, that intensity was essential if he was to make the point against a deadening consensus—just as it had been years earlier against Maurice Duplessis in Catholic Quebec. Now, going into a fourth decade, Trudeau deeply affected Canada and Canadians. Charlottetown was his final public performance; it provoked, angered, inspired, and ultimately convinced many. But some old friends, including Gordon Robertson, Bob Rae, and his former speechwriter André Burelle, left his circle with bitter feelings.[26]

—

"He haunts us still," the memorable opening sentence of Clarkson and McCall's biography published in 1990, proved the point as, over the following four years, Trudeau's memoirs and an accompanying television "mini-series" became wildly popular. Even a collection of dense essays on "the just society," with Trudeau merely as co-editor, had perched on the top of bestseller lists for weeks. His publisher and his colleague Ivan Head persuaded him to write a history of his international work, entitled *The Canadian Way*, which was in part a response to Granatstein and Bothwell's *Pirouette*, an analysis of foreign policy under Trudeau, and in part a sustained attack on the Department of External Affairs, which, Trudeau and Head believed, had too often undermined their initiatives.

The *Memoirs* were disappointing. They showed signs of haste and, more surprisingly, demonstrated surprisingly little reflection about his life and accomplishments. Former press secretary Dick O'Hagan had urged Trudeau to write memoirs many times, and he now believes that Trudeau was unwilling to confront his own past, his early nationalism and flirtation with separatism, his private fears, and the contradictions in his views. Many argue that the handsome royalties Trudeau received for the book and the television series provoked him to write and to appear on screen, but the deadlines produced a lightweight product where style trumped substance. As someone who has pored over the early writings of Trudeau, I would add that Trudeau always had difficulty in writing sustained prose. He fussed over every word, changed commas constantly, and revised endlessly. Whatever the deficiency of his memoirs and later appearances, they clearly demonstrate that he was enormously proud of his accomplishments: his polemics against Meech, Mulroney, Charlottetown, Bourassa, and Bouchard all reveal his profound sense of having created a legacy. When Jack Granatstein finally managed to get an interview with Trudeau—in exchange for lunch at Montreal's famed Ritz-Carlton—Trudeau turned on him at the end of dessert. "Why did you say I had corrupted the bureaucracy with patronage appointments?" he asked. Baffled, his host claimed ignorance, but Trudeau immediately referred to page 278 of *The Ottawa Men*, where Granatstein had questioned the recent "politicization" of the civil service. Trudeau had vowed to live in the present, look to the future, and shake off history's cobwebs; but in the nineties the evidence suggests that his legacy mattered greatly to him.[27]

The past mattered ever more as old friends disappeared. François Hertel (the *nom de plume* for Rudolph Dubé), long ago his nationalist mentor and principal confidant, died in 1985. Three years later it was Jean Marchand, whose relationship with Trudeau had survived much buffeting in the seventies. In 1992 Trudeau dedicated *Towards a Just Society* to Marchand: "He died before being able to contribute to the present volume; but the history written here would not have happened, had it not been for the extraordinary man of action that was Jean Marchand." Trudeau himself seemed to cling to the young, and he became closer than ever before to Senator Jacques Hébert, who gained national attention (and a visit from Trudeau) in 1986 when he fasted in the antechamber of the Senate to force the Mulroney government to restore funding to Katimavik, a youth program he had founded with Trudeau's encouragement. Pierre also focused ever more intensely on his sons. Writer Bruce Powe, who met him frequently for lunch during his retirement and wrote a thoughtful book about those meetings, told how Trudeau recalled those times when the boys were "around ten, eleven, thirteen" and he would read to them—Rousseau, poetry, Stendhal, Tolstoy, and many others. Those times were "one of the happiest periods of my life," he mused. But boys grow up, brief moments of their past together remain as memory, and sadness often abides. Perhaps that was one source of Trudeau's intermittent anger in these years.[28]

Once, in the early nineties, the boys got a call to come home for an urgent family meeting. Trudeau had news: he was becoming a father again. He had worked closely with constitutional lawyer Deborah Coyne after she became the adviser on the Meech Lake Accord to Premier Clyde Wells. She and Trudeau had a child together, Sarah Elisabeth Coyne, whose birth was registered on May 5, 1991, at St. John's, with Trudeau listed as the father. The news soon spread, first to the scandal magazine *Frank* and then to the national press on September 6. Both Coyne and Trudeau refused to comment. Trudeau's age, seventy-one, attracted particular attention in the cartoons and media reports, and it weighed on him when he met with his sons. So once again he strode over the boundaries of the generations between them and, that night, read to them from Alfred, Lord Tennyson's magnificent "Ulysses," with the hero on his final voyage, still searching for new experience as he struggles against the tightening bindings of time:

> Old age hath yet his honour and his toil.
> Death closes all; something ere the end,
> Some work of noble note, may yet be done,
> . . . Come, my friend,
> 'Tis not too late to seek a newer world.
> Push off, and sitting well in order smite
> The sounding furrows; for my purpose holds
> To sail beyond the sunset, and the baths
> Of all the western stars, until I die.

. . .

> Tho' much is taken, much abides; and tho'
> We are not now that strength which in old days
> Moved earth and heaven, that which we are, we are,—
> One equal temper of heroic hearts,
> Made weak by time and fate, but strong in will
> To strive, to seek, to find, and not to yield.

Striving, seeking, still finding, Trudeau began his last decade with a new life to share.[29]

Justin was now studying at McGill University, just down the street from Trudeau's home. Sacha was finishing at Brébeuf, where he vigorously debated his fellow students about Quebec and Canada, and his father in the evenings about democracy and anarchism—to which he was increasingly attracted. Trudeau, ever the questioner, responded with a vigorous defence of democracy and the free market and, more effectively, urged Sacha to read Dostoevsky, where he learned about the moral greyness of anarchism. And Michel, who seemed a blend of his two brothers, was also at Brébeuf, enduring the slings of the separatists as his father battled once again in the dirtiest trenches.

In 1993, when the Liberals returned to power, Trudeau praised Jean Chrétien unreservedly in his memoirs—something he had not always done. He charged "that those Quebecers who denigrate the man and his style do so because they don't like what he is saying in defence of Canada." The volume appeared just before Chrétien became prime minister, but Trudeau's influence weighed surprisingly lightly on the new government. The official Opposition was now the Bloc Québécois under its leader Lucien Bouchard, and the third party was the Reform Party—a strong voice of western Canadian alienation. Both parties virulently attacked the results of Trudeau's years in power, and Chrétien's government responded by moving away from past wars—not only

Meech and Charlottetown but also the economic policies of the seventies and eighties, which had produced a large, debilitating public debt. Chrétien told his caucus that never again must the party be smeared as the "tax and spend" Liberals. Trudeau's legacy remained in the shades.[30]

In September 1994 Jacques Parizeau became premier of Quebec. A decade earlier he had stepped away from the Parti Québécois when Lévesque and his successor, Pierre-Marc Johnson, moved toward conciliation with the rest of Canada. In his campaign, Parizeau had unambiguously promised a referendum on separation within a year—a sensible move, given the simmering animosity in Quebec against the recent failures of Meech and Charlottetown and the success of Bouchard in the federal election. True to his word, Parizeau called a referendum for October 30, 1995. Initially, the polls favoured the federalists, but then they suddenly swung toward the sovereignists. The *non* side rallied its forces, and in a huge wave of emotion, premiers, politicians, and ordinary citizens from all parts of Canada descended on Montreal on October 27, where they staged a "unity rally" with over one hundred thousand people crowded into the streets. But no one called on Trudeau to make a speech on Canadian unity—his "magnificent obsession"—or even to join the current leaders on the stage. Alone and rejected, the once fiery orator watched the massive rally in the square below from his office window at Heenan Blaikie's office, perched high above Avenue René Lévesque, where anti-separatists gathered for the rally. That evening Canadians learned that the referendum result was dangerously close—50.58 percent voted no; 49.42 percent, yes.

This near disaster was too much for Trudeau. He turned away from public life, telling Bruce Powe that his dearest hope now was that his children would remember him. He visited Sarah regularly in Toronto, where Deborah Coyne was now living, taking her to the swings in the local park and sometimes on short trips.* He still travelled, and even took on the rapids during canoe trips, but time and fate had finally made him weaker. He began to notice that his extraordinary memory was failing. "What is this thing?" he asked an old friend as he pointed at the bread basket before him. He attended a Toronto celebration of the launch of a new *Cité libre* in January 1998, and when asked why he did not speak, he said openly: "I have no memory." One of those present, Catherine Annau, who made the notable film *Just Watch Me: Trudeau and the Seventies Generation*, recalls the evening when, in her words, the room held "a veritable Who's Who of the English-Canadian cultural and intellectual establishment—of about thirty years ago." She joined the long receiving line, but her "exchange with the Great Man was for all intents and purposes banal." He seemed shrunken and old, but then, as he shook her hand, "a slight smile crossed his lips and a distant twinkle" appeared in his eyes. Some instincts are never forgotten.[31]

His sadness had deepened when Gérard Pelletier died of cancer on June 22, 1997; Trudeau was now the last of the three wise men who had fought Duplessis together at Asbestos, joined ranks to remake Ottawa in the sixties, and battled against separatism in the decades that followed. Pelletier was, he told those gathered at the funeral, "My guide and my mentor. . . . It is a part of my soul that has just departed and that will be waiting for me."[32]

But worse came on the afternoon of November 13, 1998, when his beloved youngest son, Michel, was swept by an avalanche into a lake in British Columbia's Kokanee Glacier Provincial Park,

---

* Alexandre Trudeau commented: "From the little I saw of his interactions with Sarah, he was incredibly gentle towards the little girl, if a little awkward. A grown daughter would have surely made for a beautiful presence in his later life."

where he was skiing with friends. He struggled briefly to free himself from his gear, they reported, before sinking forever into the lake's depths. A week later an ashen old man held by his two surviving sons, with his stricken former wife beside him, mourned Michel in Saint-Viateur in Outremont, the church where he had prayed since childhood. For a time he prayed no more, torn by doubts about a God who would take Michel and leave the wretched body that held his weary soul. He struggled with his faith, talked to his priests, began to believe once more, and finally took refuge once again in the consolation of his faith and its Church.[33]

Then cancer began to spread from his prostate gland through his body, while the Parkinson's disease he had developed a few years earlier advanced and rendered his once mobile face an expressionless mask. He knew the time left to him was fleeting. He began to say goodbye to those who mattered most to him, often at lunch, where he talked about times past, memories shared, and deeds done. Generally, he was reclusive, though he enjoyed visiting writer Nancy Southam in her converted fire hall nearby, where interesting people, including poet-muse Leonard Cohen, often dropped by. Cohen sketched him one day and wrote a short poem about Pierre, whom he admired enormously. On April 6, 1998, *Maclean's* ran a story on "Trudeau, 30 Years Later." His impact on Canada was acknowledged to be enormous, although his influence on the current Liberal government in Ottawa was correctly said to be limited. Acquaintances reported that he rarely had visitors to his home, no longer liked to drive, spoke more slowly, and wore clothes that were somewhat tattered. "Incredibly," one acquaintance said, "he seems . . . to be mellowing." When former Bourassa Cabinet minister William Tetley asked to see him to discuss a book he was writing about the October Crisis, they went to lunch on August 29, 1999, at a Chinese restaurant. He began by talking about Michel and his interest in the environment. However, as Tetley read his own diary entries, Trudeau filled in details, his long-term memory still surprisingly sharp, his anger still palpable. But, Tetley said, he was "never bitter, nor mean or noisy, but very fair, reasonable, quiet and calm." He said that, after lunch, he would walk home up the 102 stairs of the Avenue du Musée. Perhaps he did, but not for much longer.[34]

In 1999 the Canadian Press named Trudeau the "newsmaker of the century."* He refused an interview but wrote a letter saying that he was "at once surprised and quite pleased with the information." Then, in the late summer of 2000, rumours swept the country

----

* Rating prime ministers became a popular sport for pollsters, journalists, and historians as the century ended and a new millennium arrived. Two eminent and playful historians, J.L. Granatstein and Norman Hillmer, asked twenty-six of their academic colleagues to rate the Canadian prime ministers. Trudeau came fifth, behind King, Macdonald, Laurier, and St. Laurent (*Prime Ministers: Ranking Canada's Leaders* [Toronto: HarperCollins, 2000]). However, an Ekos poll in December 2002 found that 32 percent of the respondents considered Trudeau "the greatest Canadian." Cancer victim Terry Fox was second, with 6 percent, while Pearson and Lévesque tied at 3 percent (http://www.canadainfolink.ca/pms.htm). In 2004 the CBC ran an extensive contest, asking Canadians to identify the "greatest Canadian." Trudeau had an early lead but fell behind when, reportedly, environmentalist David Suzuki, a supporter of the NDP, asked his supporters to cast their votes for former NDP leader Tommy Douglas—who won. Trudeau finished third behind Douglas and Fox, the highest of the prime ministers. Journalist Rex Murphy "made the case" for Trudeau (http://www.cbc.ca/greatest/). Finally, in the summer of 2007, the *Beaver* asked readers to identify the worst Canadian. With over fifteen thousand votes cast, Trudeau won over serial killer Clifford Olson, sexual deviate Paul Bernardo, and the runner-up—Stephen Harper, the Conservative prime minister of the time. For friends and foes, Trudeau mattered. *The Beaver: Canada's History Magazine* 87, no. 4 (Aug./Sept. 2007).

that Trudeau was gravely ill. People clustered more than they normally did outside the Maison Cormier, now forever Trudeau's home. Margaret was at his side once more, with Sacha and Justin, when he died on September 28, 2000. Pollster Michael Adams had warned that Canadians were not prepared for the death of Pierre Trudeau and, emotionally, it came as a shock. Peter Mansbridge interrupted the CBC coverage of the Summer Olympics to announce Trudeau's death, and the games vanished as Canadian evening television filled with images of Trudeau. John Ralston Saul would later write that we all think we know him, but "much of that myth of knowing has to do with how we see ourselves through the mirror of his long years of power."

For most Canadians, Trudeau is forever linked with remaking a country where anglophone prime ministers spoke no French, where public servants could not serve a quarter of the population in their own language, where politicians could not break from constitutional links with Britain, where courts shied away from activism, where foreign leaders were not challenged, where there were no separatists in the House of Commons, and where great existential challenges of the nation's future had not been faced for over a century. Others, such as the lawyer Guy Pratte, argued that his vision was outmoded, his approach damaging, and his legacy corrupted. He was, Pratte wrote in 1998, a "failure as a leader." Comparing Trudeau with Lincoln, Pratte asserted that Trudeau lacked Lincoln's pragmatism, generosity of outlook, and willingness to compromise. But history changes focus: for the first eighty years after Lincoln's death, historians chipped away at Lincoln's leadership, excoriated the way his generals laid waste the South, and surrounded their stories with the spirit of Scarlett O'Hara in *Gone with the Wind*. Only when the civil rights movement and the Supreme Court finally gave meaning to equal rights did the clouds reveal Lincoln in his pristine greatness. Trudeau's death removed some of the mists from the mirror, but later Canadians will see his stature even more clearly.[35]

Many responses were elegiac, others critical, but few were bland. Bouquets of flowers immediately appeared outside 1418 Avenue des Pins. Chrétien returned home from Jamaica to the House of Commons, where leaders paid tribute to Trudeau and some MPs wore red roses in his memory. Joe Clark, now leading a Conservative rump, spoke warmly, although a future Conservative leader, Stephen Harper, then head of the National Citizens Coalition, wrote in the *National Post* that Trudeau had "flailed from one pet policy to another" and, when faced with Nazism and fascism, "took a pass." But he was a rare dissenter. Trudeau would have smiled as most of his old enemies dulled their barbs, and he would have enjoyed a *New York Times* tribute in which the Canadian-born journalist Rick Marin talked about his first meeting with "this hip-looking old guy" who walked into a Manhattan dance hall "with a gorgeous chick on each arm." He had "made Canada cool." Trudeau, he wrote, "had style. Almost everything about him was the antithesis of the two men [Al Gore and George W. Bush] jogging for the presidency in the United States." Small wonder, he concluded, that Canadians had "fanatically mourned" this man. And the mourning, if not fanatical, was extraordinary by any standard, and completely unpredicted and unprecedented in Canadian political history. Trudeau mattered.[36]

Thousands flocked to the Hall of Honour in Parliament's Centre Block, where Trudeau's body lay in state until it was taken from the Hill as a band played "Auld Lang Syne." Then, as a train bore his casket from Ottawa to Montreal, crowds unexpectedly appeared in small towns, at level crossings, and in the wasteland along the Ottawa River. In Montreal his casket lay at City Hall, where thousands more lined up to pay their respects before the funeral on October 3, 2000, at Montreal's Notre-Dame Basilica. Three thousand people crowded into the church, including Margaret, with their two remaining sons, and Deborah Coyne, with Sarah. Dignitaries mingled with former and current ministers,

MPs with celebrities, and Leonard Cohen appeared as an honorary pallbearer. Fidel Castro was the sole head of state in attendance, although two of Trudeau's friends represented, respectively, the United States and Great Britain: former Democratic president Jimmy Carter and former Conservative prime minister Edward Heath. Above them in the balconies were others, mostly ordinary folks and young people like my fourteen-year-old son, who had travelled from a distance, stood before the basilica in the cool autumn air since midnight, and finally found their way to a lofty perch, bearing proudly the beige funeral program with a single rose below the inscription "Pierre Elliott Trudeau, 1919–2000." Chrétien read the liturgy of the Word, and Sacha followed with a passage from the Book of Daniel. Roy Heenan and Jacques Hébert gave eulogies, and then it was Justin's turn.

Justin talked about what Pierre Trudeau meant as a father, how the sons knew they were "the luckiest kids in the world." He gave us "a lot of tools," he said: "We were taught to take nothing for granted. He doted on us but didn't indulge. . . . He encouraged us to push ourselves, to test limits, to challenge anyone and anything." Justin recalled that his dad taught him when he was eight years old that he should not mock Joe Clark, that no one should "attack the individual" but should show "respect," even while disagreeing with opinions. From the front pews of the church, Clark, whom Trudeau came to know was a decent man, nodded his head and smiled.

Trudeau demanded much from his sons, but Justin thanked him "for having loved us so much." Echoing Trudeau's essay on canoeing written in the forties, he ended:

"My father's fundamental belief never came from a textbook. It stemmed from his deep love for and faith in all Canadians, and over the past few days, with every card, every rose, every tear, every wave and every pirouette, you returned his love. It means the world to Sacha and me. Thank you.

"We have gathered from coast to coast to coast, from one ocean to another, united in our grief, to say good bye. But this is not the end. He left politics in '84. But he came back for Meech. He came back for Charlottetown. He came back to remind us of who we are and what we're all capable of. But he won't be coming back anymore. It's all up to us, all of us, now.

"The woods are lovely, dark and deep. He has kept his promises and earned his sleep.

"*Je t'aime Papa.*"

Justin then came down to the flag-draped casket, bent to reach out to his father one last time, and placed a rose there for him.

As Justin and Sacha signed the register, the organ burst forth with Mozart's "Lacrymosa." Cardinal Turcotte bade farewell, having conveyed "Pierre Elliott Trudeau to his rest," and prayed that "all that for him was great and holy" would be "respected and preserved" and that "any evil he may have done be pardoned."

The service ended with "O Canada."[37]

After Michel's death, 1998.

Through the following year, Trudeau still walked to his office at Heenan Blaikie. Montrealers respected his privacy and rarely bothered him.

The last time on Parliament Hill.

A family united in grief. Justin's eulogy gave voice to the love and sadness felt by mourners across the country, while Sacha spoke with clear strength the words from the Book of Daniel: "Let him be drenched with the dew of heaven, let him share the grass of the earth with all humankind."

Nine-year-old Sarah Coyne weeps at her father's funeral.

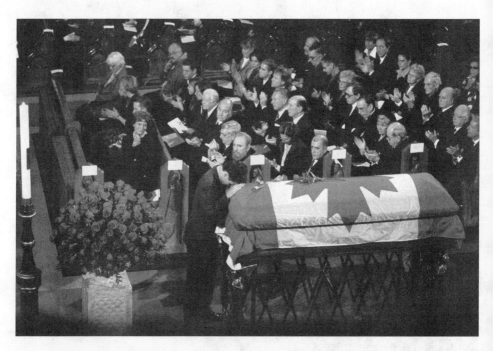

A tearful Margaret looks on as Justin weeps at his father's casket. Seated next to Margaret are Alexandre "Sacha" Trudeau, Deborah and Sarah Coyne, and Suzette Rouleau (Trudeau's sister). At Justin's left is Fidel Castro, Governor General Romeo Leblanc, The Aga Khan, and President Jimmy Carter. Sitting in the final row are Leonard Cohen and two old friends of Trudeau's, Hon. Jacques Hébert and Hon. Jean-Louis Roux, among others.

NOTES

A complete bibliography for both volumes of *The Life of Pierre Elliott Trudeau* may be found on the following websites: http://www.cigionline.org/person/john-english and http://www.randomhouse.ca

Papers, such as the Trudeau Papers, appear in abbreviated form in the notes below. The key to these and other abbreviations is as follows:

ABP Albert Breton Papers
ALP Arthur Laing Papers
ALoP Arthur Lower Papers
AP Abbott Papers
CP Cadieux Papers
EAP External Affairs Papers
GP Gillespie Papers
LAC Library and Archives Canada
LPP Liberal Party Papers
MacEP MacEachen Papers
MP McLuhan Papers
MSP Michael Shenstone Papers
NP Nixon Papers
PCO Privy Council Office
QUA Queen's University Archives
TP Trudeau Papers
TuP Turner Papers
WSP William Seidman Papers

CHAPTER ONE: TAKING POWER

1. *Calgary Herald*, April 8, 1968; Jennifer Rae quoted in Nancy Southam, ed., *Pierre: Colleagues and Friends Talk about the Trudeau They Knew* (Toronto: McClelland and Stewart, 2005), 242; and Margaret Trudeau, *Beyond Reason* (New York and London: Paddington Press, 1979), 29. The importance of Trudeau as a "cultural" phenomenon is brilliantly explored in Paul Litt, "Trudeaumania: Participatory Democracy in the Mass-Mediated Nation," *The Canadian Historical Review* 89 (March 2008): 27–53. Litt notes that "sex denoted Trudeau's radical freedom as an individual. Uninhibited by spouse and family, he was free to consume it." It was a mark of the fact that Trudeau was "with it" (41).

2. Bob Rae, *From Protest to Power: Personal Reflections on a Life in Politics* (1996; repr., Toronto: Penguin, 1997), 40–41; B.W. Powe, *Mystic Trudeau: The Fire and the Rose* (Toronto: Thomas Allen, 2007), 217; *Spectator*, June 28, 1968, 881–82; Peter C. Newman in *Toronto Daily Star*, April 8, 1968; Ramsay Cook, *The Teeth of Time: Remembering Pierre Trudeau* (Montreal and Kingston: McGill–Queen's University Press, 2006), 42. Cook's excellent book makes it clear that William Kilbourn played a much less central role in the Toronto petition than I suggested in volume 1.

3. Pearson made the comment to Bruce Hutchison. Interview with Bruce Hutchison, June 1989. The cartoon may be found in Michael Cowley, *Sex and the Single Prime Minister: A Study in Liberal Lovemaking* (Toronto: Greywood, 1968), np. Pearson's brother-in-law, Herbert Moody, recalled that when Pearson visited in the summer of 1968, the former prime minister became irritated when Maryon and his own wife constantly extolled Trudeau's virtues. Pearson dismissed Trudeau as a centralist and deplored their enthusiasm. Interview with Herbert Moody, June 1989.

4. *Le Devoir*, April 3, 1968.

5. Ibid.

6. Zink collected his columns in *Trudeaucracy* (Toronto: Toronto Sun, 1972), a book in which he claims he invented the term "Trudeaumania."

7. The critiques by Rioux, Dumont, and Vadeboncoeur were collected in André Potvin, Michel Letourneux, and Robert Smith, *L'Anti-Trudeau: Choix de textes* (Montréal: Éditions Parti-pris, 1972). Samples of Zink's

writings may be found in his *Trudeaucracy*. Ryan's defence of Trudeau is found in *Le Devoir*, May 25, 1968.

8. On Trudeau and his mother, see the first volume of this biography, *Citizen of the World* (Toronto: Knopf Canada, 2006), 209–19. The description of his mother at this time is the product of several conversations with family members and friends. On the visit, see *Montreal Gazette*, April 10, 1968.

9. Cabinet discussions of April 17, 19, 20, and 22, 1968. RG2, PCO, Series A-5-a, vol. 6338, LAC; *Montreal Gazette*, April 23, 1968; Pierre Trudeau, *Memoirs* (Toronto: McClelland and Stewart, 1993), 93–98; and Paul Martin, *So Many Worlds*, vol. 2 of *A Very Public Life* (Toronto: Deneau, 1985), 634.

10. The quotations are from Winters himself, who was interviewed by Martin Sullivan in *Mandate '68* (Toronto: Doubleday, 1968), 381.

11. Richard Gwyn gives an excellent description of Trudeau's staff and friends in "Sorcerer's Apprentice," chapter 5 of his *Northern Magus: Pierre Trudeau and Canadians* (Toronto: McClelland and Stewart, 1980). The quotation and the description of the "standpat" Cabinet are found in John Saywell, ed., *Canadian Annual Review for 1968* (Toronto: University of Toronto Press, 1969), 29–30.

12. Cabinet discussions of April 17, 19, 20, and 22, 1968. RG2, PCO, Series A-5-a, vol. 6338, LAC.

13. Trudeau, *Memoirs*, 93–98; and Martin, *So Many Worlds*, 634.

14. *Montreal Gazette*, April 23–24, 1968; and Trudeau, *Memoirs*, 93–98.

15. Suzette Trudeau is quoted in Catherine Breslin, "The Other Trudeaus," *Chatelaine*, Oct. 1969, 87. The song debuted on a Montreal CBC-TV show hosted by Trudeau critic Laurier LaPierre and Trudeau fan Patrick Watson and is quoted in Litt, "Trudeaumania," 39; McLuhan on the tribal society is quoted in W. Terrence Gordon, *Marshall McLuhan: Escape into Understanding* (Toronto: Stoddart, 1997), 235. The letter on the debate is found in Marie Molinaro, Corinne McLuhan, and William Toye, eds., *Letters of Marshall McLuhan* (Toronto: Oxford University Press, 1987), 352–54. An interesting analysis of McLuhan's attraction to the Trudeau phenomenon is found in Arthur Kroker, http://www.ctheory.net/articles.aspx?id=70. He traces McLuhan's approach to understanding media to his Catholic humanism.

16. Walter Stewart, *The Life and Times of Tommy Douglas* (Toronto: McArthur and Company, 2003), 273. Descriptions of the campaigns are based on

interviews with campaign advisers Ramsay Cook, Gordon Gibson, Jacques Hébert, Marc Lalonde, Tim Porteous, Richard Stanbury, and several of Trudeau's Cabinet ministers.

17. Trudeau, *Memoirs*, 100–101. The best accounts of the campaign are in Saywell, ed., *Canadian Annual Review for 1968*; and Sullivan, *Mandate '68*.

18. Joe McGinniss, *The Selling of the President 1968* (New York: Simon and Schuster, 1969). Trudeau's fake fall is described by Bernard Dubé in *Montreal Gazette*, April 9, 1968.

19. Stewart, *Tommy Douglas*, 272.

20. *Globe and Mail*, April 9, May 22, 1968.

21. Pierre Trudeau, Personal Journal 1938, Jan. 1, June 19, 1938, TP, MG 26 02, vol. 39, file 9, LAC.

22. Cabinet Conclusions, RG2, PCO, Series A-5-a, vol. 6323, July 25, 1967, LAC.

23. Assessment of de Gaulle's opinion by Canadian officials in France quoted by David Meren in "*Les Sanglots longs de la violence de l'automne:* French Diplomacy Reacts to the October Crisis," *The Canadian Historical Review* 88 (Dec. 2007): 626.

24. Cook, *The Teeth of Time*, 74.

25. Conversation with Barney Danson, May 2007. The story about Danson's opponent's comment is found in Barney Danson with Curtis Fahey, *Not Bad for a Sergeant: The Memoirs of Barney Danson* (Toronto: Dundurn, 2002), 90; Iglauer's impression was confirmed by Trudeau aide Tim Porteous in conversations with him in September 2007. Edith Iglauer in Southam, ed., *Pierre*, 82–83. Pearson adviser Keith Davey, who had been excluded from the campaign, was even brought in to help. See Martin, *A Very Public Life*, 634.

26. Richard Stanbury Diary, privately held, June 1968.

27. Quoted and described in Donald Peacock, *Journey to Power: The Story of a Canadian Election* (Toronto: Ryerson, 1968), 368.

28. Comments made by Martin Sullivan, who travelled with Trudeau during the campaign. See Sullivan's *Mandate '68*, 313. Interview with John Nichol, Aug. 2005. For a description of the Nichol confrontation, see Christina McCall-Newman, *Grits: An Intimate Portrait of the Liberal Party* (Toronto: Macmillan, 1982), 118.

29. *Gazette*, June 20, 1968.

30. A summary of where the newspapers stood is found in Saywell, ed., *Canadian Annual Review for 1968*, 43–44. The summary notes that five English-language papers shifted from their 1965 Conservative support to the Liberals. Among them was the influential *Globe and Mail*. Interview with Richard Stanbury, Sept. 2006.

31. These figures are taken from the charts at the end of John Meisel, *Working Papers on Canadian Politics*, 2nd ed. (Montreal and London: McGill–Queen's University Press, 1975).

32. Gallup poll analysis from Saywell, ed., *Canadian Annual Review for 1968*, 62–66; Ryan in *Le Devoir*, June 17, 1968. *Elected Seats:* PC 72 (27.3%), L 155 (58.7%), NDP 22 (8.3%), Ralliement des Créditistes (RC) 14 (5.3%), Other 1 (0.4%). *Popular Vote:* PC 2,554,765 (31.4%), L 3,696,875 (45.5%), NDP 1,378,389 (17%), SC 64,029 (0.8%), Ralliement des Créditistes (RC) 359,885 (4.4%), Others 71,895 (0.9%).

33. *Globe and Mail*, June 26, 1968. The front page includes a group of quotations from a variety of opposition politicians under the title "All running against Trudeau and Trudeau beat us all." Part of the account is drawn from Peacock, who was with Trudeau in the Château Laurier suite. *Journey to Power*, 381–82.

34. Saywell, ed., *Canadian Annual Review for 1968*, 65.

35. John Duffy, *Fights of Our Lives: Elections, Leadership, and the Making of Canada* (Toronto: Harper Collins, 2002).

36. *Kitchener-Waterloo Record*, May 26, 1968; "Santa Claus" speech quoted in George Radwanski, *Trudeau* (Toronto: Macmillan, 1978), 108–9.

37. In his analysis of Trudeaumania, Litt writes: "Those who supported Trudeau most strongly were the very people who were most immersed in mass media and popular culture and most aware of it. . . . Trudeau and the Trudeauphiles communed in their shared distrust of their means of communication with one another, even as they used it expertly to achieve their mutual goals." "Trudeaumania," 51.

CHAPTER TWO: NEW WINE IN NEW BOTTLES

1. Kurlansky, *1968: The Year That Rocked the World* (Toronto: Random House, 2005), 351, 378. Fulford in *National Post*, Jan. 26, 2008. Fulford

was comparing Trudeau to Barack Obama. Kurlansky wrongly claims that Trudeau was forty-six in 1968. The error endured.

2. For a good analysis, see Eric Koch, *Inside Seven Days: The Show That Shook the Nation* (Scarborough: Prentice-Hall, 1986).

3. Paul Rutherford, *When Television Was Young: Primetime Canada 1952–1967* (Toronto: University of Toronto Press, 1990), 430–33. These pages are the finest description of the impact of Trudeau's effective use of television.

4. Joe McGinniss, *The Selling of the President 1968* (New York: Simon and Schuster, 1969); and George Radwanski, *Trudeau* (Toronto: Macmillan, 1978), 115.

5. Pierre Trudeau, "Federalism, Nationalism, and Reason," in Trudeau, *Federalism and the French Canadians* (1968; repr., Toronto: Macmillan, 1977), 203.

6. Albert Breton, Raymond Breton, Claude Bruneau, Yvon Gauthier, Marc Lalonde, Maurice Pinard, and Pierre Trudeau, "Pour une politique fonctionnelle," *Cité libre*, May 1964, 11–17; "An Appeal for Realism in Politics," *Canadian Forum*, May 1964, 29–33. The best description of the background is found in comments by Marc Lalonde in Robert Bothwell, *Canada and Quebec: One Country, Two Histories*, rev. ed. (Vancouver: University of British Columbia Press, 1998), 125. Cabinet discussions of April 17, 19, 20, and 22, 1968. RG2, PCO, Series A-5-a, vol. 6338, LAC; *Montreal Gazette*, April 23, 1968; Pierre Trudeau, *Memoirs* (Toronto: McClelland and Stewart, 1993), 93–98; and Paul Martin, *So Many Worlds*, vol. 2 of *A Very Public Life* (Toronto: Deneau, 1985), 634.

7. Peter C. Newman, *The Distemper of Our Times: Canadian Politics in Transition, 1963–1968* (1968; repr., Toronto: McClelland and Stewart, 1990), 109; interview with Marc Lalonde, Aug. 2007.

8. Cabinet Conclusions, http://www.collectionscanada.ca/db/gad/inv/-002i1e.htmRG2, PCO, Series A-5-a , vol. 6338, July 8, 1968, LAC.

9. Trudeau, *Memoirs*, 95–96. When I interviewed Lord Trend for a biography of Lester Pearson, he commented on how often he had met with Michael Pitfield, whom he described as keenly interested in government reform matters.

10. Robert Bothwell, Ian Drummond, and John English, *Power, Politics, and*

Provincialism: Canada since 1945 (Toronto: University of Toronto Press, 1981), 348–49; Turner quoted in Richard Gwyn, *Northern Magus: Pierre Trudeau and Canadians* (Toronto: McClelland and Stewart, 1980), 87; Radwanski, *Trudeau*, 345ff.; J.W. Pickersgill, *Seeing Canada Whole: A Memoir* (Markham, Ont.: Fitzhenry and Whiteside, 1994), 798; interviews with Allan MacEachen, Paul Martin, John Turner, J.W. Pickersgill (the author's landlord during the early 1970s in Ottawa); and collective interviews conducted by Library and Archives Canada. Gordon Robertson's comment and Trudeau's comment about going overboard are found in Gordon Robertson, *Memoirs of a Very Civil Servant: Mackenzie King to Pierre Trudeau* (Toronto: University of Toronto Press, 2000), 256. The fullest account of the attempt to use scientific approaches to government is found in Jason Churchill, "The Limits of Influence: The Club of Rome and Canada, 1968–1988" (PhD diss., University of Waterloo, 2005).

11. James Patterson, *Grand Expectations: The United States, 1945–1974* (New York: Oxford University Press, 1996), 682.

12. Rick Perlstein, *Nixonland: The Rise of a President and the Fracturing of America* (New York: Scribner, 2008), 747–78. Maureen O'Neil made these comments in 2008 at her retirement dinner from the presidency of the International Development Research Centre, itself an institution that represented the innovative spirit of Ottawa in those years.

13. John Meisel, *Working Papers on Canadian Politics*, 2nd ed. (Montreal and London: McGill–Queen's University Press, 1975), 25.

14. *Le Devoir*, July 8, 1968.

15. Edith Iglauer, "Prime Minister/Premier Ministre," *New Yorker*, July 5, 1969. The trip is described in *Globe and Mail*, July 20 and July 30, 1968. The latter has three excellent photographs of the trip. Years later, Iglauer published a delightful article recalling an informal dinner party she gave for Trudeau at her New York apartment, where he unexpectedly arrived with the glamorous Barbra Streisand on his arm. See http://www.geist.com/stories/prime-minister-accepts.

16. There is a good description of the northern trip in Martin Sullivan, *Mandate '68* (Toronto: Doubleday, 1968), 421–22. Cabinet discussions for July and August are in http://www.collectionscanada.ca/db/gad/inv/002i1e.htmRG2, PCO, Series A-5-a, vol. 6338, LAC.

17. A brilliant analysis of the recommendation's novel and "academic" character was given by the distinguished Harvard tax economist Richard Musgrave. "The Carter Commission Report," *Canadian Journal of Economics/ Revue canadienne d'économique* 1, no. 1, suppl. (Feb. 1968), 159–82.

18. There is an enormous literature on the subject of de Gaulle and Quebec. Eldon Black, a former Canadian diplomat, has written a scholarly study, *Direct Intervention: Canada-France Relations 1967–1974* (Ottawa: Carleton University Press, 1996). A more controversial study based upon extensive research in French and Canadian archives is J.F. Bosher, *The Gaullist Attack on Canada: 1967–1997* (Montreal and Kingston: McGill–Queen's University Press, 2000). Bosher, a distinguished French historian, personally knew some of the "agents," and this acquaintance intensified his anger at what he regards as outrageous interference in the affairs of a sovereign nation. Claude Morin, probably the principal agent of Quebec's international policy, has written extensively on the subject. See especially *L'Art de l'impossible: La diplomatie québécoise depuis 1960* (Montréal: Boréal, 1999). A useful summary of the relationship is found in Frédéric Bastien, *Le Poids de la coopération: Le rapport France-Québec* (Montréal: Québec Amérique, 2006). The quotation summarizing de Gaulle's view of Trudeau is found in David Meren, "*Les Sanglots longs de la violence de l'automne:* French Diplomacy Reacts to the October Crisis," *The Canadian Historical Review* 88 (Dec. 2007): 35. Meren's footnotes offer a full bibliography on the subject.

19. Jim Coutts, "Trudeau in Power: A View from inside the Prime Minister's Office," in Andrew Cohen and J.L.Granatstein, eds., *Trudeau's Shadow: The Life and Legacy of Pierre Elliott Trudeau* (Toronto: Random House, 1998), 151–53. Coutts expands on these views in an outstanding 2003 article on Canadian politics, which can be found at http://www.irpp.org/po/archive/ p01103.htm#coutts. Conversation with Jim Coutts, Dec. 2008.

20. The existence of such a group was the source of lively debate among former ministers at the joint interview conducted under the auspices of Library and Archives Canada. The charge that such a group existed was made by Mitchell Sharp. André Ouellet angrily denied it. Other ministers commented, with the prevailing view being that such a "Quebec" group existed and was important in Cabinet operations.

21. Daniel Cappon, "Whom Should Trudeau Marry?" *Chatelaine*, July 1969, 22–23, 56.

22. Ian MacEwan, *On Chesil Beach* (Toronto: Knopf Canada, 2007), 6; conversation with Carroll Guérin, Aug. 2007 and July 2009.

23. Ibid.; Jennifer Rae in Nancy Southam, ed., *Pierre: Colleagues and Friends Talk about the Trudeau They Knew* (Toronto: McClelland and Stewart, 2005), 242–43.

24. A recent unofficial biography has many details on Trudeau. Christopher Anderson, *Barbra: The Way She Is* (New York: William Morrow, 2006), 180, 191–95. Barbra Streisand wrote about their relationship in Southam, ed., *Pierre*, 244–45, and this is the source of the comment on their London meeting. Interview with Tim Porteous, Sept. 2007. Most of the information here derives from an interview with Ms. Streisand in July 2009.

25. Streisand interview, ibid; Anderson, *Barbra*, 192–93; and Streisand in Southam, ed., *Pierre*, 245. Interview with Marc Lalonde, Aug. 2007.

26. Anderson, *Barbra*, 193–95. Streisand to Trudeau, nd [April 1970], and Streisand to Trudeau, Oct. 19, 1970, TP, MG 26 020, vol. 53, file 15, LAC.

27. Margaret Trudeau, *Beyond Reason* (New York and London: Paddington Press, 1979), 13, 40–44, 48–49.

28. Ibid., 48; *Ottawa Citizen*, Dec. 23, 1969. I viewed the event on YouTube at http://www.youtube.com/results?search=related&search_query=Lennon%200no%20Trudeau&v=bXXpiRmTz98.

29. John English, *Citizen of the World* (Toronto: Knopf Canada, 2006), chaps. 5 and 6, cover Trudeau's views. The notes for Couchiching are found in TP, MG 26 02, vol. 12, file 17, LAC.

30. Pierre Trudeau, "International Development as a Requisite for Peace," *External Affairs* (June 1968): 248–49. The best account of the period informed by interviews and multinational research is Robert Bothwell, *Alliance and Illusion: Canada and the World, 1945–1984* (Vancouver: University of British Columbia Press, 2007), chap. 15. Trudeau's own account of his foreign policy is contained in Ivan Head and Pierre Trudeau, *The Canadian Way: Shaping Canada's Foreign Policy, 1968–1984* (Toronto: McClelland and Stewart, 1995). The book is organized by themes, and Head appears to have been the author of most of the material. The standard account of Trudeau's foreign policy is

J.L. Granatstein and Robert Bothwell, *Pirouette: Pierre Trudeau and Canadian Foreign Policy* (Toronto: University of Toronto Press, 1990), a book that Trudeau and Head studiously ignore in their volume. There are many contemporary accounts of the foreign policy review, the best of which are Bruce Thordarson, *Trudeau and Foreign Policy: A Study in Decision-Making* (Toronto: Oxford University Press, 1972) and Peter Dobell, *Canada's Search for New Roles: Foreign Policy in the Trudeau Era* (London: Published for the Royal Institute of International Affairs by Oxford University Press, 1972, p.752). Mitchell Sharp, with the assistance of Robert Bothwell, wrote *Which Reminds Me . . . : A Memoir* (Toronto: University of Toronto Press, 1994). Linda Freeman's assessment of Trudeau can be found in her *Ambiguous Champion: Canada and South Africa in the Trudeau and Mulroney Years* (Toronto: University of Toronto Press, 1997), 284–88. I have also benefited greatly from access to several unpublished works, including the official history of the Department of Foreign Affairs and International Trade and the memoirs of Geoffrey Murray, who was active in the foreign policy review.

31. Ivan Head to Trudeau, March 5, 1968, TP, MG 26 020, vol. 21, file 17, LAC.

32. Cadieux's comments on Trudeau and External Affairs: interview with Michel Gauvin, April 1994. I also met several times with Marcel Cadieux during the 1980s, and he expressed these same opinions to me at the time. Quotation from Marcel Cadieux: Memorandum, June 5, 1968, CP, MG 31, E31, vol. 4, LAC. Bosher discusses Cadieux's relationship with Pearson and Trudeau in Bosher, *Gaullist Attack*, 66–97. On the department's weaknesses, see Gilles Lalonde, *The Department of External Affairs and Biculturalism*, vol. 3 of *Studies of the Royal Commission on Bilingualism and Biculturalism* (Ottawa: Information Canada, 1968). Coutts made the comment about Head in a conversation, Dec. 2007. Much of this discussion is drawn from my paper "Two Heads Are Better Than One," which I presented at the Department of Foreign Affairs, Dec. 18, 2008.

33. Charles Ritchie, *Storm Signals: More Undiplomatic Diaries, 1962–1971* (Toronto: Macmillan, 1983), 113–14.

34. Escott Reid to Trudeau, March 28, 1968, TP, MG 26 020, vol. 21, file 17, LAC. David Golden wrote a note in this same file that proposes an even more abrupt withdrawal of Canadian forces from NATO.

35. Mr. Gotlieb made these arguments in an interestingly titled document, "The Style of Canadian Diplomacy," that he wrote for Trudeau in 1968. He also kindly provided me with some of the documents he wrote for Trudeau.

36. Bothwell, *Alliance and Illusion*, 288–90; "Meeting in Room 340S, Dec. 9th," Dec. 13, 1969, MSP, MG 35 B61, vol. 3, LAC; Geoffrey Murray, "The Foreign Policy Review Process, 1967–1972" (in my possession from Mr. Murray); Cadieux Diary, Dec. 1968–March 1969, CP, MG 31 E31, vol. 5, LAC; and Head and Trudeau, *Canadian Way*, 66–69.

37. Cabinet Conclusions, RG2, PCO, Series A-5-a, vol. 6340, April 17, 1969, LAC; Bothwell, *Alliance and Illusion*, 289, on the reactions, including the advice to Kissinger to take it easy on the Canadians; Bosher, *Gaullist Attack*, 97; and Granatstein and Bothwell, *Pirouette*, 28.

38. Head and Trudeau, *Canadian Way*, 68–69.

39. Granatstein in *Canadian Annual Review for 1968*, 261ff. The summary of press reports is excellent. Canada, *House of Commons Debates* (10 Sept. 1968); Walter Stewart, *Shrug: Trudeau in Power* (Toronto: New Press, 1971), 110; Bothwell, *Alliance and Illusion*, 307. Note that Stewart and Granatstein have slightly different wordings for the comment made to the CBC interviewer, with Stewart claiming that Trudeau said, "peculiar questions."

40. Trudeau, *Memoirs*, 346, 348; Freeman, *Ambiguous Champion*; conversation with Robert Fowler, Feb. 2008; and Bothwell, *Alliance and Illusion*, 304ff.

41. Freeman, *Ambiguous Champion*, 285. In interviews Mr. Gotlieb has emphasized the "realist" approach of the early Trudeau, and his memoranda for Trudeau confirm that he urged such an approach.

42. Executive Briefing, "Arrival Ceremony for the Right Honorable The Prime Minister of Canada and Mrs. Pierre Elliott Trudeau," with attached briefing on Head probably produced in 1975. Jimmy Carter Presidential Library, White House Central File, CO 28, 1/20/77-2/28/77.

43. Trudeau, *Memoirs*, 202; Macdonald to Sharp, RG 25, vol. 8837, file 20-1-2STAFEUR 8, LAC; and *Foreign Policy for Canadians* (Ottawa: Information Canada, 1970). The department history is found at http://www.dfait-maeci.gc.ca/hist/canada9-en.asp.

44. Sharp, *Which Reminds Me*, 202–4; the newspaper comment occurred in a television interview and is quoted in Stewart, *Shrug*, 107–8.

45. *Time*, Cdn. ed., Jan. 24, 1969, 22; *Globe and Mail*, Jan. 6, 1969.
46. Tony Benn, *The Benn Diaries 1940–1990*, ed. Ruth Winstone (London: Arrow, 1996), 211. The Rittinghausen correspondence and clippings are found in TP, MG 26 020, vol. 10, file 54, LAC. *Ottawa Citizen*, Jan. 17, 1969.
47. *Le Devoir*, Jan.15, 1969; and Ritchie, *Storm Signals*, 124. Canadian opinions of Trudeau's behaviours, which seem evenly divided, were recorded and preserved by the CBC at http://archives.cbc.ca/on_this_day/01/16/. One of the students present at the Westminster meeting was John MacNaughton, the son of an Ontario Progressive Conservative minister. He confirms the strong impression Trudeau made on the gathering.
48. See assessments in *Montreal Star*, Jan. 14, 1969; *Ottawa Citizen*, Dec. 23, 1969; and Ritchie, *Storm Signals*, 139 (entry of Dec. 11, 1969).
49. Allan Gotlieb, "Some Reflections on Canadian Foreign Policy," nd [1968], given to me by Mr. Gotlieb. Thomas Axworthy, "'To Stand Not So High Perhaps but Always Alone': The Foreign Policy of Pierre Elliott Trudeau," in *Towards a Just Society: The Trudeau Years*, ed. Thomas S. Axworthy and Pierre Elliott Trudeau (Markham, Ont.: Viking, 1990), 19. Axworthy writes: "Any sensible foreign policy contains elements of both power and principle. Idealism without an accurate assessment of the underlying realities of power becomes mere preaching."

CHAPTER THREE: THE OCTOBER CRISIS
1. Robert Bothwell, *Alliance and Illusion: Canada and the World, 1945–1984* (Vancouver: University of British Columbia Press, 2007), 300–301; and Peter C. Newman, *Here Be Dragons: Telling Tales of People, Passion, and Power* (Toronto: McClelland and Stewart, 2004), 341–42.
2. *Le Devoir*, Feb. 15, 1969; *Globe and Mail*, Feb. 17, 1969.
3. On the Johnsons, see Benoît Gignac, *Le Destin Johnson: Une famille, trois premiers ministres* (Montréal: Stanké, 2007), 103. The most personal attack by Vadeboncoeur on Trudeau is found in André Potvin, Michel Letourneux, and Robert Smith, *L'Anti-Trudeau: Choix de textes* (Montréal: Éditions Parti-pris, 1972), 75–79, which also includes several critical articles by Trudeau's former colleagues, sociologists Fernand Dumont and Marcel Rioux. Jacques Parizeau's decision to join the Parti Québécois is covered well in Pierre Duchesne, *Le Croisé*, vol. 1 of *Jacques Parizeau: Biographie*

1930–1970 (Montréal: Québec-Amérique, 2001), 473ff. The English-Canadian historian of the left Ian McKay writes: "Not just a thriving left wing press but also a mass media alive with neo-Marxist and *indépendantiste* ideas testified to a socialist cultural ferment [in Quebec] unparalleled in Canadian left history except by the radical labour upsurge of 1917–22." *Rebels, Reds, Radicals: Rethinking Canada's Left History* (Toronto: Between the Lines, 2005), 187.

4. Gouin to Trudeau, nd [1969]. TP, MG 26 01, vol. 48, file 1, LAC.

5. *Winnipeg Free Press*, June 11, 1969; *Edmonton Journal*, July 18, 1969; and Irving, quoted in Nancy Southam, ed., *Pierre: Colleagues and Friends Talk about the Trudeau They Knew* (Toronto: McClelland and Stewart, 2005), 110–11.

6. The break with Hertel is discussed in detail in the first volume of this biography, 388–90. Trudeau's description of the reasons why he asked the police to investigate is contained in his interview with Jean Lépine, April 20, 1992. TP, MG 26 03, vol. 23, file 5, LAC. Trudeau also decided to gain information on the financing of separatism and separatist influence in the public service: see Pierre Trudeau, *Memoirs* (Toronto: McClelland and Stewart, 1993), 130–31. Two major reports later dealt with the RCMP's activities in Quebec related to alleged threats of violence. The Lévesque government appointed Jean-François Duchaîne, whose commission produced his *Rapport sur les événements d'octobre 1970* (Québec: Ministry of Justice, 1981), and the Trudeau government appointed D.C. McDonald, who issued a report entitled *Certain R.C.M.P. Activities and the Question of Governmental Knowledge*, Third Report of the Commission of Inquiry concerning Certain Activities of the Royal Canadian Mounted Police, 1981 (Ottawa: Canadian Government Publishing Centre, 1981).

7. On the continuing French interest, see David Meren, "*Les Sanglots longs de la violence de l'automne*: French Diplomacy Reacts to the October Crisis," *The Canadian Historical Review* (Dec. 2007): 625–27. Polls are listed in John Saywell, *Quebec 70: A Documentary Narrative* (Toronto: University of Toronto Press, 1971), 10–12.

8. On Liberal support, ibid.; interview with Marc Lalonde, Aug. 2007. On the offer to Lévesque, see Duchesne, *Le Croisé*, 599–605, and Bothwell, *Alliance and Illusion*, 301.

654 NOTES TO CHAPTER THREE

9. The quotation and the election results are found in Saywell, *Quebec 70*, 22–23.

10. Ibid., 26.

11. Meren, *"Les Sanglots longs,"* describes the memorandum to French foreign minister Maurice Schumann, in which the divisions in the Bourassa government are discussed, 627–68.

12. Trudeau, *Memoirs*, 134.

13. Trudeau, *Memoirs*, 128–44; Canada, House of Commons Debates (6 Oct. 1970). There is a vast literature on the so-called October Crisis. On the FLQ see especially Louis Fournier, *FLQ: Histoire d'un mouvement clandestin*, 2nd ed. (Montréal: Éditions Lanctôt, 1998). A most recent valuable study based on a contemporary diary is William Tetley, *The October Crisis: An Insider's View* (Montreal and Kingston: McGill–Queen's University Press, 2006). Tetley offers a valuable bibliography and commentary on the crisis. He has also placed much of his research and relevant documents on the Internet. Included is a dispute between him and prominent journalist Lysiane Gagnon over an article she published in the *Beaver* on the October Crisis. The journal would not let Tetley publish the full reply that he makes available on the Internet at http://www.mcgill.ca/maritimelaw/crisis/.

14. The translation of the manifesto is from Saywell, *Quebec 70*, 46. On Trudeau's disagreement with Sharp, see Trudeau, *Memoirs*, 135. Sharp confirmed Trudeau's continuing dismay in an interview with me, July 2002.

15. Gérard Pelletier, quoted in Anthony Westell, *Paradox: Trudeau as Prime Minister* (Scarborough: Prentice-Hall, 1972), 239. Gérard Pelletier, *The October Crisis*, trans. Joyce Marshall (Toronto: McClelland and Stewart, 1971), 23.

16. Trudeau, *Memoirs*, 136.

17. See Carole de Vault and William Johnson, *Toute Ma Vérité: Les Confessions de l'agent S.A.T. 945–171* (Montréal: Stanké, 1981), 102ff.; Duchesne, *Le Croisé*, 546–51; and (for the shooting) Gordon Robertson, *Memoirs of a Very Civil Servant: Mackenzie King to Pierre Trudeau* (Toronto: University of Toronto Press, 2000), 264. Alastair Gillespie, an MP but not yet a minister, opened his apartment door and immediately confronted a guard who

pointed his gun at him and demanded to know his intentions. Gillespie's neighbour was a minister who had received protection the previous evening. Jean Chrétien recalls that the guards were hidden in his garage. Conversations with Chrétien in March 2009 and Gillespie in Feb. 2009.

18. This version is taken from Saywell, *Quebec 70*, 71–73, which includes the entire exchange. It can be seen on http://archives.cbc.ca/politics/civil_unrest/topics/101/. This site has several other clips dealing with the October Crisis.

19. Tetley, *October Crisis*, 203. Tetley, now the hardliner, noted that "Trudeau has made an excellent speech on 'bleeding hearts' and holding the line. It is taped and is going to be played to us in Cabinet."

20. Saywell, *Quebec 70*, 73–74; Trudeau, *Memoirs*, 139–41, where he lists all the signatories; and *Le Devoir*, Oct. 30, 1970, where Ryan describes the circumstances of the case. See also the important account in Newman, *Here Be Dragons*, chap. 12; and Fernand Dumont, *La Vigile du Québec, Octobre 1970: L'Impasse?* (Montréal: Hurtubise, 1971), in which Trudeau is accused of treating Quebec francophones as imbeciles (193).

21. *Montreal Gazette*, Oct. 16, 1970; *Le Devoir*, Oct. 16, 1970; Paul Litt, draft biography of John Turner (I am indebted to Dr. Litt for this manuscript, which draws on Turner's private papers); Tetley, *October Crisis*; and interview with Allan MacEachen, Oct. 2003. Mr. MacEachen said that Marchand was highly influential and overwrought.

22. Cabinet Conclusions, RG2, PCO, Series A-5-1, vol. 6359, Oct. 15, 1970, LAC; Eric Kierans with Walter Stewart, *Remembering* (Toronto: Stoddart, 2001), 181.

23. Drapeau's biographers Brian McKenna and Susan Purcell argue that Drapeau played "only an indirect role in the day-to-day decisions during the October Crisis." He was preoccupied with the municipal elections. He did use the situation to his political advantage, particularly after October 15. *Drapeau* (Toronto: Clarke Irwin, 1980), 236.

24. Cabinet Conclusions, RG2, PCO, Series A-5-1, vol. 6359, Oct. 15, 1970, LAC.

25. Ibid.; Kierans with Stewart, *Remembering*, 180ff.

26. Cabinet Conclusions, RG2, PCO, Series A-5-1, vol. 6359, Oct. 15, 1970, LAC. Dr. Litt's account (see note 21) supports this view of Turner's role.

27. The website created by William Tetley at McGill contains all the major documents dealing with the crisis. See http://www.mcgill.ca/files/maritimelaw/K.doc.

28. *Montreal Gazette*, Oct. 19, 1970.

29. Duchesne, *Le Croisé*, 550–52; Douglas in Canada, *House of Commons Debates* (16 Oct. 1970); and Trudeau, *Memoirs*, 143. The difficulties Robert Stanfield, the Conservative leader, faced are described well in Geoffrey Stevens, *Stanfield* (Toronto: McClelland and Stewart, 1973), 241. Stanfield received contrary advice from two assistants, one who urged a "civil rights stand" and another who urged a strong stand with Canadians against terrorism. The Trudeau-Douglas debate reflected these differences and the debate persists between these positions. The October Crisis occupies a remarkable twenty-two pages in Trudeau's memoirs. Trudeau points out, for example, that René Lévesque had said, "One day the police and the army will be gone and Trudeau's stupidity will not have prevented more kidnappings." But Trudeau asserts correctly that the kidnappings did stop and that even Pierre Vallières urged separatists to abandon violence soon after 1970. Trudeau dismisses the diary entries of Cabinet minister Don Jamieson, which are often cited by critics as proof that Trudeau's invocation of the War Measures Act was an attempt to smash separatism. Those entries, Trudeau insists, are unreliable because Jamieson was absent for much of the time and did not participate in the "crucial exchanges" "during which our reasons for invoking the *War Measures Act* were put forward and the attitude the government had decided to take was defined." The Cabinet record appears to bear out Trudeau's point about Jamieson. That same record does illustrate his personal and political disdain for Lévesque at the time. The impact of those "crucial exchanges" is clear in the declassified Cabinet records, which reveal how those in the Cabinet who, like Douglas, wanted parliamentary approval and special legislation gave way to Marchand's argument that only the War Measures Act would permit the actions necessary to blunt the "deterioration."

30. For an interview with Cross on his experiences in Montreal, see www.chu.cam.ac.uk/archives/collections/BDOHP/Cross.pdf.

31. Robertson, *Civil Servant*, 264.

32. Kierans with Stewart, *Remembering*, 180.

33. Turner, quoted in Litt's Turner draft biography (see note 21). The remark by Otto Lang was made to me in a personal conversation in 2005. Robertson's argument is found in Robertson, *Civil Servant*, 256.

34. The controversy over the October 15 petition is covered well in William Tetley, who presents both sides of the issue, although he is critical of Ryan and Lévesque. Peter C. Newman describes how Lalonde and Trudeau himself leaked the information about Ryan's "provisional government" to him, and he indicates that he feels he was betrayed and used by them. Tetley, *October Crisis*, 121–27; Newman, *Here Be Dragons*, chap. 12.

35. Tetley, *October Crisis*, 120–31. René Lévesque, *Memoirs*, trans. Philip Stratford (Toronto: McClelland and Stewart, 1986), 245.

36. See Tetley, *October Crisis*, chap. 13, for Ryan's arguments, an examination of the debate, and a presentation of the evidence. This section owes a considerable debt to his account. See also Lévesque, *Memoirs*, 245. Separately, this interpretation depends on a discussion of the October Crisis by several leading Liberal senators and Liberal MPs from the period, held at the University Club, Toronto, May 24, 2007, and interviews with several others close to Trudeau at the time, notably Marc Lalonde, Tim Porteous, Margaret Trudeau, Carroll Guérin, Otto Lang, Ramsay Cook, Albert Breton, and John Turner. Paul Litt's draft biography of John Turner (see note 21) clearly disputes the view advanced by journalist Doug Fisher and, in passing, by Peter C. Newman in his memoirs, *Here Be Dragons*, that Turner dissented from the path taken and that his differences would become apparent when his papers were released. His biographer had full access to his papers.

37. Duchesne, *Le Croisé*, 561, based on an interview with Louise Harel, Sept. 26, 2000; and Trudeau in "Entrevue entre M. Trudeau et M. Lépine, [M. Lépine interview], April 29, 1992." TP, MG 26 03, vol. 23, file 5, LAC. The later comments of Lalonde and Pelletier are reported in L. Ian MacDonald, *From Bourassa to Bourassa: Wilderness to Restoration*, 2nd ed. (Montreal and Kingston: McGill–Queen's University Press, 2002), 154–56.

38. Based on an interview with Parizeau and the interview with Harel (see note 37); Parizeau, quoted in Duchesne, *Le Croisé*, 561.

39. Ramsay Cook, *The Teeth of Time: Remembering Pierre Elliott Trudeau* (Montreal and Kingston: McGill–Queen's University Press, 2006), chap. 4; and J.L. Granatstein, "Changing Positions," in Andrew Cohen and

J.L. Granatstein, eds., *Trudeau's Shadow: The Life and Legacy of Pierre Elliott Trudeau* (Toronto: Random House, 1998), 298–305.

40. Margaret Trudeau, *Beyond Reason* (New York and London: Paddington Press, 1979), 64. Margaret confirmed this story in a conversation with me in February 2006. British prime minister Edward Heath reported to senior ministers after meeting Trudeau in December 1970 that Mr. Trudeau "had struck him as being considerably older and more subdued. The kidnapping experiences had clearly told on him; and he was greatly relieved that Mr. Cross had been freed." "The Prime Minister's Visits to Ottawa and Washington: Note of a meeting held at 10 Downing Street on 21 December 1970 at 3 p.m.," PREM 15/7/1 22808, National Archives of the United Kingdom.

CHAPTER FOUR: REASON AND PASSION

1. Snow's comments are in Nancy Southam, ed., *Pierre: Colleagues and Friends Talk about the Trudeau They Knew* (Toronto: McClelland and Stewart, 2005), 124–25, and Leclerc's were made for the CBC and are at http://www.cbc.ca/arts/photoessay/that60s-show/index2.html. Wieland herself comments on *Reason over Passion* in an interview: Kristy Holmes-Moss, "Interview and Notes on Reason over Passion and Pierre Vallières," *Canadian Journal of Film Studies* 15 (fall 2006): 114–17.
2. Holmes-Moss, "Interview and Notes."
3. Ryan, in *Le Devoir*, May 1, 1971.
4. Denis Smith, *Bleeding Hearts, Bleeding Country* (Edmonton: Hurtig, 1971). The interview with Trudeau is found in George Radwanski, *Trudeau* (Toronto: Macmillan, 1978), 329–30.
5. I would like to thank Dr. Cook for giving me his private memorandum on the evening's discussions and for drawing my attention to Eli Mandel's poem. See his full account of the meeting in his *Teeth of Time: Remembering Pierre Elliott Trudeau* (Montreal and Kingston: McGill–Queen's University Press, 2006), 110–22. Mandel's verse is an excerpt from "Political Speech (for PET)" and appeared in *Dreaming Backwards: The Selected Poetry of Eli Mandel* (Don Mills, Ont.: General, 1981), 79. The quotation about the need to be strong is found in Pierre Trudeau, *Memoirs* (Toronto: McClelland and Stewart, 1993), 151.

Dr. Donald Wright kindly gave me the Lower letter to fellow historian George Stanley (Arthur Lower to George Stanley, Nov. 10, 1970, QUA, Collection 5072, ALoP, box 5, A75). This description of the meeting is also influenced by the recollections of the distinguished economist Albert Breton, who told me about it shortly after it occurred. We have discussed the meeting since, but I vividly remember Breton's anger concerning the comments of some of the participants. He claimed then that Trudeau shared that anger.

6. Trudeau, *Memoirs*, 150–51.

7. Geoff Pevere and Greig Dymond, *Mondo Canuck: A Canadian Pop Culture Odyssey* (Toronto: Prentice-Hall, 1996), 221.

8. William Tetley, *The October Crisis, 1970: An Insider's View* (Montreal and Kingston: McGill–Queen's University Press, 2006), 217–18. After the October Crisis, Tetley encountered Trudeau at a reception in Trudeau's riding, where according to Tetley, Trudeau did suffer fools gladly. He thanked Tetley for his help. Tetley wrote: "Actually I think we did the good work and he helped, but he is charming and fair." Tetley, *October Crisis*, 220.

9. Pierre Vallières, *L'Urgence de choisir: essai* (Montréal: Éditions Parti-pris, 1971).

10. The cartoon was published in the *Ottawa Citizen* on November 2, 1970, and is found in John Saywell, *Quebec 70: A Documentary Narrative* (Toronto: University of Toronto Press, 1971), 95.

11. Quoted in Anne Carney, "Trudeau Unveiled: Growing Up Private with Mama, the Jesuits, and the Conscience of the Rich," *Maclean's*, Feb. 1972, 68.

12. The interviews with Lundrigan, Alexander, and Trudeau may be viewed on the CBC Digital Archives, and the quotations used are taken from my viewing of these at http://archives.cbc.ca/on_this_day/02/16/. See also *Globe and Mail* and *Montreal Star*, Feb. 17, 1971. Many Liberals thought that Trudeau came out of the incident well, but Trudeau did not see "much humour in it himself." Richard Stanbury Diary, privately held, March 4, 1971.

13. The best recent treatment of the law and its context is Ross Lambertson, *Repression and Resistance: Canadian Human Rights Activists* (Toronto: University of Toronto Press, 2005), chap. 1. There is also a good collection of writings on the Padlock Law at http://faculty.marianopolis.edu/ c.belanger/quebechistory/docs/Laloiducadenas-Duplessisetlefascisme.html.

14. Wright to Smith, May 20, 1939, quoted in Philip Girard, *Bora Laskin: Bringing Law to Life* (Toronto: University of Toronto Press for the Osgoode Society, 2005), 106.
15. The quotations and interpretation draw directly from James Walker, *"Race," Rights, and the Law in the Supreme Court of Canada: Historical Case Studies* (Toronto: The Osgoode Society, 1997), 278.
16. Christopher MacLennan, *Towards the Charter: Canadians and the Demand for a National Bill of Rights, 1929–1960* (Montreal and Kingston: McGill–Queen's University Press, 2003).
17. For example, Scott gained his reputation in *Roncarelli v. Duplessis,* where a Jehovah's Witness restaurant owner lost his liquor licence because of Duplessis's Padlock Law, and the *Lady Chatterley's Lover* case, in which censorship of D.H. Lawrence's celebration of illicit love was overturned.
18. Pierre Trudeau, *Federalism and the French Canadians* (Toronto: Macmillan, 1968), xxi–xxii.
19. See Mark MacGuigan, "The Political Freedom of Catholics," in *Brief to the Bishops: Canadian Catholic Laymen Speak Their Minds*, ed. Paul Harris (Toronto: Longmans Canada, 1965), 18–25. Later, MacGuigan published a controversial study, *Abortion, Conscience, and Democracy* (Toronto: Hounslow, 1994), which Trudeau read closely and with approval. It is thoroughly consistent with MacGuigan's 1965 brief, which attacked the role of ecclesiastical authorities in public debates. In conversations with MacGuigan—I am his literary executor—he reported on Trudeau's numerous conversations that revealed the former prime minister's agreement with MacGuigan's liberal views on the abortion question. A strong attack on the role of these prominent Catholics in the abortion debate is found in Alphonse de Valk, *Lang, Lalonde, Trudeau, Turner: Abortion* (Battleford, Sask.: Marian Press, 1975). De Valk argued prophetically that "as long as one party is convinced that abortion is a criminal act which must be publicly condemned because it is the termination of human life innocent of any crime and is, therefore, against both reason and God, the other side must attempt to silence that view. It cannot rest until it has succeeded in doing so, for the simple reason that human beings cannot live in the same society over any length of time with views which are contradictory

in matters of life and death" (de Valk, *Abortion,* 18). MacGuigan, not surprisingly, fundamentally disagreed.

20. Richard Gwyn, "Prologue," in John English, Richard Gwyn, and P. Whitney Lackenbauer, eds., *The Hidden Pierre Elliott Trudeau: The Faith behind the Politics* (Ottawa: Novalis, 2004), 11; Margaret Trudeau, *Beyond Reason* (New York and London: Paddington Press, 1979), 55.

21. *Le Devoir* indicated on September 11, 1968, that many MPs would find it difficult to have the omnibus bill broken up because it would require them to vote a single "yes" or "no" on such diverse issues as homosexuality, abortion, and gun control. However, the Cabinet discussions of July and August contained no references to the omnibus bill. Trudeau's comments are in Cabinet Conclusions, RG2, PCO, Series A-5-a, vol. 6368, Sept. 5, 1968, LAC.

22. For both sides of the abortion debate, see John Turner, "Faith and Politics," in English, Gwyn, and Lackenbauer, *Hidden Pierre,* 111–16, and Bernard Daly, "Trudeau and the Bedrooms of the Nation: The Canadian Bishops' Involvement," in ibid., 135–40. *Humanae Vitae* is found at http://www.vatican.va/holy_father/paul_vi/encyclicals/documents/ hf_p-vi_enc_25071968_humanae-vitae_en.html. The Canadian ecclesiastical reaction is described in *Le Devoir,* Sept. 26, 1968.

23. Turner, "Faith and Politics," 115–16; Daly, "Trudeau and the Bedrooms of the Nation," 135–40.

24. Turner, "Faith and Politics," 113; J.A. Scollin, Director, Criminal Law Section, Department of Justice, to J.W. Goodwin, May 15, 1969, Department of Justice, RG13, vol. 2965, file 185300-149-1, LAC. Trudeau's comments on divorce are found in Canada, *House of Commons Debates* (4 Dec. 1967). I would like to thank Paul Litt, Turner's biographer, for these references. The concern about the Pope is found in Ambassador Crean (Rome) to Marcel Cadieux, Jan. 20, 1969, External Affairs RG25, box 10104, file 20-CDa-9-Trudeau, Part 1, LAC.

25. Ian Coates to John Turner, May 13, 1969, Department of Justice, RG13, vol. 2965, file 185300-149-1, LAC. Turner's comments are found in Canada, *House of Commons Debates* (17 April 1969), and Diefenbaker and Caouette are quoted in Turner, "Faith and Politics," 116.

26. Andrew Thompson, "Slow to Leave the Bedrooms of the Nation: Trudeau and the Modernizing of Canadian Law, 1967–1968," in English, Gwyn, and Lackenbauer, *Hidden Pierre*, 125.The conference upon which this book was based included an extended debate on the true nature of the abortion reform, with most Catholics emphasizing it was revolutionary and others less convinced it was so revolutionary. Although I am not a Catholic, I tend to agree with their argument on this point: the change was significant.

27. Conversation with Henry Kissinger, March 2008.

28. Report on the conference is found in EAP, RG25, box 10105, file 20-CD4-9-Trudeau P.e. FP(2).

29. The quotations are found in Brian Shaw, *The Gospel according to Saint Pierre* (Richmond Hill, Ont.: Pocket Books, 1969), 77, 240.

30. Trudeau, *Beyond Reason*, 51–54; interview with Margaret Trudeau, Feb. 2006.

31. Ibid., 54–55. His travel agenda is found in TP, MG 26 020, vol. 17, files 11–12, LAC. Trudeau wrote the preface to MacInnis's book *Underwater Man* (New York: Dodd, Mead, 1975). MacInnis remained a good friend of Trudeau. Conversation with Joe MacInnis, July 2009.

32. Interviews with Carroll Guérin, May–Aug. 2007 and July 2009. Ms. Guérin gave me copies of the letter described and some other relevant information.

33. Trudeau, *Beyond Reason*, 57–60; interview with Margaret Trudeau, Feb. 2006.

34. The reference to a November meeting with Streisand is in TP, MG 26 020, vol. 53, file 15, LAC; Trudeau, *Beyond Reason*, 65–66.

35. James Sinclair to Trudeau, Dec. 20, 1970, TP, MG 26 02, vol. 53, file 10, LAC; Trudeau, *Beyond Reason*, 67–70.

36. Speech described in *Ottawa Journal*, March 5, 1971.

37. Trudeau, *Beyond Reason*, 74; interviews with Margaret Trudeau (Feb. 2006), Madeleine Gobeil (May 2006), Carroll Guérin (Aug. 2007), and Marc Lalonde (Aug. 2007); confidential discussions.

38. Trudeau, *Beyond Reason*, 77–80; interview with Margaret Trudeau, Feb. 2006.

39. *Ottawa Journal*, March 5, 1971; *Vancouver Sun*, March 5, 1971; *Le Devoir*, March 8, 1971; and *Globe and Mail*, March 6, 1971.

Chapter Five: Victoria's Failure

1. Richard Simeon, *Federal-Provincial Diplomacy: The Making of Recent Policy in Canada* (Toronto: University of Toronto Press, 1972). See also Gordon Robertson, *Memoirs of a Very Civil Servant: Mackenzie King to Pierre Trudeau* (Toronto: University of Toronto Press, 2000), chap. 13. The Quebec argument is presented in Claude Morin, *Quebec versus Ottawa: The Struggle for Self-Government 1960–1972* (Toronto: University of Toronto Press, 1976). This tome incorporates and adds to two earlier works in French by Morin, who was the lead Quebec civil servant in the negotiations during the period described. He states in his preface that the English version of the book will reveal why Quebec turned to sovereignty as a result of the "struggle" in which he fought for Quebec against the federal government.

2. Philip Girard, *Bora Laskin: Bringing Law to Life* (Toronto: University of Toronto Press for the Osgoode Society, 2005), 368–69.

3. Pierre Trudeau, *Memoirs* (Toronto: McClelland and Stewart, 1993), 230.

4. Trudeau's classic article was "Les Octrois fédéraux aux universités," *Cité libre*, Feb. 1957, 9–31. See the discussion of his attitude in John English, *Citizen of the World*, vol. 1 of *The Life of Pierre Elliott Trudeau* (Toronto: Knopf Canada, 2006), 315–16.

5. See Pierre Trudeau, "The Values of a Just Society," 362, and Thomas Shoyama, "Fiscal Federalism in Evolution," in *Towards a Just Society: The Trudeau Years*, ed. Thomas S. Axworthy and Pierre Elliott Trudeau (Markham, Ont.: Viking, 1990), 226–34.

6. Robertson, *Civil Servant*, 272ff.; John Saywell, ed., *Canadian Annual Review of Public Affairs 1971* (Toronto: University of Toronto Press, 1972), 46–47; and interview with Marc Lalonde, Aug. 2007. A good contemporary account, deeply informed by prominent sources, is Anthony Westell, *Paradox: Trudeau as Prime Minister* (Scarborough: Prentice-Hall, 1972), chap. 1.

7. Gordon Gibson to Marc Lalonde, May 10, 1971, TP, MG 26 03, vol. 121, file 313.05, LAC. This memorandum attaches a *Le Devoir* editorial reporting on a statement by prominent intellectual Fernand Dumont, who had written that future historians would charge Trudeau with breaking up Canada. Trudeau said the comments were amusing, since his old acquaintance Dumont wanted Canada to break up.

8. Robertson, *Civil Servant*, 272ff.; Saywell, ed., *Canadian Annual Review 1971*, 46–47; and interview with Marc Lalonde, Aug. 2007.

9. Robertson, *Civil Servant*, 277–82; Saywell, ed., *Canadian Annual Review 1971*, 58–59.

10. Turner to Mr. Cummings, June 30, 1971, TUP, MG 26 Q4, vol. 6, file 11, LAC. (I am indebted to Paul Litt, Turner's biographer, for this reference); Trudeau, *Memoirs*, 233–34; and *Le Devoir*, June 22, 23, 1971. Bourassa's aide Charles Denis points out that all the advice Bourassa received was against acceptance and argues that Trudeau overemphasized the extent of agreement at Victoria (Charles Denis, *Robert Bourassa: La Passion de la politique* [Montréal: Fides, 2006], 148–51). Unlike Trudeau, Bourassa courted Ryan assiduously. According to L. Ian MacDonald, Bourassa only once failed to consult Ryan on an important decision—the result being a blistering editorial from Ryan the following morning. Bourassa never made the mistake again. L. Ian MacDonald, *From Bourassa to Bourassa: Wilderness to Restoration*, 2nd ed. (Montreal and Kingston: McGill–Queen's University Press, 2002), 6.

11. *Globe and Mail*, June 23, 1971.

12. On the Quebec labour movement and the CEQ, see Ralph Guentzel, "'Pour un pays à la mesure des aspirations des travailleurs québécois': L'aile socialiste du mouvement syndical québécois et l'indépendantisme (1972–1982)," in Michel Sarra-Bournet, ed., *Les Nationalismes au Québec du XIXème au XXIème siècle* (Québec: Les Presses de l'Université Laval, 2001), 158; *Le Devoir*, Sept. 16, 1971.

13. Trudeau quoted in Westell, *Paradox*, 49; Beetz, "Memorandum pour le Premier Ministre," June 12, 1972, TP, MG 26 020, vol. 23, file 12, LAC. This file contains other memoranda by Beetz, including one written on Feb. 15, 1972, where he uses the term *"les grands feudataires."*

14. Morin, *Quebec versus Ottawa*, 161.

15. Ibid.

16. Raymond Blake, "Social Policy and Constitutional Reform: The Case of Canada's Family Allowance Program in the 1970s," public policy paper 52, Saskatchewan Institute of Public Policy, Dec. 2007.

17. Trudeau, *Memoirs*, 232.

18. Stephen Clarkson and Christina McCall, *The Magnificent Obsession*, vol. 1 of

Trudeau and Our Times (Toronto: McClelland and Stewart, 1990), 124; interview with John Turner, May 2003; Dion quoted in Saywell, ed., *Canadian Annual Review 1971*, 76; and tapes of collective interview with colleagues of Trudeau, Dec. 9, 2002; March 5, 2003; and March 17, 2003, LAC.

19. Claude Lemelin in *Le Devoir*, July 21, 1972. Studies of official bilingualism have revealed that support for French education outside Quebec grew significantly after the Official Languages Act was passed. And despite much criticism of the act itself in the media in Quebec, the support for official bilingualism was extremely high in Quebec: 98 percent of francophones polled in 2002 said that it was "very important" or "important" to them. The percentage elsewhere varied from a high of 76 percent in Atlantic Canada to 63 percent in British Columbia. Andrew Parkin and André Turcotte, *Le Bilinguisme: Appartient-il au passé ou à l'avenir?* (Ottawa: Centre de recherche et d'information sur le Canada, March 2004). Susan Trofimenkoff, *The Dream of Nation: A Social and Intellectual History of Quebec* (Toronto: Gage, 1983), is the source of the statistics on the doubling of the francophone percentage in the military and the public service. Trudeau's description of the "English Only" atmosphere is in his *Memoirs*, 119.

20. See *Le Devoir*, Oct. 9, 1971; Fernand Dumont in *Le Devoir*, Oct. 26, 1971; Christian Dufour, *A Canadian Challenge: Le Défi québécois* (Lantiville, B.C.: Oolichan, 1989); McRoberts criticizes Trudeau's multiculturalism in an interview with Robert Bothwell in Bothwell, *Canada and Quebec: One Country, Two Histories*, rev. ed. (Vancouver: University of British Columbia Press, 1995), 235–36; Arthur Schlesinger, *The Disunity of America: Reflections of a Multicultural Society*, rev. ed. (New York: Norton, 1998); Neil Bissoondath, *Selling Illusions: The Cult of Multiculturalism in Canada*, rev. ed. (Toronto: Penguin, 2002); Ian Buruma, *Murder in Amsterdam: Liberal Europe, Islam, and the Limits of Tolerance* (Toronto: Penguin, 2006); Kwame Anthony Appiah prefers the term "cosmopolitanism," one that resonates with some of Trudeau's earlier writings and with the sign on his dorm-room door at Harvard, which declared him a "citizen of the world" (see *Cosmopolitanism: Ethics in a World of Strangers* [New York: Norton, 2007], xiii); Charles Taylor, *The Malaise of Modernity* (Toronto: Anansi, 1991); Gérard Bouchard and Charles Taylor,

Commission de consultation sur les pratiques d'accommodement reliées aux différences culturelles (Québec: Government of Quebec, 2008); and Will Kymlicka, *Multicultural Citizenship* (Oxford: Clarendon, 1995). Putnam's presentation, which argues for short- to medium-term *"anomie"* but for longer-term benefits based on American historical experience, is found in *"E Pluribus Unum:* Diversity and Community in the Twenty-First Century: The 2006 Johan Skytte Prize Lecture," *Scandinavian Political Studies* 30 (2007), 137–74. *Toronto Star* reported Helliwell's research with the title "Toronto, the Sad?" (Dec. 30, 2007). It pointed out that Toronto did not make the top ten of Canadian cities. Saint John was first, followed by a group of smaller cities. Helliwell emphasizes the importance of government action in integrating immigrants into their new society, and he develops contrasts between Canada and the United States in this respect, using evidence such as how quickly immigrants become citizens and how many adopt hyphenated identities. His work is part of the larger Social Interactions, Identity, and Well-Being project of the Canadian Institute for Advanced Research. A recent edited collection (Will Kymlicka and Keith Banting, eds., *Multiculturalism and the Welfare State: Recognition and Redistribution in Contemporary Democracies* [New York: Oxford University Press, 2006]) points out the international context of the debate over the impact of multiculturalism on the sense of collectivity, which some argue is necessary in the "welfare state." The essays in the book suggest that the jury is still out on the question of the impact of multiculturalism on redistribution and the welfare state.

21. See Mildred Schwartz, *Public Opinion and Canadian Identity* (Scarborough: Fitzhenry and Whiteside, 1967), 86–88.

22. On the multicultural concern in the Pearson years, see J.L. Granatstein, *Canada 1957–1967: The Years of Uncertainty and Innovation* (Toronto: McClelland and Stewart, 1986), 248. Jean Burnet's *Canadian Encyclopedia* entry on multiculturalism states specifically that the term "came into vogue in the 1960s to counter 'biculturalism'" (http://www.thecanadianencyclope-dia.com/index.cfm?PgNm=TCE&Params=A1ARTA0005511). Conservative senator Paul Yuzyk, a Manitoban of Ukrainian extraction, claimed that he developed the term in 1964 in response to the royal commission. The speech describing Yuzyk's claim (made by Senator Rhéal

Bélisle) is in Canada, *Senate Debates* (July 24, 1986). Yuzyk's commemorative website emphasizes his contributions to multiculturalism and to the Ukrainian community: http://www.yuzyk.com/biog-e.shtml.

23. The formal title of the White Paper is *Statement of the Government of Canada on Indian Policy, 1969, Presented to the First Session of the Twenty-Eighth Parliament by the Honourable Jean Chrétien* (Ottawa: Queen's Printer, 1969), v.

24. The Cabinet debate is found in Cabinet Conclusions, RG2, PCO, Series A-5-1, vol. 6381, Sept. 23, 1971, LAC; Canada, *House of Commons Debates* (8 Oct. 1971).

25. John Saywell, ed., *Canadian Annual Review 1971*, 96–98; *Toronto Daily Star*, Oct. 9, 1971; and *Le Devoir*, Oct. 9, 1971.

CHAPTER SIX: THE PARTY IS OVER

1. The Gallup polling data reveal that Liberal support remained fairly solid until the October Crisis. After that it diminished, followed by a sudden drop in late 1971. In August 1971, the results had been 42 percent Liberal, 24 percent Conservative, 24 percent NDP, and 10 percent Créditiste/other. The results are found in John Saywell, ed., *Canadian Annual Review of Public Affairs 1971* (Toronto: University of Toronto Press, 1972), 19.

2. Joseph Wearing, *The L-Shaped Party: The Liberal Party of Canada 1958–1980* (Toronto: McGraw-Hill Ryerson, 1981), 187–88.

3. Ibid., 192.

4. Ibid., 162–63; Richard Gwyn, who worked in Eric Kierans' office in the early 1970s, says that Davey's "consuming passion wasn't so much programs as the *programming of programs.* . . ." (*The Northern Magus: Pierre Trudeau and Canadians* [Toronto: McClelland and Stewart, 1980], 83). The influence of Davey is evident in LPC, MG 28-IV3, vol. 1083, LAC. Richard Stanbury Diary, privately held, personal copy given to me by its author.

5. See John English, *Citizen of the World*, vol. 1 of *The Life of Pierre Elliott Trudeau* (Toronto: Knopf Canada, 2006), 312–24.

6. Stanbury Diary, Oct. 2, 1969; James Robertson, "The Canadian Electoral System" (briefing paper); Parliamentary Information and Research Service, BP437-E, Library of Parliament.

7. Wearing, *L-Shaped Party*, 163. For the transcript of Trudeau's fascinating remarks to the Harrison Hot Springs conference, see Tom Hockin, ed., *Apex of Power: The Prime Minister and Political Leadership in Canada* (Scarborough: Prentice-Hall, 1971), 97–100. Stanbury Diary, June 10, 1970.

8. Stanbury Diary, Sept. 15, 1971; Wearing, *L-Shaped Party*, 169–71; *Toronto Star*, Nov. 22, 1970; and conversation with Allen Linden in early eighties.

9. Tony Judt, *Postwar: A History of Europe since 1945* (New York: Penguin, 2005), 478.

10. Marc Lalonde, "The Changing Role of the Prime Minister's Office," *Canadian Public Administration* (winter 1971): 511; Arthur Schlesinger, *The Imperial Presidency* (Boston: Houghton Mifflin, 1973); and Gordon Robertson, "The Changing Role of the Privy Council Office," *Canadian Public Administration* (winter 1971), which argued that there was far more responsibility and accountability with Trudeau than with Mackenzie King, who "would have preferred to hold everything close to his chest to be brought out for consideration as, when and how he preferred, with his ministers taken by surprise and circulated well in advance" (488). Robert McKenzie's influential study of the "iron law of oligarchy" within British political parties implicitly points to the centralization that occurs with the parties themselves and, therefore, with parties in power (*British Political Parties: The Distribution of Power within the Conservative and Labour Parties*, 2nd ed. [London: Heinemann, 1963]). Interview with Marc Lalonde, Aug. 2007.

11. Donald Savoie, *Court Government and the Collapse of Accountability in Canada and the United Kingdom* (Toronto: University of Toronto Press, 2008); Jeffrey Simpson, *The Friendly Dictatorship* (Toronto: McClelland and Stewart, 2001); Hockin, ed., *Apex of Power*; and Edward Goldenberg, *The Way It Works: Inside Ottawa* (Toronto: McClelland and Stewart, 2006), 388. A contemporary attack is Walter Stewart, *Shrug: Trudeau in Power* (Toronto: New Press, 1971). The socialist Stewart vilified Trudeau's "presidential" style of government, arguing that he preferred "parliamentary democracy, with all its sloppiness, its tedium, even its name-calling, to the single-minded rule of an overbearing man. . . . Unless some of the power is wrested away from the Supergroup, the Prime Minister will soon live in that happiest of all political worlds, the one without an opposition" (3).

12. The survey, "Attitudes about Trudeau, October 1970," is found in ALP, MG 32 C-36, vol. 1, file 2, LAC. Christina McCall-Newman, *Grits: An Intimate Portrait of the Liberal Party* (Toronto: Macmillan, 1982), 126. Pickersgill expressed his bitterness to me personally many times during this period.

13. Henry Lawless, "Correspondence Analysis—July 1969," TP, MG 26 03, vol. 290, file 319-1, LAC.

14. "Attitudes about Trudeau." Emphasis in quote is in the original.

15. Charles Trudeau to Pierre Trudeau, June 20, 1971, TP, MG 26 02, vol. 53, file 28, LAC.

16. Robert Bothwell, Ian Drummond, and John English, *Canada since 1945: Power, Politics, and Provincialism* (Toronto: University of Toronto Press, 1981), 16–17.

17. Alan Greenspan, *The Age of Turbulence: Adventures in a New World* (New York: Penguin, 2007), 61.

18. Trowbridge, quoted in Alfred Eckes, *Opening America's Market: U.S. Foreign Trade Policy since 1776* (Chapel Hill and London: University of North Carolina Press, 1995), 199. See also Thomas Zeiler, *American Trade and Power in the 1960s* (New York: Columbia University Press, 1992).

19. Trudeau, quoted in Anthony Westell, *Paradox: Trudeau as Prime Minister* (Scarborough: Prentice-Hall, 1972), 147.

20. Bulloch gives the history of his crusade, complete with the bathtub incident, in http://www.cfib.ca/legis/ontario/pdf/on0212.pdf. See also I. H. Asper, *The Benson Iceberg: A Critical Analysis of the White Paper on Tax Reform in Canada* (Toronto: Clarke, Irwin, 1970), xv.

21. Danson to Trudeau, Nov. 30, 1970, GP, MG 32 C-86, vol. 1, file 6, LAC.

22. Saywell, ed., *Canadian Annual Review 1971*, 18–19; Canada, *House of Commons Debates* (17 Dec. 1971).

23. The quotation and the description of the Waffle's role is from Ian McKay, *Rebels, Reds, Radicals: Rethinking Canada's Left History* (Toronto: Between the Lines, 2005), 188–89; Westell, *Paradox*, 1, 3.

24. The Australian objections are found in "Discussions with Canadian Prime Minister, Mr. Pierre Trudeau," Cabinet Minutes, May 19, 1970, Series A5852, C0821, National Archives of Australia. The paper incident and Nixon's concurrent efforts are described in Margaret MacMillan, *Nixon in China: The Week That Changed the World* (Toronto: Viking Canada,

2006), 166–67. See also the account in Robert Bothwell, *Alliance and Illusion: Canada and the World, 1945–1984* (Vancouver: University of British Columbia Press, 2007), 308–11. In his memorandum indicating that agreement had been reached, Under-secretary of State for External Affairs Ed Ritchie worried that Taiwan was being forgotten and isolated, but Trudeau seemed much less concerned. Ritchie to "all departments," Oct. 13, 1970, EAP, RG 25, file 10840, dossier 20-1-2PRC, vol. 10, LAC. Much background on the China recognition is found in Paul Evans and B. Michael Frolic, eds., *Reluctant Adversaries: Canada and the People's Republic of China 1949–1970* (Toronto: University of Toronto Press, 1991), especially Section 8, which concentrates on Trudeau's personal and political reasons for desiring recognition. The Finance Department had reservations, and the problem of Taiwan was acknowledged but largely ignored.

25. For opposing views on Trudeau's role in Africa, see Ivan Head and Pierre Trudeau, *The Canadian Way: Shaping Canada's Foreign Policy, 1968–1984* (Toronto: McClelland and Stewart, 1995), 107–15, and Linda Freeman, *The Ambiguous Champion: Canada and South Africa in the Trudeau and Mulroney Years* (Toronto: University of Toronto Press, 1997). On Lee Kuan Yew: conversation with former high commissioner to Singapore Barry Carin, March 2008. Carin said that Lee Kuan Yew had no interest in Canada apart from Trudeau.

26. Ford reacts critically in his memoir, *Our Man in Moscow: A Diplomat's Reflections on the Soviet Union* (Toronto: University of Toronto Press, 1989), 119. There is a good summary of the negative Canadian press reaction in Saywell, ed., *Canadian Annual Review 1971*, 258–60.

27. Trudeau's comment is quoted and assessed in Leigh Sarty, "A Handshake across the Pole: Canadian-Soviet Relations in the Era of Détente," in *Canada and the Soviet Experiment: Essays on Canadian Encounters with Russia and the Soviet Union, 1990–1991*, ed. David Davies (Waterloo: Centre on Foreign Policy and Federalism, 1993), 133n37. The article is the best assessment of Trudeau's behaviour during the visit.

28. Ibid. Sarty translates part of the editorial in which *Pravda* denounced Trudeau's critics as "local champions of 'Cold War,' supported by all kinds of reactionary émigré rabble and unbeaten Hitlerite stooges" in Canada.

Trudeau was praised for his search for "new friends and trading partners to strengthen [Canada's] independence" (125).

29. The two versions are in NP, box 750, 34452, National Archives, Washington. The final was sent on November 23, 1971. The quotation is from the Nixon Tapes, Rmn e5341, July 6, 1971, National Archives, Washington.

30. American Embassy, Ottawa, to Secretary of Defense Melvin Laird, May 27, 1969, White House Situation Room files, box 670 Canada, National Archives, Washington. See http://www.gwu.edu/~nsarchiv/japan/schaller.htm, in which American diplomatic historian Michael Schaller has summarized the mood in Washington based on archival materials in a report for the National Security Archive.

31. The *Canadian Forum* editors published Gray's report and a commentary on it as A *Citizen's Guide to the Gray Report Prepared by The Canadian Forum* (Toronto: New Press, 1971).

32. The full tape of the meeting between Nixon, Kissinger, and Trudeau was released in December 2008. The excerpts here have been taken from a CBC news clip, which can be heard electronically at http://www.thestar.com/Article/550024. The tape also reveals the instructions to Haldeman. A good discussion of the impact of Nixon's economic policies on Canada is found in Bruce Muirhead, *Dancing around the Elephant: Creating a Prosperous Canada in an Era of American Dominance* (Toronto: University of Toronto Press, 2005).

33. Trudeau's report to Cabinet on the visit occurred on December 12, 1971. It concentrated on the Auto Pact and was generally upbeat (RG2, PCO, Series-5-a, vol. 6381, LAC). The best discussion of Nixon's policies and Canada's response is in Bothwell, *Alliance and Illusion*, 319ff.

34. Trudeau made the remark to the Press Club in Washington on March 26, 1969. Quoted in *Globe and Mail*, March 27, 1969.

35. National Security Council Trip Files. President's Visit (April 17–19/72), box 471, National Archives, Washington.

36. Norman Hillmer and J.L. Granatstein, *Empire to Umpire: Canada and the World to the 1990s* (Toronto: Copp Clark, 1994), 296–99. Nixon Tapes, Rmn_734, Dec. 11, 1971, National Archives, Washington; *New York Times*, June 19, 1972.

37. These views are expressed in Bothwell, Drummond, and English, *Canada since 1945*, 410. See also a critique from the left in Alvin Finkel, *Our Lives* (Toronto: Lorimer, 1997), 139ff. Joel Bell, one of the authors of the Trudeau government's industrial policy, says that "In the end . . . the government came to feel that projects were being carried out whose justification lay too much in the virtue of their regional location and not enough in their industrial logic" (Joel Bell, "Industrial Policy in a Changing World," in Thomas S. Axworthy and Pierre Elliott Trudeau, eds., *Towards a Just Society: The Trudeau Years* [Markham, Ont.: Viking, 1990], 91). In the same book, Lloyd Axworthy defends regional development policy but admits that DREE had major "problems." He argues that later policies were successful, particularly in Manitoba ("Regional Development: Innovations in the West," in Axworthy and Trudeau, eds., *Towards a Just Society*, 249ff.).

38. Trudeau to John Godfrey, Feb. 14, 1972, ALP, MG 32 C-86, vol. 1, file 12, LAC; John Gray, "The View from Ottawa," *Maclean's*, Jan. 1972, 4; and Jerome Caminada, "Canada's Struggle for Identity," *Times* (London), Feb. 17, 1972.

39. Paul Litt, draft biography of John Turner, chap. 9; Stanbury Diary, Sept. 1, 1971. See also Wearing, *L-Shaped Party*.

CHAPTER SEVEN: THE LAND IS NOT STRONG

1. Gordon Gibson to Trudeau, Sept. 9, 1969, TP, MG 26 07, vol. 121, file 313.05, LAC. Trudeau wrote, "Hell, No," on the list of appointments that contained the other meetings mentioned.

2. Weiss's remarks are in ALP, MG 32 B22, vol. 30.

3. *New York Times*, Sept. 14, 1972.

4. "The Prime Minister confirmed that it was still his intention to hold a regular Cabinet meeting each week. He added that the odd case might occur where it might be feasible to hold a Cabinet meeting outside of Ottawa, provided that 4 or 5 other ministers were available." Cabinet Conclusions, RG2, PCO, Series-A-5-a, vol. 6395, Sept. 7, 1972, LAC.

5. The farmer story is from Christina McCall-Newman, *Grits: An Intimate Portrait of the Liberal Party* (Toronto: Macmillan, 1982), 130. Interviews with Trudeau ministers, University Club, Toronto, May 24, 2007; Lynch, quoted in *Ottawa Citizen*, Oct. 26, 1972.

6. Eric Kierans with Walter Stewart, *Remembering* (Toronto: Stoddart, 2001), 202–3; Denis Smith, *Gentle Patriot: A Political Biography of Walter Gordon* (Edmonton: Hurtig, 1973), 252–53; and Walter Gordon, "Last Chance for Canada," *Maclean's,* Sept. 1972, 72.
7. Conversation with Kathy Robinson, May 2008.
8. The changes in the Unemployment Insurance Act in 1971 expanded coverage "to nearly all members of the labour force, including teachers, public servants, the armed forces and higher income earners." Claimants also received benefits much earlier, and pregnant women could collect up to fifteen weeks of maternity benefits. Changes in 1972 brought higher costs for employers, which irritated business groups (*Canada Year Book, 1980–81* [Ottawa: Dept. of Supply and Services, 1981], 263, 269). The leading historian of unemployment insurance, James Struthers, described the changes as dramatic: "Over its 69-year history, UI has oscillated between these two competing poles of social protection and moral hazard. Until 1975 social protection dominated. During years of prosperity, eligibility for UI was gradually broadened and benefits levels were increased, slowly throughout the 1950s when seasonal workers were added to the scheme, and explosively between 1971 and 1975 when UI was liberalized to cover 96 percent of the labour force. Only eight weeks of work in a year were needed to make a claim, and benefits reached 66 percent of insurable earnings." *Globe and Mail,* April 15, 2009.
9. Stanbury Diary, privately held, Oct. 5, 1972; Heather Balodis to Alastair Gillespie, Sept. 18, 1972; and Gillespie to Balodis, Sept. 27, 1982, GP, vol. 34, file Letters and Reply, LAC. In his reply to Balodis's very specific letter, Gillespie pointed out that the number of investigators was being significantly increased, that business was being encouraged to ensure compliance, and that "90% of the persons who lose their jobs" face "real hardship." He pointed out that "it is the cheaters, the fraction of people who are taking advantage of the scheme, which angers us all and which smears the most human and comprehensive scheme that I know of." Of the Balodis complaints, three were clearly "abuses" in her view, but their actions were fully within the law, as in the case of someone who "hopes to work part-time, receiving payment in cash so that her UIC cheques will not be diminished." The Mackasey reforms were controversial within the Cabinet and remain

so. Many years later Charles Caccia, whom many regard as the most left-wing member of the Trudeau Cabinet, told me that he thought Trudeau let Mackasey go too far. He did not understand why greater attention had not been paid to the problems that might be created by extending benefits to seasonal workers.

10. The Liberal candidate's address is quoted in George Radwanski, *Trudeau* (Toronto: Macmillan, 1978), 259.

11. Joseph Wearing, *The L-Shaped Party: The Liberal Party of Canada 1958–1980* (Toronto: McGraw-Hill Ryerson, 1981), 199; Pierre Trudeau, *Memoirs* (Toronto: McClelland and Stewart, 1993), 158–60; and Radwanski, *Trudeau*, 264.

12. Stanbury Diary, Oct. 27, 1972; Wearing, *L-Shaped Party*, 196–97; and interviews with Trudeau ministers, University Club, Toronto, May 24, 2007.

13. The description and comments about the hotel room and party are from the October 31 entry in the Stanbury Diary.

14. The quotation from "Desiderata" is in *New York Times*, Oct. 31, 1972. See also *Toronto Star*, Nov. 1, 1972.

15. Interview with Alastair Gillespie, Sept. 2007; Stanbury Diary, Oct. 31, 1972.

16. *Globe and Mail*, Nov. 3, 1972.

17. I owe the references to the calls for resignation by Ross Whicher and Bill Lee to Paul Litt's forthcoming biography of John Turner. Andras was himself bitter: a small businessperson, he annoyed Stanbury in the early morning of October 31, when he and John Nichol, a former party president, "got on the phone with [B.C. Senator] George van Roggen and started talking about the necessity for getting rid of all the socialism in the party." Stanbury Diary, Nov. 1, 1972.

18. Ibid.

19. Cabinet Conclusions, RG2, PCO, Series A-5-a, vol. 6395, Sept. 7, 1972, LAC; Margaret Trudeau, *Beyond Reason* (New York and London: Paddington Press, 1979), 116; and interview with Margaret Trudeau, Feb. 2006.

20. Wearing, *L-Shaped Party*, 199.

21. Trudeau, *Memoirs*, 158–60; Radwanski, *Trudeau*, 264.

22. Pepin had narrowly lost his riding but refused to appeal to a judge.

Marchand and others believed the party should do so. Stanbury asked
Trudeau to intercede and to ask Pepin to permit the party to launch the
appeal. Trudeau said he would do so, though he wanted to make sure that
Pepin did not "take a public stand against us." Pepin refused, arguing that it
would appear, in the eyes of separatists, that a bought Liberal judge was
paying off the party. Stanbury Diary, Nov. 10, 1972.

23. On Pepin, interview with Sheila Mary Pepin, Aug. 2007. Interview with
Herb Gray, July 2007. Trudeau's negative views on Davis and especially
Richardson were well known to colleagues. Conversation with Albert
Breton, Feb. 2006.

24. On the Cabinet meetings, see interviews with Trudeau ministers and associates at Library and Archives Canada, Dec. 9, 2002, and March 5 and 17,
2003. Whelan's admiration for Trudeau is evident in his own memoir,
Whelan: The Man in the Green Stetson (Toronto: Irwin, 1986).

25. An excellent study of the fitful approach to the reform of non-
pharmaceutical drug policy is Marcel Martel, *Not This Time: Canadian
Public Policy and the Marijuana Question, 1961–1975* (Toronto: University
of Toronto Press, 2006). The title confirms the interpretation presented in
this section.

26. Stanbury Diary, Nov. 9, 1972; Wearing, *L-Shaped Party*, 199.

27. McCall-Newman, *Grits*, 149.

28. I am deeply indebted to my former student Professor Stephen Azzi, whose
work on Walter Gordon has illuminated the profound ties between Gordon
and the *Toronto Star: Walter Gordon and the Rise of Canadian Nationalism*
(Kingston and Montreal: McGill–Queen's University Press, 1999).

29. Davey claims that Trudeau was having fun at the dinner, but it is more
likely that McCall's account is the accurate one. See Keith Davey,
The Rainmaker: A Passion for Politics (Toronto: Stoddart, 1986), 162–63,
and McCall-Newman, *Grits*, 149–50. Interview with Marc Lalonde,
Aug. 2007; interview with Tony Abbott, Aug. 2005.

30. *Toronto Star*, Jan. 5, 1972; *Globe and Mail*, Jan. 4, 1972. "IDB" stands for
the Industrial Development Bank, and "UIP" for the Unemployment
Insurance Program. On Trudeau's new attention to the monarchy,
see John Muggeridge, "Why Trudeau, in 1973, Became a Monarchist,"
Saturday Night, Jan. 1974.

31. The interviewer was George Radwanski. See his *Trudeau*, 270.
    Richard Gwyn, *The Northern Magus: Pierre Trudeau and Canadians*
    (Toronto: McClelland and Stewart, 1980), chap.13. He points out
    that by 1976, it was no longer appropriate to tell bilingualism jokes
    such as the one about the lifeguard who let people drown because,
    although he knew the word *nager* (to swim), he did not know how to
    swim. Trudeau's commitment, described so well by Gwyn, is obvious
    in a letter he sent to his Cabinet on April 19, 1973, in which he com-
    plains that despite new rules promulgated in February 1970 regarding
    the use of French and English in the operations of Cabinet,
    "the number of documents submitted in French, while it has
    increased, remains small." Moreover, "the language of discussion
    is predominantly English." Trudeau asks that departments submitting
    documents through their ministers should have the titles in French
    and English. While expressing himself as willing to listen to "difficulties"
    this might create, Trudeau adds: "It is particularly important in this
    context that Ministers and Cabinet take every opportunity to use both
    languages consistent with the efficient and timely discharge of their
    responsibilities." Trudeau to Alastair Gillespie, April 19, 1973,
    GP, vol. 144, file "Correspondence with PM 1-11-1," LAC.
32. John Saywell, ed., *Canadian Annual Review of Politics and Public Affairs
    1976* (Toronto: University of Toronto Press, 1977), 83–44, describes the
    Spicer report on official languages and the reaction.
33. Gwyn, *Northern Magus*, 219–20. Spicer, who became language commis-
    sioner in 1970, traces his long career in defence of bilingualism while
    expressing his doubts about the approach in his memoir *Life Sentences:
    Memoirs of an Incorrigible Canadian* (Toronto: McClelland and Stewart,
    2004). Spicer's successor, Graham Fraser, has written a work on the official
    language policy: *Sorry I Don't Speak French: Confronting the Canadian
    Crisis That Won't Go Away* (Toronto: McClelland and Stewart, 2006). The
    classic attack on Trudeau's policy was written by a former military officer,
    J.V. Andrew: *Bilingual Today, French Tomorrow* (Richmond Hill, Ont.:
    BMG, 1977). The sales of the last book probably exceeded those of all
    others listed in this note. On the roots of the air dispute, see Sandford
    Borins, *The Language of the Skies: The Bilingual Air Traffic Control*

Conflict in Canada (Montreal and Kingston: McGill–Queen's University Press, 1983). John Meisel, *Working Papers on Canadian Politics*, 2nd ed. (Montreal and London: McGill–Queen's University Press, 1975), 218–19.

34. Meisel, *Canadian Politics*, 222.

35. The instructions to embassies are in Tim Porteous to Jean Coté, External Affairs, March 29, 1971, TP, MG 26 07, vol. 121, file 313.09, LAC. See McCall-Newman, *Grits*, 157, in which Margaret is reported as complaining about Roberts's strong enforcement. Margaret acknowledged that Roberts was enforcing the existing rules but complained bitterly about McCall-Newman's persistence in trying to get an interview with her on a Russian trip. Margaret said the result was "bitter journalism" directed against her by McCall-Newman. See Trudeau, *Beyond Reason*, 105.

36. Ibid., 111.

37. Ibid., 99, 114. In an interview in February 2006, Margaret Trudeau confirmed these impressions and remarks, which were presented in *Beyond Reason*.

38. Ibid., 115.

39. In his biography of Yakovlev, Christopher Shulgan points out that Wikipedia in 2008 claimed that Alexandre was named after Yakovlev. He disputes the story, pointing out that Yakovlev had only recently arrived and had not yet established a close relationship with Trudeau. He also notes that Yakovlev's memoirs indicate that Lyudmila Kosygina, the daughter of Soviet premier Alexei Kosygin, who had met Margaret Trudeau and befriended her on the Trudeaus' Soviet visit in 1971, had suggested the name. When Pierre and Margaret were discussing nicknames, Trudeau said that Alexandre could be nicknamed "Sacha." Margaret didn't believe him, so Trudeau told her to call Yakovlev, which she did. Yakovlev confirmed that, indeed, Alexandre could be "Sacha," and the nickname stuck. Alexandre Trudeau himself says that he was "named after Yakovlev," which is essentially what the Wikipedia story claims. In essence, the mists of memory cloud the issue. See Christopher Shulgan, *The Soviet Ambassador: The Making of the Radical behind Perestroika* (Toronto: McClelland and Stewart, 2008), 179. Conversation with Alexandre Trudeau, April 2007. The Wikipedia entry is http://en.wikipedia.org/wiki/Alexandre_Trudeau.

40. Trudeau, *Beyond Reason*, 133–34; interview with Margaret Trudeau, Feb. 2006.

41. Arthur Erickson would play a large role in Trudeau's life after this initial experience. The many letters sent between Trudeau and Erickson are in TP, MG 26 020, vol. 2, LAC.

42. See Shulgan, *Soviet Ambassador*, 179–80.

43. This section draws on Trudeau, *Beyond Reason*, 134–37, and Radwanski, *Trudeau*, which is especially valuable because the first chapter follows Trudeau in a typical day at the office. Other sources include McCall-Newman, *Grits*, 133, and interviews with Margaret Trudeau and Justin Trudeau, as well as Jim Coutts, Robert Murdoch, Tim Porteous, Jacques Hébert, Albert Breton, Marc Lalonde, and several others who interacted with the Trudeaus in those times.

44. Trudeau, *Beyond Reason*, 136.

45. Ibid., 120–22, 136.

CHAPTER EIGHT: THE STRANGE REBIRTH OF PIERRE TRUDEAU

1. Document in ABP, privately held.

2. Alastair Gillespie, "Memorandum to Self: Notes on Hudson Institute Seminar, Aug. 22, 1972," GP, vol. 46, file "associations e21," LAC; interview with John Kenneth Galbraith, Oct. 2005; and Jason Churchill, "The Limits to Influence: The Club of Rome and Canada 1968 to 1988" (PhD diss., University of Waterloo, 2006), 132ff. Trudeau remarked on his interest in the Club of Rome but dissociated himself from *The Limits to Growth: A Report for the Club of Rome's Project on the Predicament of Mankind* (New York: Universe, 1972), whose conclusions had become discredited, in a conversation with American ambassador Thomas Enders in 1976. "Conversation with Trudeau August 1976," WSP, Economic Policy Board, files 1974–77, box 224, file 7660247, Ambassador Enders, Gerald R. Ford Presidential Library.

3. Albert Breton, "For the Prime Minister: A Personal Reading of Current Economic Events," Nov. 12, 1971, ABP, privately held. The memorandum was circulated to the PCO and PMO only, and even then, only to the most senior officials: Lalonde, Head, Pitfield, Robertson, Crowe, Hudon, and Davey.

4. *Toronto Star*, Jan. 29, 1972.
5. Turner made these comments on an index card (cited by Paul Litt in his draft biography of John Turner). The finest treatment of the international ramifications of the political situation are found in Robert Bothwell, *Alliance and Illusion: Canada and the World, 1945–1984* (Vancouver: University of British Columbia Press, 2007), chap.17.
6. On Nixon's reaction, see Helmut Sonnenfeldt to Henry Kissinger, Jan. 17, 1973, NP, NSC files, box 750, file "Canada, Trudeau," National Archives, Washington. Richard Gwyn's *Northern Magus: Pierre Trudeau and Canadians* (Toronto: McClelland and Stewart, 1980) captures exceptionally well the tensions within the government during this period. Written before archival documents became available, his chapter 9 on the 1972–74 period remains the best account of the Trudeau minority.
7. "Cutting the Corporate Income Tax," Breton to Trudeau, Jan. 19, 1973, ABP; "The Elasticity of the Tax Base," Breton to Trudeau, March 1, 1973, ABP; *Toronto Star*, Feb. 20, 1973; *Globe and Mail*, Feb. 20, 1973; and Litt, Turner draft biography. Cabinet discussion (including the discussion of Feb. 13, 1974) is found in RG2, PCO, Series A-5-a, vol. 6422, LAC.
8. Ron Graham, *One-Eyed Kings: Promise and Illusion in Canadian Politics* (Toronto: Collins, 1986), 203.
9. The best account of this period is found in Douglas Hartle, *The Expenditure Budget Process in the Government of Canada* (Toronto: Canadian Tax Foundation, 1978). Breton to Trudeau, April 9, 1973, ABP.
10. Breton to Trudeau, May 5, 1973, ABP; "Entrevue entre M. Trudeau et M. Lépine" [M. Lépine interview], May 5, 1992, TP, MG 26 020, vol. 23, file 8, part 1, LAC.
11. Quotations from draft memoirs of Alastair Gillespie and conversations with Gillespie. The *Barron's* quotation is from Gwyn, *Northern Magus*, 304. In 1981 Ian Drummond, the outstanding Canadian economic historian of his generation, assessed FIRA's effectiveness: "What FIRA actually meant was hard to say. Naturally its promoters thought it did not go far enough, while many Canadian economists and businessmen thought it went rather too far." He pointed out that it became more unpredictable in the later

1970s, but that it did approve more than two-thirds of all applications. See Robert Bothwell, Ian Drummond, and John English, *Canada since 1945: Power, Politics, and Provincialism* (Toronto: University of Toronto Press, 1981), 416–17.

12. In their biography of C.D. Howe, Robert Bothwell and William Kilbourn describe how he received the nickname "Minister of Everything." Howe, they write, "was informed of what was happening or what was about to happen everywhere in Canada. To Canadian business, Howe was synonymous with 'Ottawa.'" *C.D. Howe: A Biography* (Toronto: McClelland and Stewart, 1979), 262.

13. Gerald Friesen, *The Canadian Prairies: A History* (Toronto: University of Toronto Press, 1984), 443, 445.

14. Douglas Owram, "The Perfect Storm: The National Energy Program and the Failure of Federal-Provincial Relations," in *Forging Alberta's Constitutional Framework*, ed. Richard Connors and John Law (Edmonton: University of Alberta Press, 2005), 404–5. See also Allan Hustak, *Peter Lougheed: A Biography* (Toronto: McClelland and Stewart, 1979).

15. OECD delegation, Paris, to External Affairs, May 2, 1973, GP, R1526, vol. 35, file Trade Issues, LAC; "Notes for the Prime Minister's Opening Remarks at the Western Economic Opportunities Conference," Calgary, Alta., July 24, 1973.

16. Cabinet Conclusions, RG2, PCO, Series A-5-a, vol. 6422, Oct. 31, 1973. On the uncertainty about supply, see Tammy Nemeth, "Continental Drift: Canada-U.S. Oil and Gas Relations, 1958–1974" (PhD diss., University of British Columbia, 2007), 316n166.

17. Cabinet Conclusions, ibid., Nov. 22 and 27, 1973.

18. Ibid., Dec. 12, 1973. Nemeth's thesis (see note 16) suggests more continuity in policy than the Cabinet minutes suggest. The Cabinet debates indicate considerable confusion and reaction to events. Earlier, G. Bruce Doern and Glen Toner had emphasized how the government "reeled" from crisis to crisis, with little sense of where actions would lead. G. Bruce Doern and Glen Toner, *The Politics of Energy: The Development and Implementation of the NEP* (Toronto: Methuen, 1985), 91.

19. Comments in J.T. Saywell, ed., *Canadian Annual Review of Politics and Public Affairs 1974* (Toronto: University of Toronto Press, 1975), 92–98.

20. Lawrence LeDuc, "The Measurement of Public Opinion," in *Canada at the Polls: The General Election of 1974*, ed. Howard Penniman (Washington, D.C.: American Enterprise Institute for Public Policy Research, 1975), 230. The graph on that page is derived from Gallup surveys. Colin Kenny to Trudeau, Nov. 16, 1973, TP, MG 26 07, vol. 121, file 313-05, 1973–75, LAC.

21. Pierre Trudeau, *Memoirs* (Toronto: McClelland and Stewart, 1993), 209–10; Margaret Trudeau, *Beyond Reason* (New York and London: Paddington Press, 1979), 184; and *New York Times*, Oct. 14, 1973. On the trade advantages, see Karen Minden, "Politics and Business: The Canada-China Wheat Trade 1960–1984," in *Canadian Agriculture in a Global Context*, ed. Irene Knell and John English (Waterloo: University of Waterloo Press), 103–22. Minden demonstrates how Canada had advantages over other traders such as Australia and the United States that can be explained only by Chinese political favouritism. Alexandre Trudeau confirms the often-quoted remark that Trudeau considered Chou the most impressive.

22. Michael Manley, quoted in Trudeau, *Memoirs*, 166; *New York Times*, Nov. 18, 1973.

23. *Canada Year Book 1978–79* (Ottawa: Ministry of Supply and Services, 1978), 361–62, 864.

24. See the excellent account in Saywell, ed., *Canadian Annual Review 1974*, 98ff., which includes correspondence between Lougheed and Trudeau.

25. Ibid.,103–7. The letter is remarkably detailed and long.

26. Ibid., 23. Canada, *House of Commons Debates* (7–8 May 1974). Trudeau admitted in his *Memoirs* that he had engineered the defeat: "If it's called manipulative, then so be it. I had learned in 1972 that I almost threw the election away because I had been too theoretical, too unconscious of the need for a political machine, too oblivious to the need of the people working for us and to the need for the stimulation of the party. So I wasn't about to commit the same mistake in 1974" (177).

27. Davey, quoted in George Radwanski, *Trudeau* (Toronto: Macmillan, 1978), 284.

28. *Toronto Star*, June 5, 1974; Saywell, ed., *Canadian Annual Review 1974*, 38–39; and LeDuc, "Measurement of Public Opinion," 239.

29. *Toronto Star,* June 1, 1974; Trudeau, *Beyond Reason,* 166–75; and conversations with Jim Coutts, Bob Murdoch, Keith Davey, and Margaret Trudeau.

30. *Montreal Gazette,* June 5, 1974; Saywell, ed., *Canadian Annual Review 1974,* 46–49; and Paul Desmarais to Trudeau, nd [June 1974], TP, MG 26 020, vol. 17, file 14, LAC. After the election, Trudeau visited the Desmarais estate on Anticosti Island, accompanied by Justin and Pierre's brother, Charles. Trudeau told Desmarais that "your two sons, Paul and André, impressed me by their kindness and because their help allowed us fully to enjoy this brief holiday." Trudeau to Desmarais, Aug. 20, 1974, TP, MG 26 020, vol. 17, file 13, LAC.

31. Joe Wearing, a well-informed analyst with close Liberal ties, says that "such a campaign was not without its tensions, however: the campaign committee was reportedly upset with the overwhelming emphasis on the leader and, according to one assessment, 'the whole campaign would have come apart if it had gone on for another week.'" The footnotes for this quotation reference interviews with Jerry Grafstein and Blair Williams, both members of the committee. Joseph Wearing, *The L-Shaped Party: The Liberal Party of Canada* (Toronto: McGraw-Hill Ryerson, 1981), 203.

32. Stephen Clarkson, "Pierre Trudeau and the Liberal Party: The Jockey and the Horse," in *Canada at the Polls,* ed. Penniman, 84–86.

33. LeDuc, "Measurement of Public Opinion," 232. Fifty-seven percent agreed that Trudeau had changed.

34. The election results are in William Irvine, "An Overview of the 1974 Federal Election in Canada," chap 2. in *Canada at the Polls,* ed. Penniman. See also Saywell, ed., *Canadian Annual Review 1974,* 70 (Davey quotation), and Trudeau, *Beyond Reason,* 174–75. A later academic study supports the view that leadership was a factor, but perhaps it was more the appearance of weaker leadership by Stanfield than strong leadership by Trudeau. Trudeau did not run ahead of the Liberal Party itself in this campaign, although he would do so in 1979. See Wearing, *L-Shaped Party,* 204, and J.H. Pammett et al., "The Perception and Impact of Issues in the 1974 Federal Election," *Canadian Journal of Political Science* 10 (1977): 94–126.

35. Trudeau, *Beyond Reason,* 174–75.

CHAPTER NINE: MID-TERM PROMISE

1. Rebecca DiFilippo, "Margaret Trudeau: Bipolar Disorder Drove Her Despair, Fired Her Courage," *Moods*, fall 2006, 49. See also "The Trudeaus Today: Margaret, Justin and Alexandre Unite to Share Heartfelt Memories and Discuss Their Humanitarian Achievements," *Hello*, Sept. 7, 2006, 70–80. Ms. Trudeau publicly revealed her illness at a May 5, 2006, press conference at the Royal Ottawa Hospital. She told the press that she dealt with her mood swings secretly: "It was never talked about in those days and barely recognized, no matter what sector of society you lived in. And so, in the public eye and under public scrutiny, I tried to manage as best I could" (*Ottawa Citizen*, May 6, 2006). She also gave an extensive interview to Anne Kingston for a *Maclean's* article (May 19, 2006). In that interview, Ms. Trudeau indicated that she had first been diagnosed with bipolar disease in 2000. Interview with Margaret Trudeau, June 2009.

2. Margaret Trudeau, *Beyond Reason* (New York and London: Paddington Press, 1979), 166–67. Trudeau confirms this account in Pierre Trudeau, *Memoirs* (Toronto: McClelland and Stewart, 1993), 178–79. Trudeau's campaign team was worried about the approach until Margaret's presence began attracting favourable press. She jousted particularly with Ivan Head but liked some Trudeau assistants, notably Bob Murdoch, who had known Margaret and her family earlier. Interview with Margaret Trudeau, Feb. 2006; conversations with several members of the Trudeau campaign in 1974.

3. Trudeau, *Beyond Reason*, 193; Anne Kingston interview, *Maclean's*, May 19, 2006. The comment on the "tunnel of darkness" is from *Ottawa Citizen*, May 6, 2006.

4. Trudeau, *Beyond Reason*, 166. Margaret's depression after Sacha's birth had a deep impact on Pierre, according to one story told by Peter C. Newman. Trudeau, accompanied by Stuart Hodgson, commissioner of the Northwest Territories, flew over the North Pole in the winter of 1974. Trudeau took over flying the plane as they passed over the Pole, and Hodgson made arrangements for him to speak to Margaret, who was in Ottawa. The Trudeau housekeeper answered an excited Trudeau. Then, Newman continues, Trudeau told Hodgson that Margaret would not speak

with him, and he "sobbed." Hodgson asked gently, "Why did you marry her?" "Because I love her, I truly love her," Trudeau replied. Peter C. Newman, *Here Be Dragons: Telling Tales of People, Passion, and Power* (Toronto: McClelland and Stewart, 2004), 337.

5. Keith Davey, *The Rainmaker: A Passion for Politics* (Toronto: Stoddart, 1986), 165; Richard Gwyn, *The Northern Magus: Pierre Trudeau and Canadians* (Toronto: McClelland and Stewart, 1980), 186; Paul Litt, draft biography of John Turner; and conversation with John Turner, Sept. 2008. Turner would report regularly to Cabinet on his dealings with U.S. Treasury Secretary George Shultz. See Cabinet Conclusions, RG2, PCO, Series A-5-a, vol. 6422, Aug. 1, 1973.

6. Mitchell Sharp, *Which Reminds Me . . . : A Memoir* (Toronto: University of Toronto Press, 1994), 166; Davey, *Rainmaker*, 187; and numerous conversations with J.W. Pickersgill, 1974. I lived in Mr. Pickersgill's house during the election campaign and heard his reports on Reisman, with whom he agreed in many respects.

7. On Reisman and the election, see Christina McCall-Newman, *Grits: An Intimate Portrait of the Liberal Party* (Toronto: Macmillan, 1982), 223–25. Breton to Trudeau, Dec. 21, 1972, ABP, privately held.

8. The Trudeau decision, which Turner questioned, is described in Cabinet Conclusions, RG2, Series A-5-a, vol. 6436, Nov. 14, 1974. See also Stephen Clarkson and Christina McCall, *The Heroic Delusion*, vol. 2 of *Trudeau and Our Times* (Toronto: McClelland and Stewart, 1994), 112–14.

9. J.T. Saywell, ed., *Canadian Annual Review of Politics and Public Affairs 1974* (Toronto: University of Toronto Press, 1975), 346ff.

10. McLuhan to Trudeau, Aug. 14, 1973, with attachment, TP, MG 26 020, vol. 9, file 32, LAC (emphasis in original). McLuhan's approach to inflation bears comparison with that of John Kenneth Galbraith, who influenced Trudeau's thinking at this time. Galbraith emphasized the role of advertising in creating artificial needs and tried to understand the impact of communications. McLuhan related inflation to the new economy as he understood it: "In order to understand inflation in a world of instantaneous and universal information it is necessary to see the old hardware of products and prices as they now interface with the new hidden ground of worldwide and instant information. It is not only a new ball-game it is a

new ball-park with new ground rules when the old industrial production of hardware technology is suddenly located *inside* an environment of simultaneous electric information. The phrase 'making money' came in at the beginning of the twentieth century along with 'making news.' Both are aspects of the same information process. At electric speed, time and space are greatly abridged, if not altogether eliminated" (emphasis in original).

11. G. Bruce Doern and Glen Toner, *The Politics of Energy: The Development and Implementation of the NEP* (Toronto: Methuen, 1985), 88ff.; Cabinet Conclusions, RG2, Series A-5-a, vol. 6436, Jan. 17, 1974, LAC; and Tammy Nemeth, "Continental Drift: Canada-U.S. Oil and Gas Relations, 1958–1974" (PhD diss., University of British Columbia, 2007), chap. 4.

12. *New York Times*, July 10, 1974. Unemployment was a low 4.9 percent in June 1974, and Saywell, ed., *Canadian Annual Review 1974* summarized the year as one in which "the Canadian economy performed reasonably well" (346).

13. The statistics on divorce are from *Canada Year Book, 1978–79* (Ottawa: Ministry of Supply and Services, 1978), 167; those on abortion, from Statistics Canada: http://cansim2.statcan.ca/cgi-win/cnsmcgi.pgm?regtkt=&C2Sub=HEALTH&ARRAYID=1069013&C2DB=&VEC=&LANG=E&SrchVer=&ChunkSize=&SDDSLOC=&ROOTDIR=CII/&RESULTTEMPLATE=CII/CII_PICK&ARRAY_PICK=1&SDDSID=&SDDSDESC=. On Morgentaler, Trudeau, and Lang, see articles by Andrew Thompson and Otto Lang in *The Hidden Pierre Elliott Trudeau: The Faith behind the Politics*, ed. John English, Richard Gwyn, and P. Whitney Lackenbauer (Ottawa: Novalis, 2004). Cabinet responses to the Morgentaler decision can be seen in Cabinet Conclusions, RG2, Series A-5-a, vol. 6457, June 26 and July 3, 1975. Trudeau expressed concern that the overturning of the Morgentaler decision was leading to a questioning of the jury system.

14. Canada, *House of Commons Debates* (14 July 1976). Capital punishment was retained for treason and military crimes, but it was removed from the Criminal Code and replaced by twenty-five-year mandatory sentences for first-degree murder (*Globe and Mail*, June 23, 1976). There is a full account of the debate in John Saywell, ed., *Canadian Annual Review of Politics and Public Affairs 1976* (Toronto: University of Toronto Press,

1977), 9–12. The Gwyn description and the Gallup poll results are contained in this account.

15. Henry Kissinger, *White House Years* (Boston and Toronto: Little, Brown, 1979), 384–85, and National Security Advisers, Memoranda and Conversations, box 7, Gerald Ford, Kissinger, and Scowcroft, Dec. 3, 1974, Gerald R. Ford Presidential Library. See also Nixon presidential tapes, rmn e534a, July 6, 1971; rmn _625b, Nov. 10, 1971; rmn_629a, Dec. 11, 1971; and rmne759_10, Aug. 19, 1972. See the fine assessment of the relationship in Robert Bothwell, *Alliance and Illusion: Canada and the World, 1945–1984* (Vancouver: University of British Columbia Press, 2007), 314ff.

16. Ivan Head and Pierre Trudeau, *The Canadian Way: Shaping Canada's Foreign Policy, 1968–1984* (Toronto: McClelland and Stewart, 1995), 39.

17. In his study of parliamentary reform, Thomas Axworthy puts the Canadian situation within an international context. While deploring Trudeau's famous remark about MPs being "nobodies" fifty yards from Parliament Hill, Axworthy credits Trudeau with several reforms: "There can be little doubt that the enduring parliamentary legacy of the Trudeau era is embedding the committee system and giving the government Standing Order 75-C for time allocation." *Everything Old Is New Again: Observations on Parliamentary Reform* (Kingston: The Centre for the Study of Democracy, Queen's University, 2008), 47.

18. Stanfield is quoted in Saywell, ed., *Canadian Annual Review 1974*, 56–57. See also Matthew Hayday, *Bilingual Today, United Tomorrow: Official Languages in Education and Canadian Federalism* (Montreal and Kingston: McGill–Queen's University Press, 2005), 181. See especially chapter 3, where he discusses the period 1970–76.

19. Peter Desbarats, "Future Canadians May Regard Trudeau as a Success," *Saturday Night*, June 1975, 9–12.

20. Claude Ryan, "The Three Doves Ten Years Later," in *The Trudeau Decade*, ed. Rick Butler and Jean-Guy Carrier (Toronto: Doubleday, 1979), 290–91. [Originally published in French in *Le Devoir*, June 10, 1975.]

21. George Radwanski, *Trudeau* (Toronto: Macmillan, 1978), 345–46, 350. Radwanski's last chapter is entitled "A Leader Unfulfilled." He dates his introduction January 1978.

22. Canada, *House of Commons Debates* (22 Jan. 1975); John Saywell, ed., *Canadian Annual Review of Politics and Public Affairs 1975* (Toronto: University of Toronto Press, 1976), 7, 87–88; Marchand to Trudeau, July 11, 1975, TP, MG 26 020, vol. 8, file 20, LAC; interviews with Marc Lalonde (Aug. 2007), Alexandre Trudeau (April 2007), Jacques Hébert (July 2007); and conversations with Pauline Bothwell. The comments on the hospital visit are in Saywell, ed., *Canadian Annual Review 1975*, 88. The police report on Marchand is found with Trudeau's annotations in TP, MG 26 020, vol. 8, file 20, LAC. According to the police report there was a female companion with Marchand. Her presence was the apparent reason for his decision not to use the government chauffeur and for his erratic behaviour when he struck the other car.

23. Interview with Herb Gray, July 2007. Trudeau personally assured Gray that it was not Michael Pitfield, Gray's former deputy minister, who had spoken against Gray. On Davey and the Cabinet, see Davey, *Rainmaker*, 192.

24. I discussed this Liberal tradition and Trudeau's role in international affairs in my article "In the Liberal Tradition: Lloyd Axworthy and Canadian Foreign Policy," in Canada among Nations 2001: *The Axworthy Legacy*, ed. Fen Hampson, Norman Hillmer, and Maureen Molot (Toronto: Oxford University Press, 2001), 89–93.

25. James Eayrs, "Defining a New Place for Canada in the Hierarchy of World Power," *International Perspectives* (May/June 1975): 24; Bothwell, *Alliance and Illusion*, 346–48; and J.L. Granatstein and Robert Bothwell, *Pirouette: Pierre Trudeau and Canadian Foreign Policy* (Toronto: University of Toronto Press, 1990), chap. 6.

26. Peter Hayman, British High Commission, Ottawa, to Hon. H.A.A. Hankey, Foreign and Commonwealth Office, July 15, 1971, FCO 82/17.122837, National Archives of the United Kingdom. Granatstein and Bothwell, *Pirouette*, 164. I have also discussed the Third Option with Dupuy, who remained an enthusiast for the contractual link for many years.

27. The foreign policy speech was given to the Canadian Jewish Congress, June 16, 1974. EAP, file 20-2-2-1, vol. 8821, LAC. The Chinese speech is quoted in Eayrs, "Defining a New Place for Canada," 24.

28. In the universities, the writings of Argentinian economist and international public servant Raúl Prebisch gained significant influence, especially in

Canada, where a neo-Marxist cadre of political scientists found Prebisch's theory of the economic dependency of the periphery on the centre to be illuminating. Trudeau thought these were little more than academic musings, for which he had increasingly less respect.

29. Trudeau to MacEachen, Sept. 4, 1974, quoted in draft history of the Department of External Affairs.

30. Robinson had justifiably earned great admiration for his ability to act as foreign policy adviser to the difficult John Diefenbaker, and he had good friends in the government, notably his fellow cricket players Alastair Gillespie and Donald Macdonald. Basil Robinson wrote the finest study of Diefenbaker's foreign policy: *Diefenbaker's World: A Populist in Foreign Affairs* (Toronto: University of Toronto Press, 1988). The book indicates that Robinson's time with Diefenbaker prepared him well for the equally difficult struggles with Head and, to a lesser degree, Trudeau.

31. The comment about Head and the "spy" is found in the draft history of the Department of External Affairs and is made by the "spy" himself: Norman Riddell.

32. Canadian Embassy, Denmark, to Under-Secretary of State for External Affairs, with attachment, June 6, 1975, EAP, RG 25, vol. 9246, file 20-CDA-9-Trudeau/SCAN, LAC; Ivan Head to Basil Robinson, May 12, 1975, ibid. Head attended the meeting, along with John Halstead, who was deputy under-secretary. Trudeau's press secretary, Pierre O'Neill, and his executive assistant, Bob Murdoch, were also in attendance.

33. Trudeau had played a role in changing the structure of the Commonwealth meetings, particularly at the meeting in Ottawa in 1973. He emphasized informality and careful preparation, including visits by Head to the member countries before the meeting. See Bothwell, *Alliance and Illusion*, 350.

34. Canadian Embassy, Denmark, to Under-Secretary of State for External Affairs, with attachment, June 6, 1975, EAP, RG 25, vol. 9246, file 20-CDA-9-Trudeau/SCAN, LAC; Ivan Head to Basil Robinson, May 12, 1975, ibid.

35. Head and Trudeau, *Canadian Way*, 147. Speech in TP, MG 26 020, vol. 741, box 241, file Trudeau, Pierre corresp., news release, LAC.

36. Mitchell Sharp, Acting Secretary of State for External Affairs, to Trudeau, Dec. 16, 1975, EAP, RG 25, vol. 9246, file 20-1-2USA, LAC.

37. Cabinet Conclusions, RG2, PCO, Series A-5-a, vol. 6456, June 19, July 10, and July 24, 1975; *Canadian Annual Review 1975*, 290–94; *Toronto Star*, July 16, 1975; and conversations with Barney Danson and Allan Gotlieb. John Holmes, a retired diplomat, director of the Canadian Institute of International Affairs, and widely regarded as the leading analyst of Canadian foreign policy, deplored Trudeau's decision. He was quoted in the Canadian edition of *Time* (Aug. 4, 1975) as saying: "Canada has set a very unfortunate precedent. The tragedy is that well-meaning people in Toronto and Ontario are encouraging rather than discouraging terrorism. The media have misrepresented the Palestine Liberation Organization. It is a fragmented organization. The moderates who are in control are themselves fighting to rid it of terrorist factions. To get a settlement in the Middle East, Israel will have to deal with the Palestinians, and who is going to represent them? By giving the Palestinians a platform, it removes some of the frustrations." Holmes told me at the time that in response to his comment, he received much criticism, suggesting he was soft on terrorism and even anti-Semitic.

38. Head and Trudeau, *Canadian Way*. Trudeau speaks about his poor relationship with Begin in his *Memoirs*, 217–18. When he discussed Begin with his friend Gale Zoë Garnett in 1981, he expressed his deep dislike of the man. Trudeau was also influenced by the fact that Likud was a religiously based party, while Labour was secular. Gale Zoë Garnett to Trudeau, June 11, 1981, TP, MG 26 020, vol. 4, file 4-42, LAC; conversation with Gale Zoë Garnett, Sept. 2007.

39. Peter Hajnal, in *The G8 System and the G20: Evolution, Role, and Documentation* (Aldershot: Ashgate, 2007), uses recently opened archival sources to trace the formation of the institution. This account also relies on Bothwell, *Alliance and Illusion*, 348–50, and Head and Trudeau, *Canadian Way*, 196–97. Head and Trudeau report that Trudeau was "critical of the department . . . when some senior officials employed in public statements the very kind of language to which he objected . . . [and] regarded as undignified and counterproductive" (197). Paul Martin, *The London Diaries, 1975–1979* (Ottawa: University of Ottawa Press,

1988), 70–92, has excellent reporting on the emerging effort to exclude Canada from the new organization. The important American documents are Helmut Sonnenfeldt, Memorandum of Conversation with Canadian Ambassador Jake Warren, Oct. 22, 1975, and Mack Johnson, U.S. Embassy, Ottawa, to State Dept., Oct. 31, 1975 (Ford Papers, NSA Presidential Country Files, box 3, Gerald R. Ford Presidential Library). On the Canadian side, the documents are found in RG 25, box 14123, file 3504-ESC, LAC, notably a Head "Memorandum for File" of October 3, 1975. On Puerto Rico, see "Report by Peter Towe on Preparatory Discussion for Puerto Rico Economic Summit," June 14, 1976. The British position has been described as supportive, but the Martin diaries, as well as the External Affairs papers, make it clear that the British hesitated for fear of irritating the French, with whom relations were not good at the time. Apart from the general attitude to Canada, the French clearly opposed the notion of a second North American representative, and they anticipated, correctly, that Canada shared the American view on currency exchange issues.

40. Thomas Courchene, "Proposals for a New National Policy," in *In Pursuit of the Public Good: Essays in Honour of Allan J. MacEachen*, ed. Tom Kent (Montreal and Kingston: McGill–Queen's University Press, 1997), 75, and Richard Harris, "Canadian Economic Growth: Perspective and Prospects," in ibid., 124–25.

41. The assessment of the ministers is based on my reading of Cabinet Conclusions, interviews (which are less reliable), and documentation of the time. The quotation describing Hayek is from a sympathetic study of the conservative revolution by Daniel Yergin and Joseph Stanislaw, *The Commanding Heights: The Battle for the World Economy* (New York: Touchstone Books, 2002), 80.

CHAPTER TEN: WRONG TURNS

1. On Finance's position, see Douglas Hartle, *The Expenditure Budget Process in the Government of Canada* (Toronto: Canadian Tax Foundation, 1978), 6–12, which emphasizes the department's anti-interventionist stand. Ron Graham, *One-Eyed Kings: Promise and Illusion in Canadian Politics* (Toronto: Collins, 1986), 203, 210–11; and Paul Litt, draft biography of

John Turner. A useful biography of Galbraith, which illustrates his influence on Trudeau's language and thought, is Richard Parker, *John Kenneth
Galbraith: His Life, His Politics, His Economics* (New York: Farrar, Straus,
and Giroux, 2005). Parker views *Economics and the Public Purpose* (New
York: Houghton Mifflin, 1973) as the product of Galbraith's disillusionment with American capitalism and public policy after Vietnam, Nixon,
and the financial crises of the early seventies. He agrees that Galbraith
became a socialist at this time.

2. Albert Breton, "Memorandum for the Prime Minister. Do Markets Work?"
Jan. 16, 1976 (ABP, privately held). An excellent summary of Galbraith's
own recognition late in life that his concept of the corporation failed to
take into account international competition and its altered form is found in
a review of Richard Parker by Keynes' biographer Robert Skidelsky,
http://skidelskyr.com/index.php?id=2,85,0,0,1,0

3. The statistics are taken from John Saywell, ed., *Canadian Annual Review of
Politics and Public Affairs 1975* (Toronto: University of Toronto Press, 1976),
6, 313ff., and Robert Bothwell, Ian Drummond, and John English, *Canada
since 1945: Power, Politics, and Provincialism* (Toronto: University of Toronto
Press, 1981), chap. 33. The Whelan comment about farmers' exemptions is
in Cabinet Conclusions, RG2, PCO, Series A-5-a, vol. 6456, LAC.

4. Cabinet Conclusions, May 22 and June 18, 1975, ibid. Litt, Turner draft
biography.

5. On Reisman, see Stephen Clarkson and Christina McCall, *The Heroic
Delusion*, vol. 2 of *Trudeau and Our Times* (Toronto: McClelland and
Stewart, 1994), 112–13, 122. The account is based on comments Reisman
made soon after his resignation. An excellent brief summary of the growth
and restructuring of the Canadian social welfare system from the perspec-
tive of the mid-nineties is found in Ken Battle, "Back to the Future:
Reforming Social Policy in Canada," in *In Pursuit of the Public Good:
Essays in Honour of Allan J. MacEachen*, ed. Tom Kent (Montreal and
Kingston: McGill–Queen's University Press, 1997), 35–43. There are
numerous contemporary descriptions of the creation of the Canadian
welfare state, notably Dennis Guest, *The Emergence of Social Security in
Canada* (Vancouver: University of British Columbia Press, 1980); Rodney
Haddow, *Poverty Reform in Canada, 1958–1978* (Montreal and Kingston:

McGill–Queen's University Press, 1978); and Richard Van Loon, "Reforming Welfare in Canada," *Public Policy* (fall 1979): 469–504.

6. On Grandy's and Reisman's resignations, conversations with their former ministers Alastair Gillespie and John Turner. On Morris's statement, see Saywell, ed., *Canadian Annual Review 1975*, 328. On the oil business and government, see Peter Foster, *The Blue-Eyed Sheiks: The Canadian Oil Establishment* (Toronto: Collins, 1979), 151—an early inside account of the period, which has stood the test of time well.

7. The well-informed journalist W.A. Wilson claimed that Turner's resentment of the "slighting way" Trudeau treated Reisman's resignation became a reason for his own resignation (*Montreal Star*, Jan. 27, 1976). Wilson's views are described in Saywell, ed., *Canadian Annual Review 1975*, 336. It notes also that business economists were, on the whole, positive. Breton wrote to Trudeau on June 27, 1975, criticizing the budget: "Inflation to-day is very different than it was only 18 months or even 12 months ago. Excess demand plays no role now; demand shift plays a very minor role; shortages for the same reasons are unimportant; there is enough unemployment in the private sector to dampen demands there. The new challenge is cost-push in the public sector and inflationary expectations." ABP.

8. As a spectator in that crowd, I can affirm this account. See Jack Cahill, *John Turner, the Long Run: A Biography* (Toronto: McClelland and Stewart, 1984), 182; George Radwanski, *Trudeau* (Toronto: Macmillan, 1978), 224–26; and Vic Mackie, *Montreal Star*, Oct. 11, 1975. An interview with Trudeau at the time of the resignation is recorded on a CBC tape, showing him in a colourful sports shirt and white jeans, and includes comments by Turner about the cryptic nature of his letter (http://archives.cbc.ca/politics/prime_ministers/clips/13005/).

9. *Globe and Mail*, Sept. 12, 1975.

10. Christina McCall-Newman, *Grits: An Intimate Portrait of the Liberal Party* (Toronto: Macmillan, 1982), 230.

11. *Globe and Mail*, Oct. 10 and Oct. 14, 1975; Radwanski, *Trudeau*, 198–99.

12. Keith Davey, *The Rainmaker: A Passion for Politics* (Toronto: Stoddart, 1986), 201. Davey wrongly claims that the Anti-Inflation Board received "an overwhelmingly positive public response. And the prime minister's

credibility remained intact with all but his most virulent critics." Stewart, an economist and former civil servant, obviously disagrees. Ian Stewart, "Global Transformation and Economic Policy," in *Towards a Just Society: The Trudeau Years*, ed. Thomas S. Axworthy and Pierre Elliott Trudeau (Markham, Ont.: Viking, 1990), 158.

13. On Hochelaga and Juneau, see *Le Devoir*, Oct. 17, 1975. On the presidency, see Joseph Wearing, *The L-Shaped Party: The Liberal Party of Canada 1958–1980* (Toronto: McGraw-Hill Ryerson, 1981), 205–6, where it is claimed that the appointment of Gerry Robinson as national director of the party by Keith Davey without adequate consultation was the major cause of the rebellion, although Christina McCall claims the major cause was general dissatisfaction with Turner's resignation and the party's overall troubles (McCall-Newman, *Grits*, 365). Interviews with many of the key figures, including Davey, suggest that McCall was correct. Davey himself claims he did not want the job and the appointment of Robinson actually took place after the fuss about his potential presidency. Davey, *Rainmaker*, 202–3. The description of the scandals is drawn from the excellent account in Saywell, ed., *Canadian Annual Review 1975*, 93–95, which reprints the full interview of Lalonde with Malling.

14. John Updike, *Memories of the Ford Administration: A Novel* (New York: Knopf, 1992).

15. Davey tells the swimming pool story in *Rainmaker*, 193–95, but identifies only two donors apart from Trudeau, one being "Honest Ed" Mirvish. Cossitt's biography and his attack on Trudeau are found in Jonathan Manthorpe's "The Tory Scourge of Sussex Drive," *Globe and Mail*, May 31, 1975. See also Canada, *House of Commons Debates* (11 April and 5 June 1975). On the pay increase, see Saywell, ed., *Canadian Annual Review 1975*, 16–18; Canada, *House of Commons Debates* (19–30 April 1975); *Toronto Star*, April 11, 1975; and *Globe and Mail*, April 11, 1975. The Davey Papers indicate how significant the "rainmaker" considered Cossitt's attacks to be.

16. Scott Young, "Price of a PM," *Globe and Mail*, Aug. 5, 1975. Cossitt made his allegations about expenses incurred by Trudeau in the House of Commons during the debate on the budget. Cossitt and Young corresponded about the allegations.

17. The interview is found in Saywell, ed., *Canadian Annual Review 1975*, 96–98, along with Cossitt's attack.

18. Ibid., 98; and John Saywell, ed., *Canadian Annual Review of Politics and Public Affairs 1976* (Toronto: University of Toronto Press, 1977), which reports on the Leeds Federal Liberal Association letter. See also Lang in *Globe and Mail*, Jan. 9, 1976. The meeting at the Toronto Club is reported in an account in the *Globe* that same day. Gillespie's own account of the meeting is found in "Memorandum to file," Jan. 13, 1976, GP, vol. 240, file 225, Gillespie meeting. LAC. An extensive description by Ed Cowan is found in *New York Times*, Jan. 19, 1976. The group Gillespie addressed was a powerful collection of Toronto business leaders. Besides Corrigan and Macdonald, it included Rod Bilodeau, the chair of Honeywell; Molson president James T. Black; Roy Bennett, president of Ford; Guy French, president of American Can; Richard Thomson, president of Toronto-Dominion Bank; Peter Gordon, president of Stelco; Ted Medland, chair of Wood Gundy; and a representative of INCO.

19. The full text of Trudeau's speech is in *Globe and Mail*, Jan. 20, 1976. The speech is wrongly reported as having occurred on January 19 in Saywell, ed., *Canadian Annual Review 1976*, which nevertheless has a good summary of the reaction (on pages 138–40). MPs, ministers, and the Prime Minister's Office were deluged with letters, as were newspapers. See also Pierre Trudeau, *Memoirs* (Toronto: McClelland and Stewart, 1993), 197–98.

20. Trudeau makes the comment about Galbraith in his *Memoirs*, 197–98. Galbraith confirmed the story to me before his death. Conversation with Don Johnston. The history of Parc Belmont describes Trudeau's challenge to the board chair on the ground of irregularities but does not document his full involvement. Steve Proulx, *Les Saisons du Parc Belmont 1923–1983* (Outremont: Libre Expression, 2005), 122–24. The extensive Belmont records are in TP, MG 26 01, vol. 2, files 2-5 to 2-12, LAC. When Belmont was sold in the mid-seventies for $2.4 million, the Trudeaus owned 146 of 480 shares.

21. Alexandre Trudeau expressed this view to me in June 2009. He said his father also believed that business demanded freedom to act but then the same businesses came to him for assistance. This approach angered his father.

22. H.I. Macdonald, "Economic Policy: Can We Manage the Economy Any More," *Canadian Public Policy: Analyse de politiques* (autumn 1976): 4–5. Robert Campbell, *Grand Illusion: The Politics of the Keynesian Experience in Canada, 1945–1975* (Peterborough, Ont.: Broadview, 1987), argues that pure Keynesian approaches never did apply in Canada and that it was an "illusion" to believe they did. Certainly, in the sixties, policy makers stretched understanding of the concept beyond any that Keynes would have recognized.

23. Enders to Sec. State, Washington, Aug. 12, 1976, National Security Adviser Presidential Country Files for Europe and Canada, box 3, Gerald R. Ford Presidential Library.

24. Ibid. On Schmidt and his admiration for, and similarities to, Trudeau, see Trudeau, *Memoirs*, 200. Their correspondence was warm right from the start. Schmidt indicates that Trudeau impressed him on their first meeting, and Trudeau especially welcomed Schmidt's support for Canada as a member of the G7.

25. The best description of the change of mood, from which this account is taken, is found in Foster, *Blue-Eyed Sheiks*, 43–45. On the firms and the oil sands, see pages 78ff. The federal document describing the problems for the consuming provinces is *An Energy Strategy for Canada: Policies for Self Reliance* (Ottawa: Dept. of Supply and Services, 1976), 31–40.

26. Trudeau's speech is excerpted and Bourassa's comment is reported in Saywell, ed., *Canadian Annual Review 1975*, 70–71.

27. On Choquette and his party, see *Le Devoir*, Nov. 11, 1975. For the events of 1975, see the chapter on Quebec by Jean-Charles Bonenfant in Saywell, ed., *Canadian Annual Review 1975*, 146–61. Trudeau's comments on Bill 22 are in his *Memoirs*, 234. See also Robert Bothwell, *Canada and Quebec: One Country, Two Histories*, rev. ed. (Vancouver: University of British Columbia Press, 1998), chap.8, and Don Murray and Vera Murray, *De Bourassa à Lévesque* (Montréal: Quinze, 1978).

28. Québec, *Commission d'enquête sur l'exercice de la liberté syndicale dans l'industrie de la construction* (Québec: Éditeur officiel du Québec, 1975), 176; Forget, quoted in Bothwell, *Canada and Quebec,*152.

29. The original account is in *Le Soleil*, March 6, 1975. A full description of the context is found in Gérard Bergeron, *Notre Miroir à deux faces* (Montréal: Québec Amérique, 1985), 149.

30. *Globe and Mail*, April 14, 1974.

31. The letters are found in Saywell, ed., *Canadian Annual Review 1976*, 73–74, which has an excellent account of the controversy and press reaction. The definitive study, which upholds the government's position, is Sandford Borins, *The Language of the Skies: The Bilingual Air Traffic Control Conflict in Canada* (Montreal and Kingston: McGill–Queen's University Press, 1983).

32. L. Ian MacDonald, *From Bourassa to Bourassa: Wilderness to Restoration*, 2nd ed. (Montreal and Kingston: McGill–Queen's University Press, 2002), ix–x. The description of the meeting between Bourassa and Trudeau in the Hilton Hotel in Quebec City, arranged by Charles Denis, who was an adviser to Bourassa, is found in Charles Denis, *Robert Bourassa: La Passion de la politique* (Montréal: Fides, 2006), 344–45. Trudeau, quoted in Denis, *Bourassa*, 349.

33. René Lévesque, *Memoirs*, trans. Philip Stratford (Toronto: McClelland and Stewart, 1986), 265.

34. MacDonald, *Bourassa to Bourassa*, ix–x. Polling figures and a description of the resurgence of the Union nationale are found in Saywell, ed., *Canadian Annual Review 1976*, 118–23.

35. Bergeron, *Notre Miroir*, 148; Pierre Godin, *René Lévesque: Un Homme et son rêve 1922–1987* (Montréal: Boréal, 2007), 316. Claude Forget, a Bourassa minister, agreed. He thought Trudeau's remark about Bourassa as a "hot dog eater" was a "tremendous slight." He told Bourassa: "Everybody in your government feels personally insulted if you are insulted, and we want you to say something and bite back." Bourassa refused to respond. Quoted in Bothwell, *Canada and Quebec*, 152.

36. Lévesque's comments on Nov. 15, 1976, are taken from his *Memoirs*, 275. Trudeau's speech that night is from *Montreal Gazette*, Nov. 16, 1976.

37. Bergeron, *Notre Miroir*, 148; Trudeau, *Memoirs*, 240–41. In the original interview, Trudeau made the "fat in the fire" comment. Trudeau interview with Ron Graham, May 7, 1991, TP, MG 26 03, vol. 23, file 10, LAC.

38. Margaret Trudeau, *Beyond Reason* (New York and London: Paddington Press, 1979), 185–86, in which the bad state of the marriage in the fall of 1976 is described; conversation with Margaret Trudeau, June 2009.

CHAPTER ELEVEN: BEYOND REASON

1. Linda Griffiths with Paul Thompson, *Maggie and Pierre: A Fantasy of Love, Politics, and the Media* (Toronto, Vancouver, and Los Angeles: Talonbooks, 1980), 11, 19. The play was previewed in the Backspace at Theatre Passe Muraille in Toronto on November 30, 1979. It opened in the Mainspace at the theatre on Valentine's Day, 1980, with Linda Griffiths playing Margaret, Pierre—and Henry, a journalist commentator. Griffiths' later comments are in her "The Lover: Dancing with Trudeau," in *Trudeau's Shadow: The Life and Legacy of Pierre Elliott Trudeau*, ed. Andrew Cohen and J.L. Granatstein (Toronto: Random House, 1998), 45. Griffiths modified her harsh view of Trudeau because of comments from friends. Interview with Gale Zoë Garnett, Oct. 2007. In her book *Consequences*, Margaret included a photo of Linda Griffiths in the play. The caption reads: "I was filled with admiration for Linda Griffiths' performance in her play MAGGIE & PIERRE" (Toronto: McClelland and Stewart, 1982), 107.

2. Margaret Trudeau, *Beyond Reason* (New York and London: Paddington Press, 1979); Pierre Trudeau, *Memoirs* (Toronto: McClelland and Stewart, 1993), 179, 184.

3. Stephen Clarkson and Christina McCall, *The Magnificent Obsession*, vol. 1 of *Trudeau and Our Times* (Toronto: McClelland and Stewart, 1990), 136. Rick Butler and Jean-Guy Carrier, *The Trudeau Decade* (Toronto: Doubleday, 1979) includes an editorial by Michel Roy of *Le Devoir* of June 4, 1977, analyzing the difference in coverage between English and French Canada, 352–53. For another point of view, see *Globe and Mail*, Sept. 25, 1974. J.T. Saywell, ed., *Canadian Annual Review of Politics and Public Affairs 1974* (Toronto: University of Toronto Press, 1975) makes only a short reference to Margaret's presence in the campaign and none to her troubles in the fall. Between September 1, 1974, and June 11, 1977, the *Globe and Mail* website has 2,101 hits for "Margaret Trudeau."

4. Trudeau, *Beyond Reason*, 184. The transcript of the interview is found in *Globe and Mail*, Oct. 28, 1974. On November 5, the leading *Globe* columnist Geoffrey Stevens criticized the interview for its contradictions.

5. Simone Florence, Creeds, Aug. 5, 1974, TP, MG 26 020, vol. 17, file 5, LAC. The file also contains bills for clothing, which appear to be totals.

They are $3,654.24 at Holt Renfrew and $4,522.57 at Creeds. Nancy Pitfield
is described by Margaret as her "closest friend" at the time (*Beyond Reason*,
168). Conversation with Marc Lalonde, Oct. 2006; conversation with Carroll
Guérin, Aug. 2007; several confidential sources. Margaret Trudeau.

6. Ottawa to Copenhagen, May 20, 1975, EAP, RG25, vol. 9246, file 20-CDA-
9-Trudeau-Scan, LAC; interview with Margaret Trudeau, Feb. 2006. In 1975
Trudeau was away on official trips from February 26 to March 15 in Europe,
April 24 to May 7 in the Caribbean, May 27 to June 1 in Europe, and July 28
to August 5 in Finland and Poland, and he made an official visit to
Washington on October 23. There were additional private trips with King
Hussein of Jordan, whose wife was a close friend of Margaret, and there
were several other private trips. The *New Yorker* has placed *Fear of Flying*,
which has sold eighteen million copies, in the "canon" of major literature.
See Rebecca Mead, "Still Flying," *New Yorker*, April 14, 2008, 23.

7. Margaret Trudeau describes the visit in *Beyond Reason*, 143ff. The problems are noted in H.B. Robinson, "Memorandum for the Minister," Jan. 8,
1976, EAP, RG 25, vol. 11089, file 21-3-Angola, LAC. A full account of the
visit is found in Robert Wright, *Three Nights in Havana: Pierre Trudeau,
Fidel Castro, and the Cold War World* (Toronto: Harper Collins, 2007).

8. Hyndman, quoted in Wright, *Three Nights in Havana*, 169. Hyndman
recalled that "Pierre was very, very sensitive to her, doing a great deal to
cope with the pressures that were on her, and to keep the two of them
together." The Castro quotation comes from Trudeau, *Beyond Reason*, 148.
I discussed Castro with Ms. Trudeau in Havana in February 2006, the thir-
tieth anniversary of the trip. She remarked that Castro always spoke English
with her, though he insisted on Spanish with others and though Pierre
spoke fluent Spanish. Trudeau was surprised to discover that Castro,
despite heavy smoking, could hold his breath for a full minute underwater
while spearfishing. Contrary to expectations, the prime minister found
Castro was "very thoughtful and didn't overindulge in monologues; he
would throw out questions and be prepared to have an exchange of views
with you." Jesuitical, one might say. Trudeau, *Memoirs*, 210.

9. Trudeau, *Beyond Reason*, 144.

10. Ibid., 146–49.

11. Ibid., 150–51; *Globe and Mail*, Feb. 3, 1976.

12. Trudeau, *Beyond Reason*, 159–60.
13. Ibid., 157–58; confidential interviews; and *New York Times*, Dec. 30, 2006.
14. Quoted in Trudeau, *Beyond Reason*, 182–83.
15. John Saywell, ed., *Canadian Annual Review of Politics and Public Affairs 1977* (Toronto: University of Toronto Press, 1979), simply reported that "Pierre Trudeau suffered a personal tragedy when at the end of May his wife Margaret formally separated from him leaving their three children with the prime minister." Trudeau had begun the year behind the Conservatives by ten points, but in June his party led, with 51 percent support (compared to 27 percent support for the Conservatives) (31, 37). The Conservative *Toronto Sun* was especially focused on the Trudeau separation, as was the *Journal de Montréal*, which broke with the discretion observed by most of the francophone press.
16. Trip with Sinclair: TP, MG 26 020, vol. 17, file 13, LAC. Margaret's father consistently supported Trudeau, not only in this period but also after their separation. The comment on Trudeau's body and his age is from Sheena Paterson and Mary McEwan, "Margaret Trudeau's Struggle for Identity: Victor or Victim?," *Chatelaine*, Aug. 1977, 92. Quotation from Trudeau, *Beyond Reason*, 160. Jordan trip and the "detestable" description, ibid., 156. Incident with quilt, ibid., 186. Interview with Peter C. Newman, *Maclean's*, Oct. 20, 1975, 6.
17. Warren's comments are found in Warren to Ottawa, Feb. 4, 1977, RG 25, vol. 9246, file 20-CDA-9-Trudeau-USA, LAC; interview with Arthur Erickson, Sept. 2007. The details of the dinner are found in Records of the First Lady, Mary Hoyt file, box 20, Jimmy Carter Presidential Library. Interview with Jimmy Carter, April 2008; *Washington Post*, Feb. 22, 1977; and *Globe and Mail*, Feb. 21–25, 1977 (editorial on the 25th). Report on press coverage: Canadian Consulate, New York, to External Affairs, March 1, 1977, RG 25, vol. 9246, file 20-CDA-9-Trudeau-USA, LAC.
18. The Carter letter is found in Records of the First Lady, Mary Hoyt file, box 20, Jimmy Carter Presidential Library. Trudeau, *Beyond Reason*, 189. The Trudeau reply, dated March 4, is found in EAP, RG25, vol. 9246, file 20-Cda-9-Trudeau-USA, LAC.
19. Margaret is the source of the story on the Stones' visit to her suite and the hash smoking (*Beyond Reason*, 191). Wasserman's apology for his

erroneous remarks and Jagger's comment are reported in *Globe and Mail*, March 10, 1977.

20. Patrick Gossage, *Close to the Charisma: My Years between the Press and Pierre Elliott Trudeau* (Halifax: Goodread Biographies, 1987; original, 1986), 66. His diary gives an excellent account of the way the marriage breakdown was received by the press. The text of the news release is found in Trudeau, *Beyond Reason*, 193. Interview with Patrick Gossage, May 2009.

21. Gossage, *Close to the Charisma*, 64–69; *Globe and Mail*, May 30, 1977.

22. Gossage, *Close to the Charisma*, 68; Clarkson and McCall, *Magnificent Obsession*, 136; and George Radwanski, *Trudeau* (Toronto: Macmillan, 1978), 310. I spoke with or interviewed most of Trudeau's principal assistants at the time: Jim Coutts, Bob Murdoch, Tom Axworthy, Keith Davey, Rémi Bujold, Albert Breton, and ministers who were close to him, including André Ouellet, Donald Macdonald, Alastair Gillespie, Mitchell Sharp, and several other people who knew the situation well. The interviews with Library and Archives Canada staff also touch upon the question, although participants, including Marie-Hélène Fox, who dealt with Margaret's correspondence, did not comment directly. All agree that Trudeau's sang-froid was remarkable given the circumstances, and they tend to emphasize this quality rather than his difficulties.

23. The Gallup poll results, as well as the earlier poll on Turner and musings about Trudeau's departure, are found in Saywell, ed., *Canadian Annual Review*, 30–31. Trudeau had literally thousands of letters of "sympathy" after the divorce was announced. Margaret indicates that most of the letters sent to her were extremely hostile. Interview with Margaret Trudeau, Feb. 2006. The Trudeau letters are scattered throughout TP, MG 26 020, LAC.

24. The values of Quebec-based stocks were traced in *Toronto Star*, April 12, 1977, and the head office departures are described in Saywell, ed., *Canadian Annual Review 1977*, 58. The Reston article and the report on the stock market drop are in *New York Times*, Jan. 26, 1977, and another report on stocks appeared on Jan. 28, 1976. On the tension between union and working-class support and the need to reassure a business community integrated within North America, see William Coleman, *The Independence*

Movement in Quebec 1945–1980 (Toronto: University of Toronto Press, 1984), 225–28.

25. *Montreal Gazette*, Jan. 29, 1977. Description of Lévesque as "tired" and "shaken" is in *Globe and Mail*, Feb. 9, 1977. Quebec Chamber of Commerce speech: *Le Soleil*, Jan. 29, 1977.

26. Cabinet Conclusions, RG 2, PCO, Series A-5-a, vol. 6496, Dec. 9, 1976, LAC; interview with Patrick Gossage, June 2009.

27. Comment on press conference: External Affairs to several consulates and embassies, February 14, 1977, EAP, RG25, vol. 9246, file 20-CDA-9-Trudeau-USA, LAC.

28. "Remarks by the Prime Minister to a Joint Session of the United States Congress, Washington, D.C., February 22, 1977," personal copy; *New York Times*, Feb. 23, 1977. A fine contemporary account of the relationship between leaders is Lawrence Martin's *The Presidents and the Prime Ministers: Washington and Ottawa Face to Face: The Myth of Bilateral Bliss 1867–1982* (Toronto: Doubleday Canada, 1982).

29. *Le Devoir*, Feb. 23, 1977.

30. *New York Times*, Jan. 26, 1977.

31. The *Toronto Star* ran its op-ed stories between Nov. 27 and Dec. 2, 1976. The letters exchanged between Lougheed and Trudeau and the views of Clark and Broadbent are described in John Saywell, ed., *Canadian Annual Review of Politics and Public Affairs 1976* (Toronto: University of Toronto Press, 1977), 129ff. The comment to the student from Alberta is in "Transcript of the Prime Minister's Remarks at Question & Answer Session with Students—Oxford University, England," Government Publications, University of Waterloo Library.

32. The Liberal MPs were identified in *La Presse* on Nov. 18 as Pierre De Bané, Claude Lachance, Gérard Loiselle, Claude Tessier, and Marcel Prud'homme. Trudeau's comments from a TV interview are found in Saywell, ed., *Canadian Annual Review 1976*, 136.

33. Saywell, ed., *Canadian Annual Review 1977*, summarizes and compares the polls, 64–66, while the extensive Gallup poll is presented in *The Canadian*, April 8, 1977.

34. Christina McCall's original article, "The Exotic Mindscape of Pierre Trudeau," was published in the Jan./Feb. 1977 issue of *Saturday Night* and

is reprinted in Stephen Clarkson, ed., *My Life as a Dame: The Personal and Political in the Writings of Christina McCall* (Toronto: House of Anansi, 2008), 295.

CHAPTER TWELVE: OFF THE TRACK

1. Pierre Trudeau, *Memoirs* (Toronto: McClelland and Stewart, 1993). Breton strongly opposed the controls and wrote on September 5, 1975, that "a consideration of current proposals to control prices and wages makes very clear by hindsight that your Government made the right decisions in the last two years not to have wage and price controls. Had we had them, with exemptions for food, imports, land, energy, regulated prices, excise taxes, and possibly a few other things such as exports and rents on new buildings, the price picture would not be very different than it is now, and the Government would not only look bad, it would have discredited itself." "Memorandum for the Prime Minister," ABP, privately held. He had the grace not to remind others that he was right. Breton accepted the mone-tarist argument that money supply was critical to inflationary pressures in society, and he also emphasized the role of monopolists and public-sector unions, as well as the Bank of Canada's excessive concern about the exchange rate, which if cleanly floated, would influence prices. He shared some of the views of the monetarist Milton Friedman, who attacked Trudeau in a Feb. 17, 1977, CBC TV interview. Friedman said neither big business nor trade unions were responsible for inflation. Moreover, the problem was not "to get self-control of the people." He dismissed Trudeau's analysis of the causes and added: "There is only one place where inflation is made in Canada and that's Ottawa." Transcript attached to Peter Cooke to Bob Murdoch, April 5, 1977, TP, MG 26 020, vol. 32, file 1, LAC.

2. Canada, *House of Commons Debates* (25 April 1976); *Globe and Mail*, Sept. 15, 25, 1976. Keith Davey took credit for securing Mackasey's earlier return to the Cabinet in 1974, arguing that the popular minister repre-sented blue-collar Canada. Davey said that when he met with both men to discuss this possibility, Trudeau told Mackasey that he was bringing him back to "do whatever Keith asks you to do during this campaign." Mackasey grinned and said, "Ah, come on, Pierre. You know you're bringing me back for another reason. It's because you like me!" He did. Keith Davey,

The Rainmaker: A Passion for Politics (Toronto: Stoddart, 1986), 209.

3. See John Saywell, ed., *Canadian Annual Review of Politics and Public Affairs 1976* (Toronto: University of Toronto Press, 1977), 142ff., for a description of the Cabinet shuffle. *Toronto Star*, Sept. 15, 1976. On Richardson and by-elections, see *Globe and Mail*, Oct. 14, 19, 1976. On Herbert, see *Montreal Gazette*, Nov. 16, 1976.

4. Joyal expressed his dissent in a November 24 speech. *Le Devoir*, Nov. 25, 1976. The dissenters in English Canada were frequently found in the *Canadian Forum*, which Denis Smith, a strong critic of Trudeau, edited between 1975 and 1979.

5. Burelle became Trudeau's French speechwriter in 1977 and has written an important account of his work. He later became a strong critic of Trudeau's constitutional approach. *Pierre Elliott Trudeau: L'Intellectuel et la Politique* (Montréal: Fides, 2005). On McRoberts and Laforest, see their comments on Trudeau in Robert Bothwell, *Canada and Quebec: One Country, Two Histories*, rev. ed. (Vancouver: University of British Columbia Press, 1998), 235–36.

6. The 1977 polls are summarized and presented in John Saywell, ed., *Canadian Annual Review of Politics and Public Affairs 1977* (Toronto: University of Toronto Press, 1979), 50ff.

7. On Lavoie, see *Le Devoir*, June 14, 1977. On Horner's wooing, see Davey, *Rainmaker*, 215ff. Saywell, ed., *Canadian Annual Review 1977*, 35–36. *Globe and Mail*, April 21, 1977.

8. *Globe and Mail*, May 25, 27, 1977.

9. Patrick Gossage, *Close to the Charisma: My Years between the Press and Pierre Elliott Trudeau* (Halifax: Goodread Biographies, 1987), 78, 82; *Times* (London), May 6, 1977. Paul Martin's diary indicates that Trudeau was upset during the trip because of his marital difficulties; still, he wanted to meet British intellectuals and others who could help him with problems of the economy (Paul Martin, *The London Diaries, 1975–1979* [Ottawa: University of Ottawa Press, 1988], 248ff.). The *Times* did not take note of Trudeau's pirouette, although it appeared on the front pages of Canadian newspapers.

10. Judith Maxwell, *Policy Review and Outlook, 1977: An Agenda for Change* (Montreal: C.D. Howe Research Institute, 1977), 27. The comment on 1976 is in J.H. Perry, *A Fiscal History of Canada—The Postwar Years* (Toronto: Canadian Tax Foundation, 1989), 82.

11. Martin, *London Diaries*, 253, 269; Colin Kenny in Gossage, *Close to the Charisma*, 88–89. On Pepin-Robarts, McDonald, and Atomic Energy of Canada, see *Globe and Mail*, July 5–9. Interview with Gerry Robinson, July 2008.

12. Martin, *London Diaries*, 281.

13. Gossage, *Close to the Charisma*, 89–90. Alain Stanké was given several interviews with Trudeau, which were telecast in 1977. He published a partial transcript, *Pierre Elliott Trudeau: Portrait intime* (St. Léonard: Alain Stanké, 1977).

14. Davey, *Rainmaker*, 220. Davey undermines his argument by telling a joke about caucus: "What do you call a group of geese? A flock. What do you call a group of cows? A herd. What do you call a group of doves? A caucus," ibid. Gossage, *Close to the Charisma*, 89–90. Hugh Winsor gave a full analysis of the reasons and rumours surrounding the decision about an election in *Globe and Mail*, Aug. 31, 1977. Richard Gwyn makes the argument that Lévesque won the first engagement with Trudeau through the Charter of the French Language, which was popular in Quebec, and thereafter Trudeau feared an election where language issues would predominate. Although the Cabinet discussions reportedly reveal resentment of the charter and include comments about the danger of running an election on bilingualism alone, the language issue is but one of several factors the ministers considered. The sources of Gywn's Cabinet conclusions are not available after 1976. Richard Gwyn, *The Northern Magus: Pierre Trudeau and Canadians* (Toronto: McClelland and Stewart, 1980), 246ff.

15. Trudeau to McLuhan, July 25, 1977, TP, MG 26 020, vol. 9, file 9-8, LAC; D'Iberville Fortier to Trudeau, May 30, 1977; and Trudeau to Fortier, July 8, 1977, ibid., vol. 4.

16. Jim Coutts, "Trudeau in Power: A View from inside the Prime Minister's Office," in *Trudeau's Shadow: The Life and Legacy of Pierre Elliott Trudeau*, ed. Andrew Cohen and J.L. Granatstein (Toronto: Random House, 1998), 149.

17. Polls and discussion of the Cabinet shuffle are found in Saywell, ed., *Canadian Annual Review 1977*, 31–39. On Allmand, see *Globe and Mail*, Sept. 17, 1977.

18. When Trudeau spoke with Martin on June 16, he said that Macdonald, his

best minister, would probably leave politics. Martin told him that he was
not giving ministers the "fullest opportunity to become personalities in
their own right." Martin, *London Diaries*, 270. Bouey's warning is reported
in *Globe and Mail*, Sept. 17, 1977. For a discussion of the value of the
Canadian dollar, see *Financial Post*, Oct. 14 and Oct. 24, 1977.

19. Bégin is quoted in Saywell, ed., *Canadian Annual Review 1977*, 26–27;
Hugessen in *Montreal Gazette*, Dec. 10, 1977.

20. Gossage, *Close to the Charisma*, 93.

21. George Radwanski, *Trudeau* (Toronto: Macmillan, 1978), Author's Note
and chap. 1.

22. Ibid., 213–14.

23. Ibid., 345–55. Ramsay Cook, "'I never thought I could be as proud . . .':
The Trudeau-Lévesque Debate," in *Towards a Just Society: The Trudeau
Years*, ed. Thomas S. Axworthy and Pierre Elliott Trudeau (Markham,
Ont.: Viking, 1990), 343–44.

24. Trudeau, *Memoirs*, 250.

25. For a critical assessment of the change, see Robert Bothwell, Ian
Drummond, and John English, *Canada since 1945: Power, Politics, and
Provincialism* (Toronto: University of Toronto Press, 1981), 382. See also
Saywell, ed., *Canadian Annual Review 1977*, 110–11, and Canada, *House
of Commons Debates* (15 Feb. 1977). Pickersgill made the comments many
times to me personally in the late eighties and early nineties, when he broke
strongly with Trudeau. Keith Banting points out that federal systems have a
"conservative" influence on the expansion of welfare programs, although
this influence was broken by the war years and by the development of a
"bifurcated" welfare system in Canada, where health remained with the
provinces and income security with the federal government. *The Welfare
State and Canadian Federalism* (Kingston and Montreal: McGill–Queen's
University Press, 1982), 173–74.

26. Gordon Robertson, *Memoirs of a Very Civil Servant: Mackenzie King to
Pierre Trudeau* (Toronto: University of Toronto Press, 2000), 292–93;
Le Devoir, Nov. 25, 1977; *Globe and Mail*, Nov. 29, 1977. Trudeau was
able to announce the Quebec members of the task force only in late
August: journalist Solange Chaput-Rolland and constitutional lawyer
Gérald Beaudoin, who later became a Conservative senator.

27. The description of the premiers' conference and the letters between Trudeau and Lévesque are found in Saywell, ed., *Canadian Annual Review 1977*, 90–101. For a critical review of the letters, see Gwyn, *Northern Magus*, 248–49. Trudeau had worked with Dumont, a major figure in Quebec intellectual life, in the fifties.

28. *Globe and Mail*, Oct. 7, 1977.

29. Gossage, *Close to the Charisma*, 109–17.

30. Pierre Bouchard and Sylvie Beauchamp-Achim, *Le Français: Langue des commerces et des services publics—Le point de vue de la clientèle*, Dossier du Conseil de la langue française no. 5 (Québec: Conseil de la langue française, 1978); Pierre O' Neill and Jacques Benjamin, *Les Mandarins du pouvoir: L'Exercice du pouvoir au Québec de Jean Lesage à René Lévesque* (Montréal: Éditions Québec Amérique, 1978), 193. By 1978 the provincial and federal Liberals had markedly different attitudes on the language issue. The Trudeau government's decision not to refer Quebec's Bill 101 to the Supreme Court was based on several studies that indicated the considerable sympathy among francophones in Quebec for the language legislation. The studies also reveal a split between anglophone Liberal politicians in Quebec and their counterparts in other provinces who were not as passionate in their opposition. See, for example, David Rayside, "Federalism and the Party System: Provincial and Federal Liberals in the Province of Quebec," *Canadian Journal of Political Science* (Sept. 1978): 499–528.

31. The story is related in Gwyn, *Northern Magus*, 249. Gossage does not report it in his diary. Gossage notes only that he had "drinks" with journalists and others. Nor is the story mentioned in any press accounts of the time. However, the spirit is surely accurate even if the tale may be a bit tall.

32. Martin, *London Diaries*, 346–47.

33. Gossage, *Close to the Charisma*, 124–26, reports on the unexpected booing and the decision to hold off. For the picture of Justin and Sacha, see *Globe and Mail*, April 24, 1978. For the McLuhan portrait, see TP, MG 26 020, vol. 8, file 9-29, LAC.

34. Consul General, New York, to Ottawa, March 27, 1978, RG25, vol. 9246, file 20-CDA-9-Trudeau-USA (6), LAC; *New York Times*, March 23, 1978.

35. *New York Times*, March 23, 1978; Davey, *Rainmaker*, 233–34; and Trudeau

to Schmidt, with comments, Archiv der soziale Demokratie, Dep. HS, Mappe 8807.

36. Robert Putnam and Nicholas Bayne, *Hanging Together: Cooperation and Conflict in the Seven-Power Summits*. Revised edition (Cambridge: Harvard University Press, 1987).The rating and the description are found in Peter Hajnal, *The G8 System and the G20: Evolution, Role and Documentation* (Aldershot, England: Ashgate, 2007), 55.

37. "Notes for a Toast to be Proposed by the Prime Minister at Chancellor Schmidt's Dinner in His Honour, July 18, 1978, Archiv der soziale Demokratie, Dep. HS , Mappe 8807. Fred Bergsten of the Institute of International Economics has also pointed to the Bonn Summit as a model for economic convergence: http://www.iie.com/publications/papers/paper.cfm?ResearchID=275.

38. Gossage, *Close to the Charisma*, 144; *Toronto Star*, Aug. 2, 1978. Fotheringham, in *Maclean's*, Sept. 18, 1978, 68. In his *Memoirs*, Trudeau claims that he called Chrétien before he announced the measures (199–200), but Edward Goldenberg denies this in *The Way It Works: Inside Ottawa* (Toronto: McClelland and Stewart, 2006), 118–19, as did Chrétien in a conversation with me. Goldenberg suggested to me that Chrétien may have been deliberately excluded because of PMO fear that he would oppose the actions. Keith Davey indicates that in addition to himself, Jim Coutts, Michael Pitfield, Marc Lalonde, and Allan MacEachen were part of the "exercise" (*Rainmaker*, 234).

39. *Observer*, March 30, 1978; Sandra Gwyn, "Where Are You, Mike Pearson, Now That We Need You? Decline and Fall of Canada's Foreign Policy," *Saturday Night*, April 1978, 27–35; and Anne-Marie Mosey, "The Canadian Foreign Service in the 21st Century," NPSIA Occasional Paper No. 45, Jan. 2005, http://www.carleton.ca/csds/occasional_papers/NPSIA-45.pdf. Enders' comment is found in the briefing book for President Carter for the Trudeau visit in February 1977. Brzezinski Materials, NSA VIP file, Canada PM Trudeau Briefing Book, Feb. 1977, Jimmy Carter Presidential Library.

40. On Canada and India and the nuclear relationship, see Ryan Touhey, *Dealing with the Peacock: India and Canadian Foreign Policy*. Unpublished doctoral thesis, University of Waterloo, 2007. Carter conversation in Washington Embassy to Ottawa, Feb. 21, 1977, RG25, vol. 9246, file

20-CDA-9-Trudeau-USA, LAC. On India's opinion on exploding the atomic device, see New Delhi to Ottawa, June 11, 1974, ibid., file 23-1-India.

41. The speech is found in Pierre Elliott Trudeau, *Lifting the Shadow of War*, ed. C. David Crenna (Edmonton: Hurtig, 1987), 25–38.

42. Robert Bothwell, *Alliance and Illusion: Canada and the World, 1945–1984* (Vancouver: University of British Columbia Press, 2007), 283–84. The academic criticism is found in Trevor Findlay, "Canada and the Nuclear Club," in Jean Daudelin and Daniel Schwanen, eds., Canada among Nations 2007: *What Room for Manoeuvre?* (Montreal and Kingston: McGill–Queen's University Press, 2008), 204–206. *Toronto Star* and *Le Devoir*, May 27, 1978; Geoffrey Stevens, "A Pretentious Speech," *Globe and Mail*, May 30, 1978.

43. On the respect for Trudeau, see Ivan Head and Pierre Trudeau, *The Canadian Way: Shaping Canada's Foreign Policy, 1968–1984* (Toronto: McClelland and Stewart, 1995), 303. Ivan Head to John O'Manique, Norman Paterson School, April 17 and June 4, 1979, and O'Manique to Head, May 7, 1979 (copies given to me by Head); Bothwell, *Alliance and Illusion*, 303.

44. "Transcript of the Prime Minister's Press Conference-Ottawa-May 23, 1978," PMO, RG2-19c, vol. 2736, LAC.

45. Davey, *Rainmaker*, 234–35; Gossage, *Close to the Charisma*, 151 (report on interpretations in the press); *Toronto Star*, Oct. 17, 1978; and Alastair Gillespie, "Made in Canada," draft manuscript courtesy of the author.

46. Gillespie, "Made in Canada"; interview with Alastair Gillespie, May 2008; and interviews with Richard O'Hagan, Jim Coutts, Donald Macdonald, and Richard Stanbury. In an earlier article, I claimed that John Turner was responsible for the newsletters issued by his firm, McMillan Binch, but he responded that his partner William Macdonald was the author. However, simply because of his presence in the firm and the information conveyed in the newsletters, Turner was inevitably associated with these articles. Paul Litt, draft biography of John Turner, chap. 12. Don McGillivray, in *Ottawa Citizen*, Aug. 25, 1978. Marie Josée Drouin and B. Bruce-Briggs, *Canada Has a Future* (Toronto: McClelland and Stewart, 1978), 44. Mme Drouin had close ties with senior Liberals. She later became associated with neo-conservatives through her marriage to Wall Street businessman Henry Kravis.

47. For Latouche's comment and the description of the success of the PQ government, see Martine Tremblay, *Derrière les portes closes: René Lévesque et l'exercice du pouvoir (1976–1985)* (Montréal: Québec Amérique, 2006), 199–200.

48. Lévesque is quoted in *Globe and Mail*, Jan. 26, 1979. Interview with Mary Pepin, Aug. 2007. Forsey's comments are found in *Toronto Star*, July 21, 1978; Diefenbaker's are in *Toronto Star*, July 12, 1978. I owe these references to Matthew Stubbings, "The Defeat of Bill C-60." Paper for History 602, University of Waterloo (winter 2009).

49. The report on the Constitutional conference is in R.B. Byers, ed., *Canadian Annual Review of Politics and Public Affairs 1979* (Toronto: University of Toronto Press, 1981), 88ff.

50. Davey to "All Liberal Candidates," March 29, 1979, Keith Davey Fonds, box 22, file 13, Victoria University Archives; Byers, ed., *Canadian Annual Review 1979*; interviews with participants.

51. I was present at the Kitchener event, where I met Trudeau for the first time. B.W. Powe, *Mystic Trudeau: The Fire and the Rose* (Toronto: Thomas Allen, 2007), 142.

52. Quotation in *Trudeau Albums*, Karen Alliston, Rick Archbold, Jennifer Glossop, Alison Maclean, Ivon Owen, eds. (Toronto: Penguin, 2000), 112. On election night, see Davey, *Rainmaker*, 242.

Election results 1979:
Canadian Annual Review of Politics and Public Affairs 1979, 43–45

Federal Seat Distribution

	Liberal	PC	NDP	Other
Nfld.	4	2	1	0
N.S.	2	8	1	0
N.B.	6	4	0	0
P.E.I.	0	4	0	0
Que.	67	2	0	6
Ont.	32	57	6	0
Man.	2	7	5	0

	Liberal	PC	NDP	Other
Sask.	0	10	4	0
Alta.	0	21	0	0
B.C.	1	19	8	0
Yukon & N.W.T.	0	2	1	0
Total	114	136	26	6

Popular Vote %

	Liberal	PC	NDP	Other
Nfld.	41	30	30	0
N.S.	36	45	19	0
N.B.	45	40	15	0
P.E.I.	41	53	7	0
Que.	62	14	5	19
Ont.	37	42	21	1
Man.	24	43	33	1
Sask.	22	41	36	1
Alta.	22	66	10	2
B.C.	23	44	32	1
Yukon & N.W.T.	33	37	29	1
Total	40	36	18	6

CHAPTER THIRTEEN: THE FALL OF PIERRE TRUDEAU

1. The remarks on election night are found in *Globe and Mail*, May 24,
   1979; *Chicago Tribune*, May 24, 1979; and *Los Angeles Times*,
   May 24, 1979. The quotation about the picnic is from Margaret Trudeau,
   Beyond Reason (New York and London: Paddington Press, 1979), 201.
   Much of the following section derives from interviews with family
   members and friends. Margaret Trudeau also gave an extended interview
   about her reaction to the changed circumstances and the Studio 54 interview to Celeste Fremon, "Margaret Trudeau," *Playgirl*, Sept. 1979, 116.
2. Trudeau, *Beyond Reason*, 201–2. Interview with Jane and Hugh Faulkner,

Aug. 2008. Margaret says that after the separation, her "relationship with the children and with Pierre was growing more healthy by the week. My independence and my attempts to work were giving me a far more balanced attitude to motherhood," ibid., 195.

3. The comments occurred at a meeting with several Trudeau assistants and other aides at the National Archives of Canada, March 17, 2003, which I organized and recorded.

4. Heidi Bennet tells this story in Nancy Southam, ed., *Pierre: Colleagues and Friends Talk about the Trudeau They Knew* (Toronto: McClelland and Stewart, 2005), 158–59.

5. The wonderful account of their time as nannies is found in ibid., 151–58. The story of the swimming pool is Kimberley-Kemper's account (153).

6. Interview with Alexandre Trudeau, June 2009.

7. Interview with Alastair Gillespie, July 2008.

8. Harrington Lake is described in Southam, *Pierre*, 151–52; Bennet's words: ibid., 159–60. In their biography of Trudeau, Stephen Clarkson and Christina McCall report one particular incident involving the staff and Margaret after the election defeat of May 22, 1979. Margaret was holding "an impromptu farewell" for staff and was urging two of the Mounties to throw Trudeau into the pool. He resisted and clung to the door, but their brute force won and Trudeau was thrown, clothes and all, into the drink. They cite a confidential source. Stephen Clarkson and Christina McCall, *The Magnificent Obsession*, vol. 1 of *Trudeau and Our Times* (Toronto: McClelland and Stewart, 1990), 146. Interview with Patrick Gossage, June 2009.

9. *Montreal Star*, June 5, 1979. I would like to thank the Rt. Hon. Paul Martin and Sheila Martin for permitting me to "walk through" 24 Sussex Drive and the Hon. Bill Graham and Kathy Graham for allowing me to do the same at Stornoway. The descriptions reflect my own personal preferences as well as some comments from former residents of both places. Interview with Justin Trudeau, Sept. 2007. Justin said the children loved 24 Sussex, even though their mother did not.

10. Liona Boyd, *In My Own Key: My Life in Love and Music* (Toronto: Stoddart, 1998), 137–39.

11. Ibid., 138–40; Trudeau to Boyd, Nov. 17, 1976, TP, MG 26 020, vol. 2, file 40, LAC. Canadian High Commissioner to the United Kingdom

Paul Martin, who accompanied Callaghan, complained bitterly in his diary about the poor press coverage for Callaghan. Boyd similarly wondered why the press did not notice her presence at so many events. Paul Martin, *The London Diaries: 1975–1979* (Ottawa: University of Ottawa Press, 1988), 168–70.

12. Boyd, *In My Own Key*, 143–44, 214–15; interview with Arthur Erickson, Sept. 2007. Confidential interviews revealed that the Trudeau family and close friends were very angry with Boyd's account, which they told me they regarded as unfair to both Margaret and Pierre, and at times inaccurate.

13. Boyd, *In My Own Key*, 138ff.; confidential interviews.

14. Keith Davey, *The Rainmaker: A Passion for Politics* (Toronto: Stoddart, 1986), 211. Davey says that Bennett was a friend of Margaret Trudeau. However, in a later comment, Bennett wrote that she and Trudeau had met in 1968 at the annual St. Mary's Ball in Montreal, at which Trudeau was the guest of honour. He "charmed" Bennett "with his boyish smile and wouldn't let me go, saying, 'Don't stop. Let's keep dancing.' We were so intent on each other's sparkly eyes that no one dared cut in. I felt giddy and free as we danced and flirted." They felt an "immediate connection." Southam, *Pierre*, 252.

15. See Jane O'Hara, "Heady Day," *Maclean's*, April 6, 1998, 30, for Margaret's comments on the separation agreement. See also Trudeau, *Beyond Reason*, 193, on the black eye and the "intolerable" description.

16. On the suits at Studio 267, see Albert Morton to Trudeau, bills dated June 1981, and letters of Nov. 26 and July 16, 1983, TP, MG2 6 020, vol. 9, file 9-3, LAC. The Margot Kidder interview and Kidder comments are in Southam, *Pierre*, 255. Trudeau's papers reveal that he maintained warm relationships with many women while he was married to Margaret. He had a diverse list of female correspondents, and many continued to write. Although none of the letters indicate any impropriety, his salutations were often very warm.

17. Kidder interview and Kidder in Southam, *Pierre*, 255; interview with Gale Zoë Garnett, April 2008; Boyd, *In My Own Key*, 141; and Buffy Sainte-Marie to Trudeau, Nov. 20, 1977, TP, MG 26 020, vol. 11, file 11-9, LAC. A very good compilation of comments made about Trudeau *"l'objet"* (Trudeau as object) is found in François-Xavier Simard, *Le Vrai Visage de*

Pierre Elliott Trudeau (Montréal: Les Éditions des Intouchables, 2006), chap. 6. Simard has collected a fascinating group of quotations dealing with Trudeau and women and men.

18. Jeffrey Simpson, *Discipline of Power: The Conservative Interlude and the Liberal Restoration* (Toronto: University of Toronto Press, 1996); *Globe and Mail*, July 20, 1979; and Richard Gwyn, *The Northern Magus: Pierre Trudeau and Canadians* (Toronto: McClelland and Stewart, 1980), 336.

19. Based on discussions with John Godfrey and David Silcox and Godfrey's account of the trip in *The Hidden Pierre Elliott Trudeau: The Faith behind the Politics*, ed. John English, Richard Gwyn, and P. Whitney Lackenbauer (Ottawa: Novalis, 2004), 175–76.

20. Interview with Alexandre Trudeau, June 2009. Quotation from introduction by Alexandre Trudeau to Pierre Trudeau and Jacques Hébert, *Two Innocents in Red China* (1961; repr., Vancouver: Douglas and McIntyre, 2007), 2–3.

21. Patrick Gossage, *Close to the Charisma: My Years between the Press and Pierre Elliott Trudeau* (Halifax: Goodread Biographies, 1987), 182–83.

22. Conversation with Jim Coutts. Paul Martin learned in London of Trudeau's insistence on Marchand and was troubled. He wrote in his diary: "In any event, Marchand would be a disaster. Perrault has done well [as Senate leader]. Is it true that he was closed out of a meeting of the Liberal shadow Cabinet? . . . Marchand has had trouble wherever he has moved. It would be a mistake to make him Senate leader." Paul Martin, *London Diaries*, 565–66. Martin is atypically silent on Trudeau's defeat.

23. Gwyn, *Northern Magus*, 337ff., covers this period well; interview with Arthur Erickson, Sept. 2007. *Globe and Mail*, Oct. 11, 1979. The "boa constrictor" comment is found in Geoffrey Stevens' column; the description of Trudeau's first question is in the news story. Canada, *House of Commons Debates* (10 and 30 Oct. 1979).

24. The best account of this period is Jeffrey Simpson's *Discipline of Power*, upon which this summary paragraph is based. There is also a fine description of the energy problems in R.B. Byers, ed., *Canadian Annual Review of Politics and Public Affairs 1979* (Toronto: University of Toronto Press, 1981), 90–97 (page 79 for Gallup polls for year).

25. *Globe and Mail*, Nov. 14, 1979; Canada, *House of Commons Debates* (13 Nov. 1979). The CBC clip with Trudeau, Duffy, and Nash is on the CBC digital archives site: http://archives.cbc.ca/politics/parties_leaders/clips/13255/.
26. Gossage, *Close to the Charisma*, 184–85.
27. Ibid.; Gwyn, *Northern Magus*, 340–41. The video of the press conference can be found at http://archives.cbc.ca/politics/prime_ministers/clips/13256/.
28. The House of Commons exchanges can be found at ibid.
29. Gwyn, *Northern Magus*, 341.
30. Michel Roy, *Le Devoir*, Nov. 26, 1979. Gossage, *Close to the Charisma*, 187; *Globe and Mail*, Nov. 22, 1979. Reactions are summarized in Byers, ed., *Canadian Annual Review 1979*, 56–57. The *Maclean's* article "An Era Ends," by Robert Lewis and Susan Riley, is typical in its brief attention to the Trudeau resignation, followed by extensive speculation on his successor (Dec. 3, 1979, 25–26).
31. The Gregg memorandum is found in Simpson, *Discipline of Power*, 86. Reg Whitaker, "Reason, Passion, and Interest: Pierre Trudeau's Eternal Liberal Triangle," *Canadian Journal of Political and Social Theory/Revue canadienne de théorie politique et sociale* (winter 1980): 28. Whitaker (30n18) argues that the limitations of Trudeau's understanding of popular sovereignty were ironically revealed when Clark won a majority with 4 percent less of the vote. He claims that it was "curious" that Trudeau was silent about this fact. He wasn't: he attacked the result and called for proportional representation in his farewell address to his constituency.
32. George Radwanski, *Trudeau* (Toronto: Macmillan, 1978). Chap. 16 is entitled "A Leader Unfulfilled." A good summary of the RCMP Security Service is found in Philip Rosen, "The Canadian Security Intelligence Service," Library of Parliament Document 84-27E; Trudeau to Kenneth McNaught, Nov. 16, 1979, TP, MG 26 020, vol. 22, file 13, LAC. The document McNaught sent to Trudeau was produced by Dr. Martin Friedland, professor of law at the University of Toronto.
33. Tony Judt, *Postwar: A History of Europe since 1945* (New York: Penguin, 2005), 447.
34. Whitaker, "Reason, Passion, and Interest," 31n50. On the PQ and the referendum, discussion is in Martine Tremblay, *Derrière les portes closes: René*

Lévesque et l'exercice du pouvoir (1976–1985) (Montréal: Québec Amérique, 2006), 221. Pierre Vallières, *L'Urgence de choisir: essai* (Montréal: Éditions Parti-Pris, 1972).

35. Lévesque's comments in May 1979 about the advantages for separatists caused by the departure of Trudeau are found in *La Presse*, Nov. 22, 1979. Tremblay describes the later return of Trudeau as a profound shock, which had "un impact majeur sur la campagne référendaire." Tremblay, *Derrière les portes closes*, 236.

36. Interview with Hugh Faulkner, Aug. 2008. When a female friend from Calgary wrote to Trudeau in 1980, expressing familiar grievances, he replied:

> I am glad your feet are back on the ground if that is where you want them. But I am not sure that that is your best place. On oil and gas I must respect your expertise. But I am a bit sad that on East and West you speak in clichés: Ontario's wealth, freight rates, rules of the game, treated as a colony, unwise to continue. . . .
>
> You are a special stranger, and I am sad. I do not hear the Canadian in you. Is Alberta really so poor, so oppressed? Why are so many of you miserable? But joyeux noel, happy new year anyway.

TP, MG 26 020, vol. 3, file 3-44. Statistics on unemployment: *Canada Year Book, 1978–79* (Ottawa: Ministry of Supply and Services, 1978), 362.

37. Kenneth Norrie, Douglas Owram, and J.C. Herbert Emery, *A History of the Canadian Economy*, 4th ed. (Toronto: Thomson Nelson, 2008), 404, 415. On the standard of living, see Pierre Fortin, *The Canadian Standard of Living: Is There a Way Up?* (Toronto: C.D. Howe Institute, 1999), and on the oil sands, see Paul Chastko, *Developing Alberta's Oil Sands: From Karl Clark to Kyoto* (Calgary: University of Calgary Press, 2004). Chastko is generally critical of Ottawa but acknowledges the importance of the 1975 intervention in the financing crisis of the oil sands. Some details in this passage are from a student paper: Bob Shields, "The Oil Sands: A Business History, 1973–1975," paper for History 602, University of Waterloo, April 2009.

38. Trevor Findlay, "Canada and the Nuclear Club," in *Canada among Nations 2007: What Room for Manoeuvre?*, ed. Jean Daudelin and Daniel

Schwanen (Montreal and Kingston: McGill–Queen's University Press, 2008), 206.

39. Allan Gotlieb, *The Washington Diaries: 1981–1989* (Toronto: McClelland & Stewart, 2006).

40. These judgments are based on conversations with former Canadian high commissioner to Singapore Barry Carin, former Mexican official Andrés Rozental, former German official (and Schmidt assistant) Hans Gunter Sullima, Lord Trend of Britain, former high commissioner to Britain Paul Martin (a view reflected in his published diaries), and many Canadian officials who worked with Trudeau. Trudeau's letter to Schmidt after his 1979 defeat is exceptional for the handwritten additions, which expressed the hope that they would keep in touch and offered thanks for "our personal talks." Trudeau to Schmidt, June 22, 1979, Depost HS Mappe 6600, Archives of Germany.

41. Catherine Annau, *Just Watch Me: Trudeau and the 70's Generation* (National Film Board of Canada, 1999).

CHAPTER FOURTEEN: TRUDEAU REDUX

1. Jeffrey Simpson, *Discipline of Power: The Conservative Interlude and the Liberal Restoration* (Toronto: University of Toronto Press, 1996), 118, 228ff.; *Ottawa Citizen*, Nov. 23, 1979. Regarding Turner and Macdonald, see R.B. Byers, ed., *Canadian Annual Review of Politics and Public Affairs 1979* (Toronto: University of Toronto Press, 1981), 57.

2. Campagnolo to Trudeau, Nov. 28, 1979, TP, MG 26 020, vol. 2, file 62, LAC; Danson to Trudeau, Nov. 21, 1979, ibid.

3. The best account of the fall of the Conservatives remains the first chapter of Simpson's *Discipline of Power*. My account also draws upon conversations with Allan MacEachen, Marc Lalonde, Jim Coutts, Flora MacDonald, Geoffrey Stevens, Mark MacGuigan, Herb Gray, Bob Rae, Ed Broadbent, and several others present at the time.

4. See Byers, ed., *Canadian Annual Review 1979*, 79–80, and the detailed account in Simpson, *Discipline of Power*, 33–47. Sheppard makes his comment in *Globe and Mail*, Dec. 14, 1979. Trudeau's comment is in his memoirs (Trudeau, *Memoirs* [Toronto: McClelland and Stewart, 1993]), 264. Keith Davey gives his account in *The Rainmaker: A Passion for Politics*

(Toronto: Stoddart, 1986), 261ff. Richard Gwyn provides a lively commentary in *The Northern Magus: Pierre Trudeau and Canadians* (Toronto: McClelland and Stewart, 1980), 349ff., which is based on contemporary recollection and conversations. Comments about Liberal presidents and phone calls are based on personal recollection. I was president of the Kitchener Federal Liberal Association when the government fell and was personally called about the constituency's views. The constituency was strongly opposed to Trudeau's return, but I was not. In discussion with other Ontario Liberals, it appeared to me that the split was principally between conservative and liberal factions of the party, with the former favouring a leadership convention. There continued to be hope that John Turner would reverse his decision, a view expressed to me by two Liberal MPs.

5. Christina McCall and Stephen Clarkson, *The Heroic Delusion*, vol. 2 of *Trudeau and Our Times* (Toronto: McClelland and Stewart, 1994), 229. A story in *Montreal Gazette*, Dec. 17, 1979, alleged that Buchanan was lobbying Ontario Liberals against Trudeau. In his role as MP responsible for Ontario organization, he had the responsibility to test opinions. However, he was well known as one who thought Trudeau should resign, and the calls were interpreted by many as an attempt to get support for his views. When Buchanan told Trudeau about his findings, which indicated strong opposition to Trudeau, the conversation permanently affected his position with Trudeau, who would not put Buchanan in the Cabinet after the election.

6. Trudeau sums up his "friends'" reaction with this statement. *Memoirs*, 268.

7. This account is taken from Trudeau's *Memoirs*, 267–68. A somewhat different version is found in Davey, *Rainmaker*, 264, where Coutts is presented as persuading Trudeau, the following morning, to run. The same account, with a comment by Coutts that he did not know of Trudeau's decision until the press conference, is found in Gwyn, *Northern Magus*, 352. The best description is in Simpson, *Discipline of Power*, 33–47, which has the same account as Davey—indicating that Trudeau told Coutts at 8:30 a.m. that he was not running.

8. Simpson, *Discipline of Power*, 46–47; *Globe and Mail*, Dec. 19, 1979; . Patrick Gossage, *Close to the Charisma: My Years between the Press and Pierre Elliott Trudeau* (Halifax: Goodread Biographies, 1987), 188–89.

9. Grafstein's trip to Harry Rosen and the approach to the campaign are described in campaign chronicler John Duffy's *Fights of Our Lives: Elections, Leadership, and the Making of Canada* (Toronto: HarperCollins, 2002), 292.

10. Davey wrote in his memoirs that the Liberal campaign was principally about Joe Clark: "However, it was equally clear that this was not the campaign where our leader should be in the front of the window. Whether or not it was Pierre Trudeau—but especially because it *was* Pierre Trudeau" (*Rainmaker*, 265). The information on the relations with the press is drawn from Gossage, *Close to the Charisma*, 193–95. Gossage made his comment about the poetry wars to me in an interview, June 2009. The best academic study of the elections of 1979 and 1980 is Howard Penniman, ed., *Canada at the Polls, 1979 and 1980: A Study of the General Elections* (Washington, D.C.: American Enterprise Institute for Public Policy Research, 1981), although it concentrates on the 1979 election. Robert Bothwell wrote an excellent summary of the 1979 and 1980 elections for Historica, the Canadian historical organization: http://www.histori.ca/prodev/article.do?id=15406.

11. Both Davey and Gossage describe the incident, at 269 and 194, respectively. Neither is sure whether or not Trudeau used the wrong name intentionally.

12. Gossage, *Close to the Charisma*, 190–91. Other comments are based on conversations with Lorna Marsden, Allan MacEachen, and Tom Axworthy. See also Clarkson and McCall, *Heroic Delusion*, 156–57, including a good description of Marsden's influence on pages 306–12. The letter to Trudeau's friend was cited in chapter 13, note 34. TP, MG 26 020, vol. 3, file 3-44.

13. Davey, *Rainmaker*, 270. Liberal strategist John Duffy emphasizes how the East-West division became a central feature of Canadian politics. He describes the 1979 campaign in detail in his *Fights of Our Lives*, 291ff. Byers, ed., *Canadian Annual Review 1979*, 43–45.

14. The CBC election night clip can be seen at http://archives.cbc.ca/on_this_day/02/18/. Trudeau's comments are in his *Memoirs*, 270.

15. On the washroom story, see Gossage, *Close to the Charisma*, 195. The Quebec government statement was published as *Québec-Canada: A New Deal: The Quebec Government Proposal for a New Partnership between Equals, Sovereignty-Association* (Quebec: Government of Quebec, 1979). The polls are discussed in Byers, ed., *Canadian Annual Review 1979*, 103–4. Three of four polls taken in 1979 indicated a lead for the "yes" side. The lack

of clarity in the wording of questions in the polls makes it difficult to judge their validity. However, the discussion indicates that the Quebec government was moderately optimistic about the result before Trudeau's return. See Martine Tremblay, *Derrière les portes closes: René Lévesque et l'exercice du pouvoir (1976–1985)* (Montréal: Québec Amérique, 2006), 236.

16. Edward McWhinney, *Canada and the Constitution 1979–1982: Patriation and the Charter of Rights* (Toronto: University of Toronto Press, 1982), 32; Léon Dion, *Le Québec et le Canada: Les Voies de l'Avenir* (Montréal: Les Éditions Québécor, 1980); and André Burelle, *Pierre Elliott Trudeau: L'Intellectuel et la Politique* (Montréal: Fides, 2005), 424. The *livre beige* is described in *Le Devoir*, Jan. 11, 1980; and Ryan discusses it with journalist Denise Bombardier on http://archives.radio-canada.ca/emissions/523-7461/ page/1/, an interview which illustrates well Ryan's seriousness as well as his clarity in exposition.

17. Trudeau discusses the offer in his *Memoirs*. He says he respected Broadbent but that they were not close, a view shared by Broadbent. A photograph of the meeting appears in Trudeau, *Memoirs*, 272–73. Interview with Bob Rae, Sept. 2005. Quotations from Judy Steed, *Ed Broadbent: The Pursuit of Power* (1988; repr., Markham, Ont.: Penguin, 1989), 240–41. Rae told Steed in the late 1980s: "The party was not in good spirits, facing another four years of Trudeau. We were in an awfully tough position" (243).

18. Trudeau, *Memoirs*, 277; L. Ian MacDonald, *From Bourassa to Bourassa: Wilderness to Restoration*, 2nd ed. (Montreal and Kingston: McGill-Queen's University Press, 2002), 98; *La Presse*, March 31, 1980; poll results are summarized in *Globe and Mail*, April 12, 1980. Gérard Bergeron, *Notre Miroir à deux faces* (Montréal: Québec Amérique, 1985), 218.

19. Their first encounter is described in detail in vol. 1 of this biography. *The Champions* (1994) is a brilliant 1994 CBC and National Film Board documentary in three parts, dealing with the relationship between Trudeau and Lévesque. Part 3 is a major source for this chapter.

20. Quoted in Gérard Pelletier, *Years of Impatience, 1950–1960*, trans. Alan Brown (1983; repr., Toronto, Methuen, 1984), 119.

21. Canada, *House of Commons Debates* (15 April 1980). The photograph is in *Globe and Mail*, April 16, 1980. For criticisms of Trudeau's approach, see *Le Devoir*, April 16, 1980.

22. The phenomenon has attracted scholarly attention from feminists. See Naomi Black, "Les Yvettes: Qui sont-elles?" in *Thérèse Casgrain: Une Femme tenace et engagée*, ed. Anita Caron and Lorraine Archambault (Sainte-Foy: Presses de l'Université du Québec, 1992), 165–69, and Micheline Dumont, "Les Yvettes ont permis aux femmes entrer dans l'histoire politique québécoise," *L'Action nationale*, Oct. 1991, 40–44. An excellent account also appears in MacDonald, *Bourassa to Bourassa*, chap.10. There is an enormous literature concentrating on the referendum. An excellent bibliography has been compiled by the library of Quebec's National Assembly: http://www.assnat.qc.ca/fra/Bibliotheque/publications/thematiques/btHs.pdf.

23. Library and Archives Canada chose to place the speech on their website as emblematic of addresses by prime ministers: http://www.collectionscanada.gc.ca/primeministers/h4-4083-e.html. MacDonald, *Bourassa to Bourassa*, 169–70. MacDonald's emotions are described in Gossage, *Close to the Charisma*, 197. Trudeau's essay, "The Ascetic in a Canoe," is found in his *Against the Current: Selected Writings 1939–1996*, ed. Gérard Pelletier (Toronto: McClelland and Stewart, 1996), 9–12.

24. Bergeron is one of many who made this assertion. *Globe and Mail* columnist Stevens was a consistent critic of the injection of constitutional reform into the debate. He also took strong objection to an angry attack on Quebec intellectuals and the media by Liberal MP André Ouellet. *Globe and Mail*, April 17, 1980.

25. This account of the meeting is based on MacDonald, *Bourassa to Bourassa*, 172ff., and on conversations with Jim Coutts, Eddie Goldenberg, and Jean Chrétien.

26. MacDonald, *Bourassa to Bourassa*. The description of the rallies comes from websites where Lévesque's and Ryan's speeches are posted: http://archives.cbc.ca/on_this_day/05/20/776/ and http://archives.cbc.ca/on_this_day/05/20/5600/, respectively. Ryan's aggressiveness contrasts sharply with Lévesque's dejection. Trudeau's description of his mood is from his *Memoirs*, 283–84.

27 . Gossage, *Close to the Charisma*, 198; Trudeau, *Memoirs*, 284.

CHAPTER FIFTEEN: CLOSING THE DEAL

1. The literature on the constitutional process in the early 1980s is vast and replete with controversy. Trudeau discusses the debate in his *Memoirs* (Toronto: McClelland and Stewart, 1993), part 4, and Chrétien has described his role in *Straight from the Heart* (1985; repr., Toronto: Key Porter Books, 2007), chap. 6. Brian Mulroney has commented on the Trudeau process, which in the initial stages he had supported, unlike Joe Clark and Peter Lougheed (Brian Mulroney, *Memoirs 1939–1993* [Toronto: McClelland and Stewart, 2007], 508–11). Lévesque's major biographer, Pierre Godin, discusses the subject at length in the relevant volume (*René Lévesque: L'Homme brisé [1980–1987]* [Montréal: Boréal, 2005]), as does Martine Tremblay, *Derrière les portes closes: René Lévesque et l'exercice du pouvoir (1976–1985)* (Montréal: Québec Amérique, 2006), which has an excellent bibliography covering francophone sources. Saskatchewan premier Allan Blakeney discusses his own important role in *An Honourable Calling: Political Memoirs* (Toronto: University of Toronto Press, 2008). A valuable contemporary edited collection, which is largely critical, is Keith Banting and Richard Simeon, eds., *And No One Cheered: Federalism, Democracy, and the Constitution Act* (Toronto: Methuen, 1983). The best contemporary history, based on exceptional access to most of the principals, is Robert Sheppard and Michael Valpy, *The National Deal: The Fight for a Canadian Constitution* (Toronto: Fleet, 1982). Judy Steed's biography of Ed Broadbent has an excellent account of the trouble the constitutional "wars" caused the New Democrats: Judy Steed, *Ed Broadbent: The Pursuit of Power* (1988; repr., Markham, Ont.: Penguin, 1989), chap. 7. The ghostwriter for Trudeau and Chrétien, Ron Graham, has written a well-informed account of the political dealings and impacts in *One-Eyed Kings: Promise and Illusion in Canadian Politics* (Toronto: Collins, 1986). Trudeau's speechwriter André Burelle not only traces his own dissent from Trudeau's approach but also provides considerable documentary evidence from his own papers in *Pierre Elliott Trudeau: L'Intellectuel et la Politique* (Montréal: Fides, 2005). Stephen Clarkson and Christina McCall wrote an award-winning account of Trudeau and the Constitution: Stephen Clarkson and Christina McCall, *The Magnificent Obsession*, vol. 1 of *Trudeau and Our Times* (Toronto: McClelland and

Stewart, 1990), part 2, and Philip Girard covers the judicial controversies well in his fine biography of Chief Justice Bora Laskin: *Bora Laskin: Bringing Law to Life* (Toronto: University of Toronto Press for the Osgoode Society, 2005). Donald Brittain's 1994 documentary, *The Champions*, made for the CBC and the National Film Board, is an excellent source, with superb interviews with the principal figures.

2. The quotations from Axworthy are found in Graham, *One-Eyed Kings*, 60, 64. Graham gives a superb account of the mood when Trudeau returned to power. Mr. Axworthy confirmed his impressions in a discussion in July 2005.

3. Mark MacGuigan, *An Inside Look at External Affairs during the Trudeau Years: The Memoirs of Mark MacGuigan*, ed. P. Whitney Lackenbauer (Calgary: University of Calgary Press, 2002). I served as Mr. MacGuigan's literary executor and had several conversations with him about this manuscript before he died. The comment quoted was made frequently in those discussions.

4. *Globe and Mail*, March 4, 1980.

5. Graham, *One-Eyed Kings*, section 1, and Donald Johnston, *Up the Hill* (Montreal and Toronto: Optimum, 1986).

6. Interview with Don Johnston, June 2009. When I described the meetings I held with former Trudeau ministers at Library and Archives Canada to Tom Axworthy, he commented that the divisions were exactly the same as they had been when they were in government.

7. Thomas S. Axworthy and Pierre Elliott Trudeau, eds., *Towards a Just Society: The Trudeau Years* (Markham, Ont.: Viking, 1990), 5. In addition to Axworthy and Trudeau, Marc Lalonde, Trudeau adviser Joel Bell, finance and Bank of Canada official Ian Stewart, Jacques Hébert, Environment Minister John Roberts, Jim Coutts, Gérard Pelletier, Finance Deputy Minister Thomas Shoyama, Lloyd Axworthy, party official and later Senator Lorna Marsden, Jean Chrétien, and York University historians and Trudeau supporters Fernand Ouellet and Ramsay Cook were contributors.

8. Stephen Clarkson, *Canada and the Reagan Challenge* (Toronto: Lorimer, 1985) is essentially a contemporary defence of the Trudeau resistance to the challenge, while Peter Foster, *The Sorcerer's Apprentices: Canada's Super-Bureaucrats and the Energy Mess* (Toronto: Collins, 1982) is a contemporary attack on Trudeau's economic policies, which he blames on

Trudeau's style of government, the influence of John Kenneth Galbraith, and an elite group of bureaucrats in Ottawa. An exchange between Keith Davey and Trudeau, in which the latter indicates that he has read and absorbed Coleman's arguments, is found in Davey to Trudeau, Feb. 21, 1973, TP, MG 26 07, vol. 290, file 319-14, LAC.

9. Trudeau and Carter had developed a warm friendship at G7 meetings, and despite Joe Clark's opposition to economic nationalism, the Americans seemed to prefer the familiar Trudeau. An assessment just before the 1980 election noted that in "the likelier event of a Liberal victory, Trudeau will also support US initiatives in Iran and Afghanistan. He has even attacked Clark for not doing enough in support of the United States. He, too, advocates an Olympic boycott as long as other Western allies go along. Trudeau's support for Western solidarity reflects his desire to be identified with an issue with strong popular support in Canada." However, the report did note that "Trudeau would differ from Clark mainly on economic policy—he would definitely be a more difficult bargaining partner for the United States." Brzezinski material, box 7, file Canada 10/79-1/81, Jimmy Carter Presidential Library. Reagan shared Trudeau's concerns about the Carter embargo. He wrote in his diary on Feb. 4, 1981: "I've always felt [the grain embargo] hurt our farmers worse than it hurt Soviets. Many of our allies . . . filled the gap & supplied Soviets." *The Reagan Diaries*, ed. Douglas Brinkley (New York: HarperCollins, 2007), 2.

10. Quoted in Christopher Shulgan, *The Soviet Ambassador: The Making of the Radical behind Perestroika* (Toronto: McClelland and Stewart, 2008), 240. Shulgan's book is an excellent description of the friendship between Trudeau and Yakovlev, who deeply influenced Soviet policy in the eighties.

11. Quoted in Pierre Godin, *René Lévesque: Un Homme et son rêve 1922–1987* (Montréal: Boréal, 2007), 473. Despite this anecdote, Godin dates Lévesque's demise from the day of the referendum defeat. However, Lévesque confidante Martine Tremblay strongly dissents in *Derrière les portes closes*, 248.

12. A good account of the meeting is found in Sheppard and Valpy, *National Deal*, 40–42. This book remains the fullest treatment of the constitutional process.

13. *Globe and Mail*, June 10, 1980; *Ottawa Citizen*, June 10, 1980.

14. Trudeau's conversation with Stephen Clarkson and Christina McCall, Dec. 11, 1986, quoted in *Magnificent Obsession*, 282–83. Kirby had been an opponent of Trudeau's return in 1979, but he was not then a major figure and Trudeau appears not to have known of his opposition. Confidential sources. The description of the Christmas card is from Patrick Gossage, *Close to the Charisma: My Years between the Press and Pierre Elliott Trudeau* (Halifax: Goodread Biographies, 1987), 239. On the origins of the Machiavelli statement, see Sheppard and Valpy, *National Deal*, 7.

15. Quoted in Burelle, *Pierre Elliott Trudeau*, 267. On pages 262 to 294, Burelle reproduces the documents in which Trudeau stroked out every reference to "nation."

16. Trudeau's comment about Robertson was made to Stephen Clarkson and Christina McCall in December 1986 (*Magnificent Obsession*, 280–81). Conversation with Robert Fowler. For Gordon Robertson's response to Trudeau's comments, see *Memoirs of a Very Civil Servant: Mackenzie King to Pierre Trudeau* (Toronto: University of Toronto Press, 2000). While clearly offended, he agrees with their substance. He was not appropriate and, accordingly, refused to advise: "No one who had worked with Mackenzie King, Louis St. Laurent, or Lester Pearson could believe that a power play, however successful in the short term, was the way to solve a constitutional problem" (321–22).

17. Sheppard and Valpy, *National Deal*, 53–54; Steed, *Ed Broadbent*, 244. The formal title of the Kirby memorandum is "Report to Cabinet on Constitutional Discussions, Summer 1980, and the Outlook for the First Ministers Conference and Beyond, August 30, 1980." The Kirby document is now available online at http://faculty.marianopolis.edu/ c.belanger/QuebecHistory/docs/1982/17.htm. It contains the quotation from Machiavelli that he placed on the front of his Christmas card.

18. The descriptions of participants' religious faiths are from *The Canadian Parliamentary Guide 1981* (Ottawa: Normandin, 1981), and the national figures are from *Canada Year Book, 1980–81* (Ottawa: Ministry of Supply and Services, 1991), and from *Globe and Mail* and *Le Devoir*, Sept. 8–11, 1980. On Lougheed and Davis, see Allan Hustak, *Peter Lougheed: A Biography* (Toronto: McClelland and Stewart, 1979), 144.

19. The description of the conference and the quotations are from the following sources: http://archives.cbc.ca/politics/constitution/clips/6041/; Donald Brittain's extraordinary documentary, *The Champions*, part 3, which superbly captures the tensions at the conference table; *Globe and Mail*, Sept. 8–11, 1980; and *Ottawa Citizen*, which was the first recipient of the leaked "Kirby Memorandum."

20. Quotations are in Clarkson and McCall, *Magnificent Obsession*, 291. See also Trudeau, *Memoirs*, 308–10, and "Interview between Mr. Trudeau and Mr. Graham," May 4, 1992, TP, MG 26 03, vol. 23, file 7, LAC.

21. The names of the dissenters soon leaked out despite Cabinet secrecy. See David Milne, *The New Canadian Constitution* (Toronto: Lorimer, 1982), 77. These names have also been confirmed in confidential interviews, although it seems clear that others had hesitations that were not expressed.

22. Bob Rae's brother John was an aide to Jean Chrétien and a close friend of Eddie Goldenberg, who played a central role in the constitutional initiative. Through them, Bob came to know the team in the Langevin Block who "quarterbacked" the effort. A quarter-century later, the same group facilitated Bob Rae's entry into the Liberal Party, surrounded him at the Montreal Convention Centre, where the 2006 Liberal leadership convention was held, and almost made him leader of the Liberal Party. On the referendum idea, which André Burelle strongly favoured, see Burelle, *Pierre Elliott Trudeau*, 295–300. A full description of the "team" on the bureaucratic and political side, which emphasizes the importance of Goldenberg, is found in Sheppard and Valpy, *National Deal*, 72–73.

23. Steed, *Ed Broadbent*, 245. Conversation with Bob Rae.

24. Quotations are from *Globe and Mail*, Oct. 3–4, 1980, which contains, on October 3, the statements by the federal leaders. For Quebec, see *Le Devoir*, Oct. 3, 1980. Trudeau's offensive led to a postponed election in Quebec (see Tremblay, *Derrière les portes closes*, 252–53).

25. On the criticism by Chamber president Sam Hughes, see *Toronto Star*, Oct. 3, 1980. Brian Mulroney's speech is described in Mulroney's *Memoirs*, 203. Mulroney's support for the patriation and the charter is acknowledged (511), although Clark is given credit for "a marvelous fight in the House opposing Trudeau's constitutional plans—probably his finest moment as leader" (208).

26. Craig Brown's classic study of the national policy is *Canada's National Policy 1883–1900: A Study in Canadian-American Relations* (Princeton: Princeton University Press, 1964). Lalonde's essay is in Axworthy and Trudeau, eds., *Towards a Just Society*, chap. 2. The quotation about Alberta is from Stephen Clarkson and Christina McCall, *The Heroic Delusion*, vol. 2 of *Trudeau and Our Times* (Toronto: McClelland and Stewart, 1994), 176.

27. The description of Lougheed's opposition to Victoria is found in Hustak, *Lougheed*, 144–45. The National Energy Program has had surprisingly little scholarly attention. An early and very critical analysis, which contains invaluable detail, is Foster's *Sorcerer's Apprentices*. Clarkson and McCall, *Heroic Delusion*, chap. 5, is more favourable, and part 2 of Axworthy and Trudeau, eds., *Towards a Just Society*, is, unsurprisingly, highly favourable to the policy while admitting that the unexpected drop in the oil price complicated matters. The best source remains G. Bruce Doern and Glen Toner, *The Politics of Energy: The Development and Implementation of the NEP* (Toronto: Methuen, 1985).

28. Quoted in Edmund Morris, *Dutch: A Memoir of Ronald Reagan* (New York: Random House, 1999), 411.

29. *Alberta Report's* views are quoted in James Laxer, *Canada's Economic Strategy* (Toronto: McClelland and Stewart, 1981), 178–79. This contemporary work is especially valuable on the split between the western and eastern branches of the NDP. One casualty of the NEP, Dome Petroleum, is covered in Jim Lyon, *Dome: The Rise and Fall of the House That Jack Built* (Toronto: Macmillan, 1983).

30. The relationship between the financial needs and the energy policy is explained well in Doern and Toner, *The Politics of Energy*, chap. 6. Interviews with Marshall Crowe, Jan. 2008, and Marc Lalonde, Oct. 2005. As an additional enticement to the West, the federal government established a Western Development Fund chaired by Manitoban Lloyd Axworthy. It was to recycle some of the additional revenues accruing to the federal government for western projects on the model of similar programs for eastern Canada.

31. Chrétien believes that Lougheed developed a warm regard for him when he assisted in the bailout of the oil sands in 1975. On Blakeney, see Chrétien, *Straight from the Heart*, 157.

32. There is an excellent account of the Winnipeg meeting in Clarkson and McCall, *Heroic Delusion*, 179–80. Details of the negotiations throughout the year are found in R.B. Byers, ed., *Canadian Annual Review of Politics and Public Affairs 1981* (Toronto: University of Toronto Press, 1984), 157–65.

33. Canada, *House of Commons Debates* (9 July 1981). According to Jim Lyon, whose source was Dome CEO Jack Gallagher, "Lalonde was on the phone almost daily to Dome as the launching date approached, and he flew to Alberta especially to appear with Jack Gallagher when Dome Canada was unveiled at a press conference" (*Dome*, 9). Dome Canada was the vehicle allowing Dome Petroleum to take advantage of the grants for frontier exploration. Interview with Marc Lalonde, Oct. 2005.

34. These statistics are drawn from the extensive and excellent discussion found in Doern and Toner, *The Politics of Energy*, chap. 9. *Globe and Mail*, Sept. 2, 1981, also provided detail. The photograph is reproduced in Trudeau, *Memoirs*, 295.

35. John F. Helliwell, M.E. MacGregor, and A. Plourde, "The National Energy Program Meets Falling World Oil Prices," *Canadian Public Policy/Analyse de Politiques*, vol. IX, No. 3 (Sept. 1983): 294.

36. These comments were made in an interview with Lougheed on the anniversary of the passage of the Canadian Charter of Rights and Freedoms. See www.collectionscanada.ca/rights-and-freedoms/ 023021-144-e.html.

37. See Edward McWhinney, *Canada and the Constitution 1979–1982: Patriation and the Charter of Rights* (Toronto: University of Toronto Press, 1982), 50. For the contrary view, see Martha Jackman, "Canadian Charter Equality at 20: Reflections of a Card Carrying Member of the Court Party," *Policy Options* (Dec. 2005–Jan. 2006): 72–77, and Louise Arbour, "Beyond Self-Congratulations: The Charter at 25 in an International Perspective" (paper presented at "A Tribute to Chief Justice Roy McMurtry," Toronto, April 12, 2007). Canada, *House of Commons Debates* (23 March 1981).

38. The provincial challenges are described in Sheppard and Valpy, *The National Deal*, 229ff; and Byers, ed., *Canadian Annual Review 1981*, 35, which has extensive quotations from the judgments.

39. *New York Times*, April 3, 1981. See also Byers, ed., *Canadian Annual Review 1981*, 38ff.

40. Canada, *House of Commons Debates* (23 March 1981). The court decisions are conveniently presented in McWhinney, *Patriation and the
Charter of Rights*, Appendix G.

41. The best account is in Girard, *Bora Laskin*, chap. 22.

42. On the Quebec election and Ryan's response, see Byers, ed., *Canadian
Annual Review 1981*, 373–36. Trudeau's comments are from an interview
he gave to other press members when the CBC refused to grant him free
air time after the provincial accord. *Globe and Mail*, April 17, 1981. On
the British reaction, see McWhinney, *Patriation and the Charter of Rights*,
chap. 7. Quotation on General Gordon is on page 66.

43. Canada, *House of Commons Debates* (6 Feb. 1981). MacGuigan, *Inside
Look*, 92–93. Conversations with Mark MacGuigan; Paul Martin, Sr.;
and Don Jamieson (then Canadian high commissioner to the U.K.) at
Cambridge Institute, summer 1981. *Ottawa Citizen*, Feb. 7, 1981.
Confidential interview.

44. On the conference in Cambridge, see Girard, *Bora Laskin*, 508–9.
I attended the conference, and the personal impressions are my own.

45. Burelle, *Pierre Elliott Trudeau*, 80–81, 333–34. Burelle's invaluable
book contains the exchanges between Pelletier and him concerning
the meetings.

46. Trudeau, *Memoirs*, 316. On Trudeau's frustration, see Chrétien, *Straight
from the Heart*, 181. Trudeau asked Chrétien, when they sat together in the
Commons, "if . . . [Chrétien] had heard when the decision was coming,
and he seemed uncomfortable in having his schedule [to have the pact
signed on Canada Day 1981] upset."

47. Sheppard and Valpy, *National Deal*, 256–58. Kirby's central role is
described in detail in this book, for which Kirby is a key source.

48. The account of Lévesque is taken from Godin, *L'Homme brisé*, chap. 14,
which has wonderful detail and a good discussion of those who made up
the Quebec delegation. On Claude Morin, see his *Lendemains piégés:
Du référendum à la nuit des longs couteaux* (Montréal: Boréal, 1988),
289–99. Chrétien, *Straight from the Heart*, 182–83. Peckford is quoted in
Byers, ed., *Canadian Annual Review 1981*, 57.

49. Chrétien, *Straight from the Heart*, 185. Clarkson and McCall have
some excellent material in their account of the deal based on interviews

with principals, notably Trudeau himself (*Heroic Delusion*, 380–85). Mr. Chrétien has confirmed the substance of this account.

50. Charron made the comment in the CBC/NFB film documentary *The Champions*, part 3. Lévesque biographer Pierre Godin has commented that the statement about what each represented was often made by Lévesque.

CHAPTER SIXTEEN: HARD TIMES

1. *Globe and Mail*, Oct. 24, 1981; *New York Times*, Aug. 22, 1982.

2. Davis is quoted in R. B. Byers, ed., *Canadian Annual Review of Politics and Public Affairs 1982* (Toronto: University of Toronto Press, 1984), 67. Trudeau, quoted in *Montreal Gazette*, Nov. 6, 1981. Trudeau interview with David Frost, Feb. 23, 1982, TP, MG 26 013, LAC.

3. Keith Banting and Richard Simeon, *And No One Cheered: Federalism, Democracy, and the Constitution Act* (Toronto: Methuen, 1983); Eugene Forsey, *Globe and Mail*, Nov. 21, 1981.

4. Judy Erola made her comment at my interview-meeting with former Trudeau ministers at Library and Archives Canada, Dec. 9, 2002, in response to my question about the success of the November meeting. Other ministers present did not contest her analysis. Trudeau's embarrassing admission is found in Canada, *House of Commons Debates* (6 Dec. 1981). Chrétien's comment is in his *Straight from the Heart* (1985; repr., Toronto: Key Porter Books, 2007), 189. See also Penney Kome, *The Taking of Twenty-Eight: Women Challenge the Constitution* (Toronto: Women's Press, 1983), and F.L. Morton and Avril Allen, "Feminists and the Courts: Measuring Success in Interest Group Litigation in Canada," *Canadian Journal of Political Science/Revue canadienne de science politique* 34 (2001): 55–84.

5. Judy Steed, *Ed Broadbent: The Pursuit of Power* (1988; repr., Markham, Ont.: Penguin, 1989), 252.

6. On the leak, see *Toronto Star*, Nov. 19, 1981. Lougheed's family history is covered in Allan Hustak, *Peter Lougheed: A Biography* (Toronto: McClelland and Stewart, 1979), 12. See also the biography of William Hardisty by Jennifer Brown in *The Dictionary of Canadian Biography Online*: http://www.biographi.ca/009004-119.01-e.php?&id_nbr=5566&interval=25&&PHPSESSID=s1mgens3hav4bjusctlf220n02.

The revision occurred in the Constitution, not the charter, and the implications have caused some debate.

7. On Côté, see Pierre Godin, *René Lévesque: L'Homme brisé (1980–1987)* (Montréal: Boréal, 2005), 187–88. Chaps. 16 and 17 give a full account, based on extensive interviews. For a complementary account, which differs from Godin, particularly on Lévesque's stability in this period, see the analysis by Lévesque's aide Martine Tremblay: *Derrière les portes closes: René Lévesque et l'exercice du pouvoir (1976–1985)* (Montréal: Éditions Québec Amérique, 2006), 270–73. Constitutional adviser Claude Morin places the events in context in his *Lendemains piégés: Du référendum à la nuit des longs couteaux* (Montréal: Boréal, 1988), while Claude Charron describes his experiences in *Désobéir* (Montréal: VLB Éditeur, 1983). On page 53, he describes the exchange between Trudeau and Lévesque. Trudeau speechwriter André Burelle was a strong critic of the course chosen by Trudeau, especially the acceptance of the notwithstanding clause. He nevertheless drafted the speeches to be given if the constitutional conference failed or if it succeeded. They are contained in his *Pierre Elliott Trudeau: L'Intellectuel et la Politique* (Montréal: Fides, 2005), 357–61. The reactions of Trudeau and Lévesque, as well as the celebratory air among non-Quebec premiers, are captured in a CBC archives clip: http://archives.cbc.ca/politics/constitution/topics/1092/.

8. *Journal des débats*, Assemblée nationale, Nov. 9, 1981; *Toronto Star*, Dec. 3, 1981.

9. The full text of the exchanges is found in Byers, ed., *Canadian Annual Review of Politics and Public Affairs 1981* (Toronto: University of Toronto Press, 1984), 79–85. It is also available, along with the Quebec National Assembly resolution, at http://faculty.marianopolis.edu/ c.belanger/ quebechistory/docs/patriate/index.htm.

10. René Lévesque, *Memoirs*, trans. Philip Stratford (Toronto: McClelland and Stewart, 1986), 24–25.

11. Ibid., 325–26.

12. Morin, *Lendemains piégés*, 301–2. The referendum options are discussed in Roy Romanow, *Canada—Notwithstanding: The Making of the Constitution 1976–1982* (Toronto: Carswell/Methuen, 1984), 193–207.

13. *Montreal Gazette*, Nov. 3, 1981; *Globe and Mail*, Nov. 3, 1981; *Le Devoir*, Nov. 6, 1981. Corinne Côté, Lévesque's wife, would not greet Trudeau at

the visitation. Trudeau at the visitation is described by Godin, *Lévesque: L'Homme brisé*, 532–33. Interview with Jacques Hébert, Aug. 2007.

14. Pierre Elliott Trudeau, *Memoirs* (Toronto: McClelland & Stewart, 1993); "Entrevue entre M. Trudeau et M. Lépine," May 11, 1992, TP, MG 26 03, vol. 23, file 11, LAC; Cook to Trudeau, Nov. 8, 1981, and Trudeau to Cook, Nov. 30, 1981, TP, MG 26 020, vol. 3, file 20, LAC; Frank Scott to Trudeau, Dec. 11, 1981, TP, MG 26 020, vol. 11, file 23, LAC.

15. Chrétien, *Straight from the Heart*, 187–88. Cook to Trudeau, Sept. 28, 1983, TP, MG 26 020, vol. 3, file 20, LAC. Cook made Trudeau's point in his essay "Has the Quiet Revolution Finally Ended," *Queen's Quarterly* 90, no. 2 (summer 1983): 336. He enclosed the article in the letter. Mulroney's attack on Trudeau is found throughout his memoirs, but his specific criticisms of the November 1981 agreement and its reception in Quebec by its politicians are found in Brian Mulroney, *Memoirs 1939–1993* (Toronto: McClelland and Stewart, 2007), 511–14.

16. "Entrevue entre M. Trudeau et M. Lépine," May 11, 1992, TP, MG 26 03, vol. 23, file 11, LAC.

17. Godin, *L'Homme brisé*. On pages 529–30, he quotes Romanow making the comment upon the death of Lévesque. The same quotation appears in *Globe and Mail*, Nov. 3, 1987, and he made a similar comment on November 5, 1981 (*Globe and Mail*, Nov. 6, 1981). Godin's statement about their mutual significance is in his biography of Lévesque in the *Dictionary of Canadian Biography*, which is soon to appear on the website of Library and Archives Canada.

18. This account draws on *Ottawa Citizen*, April 19, 1982; *Globe and Mail*, April 19–20, 1982; and Robert Sheppard and Michael Valpy, *The National Deal: The Fight for a Canadian Constitution* (Toronto: Fleet, 1982), 320–21, which gives a most ambivalent appraisal of the work of the premiers and Trudeau.

19. The full polling results are given in Byers, ed., *Canadian Annual Review 1981*, 139. Patrick Gossage, *Close to the Charisma: My Years between the Press and Pierre Trudeau* (Halifax: Goodread Biographies, 1987), 237–38.

20. Monica Gaylord to Trudeau, June 13, 1982, TP, MG 26 020, vol. 5, file 5-2, LAC.

21. Interview with Justin Trudeau, Aug. 2007. Interview with Gale Zoë Garnett, April 2008. Justin's young friend is Shauna Hardy—quoted in Nancy

Southam, ed., *Pierre: Colleagues and Friends Talk about the Trudeau They Knew* (Toronto: McClelland and Stewart, 2005), 301–2. Sociologist Annette Lareau has called this stage of development in a child's life an atmosphere of "concerted cultivation": see *Unequal Childhoods: Class, Race, and Family Life* (Berkeley: University of California Press, 2003). I was drawn to this work by reading Malcolm Gladwell, *Outliers: The Story of Success* (New York: Little, Brown, 2008), chap. 4.

22. Margaret Trudeau, *Consequences* (Toronto: McClelland and Stewart, 1982), 134, 175–76. Interviews with Margaret Trudeau, Jane Faulkner, Justin Trudeau, Alexandre Trudeau, and confidential interviews.

23. Ibid.; and Trudeau, *Consequences*, 177.

24. Boutros-Ghali's story is also found in Southam, ed., *Pierre*, 303. The superb account of the visit to Saudi Arabia is written by Norman Webster and is in *Globe and Mail*, Nov. 20, 1980. On the special seats, see the comments by Justin's friend Jeff Gillin in Southam, ed., *Pierre*, 312.

25. Trudeau, *Consequences*, 78–79. Conversation with Marc Lalonde.

26. Trudeau, *Consequences*, 80; Allan Gotlieb, *The Washington Diaries: 1981–1989* (Toronto: McClelland and Stewart, 2006), 263–64; conversations with Jacques Roy and Paul Heinbecker. This general description of Trudeau's many intimate women friends is drawn from the correspondence, which is found in many files in TP, MG 26 020, LAC.

27. Kidder to Trudeau, March 30, 1983, TP, MG 26 020, vol. 6, file 7.3, LAC; Trudeau to Garnett, Christmas 1981, TP, MG 26 020, vol. 4, file 4.2, LAC; and Garnett to Trudeau, Feb. 3 and Feb. 9, 1981, ibid.

28. Garnett to Trudeau, June 12, June 14, and Nov. 9, 1981, TP, MG 26 020, vol. 4, file 44, LAC.

29. Trudeau to Garnett, Christmas 1982; Garnett to Trudeau, Sept. 23, 1982, and May 30 and July 9, 1983 (emphasis in original quotations). Interview with Gale Zoë Garnett, Sept. 2008.

30. Embassy, Athens, to External Affairs, June 22, 1983, TP, MG 26 020, vol. 4, file 44, LAC; External Affairs to Embassy, Athens, June 22, 1983, ibid.; Garnett to Trudeau, May 30 and June 3, 1983, ibid. Interview with Garnett, ibid.

31. Garnett to Trudeau, June 29, 1982, ibid.

32. Volcker is quoted in Daniel Yergin and Joseph Stanislaw, *The Commanding*

Heights: The Battle for the World Economy (New York: Touchstone Books, 2002), 348.

33. Canada, *House of Commons Debates* (12 Nov. 1981). An excellent summary of the budget and, in particular, of the lobbying effort is found in Byers, ed., *Canadian Annual Review 1981*, 255–65. In his study *The Welfare State and Canadian Federalism* (Kingston and Montreal: McGill–Queen's University Press, 1982), Keith Banting traces income security payments per capita and indicates how such payments became an increasingly important component of personal income. For example, in 1964 such payments made up 15.5 percent of total personal income in Newfoundland. By 1978 such payments were 29.4 percent. In MacEachen's Nova Scotia, they had risen from 12.2 to 18.4 percent; in New Brunswick, from 13.3 to 20.9 percent; and in Quebec they grew from only 8.95 to 16.5 percent. Alberta grew only from 9.1 to 10.7 percent and Ontario from 6.9 to 10.8 percent. In these figures reside many political explanations (100–101).

34. Byers, ed., *Canadian Annual Review 1981*, 108–9; Ian Stewart, "Global Transformation and Economic Policy," in Axworthy and Trudeau, eds., *Towards a Just Society: The Trudeau Years* (Markham, Ont.: Viking, 1990), 166. See also the essays by Marc Lalonde and Joel Bell in this collection.

35. Comment made at Rideau Club luncheon on Trudeau, April 8, 2009. Several other Trudeau-era officials did not disagree with Mme Bégin's statement.

36. Agriculture Minister Eugene Whelan attacked MacEachen in a public address. Trudeau, in Whelan's words, "took me aside and said, 'You can say anything you like about the banks, but leave MacEachen out of it. He's one of us.'" Eugene Whelan with Rick Archbold, *Whelan: The Man in the Green Stetson* (Toronto: Irwin, 1986), 228. Whelan takes many shots at his Cabinet colleagues whom he perceived as less progressive, notably Don Johnston.

37. Interview with Marshall Crowe, Jan. 2008. Michael Bliss, *Right Honourable Men: The Descent of Canadian Politics from Macdonald to Mulroney* (Toronto: Harper Perennial 1995), 271. Bliss's fuller comments on the problems of the NEP from the perspective of the Canadian business community are found in *Northern Business: Five Centuries of Canadian Business* (Toronto: McClelland and Stewart, 1987), 541.

38. The Gallagher discussion is in a series of rough notes from the Dec. 1, 1980, meeting found in TP, MG 26, vol. 265, file 1, LAC. The Trudeau and Lalonde speeches are described in Byers, ed., *Canadian Annual Review 1981*, 318.

39. Alonzo Hamby, a historian of American liberalism, points out that in the seventies, "Nixon's neo-conservatism had hardly gotten beyond resentment of the New Class [bureaucrats and technocrats] and the practice of social politics," but "Reagan's was much more comprehensive in its program-matic definition, highly developed in its ideological base, and determined in its objectives." See Hamby, *Liberalism and Its Challengers: F.D.R. to Reagan* (New York: Oxford University Press, 1985), 353.

40. Marc Lalonde, "Riding the Storm: Energy Policy," in *Towards a Just Society: The Trudeau Years*, ed. Thomas S. Axworthy and Pierre Elliott Trudeau (Markham, Ont.: Viking, 1990), 114–19. Figures on the sovereign wealth funds are from http://www.swfinstitute.org/fund/alberta.php. The figures for the Norwegian fund at the end of 2008 are US$301 billion, compared with US$14.9 billion for Alberta.

41. G. Bruce Doern, "The Mega-Project Episode and the Formulation of Canadian Economic Development Policy," *Canadian Public Administration* 26, no. 2 (summer 1993): 223. Doern's major work was written with Glen Toner: *The Politics of Energy: The Development and Implementation of the NEP* (Toronto: Methuen, 1985). There is also much valuable commentary in Timothy Lewis, *In the Long Run We're All Dead: The Canadian Turn to Fiscal Restraint* (Vancouver: University of British Columbia Press, 2004), especially pages 75ff.

42. According to Dr. Richard Bird, in the period from 1959 to 1977 the provinces accounted for most of the growth of expenditures on a National Account basis. Specifically, the provinces accounted for 41 percent of growth, while local government accounted for 26 percent and the federal government only 12 percent. However, much of the provincial growth came from provinces responding to shared-cost programs encouraged by the federal government, notably medicare. There was a reversal between 1977 and 1986, according to J.H. Perry, which saw the federal proportion stand at 53 percent, the provinces at 47 percent, and an actual decline at the local level. Richard Bird, *Financing Canadian Government:*

A *Quantitative Overview* (Toronto: Canadian Tax Foundation, 1979),
20–32; J.H. Perry, A *Fiscal History of Canada: The Postwar Years* (Toronto:
Canadian Tax Foundation, 1989), 419.

43. Kenneth Norrie and Douglas Owram, A *History of the Canadian Economy*
(Toronto: Harcourt Brace Jovanovich, 1991), 606.

44. Clarence Barber and John McCallum, *Controlling Inflation: Learning
from Experience in Canada, Europe, and Japan* (Ottawa: Canadian
Institute for Economic Policy, 1982), 109.

45. Monica Gaylord to Trudeau, Sept. 11, 1982, TP, MG 26 020, vol. 5,
file 5.2, LAC; Lewis, *In the Long Run*, 78–80.

46. "Prime Minister's Address to the Nation on the Economy," June 28, 1983,
MG 32, Family Papers of Maurice Sauvé fonds B-4, vol. 132, LAC.

47. The quotation about policy is found in the best account of the fall of
Clark and the rise of Mulroney: Patrick Martin, Allan Gregg, and George
Perlin, *Contenders: The Tory Quest for Power* (Scarborough, Ont.:
Prentice-Hall, 1983), 92. This well-informed account draws on the
polling data of Allan Gregg, who was a leading Conservative pollster.
Mulroney published a campaign policy statement where he spoke about
special status and other policy positions: *Where I Stand* (Toronto:
McClelland and Stewart, 1983).

48. The figures on Gross Health Expenditures are from Perry, *Fiscal History of
Canada*, 648. On the background of the Canada Health Act, see ibid.,
655–58, and R.B. Byers, ed., *Canadian Annual Review of Politics and
Public Affairs 1983* (Toronto: University of Toronto Press), 23–24.

49. *Globe and Mail*, Dec. 15, 1983.

50. The best account of the party during this period is found in Stephen
Clarkson, *The Big Red Machine: How the Liberal Party Dominates
Canadian Politics* (Vancouver: University of British Columbia Press, 2005),
which illustrates how the conservative and young Grindstone Group,
created by a group of Liberal dissidents, played an increasingly important
role in the eighties.

CHAPTER SEVENTEEN: PEACE AT LAST

1. Robert Bothwell, *Alliance and Illusion: Canada and the World, 1945–1984*
(Vancouver: University of British Columbia Press, 2007), 277.

2. The best accounts of Trudeau's early approaches to foreign policy can be found in Bothwell, ibid., and a contemporary book by Peter Dobell, a former External Affairs officer. Dobell wrote the aptly titled *Canada's Search for New Roles: Foreign Policy in the Trudeau Era* (London: Published for the Royal Institute of International Affairs by Oxford University Press, 1972). He undertook to write the book when he believed that Trudeau was fundamentally altering the directions of Canadian foreign policy. He was particularly disturbed by a statement concerning Trudeau's approach that he believed rejected too decisively the Pearsonian tradition—and was startled to learn that amongst its authors were two friends and young foreign affairs officers, Max Yalden and Allan Gotlieb. Conversation with Peter Dobell, April 2008.

3. Granatstein, quoted in John Saywell, ed., *Canadian Annual Review for 1968* (Toronto: University of Toronto Press, 1969), 249. In his essay "All Things to All Men: Triservice Unification," in *An Independent Foreign Policy for Canada?*, ed. Stephen Clarkson (Toronto: McClelland and Stewart, 1968), Granatstein writes, "To this observer, unification [of the armed forces] regrettably does not seem to imply Canadian withdrawal from NATO" (137).

4. Cabinet Conclusions, RG2, PCO, Series A-5-a, vol. 6340, March 29, 1969, LAC; Canada, *House of Commons Debates* (24 Oct. 1969); interview with Marshall Crowe, Jan. 2009.

5. Trudeau, quoted in John Saywell, ed., *Canadian Annual Review of Public Affairs 1971* (Toronto: University of Toronto Press, 1972), 258. See a slightly different version in Leigh Sarty, "A Handshake across the Pole: Canadian Soviet Relations during the Era of Détente," in *Canada and the Soviet Experiment: Essays on Canadian Encounters with Russia and the Soviet Union, 1900–1991*, ed. David Davies (Waterloo: Centre on Foreign Policy and Federalism, 1991), 124–26.

6. Ivan Head and Pierre Trudeau, *The Canadian Way: Shaping Canada's Foreign Policy, 1968–1984* (Toronto: McClelland and Stewart, 1995).

7. Robert Bothwell, Ian Drummond, and John English, *Canada since 1945: Power, Politics, and Provincialism* (Toronto: University of Toronto Press, 1981), 378. Harald Von Riekhoff, "The Impact of Prime Minister Trudeau on Foreign Policy," *International Journal* 33 (spring 1978): 267–86.

8. For the argument for Canadian successes in specific areas, see David
   Dewitt and John Kirton, *Canada as a Principal Power: A Study in Foreign
   Policy and International Relations* (Toronto: Wiley, 1983). The standard
   study of Trudeau's foreign policy, J.L. Granatstein and Robert Bothwell,
   Pirouette: Pierre Trudeau and Canadian Foreign Policy (Toronto: University
   of Toronto Press, 1990), is more critical but does acknowledge Canada's
   successful promotion of its interests in the seventies.

9. Brzezinski's advice is in Brzezinski file, NSA, Canada 2.21-23-77, box 5,
   Jimmy Carter Presidential Library. The toasts are found in Staff Offices,
   box 1, file 2.21.77, Visit Prime Minister Trudeau, Jimmy Carter
   Presidential Library. Carter writes in his memoirs: "Shortly after arriving [at
   the 1980 summit] I had an unbelievable meeting with Helmut Schmidt . . .
   ranting and raving about a letter that I had written him which was a well-
   advised message. He claimed that he was insulted." Jimmy Carter, *Keeping
   Faith: Memoirs of a President* (New York: Bantam, 1981), 536–37.

10. John Campbell, *The Iron Lady*, vol. 2 of *Margaret Thatcher* (London:
    Pimlico, 2004), 319; Margaret Thatcher, *The Downing Street Years*
    (New York: HarperCollins, 1993), 168.

11. Trudeau and Head describe the plans for Montebello and Cancún in
    Canadian Way, 158ff. The major study of Canadian development assis-
    tance points out that Canadian "ODA" rose from $122.35 million in
    1965–66 to $903.51 million in 1975–76. David Morrison, *Aid and Ebb
    Tide: A History of CIDA and Canadian Development Assistance* (Waterloo:
    Wilfrid Laurier University Press, 1998), 8. Comments on Head's role and
    the reasons for his departure were discussed by several of Trudeau's former
    assistants at a special interview/dinner organized by Library and Archives
    Canada, March 17, 2003. When I questioned why Head had left the Prime
    Minister's Office, the general view was that it was his own choice and that
    his influence remained large.

12. MacGuigan's posthumous memoir of his years as external affairs minister
    details the many interventions. See Mark MacGuigan, *An Inside
    Look at External Affairs during the Trudeau Years: The Memoirs of Mark
    MacGuigan*, ed. P. Whitney Lackenbauer (Calgary: University of Calgary
    Press, 2002). He describes his frustration with Trudeau's interventions
    and his differences on East-West matters in chap. 2. The full version is

available in Fonds John English, University of Waterloo Archives. Robert Bothwell has written that "MacGuigan was not close to Trudeau, and the prime minister often seemed to respect neither his political position nor his policy. MacGuigan swallowed hard." Bothwell, *Alliance and Illusion*, 377.

13. John Gaddis, *The Cold War: A New History* (New York: Penguin, 2005), 211–12.

14. On the meetings, see Roy Rempel, *Counterweights: The Failure of Canada's German and European Policy, 1955–1995* (Montreal and Kingston: McGill–Queen's University Press, 1996), 87. Trudeau wrote to Schmidt on July 21, 1978, upon his return from Germany: "During the two days we spent sailing, we had the opportunity to go more deeply into the issues confronting us in the world at large and we discussed the relations between the Federal Republic and Canada. On both counts I was gratified to note the large degree of convergence in our approach." He added: "You are becoming a familiar figure to Canadians, and I am sure each visit will bring you a warmer welcome than the last." Archiv der sozialen Demokratie, file L-E-K Schmidt. I would like to thank Dr. Wilhelm Bleek for this reference. With Roy Rempel and Hans Stallman, he has written an excellent account of the friendship between Trudeau and Schmidt, "Die Männerfreundschaft zwischen zwei politischen Kapitänen," *Zeitschrift für Kanada Studien* 20, no. 2 (2000): 62–86. On Schmidt's view of Carter, see Helmut Schmidt, *Men and Powers: A Political Retrospective*, trans. Ruth Hein (New York: Random House, 1989), 181–87. In a note to Carter's National Security Adviser Zbigniew Brzezinski, an official reported that "this Federal Chancellor and many, many Germans believe this American Administration does not understand the FRG's problems" (underlining in original). Robert Blackwill to Brzezinski, Oct. 12, 1979, NSF Brzezinski, President's Correspondence with Foreign Leaders, box 7, Jimmy Carter Presidential Library.

15. See Rempel, *Counterweights*, 98. John Halstead, Canada's leading authority on Germany at the time, confirmed the importance of Schmidt's influence in a conversation with me.

16. These statistics are taken from the best account of Canadian development spending and policy: Morrison, *Aid and Ebb Tide*, 453–54.

17. *In the Canadian Interest? Third World Development in the 1980s* (Ottawa: The North-South Institute, 1980). Another analysis of Trudeau's performance claims that "Canada's relations with the Third World were better conceived, and worse managed, than they deserved to be." Nevertheless, Jack Granatstein and Robert Bothwell conclude: "The balance is, nevertheless, ever so slightly favourable." *Pirouette*, 307.

18. An excellent example of criticism at the time is Robert Carty and Virginia Smith, *Perpetuating Poverty: The Political Economy of Canadian Foreign Aid* (Toronto: Between the Lines, 1981). Another excellent analysis, which discusses these criticisms, is Kim Nossal, "Personal Diplomacy and National Behaviour: Trudeau's North-South Initiatives," *Dalhousie Review* 62 (summer 1982): 278–91. MacGuigan's comments are found in his *Inside Look*, 76.

19. The trips are described in R.B. Byers, ed., *Canadian Annual Review of Politics and Public Affairs 1981* (Toronto: University of Toronto Press, 1984), 311–12. The road to Cancún is described in Head and Trudeau, *Canadian Way*, 158ff.

20. Bernard Wood, "Canada's Views on North-South Negotiations," *Third World Quarterly* 3 (Oct. 1981): 651.

21. Canada, *House of Commons Debates* (15 June 1981).

22. Schmidt, *Men and Powers*, 246. On Schmidt's and Reagan's initial views of Mitterrand, see *Globe and Mail*, July 16, 1981, reporting a comment of a German official indicating that Schmidt thought Mitterrand a pinko, and Edmund Morris, *Dutch: A Memoir of Ronald Reagan* (New York: Random House, 1999), 442. On Thatcher and Reagan on the White House lawn, see Campbell, *Iron Lady*, 263. John Kirton interview with Henry Rau, former National Security Council official, May 7, 2004 (http://www.g8.utoronto.ca/oralhistory/nau040507.html). The G8 Centre at Trinity University, Toronto, is an excellent repository of literature on the institution and summit outcomes. See also Peter Hajnal, *The G8 System and the G20: Evolution, Role, and Documentation* (Aldershot, England: Ashgate, 2007), which is a product of the Centre.

23. Tony Judt, *Postwar: A History of Europe since 1945* (New York: Penguin, 2005), 549. The anecdote about Thatcher and Mitterrand is found in Morris, *Dutch*, 442.

24. Robert Putnam and Nicholas Bayne evaluate the summits since the first at Rambouillet in 1975 in *Hanging Together: Cooperation and Conflict in the Seven-Power Summits*, rev. ed. (Cambridge: Harvard University Press, 1987). On the Japanese prime minister dozing and Trudeau playing with the rose, see Jacques Attali, *Verbatim*, vol. 1 of *Chronique des années 1981–1986* (Paris: Fayard, 1993), 62–63. The story on the Middle East was told to me at the time by external affairs minister Mark MacGuigan. Separately, Marc Lalonde and David Smith, a Liberal activist and MP between 1980 and 1984, have confirmed the story, as has Eddie Goldenberg, Jean Chrétien's assistant at the time.

25. Pierre Trudeau, *Memoirs* (Toronto: McClelland and Stewart, 1993), 332, for anecdote about Reagan, which is repeated in slightly different form in Morris, *Dutch*, 442–43. The Reagan view of Mitterrand is found in ibid., 442. For Schmidt's favourable assessment of Reagan, see his *Men and Powers*, 245. The comment about Reagan's "obsession with communism" is in Trudeau, *Memoirs*, 329.

26. Conversation with Dr. David Cameron, who worked at the Privy Council Office during the constitutional crisis, April 2009.

27. Bothwell and Granatstein, *Pirouette*, 322–23; Morris, *Dutch*, 442–43; Campbell, *Iron Lady*, 264; and the memoir of the period by the controversial French politician Jacques Attali, who was present: *Verbatim*, 59–104.

28. Office of the Prime Minister, "Prime Minister's Statement at Joint Press Conference by Heads of Delegation in the Opera of the National Arts Centre, Ottawa, Tuesday, July 21, 1981," personal copy.

29. "Memorandum of Conversation," July 16, 1981, Meese Files LOC1/9/10/3, Ronald Reagan Presidential Library.

30. External Affairs, "A speech by the Right Honourable Pierre Elliott Trudeau, Prime Minister, to the United Nations Conference on Energy," Nairobi, Kenya, Aug. 11, 1981, Statements and Speeches No. 81/22.

31. Alexander Haig, "Memorandum for: The President," on "Your Meetings with Other Heads of State or Government in Cancun, October 21–24," Oct, 2, 1981, Meese Files, LOC1/9/10/3, Ronald Reagan Presidential Library; Campbell, *Iron Lady*, 341; Thatcher, *Downing Street*, 170. Trudeau's private comments to the Commonwealth Conference are found in PM Delegation to External, Ottawa, Oct. 8, 1981, EAP, RG 25,

Commonwealth Heads of Government Meeting, 1981, vol. 11092, file 23-3-1981, (LAC), and his public remarks are in Byers, ed., *Canadian Annual Review*, 314.

32. Campbell, *Iron Lady*, 341; Thatcher, *Downing Street*, 170. Trudeau has two full pages of colour photographs of Cancún in his *Memoirs*, 304–5.

33. Head and Trudeau, *Canadian Way*, 159–60. Conversations with Mexican representative Andrés Rozental and German representative Hans Sulimma, Oct. 2008.

34. Allan Gotlieb, *The Washington Diaries: 1981–1989* (Toronto: McClelland and Stewart, 2006), 12–13. The threat to Canadian membership in the G7 is discussed in Granatstein and Bothwell, *Pirouette*, 324.

35. Canada, *House of Commons Debates* (18 Dec. 1981). See MacGuigan, *Inside Look*, 56, for the favourable reaction from the Poles.

36. Notre Dame University speech, May 17, 1981. *Public Papers of the President of the United States: Ronald Reagan, 1981* (Washington, D.C.: Government Printing Office, 1982), 434.

37. Gotlieb, *Washington Diaries*, 61.

38. The speech is reprinted in Pierre Elliott Trudeau, *Lifting the Shadow of War*, ed. C. David Crenna (Edmonton: Hurtig, 1987), 40–43.

39. Gotlieb, *Washington Diaries*, 66; MacGuigan, *Inside Look*, 58; Alexander Haig, *Caveat: Realism, Reagan, and Foreign Policy* (New York: Scribner, 1984), 309.

40. The best account of the period is found in Granatstein and Bothwell, *Pirouette*, chap. 12. The impact of the *National Review* article is discussed on pages 328–29. Zink's article is "The Unpenetrated Problem of Pierre Trudeau," *National Review*, June 25, 1982, 751–76. The Gotlieb exchange with Deaver is in *Washington Diaries*, 72. The Pitfield, MacGuigan, Gotlieb effort to conciliate the Americans can be followed in Gotlieb (73ff.) and is described by MacGuigan in *Inside Look*, 122–23.

41. A recent history details the cruise missile issue. See John Murray Clearwater, *"Just Dummies": Cruise Missile Testing in Canada* (Calgary: University of Calgary Press, 2006).

42. The description of the Soviet Union as an "evil empire" was not original, as Reagan's biographer points out, but its use by the president had a dramatic impact. See Morris, *Dutch*, 472–73.

43. Trudeau, *Memoirs*, 334.

44. Jewett's comments and the chanting demonstrators may be heard on the CBC Archives report by reporter Mike Duffy at http://archives.cbc.ca/war_conflict/defence/clips/1040/.

45. MacEachen to Shultz, MacEP, July 15, 1983, MG 35 A 67, vol. 806, LAC. Verification was an area of Canadian expertise at the time. It referred to the ability of each side to confirm the other's promises through electronic surveillance, intelligence, and disclosure.

46. Conversation with Gale Zoë Garnett, May 2008. Gotlieb, *Washington Diaries*, 147–49; conversations with Paul Heinbecker, Jacques Roy, and John Seibert, Canadian foreign service officers at the residence; interview with Margot Kidder.

47. Margot Kidder to Trudeau, May 12, May 17, and nd, 1983, TP, MG 26 020, vol. 6, file 7-3, LAC. Interview with Margot Kidder.

48. This description comes from the excellent study of the Yakovlev-Trudeau relationship by Christopher Shulgan, a relationship which Mark MacGuigan said was "a private preserve" for Trudeau (MacGuigan, *Inside Look*, 9). Shulgan, *The Soviet Ambassador: The Making of the Radical behind Perestroika* (Toronto: McClelland and Stewart, 2008), 248.

49. There is an excellent account in Shulgan, 248ff. See also the account of the meeting in "Prime Minister's Discussions with Mr. Gorbachev, May 18, 1983," EAP, RG 25, vol. 8704, file 20-USSR-9, LAC. The report of Trudeau's comments surprised Gotlieb, who had increasingly come to believe Trudeau was too soft on the Soviets. He wrote in his diary: "Trudeau the hardliner. Go figure." *Washington Diaries*, 159.

50. *New York Times*, March 9, 1983; Gaddis, *Cold War*, 224–25.

51. Description of Trudeau is in *New York Times*, March 9, 1983.

52. Thatcher and the prepared draft are described in Thatcher, *Downing Street*, 300, and the Reagans' movie night in Morris, *Dutch*, 485.

53. The Gotlieb account is in *Washington Diaries*, 160–62. Trudeau's account in Head and Trudeau, *Canadian Way*, is surprisingly brief but takes credit for the statement quoted, 296–97. There are also good accounts in Christina McCall and Stephen Clarkson, *The Heroic Delusion*, vol. 2 of *Trudeau and Our Times* (Toronto: McClelland and Stewart, 1994), 358–59; Morris, *Dutch*, 485–47; and Bothwell, *Alliance and Illusion*, 384.

54. Trudeau, *Memoirs*, 335–36.

55. Washington Embassy to Ottawa, Sept. 1, 1983; Pearson to Ottawa, Sept 1, 1983, MacEP, MG 35 A67, vol. 806, LAC. See *Globe and Mail*, Sept. 5, 1983, for details of reaction.

56. The MacEachen file above has strong evidence of the differences between Trudeau and MacEachen on the KAL incident. Trudeau's comments to Hersh are in Seymour Hersh, *"The Target Is Destroyed": What Really Happened to Flight 007 and What America Knew about It* (New York: Random House, 1986), 245; and Thomas S. Axworthy and Pierre Trudeau, eds., *Towards a Just Society: The Trudeau Years* (1990; repr., Toronto: Penguin, 1992), 90. Bothwell and Granatstein, *Pirouette*, 364, describe the reaction to Trudeau's description of the incident as an accident.

57. The following section relies on an unpublished article by Foreign Affairs official historian Greg Donaghy, "The 'Ghost of Peace': Pierre Trudeau's Search for Peace, 1982–84," which Dr. Donaghy has kindly lent me. It refers to confidential documents that I am unable to consult. See also Head and Trudeau, *Canadian Way*, 297ff.

58. Patrick Gossage was brought back from Washington, where he had been a press secretary at the Canadian Embassy, to assist with the press. He reported on the Oct. 7 meeting in *Close to the Charisma: My Years between the Press and Pierre Elliott Trudeau* (Halifax: Goodread Biographies, 1987), 255. Gotlieb, *Washington Diaries*, 179.

59. The speech is published and edited "by Mr. Trudeau to improve its clarity," in Trudeau, *Lifting the Shadow*, 75–80.

60. *Globe and Mail*, Oct. 27–28, 1983.

61. Granatstein and Bothwell, *Pirouette*, 369. Thatcher is quoted in Donaghy, "'Ghost of Peace.'"

62. The Chinese meeting is treated briefly without comment in Head and Trudeau, *Canadian Way*, 305. Geoffrey Pearson, who accompanied Trudeau, was appalled by the meeting and dismissive of Trudeau's perform-ance (personal memory of conversation). Geoffrey Pearson has described his travels with Trudeau to China and has attached documents he wrote at the time in *Anecdotage* (privately published, 2007), 49–50. Richard and Sandra Gwyn, "The Politics of Peace," *Saturday Night*, May 1984, is the

best contemporary article on the initiative and is based on interviews with confidential sources.

63. Gossage, *Close to the Charisma*, 255; Roy MacLaren, *Honourable Mentions: The Uncommon Diary of an M.P.* (Toronto: Deneau, 1986), 165; and Donaghy, "'Ghost of Peace.'"

64. Regarding Reagan and *The Day After*, see Morris, *Dutch*, 46. James Mann, *The Rebellion of Ronald Reagan: A History of the End of the Cold War* (Viking: New York, 2009). Neither Canada nor Trudeau is mentioned in the book, which demonstrates Reagan's strong antinuclear views, views that were opposed strenuously by Henry Kissinger and Richard Nixon, among others. Eric Hobsbawm, *The Age of Extremes: The Short Twentieth Century, 1914–1991* (1994; repr., London: Abacus, 1995), 250.

65. Gossage, *Close to the Charisma*, 256ff.; Gotlieb, *Washington Diaries*, 193–94.

66. Trudeau's comments on Fowler, "Memorandum for the Prime Minister," Dec. 22, 1984, PCO file U-4-5, quoted in Donaghy, "'Ghost of Peace.'" Correspondence with Gale Zoë Garnett, July 2009.

67. MacEachen made the remarks at a collective interview with Trudeau ministers, Library and Archives Canada, Dec. 9, 2002.

68. Conversations with Kidder and Garnett; "Kathleen and Jimmy" Sinclair to Trudeau, Jan. 14, 1984, TP, MG 26 020, vol. 17, file 17-6, LAC; Gossage, *Close to the Charisma*, 263; Pascale Hébert to Trudeau, Oct. 30, 1983, TP, MG 26 020, vol. 6, file 6-7, LAC; Jacques Hébert to Trudeau, Dec. 20, 1983, ibid. The book dedicated to Palme is Trudeau, *Lifting the Shadow*.

69. Trudeau, *Memoirs*, 142.

CHAPTER EIGHTEEN: HIS WAY

1. Ronald Reagan, *The Reagan Diaries*, ed. Douglas Brinkley (New York: HarperCollins, 2007), 246; Donald Jamieson, *No Place for Fools: The Political Memoirs of Don Jamieson*, ed. Carmelita McGrath, vol. 1 (St. John's: Breakwater, 1989), 11.

2. Jamieson, *No Place for Fools*, 12–14. Interview with Alexandre Trudeau, June 2009. The quotation about Trudeau in the snowstorm is from *Ottawa Citizen*, March 1, 1984. French politician Jacques Attali's fascinating memoir of the period relates a conversation between Prime Minister

Thatcher and President Mitterrand: Trudeau had told her, she claimed, that his peace initiative resulted from his concern about the coming Canadian election. Mitterrand responded that the cruise missile decision was very difficult for Trudeau, but Thatcher had no patience with the argument. Trudeau had not defended the cruise effectively, she scoffed, and besides, he did not have the right to raise such doubts when Canada spent only 2 percent of its GDP on defence (*Verbatim*, vol. 1 of *Chronique des années 1981–1986* (Paris: Fayard, 1993), 522. Thatcher does not mention her disciplining of Trudeau in her memoirs, though she acknowledges that he informed her during her September 1983 visit to Canada that Mikhail Gorbachev was someone to watch. Margaret Thatcher, *The Downing Street Years* (New York: HarperCollins, 1993), 320–21.

3. These assessments are taken from *Ottawa Citizen*, March 1, 1984; *Globe and Mail*, March 1, 1984; and *Montreal Gazette*, March 1, 1984.

4. Kidder to Trudeau, May 4, 1974, and undated postcard, TP, MG 26 020, vol. 6, file 7-3, LAC. Sandra and Richard Gwyn, "The Politics of Peace," *Saturday Night*, May 1984, 19. Geoffrey Pearson to Trudeau, June 28, 1984, personal copy of Geoffrey Pearson.

5. Michael Tucker, "Trudeau and the Politics of Peace," *International Perspectives* (May–June 1984): 7–10; Adam Bromke and Kim Nossal, "Trudeau Rides the 'Third Rail,'" ibid., 3–6. The second article is more sharply critical and reflects opinion within the department, as a recent unpublished paper by Greg Donaghy, head of the Historical Division of Foreign Affairs, confirms. The articles credit Trudeau for awakening Canadians to international issues but argue that resources and preparation were inadequate and that "quiet diplomacy" could have been more effective—a view Trudeau strongly opposed in his memoirs (*Memoirs* [Toronto: McClelland and Stewart, 1993], 340–41) and in his speech to the Albert Einstein Peace Prize Foundation on November 13, 1983, which is published, with an introduction by David Crenna, in *Lifting the Shadow of War*, ed. C. David Crenna (Edmonton: Hurtig, 1987), 116–21.

6. Apps is quoted in *Toronto Star*, June 17, 1984. Chrétien is quoted in Ron Graham, *One-Eyed Kings: Promise and Illusion in Canadian Politics* (Toronto: Collins, 1986), 217. I attended the convention as a delegate and many impressions are my own.

7. Davey to Anka, April 2, 1984; Asper to Davey, March 12, 1984. Keith Davey Papers, box 32, file 36, Victoria University Library.
8. Davey to Anka, April 2, 1984; Davey to Streisand, May 4, 1984; ibid.
9. *Globe and Mail,* June 14, 1984.
10. Ian Brown's article was in the entertainment section of *Globe and Mail,* June 16, 1984. The Trudeau transcript is from *Toronto Star,* June 15, 1984.
11. *Toronto Star,* June 15, 1984; personal notes; *Globe and Mail,* June 16–17, 1984.
12. Kennedy's moving speech to the Democratic convention in 1980 ends with these lines: "For all those whose cares have been our concern, the work goes on, the cause endures, the hope still lives, and the dream shall never die." I'd like to thank Jack Cunningham, a University of Toronto doctoral student, who pointed out the similarities, which are obviously not coincidental. Gordon's denunciation of Trudeau is found in Denis Smith, *Gentle Patriot: A Political Biography of Walter Gordon* (Edmonton: Hurtig, 1973), 253–53.
13. Michel Vastel, *Trudeau: Le Québécois* (Montréal: Les Éditions de l'Homme, 2000), 273ff.; Brian Mulroney, *Memoirs 1939–1993* (Toronto: McClelland and Stewart, 2007), 301. On Gregg, see Christina McCall and Stephen Clarkson, *The Heroic Delusion,* vol. 2 of *Trudeau and Our Times* (Toronto: McClelland and Stewart, 1994), 419. Peter C. Newman, *The Secret Mulroney Tapes: Unguarded Confessions of a Prime Minister* (Toronto: Random House, 2005), 80–81; Allan Gotlieb, *The Washington Diaries: 1981–1989* (Toronto: McClelland and Stewart, 2006), 226–27.
14. Photographs of the living room and Cormier-designed furniture and the multilevel exterior are found in *Ernest Cormier and the Université de Montréal,* ed. Isabelle Gournay (Montréal: Centre Canadien d'Architecture/ Canadian Centre for Architecture, 1990), 79. Cormier had taken excess materials from the university and incorporated them into his home.
15. Personal memory of discussion with archivists, Aug.1984. Interview with Alexandre Trudeau, June 2009. There are numerous memoirs of Trudeau's retirement years in *Pierre: Colleagues and Friends Talk about the Trudeau They Knew,* ed. Nancy Southam (Toronto: McClelland and Stewart, 2005), especially chap. 15, "Papa."

16. Robert Simmonds' comments are found in Southam, *Pierre*, 119. Interview with Jim Coutts, April 2009; Trudeau, *Memoirs*, 348.

17. Brooke Johnson, *Trudeau Stories*, copy provided by author. Conversation with Brooke Johnson, Nov. 2008.

18. Ibid. The reports written by Trudeau can be found in full on the website of the InterAction Council: http://interactioncouncil.org/. Tom Axworthy accompanied Trudeau and helped with the reports. He testifies to the enormous influence of Helmut Schmidt on this organization and on Trudeau. Conversation with Tom Axworthy, Feb. 2009. Bartleman discussed the Cuba intervention by Trudeau with me in Jan. 2007, and while Trudeau's influence is unclear the conversation between Trudeau and Castro most certainly occurred.

19. Alexandre Trudeau, "Introduction," to Pierre Trudeau and Jacques Hébert, *Two Innocents in Red China*, ed. Alexandre Trudeau (Vancouver and Toronto: Douglas and McIntyre, 2007; original 1961),11–12. My comments here derive from discussions and correspondence on the subject with Alexandre Trudeau. For a debate about the influence of Catholicism and Trudeau's attraction to "authoritarian" approaches, see the comments in John English, Richard Gwyn, and P. Whitney Lackenbauer, eds., *The Hidden Pierre Trudeau: The Faith behind the Politics* (Ottawa: Novalis, 2004), particularly the exchanges between the philosopher of religion Gregory Baum and religious sociologist David Seljack (145–50). Tom Axworthy commented: "I think [Trudeau] was rather agnostic about the use of the state, except as a means to try to expand human freedom; restricting in one case, but allowing it to exercise some measure of regulation on the market on the other" (150).

20. There are numerous accounts of these events. Trudeau, *Memoirs*, 358ff.; Mulroney, *Memoirs*, 508–28; André Burelle, *Pierre Elliott Trudeau: L'Intellectuel et la Politique* (Montréal: Fides, 2005), section 7; L. Ian MacDonald, *From Bourassa to Bourassa: Wilderness to Restoration*, 2nd ed. (Montreal and Kingston: McGill–Queen's University Press, 2002), chap. 22; Clarkson and McCall, *Heroic Delusion*, 425ff.; and especially Trudeau's articles in *Toronto Star* and *La Presse*, May 27, 1987, and his interview with Barbara Frum on CBC at http://archives.cbc.ca/arts_entertainment/media/topics/368-2083/. More generally, see the fullest account in

Andrew Cohen, A *Deal Undone: The Making and Breaking of the Meech Lake Accord* (Vancouver: Douglas and McIntyre, 1990).

21. *Montreal Gazette*, March 30, 1988; and *Globe and Mail*, March 30, 1988.

22. Michael Bliss, quoted in Robert Bothwell, *Canada and Quebec: One Country, Two Histories*, rev. ed. (Vancouver: University of British Columbia Press, 1998), 193; Mulroney, *Memoirs*, 767.

23. The *Canadian Encyclopedia* article on Bill 178, the Quebec language bill limiting the use of English, is found at http://www.thecanadian-encyclopedia.com/index.cfm?PgNm=TCE&Params=A1ARTA0009100. Interview with Paul Martin, May 2009.

24. The speech was published as *Fatal Tilt: Speaking Out about Sovereignty* (Toronto: HarperCollins, 1991), 16. For Dickson's reaction, see Robert J. Sharpe and Kent Roach, *Brian Dickson: A Judge's Journey* (Toronto: University of Toronto Press, 2003), 279–81.

25. The *Maclean's* article was reprinted in Pierre Elliott Trudeau, *Against the Current: Selected Writings, 1939–1996*, ed. Gérard Pelletier (Toronto: McClelland and Stewart, 1996), 262–74. Vastel, *Trudeau*, 297, discusses the impact of Trudeau, which is confirmed in the definitive academic study by Richard Johnston et al., *The Challenge of Direct Democracy: The 1992 Canadian Referendum* (Montreal and Kingston: McGill–Queen's University Press, 1996). Mulroney's comments are in his *Memoirs*, 955. Bob Rae's comments are in Susan Delacourt, *United We Fall: The Crisis of Democracy in Canada* (Toronto: Viking, 1993), 183–84. Delacourt's book is the best account of Charlottetown's failure.

26. From the *Maclean's* article in Pelletier, ed., *Against the Current*, 274.

27. Stephen Clarkson and Christina McCall, *The Magnificent Obsession*, vol. 1 of *Trudeau and Our Times* (Toronto: McClelland and Stewart, 1990), 9; conversation with Richard O'Hagan, May 2009; Thomas S. Axworthy and Pierre Elliott Trudeau, eds., *Towards a Just Society: The Trudeau Years* (Markham, Ont.: Viking, 1990); Ivan Head and Pierre Trudeau, *The Canadian Way: Shaping Canada's Foreign Policy, 1968–1984* (Toronto: McClelland and Stewart, 1995); J.L. Granatstein and Robert Bothwell, *Pirouette: Pierre Trudeau and Canadian Foreign Policy* (Toronto: University of Toronto Press, 1990); Trudeau, *Memoirs*; J.L. Granatstein, *The Ottawa Men: The Civil Service Mandarins 1935–1957* (Toronto: Oxford University

Press, 1982), 278. After praising earlier prime ministers, including
Diefenbaker, for respecting the impartiality and independence of the civil
service, Granatstein wrote: "Whether such a judgement could now be
made—after almost a decade and a half of Trudeau government, and the
politicization of the bureaucracy from the office of the Clerk of the Privy
Council downward—is much less certain."

28. Interview with Jacques Hébert, Feb. 2006. Powe wrote about the children
in "The Lion in Winter," in *Trudeau's Shadow: The Life and Legacy of
Pierre Elliott Trudeau*, ed. Andrew Cohen and J.L. Granatstein (Toronto:
Random House, 1998), 401. See also B.W. Powe, *The Mystic Trudeau:
The Fire and the Rose* (Toronto: Thomas Allen, 2007).

29. *Globe and Mail*, Sept. 6, 1991; interview with Alexandre Trudeau, June 2009.

30. Trudeau makes the comment in a caption beside a photograph of himself
and Chrétien taken in 1990 (*Memoirs*, 365). The Chrétien caucus
comment is from personal memory.

31. Catherine Annau, "The Sphinx," in *Trudeau Albums*, Karen Alliston, Rick
Archbold, Jennifer Glossop, Alison Maclean, Ivon Owen, eds. (Toronto:
Penguin, 2000), 145.

32. *Le Devoir*, June 28, 1997. The comments about the impact of Pelletier's
death are made by all who knew both men well.

33. On his questioning of his faith after Michel's death, see Ron Graham,
"The Unending Spiritual Search," in *Hidden Pierre*, ed. English, Gwyn, and
Lackenbauer, 103. Confidential interviews.

34. Tetley's account appeared in *Toronto Star*, Sept. 28, 2001. *Maclean's* was
consulted online at http://thecanadianencyclopedia.com/
index.cfm?PgNm=TCE&Params=M1ARTM0011606.

35. *Montreal Gazette*, Sept. 29, 2000; *Le Devoir*, Sept. 29, 2000. The
"newsmaker of the year" poll and Trudeau's response are described in
Trudeau Albums, 156. John Ralston Saul's introduction to Nino Ricci,
Pierre Elliott Trudeau (Toronto: Penguin, 2009), xiii. The comparison with
Lincoln is in Guy Pratte, "What Makes a Country? Trudeau's Failure as a
Leader," in Cohen and Granatstein, eds., *Trudeau's Shadow*, 356–66.

36. *National Post*, Oct. 5, 2000; *New York Times*, Oct. 6, 2000.

37. "Pierre Elliott Trudeau 1919–2000," Notre-Dame Basilica of Montreal,
personal copy. Justin Trudeau eulogy, *Toronto Star*, Oct. 4, 2000.

ACKNOWLEDGMENTS

—

I must first thank the family of Pierre Elliott Trudeau and the executors of his estate for asking me to write this biography. The Trudeau family is deeply interested in and knowledgeable about history, literature, and, of course, Canadian politics. They gave me full access to Trudeau's personal papers, which form the core of this volume. Justin Trudeau and Sophie Grégoire, Alexandre Trudeau and Zoë Bedos, and Margaret Trudeau have all shared their memories and offered hospitality as I carried out my research, and I thank them for their generosity and for the complete freedom to write what I believe to be true about Pierre Trudeau.

As with volume 1, this volume has benefited from the generous support of the Social Sciences and Humanities Research Council, which permitted me to employ several of my doctoral students to assist me in the creation of this book: Matthew Bunch, Jason Churchill, Beatrice Orchard, Andrew Thompson, and Ryan Touhey. Their own thesis research contributed greatly to this tome.

I have dedicated this volume to my brother, who was an active member of the New Democratic Party when Pierre Trudeau was prime minister. My mother always supported the Liberal Party and Trudeau, while my father always cancelled out her vote until he, too, finally voted Liberal when I became a candidate. By that time, however, Trudeau was out of politics. I learned from them that different political opinions have legitimacy and that differences in politics do not mean that people cannot have a happy marriage, which my parents certainly did. I also owe much to my wife, Hilde, who died of cancer just as I was completing volume 1, and to my son, Jonathan, who follows politics closely and diligently checks my facts about the past and the present. I would also like to thank my mother-in-law, Barbara Abt, and my sister-in-law, Linda Abt, for their support, and Angela Granic for her great assistance.

Many friends, colleagues, and associates have been enormously helpful in the writing of these two volumes. Although I did not know Pierre Trudeau—I met him a few times, but he would not have recognized me had I walked past him—my own life has often intersected with his work and his associates. It is surely a commentary on Trudeau's relationship with his political party that even though I was a constituency president and a campaign chair from 1977 to 1980, I spoke with him only once—during the week before he resigned. I served again as a constituency president in his last government, but I never met him or talked to him during those years. Nevertheless, I have known many of his Cabinet ministers and his chief political strategists for over three decades, and some of his closest and most influential friends for almost four decades. I have attended political conventions where his influence dominated, and like all Canadians, I watched Pierre Trudeau as his extraordinary career deeply affected our lives.

My sources for this book are, therefore, often personal memory and impressions, formed long ago but mediated by time and historical interpretation. Several years ago I heard the anger of Jack Pickersgill, for example, a Liberal political giant of an earlier time who had profound doubts about some of the paths Trudeau followed. I was privileged in the mid-seventies to hear a lively debate about Trudeau's merits between Paul Martin and Allan

MacEachen, fuelled by fine scotch. These two astute and experienced politicians deeply disagreed, with Martin, then Canada's high commissioner to the United Kingdom, arguing for the prosecution while his minister, MacEachen, defended Trudeau with expected eloquence and surprising affection. Later, I encountered many members of Trudeau's immediate staff—drivers, secretaries, assistants, and guards—who shared MacEachen's fondness for Trudeau as a person, based on their respect for a decent, caring, and fair human being. Leaders from Mao through Churchill have been exposed in harsh light by physicians, valets, and others who attended the daily needs of their great employers. For Trudeau, the opposite seems true, as Nancy Southam's valuable collection of personal memories of the former prime minister clearly demonstrates.

As a generalization, the same structure of remembrance fits the Liberal Party during the period when Trudeau was predominant. His popularity was strongest among the rank and file, particularly within ethnic communities, while his chief detractors were often found among the higher officers of government and party. As I researched and wrote this book, I found that even as I read Trudeau's documents and speeches, I also recalled long-ago conversations in which prominent Liberals tore into Trudeau and blamed the party's woes on his record. They provided a necessary check on any biographer's natural tendency to accept the protagonist's arguments or frame of mind, and, like the debates in my own family, I hope they have introduced some balance into my understanding of the former prime minister.

In formulating my impressions of Trudeau and his impact on Canadian politics and life, I am indebted to many people, including those who worked with me in my own political life: David Cooke, Jim Breithaupt, Elaine and Roly Rees, Betty and Peter Sims, Mary and Jim Guy, Shawky and Kathie Fahel, the late Walter Muzyka, Irene Sage, the late Vir Handa, Constantine Victoros, Munif Dakkak, Chris Karakokinos, the late Andy Borovilos,

Steve Skropolis, Don and Katie Thomson, Noreen and Pat Flynn, Louise and Paul Puopolo, Janice Bryson, Jean Reilly, Wendy Angel and John Shewchuk, James Howe, Joan Euler, Basheer Habib, Marianne Apostolache, the late Tim Fitzpatrick, Merv Villemaire, Andrew and Nancy Telegdi, Janko Peric, Bryan Stortz, Pat Rutter, Jamie Martin, Dalbir Sidhu, Prakash Ahuja, Herb Epp, John Milloy, the late John Sweeney, Sue King, Carl Zehr, Jim Erb, Ray Simonson, Chris Farley, Mike Carty, the late Doug and Linda McDowell, Karen Redman, and Berry Vrbanovic.

I would also like to thank the institutions that have supported me during the writing of this book. I entered the University of Waterloo as a student in the sixties and have been a professor there since the early seventies. It has provided a firm base for research and teaching, and I have the greatest respect for it as an extraordinary institution. My personal debts are too many to list, but I must acknowledge the support of my departmental chairs and good friends Pat Harrigan and Andrew Hunt; their superb assistants Nancy Birss, Donna Lang, and the inimitable Irene Majer; my deans Bob Kerton and Ken Coates; Provost Amit Chakma; and Trudeau's friend and neighbour who is now my president, David Johnston. Ken McLaughlin worked with me in many capacities while I was writing this book, most recently at the Centre for International Governance Innovation (CIGI), where I serve as executive director.

At CIGI, I owe a great debt to my assistant, Lena Yost, who has helped me in so many ways for many years, and to her summer replacement, the effervescent Jen Beckermann; I also want to thank my many colleagues there: Daniel Schwanen, who stepped in as acting director for a year while I worked on this book; Andy Cooper, my deputy director and long-time collaborator; and Paul Heinbecker, who always offered a corrective view based on his distinguished service as a Canadian diplomat and Brian Mulroney's chief foreign policy adviser. Alison De Muy and her partner,

Andrew Thompson, read the manuscript, and many others helped in diverse ways. I would especially like to thank Jim Balsillie, the chair and founder of CIGI, who has generously given his time, vitality, and intellectual drive to guide me as I set up this foreign affairs think tank, which, in many ways, reflects Trudeau's own view that we must now all become citizens of the world. Board members Scott Burk, Ken Cork, Cosimo Fiorenza, Dennis Kavelman, and Joy Roberts have also been supportive, as have government representatives Drew Fagan and Graham Shantz.

More recently I have served as the general editor of the *Dictionary of Canadian Biography / Dictionnaire biographique du Canada* (DCB/DBC), where Robert Fraser, Willadean Leo, Geocelyne Meyers, and Loretta James are the excellent staff backing my work. My collaborator at Université Laval is Réal Bélanger, Laurier's biographer, who once worked closely with Robert Bourassa. His wise counsel, enormous knowledge of Quebec history, and warm friendship have sustained me often. I also owe a great debt to my predecessor at the DCB, Ramsay Cook, who has written a splendid personal memoir of his own interaction with Pierre Trudeau; like Cook himself, it is wise, generous, and intellectually first class.

Many others who have written about Trudeau have provided a solid foundation on which to build this biography. There are now dozens of books on Trudeau, but special mention should be made of Stephen Clarkson and Christina McCall's two-volume *Trudeau and Our Times*, which is magisterial in its scope; Richard Gwyn's *Northern Magus*, an early classic; George Radwanski's *Trudeau*, based on the best contemporary interviews with Trudeau; Anthony Westell's *Paradox*, an insightful tract; Monique and Max Nemni's much-needed intellectual biography of Trudeau, *Young Trudeau*; Michel Vastel's provocative *Trudeau: Le Québécois*; André Burelle's highly critical *Pierre Trudeau: L'Intellectuel et la Politique*; and two recent personal accounts of Trudeau—Bruce Powe's

Mystic Trudeau: The Fire and the Rose and Nino Ricci's *Pierre Elliott Trudeau*. Readers of this second volume will recognize the importance of three published diaries—by Paul Martin Sr.; Trudeau aide Patrick Gossage; and Liberal MP Roy MacLaren. I also owe an enormous debt to the National Film Board and especially the CBC/Radio-Canada, whose archives contain a remarkable visual record of Trudeau, which I consulted frequently. Interestingly, when my short biography of Trudeau for the DCB/DBC volume on Canada's prime ministers was edited by the fine editorial team at Laval, they checked the Trudeau quotations against the visual or audio record in the CBC archive, and many times the print record was not identical with what Trudeau actually said. After that experience, I have tried, in my research for this volume, to check the electronic records against the print, again with similar results.

Many of Trudeau's colleagues have written or are writing their own accounts of the period, and I have benefited from discussions with them. Again my bibliography, available online, provides a full list, but I must mention several works here because of their particular significance. Alastair Gillespie, a senior Trudeau minister in the seventies, has the best-organized papers on the period. I have been assisted greatly by full access to these documents and by the generous collaboration of Irene Sage, Gillespie's co-author and my former assistant and close friend. Paul Litt, who is writing a major biography of John Turner, allowed me to read his manuscript, and it has been extremely important in helping me to understand the period and the Turner-Trudeau relationship. Allan MacEachen has been working on his memoirs, and two of my former doctoral students (now colleagues at the University of Waterloo), Andrew Thompson and Ryan Touhey, worked on his papers—to both their and my benefit. Another former student, Greg Donaghy, now head of the historical division of the Department of Foreign Affairs, has been extremely helpful as always, particularly in giving me his own fine essay on Trudeau's peace initiative. Dick Stanbury gave me a copy of his invaluable diary and participated in a "collective interview" with nine former ministers in Toronto. Library and Archives Canada, under the inspired leadership of Ian Wilson, collaborated with me in four more interviews of this type, and all of these meetings, through the active participation of Trudeau's ministers, senior assistants, and office staff, provided exceptionally valuable material on Trudeau.

Robert Bothwell, the leading historian of Canadian foreign policy and a friend since the day four decades ago when we met and discovered that we both intended to write a doctoral thesis on the same subject, appears regularly in the notes to this book and, even more frequently, as an influence on my assessment of events. We have shared research notes and interview records over the years, and they assisted me in my work. I also owe thanks to several others who have given me information: Don Avery, Jack Granatstein, Norman Hillmer, Stephen Azzi, Donald Wright, Joan Euler, and the late Geoffrey Pearson.

When I began this project, my good friend and distinguished diplomat Geoffrey Pearson, who was not an admirer of Trudeau, advised me not to "touch it." Whether I was wise to ignore his advice is for readers to decide, but the experience of writing these two volumes has been made much more rewarding because of the splendid people who have worked closely with me during the last seven years. My principal assistant has been Jonathan Minnes, who, while a history student at Wilfrid Laurier University, has checked my notes, corrected proofs, visited archives, and helped out with hundreds of small tasks. Nicolas Rouleau, an exceptional young man who is now in India, assisted with research and, more recently, with translation. Others who have worked on the project include Eleni Crespi, Ian Haight, Sean House, Alexis Landry, Alex Lund, Brodie Ross, and, indirectly, students in my graduate course who focused on the Trudeau period.

Finally, I, like so many other Canadian authors, owe an enormous debt to my publisher, Louise Dennys, whose emails at 2:30 a.m. remind me not only of her diligent ways but also of her great commitment to the project. Rosemary Shipton, the best historical editor in Canada, who regularly turns dross into elegant prose and insightful observation, has edited both volumes. They are so much better because her incomparable editorial skills touched the manuscript firmly. My agent, Linda McKnight, is always a reservoir of common sense and knowledge about Canadian publishing. I must confess that I came to enjoy missing a deadline because it would occasion a meeting that brought together these brilliant but kind women, who rebuked me gently, entertained me with stories, and sent me back to the manuscript with a renewed energy. Kathryn Dean has been a superb copyeditor; Gena Gorrell—excellent in all matters editorial—was in this case our reliable proofreader; and Professor Barney Gilmore proved himself again the finest of indexers. And at Knopf Canada a team of talented editorial and production specialists has turned the manuscript into a book: Deirdre Molina, the Senior Managing Editor who somehow keeps projects on schedule with a firm but courteous hand; Michelle MacAleese, who diligently and intelligently tracked down and obtained the illustrations and permissions; Zoë Bercovici, who assisted her most ably; Amanda Lewis, who conscientiously and skillfully entered the final corrections; Carla Kean, who calmly met all the deadlines through the production process; and Nina Ber-Donkor, Louise's Executive Assistant, who was always helpful. *Just Watch Me* is the fourth book I've published with Louise Dennys's team, and I can't imagine a better publishing experience.

John English
Kitchener, Ontario
June 2009

PHOTO CREDITS/PERMISSIONS

Page iii (top) © Getty Images Hulton Archive/David Montgomery; (bottom left) © The Canadian Press/Charles Mitchell; (bottom right) © Library and Archives Canada accession number C-112617

Page iv Courtesy of Margaret Trudeau

INSERT FIVE

Page i © The Canadian Press/Rod Ivor

Page ii (top) © The Canadian Press/Gary Hershorn; (middle) © The Toronto Star/Boris Spremo; (bottom) Courtesy of Gale Zoë Garnett

Page iii (top) © The Canadian Press/Fred Chartrand; (bottom) © The Canadian Press/Robert Cooper

Page iv (top) © The Canadian Press/Drew Gragg; (bottom) The Gazette/ Mike Aislin

INSERT SIX

Page i © Jean-Marc Carisse

Page ii (top) © The Canadian Press/Bill Grimshaw; (bottom) © The Canadian Press

Page iii (top) © The Canadian Press/Fred Chartrand; (bottom) © Library and Archives Canada accession number PA-141503

Page iv (top) © The Canadian Press/Peter Bregg; (bottom left) © The Canadian Press/Gail Harvey; (bottom right) Courtesy of the Author

INSERT SEVEN

Page i (top series) © Jean-Marc Carisse; (bottom) © The Canadian Press

Page ii (top) © Jean-Marc Carisse; (bottom) © The Canadian Press/ Andrew Vaughan

Page iii (top left) © Jean-Marc Carisse; (top right) Courtesy of the Author; (bottom) © Jean-Marc Carisse

Page iv (top) © Jean-Marc Carisse; (bottom) © Jean-Marc Carisse

INSERT EIGHT

Page i (top) © The Canadian Press/Ryan Remiorz; (bottom) © The Canadian Press/Ryan Remiorz

Page ii © The Canadian Press/Aaron Harris

PERMISSIONS

The author has made every effort to locate and contact all the holders of copy
written material reproduced in this book, and expresses grateful acknowledgment
for permission to reproduce from the following previously published material:

Gossage, Patrick. *Close to the Charisma: My Years between the Press and
   Pierre Elliott Trudeau* (Halifax: Goodread Biographies), 1987.
Griffiths, Linda and Paul Thompson. *Maggie and Pierre: A Fantasy of Love,
   Politics and the Media* (Vancouver: Talon Books), 1980.
Head, Ivan L and Pierre Elliott Trudeau. *The Canadian Way: Shaping Canada's
   Foreign Policy, 1968–1984* (Toronto: McClelland & Stewart), 1995.
The Estate of Eli Mandel
Mandel, Eli. "Political Speech (for PET)", *Dreaming backwards, 1954–1981:
   The selected poetry of Eli Mandel* (Toronto: General Publishing Co.), 1981
Morin, Claude. *Quebec versus Ottawa: The Struggle for Self-Government
   1960–1972* (Toronto: University of Toronto Press), 1976.
McWhinney, Edward. *Canada and the Constitution 1979–1982: Partriation
   and the Charter of Rights* (Toronto: University of Toronto Press), 1982.
Ritchie, Charles. *Storm Signals More Undiplomatic Diaries, 1962–1971*
   (Toronto: McClelland & Stewart), 2001.
The Estate of Pierre Elliott Trudeau
Trudeau, Pierre. *Memoirs* (Toronto: McClelland & Stewart), 1993.

INDEX

Buckley, Pat, 397
Buckley, William, 582
budgets and finance, federal-provincial
    differences and, 133–35
Bulloch, John, 161
Burelle, André, 345, 446, 458, 472–73,
    501–2, 626
Burney, Derek, 562
Burt, Richard, 599–600
Burton, Edgar, 293
Burton, Pierre, 227–28
Buruma, Ian, 142
Bush, George W., 636
the business community. See Bay Street
    (business lobby), 466
Byfield, Ted, 484
Byng, Governor General Lord, 187

Caccia, Charles, 288
Cadieux, Fernand, 38–39
Cadieux, Léo, 63, 558
Cadieux, Marcel, 59–60, 62, 73
Cafik, Norm, 355, 404
Cahill, Jack, 282
Cairns, Alan, 144
Caldicott, Helen, 587, 589, 592
Callaghan, James, 399, 421
Callwood, June, 5, 612
Caminada, Jerome, 173–74
Camp, Dalton, 180
Campagnolo, Iona, 400, 404, 429–30, 612
Canada,
    agrees to local U.S. testing of cruise
        missiles, 583–87, 589
    as an ambivalent NATO member.
        See NATO, Canada's ambivalent
        participation in
    anti-discriminatory court rulings in, 109
    defense spending in, 584–86
    developmental assistance by, 59, 65,
        67, 378
    ends its nuclear role, 64, 69
    federal vs. provincial powers in, 130–39
        (see also Constitution [Canadian])
    federalism and, 8, 446
    an "identity" crisis within, 375
    1970s standards of living in, 382
    Parliament of approves patriation by
        huge margin, 516–17

profoundly affected by distant world
    events, 202
proposed eventual relationship with
    Quebec unclear, 362–64
regional inequities in, 171, 216, 226,
    231, 245, 424, 485, 546
regional rivalries within, 139, 189, 371
    (see also Alberta; Quebec)
rising nationalism in, 36
western disaffection in, 107, 200–201,
    223, 423, 488 (see also the [federal]
    Liberal Party, western Canada weak-
    nesses of)
See also Alberta; Quebec (province of);
    and particular topics (e.g.,
    bilingualism)
Canada Development Corporation, 219
Canada Has a Future (book), 382
Canada Pension Plan, 138, 158
Canada-U.S. Auto Pact, 167, 252
Canadian Annual Review of Politics and
    Public Affairs, 322
Canadian Club of Ottawa, 294–95
Canadian Conference of Catholic
    Bishops, 114–15
Canadian Council for Fair Taxation, 161
Canadian dollar, 277, 356, 371, 541
Canadian foreign policy, reviewed by
    Trudeau's govt., 57
The Canadian Forum, 37–38, 167
Canadian Human Rights Commission, 380
Canadian International Development
    Agency (CIDA), 65, 563
Canadian Manufacturers' Association
    (CMA), 293–94
Canadian Radio-Television Commission.
    See CRTC
Canadian Unity, task force concerned
    with, 351–52
The Canadian Way (memoir by Head and
    Trudeau), 65, 252, 378, 560, 627
Canairelief, Canada's lukewarm support
    of, 66
Caouette, Réal, 25, 27, 116
capital punishment, Canada's outlawing
    of, 250–51
Cardinal, Harold, 144
Carstairs, Sharon, 622
Carter, Bishop Alex, 114

negotiates the Charlottetown Accord,
624
objects fiercely to Liberal's patriation
plans, 481–82, 494
party dissatisfaction with, 527
performs well in 1979 TV debate, 386
praises Trudeau, 636
replaced by Brian Mulroney as leader,
551
supports outlawing capital punishment,
251
urges greater provincial powers, 336
western Canada difficulties of, 423, 482
his worsening relations with Bill Davis,
428, 546
Clark, S.D., 486
Clarkson, Stephen, 139, 311, 328, 434,
441, 467, 613, 627
Cliche, Robert, 23, 302
Clinton, Hilary Rodham, 324
Clinton, William J. (Bill), 324
Club of Rome, 211–12, 298
CNTU (Quebec labour federation), 79
Cohen, Leonard, 633, 637
Cohen, Mickey, 486
Coleman, James, 467
Collins, Doug, 430
Colville, Hazel, 309
Commission on International
Development (Canada, 1969), 378
Committee for an Independent Canada
(CIC), 181–82
Commonwealth Conferences, 70, 164–65,
230, 263, 350, 376, 559, 580, 597
Commonwealth Heads of Government
Meeting (1981), 567, 575
Confederation of Tomorrow Conference
(1967), 129–30
Conference on New and Renewable
Sources of Energy, 574
Conlon, Mary Ann, 235
Connally, John, 167
Consequences (book), 310
Conservative Party, 428–29, 432, 440, 615
the Constitution (Canadian)
an amending formula for, 134, 481,
494–95
historical Quebec opposition to
patriation of, 523, 526

Liberal changes proposed to, 470, 481
the patriation of, 138, 305–6, 418,
457–58, 567, 611
proposed social policies of, 134–36
provincially requested changes to,
470–71, 499
Quebec and, 49, 341
reforms of, 107–8, 129–38, 341
Supreme Court ruling re proposed
changes to, 384
Trudeau threatens unilateral patriation
of, 303, 448, 472, 474–75, 477–79
The Constitution and the People of
Canada (document), 131
Constitutional conference with premiers
called by Trudeau, 504–7
Continuing Committee of the Ministers,
471
Conversation with Canadians (collected
speeches), 184
Cook, Ramsay, 5, 24–25, 38, 96, 100–101,
361, 523–25
Cools, Anne, 77
Corman, Cis, 52
Cormier, Ernest, 401, 499
corporations, public mistrust of the
powers of, 290–92, 296. See also
Foreign Investment Review Agency
(Canada); multinational corporate
control of Canadian assets
Corrigan, Harold, 293–94
Cossitt, Tom, 287–89, 293
Cotchet, Tim, 406
Coté, Corinne, 515
Council of Foreign Relations (New York),
370
Courchene, Tom, 271
Coutts, Jim, 156, 197, 228, 234, 287, 379,
386–87, 397, 438, 458, 467, 528,
609, 615, 626
acts as PM's principal secretary, 259,
358, 374, 405, 408–9
approaches Mulroney for Trudeau's
cabinet, 306–7, 551
assesses Trudeau's brand of leadership, 48
hints Trudeau will run again for leader,
433–37
his importance to Trudeau's work, 231,
528

rallies Liberals to defeat Clark's government, 431
urges Trudeau to call a 1977 election, 351–55
Couve de Murville, Maurice, 64
Coyne, Deborah, 629, 631–32, 636
Coyne, Sarah Elisabeth, 629, 631–32, 636
Créditistes, 22, 25, 30, 74, 139, 148, 386, 432
crime, as different from sinfulness, 112
Criminal Code of Canada, 8, 47, 107, 111–17, 249
Crosbie, John, 428, 430, 432, 482
Cross, James, 79–82, 90–91, 100, 151
Crow's Nest Pass shipping rates for grain, 465, 547
Crowe, Marshall, 156
CRTC (Canadian Radio-Television Commission), 285
Cullen, Bud, 404
currencies (world), turbulence in, 211

Daly, Bernard, 114–15
Danson, Barney, 25, 162, 259, 265, 381, 404, 430–31
Davey, Dorothy, 387, 442, 447
Davey, Jim, 17, 39, 41, 43, 149, 196–97
Davey, Keith, 156, 243, 257, 284–85, 287, 352–53, 355, 372, 379, 400, 411, 442, 467, 595, 609–10, 626
advises Liberal election campaigns, 197–98, 384, 386–87, 438
described, 179–80
dreams of uniting the left, 447
encourages Trudeau to stay as leader, 435–36
manages the 1974 campaign, 227, 231, 234, 237–38, 244–46
recommends selective by-elections, 380
his role in choosing the 1974 Cabinet, 259
urges a strategic resignation, 187–88
Davis, Fred, 228
Davis, Jack, 192–93, 259
Davis, William, 137, 226, 265, 364, 410, 471, 504–5, 510, 514
brokers compromise on patriation, 506
declines to run for federal party leadership, 551

in opposition to Peter Lougheed, 476–77
supported federal Liberal policies, 481, 484, 503, 546
The Day After (TV film), 598
Deaver, Michael, 582
de Bané, Pierre, 420, 429
Décarie, Thérèse Gouin. See Gouin, Thérèse
decentralization (political), regional support for, 347–48
de Gaulle, Charles, 22–23, 47, 60, 74, 77, 154, 260, 374, 615
de Grandpré, Jean, 188
de Heredia, José-Maria, 440
"democracy, participatory," 42–43, 48, 150–51, 153
Deng Xiaoping, 597–98
Denmark, Trudeau's visits to, 263
Department of Regional Economic Expansion (Canada). See DREE
Desbarats, Peter, 255–56, 330
Desbiens, Jean-Paul, 80
Deschambault, Jack, 399
Deschenes, M. et Mme René, 412
Desmarais, André, 416
Desmarais, Paul, 237
de Vault, Carole, 81, 89
Dickson, Brian, 624–25
Diefenbaker, John, 6, 13, 26, 30, 37, 155, 207, 320, 348, 384, 623
appoints Royal Commission on Energy, 220
his bill of rights, 493
civil libertarian views of, 110–11
fought for bilingualism, 254
maintains trade with China, 164
quoted, 116, 128, 149, 169
votes against MP raises, 288
Dion, Léon, 140, 445–46
Dion, Stéphane, 445
discrimination (racial), 109–10
divorce, 112, 115, 328, 400, 531
the Divorce Act (Canada), 129, 249
Doern, Bruce, 545
dollar (Canadian). See Canadian dollar
Dome Petroleum Corp., 488
Douglas, Tommy, 4, 18, 25, 29–30, 72, 90, 96
Doyle, Richard, 612

Drapeau, Jean, 27–28, 80, 86, 88, 150, 302
DREE (Department of Regional Economic Expansion), 172, 216
Drouin, Marie-Josée, 382
Drummond, Ian, 413
Drury, Charles "Bud," 13, 45, 158, 193, 343, 381
Dryden, Gordon, 195–97
Dubé, Rudolph, 628
Duchesne, Pierre, 93–94
Duffy, John, 31
Duffy, Mike, 411–12
Dufour, Christian, 142
Dumont, Fernand, 9, 85, 142, 366
Duplessis, Maurice, 38, 109, 133, 626
Dupuy, Michel, 261

Eagleburger, Lawrence, 599–600
Eagleton, Thomas, 321
Economic Club (New York), 323, 330, 370
economics
    baffling complexity of, 43, 297–98, 492
    non-rationality and volatility affecting, 247, 492–93
    provincial free-trade inside Canada and, 481
economics ("free-market"), 160, 276, 291–92, 294–95, 297–98, 301, 485, 544, 563–65
    threats posed by, 417
    urged upon the Third World, 574
economics ("Keynesian"), 43, 148, 158–59, 272, 297
economics ("supply-side"), 159
Economics and the Public Purpose (book), 274, 296
the economy, government focus on, 202, 209. See also economics; inflation; unemployment
Edmonton Journal, 489
Election Expenses Act (Canada, 1974), 151, 194, 254
election results
    1970 in Quebec, 78
    various federal, 29–30, 186, 238–39, 442–43
Elliott, William Yandell, 350
Enders, Thomas, 298–99, 376

energy, 221
    Alberta slaps new royalty rate on oil production, 231
    Canadian controls over the production and transport of, 219–27, 231
    "fair" access to, 543
    shortages of, 211, 219, 224, 476–77
    unrest due to rising prices of, 231, 260, 381
energy resources (Canadian)
    American interest in, 169
    necessary policy for, 462–63
English, John, meets Pierre Trudeau, 412–13, 752
environmental issues and awareness, 113, 264–65, 464, 559, 616–17
Erickson, Arthur, 206–7, 323, 396, 407, 533, 577–78
Erola, Judy, 465–66, 511
Established Programs Financing Act, 303, 363
Estey, W.Z. "Bud," 501
European Common Market (ECM), 160, 202, 261, 263–65
European Economic Community (EEC), 263
Evans, John, 380–81
External Affairs Department (Canada), 262, 375. See also named ministers, critics, and particularly Trudeau, Pierre Elliott

Fader, Henry, 287
Fairbairn, Joyce, 207, 360–61, 376
Fairweather, Gordon, 380
the Falkland War, 583
famine, 202
Fanon, Frantz, 90
Faribault, Marcel, 23, 26
"Farley" (typical Labrador retriever), 393
Faulkner, Hugh, 208, 391, 423–24
    defeated in 1979 election, 404
Faulkner, Jane, 208, 320, 323, 391, 401
Fauteux, Gérald, 268
Fear of Flying (book), 314
federal-provincial disputes and tensions, 45, 49, 361, 366–68
Federalism for the Future (document), 131
Financial Post, 382